SOUTH CAROLINA DEED ABSTRACTS

1773–1778

Books F-4 through X-4

Abstracted by

Brent H. Holcomb

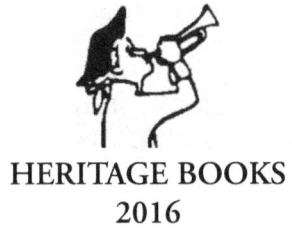

HERITAGE BOOKS
2016

HERITAGE BOOKS
AN IMPRINT OF HERITAGE BOOKS, INC.

Books, CDs, and more—Worldwide

For our listing of thousands of titles see our website
at
www.HeritageBooks.com

Published 2016 by
HERITAGE BOOKS, INC.
Publishing Division
5810 Ruatan Street
Berwyn Heights, Md. 20740

Copyright © 1994 Brent H. Holcomb

All rights reserved. No part of this book may be reproduced or transmitted in any form or by any means, electronic or mechanical, including photocopying, recording or by any information storage and retrieval system without written permission from the author, except for the inclusion of brief quotations in a review.

International Standard Book Numbers
Paperbound: 978-0-917890-12-3
Clothbound: 978-0-7884-6444-7

INTRODUCTION

This volume is a continuation of the abstracts prepared under Clara Langley of the Works Progress Administration in the 1930s and published in four volumes by Southern Historical Press. Until the establishment of county courts in South Carolina in 1785, all deeds were recorded in Charleston. The original deed books remain in the Office of the Register of Mesne Conveyance in the Charleston County Court House. I have prepared the abstracts in this volume from microfilm of those deed books. While the deeds in these deed books (F-4 through X-4) were *recorded* between 1773 and 1778, within these deed books are instruments dating from a much earlier time, some as early as 1706. Additionally, the derivation clauses in many deeds trace titles to early land grants, some during the proprietary period (prior to 1720). One will note that there are often several deed books containing deeds recorded in the same years. There are also occasional notations, especially in the case of mortgages, dated later than the recording dates of the deeds or mortgages. After the border surveys between the two Carolinas in 1764 and 1772, many lands formerly deemed to be in North Carolina fell into South Carolina. For that reason some deeds refer to lands granted by North Carolina, sometimes called "north patents." For the same reason, some deeds formerly recorded in North Carolina, particularly in Tryon County, were re-recorded in the Charleston deed books.

The old forms of lease and release were still common in the period covered by these abstracts. There is no particular significance to this form, the lease usually dated one day prior to the release. Together, the lease and release should be considered one instrument. Both lease and release have been examined for these abstracts, because the same information is not always recorded in both. Frequently, the wife signed only the release portion of the deed. The release usually gives a more complete chain of title and a more complete description of the tract conveyed in the instrument. Sometimes dower relinquishments by the wives of the grantors were recorded in a paragraph at the end of the deed or as a separate instrument following the deed and these are included. There are also separate volumes of dower relinquishments, which volumes are now preserved in the South Carolina Archives and indexed in the Archives' COM Index.

In the Colonial period, South Carolina had only four counties, which extended from the sea to the mountains: Granville, Colleton, Berkeley, and Craven. Craven County, being all of South Carolina north of the Santee River, was the largest county by area. The Santee River did not extend into the upper (western) part of South Carolina. The Congaree River may have been used as the line between Craven and Berkeley counties and further west, the Saluda River was considered an extension of the Santee River. However, sometimes the Broad River was used as the dividing line. Therefore, the area between the Broad and Saluda might be considered either Craven County or Berkeley County. The entire province was also divided into parishes. While they were not quite so meaningful in the western part of South Carolina, the parishes were fairly distinct in the coastal area. Another political division was the circuit court district. South Carolina was divided into seven such districts in 1769: Ninety Six, Camden, Cheraw, Georgetown, Charleston, Orangeburg(h), and Beaufort. Some deeds contain all three designations: county, parish, and district. These designations, coupled with the watercourses mentioned in the deeds, are helpful in determining the present-day county location of many of the lands conveyed in the colonial deeds. Maps of the counties, parishes, and districts are included herein as an aid.

As anyone familiar with early records knows, variant spellings of names are frequently the rule rather than the exception. The spelling of the name of the original grantee recorded in a deed may be quite different from the name which appears on the grant for that tract. The description of the land and names of the adjacent land owners must frequently be examined to determine the location of the land. It is my hope that these abstracts will be an aid to genealogists and historians working in South Carolina's colonial period.

Brent H. Holcomb
September 10, 1993

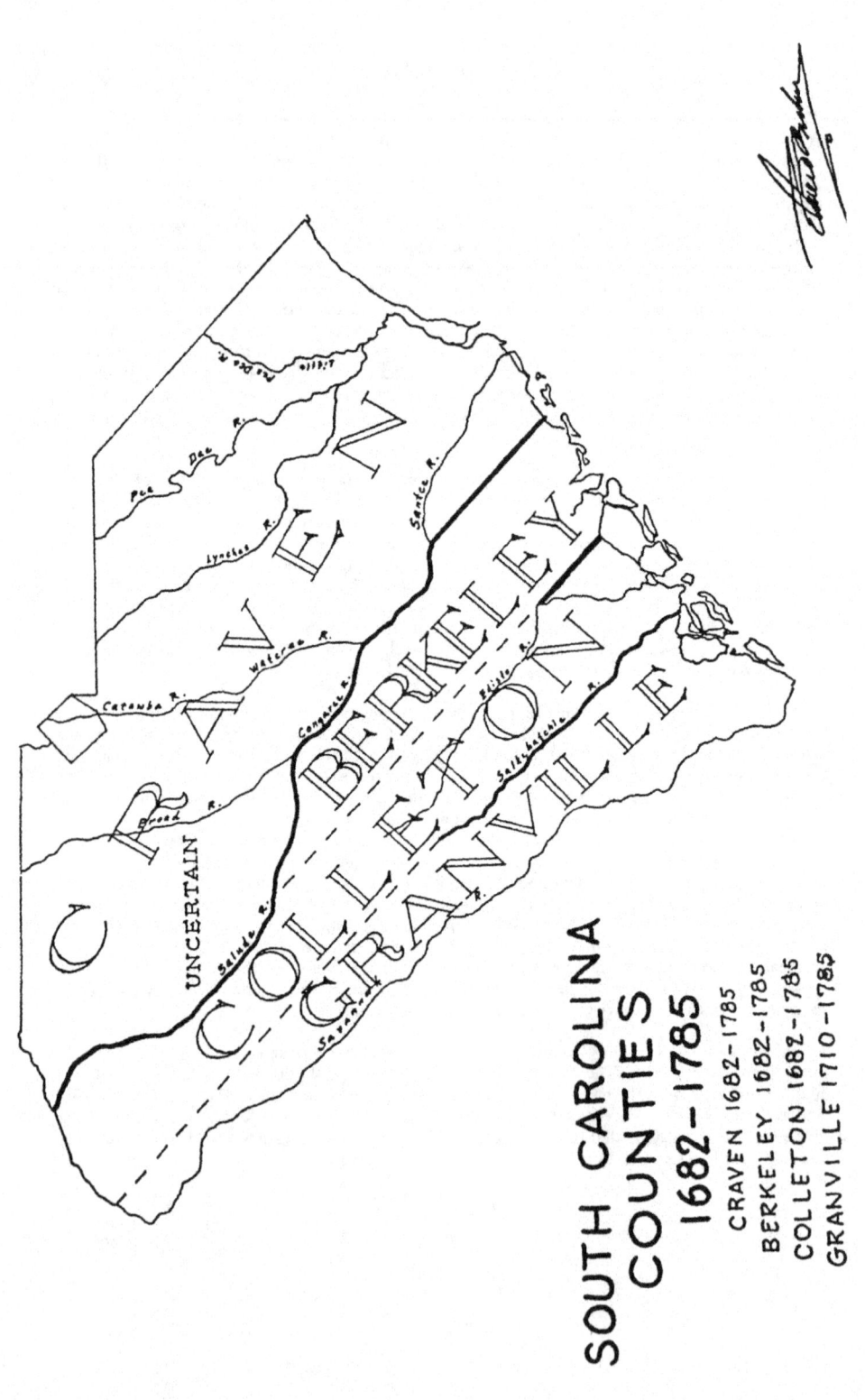

PARISHES OF SOUTH CAROLINA

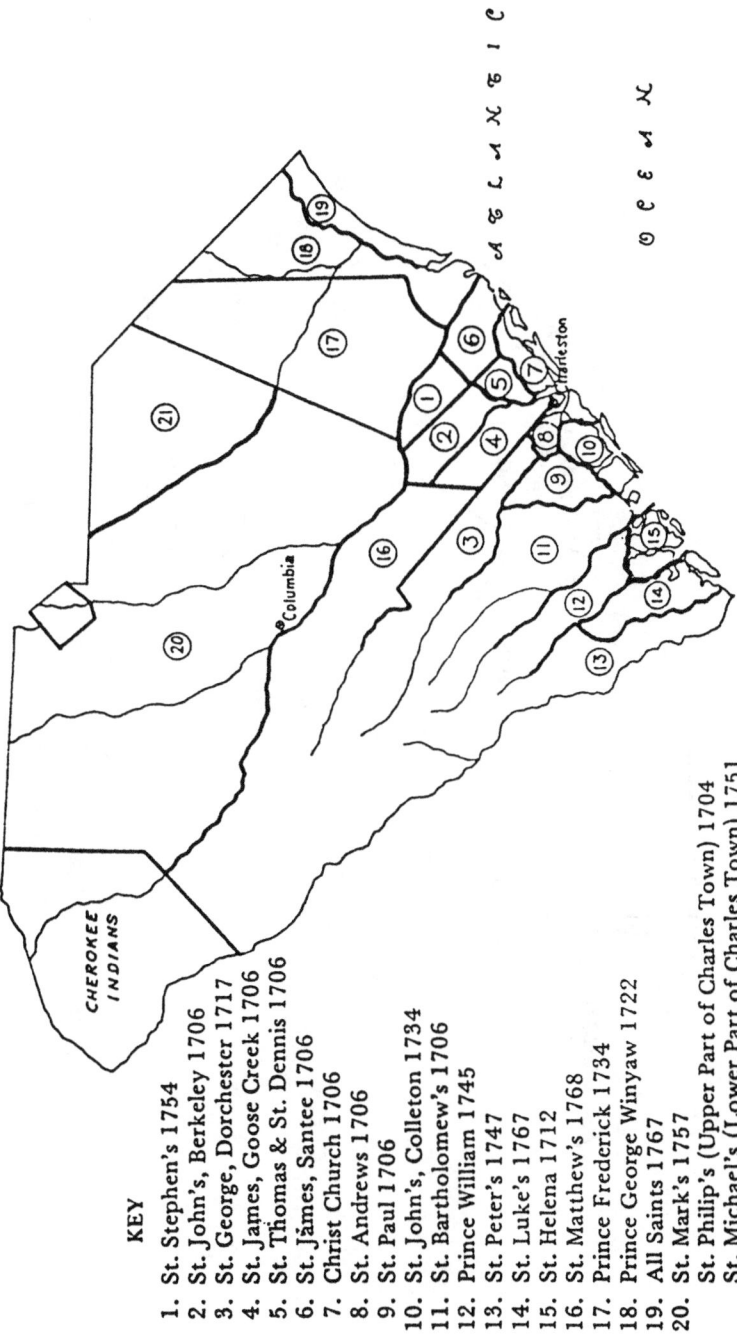

KEY
1. St. Stephen's 1754
2. St. John's, Berkeley 1706
3. St. George, Dorchester 1717
4. St. James, Goose Creek 1706
5. St. Thomas & St. Dennis 1706
6. St. James, Santee 1706
7. Christ Church 1706
8. St. Andrews 1706
9. St. Paul 1706
10. St. John's, Colleton 1734
11. St. Bartholomew's 1706
12. Prince William 1745
13. St. Peter's 1747
14. St. Luke's 1767
15. St. Helena 1712
16. St. Matthew's 1768
17. Prince Frederick 1734
18. Prince George Winyaw 1722
19. All Saints 1767
20. St. Mark's 1757
    St. Philip's (Upper Part of Charles Town) 1704
    St. Michael's (Lower Part of Charles Town) 1751

BY ELMER ORIS PARKER

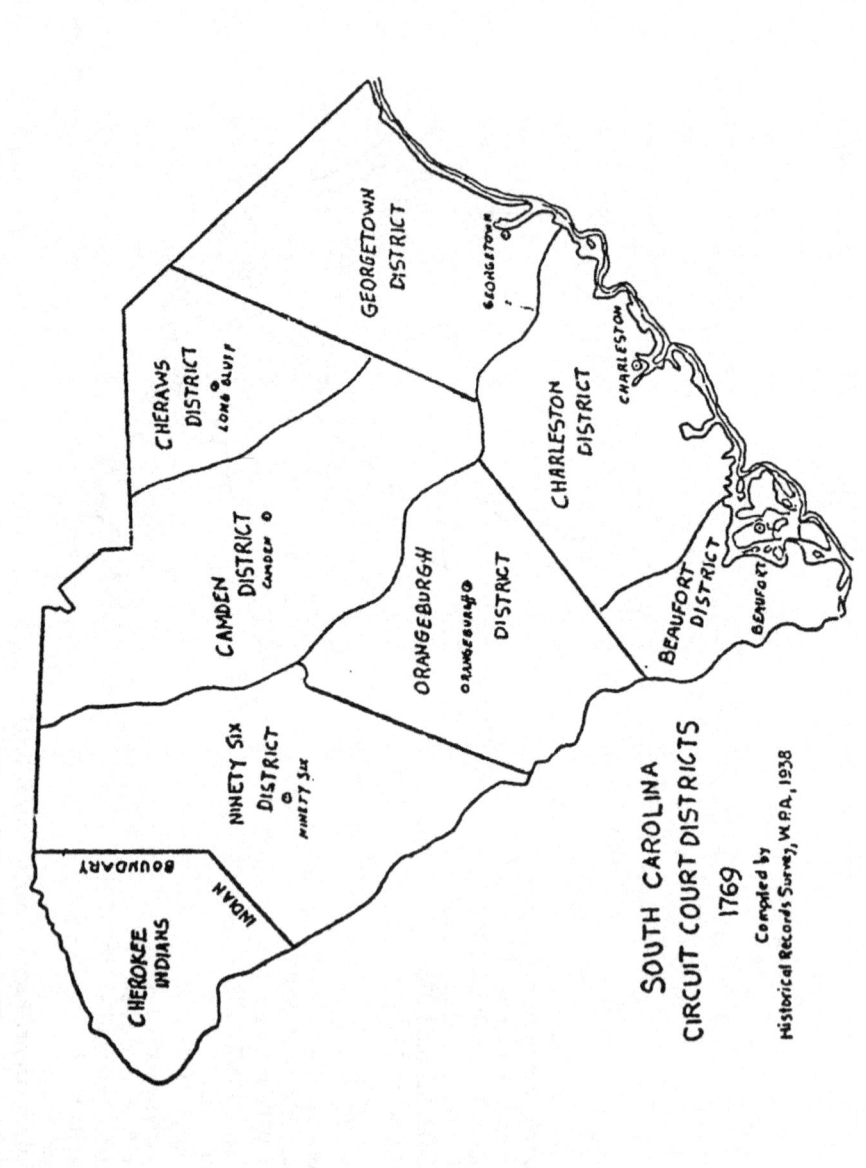

SOUTH CAROLINA DEED ABSTRACTS

F-4, 1-2: 9 Feb 1771, Samuel Williams of Craven County, Province of SC, to George Hicks of same, for £1500 current money, tract on both sides of Naked Creek, 800 acres granted to Thomas Crawford 29 April 1768 by Gov. Montague, entered in Book H No. 8, page 452, 1 July 1768, by deed from said Thomas Crawford 17 Dec 1768 to Samuel Williams. Samll Williams (LS), Martha Williams (M) (LS), Wit: Charles Bedingfield, Reuben Taylor. Proved in "Carraw" District by the oath of Reuben Taylor before Phil: Pledger, 4 March 1773. Recorded 15 June 1773.

F-4, 2-4: 7 Dec 1771, Michael Griffiths of Parish of St. Davids, Province of SC, to George Hicks, planter, of same province & parish, for £1300 current money, 300 acres being the upper part of a tract of 400 acres in the Welch Tract, surveyed for James Griffiths in his life time who was supposed to be dead before any Grant passed for the same, said 300 acres on Pee Dee, adj. John Hicks's land, and the other part of said tract of 10 acres granted to Samuel Griffiths, which said 300 acres was granted to Elizabeth Griffith widow, James Griffith, Michael Griffiths, and William Griffiths, son of James Griffiths deceased by Gov. Glenn, 28 Nov 1747; part of said 300 acres was granted by a Joint Deed by James Griffith & Elizabeth Griffith, James Griffith Junr & Mary Griffiths, 1 Dec 1760, recorded in Book C No. 3 pages 575 & 577, 90 Feb 1765 to Michael Griffith and 75 acres was sold by Samuel Griffith being the Lawfull Heir of William Griffith Deceas'd by deed of conveyance to Michl. Griffith 12 Dec 1771 not yet recorded, and 75 acres granted unto Michl. Griffith. Michael Griffiths (LS), Ann Griffiths (X) (LS), Wit: James Roe, James Hicks, William Smith. Proved in Craven County by the oath of James Hicks, 14 Nov 1772, before Arthur Hart, J.P. Recorded 15 June 1773.

F-4, 4-5: South Carolina, Grenville County. 30 Oct 1770, James Cane of province aforesaid to Thomas Waters of same, by grant from George III 19 Sept 1770 to James Cane, 150 acres on Savanna River, adj. Great Falls on said River, and vacant land, now for £100 current money to Thomas Waters. James Cane (I) (LS), Wit: Andrew Stephens, Charles Evans. Frances Cane, wife of James Cane, relinquished dower in Grenville County 30 Oct 1770 before Frederick Winter, J.P. Proved 11 April 1772 by the oath of Charles Evans before Frederick Winter, J.P. Recorded 15 June 1773.

F-4, 6-10: 8 April 1773, Barbary Everin of Charles Town, South Carolina, to Peter Black of Berkly County, for £250 current money, tract on north side Saluda River on the mouth of Beaver Dam Creek, 100 acres granted to said Barbary Everin 11 July 1754. Barbary Everin (+) (LS), Wit: Jas. Wright, John Bunkart, Peter Wealth. Proved 8 April 1773 by the oath of Peter Wealth before Thomas Grimball, Junr, Esqr., J. P., in Charles Town District. Recorded 17 June 1773.

F-4, 10-16: Lease & Release. 26 & 27 Nov 1772, the Rev. Robert Smith and Alexander Gillon of Charles Town, South Carolina, only acting and qualified Executors of last will & testament of Richard Beresford, late of said Town and province, Esquires, Deceased, to Thomas Harris, for £2410 current money, four lots in Charles Town, numbers 256, 257, 258, and 259, and said Richard Beresford did divide and lay out the said four lots into thirty smaller pieces or parcels agreeable to t plat thereof; on 8 July 1772 duly executed his last will and testament and after the several legacies, devises, and bequests, named and appointed his wife Sarah Beresford during her Widowhoood executrix and Christopher Gadsden, Thomas Smith of Broad-Street, and his sons when they respectively attain the age of twenty one years executors, to dispose of all the rest of his estate both real and personal within five years of his decease, and said Richard Beresford in some short time after he had so made and executed his said last will & testament departed this life; Robert Smith and Alexander Gillon in pursuance of the direction and after publick notice on 26 day of Nov expose to sale all that piece or parcel of land in said platt, Number One, bounding on King Street, on lands of Caleb Easton deceased. Robert Smith (LS), Alexander Gillon (LS), Wit: William Cripps, Peter Meurset. Proved in Charles Town District by the oath of Peter Meurset before William Rugeley, J.P., 9 April 1773. Sarah Beresford, widow relict of Richard Beresford, relinquished dower 27 Nov 1772. Recorded 18 June 1773.

F-4, 17-21: Lease & Release. 3 Oct 1772, Philotheos Chiffelle of Charles Town, merchant, to William Logan of same, merchant, for £4120 current money, six acres in St. Bartholomews Parish, Colleton County on Bay Street of the Village of Jacksonburgh, adj. lands lately belonging to James Postell, Pon Pon River. Philotheos Chiffelle (LS), Wit: J. Hirst, Pou Porcher Junr. Proved by the oath of Joshua Hirst before Wm. Rugeley, J.P., in Charles Town District, __ April 1773. Recorded 19 June 1773.

SOUTH CAROLINA DEED ABSTRACTS 1773-1778

F-4, 22-23: South Carolina. Articles of agreement 19 March 1773 between James Atkins of said province, planter, and William Garner also of same, whereas some time in the month of April 1772, James Atkins did sell to said William Garner a certain tract of land in St. Bartholomews Parish in Colleton County and whereas one John Mowett claims or pretends to claim part of said plantation and has in fact instituted a Bill in Chancery for the Recovery thereof, and whereas the said James Atkins hath agreed to sell the land hereafter mentioned to the said William Garner in fee simple by way of indemnity to compensate him in damage for the loss of all or any part of the said land conveyed as aforesaid should said John Mowett recover the same at law or in equity, tract of 180 acres in St. Bartholomews Parish, Colleton County on Cockholds Creek, adj. Mrs. Gibbes land, said James Atkins's land, John Rivers's land. James Atkins (LS), Wit: Patrick Turnbull, Zac. Ladson. Proved by the oath of Zacheriah Ladson before James Hamilton, J.P. 16 April 1773. Recorded 23 June 1773.

F-4, 24-27: 28 Jan 1772, Roger Pinckney, Provost Marshal of the Province of SC to Philotheos Chiffelle of Charles Town. Whereas Henry Webster of Jacksonburg was lately seized of six acres in St. Bartholomews Parish in Colleton County on Bay Street of the Village of Jacksonburg, adj. lands lately of James Postell, Pon Pon River, and by lease & release 28 & 29 April 1769 under the hand of James Stobo and also of a certain piece of land of one Road and twenty Six Perches in the same, by lease & release from George Jackson 17 & 18 Sept 1771, and said Henry Webster by a certain bond dated 1 June 1769 acknowledged himself to be bound to William Ancrum, George Ancrum & Philotheos Chiffelle of Charles Town, Merchants, for £10,000 for the payment of £5000 with interest, and in the court of common pleas at August term in 1771 said Ancrums and Philotheos Chiffelle recovered a judgment against Henry Webster, now the tract sold at publick sale for £4120. Roger Pinckney, Pro. Mar. (LS), Wit: Hopson Pinckney, Joseph Millgan.

F-4, 28-31: 28 May 1772, Lewis Committer and his wife Ratchel, Daniel Orange Bowman and his wife Barbara of St. George Parish, Berkly County, to John Fisher of Orangeburgh in St. Mathews parish, Berkly County, merchant, for £50 current money, the undivided two-thirds of 100 acres in Orangeburgh Township, Berkley County, bounding on land granted to Martin Johude, the north branch of Edisto or Pon Pon River, and vacant land, and also the undivided two-thirds of a town lott in Orangeburgh of half an acre known as number 185, bounding on number 184 granted to Hans Balzeher, on number 282 granted to Charles Hutto, on lot 286 not granted and on a street, it being the third parts of that tract of 100 acres and town lott of half an acre granted to John George Kerch 10 March 1734/4 recorded in Book FF, page 210, which said John George Kerch was the father of the above mentioned Ratchel Committer and Barbara Bowman and died intestate without male issue, leaving only three daughters Frances Owens & the above mentioned Ratchel and Barbara who are consequently his heirs at law. Lewis Committer (LS), Rachel Committer (+) (LS), Daniel Orange Boman (LS), Barbary Boman (+) (LS), Wit: Jno Pendarvis, James Dewitt, Sarah Dewitt. Proved 12 June 1772 before Lewis Golson, Esqr., J. P., in Berkley and Colleton Countys by the oath of James Dewit.

F-4, 32-33: 27 March 1770, John Rutledge, Esqr., of Charles Town, to John Fisher of Orangeburgh, merchant, for £5 money of province, 750 acres in Berkley County being the southward part of a tract of 1500 acres granted to Thomas Bee 19 Feb 1767 adj. Hugh McIntoshes, John Crieghton's, and above mentioned John Fishers land, on Edisto River, and remainder of the said authentic tract and to be divided and separated from the said original tract by a line on said River of a right line between a Cypress the corner of Henry Felders and the tract above mentioned, and a tupelow the corner of Hugh McIntoshes land and said Thomas Bees land. John Rutledge (LS), Wit: John Shapland, Benjamin Farar. (Plat included showing land of John Fisher & Luke Patrick, land laid to Joseph Booker, land laid out to John Creighton, Hugh McIntosh.) Proved 1 January 1771 by the oath of Benjamin Farar before William Thomson, J. P. Recorded 22 June 1773.

F-4, 34-36: 10 Sept 1771, William Blickenden of Colleton County, Province of SC, planter, to John Fisher of Orangeburg, merchant, by a certain grant 21 August 1767 to William Blickendin, a tract of 200 acres in Colleton County, bounding on all sides by vacant lands, recorded in Book BBB, page 200, for £170. William Blitchenden. Wit: William Mitchell, Peter Daly, John Shieder. Proved 2 July 1772 by the oath of William Mitchell before John Bowie, J.P. in Colleton County. Recorded 23 June 1773.

SOUTH CAROLINA DEED ABSTRACTS 1773-1778

F-4, 36-39: 23 Dec 1769, Jacob Jehudi of Orangeburgh Township, Berkley County, planter, to John Fisher of the Town of Orangeburg, for £20, 300 acres in Orangeburgh Township, Berkley County, bounded on land granted to John Kirch, said John Fisher, the north fork of Edisto or Pon Pon River, and also one Town Lot in Orangeburgh number 279, bounded on Number 282 granted to Isaac Hotto, number 278 granted to George Shower, number 280, on Windzor Street, all of that tract of 300 acres and town lot granted to Martin Jehudi 1 March 1734/4 and recorded in Book EE folio 205, which said Martin Jehudi was the father of above mentioned Jacob Jehudi who died intestate and he the said Jacob Jehudi being the Elder Son and Heir at Law. Jacob Jehudi (+) (LS). Wit: William Mitchell, Henry Grissendaner, Baltis Inabnit. Proved 29 Jan 1770 by the oath of William Mitchell before Christopher Rowe, Esqr., J.P. in Berkley County. Recorded 23 June 1773.

F-4, 39-40: James Atkins and William Atkins, both of Province of SC, planters, bound to William Garner of same in the sum of £15,280, 19 March 1773, to perform the covenants, etc., mentioned in certain articles of agreement between James Atkins and William Garner. James Atkins (LS), William Atkins (LS), Wit: Patrick Turnball, Zac. Ladson. Proved in Colleton County by the oath of Zecheriah Ladson before James Hamilton, J.P., 16 April 1773. Recorded 24 June 173.

F-4, 40-44: Lease & Release. 15 & 16 July 1772, Anthony Gautier (Gotier) of Savannah, Province of Georgia, and Jane his wife, to John Louis Bourquin of Purysburgh, Province of SC, Esquire, for £25 sterling, tract of land in the Township of Purysburgh, Parish of St. Peter, 50 acres, adj. land of Daniel Vernezobre, David Wicolett, and said John Lewis Bourquin. Anthoine Gautier/ Antoine Gotier (LS), Jane Gotier (X) (LS), Wit: Willm. Young, David Gotiere. Proved in Georgia by the oath of William Young of Savannah, Gent., 31 Aug 1772 before David Giroud, J.P. Recorded 25 June 1773.

F-4, 45-50: Lease & Release. 26 & 27 Apr 1773, David Maull of Charlestown, Taylor, to William Alder of the Island of Grenada (now being at Charles Town) for £700 lawful money, tract of 300 acres in Craven County on a branch of Little River called Sandy Run, bounded by land vacant at the time of the original survey (for John Toles which was 25 Feb 1768), another tract of 300 acres adj. land laid out to Joseph Johnson, being the tract of 150 acres next herein before mentioned, the original survey for John Monk which was 12 March 1768, said three several plantations or tract of land are contiguous and granted to said David Maull and are supposed in the grants thereof to be in Berkley County but found since the late survey of said province to be within the limits of Craven County. David Maull (LS), Wit: Davd. Lessly, James Moore. Proved 28 Apr 1773 by the oath of James Moore before Wm. Nisbet, J. P., Charles Town District. Recorded 26 June 1773.

F-4, 50-54: Lease & release. 15 & 16 June 1772, Jacob Zahler of St. Bartholomews Parish, Colleton County, planter, and Lewis Stapf of same, carpenter, to Daniel Strobel of same, planter, for £3000, 1500 acres In Prince Williams Parish, Granville County, adj. John MacTeers land, on Salt Catchers River, adj. land granted to James Ferguson. Jacob Zahler (LS), Lewis Stapf (LS), Wit: John Brown, Thomas Patterson. Proved by the oath of Thomas Patterson before Stephen Bull, J.P. in Granville County. Recorded 28 June 1773.

F-4, 55-57: Lease & release. 17 & 18 May 1771, Philip Pledger of Parish of St. Davids, Province of SC, to Betty Wise of same, for £5, 150 acres on North side Pedee River, adj. Thomas Wade and vacant land, granted 3 Nov 1770 to Philip Pledger. Phil Pledger (LS), Wit: N. Bedggood, Joseph Pledger, Thomas Jones. Proved by the oath of Nicholas Bedggood before Alexander Mackintosh, J.P. in Craven County. Recorded 28 June 1773.

F-4, 58-61: Lease & release. 28 & 29 April 1773, William Glen of Charles Town, merchant, to the Honorable Andrew Irvin, Esqr., for £1500, 1500 acres in Granville County on Coosawhatchie and Jully Finny Swamps, granted by George II about 29 Nov 1750 to Jonathan Russ, adj. Colonel Prioleau, Thomas Elliot. William Glen (LS), Wit: Geo. Duncan, Wills. Alder. Proved 30 April 1773 by the oath of Williams Alder before Wm. Nisbett, J.P. Recorded 29 June 1773.

F-4, 61-63: Lease & release. 15 & 16 July 1765, John Lamar of the county of Granville, Province of Sc, to George Rodgers of same, for £300 SC money, tract granted 9 Jan 1755 to John Perkins, 200 acres in Granville county on Stephens Creek, adj. John Nolloboys land. John Lamar (LS), Wit:

SOUTH CAROLINA DEED ABSTRACTS 1773-1778

Thos Roberts, William Sinquefield, Solomon Newsum. Proved 14 Oct 1772 by the oath of Solomon Newsom, Jr., before LeRoy Hammond, J.P. in Granville County. Recorded 30 June 1773.

F-4, 64-67: Lease & release. 2 & 3 March 1773, Charles Warnock of Parish of St. Marks, Province of SC, planter, and Elizabeth his wife, to Abraham Warnock of same, planter, for £200, tract granted 20 Oct 1772 to Charles Warnock, 150 acres on Duglass Swamp in St. Marks Parish, bounded on all sides by vacant land. Charles Warnock (LS), Elizabeth Warnock (LS), Wit: John Storey, Marey Storey. Proved 28 Apr 1773 by the oath of John Storey before John Egan, J.P. in Craven County. Recorded 30 June 1773.

F-4, 67-71: Lease & release. 7 & 8 Jan 1773, George Long of St. Bartholomews Parish, Province of SC, to Adam Ulmer of Prince Williams Parish, for £55, 150 acres in Granville County on Duck Branch waters of Coosawhatchie River bounded on all sides by vacant land, granted 13 May 1768 to said George Long. George Long (LS), Wit: J. Sacheveul, John Bodett. Proved 27 Feb 1773 by the oath of John Sacheveull before Thos. Hutchinson, J.P. in Colleton County. Recorded 3 July 1773.

F-4, 71-75: Lease & release. 30 June and 1 July 1769, Elias Jaudon of Prince Williams Parish, Colleton County, planter, to David Ferguson of St. Bartholomews Parish, planter, for £300, 558 acres in Colleton County in St. Bartholomews Parish, on Black Creek out of Saltcatcher River Swamp, adj. lands of John Hunt, Esqr., land laid out to William McKenzie. Elias Jaudon (LS), Wit: James Hamelton, John Lambright, Andrew Anderson. Plat included by Alex. M. Forster, D. S., "The above is a general Plat of the undermentioned Lands viz 158 acres being part of a tract laid out to Mr. Elias Jaudon for 400 acres 10 June 1765, out of which tract a prior grant to Mr. Wm. McKenzie cuts out 202[?] acres, two others tracts laid out to the sd. Elias Jaudon for 200 acres each one laid out 10 June 1766[?] and the other 30th July 1766.... 18 January 1769." Proved in Colleton County by John Lambright 13 June 1772 before James Donnom, J.P. Recorded 7 July 1773.

F-4, 75-79: Lease & release. 4 & 5 Dec 1772, Rawlins Lowndes of Charles Town, Esquire, to Rowland Rugeley of same, Gentleman, for £7350, 14 acres on Charles Town Neck in Berkley County adj. lands of said Rawlins Lowndes, line ranging the present Kitchen intersecting the Broad Road & the Lane which divides the land of Daniel Cannon from the land of said Lowndes, land late of Colonel John Smith deceased, Barnard Elliot. Rawlins Lowndes (LS), Wit: Jer'h Theus, Thos Shubrick Junr. [Proving and recording dates not indicated]

F-4, 80-82: Lease & release. 23 & 24 Jan 1769, Phillip Fagans of Berkly County, Province of SC, planter, to Jonathan Taylor of same, planter, for £200, tract granted 19 Aug 1768 to Phillip Fagans, 200 acres in the fork of Broad and Saludy Rivers on a small branch of Saludy called Bush Creek. Phillip Fagans (LS), Martha Fagans (W) (LS), Wit: Saml. Kelly, Saml. Newman. Proved by the oath of Saml. Kelly before Jas. Lindly, J.P. in Granville County, 25 Nov 1768. Recorded 10 July 1773.

F-4, 83-85: Lease & release. 13 & 14 July 1772, William Gillum of St. Marks Parish, Wheel-wright, and Hannah his wife, to Jonathan Taylor of said parish and province, farmer, for £150 current money, 250 acres in the forks between Broad and Saludy Rivers on a small branch of Bush Creek in Berkly County, part of 500 acres granted to said William Gillum 15 Feb 1769, said 250 acres adjacent to John Gilder, John Ridgdell. William Gillum (X) (LS), Hanah Gilum (X) (LS), Wit: Moses Embree, Robert Gilliam, Rachel LittleJohn. (Plat included by Jno Caldwell, D. Surv.) Proved by the affirmation of Moses Embree, one of the people called Quakers, in Craven County, 14 July 1772 before Jno Caldwell, J.P. Recorded 12 July 1773.

F-4, 86-89: Lease & release. 17 & 18 May 1773, Marmaduke Bell of Province of East Florida, to Joseph Huggins of Prince George Parish, Craven County, for £1000 current money, 311 acres on north side Santee River in Prince George Parish, Craven County, adj. land of Joseph Huggins, land granted to Joseph Huggins deceased, land granted to John Bell, said tract granted 20 June 1764 to Marmaduke Bell. Marmaduke Bell (LS), Wit: Thomas Swaine, James Campbell. Proved by the oath of Thomas Swaine before Job Rothmahler, Geo. Town District [no date]. Recorded 13 July 1773.

F-4, 90-94: 18 Sept 1771, Alexander Swinton of Prince Fredericks Parish, Craven County, planter, and Elizabeth his wife, to Margaret Swinton of Charles Town, spinster, that William Swinton father to the said Alexander and Margaret Swinton, did by his last will and testament devise to his daughter Margaret and her heirs six lots of land in George Town and province but having neglected to obtain titles for the same from the trustees to the said six lots the said Alexander Swinton did apply for and obtained deeds for the said six lots 29 March 1754 in order to comply with the intentions of his said Father and for £10 current money, lot in George Town number 18, lot number 57, lot number 176, lot number 177, lot number 200, and lot number 201. Alexr. Swinton (LS), Elizabeth Swinton (LS), Wit: Thos Potts, Peter Lequeux Junr, John Moore Junr (+). Lease proved 18 Dec 1771 by the oath of Thomas Potts before Job Rothmahler, J.P. in Craven County. Release proved 2 Oct 1771 by the oath of Peter Lequeux Junr before John Cantzon, J.P. in Craven County.

F-4, 94-95: South Carolina. George Pawley & Alexander Swinton of Winyaw in Craven County, Gent., for £10 to Archibald McDonald of same place, Gent., lot in George Town, Craven County, number 200, dated 29 March 1754. George Pawley (LS), Alexander Swinton (LS), Wit: Jno McDonald, Wm. James.

Archd. McDonald for £10 to Alexr. Swinton, lot number 200 in George Town, 19 March 1754. Archd. McDonald. Wit: Jno McDonald, Wm. James.

South Carolina, Craven County. Joseph Dubourdieu swears that altho he was not a subscribing witness to the with and above instrumts. of writing yet he was personally present and did see the execution of them and that he also saw the Subscribing witnesses (both of whom are now dead) sign their names to the same, 14 May 1772, before Job Rothmahler, J.P. Recorded 15 July 1773.

F-4, 96-99: Similar deeds from same parties for lots number 201, 177, 176, and 57 in George Town.

F-4, 100-104: Lease & release. 21 & 22 May 1773, Griffin Nunry of Craven County, Wheelwright, and Mary his wife, to John Brynan of Charles Town, Merchant, for £20 current money, 100 acres in Craven County on the North side of Peedee River adj. William Meegees land, all other sides on vacant land. Grifen Nunry (LS), Mary Nunry (X) (LS), Wit: William Kenny, Ann Green (+). Proved 31 May 1773 by the oath of William Kenney before William Nisbett, Esqr., J. P. in Charles Town Dist. Recorded 19 July 1773.

F-4, 104-108: Lease & release. 20 Dec 1770, James Wright of Turkey Creek, Craven County, Province of SC, to Isaac Sadler of same, for £700, 200 acres on Turkey Creek, granted to said James Wright by patent August 1763. James Wright (LS), Hannah Wright (LS), Wit: James Murphy, John Brown, James Brown. Proved by the oath of James Murphy before Jo. Brown, J. P. in Craven County, 13 Jan 1771. Recorded 20 July 1773.

F-4, 108-111: Lease & release in trust. 15 & 16 Oct 1771, John Mitchell of Charles Town, Gentleman, to Thomas Skottowe, Esqr., Secretary of the Province aforesaid, for £5, three acres in the Township of Orangeburgh whereon and about which the Court House and Gaol now Stands being pat and parcel of 400 acres of land originally granted to William Mitchell, father of the above named John Mitchell, and by him conveyed to the said John Mitchell by lease & release 29 & 30 May in the present year. John Mitchell (LS), Wit: Frans. Bremar, Jonathan Clarke Junr, Daniel Ferguson. Proved by the oath of Daniel Ferguson 16 Oct 1771 before John Troup, J.P. Recorded 24 July 1773.

F-4, 112-114: Lease & release. 10 March 1765, Malachia Murphey Senr. of St. Marks Parish, Province of SC, planter, to James Sanders of same place, planter, for £200 lawful money, 150 acres on NE side Pedee River in Craven County adj. lands of William Lacey, Malachia Murphey. Malachia Murfe (LS), Wit: Gid. Gibson, Jno. Gibson. Proved before Claudius Pegues, J.P. in Craven County, by the oath of Gideon Gibson, 17 March 1765. Recorded 26 July 1773.

F-4, 115-117: Lease & release. 23 & 24 April 1765, Richard Blake of Christ Church Parish, Berkly County, planter, to James Saunders of Prince Frederick Parish, Craven County, for £100 lawful money of SC, 195 acres in Craven County on SW side Peedee River in the Welsh Tract adj. said river, land laid out for John Dexter, Black Creek, and land not then laid out. Richard Blake Junr. (LS), Wit: Daniel Cannon, Jno. Calvert. Proved in Charles Town District, 3 June 1773, before Thomas Turner, J.P., by the oath of Daniel Cannon. Recorded 27 July 1773.

SOUTH CAROLINA DEED ABSTRACTS 1773-1778

F-4, 118-120: Lease & release. 26 & 27 Sept 1760, William Terrell of the Welch Tract, County of Craven, Province of SC, planter, and Anne his wife, to Robert Blair of same county & province, for £200 current money of SC, land granted 6 Dec 1744 to said William Terrell, 100 acres in Craven County bounding to the NE on Pedee River and all other sides vacant land. William Terrell (LS), Ann Ferrell (O) (LS), Wit: Mathew McCreest, William Besley. Proved by the oath of William Besely before Alexander Mackintosh, J. P. for Craven County, 19 March 1770. Recorded 27 July 1773.

F-4, 120-123: Lease & release. 24 & 25 Oct 1760, Hardy Councell of Waccamaw in Craven County, Province of SC, planter, and Betrix his wife, to Robt. Blair of same, for £400 SC money, 200 acres granted 19 Oct 1748 to said Hardy Councell adj. land of William Evans, said Hardy Councell, John Mackelmore. Hardy Councell (LS), Betrix Councell (X) (LS), Wit: John McLamore, John Scott. Proved in Craven County before William Lord, J.P., by the oath of John Scott, 1 June 1761. Recorded 17 Nov 1773.

F-4, 124-127: Lease & release. 1 & 2 Dec 1769, Allan Brown & Esther his wife of the Welch Tract in Craven County, Province of SC, planter, to Robt. Blair of same place, planter, for £150 SC money, 150 acres granted 20 Nov 1750 to John Westfield in the Welch Tract bounded on the Northwest by Pedee river adj. Godfrey Bone's land. Allan Brown (X) (LS), Esther Brown (LS), Wit: Enoch John, Francis McLemore (M). Proved in Craven County before Alexander McKintosh, J. P., by the oath of Francis McLemore, 17 March 1770. Recorded 17 Nov 1773.

F-4, 127-129: 12 Feb 1773, Lewis Stapf of Parish of Prince William, County of Granville, Province of SC, Carpenter, and Margaret his wife, to George Rentz of St. Bartholomews Parish, Colleton County, for £450 SC money, eight lots in the village of Jacksonborough in the parish of St. Bartholomew, numbers 74, 75, 76, 77, 86, 87, 89, each lot containing one hundred fee front on Markett Street, 218 feet in depth. Lewis Stapf (LS), Margaret Stapf (LS), Wit: Jno. Macter, Thos Patterson. Proved by the oath of Thos Patterson before John Hunt, Esqr., J. P. for Colleton County, 27 April 1773. Recorded 16 March 1774.

F-4, 130-133: Lease & release. 23 & 24 Nov 1773, William Wright of St. Marks Parish, SC, planter, to Asa Dinkins of St. Marks Parish, planter, for £500 SC money, 100 acres in Craven County on E side Wateree River in the High Hills of Santee, adj. land of Henry Pits, Isaac Helton, granted to William Dinkin of St. Marks Parish, 5 March 1770. William Wright (LS), Wit: David Gilbert, John Llewellen, David Jackson. Proved by the oath of David Gilbert before Wood Furman, J.P. for Craven County, 23 Nov 1773. Recorded 15 Dec 1773.

F-4, 133-136: Lease & release. 19 & 20 Nov 1773, William Dinkin of St. Marks Parish, SC, planter, to Wm. Wright of St. Marks Parish, planter, for £500 SC money, 100 acres on E side Wateree River on the High Hills of Santee adj. land of Henry Pits, Isaac Helton. William Dinkin (LS), Wit: John Llewellen, David Jackson, David Gilbert. Proved by the oath of David Gilbert before Woord Furman, J.P. for Craven County, 23 Nov 1773. Recorded 15 Dec 1773.

F-4, 136-141: Lease & release. 2 & 3 Nov 1773, David Tharin of Charles Town, SC, Gent., to John Creighton of Parish of St. James, Innholder, for £4000 SC money, 36 acres in the Parish of St. James Goose Creek, on the north side of the Great Road Leading from Charles Town, adj. land of John Wragg, Esquire, land now of Daniel Legare Senior, known by the name of the Old Quarter House. Daniel Tharin (LS), Wit: John Troup, John Giles. Proved in Charles Town District by the oath of John Troup, Esqr., before William Rugeley, J.P. Recorded 17 Jan 1774.

F-4, 141-142: 8 October 1771, Thomas Wade of Craven County, SC, to William Murrell, for £50 proc. money, land in Tryon County, North Carolina, on north side of Broad River about one Mile above Smiths ford, 100 acres granted to Henry Smith and by him conveyed to John Russell Junr of the said county, and by him conveyed to the said Thomas Smith [sic] by deed. Thos Wade (LS), Wit: Jacob Kendall Junr, Wm. Smith. North Carolina, Tryon County. The within deed and clarks certificate thereon was Duly entered in the Publick Register of said County 3 March 1772 in Book No 6. Thos Neall, Register. January Court 1772. The within Deed was proved in Open Court and Recorded in the Clarks Office. Ezekl. Polke. Recorded 17 Jan 1774.

SOUTH CAROLINA DEED ABSTRACTS 1773-1778

F-4, 142-144: 8 October 1771, Thomas Wade of Craven County, SC, to William Murrell of Gilford County, North Carolina, for £8 proc. money, land in Tryon County, North Carolina, on north side of Broad River on Howard [Howard's Creek], 250 acres granted to William Boggan 17 Nov 1764 and conveyed by deed from him to the said Thomas Wade. Thomas Wade. Wit: William Smith, Jacob Randall Junr. North Carolina Tryon County. January Court 1772. The within Deed was proved in Open Court and Recorded in the Clarks Office. Ezekl. Polke. The within deed and clarks certificate thereon was Duly entered in the Publick Register of said County 3 March 1772 in Book No 6. Thos Neall, Register. Recorded 17 Jan 1774.

F-4, 144-147: Lease & release by way of mortgage. 5 & 6 Oct 1773. James Christie of St. Pauls Parish, SC, planter, and Hepzibah his wife, to Miles Brewton of Charleston, bound in the sum of £5760 for the payment of £2880, mortgage of half a tract of 400 acres known by the name of Morris' Nook devised by the will of Thomas Elliott to his daughter Beulah the mother of the said Hepzibah in fee simple, by virtue of a writ of partition obtained from the court of common pleas of this province for Dividing between the said Hepzibah Christie by the name of Hepzibah Rose before her Marriage with the said James Christie and Beulah Fitch was allotted to the said Hepzibah as her moiety. James Christie (LS), Hephzibah Christie (LS), Wit: John Rutledge, Thos Shubrick Junr. Proved by the oath of Thos Shubrick Junr before William Rugeley, Esqr., J.P. in Berkley County, 5 Nov 1773. Recorded 18 Jan 1774.

F-4, 148-149: Alexander Adamson of Charles Town, SC, carpenter, bound to Edward Lightwood and Thomas Eveleigh of Charles Town, merchants, in the penalty of £1300 SC money, mortgage of part of a town lot in said town on which I now live on King Street, the whole of what land I bought of Christopher Fitzsimmons, also one negro slave Ben, dated 13 Jan 1773. Alexander Adamson (LS), Wit: Alexr. Horn, Tobias Cambridge. Proved in Charles Town District by the oath of Tobias Cambridge before Hopkin Price, J.P., 8 Nov 1773. Recorded 19 Jan 1774. Mortgage discharged 2 March 1774.

F-4, 149-151: 8 July 1773, Francis Wilson of Roan County, Province of North Carolina, Farmer, & Jain his wife, to John Timmons of Tyger River, Craven County, South Carolina, for £950 SC money, 1000 acres granted 26 Nov 1753 by Josiah Martin, Governor of NC, to Francis Wilson, on the north fork of Tyger River Lately of Anson County, Province of NC, by his Majestys Late Instructions has fell into the Province of SC. Francis Wilson (LS), Jain Wilson (l) (LS), Wit: Saml Hughey, Wm. Montgomery, James Wood. South Carolina, Ninety Six District. Proved by the oath of James Wood 7 Aug 1773 before William Wofford, J.P.

F-4, 152-155: Lease & release. 3 & 4 Feb 1772, Francis Brown of Parish of St. Davids, Province of SC, to John Chiles of Lunenburg County, Colony of Virginia, for £300 currency, 200 acres in the Parish of St. David, on SW side Pedee River called Savannah, granted 12 Oct 1770 to Francis Brown. Francis Brown (C) (LS), Wit: Dennis Golfen, Arthur Hart, Peter Gibbens. Proved by the oath of Arthur Hart in Craven County, SC, before Charles Augustus Steward, 23 Sept 1772. Recorded 19 Jan 1774.

F-4, 155-158: 6 March 1773, John Dooly, Eldest son of Patrick Dooly Deceased of Berkley County, Province of SC, planter, to Israel Gaunt of same province planter, for £30, 100 acres surveyed for Patrick Dooly, 2 Nov 1768, in Berkley County on a Branch of Bush River called Pallmetto branch, adj. Samuel Kelly, Israel Gaunt, John Raggins. John Dooly (LS), Wit: Thos Dooly, John Edwards, Thomas Mitchell. Proved by the oath of John Edwards before William Hausihl, J.P., 9 March 1773.

F-4, 158-161: Lease & release. 6 & 7 March 1772, Daniel Ellis of Province of Georgia, Parish of St. Pauls, to Thomas Harbit of Craven County, Province of SC, for £175, 100 acres on north side of Broad River on Brents branch, granted 7 Oct 1762 to Barbara Vanlerin, and whereas the said Barbary Vanlerin hath joined herself in Holy Matrimony unto Jacob Brown, and with the consent of his said wife did convey the said 100 acres to Gasper Nagerly by lease & release 15 & 16 March 1763. Daniel Ellis (LS), Wit:George Dawkins, James Beard, George Smith. Proved by the oath of George Dawkins 7 March 1772 before Michl. Dickert, J.P. Recorded 20 January 1772 [sic].

F-4, 161-165: Lease & release. 6 & 7 March 1772, Daniel Ellis of Province of Georgia, Parish of St. Pauls, to Thomas Harbit of Craven County, Province of SC, for £175, 50 acres in Craven County

SOUTH CAROLINA DEED ABSTRACTS 1773-1778

on north side of Broad River, adj. land of said Daniel Ellis, granted 29 Apr 1768 to Daniel Ellis, plat recorded in book CCC, page 111, and a memorial entered in Book H No. 8, page 457. Daniel Ellis, Wit: George Dawkins, James Beard, George Smith (+). Proved by the oath of George Dawkins 7 March 1772 before Michl. Dickert, J.P. Recorded 21 January 1774.

F-4, 165-166: 6 May 1773, John McKnitt Alexander of Mecklenburg Co., NC, to Hugh McCall of Craven County, SC, for £5 proc. money, 100 acres on stoney fork of Fishing Creek above the tract of land the said Hugh McCall now lives on, granted to said John McKnitt Alexander 27 Sept 1766 and number 474 duly of record. John McKnitt Alexander (LS), Wit: Saml Lusk, James Armstrong. Proved by the oath of Samuel Lusk before Dd. Gorden, J. P., 29 Nov 1773. Recorded 22 January 1774.

F-4, 166-168: 8 Sept 1772, John Miller of Parish of St. Marks, SC, planter, to John Mills of same parish, planter, for £100 SC money, 108 acres on waters of So fork of Fishing Creek and Rocky Creek in Craven County adj. land of Henry Culp, John McLilly. John Miller (LS), Wit: Hugh Whiteside, James McCluer. Proved in Craven County, SC, before James Patton, J.P., by the oath of Hugh Whiteside, 19 Sept 1772. Recorded 24 Jan 1774.

F-4, 168-170: 8 Sept 1772, Daniel Elliott and Elizabeth his wife of Parish of St. Mark, SC, planter, to John Miller of same, planter, for £100 SC money, 108 acres surveyed for Daniel Elliott 24 March 1770 on south side Fishing Creek between the lines of Archibald Elliott, James McCullouch, Joseph Gaston and George Craig. Daniel Elliott (LS), Elizabeth Elliott (E) (LS), Wit: Hugh Whiteside, Samuel Neeley. Proved in Craven County by the oath of Hugh Whiteside before James Patton, J.P., 19 Sept 1772. Recorded 24 Jan 1774.

F-4, 170-174: Lease & release. 10 & 13 July 1770, Samuel Glegney & Mary his wife of St. Marks Parish, Craven County, SC, weaver and spinster, to Archibald Paul of same, weaver, for £100, 100 acres granted to Scarborough Ginn, on a branch of Broad River called Jacksons Creek in St. Marks Parish, and Scarborough Ginn did make over her right & title to Samuel Glegney by lease and release 2 & 3 March 1768. Samuel Glegney (LS), Mary Glegney (+) (LS), Wit: Robt. Ellison, Wm. Ownes. Proved by the oath of Wm. Ownes before Robt. Ellison, a Magistrate for Comande District, 30 Oct 1773. Recorded 24 Jan 1774.

F-4, 174-178: Lease & release. 13 & 14 July 1772, Peter Horlbeck of Parish of St. George Dorchester, SC, Bricklayer, and Catherine his wife, to John Horlbeck of Charles Town, Bricklayer, for £1350, one half part of a town lott in Charles Town, number 282, now held by the said John & Peter Horlbeck as tenants, adj. land of Michael Kalteisen. Peter Horlbeck (LS), Catharine Horlbeck (LS), Wit: George Hahnbaum, John Hall. Proved in Chs. Town District by the oath of George Hahnbaum before William Rugeley, Esqr., J.P., 25 Nov 1773. Recorded 25 Jan 1774.

F-4, 179-184: Lease & release. 26 & 27 Apr 1769, Catharine Moody and James Fisher, merchant, both of Charles Town, SC, to John Swint, Cherugeon; Philip Minsing, Blacksmith; Melchior Warley, Bucher; Michael Kalteison, Innkeeper; Abraham Spidle, Tannor; Michael Booner, Butcher; Martin Miller, Bricklayer, and John Schetterle, Baker; all of Berkley County, for £2000, half lot of land in Charles Town, adj. land originally granted to Henry Simmons, and now belonging to the German Congregation in Charles Town called Lutherans, George Duhum, land belonging to the Dissenting Protestants in Charles Town called Independents, on Archdale Street, which half lot was the estate of the hon'bl Robert Fenwicke, Esqr., and was by him and Sarah his wife, conveyed to Joseph Moody of said town, merchant, now deceased, and the said Joseph Moody died seized and possessed of the said half town lot, and said became the right of the said Catharine Moody widow and relict of said Joseph Moody and James Fisher only son of Ebenezer Fisher formerly Ebenezer Moody, eldest sister to the said Joseph Moody also deceased, as heirs at law. James Fisher (LS), Catharine Moody (LS), Wit: Hugh Alison, John Wagner. Proved by the oath of John Wagner before William Rugeley, J.P. in Charles Town District, 27 Jan 1774. Recorded 27 Jan 1774.

F-4, 185-190: Lease & release. 26 & 27 May 1772, Richard Caudle of province of SC, to Frederick Winter, Esq., of same, for £225 SC money, 100 acres in Granville County on Savannah River, granted 5 March 1770 to said Richard Caudle. Wit: Wm. Waters, Jaquar Roquemore. Hannah (Anna) Caudle (H), wife of Richard Caudle, relinquished dower 1 June 1772. Proved 1 June 1772

SOUTH CAROLINA DEED ABSTRACTS 1773-1778

by the oath of Jaquer Roquemore before William Calhoun, J. P. in Granville County. Recorded 27 Jan 1774.

F-4, 191-199: Lease & release. 29 & 30 Oct 1773, Joseph Salvador, Esqr., of City of London, Kingdom of Great Britain, Merchant, by Richard Andrew Ripely, late of said city but now of Province aforesaid, Gentleman, his attorney, for £2124 to Abraham Pardo of City of London, Esqr., 1062 acres above a place called Ninety Six, part of 50,000 acres number the third tract granted to William Livingston, Esqr., of the Parish of St. Martins in the fields in the County of Middlesex, Kingdom of Great Britain, by indentures of lease & release, conveyed the said four parcels to John Hamilton, said to be late of Parish of St. George Hanover Square, County of Middlesex, but then of Charles Town, province aforesaid, esqr., and said Hamilton 27 & 28 Nov 1755 to Joseph Salvador, third and fourth tracts on Saludie River. (plat included) Joseph Salvador by his attorney Richard Andrew Rapley. Wit: Robt Williams Junr, John Lewis Gervais. Proved in Charles Town District 17 Jan 1774 by the oath of John Lewis Gervais before John Rutledge, Esquire, J.P. Recorded 1 Feb 1774.

F-4, 200-206: Lease & release. 29 & 30 Oct 1773, Joseph Salvador, Esqr., of City of London, Kingdom of Great Britain, Merchant, by Richard Andrew Ripely, late of said city but now of Province aforesaid, Gentleman, his attorney, for £3480 to Abraham Pardo of City of London, Esqr., 1638 acres above a place called Ninety Six, part of 50,000 acres number the third tract granted to William Livingston, Esqr., of the Parish of St. Martins in the fields in the County of middlesex, Kingdom of Great Britain, by indentures of lease & release, conveyed the said four parcels to John Hamilton, said to be late of Parish of St. George Hanover Square, County of Middlesex, but then of Charles Town, province aforesaid, esqr., and said Hamilton 27 & 28 Nov 1755 to Joseph Salvador, first and second tracts on Saludie River. (plat included) Joseph Salvador by his attorney Richard Andrew Rapley. Wit: Robt Williams Junr, John Lewis Gervais. Proved in Charles Town District 17 Jan 1774 by the oath of John Lewis Gervais before John Rutledge, Esquire, J.P. Recorded 1 Feb 1774.

F-4, 206-210: Lease & release. 5 & 6 Nov 1773, Patrick Gibson of the District of Ninety Six, SC, planter, and Margarey his wife, to Andrew Williamson of same, planter, for £500 SC money, 100 acres on Stephens Creek adj. land of said Patrick Gibson, and 93 acres in Granville County on waters of hard Labour Creek adj. said Patrick Gibson, David Pressley, William Dorreses land. Patrick Gibson (LS), Margarey Gibson (G) (LS), Wit: Joseph Moore, Timothy Parker. Proved by the oath of Timothy Parker before Richard Andrews Rapley, J.P. for Ninety Six District, 9 Nov 1773. Recorded 2 Feb 1774.

F-4, 210-214: Lease & release. 3 & 4 June 1773. Richard Hutchings of Orangeburgh, Province of SC, School Master to Andrew Williamson of Long Canes, SC, for £100 SC money, 100 acres in Belfast Township on the Road from the Long Cane Settlement to Charles Town, granted 27 Aug 1764 to Richard Hutchins, recorded in Book YY, page 110. Richard Hutchings (LS), Wit: George Whitefield, Timothy Parker. Proved by the oath of Timothy Parker before Richard Andrews Rapley, J.P. for Ninety Six District, 9 Nov 1773. Recorded 3 Feb 1774.

F-4, 214-218: Lease & release. 5 & 6 Nov 1773, Richard Johnston of District of Ninety Six, SC, sadler, to Andrew Williamson of same, planter, for £500 SC money, 250 ares on Savannah River adj. John Vanns, William Rogers, granted 20 June 1764 to sd. Richard Johnston, recorded in Book YY, page 16. Richard Johnson (R) (LS), Wit: Timothy Parker, Thos Lee, Wm. Hutchison. Proved by the oath of Timothy Parker before Pat. Calhoun, J.P. for Ninety Six District, 6 Nov 1773. Recorded 3 Feb 1774.

F-4, 218-220: 1 Feb 1773, David Drennen, yoeman, of Craven County, SC, to John Craig of same county & province, for £130 SC money, 172 acres, part of 418 acres on both sides Camp Creek a branch of Cataba River, granted at first to James Larrimore by patent 17 May 1754 in the county of Craven, SC. David Drennen (C) (LS), Wit: Patrick Cain, Roger Smith, James Craig. Proved in Craven County by the oath of Roger Smith before James Patton, J. P., 22 May 1773. Recorded 4 Feb 1774.

SOUTH CAROLINA DEED ABSTRACTS 1773-1778

F-4, 220-222: 6 May 1772, Henry Foster and Ann his wife in Parish of St. Marks, Craven County,SC, to William Davies, of Mecklenburg County, North Carolina, for £575, 300 acres granted by pattent unto George Douglas, 24 Sept 1754, conveyed to above named Henry Foster by deed 30 Oct 1761. Henry Foster (LS), Ann Foster (LS), Wit: John Barnet, Robert Dunlap, George Dunlap. Proved in Craven County by the oath of George Dunlap before James Patton, J. P., 6 May 1772. recorded 4 Feb 1774.

F-4, 222-227: Lease & release. 2 & 3 Nov 1753, Ralph Jones of Craven County, SC, yoeman, to John Douglas of same, yeoman, for £150 SC money, 300 acres on Cane Creek on North side Waxaws. Ralph Jones (J) (LS), Wit: Saml Wyly, Hugh Conhary/Conroy. Proved by the oath of Hugh Conhary, 27 Nov 1753, before Jared Nelson, J. P. in Craven County. Recorded 5 Feb 1774.

F-4, 227-231: Lease & release. 9 & 10 Aug 1759, John Douglas of Craven County, SC, yeoman, to George Douglas of same, yeoman, for £125 SC money, 300 acres in Craven County on Cane Creek, north side Waxaws. John Douglas (LS), Wit: Robt Ramsay, Wm. Hood, Wm. Givens. Proved 23 Aug 1759 before Thomas Simpson, Esqr., J.P., for Craven County, by the oath of William Hood. Recorded 7 Feb 1774.

F-4, 231-233: 27 March 1771, William Bolding of Tryon County, North Carolina, to Moses McCarter of same, for £250 proc. money, mortgage, lease for 100 years, £90 South currency, tract on Susey Boles Branch. William Bolding (LS), Wit: William Milbrank, Catharine Milbank (+). Proved in open court, Tryon County, April term 1771, Ezekl. Polk, C. C. Recorded in Tryon County Book No. 5, 19 July 1771. Thos Neel, Regr. Recorded 8 Feb 1774.

F-4, 233-236: Lease & release. 8 & 9 Apr 1768, John Albright Everett of Craven County, SC, cordwainer, and Jane his wife, to Andrew Salsbery of same, planter, for £200 SC money, by grant 7 Sept [year not indicated] to John Albright Everett, 150 acres in the fork of Wateree and Congaree rivers, adj. land surveyed for John Lloyd. John Albright Everett (LS), Wit: John Hamelton Junr, Benjn. Rolleson, Isaiah Eason (+). Memorial entered in the Audr Generals office Book M No. 12, page 155, 20 Apr 1773. Proved in Craven County before Philip Pearson, J.P., by the oath by Benjamin Rawlinson, 27 Feb 1773. Recorded 8 Feb 1774.

F-4, 236-238: 19 Nov 1773, Archibald Robinson and wife Sarah of Craven County, Sc, planters, to Samuel Femster of same, planter, for £150, 100 acres in Craven County on north side Broad River on Turkey Creek granted to sd. Archibald Robison 25 Oct 1764, adj. Steward Browns land. Archebald Robison (Seal), Sarah Robeson (Seal), Wit: Joseph Femster, William Clark, Margaret Robison (M). Proved in Charles Town District by the oath of Joseph Femster before William Rugeley, 2 Dec 1773. Recorded 9 Feb 1774.

F-4, 238-243: Lease & release. 6 & 7 Dec 1773, Alexander Adamson of Charles Town, SC, carpenter, and Dorothy his wife, to Samuel Bonneau of St. Stephens Parish, SC, planter, to for £5500 SC money, lott in Charles Town number 18, on King Street, adj. lot belonging to Patrick Hinds, Cato Ash. Alexander Adamson (LS), Wit: John Fullerton, Thos Grimball Junr. Proved in Chas. Town District before Thomas Turner, J.P., by the oath of Thos. Grimball Junr, 7 Dec 1773. Recorded 11 Feb 1774.

F-4, 243-252: Joseph Salvador, Esqr., of City of London, merchant, now being in the city of Bristol, by publick instrument of writing 25 Sept 1769, stating that he was invested with the property of 100,000 acres of land in the lines of platts no. 3 & 4, bounding on the North East by Saludy River & Reaching near Long Canes Settlement, adj. land of John Hamilton, Esqr., appointed Richard Andrews Rapley of the City of London, Gentleman, then on his Departure into foreign parts, to be his true and lawfull attorney, receive money from tenants on said land... also for his to dispose of 5050 acres or any part not exceeding 5050 acres, another power of attorney dated 25 Sept 1772. Joseph Salvador (LS), Wit: John Asher, John Lewis, Notary Publick. Proved by the oath of John Lewis of the City of Bristol, Kingdom of Great Britain, 6 Oct 1773. Robt Gordon, Mayor. Recorded 14 Feb 1774.

F-4, 253-255: Whereas the Lords Proprietors of the Province of SC for £10 current money did grant 29 Oct 1809 to William Rawsom and his heirs, 500 acres on Combee Island in Granville County,

SOUTH CAROLINA DEED ABSTRACTS 1773-1778

SC, adj. William Bakers land, Cusa River, on a creek and marshes, likewise for £15 to Lady Elizabeth Blake of Colleton County did convey 24 July 1711; and said Elizabeth Blake for £15 paid by William Holmes conveyed the said tract 6 Feb 1713; now **William Holmes** of Berkley County, planter, for £400 current money to **John Palmer** of Colleton County have sold this tract of 500 acres, 29 Aug 1723. William Holmes (LS), Wit: Rowd. Evans, Jacob Wright, John Field. Proved on 23 May 1724 by all three witnesses, before Thos. Jones. Recorded 14 Feb 1774. A Memorial hereof entered in the Auditors Office 17 May 1733.

F-4, 255-258: Lease & release. 1 & 2 Apr 1741, Lewis Gourdin (Gordin) of Parish of St. James Santee, Craven County, SC, planter, and Maryann his wife, to Theodore Gaillard of same, planter, for £1300 SC money, 362 acres part of 620 acres granted to Lewis Gordin 5 July 1740, on Wambaw Swamp, adj. lands of Theodore Gaillard, James Guerry, Bay Swamp, lands lately sold by said Lewis Gourdin to Tacitus Gaillard. Lewis Gourdin (LS) Maryann Gourdin (A) (LS), Wit: Paul Bruneau, James Guerry, Tacitus Gaillard. Proved before James Gendron, Esqr., J. P., by the oath of James Guerry, 16 Dec 1746. Recorded 15 Feb 1774.

F-4, 258-262: Lease & release. 21 Oct 1762, Hilarius Mankin of Charles Town, SC, to Thos Cox of Berkley County, for £100 SC money, tract in Berkley County, SC, 100 acres on a branch of Tyger River called fair forest Creek waters of Broad River. Hilarius Mankin (LS), Wit: Jacob Lehre, Abraham Pennington, Edwd. Musgrove. Proved 12 Sept 1763 by the oath of Abraham Pennington before Edward Musgrove, J.P. in Berkley County. Recorded 16 Feb 1774.

F-4, 262-264: 12 Oct 1773, Michael (alias Melicher) Lohner of the Fork in Craven County between Broad & Saludy Rivers, Farmer, for natural love and affection to his son John Lohner, 103 acres part of 153 acres between the forks of Broad and Saludy Rivers, Craven County, at that time called Berkley County, granted to said Melicker Lohner 22 Jan 1759, recorded in Book TT, page 176, adj. Pendrick coons land, John Hans Adams land, John Hand Windle. Melciker Lohner (LS), Wit: Michl. Dickert, Jordan Jasu, Margaret Dickert (M). Proved by the oath of George Adam Goun 8 April 1774 [sic] before Michl. Dickert, J.P. Recorded 16 Feb 1774.

F-4, 264-268: 4 Dec 1773, Isabella Dennison to Jacob Valk for £100 SC money, 150 acres in Berkley County on Southwest side of four hole Swamp, adj. lands of Thomas Eughstes, granted 6 Feb 1773. Isabella Dennison (O) (LS), Wit: Robert Denneson, Paul Schlatter. Proved by the oath of Paul Schlatter 6 Dec 1773 before hopkin Price, Esqr., J.P. Recorded 17 Feb 1774.

F-4, 268-270: Lease & release. 6 & 7 Feb 1771, John Dooly of Colleton County, SC, to James Muckleroy of same, for £50, 450 acres in Boonsborough Township on a small branch of Long Cane Creek, adj. land of Sarah Fee, said tract granted to Hugh Fee 30 Aug 1765. John Dooly (LS), Wit: Thos Dooly (D), William Wright, Edmund Ellis. Recorded 17 Feb 1774.

F-4, 270-271: (Lease only) 7 Dec 1767, Margaret Fee of Charles Town, SC, to John Dooly of Ninety Six, Deputy Surveyor, for four shillings, 100 acres in Boonesborough Township adj. land of Hugh Fee. Margaret Fee (LS), Wit: Danl Horsey, Philip Goode, Joseph Freemon. Recorded 17 Feb 1774.

F-4, 272-276: Lease & release. ____ 1773, Thomas Barton of Charles Town, sadler, and Mary his wife, to Robert McKewn of same [consideration not stated], 300 acres surveyed for Daniel Caine 25 Jan 1770 in Craven County, on SW side Pedee River on the Long Marsh, adj. Mr. Skeen's land, Mr. Crawford's land. Thos Barton (LS), Mary Barton (LS), Wit: Robt. Crabb, Daniel Caine. Proved 7 Dec 1773 before Thos. Phepoe, Esqr., J. P. in Charles Town District, by the oath of Robt. Crab. Recorded 19 Feb 1774.

F-4, 276-278: Charles Story of St. Marks Parish, Craven County, SC, planter, for love, good will and affection to my loving grandson Charles Warnock Junior (now a minor) son of Charles Warnock Senior, planter, by my loving daughter Elizabeth Warnock otherwise Story wife of said Charles Warnock Senior, 150 acres in St. Marks Parish, Craven County, on Douglas Swamp, granted 1 Feb 1768... dated 20 Feb 1773. Charles Story (O) (LS), Wit: Sutton Bird, Abram Warnock. Proved by the oath of Abraham Warnock before John Egan, Esqr., J.P. Recorded 19 Feb 1774.

SOUTH CAROLINA DEED ABSTRACTS 1773-1778

F-4, 278-282: Lease & release. 13 & 14 Dec 1773, Joseph Hunt of Chehaw in SC, planter, and Martha his wife, to William Harvey, Gent., of Charles Town, for £660, tract by a late resurvey 213 acres on Combahee River adj. land in possession of John Wells, Henry Hyrne. Joseph Hunt (LS), Martha Hunt (LS), Wit: Alexander Harvey, Simon Berwick. Proved in Charles Town District by the oath of Alexander Harvey before William Rugeley, J.P., 6 Dec 1773. Recorded 19 Feb 1774.

F-4, 282-287: Lease & mortgage. 7 & 8 Dec 1772, Rawlins Lowndes of Province of SC, to Rowland Rugeley of Charles Town, Esqr., mortgage in the penal sum of £1400 for payment of £7000, land on Charles Town Neck in Berkly County, adj. land of said Rawlins Lowndes, adj. land late of Col. John Smith deceased but now the late which divides the lands of said Lowndes from lands of Daniel Cannon, Barnard Elliott. Rowland Rugeley (LS), Wit: Jerh. Theus, Thos Shubrick Junr. Proved in Charles Town District by the oath of Jeremiah Theus before John Rutledge, J.P., 21 Jan 1774. Recorded 22 Feb 1774. Mortgage satisfied Dec 1775. Acknowledged 17 Feb 1818 by Thos Lowndes, Exor of Raws. Lowndes, Wit: W. B. Tucker, Register.

F-4, 288-291: Lease & release. 19 & 20 Jan 1763, Drury Dunn of Granville County, Sc, planter, to John Barnwell of same, planter, for £950 SC money, four Islands the large of which is known as Horse Island, 219 acres on a creek called Gun Bluff, near Archers Creek, three other small islands, one known as Sheep Island, 20 acres. Drury Dunn (LS), Wit: John Grayson, Peter Lavein. Proved in Granville County before Andrew Verdier, Esqr., J.P., by the oath of John Grayson. A Memorial entered in Book M No. 8, page 235 14 July 1767. Recorded 22 Feb 1774.

F-4, 291-296: Lease & release. 1 & 2 Sept 1758, John Kenard Delebere and Anne his wife, both of Granville County, Sc, to Drury Dunn of same, planter, for £850, four Islands the largest of which is known as Horse Island, 219 acres, and Sheep Island, 20 acres [same tracts as preceding deed]. John Kenard Delebare (LS), Ann Delebare (LS), Wit: John Chapman, John Thomas. Proved in Granville County before William Harvey, J.P., 20 Aug 1760. Recorded 23 Feb 1774.

F-4, 297-302: Lease & release. 3 & 4 Jan 1774, John Delasay formerly of the town of Beaufort, Province of SC, but now residing at Nismes in Frances, by his attorney John Savage of Charles Town, to Daniel DeSaussure of town of Beaufort, Merchant, for £5000 SC money, and by power of attorney dated 30 March 1772, conveys lot number 12 and a low water lot adjacent to it in Beaufort originally granted 27 Aug 1764 to George Roupell, Esqr., and by him 10 & 11 June 1765 by lease and release to said John Delasaye. John Delasye [sic] by his attorney John Savage (LS), Wit: Saml Legare, Josiah Smith Junr. Proved in Charles Town District 22 Jan 1774 before William Burrows, Esqr., J.P., by the oath of Josiah Smith Junr. Recorded 24 Feb 1774.

F-4, 302-307: Lease & release. 24 & 25 Nov 1772, Benjamin Rees of St. Marks Parish, planter, to Hugh Rees of same, planter, for £90 SC money, 50 acres granted 23 Jan 1769 to Thomas Crawford in Craven County on or near Dry Swamp, adj. land formerly laid out for said Thomas Crawford, and land laid out for James McKelver Senr; also another tract of 150 acres granted 15 Feb 1769 to said Thomas Crawford in Craven County, St. Marks Parish, on Dry Swamp, adj. land of John Hate, John Dargan. Bejn Rees (LS), Wit: Wm. Rees, Isham Rees, Edwin Rees. Proved in Camden District before John Newman Oglethorpe, J.P., by the oath of Edwin Rees, 12 Dec 1772. Recorded 26 Feb 1774.

F-4, 307-313: Lease & release. 10 & 11 July 1766, John McCall of Charles Town, SC, Merchant, and Martha his wife, to Rowland Rugeley, of same, gentleman, for £1050 SC money, 201 acres on north side Ashley River in the Parish of St. Andrew, adj. lands now or late of Charles Cantey, lands lately belonging to John Burford deceased, lands lately belonging to Henry Wood, and lands now or lately belonging to William Fuller. John McCall (LS), Martha McCall (LS), Wit: john Baker, Peter Bowra. Proved in Charles Town District by the oath of John Baker before Thos Phepoe, J. P., 12 Feb 1774. Recorded 26 Feb 1774.

F-4, 314-318: Lease & release. 5 & 6 Oct 1773, William Sneider of Charles Town, to Jacob Myers of Saxagotha Township, for £250, 150 acres on the north side of Santee (otherwise Congaree) River adj. Casper Cantz, George Bewsers's land, which tract was granted to Michael Sneider 10 Feb 1749 who was the father of said William Sneider and also died intestate leaving the said William Sneider the eldest male heir. William Sneider (X) (LS), Wit: Dl. Mazyck, Saml Cross. Proved 14 Dec 1773 before William Nisbett, Esqr., J.P., in Charles Town District by the oath of Daniel Mazyck. Recorded 26 Feb 1774.

F-4, 318-320: 19 Apr 1755, William Graves of Colleton County, Sc, planter, to Thomas Porter of St. Georges Parish, Berkley County, for £1200 SC money, 200 acres in Beechhill, St. Pauls Parish, Colleton County adj. land belonging to the heirs of Capt. Whitefield deceased, land of William Quarterman, land of sd. Thomas Porter, and Winns land. William Graves (LS), Wit: Jenry Saltus, John Stewart. Proved in Berkley County 14 Dec 1773 by the oath of Henry Saltus before John Troup, Esqr., J.P. Recorded 1 March 1774.

F-4, 320-321: 25 Sept 1773, Mary Ayres (widow of Thos. Ayres deceased) of Parish of St. Paul, province of Georgia, to David Hunter of Parish of Prince William, Granville County, SC, for £300, 500 acres on Spur Creek one of the branches of the NW fork of Long Cane, granted to said Thomas Ayres 4 ____ 1769. Mary Ayres (LS), Wit: Mathew Long, Robt. Mathews. Proved 9 Nov 1773 in Granville County, Ninety Six District, by the oath of Mathew Long before Adam Cr. Jones. Recorded 1 March 1774.

F-4, 322-325: 4 Sept 1771, Roger Pinckney, Provost Marshall of SC, to Thomas Radcliffe junior of Charles Town, Merchant, whereas Thos. Walter of Charles Town, Merchant, was Lately seized of a parcell of the Eastern Bay Lot or Lotts formerly belonging to Bernard Elliott now deceased and by his bond 23 Aug 1771 to Peter Manigault and Robert Williams Junr., of Charles Town, Gentlemen, in the sum of £30,000 and said Peter Manigault and Robert Williams Junr. in the court of common pleas in an action of debt in August term 1771 did recover a Judgement, now for £33 s8 d4, lot on Eastern Bay in or near Charles Town, adj. lot and stonehouse now in the possession of Arthur Lykes, John Champneys, Bernard Beckman. Roger Pinckney, Prov. Marsl. (LS), Wit: James Donovan, Hopson Pinckney. Proved by the oath of James Donovan before John Troup, J.P., 1 Feb 1772. Recorded 1 March 1774.

F-4, 325-330: Lease and release. 8 & 9 Feb 1769, Barnaby Cockfield of SC, planter, Alexander Martin of said province, planter, and Ann Martin his wife, to Thomas Radcliff of Charles Town, merchant, for £3200, 419 acres in Colleton County adj. lands of Mr. Dalton deceased Cockholds Creek, Mr. Cochran. Barnaby Cockfield (LS), Alexander Martin (LS), Ann Martin (LS), Wit: John Troup. Proved by the oath of John Troup, Esqr., in Charles Town District 3 March 1774 before William Rugeley, J.P. Recorded 3 March 1774.

F-4, 330-331: Barnaby Cockfield and Alexander Martin, bond concerning preceding lease and release, 9 Feb 1769. Recorded 3 March 1774.

F-4, 331-335: Lease and release. 30 & 31 Dec 1772, John Gibson of Craven County, SC, planter, to George Strother of same, for £79 currency, 150 acres granted to David Jackson 6 Nov 1751 on north side south branch of Santee river, adj. land laid out to Henry Brown, Casper Gallizer, Felix Long, Joseph Yates. John Gibson (J) (LS), Wit: Frederick Barrs, Jacob Eleber, John Gibson Junr. Proved by the oath of Jacob Eler 11 Dec 1773 before Henry Patrick, J.P. A Memorial entered in Book M. No. 12, page 451, 15 Dec 1773. Recorded 7 March 1774.

F-4, 335-338: 9 Dec 1773, George Porter of Parish of St. Paul, Colleton County,SC, planter, to Elizabeth Porter and Mary Waldron of St. Georges Parish, Berkly County, for affection to said Elizabeth Porter and Mary Waldron, his two sisters, and for their paying all his Just Debts that are or were contracted before the date of these presents, and for £200, two parcels of land formerly purchased of John & William Graves by his father Thomas Porter deceased adj. each other in parish of St. Paul, Colleton County, also 22 slaves [named], and cattle branded [marks given]. George Porter (LS), Wit: Mary Saltus, Offspring Pearce, Thos Baker. Proved by the oath of Thomas Baker before Stephen Cater, Esqr., J. P., 10 Dec 1773.

F-4, 338-342: Lease and release. 11 & 12 Jan 1773, Andrew Rembert Junr of St. Marks Parish, Sc, planter, to James Rembert of same, for £210, 70 acres on Et. side Santee River adj. land of David Brunson, Isaac Brunson, land of John Dargan called Glebe, land of Porcher; granted 2 June 1769 to sd. Andrew Rembert Junr. Andrew Rembert Junr. (LS), Wit: Josiah Gayle, Wm. Rees, Benjn.

SOUTH CAROLINA DEED ABSTRACTS 1773-1778

Rees. Proved 21 May 1773 before Wood Furman, Esqr., J.P. in Craven County, by the oath of Benjamin Rees.

F-4, 342-346: Lease and release. 24 March 1772, William Dinkins of St. Marks Parish, SC, Taylor, & Sarah his wife, to James Rembert of same, planter, for £300, 200 acres in Craven County on the high hills of Santee adj. land of Thos Jones, Wm Rees, granted __ Feb 1768 to William Denkins. William Dinkins (LS), Sarah Dinkins (LS), Wit: Isham Moore, Nathl. Moore, Wm. Moore. Proved 21 May 1773 before Wood Furman, J.P. for Craven County, by the oath of William Moore. Recorded 9 Feb 1774.

F-4, 346-350: Lease and release. 1 & 2 Apr 1772, Peter Mellet of St. Marks Parish, SC, planter, and Mary his wife, to James Rembert of same, planter, for £90 SC money, 45 acres in Craven County, St. Marks Parish, on the high Hills of Santee adj. on the Glebe land, adj. land granted to William Dinkins, Wm. Rees, land granted to James Brunson, land granted to Isaac Brunson; said plantation granted 5 June 1770 to said Peter Mellet. Peter Mellet (LS), Mary Mellet (LS), Wit:Isaac Hilton, Elizha Griffith (+). Proved 21 May 1773 before Wood Furman, Esqr., J.P., by the oath of Isaac Hilton. Recorded 10 March 1774.

F-4, 351-355: Lease and release. 23 & 24 May 1772, Peter Mellet of Craven County, SC, planter, and Mary his wife, to Abijah Rembert of St. Marks Parish, planter, for £500 SC money, 200 acres in Craven County adj. land of Joseph Kershaw, on Wateree River, John Jonym; plantation granted 7 March 1779 [sic] to John Jonym and by him conveyed to said Peter Mellet. Peter Mellet (LS), Mary Mellet (LS), Wit: Anthony Simons, James Rembert, Elisha Griffith (+). Proved 20 Nov 1773 by the oath of James Rembert before Wood Furman, Esqr., J.P. Recorded 10 Feb 1774.

F-4, 355-359: Lease and release. 3 & 4 May 1772, Brian Toland of St. Marks Parish, SC, planter, and Janeret his wife, to Abijah Rembert of same, planter, 100 acres in Craven County on South side of Wateree River, adj. said river, land laid out to Timothy Puckett. Brian Toland (M) (LS), Janerett Toland (I) (LS), Wit: Peter Mellet, Absalom Collins, James Toland. Proved by the oath of Peter Mellett before Wood Furman, Esqr., J.P., 20 Nov 1773. Recorded 11 March 1774.

F-4, 360-365: Lease and release. 17 & 18 Dec 1773, John McQueen of Charles Town, Gentleman, to David Deas of same, gentleman, for £7350, lot in Charles Town, number 60, on south side of Tradd St., adj. Meeting St.,adj. land formerly belonging to Daniel Townshend deceased, and land now belonging to Robert Williams the younger; said lot formerly belonged to William Harvey of Charles Town, gentleman, and by lease & release 5 & 6 March 1772, and William Harvey and Mary his wife to Alexander harvey their son, and Alexander Harvey by lease and release 26 * 27 Oct 1773 to said John McQueen. John McQueen (LS), Wit: Robt Williams Junr, Wm. Print. Proved in Charles Town District 3 Jan 1774 by the oath of William Print before William Burrows, Esqr., J.P. Recorded 11 March 1774.

F-4, 365-368: Lease and release. 13 Oct 1772, Henry Downs and wife Frances of Mecklenburgh County, NC, to Robert Frazer of Granville County, SC, for £68 Virginia money, 400 acres in Granville county, SC, on Sawneys Creek, vacant on all sides when surveyed, granted 18 Aug 1763 to Henry Downs. Henry Downs (LS), Frances Downs (LS), Wit: Benjn. Matthison, Susannah Cavat (S), John Pickens. Proved before James Patton, Esqr., J. P. for Craven County, by the oath of John Pickens 13 Oct 1772. Recorded 14 March 1774.

F-4, 368-371: Lease and release. 18 & 19 Oct 1771, James Brown of Parish of Prince Williams, SC, planter, to Robert Frazer of same, planter, for £175 SC money, 200 acres granted 21 June 1765 to Allexander Miller, on NW fork of Lang Cane called Sandies Creek, adj. lands of Henry Downs Junr, plat and grant recorded in Book YY page 550, lease and release acknowledged by James and Hannah Robertson to said James Brown. James Brown (LS), Wit: Robert Anderson, James Scott. Proved 19 Oct 1771 before John Pickens by the oath of James Scott & Robt. Anderson. Recorded 14 March 1774.

F-4, 372-375: Lease and release. 10 & 11 July 1740, Edward Clements of Barkley County, SC, planter, to George McNicholes of Berkley County, planter, for £100, 250 acres on west side Santee River near the SE side of Amelia Township, granted to Edward Clements. Edward Clements (EC)

SOUTH CAROLINA DEED ABSTRACTS 1773-1778

(LS), Elizabeth Clements (+) (LS), Wit: Charles ONeal, Elexr. McKelvey, John Wellstead. Proved 8 Dec 1773 by the oath of Margaret McKelvey who stated that she verily believes that one of the within subscribing witnesses Charles ONeil Deceased her Former Husband did subscribe & write his name to the within deed, before John Savage, J.P. Recorded 15 March 1774.

F-4, 375-378: Lease and release. 20 & 21 Oct 1773, John Welch eldest son and heir to James Welch deceased, and his mother Elizabeth Welch of Granville county, SC, to William Hall of same, sadler, for £800, 200 acres granted 27 March 1771 to William Harris in Granville County on Ne fork of Long Canes adj. Moses Alexander, Nathaniel Alexander, which said William Harris got in exchange from Thos harris and joining this they have now sold to Wm. Hall. John Welch (LS), Elizabeth Welch (O) (LS), Wit: Robt Anderson, John McGill. Proved 21 Oct 1773 before Alexander Cameron, J.P. in Ninety Six District, by the oath of Robert Anderson, planter. Recorded 15 March 1774.

F-4, 379-382: Lease and release. 3 & 4 Aug 1772, William Harris of Granville county, SC, planter, to James Welch of same, weaver, for £500, 200 acres in Granville County on NW fork of Long Canes adj. Moses Alexander, Nathaniel Alexander, granted to William Harris 27 March 1771. Wm. Harris Wit: John Harris, Thos Harris. Recorded 17 March 1774.

F-4, 382-384: Lease and release. 11 & 12 June 1772, Benjamin Farar of St. Mathews Parish, Berkley County, SC, to James Clark of St. Marks Parish, Craven County, for £500 SC money, 370 acres being 3/4 of 500 acres of land in St. Marks parish, Craven County, originally granted to Isaac Porcher, Esqr., 30 Sept 1736, and by divers conveyances became the property of Benjamin Farar. Benjn. Farar. Wit: Timothy Corse, Saml Clarke. Proved in Charles Town District before William Rugeley, J.P., by the oath of Saml. Clarke, 17 Dec 1773. Recorded 17 March 1774.

F-4, 385-386: John Williams of Craven county, SC, whereas by bond of even date with these presents bound to William Rees of same province, in the penal sum of £3614 SC money for the payment of £1807, on or before 1 January to sell to William Rees three negroes Vilet, Luster & George, and 675 acres on High hills Santee, 175 acres granted to Thos Jones 22 Jan 1759 also 200 granted to John Rees 10 Apr 1771, and 100 acres granted to said John Rees 7 April 1770; 100 acres granted to Benjn Rees. John Williams (LS), Wit: Saml. _____. Recorded 18 March 1774.

F-4, 386-389: 29 June 1773, Ebenezer Smith of Province of Georgia, planter, to Alexander Cheves of Ninety Six District, SC, mercht., for £200 SC money, 100 acres in Granville county on NW fork of Long Cane, adj. Henry Wilson, William Baskins, Moses Alexander, granted 22 March 1769 to Ebenezer Smith. Ebeneazer Smith. Wit: George Parks, Mathew Long. Proved by the oath of George Parks in Berkley County before Rowld. Rugeley, 17 Dec 1773. Recorded 18 March 1774.

F-4, 389-392: Lease and release. 27 & 28 Nov 1773, Lewis Motlett of Charles Town, Practitioner of Physick, to Thomas Lord of same, merchant, for £500, 300 acres in Long Cane Settlement in Granville County on Long Cane Creek adj. vacant land on all sides, granted 7 Apr 1770 and entered in the Auditors Office in Book N No. 10 page 149, 20 May 1770. Lewis Motlett (LS), Wit: Philip Henry, Richd. Latham. Proved 1 Dec 1773 before Thomas Turner, Esqr., J. P., in Charles Town District, by the oath of Philip Henry. Recorded 18 March 1774.

F-4, 393-397: Lease and release. 25 & 26 Jan 1763, William Killingsworth of Amelia Township, Berkley County, SC, planter, son, heir, and executor of William Killingsworth Senior, now deceased, to Alexander McKintosh, Esqr., of Craven county, SC, merchant, for £380 SC money, 125 acres in the Welch Tract in Craven County, SC, granted 6 Dec 1744 to Thomas Evans of Plumfield now deceased, on Pedee River, adj. land of Philip Douglass; transferred by Abel & Thomas Evans by lease & release to William Killingsworth Sr. Wm. Killingsworth (LS), Wit: David Evans, Thomas James. Proved before John Abian, J.P. in Craven County, by the oath of David Evans, 23 Apr 1764. Recorded 21 March 1774.

F-4, 397-398: 11 Apr 1773, David Evans and Catharine his wife of Craven County, SC, Parish of St. David, to Mary Harry of same parish and province, for £2000, 155 acres granted to William Hollingsworth, dated 29 Nov 1750 descended from Samuel [sic] Hollingsworth to his son Samuel Hollingsworth as his right & lawful heir and from Samuel Hollingsworth to his sister Catharine

SOUTH CAROLINA DEED ABSTRACTS 1773-1778

Evans wife to said David Evans, in the Welch Tract on Pedee River, adj. Simon Parsons, John Westfields lands, Thos Bowen, John Carter, John Evans. David Evans (LS), Catharine Evans (LS), Wit: John Hustess, John Sutton. Proved in Cheraws District before Alexander McKintosh, J.P., by the oath of John Sutton, 26 June 1773. Recorded 21 March 1774.

F-4, 398-400: 11 Apr 1773, David Evans and Catharine his wife of Craven County, SC, Parish of St. David, to Mary Harry of same parish and province, for £2000, 100 acres granted to Thomas Bowen 29 Jan 1742 descended from Thomas Bowen to his son William Bowen as his right & lawful heir and conveyed from William Bowen to Samuel Hollingsworth, by lease & release 24 & 25 Feb 1764, and from Samuel Hollingsworth to his sister Catharine Evans wife to said David Evans, in the Welch Tract adj. John Carter. David Evans (LS), Catharine Evans (LS), Wit: John Hustess, John Sutton. Proved in Cheraws District before Alexander McKintosh, J.P., by the oath of John Sutton, 26 June 1773. Recorded 22 March 1774.

F-4, 400-401: 11 Apr 1773, David Evans and Catharine his wife of Craven County, SC, Parish of St. David, to Mary Harry of same parish and province, for £2000, 100 acres granted to John Carter 24 May 1745 conveyed from John Carter to Samuel Hollingsworth, by lease & release 26 & 27 Sept 1746, and descended from Samuel Hollingsworth to his sister Catharine Evans wife to said David Evans, in the Welch Tract adj. John Evans. David Evans (LS), Catharine Evans (LS), Wit: John Hustess, John Sutton. Proved in Cheraws District before Alexander McKintosh, J.P., by the oath of John Sutton, 26 June 1773. Recorded 22 March 1774.

F-4, 401-407: Lease & release. 11 & 12 Nov 1773, Mathew Kemmerling of Amelia Township, Berkley County, SC, planter, and Margaret his wife, to Peter Manigault of Charles Town, but now occasionally residing in the Kingdom of Great Britain, Esqr., for £700, 300 acres in Amelia Township, Berkley County, adj. land granted to Joseph Joiner, Barnard Litz, John Burnh, land granted to Mary Kebler, Frederick Knapper, Andrew Hawser; said 300 acres granted 29 July 1768 to said Mathew Kimmerling. Mathw. Kimmerling (LS), Margt. Kimmerling (LS), Wit: Wm. Thompson, Malcome Clark. Proved in Charles Town District, 16 Dec 1773, before Robt. Williams Junr, J. P., by the oath of Wm. Thomson. Recorded 23 March 1774.

F-4, 407-410: 30 Dec 1773, James Johnston of Charles Town, Baker, to Charles Pinckney, of same, esquire, for £500, assigns lots leased 25 March 1771 by the Vestry & Church Wardens of Parish of St. Philip in Charleston lot number 36 on Beaufain St. to said James Johnston, and leased on 25 March 1771 the said Vestry & Church Wardens lease unto Frederick Ehney of same, shoemaker, lot number 35. James Johnston (LS), Wit: John Colcock, Charles Pinckney, Junr. Proved in Charles Town District by the oath of Charles Colcock before William Burrows, J.P., 31 Dec 1773. Recorded 23 March 1774.

F-4, 410-414: Lease & release. ____ 1773, Joseph Collins of Province of Georgia, to Thomas Bettey of Camden District, St. Marks Parish, SC, for £10, 100 acres in Amelia Township, granted 1 July 1768. Joseph Collins (I) (LS), Ann Collins. Wit: Thos Singleton, Wm. Collins, Jonathan Drake. Recorded 23 March 1774. Proved 6 Oct 1773 before Ebeneazer Smith, Esqr., J.P. in Georgia, by the oaths of William Collins & Thos Singleton. Recorded 24 March 1774.

F-4, 414-418: Lease & release. 27 & 28 Dec 1773, Robt. Hurst of Berkley County, SC, planter, & Jane his wife, to William Holliday of Charles Town, for £3500 SC money, 452 acres including an Island in the marsh in the Parish of St. James Goose Creek, on Cooper River adj. lands of Samuel Prioleau, Esqr., adj. land sold by Robert Hurst to Daniel Cannon, land now the property of William Logan, Esqr. Robert Hurst (LS) Jane Hurst (LS), Wit: Jacob Valk, Paul Schlatter. Proved 5 January 1773 before Hopkin Price, Esqr., J. p. for Charles Town District by the oath of Jacob Valk. Recorded 24 March 1774.

F-4, 419-423: Lease & release. 20 & 30 Dec 1766, Henry Hartley of Craven County, Sc, planter, & Elizabeth his wife, to William Jefferys of same, for £200 SC money, 100 acres in the low ground of the Congaree River granted 20 June 1760, adj. land of Martin Oatt, Capser Couch, Jacob Sneither, George Boozer, John Spits, William Tucker. Henry Hartley (LS), Elizabeth Hartley (LS), Wit: Henry Chappell, John Taylor, Henry Weaver (Wiver). Proved 30 Dec 1766 before William Tucker, J.P., by the oath of John Taylor. Recorded 28 March 1774.

F-4, 423-427: Lease & release. 2 & 3 June 1763, Peter Kolb of Craven county, SC, planter, to John Rogers of Cat fish, SC, planter, 250 acres in the Welch Tract, Prince Fredericks Parish, adj. Langford Owens, granted 9 Jan 1756 to Peter Kolb. Peter Kolb (LS), Wit: Wm. Watkins, James Webb. Proved before John Alran, J. P. in Craven County, by the oath of William Watkins of Prince Fredericks Parish, 22 July 1763. Recorded 29 March 1774.

F-4, 427-433: Lease & release. 18 & 19 Jan 1773, John Titmore (Ditmore) of Charles Town, Baker, & wife Elizabeth, to Adam Cusack of Berkley County, planter, for £100 SC money, 500 acres on Pedee River adj. William Little, granted 12 Oct 1770 to John Titmore. John Titmore (LS), Eliz'h Titmore (O) (LS), Wit: Wm. Fitzpatrick, Robert Smith. Proved in Berkly County before John Troup, J.P., by the oath of Robert Smith, 22 Jan 1771. Recorded 30 March 1774.

F-4, 433-438: Lease & release. 20 & 21 Sept 1773, Henry Hyrne of St. Bartholomews Parish, Colleton County, SC, Gentleman, to Solomon Harper of Prince Williams Parish, SC, planter, for £49 s15 SC money, 620 acres in Colleton County, adj. Abraham Colson, Thomas Ford, originally 7 Jan 1737 surveyed & Laid out to Stephen Nichols and on 21 May 1772 granted to sd. Henry Hyrne. Henry Hyrne (LS), Mary Ann Hyrne (LS), Wit: Richd Bohun Baker, Jno. Bellinger. Proved 23 Aug 1774 before William Nisbett, Esqr., J. P. in Charles Town District, by the oath of John Bellinger. Recorded 7 Apr 1774.

F-4, 438-443: Lease & release. 22 & 23 Oct 1773, Solomon Harper of Prince Williams Parish, Colleton County, planter, to Hannah McCants of St. Bartholomews Parish, widow, for £1340 SC money, 670 acres in Colleton County adj. land laid out to Thos Ford, originally 7 Jan 1737 surveyed and laid out to Stephen Nichols and 21 May 1772 granted to Henry Hyrne. Solomon Harper (LS), Elinor Harper (+) (LS), Wit: Jesse Day, Henry Van Bebber, John Goodbe. Proved 23 Nov 1773 before Charles Brown, Esqr., J.P. in Beaufort District, by the oath of Jesse Day. Recorded 7 Apr 1774.

F-4, 443-444: John Barnwell & Martha Barnwell of St. Helena Parish, Granville county, planter, bound to Jacob Deveaux of same parish, planter, in the sum of £4600, 16 Nov 1773, whereas by lease & release 12 & 13 Nov 1773 to Jacob Deveaux, granted tract of four Islands known by the name of Horse Island & Sheep Island, 239 acres. John Barnwell Senr (LS), Martha Barnwell (LS), Wit: William Deveaux. Recorded 7 Apr 1774.

F-4, 444-446: 27 Nov 1773, William Jones & wife Rebecca of st. Marks Parish, Craven County, sadler, to Frances Adam of same, yeoman, for £319 SC money, 100 acres part of 400 acres granted 7 May 1754 by Mathew Rowan, Gov. of North Carolina, to James Robertson & John Arnold Pender, on Camp Creek in Anson County "but since the running of the Boundary line it is fell into South Carolina" and sd. James Robertson and John Arnold Pender did grant unto Robert Gault, 100 acres of said grant, and Robert Gault did grant unto William Jones. William Jones (W) (LS), Rebecca Jones (LS), Wit: James Boyd, James Johnston, William Adams. Craven County, Camden District: proved 6 Dec 1773 by the oath of William Adams before James Simpson, J.P. Recorded 8 Apr 1774.

F-4, 446-453: Lease & release. 3 & 4 Jan 1774, Thomas Ferguson of Spoon's Savannah, St. Pauls Parish, SC, Esqr., and wife Martha which said Martha is daughter Heir at Law and Devisee of Barnabay Ryley and Neice & heir at law of John Ryley sons of Bryan Ryley late of said parish, planter, deceased, to Benjamin Elliot and Charles Elliott of same parish, esqrs., in trust for the better securing and settling the said premises after the death of said Ferguson for ten shillings, 154 acres granted by the Lords Proprietors Deputies 17 May 1701 to Thos Drayton deceased also 100 acres likewise granted on the same day to Jonathan Fitch and another tract of 470 acres granted 18 Sept 1703 to said Jonathan Fitch and a tract of 200 acres granted to James Wirxam 5 May 1704 and 150 acres granted 15 Sept 1705 to said Jonathan Fitch and 200 acres granted 15 March 1705 to said Jonathan Fitch and 200 acres granted 14 March 1705 to said Jonathan Fitch and 1150 granted 11 July 1733 to the aforesaid Bryan Ryley adj. lands of then the said Bryan Ryley, John Bull, Joseph Peacomb, Thos Sacheveral, in the whole 2424 acres being continuous at Spoon's Savannnah and all except tract of 1050 granted to said Bryan Ryley by divers mesne conveyances and devises became vested in the said Bryan Ryley who by deed in his life time and by his last will devised the same to his sons Barnaby Ryley and John Ryley whose legal representative is the said Martha; after the decease of Thomas Ferguson to the use of said Martha, Charles Ferguson, John Horry Ferguson, Benjamin Ferguson and William Cattle Ferguson, sons of said Thomas and Martha. Thos Ferguson (LS), Martha Ferguson (LS), Wit: Eliz. Web, Gabriel Manigault Jnr. Proved in Charles Town District 8 January 1774 before William Burrows, J. P., by the oath of Gabriel Manigault Junr. Recorded 9 Apr 1774.

F-4, 452-456: Lease & release. 13 & 14 1756, James Means and Rachel his wife of County of Anson [North Carolina], Shoemaker, to John Latta of same, farmer, for £40 SC money, 278 acres in Anson County, North Carolina on both sides of a fork of fair forest being a tract of patent land granted 18 Nov 1752. James Means (LS), Rachel Means (C) (LS), Wit: Henry Foster, Joseph Kelso. North Carolina, Anson County: Recorded in Book C No. 3, page 442-424 pr. Robt. Harris, Pub. Register, 5 Oct 1759. A memorial entered in the Audr. Office Book M No.12, page 452, 24 Dec 1773. Recorded 8 Apr 1774.

F-4, 457-458: 21 March 1759, John Brians of Craven County, SC, planter, to Philip Walker, planter, of same, for £200 SC money, 350 acres on South side Broad River on Thickety Creek formerly belonging to William Green. John Brians (Seal), Wit: Hugh Mcdoneld, Thos Poole. North Carolina, Anson County: The within deed is recorded in the Clerks office of Anson County. Thos Kohock, C. C. Robt. Harris, Publ. Register. North Carolina, Mecklenburgh County: Proved by the oath of Hugh McDonnel of said county, before Robt. McCleanachan, J. P. of said county, that he saw John Brian and Mary his wife sign the within deed, 8 Dec 1773. Recorded 8 Apr 1774.

F-4, 458-462: 30 & 31 Jan 1772, Peter Crim of the fork in Craven County, SC, planter, to George Dawkins of same, planter, for £800, 250 acres in the fork adj. land of George Fryer, Andrew Emmerks, tract granted to Peter Crim Senr. 6 Oct 1752 and the said Peter Crims Senr died without will his oldest son Peter Crim sells this 250 acres. Peter Crim (LS), Wit: Thos Harbirt, George Crim, Margarate Dickert (O). Proved 31 Jan 1773 by the oath of Thomas Harbert before Michl. Dickert, J.P. Recorded 12 Apr 1774.

F-4, 462-464: Lease & release. 4 & 5 Feb 1772, Peter Crim of Craven County, SC, planter, to George Dawkins of same, planter, for £550, 145 acres, Island in the Broad River, granted 7 Oct 1755 to Christopher Sherss 7 Oct 1755 and property transferred into the possession of said Peter Crims by lease and release 14 & 15 Feb 1756. Peter Crim (LS), Wit: Wm. Ballentine, Thos Harbirt, John Arnold (O). Proved __ Feb 1773 by the oath of William Ballentine before Michl. Dickert, J.P. Recorded 12 Apr 1774.

F-4, 465-469: Lease & release. 25 & 26 Jan 1770, James Cary of Berkley County, Sc, planter, and Mary his wife, to John Grumes of same, for £140 SC money, 100 acres on North wise side of Wassamasaw Swamp adj. lands now John Shingleton, and sd. Cary, said 100 acres taken out from a tract of 740 acres purchased by Cary of Joseph Porcher. James Cary (LS), Mary Cary (LS), Wit: Gilbert Gibson, John Gibson. Proved in Berkly County before John Troup, J.P., by the oath of Gilbert Gibson, 16 May 1770. Recorded 13 Apr 1774.

F-4, 470-471: Michael Kalteison of Charles Town, whereas Alexander Gillon of Charles Town, merchant, did 8 Dec instant join said Michael Kalteison in a bond to Peter Boquet of Charles Town, merchant, on the penal sum of £8000 SC money, to secure payment of £4000, mortgage of town lot on east side King Street, Number 212, lately purchased by said Peter Boquet of Peter & John Horlbeck. Michael Kalteison (LS), Alexr. Gillon (LS), Wit: Ezekiel Townsend, Thos Phepoe. Proved in Charles Town District by the oath of Ezekiel Townsend before Wm. Rugeley, J.P., 24 Jan 1774. Recorded 13 Apr 1774. Satisfied 3 June 1778 A. Gillon. Wit: G. Speed.

F-4, 472-476: Lease & release. 19 & 20 July 1773, William Wells of Parish of St. Peters, Granville county, planter, to Willoughby Pugh of same, planter, for £500 SC money, 110 acres granted to William Wells 24 Dec 1772, adj. land of Joakim Hartston, Henry Gendrat, Thomas Page, Paul Porcher. William Wells (LS), Wit: William Catterton, Hannah Catterton, Elizabeth Hair. Proved in Granville County, Pursyburgh, by the oath of William Catterton 18 January 1774 before Adrian Mayer, J.P. Recorded 13 Apr 1774.

SOUTH CAROLINA DEED ABSTRACTS 1773-1778

F-4, 476-478: 10 Sept 1740, Thos Buer of Colleton County, SC, planter, to William Melven of same carpenter, for £400; 82 acres in Colleton County adj. John Melven, John Peter, Capt. Jackson, Mrs. Didcotts. Thos Buer (LS), Wit: Jas Donom, Thos Andrew, John Derriman. Proved bin Colleton County before James Skirving, J.P., by the oath of Thos Andrew, 15 Sept 1740. Recorded 14 Apr 1774.

F-4, 478-481: 12 Jan 1773, Adrian Loyer of Town of Savannah, Georgia, Gunsmith, to Miles Brewton of Charles Town, SC., Esqr., for £2370, 190 acres part of a tract granted to one John Grenier and afterwards sold by the son & heir of the said John Greneir to the said Adrian Loyer, in the lines of Pursyburgh Township on E side of Aposce Creek in Granville County, adj. lands of Hector Beringer DeBeaufain Esqr., lands now or late of Col. Samuel Montagu, land granted to John Grenier but now belonging to the said Miles Brewton. Adrian Loyer, Wit: John Simpson, John Jamieson. Proved in Berkly County by the oath of John Simpson before James Simpson, J.P., 20 Jan 1774. Recorded 14 Apr 1774.

F-4, 481-485: Lease & release. 17 & 18 Nov 1773, William Dinkens of SC, St. Marks Parish, planter, and Sarah his wife, to John Recks of same, joiner, for £250 SC money, 200 acres in Craven County, on high Hills of Santee, granted 19 Sept 1770 to Peter Mathews, and transferred by lease & Release to William Dinkens. William Dinkens (LS), Wit: Wm. Wright, David Gilbeart. Proved by the oath of David Gilbert before Saml. Porcher, 25 Jan 1774. Recorded 14 Apr 1774.

F-4, 485-489: Lease & release. 16 Dec 1773, Paul Townsend of Charles Town, merchant, to George Eagner Junr of same, planter, for £425, 150 acres in the fork of road & Saludy Rivers on Williams Creek originally granted to Conrad Folk on a bounty warrant about 1753 adj. at the time of the original grant on all sides on vacant land. Paul Townsend (LS). Wit: John Wagner, John Salley. Proved 31 Dec 1773 before Robert Goodwin, J.P. in Charles Town District, by the oath of John Wagner. Recorded 15 Apr 1774.

F-4, 490-494: Lease & release. 25 & 26 March 1774, Honb'l William Bull, Esqr., Lt. Gov. of SC, and Hannah his wife, to White Outerbridge of Charles Town, Gentleman, for £10,000, two tenements in Charles Town on Broad St and King Street now and for many years past occupied by Thos Elfe, Late the property of Othniel Beal, Esqr., deceased, and also the low water lots fronting the bay between lands now or late of Charles Elliott and Jacob Motte Deceased, now or late the property of Othniel Beale and by him devised to his daughter Hannah Bull. Wm. Bull (LS), Hannah Bull (LS), Wit: Jas. Johnson. Proved by the oath of James Johnston, 6 May 1774 [sic], before James Trail, J.P. Recorded 16 Apr 1774. Before Edward Savage, Esqr., one of the Justices of the Court of Common Pleas, 26 March 1774, appeared Hannah wife of Honb'le William Bull, Esqr., Lot. Gov., relinquished dower.

F-4, 494-496: Lease & release. 28 & 29 March 1774, White outerbridge of Charles Town, Gentleman, to Honb'l William Bull, Lt. Gov., for £10,000, two tenements in Charles Town on Broad St and King Street now and for many years past occupied by Thos Elfe, Late the property of Othniel Beal, Esqr., deceased, and also the low water lots fronting the bay between lands now or late of Charles Elliott and Jacob Motte Deceased, now or late the property of Othniel Beale and by him devised to his daughter Hannah Bull. White Outerbridge (LS), Wit: Jas. Johnston. Proved by the oath of James Johnston, 6 May 1774 [sic], before James Trail, J.P. Recorded 16 Apr 1774.

F-4, 496-498: 27 Jan 1774, Capt. John Scott of Charles Town, to Hannah Bull wife of Honb'l William Bull, Lt. Gov., whereas the Honorable Othniel Beale, Esqr., deceased, by his last will and testament 13 July 1769 did bequeath unto said Capt. John Scott two tenements in Charles Town, release of trust. John Scott (LS), Wit: John Jeffords Junr, Solomon Milner. Proved by the oath of John Jeffords Junr 6i May 1774 before James Johnston, J. P. Recorded 17 Apr 1774.

F-4, 498-504: Lease & release. 30 Sept & 1 Oct 1771, Christopher Wilkinson of Colleton County, Sc, planter, and Elizabeth his wife, to Isaac Rippon of same, planter, for £3500, 180 acres part of 2700 acres originally granted to Joseph Morton 29 March 1700 on Marsh of Edisto River, Littenwaw Creek and another tract of 232 acres on Wadmalaw Island in colleton County, part of said 2700 acres bounding now or lately of one Henry Livingston, on Bear Bluff (plats included). Christopher Wilkinson (LS), Eliz'h Wilkinson (LS), Wit: Morton Wilkinson, Andrew Slann, Wm.

SOUTH CAROLINA DEED ABSTRACTS 1773-1778

Smelie. Proved before James Brisbane, Esqr., J.P., by the oath of Andrew Slann, 14 May 1772. Recorded 19 Apr 1774.

F-4, 504-509: Lease & mortgage. 14 & 15 Jan 1774, Samuel Wise and Jacob Valk of SC, Gentlemen, to Peter Slann of Charles Town, merchant, in penal sum of £5600, 125 acres in the Welch Tract bounding at the time of grant on Andrew Slann, Pedee River, grant recorded in Book FFF, page 129, and that tract of 130 acres in the Welch Tract bounding at the time of the grant on William Jones, Pedee River, and tract of 130 acres in Welch Tract bonding at the time of the grant on land of Andrew Slann, Pedee River, and 250 acres in Welch Tract, four several tracts granted to Andrew Slann, father of said Peter Slann. Saml Wise (LS), Jacob Valk (LS), Wit: Paul Schlatter, Richd Corbett. Proved by the oath of Richard Corbett 24 Jan 1774 before Hopkin Price, J.P. Recorded 20 Apr 1774.

F-4, 509-513: Lease & release. 1 & 2 July 1773, William Benison of Prince George Parish, SC, planter, to Benjamin Huger of Charles Town, for £2700, 1800 acres in Prince George Parish, Craven county, adj. Lazowis land, Smiths Barony, Mark Huggins land, John Skrenes land. Wm. Benison (LS), Wit: Richard Muncrieff, John Cart. Proved in Charles Town District by the oath of Richard Muncrieff 9 March 1774 before William Rugeley, J.P. Recorded 21 Apr 1774.

F-4, 514-517: Lease & release. 23 & 24 Nov 1772, Andrew Linds of Berkley County, planter, to Peter Ansminger, planter in Craven County, for £200, 400 acres on N side Broad River the waters of Cedar and Cane Creeks adj. David Moore and vacant land. Andrew Linds (+) (LS), Wit: John Alston, James Brown, Mark Davis. Proved in Craven County 16 March 1773 before Michael Dickert, J.P., by the oath of John Alston. Recorded 21 Apr 1774.

F-4, 517-521: Lease & release. 21 & 22 July 1773, Lewis Morgan of St. Peters Parish, SC, Gentleman, and Meldred his wife, to Paul Porcher of St. Peters Parish, Gentleman, for £200 SC money, 100 acres in Granville county adj. Lewis Quich. Lewis Morgan (LS), Meldred Morgan (+) (LS), Wit: Mathew McKinnie, Jno Postell. Proved in Granville County 22 July 1773 before Adrian Mayer, Esqr., J.P., by the oath of Doctor Mathew McKinnie. Recorded 22 Apr 1774.

F-4, 522-525: Lease & release. 1 & 2 Oct 1773, James Simpson of Charles Town, Attorney at Law, and Barbara his wife, to John Logan of same, gentleman, for £4410 SC money, 593 acres adj. Mr. Crolls land, Mr. Draytons land, Mr. Sullivans land. James Simpson (LS), Barbara Simpson (LS), Wit: Anne Allenby, Isaac Huger. Proved in Charles Town District by the oath of Isaac Huger before William Rugeley, J.P., 31 Jan 1774. Recorded 22 Apr 1774.

F-4, 526-528: 25 Sept 1773, John Reagon of Berkley County, SC, and Elizabeth his wife, to John Wright of same, for £100, 100 acres half of 200 acres granted 29 Apr 1768 to John Wright, on waters of Saludah known by the name of Beaver Dam Creek. John Reagon (LS), Elizabeth Reagon (A) (LS), Wit: Jos. Wright, Wm. Wright, David Mote. Proved 26 Sept 1773 by the oath of William Wright before Elias Hollingsworth, J.P. Recorded 23 Apr 1774.

F-4, 528-530: 2 Dec 1768, Peter Scott and Mary his wife of Berkley County, SC, to William Gould of same, for £100 SC money, 100 acres on a branch called Beaver dam, part of 200 acres granted to sd. Peter scott 29 Apr 1768, adj. land now or late the property of said Peter Scott. Peter Scott (P) (LS), Mary Scott (+) (LS), Wit: Joseph Wright, Dorman Nenson, Joseph King. Proved in Ninety Six District by the oath of Joseph Wright before Elias Hollingsworth, J.P., 4 Sept 1773. Recorded 25 Apr 1774.

F-4, 530-536: Lease & release. 23 & 24 Nov 1756, Benjamin Atwell of James Island, Berkley County, SC, planter, to Mary Atwell of same, for £1561 SC money, tract where said Benjamin Atwell now lives, 75 acres on said Island and is the easter part of a plantation of 100 acres originally granted by the late Sr. Nathaniel Johnson, Knt. and Gov. and rest of the Lords Proprietors, 1 Feb 1706 to one John Green (since deceased) adj. land late of John Hearne deceased, on the high Road, lands which were late of William Chapman decd, land late of Joseph Atwell, land now or late of Witter, and also Benjamin Atwell's small island plantation of 55 acres on in the Great Marshes on south side James Island, near to the northward of a certain larger Island now or late of Col.

SOUTH CAROLINA DEED ABSTRACTS 1773-1778

Robert Rivers. Benjn Atwell (LS), Wit: Thos Lamboll, Elizabeth Lamboll. Proved in Charles Town District before William Rugeley, Esqr., 4 Feb 1774. Recorded 26 Apr 1774.

F-4, 536-538: 2 Feb 1774, Thomas Harris of Charles Town, SC, Sail Maker, and Susannah his wife, to Alexr Gillon of same, merchant, said Thos Harris by his obligation bound to sd. Alexr Gillon in the penal sum of £4820 for payment of debt of £2410, mortgage of part of four town lots numbers 256, 257, 258, and 259, heretofore belonging to Richard Beresford, Esqr. Thos Harris (LS), Susanna Harris (+) (LS), Wit: Thos Phepoe, Ezekiel Townsend. Proved in Charles Town District by the oath of Ezekiel Townsend, 27 Apr 1774, before William Rugeley, J.P. Recorded 27 Apr 1774. Satisfied 7 Apr 1778. Wit: Geo: Sheedy.

F-4, 538-542: Lease & release. 9 & 10 Jan 1774, William Little of Granville county, SC, Freeholder, to John Irwin of Colleton County, sadler, for £150 SC money, 200 acres on Long Cane Creek a branch of Savannah River adj. Mathey Edwards, adj. a great survey called Salvadors, lands laid out to Moses Lindouws, granted 21 June 1765 to William Little. Wm. Little (mark) (LS), Penelephy Little (LS), Wit: John Hairston, Thos Hairston. Proved in Ninety Six District 15 Jan 1774 by the oath of John Hairston, before John Bowie, J.P. Recorded 27 Apr 1774.

F-4, 542-547: 5 Oct 1773, Roger Pinckney, Esqr., Sheriff for Charles Town District, to Gabriel Gignilliat of Parish of St. John, Berkley County, planter, whereas Edward Newman, planter, deceased, was seized at the time of his death of the following plantations containing 250 acres in St. Johns Parish, Berkley County, adj. land of Tacitus Gaillard, John Pearces, William McNichols, granted to John hay 1761, and by lease & release 25 & 26 Nov 1770 conveyed to said Edward Newman; one other plantation of 100 acres in county aforesaid adj. land of Edward Newman, Charles Cantey, Samuel Dubois, conveyed by lease & release 15 & 16 May 1771 by Samuel Richbourgh; another plantation of 250 acres in parish aforesaid adj. William McNichols, John Hay, John Pearce, Isaac Courturier, granted 27 Nov 1770 to Edward Newman; another plantation of 200 acres on Santee River Swamp in Craven County, adj. land of Samuel Duboise, Isaac Bradwell, by lease & release 30 Apr & 1 May 1771 from Samuel Duboise to said Edward Newman; and said Edward Newman was bound 1 May 1771 to Gabriel Marion & Nathaniel Bull in the sum of £2800 for payment of £1400 with lawfull interest, and in the court of common pleas did implied Adam McDonald administrator of Edward Newman deceased and recovered at August Term 1773, sold to Gabriel Gignilliat for £4310. Roger Pinckney PM (LS), Wit: Jno Harleston, Benjn Gignilliat. Proved by the oath of Benjn Gignilliat before John Troup, J. P., in Charles Town District, 9 Feb 1774. Recorded 28 Apr 1774.

F-4, 547-553: Lease & release. 2 & 3 Nov 1762, Oliver Hart of Charles Town, Gentleman and Sarah his wife, to Mary Atwell, spinster, and Icabod Atwell of same, carpenter, for £1500, western parcel of the back part of a town lot number 102, adj. lot formerly of one William Chapman deceased, part of said lot 102 lately belonging to one William Screven the younger deceased and since his death sold to one Wm. Brisbane, adj. lot devised by one Wm. Screven the Elder also lately deceased to his daughter Eleanor Screven. Oliver Hart (LS), Sarah Hart (LS), Wit: Augustine Stillman, David Stoll, David Williams. Proved by the oath of David Stoll 6 July 1763 before Wm. Brisbane, J.P. Recorded 30 Apr 1774.

F-4, 554-555: Lease. 11 Feb 1773, Lewis Stapf of Parish of Prince William, County of Granville, carpenter, and Margaret his wife, to George Rentz, for ten shillings, eight lots in Jacksonborough, 74, 75, 76, 77, 86, 87, 88, and 89. Lewis Stapf (LS), Margret Stapf (+) (LS), Wit: John Macteer, Thos Patterson. Proved by the oath of Thos Patterson before John Hunt, J.P. for Colleton County, 27 Apr 1773.

END OF BOOK F-4.

SOUTH CAROLINA DEED ABSTRACTS 1773-1778

G-4, 1-2: 21 Dec 1772, Christiana Lever, wife of Samuel Lever, Shop keeper, relinquished dower to lease & release dated 17 & 18 December instant to Elizabeth Lever, lot on Colleton Square in Charles Town, by Thos Knox Gordon, Esqr. Chief Justice of South Carolina.

G-4, 3-6: Lease & release. 13 & 14 March 1773, John Brown of Prince George Parish, SC, and Mourning his wife, to James Elks of same parish and county, 350 acres in Craven County bounded on long bay on Waccamaw Neck, Dennis Hankins land, Bellamys land, John Murrells, widow Franks; granted to John Brown 24 Nov 1767. John Brown (X) (LS), Mourning Brown (O) (LS), Wit: Dalziel Hunter, David Griffiths. Proved 28 May 1773 before William Rugeley, J. P. for Craven county, by the oath of Dalziel Hunter. Recorded 3 Aug 1773.

G-4, 6-11: 26 & 27 May 1772, Alexander Joiner of St. Marks Parish, Carpenter, to James Berry of same, carpenter, for £200 SC money, 200 acres granted 21 May 1772 to said Alexander Joiner on east side Watree River on both sides Parking Creek adj. land of John Wheeler. Alexander Joiner (+) (LS), Wit: James McCormick, William Mitchell, John Rogers. Proved by the oath of James McCormick in Craven County before Wood Furman, J.P., 21 Nov 1772. Recorded 25 Aug 1773.

G-4, 11-14: South Carolina, Colleton County. 25 Nov 1769, John Heard and wife Lydia to Thos. Yates of said county, for £200 SC money, 400 acres granted 17 Feb 1753 to William Smith on Saluda River in Berkly County, vacant on all sides, recorded in Book OO folio 162, the said William Smith dying intestate, tract fallen to John Smith eldest son, and said John Smith sold to John Heard 8 March 1768, 200 acres divided by Wm. Anderson. John Heard (LS), Lydia Heard (LS), Wit: Thos Dillon, John Heard, Edmund Ellis. Proved in Colleton County 3 Oct 1772 by the oath of Thos. Dillon before Wm. Anderson, J.P. Recorded 25 Aug 1773.

G-4, 14-17: 8 March 1768, John Smith of County of Berkley, SC, and wife Mary, to John Heard of Colleton County, for £200 SC money, 200 acres, part of 400 acres granted to William Smith 13 Feb 1753, said William Smith dying intestate, the tract of 400 acres having fallen to John Smith eldest son and sole heir at law. John Smith (LS), Mary Smith (M) (LS), Wit: Thos Heard, Ann Heard (A), James Smith. Proved 8 March 1768 by the oath of Thos. Heard before John Savage, J.P. in Berkley County.

G-4, 18-20: 27 May 1768, James Sharp of St. Bartholomews Parish, SC, merchant, to Mathias Peter of same, Baker, for £100 SC money, lot 42 in village of Jacksonburgh on King St. James Sharp (LS), Wit: Robt. Ballingall, Samuel Wise. Proved in Berkley County before Wm. Mason, J.P., by the oath of Robt. Ballingall, 30 June 1768. Recorded 26 Aug 1773.

G-4, 20-24: Lease & release. 15 & 16 Aug 1758, Jean Brown and George Jackson, Executrix & Executor of the estate of Capt. John Jackson, late of Ponpon deceased, to James Sharp, Esqr., of St. Bartholomews Parish, Colleton County, for £28 SC money, lot in Jacksonburgh, by virtue of a devise in the will of Capt. John Jackson deceased, dated 24 March 1747. Jean Brown (LS), George Jackson (LS), Wit: William Fishburn, John Smith. Recorded 25 Aug 1773.

G-4, 24-26: Lease. 14 Jan 1772, Patrick Hinds of Charles Town, cordwainer, for five shillings to Christopher Taylor, lot in St. Phillips Parish, adj. land of Christopher Fitzsimmons, said Patrick Hinds, Roger Peter Handyside[?] Hartley; part of a tract lately belonging to William Wragg, Esqr, and by him conveyed to said Patrick Hinds 16 & 17 Aug 1769. Patrick Hinds (LS), Ann Hinds (LS), Wit: John Potter, Peter Monelar. Recorded 25 Aug 1773.

G-4, 26-33: Lease & release. 12 & 13 July 1773, Samuel Fley of Charles Town, cooper, and Frances his wife, to William Lee, watchmaker, of Charles Town, for £3500 SC money, lot # 27 on South side Broad Street in Charles Town, adj. lot formerly occupied by Isaac Holmes, adj. Francis Pagget, adj. John Britton. Samuel Fley (LS), Frances Fley (LS), Wit: Joel Holmes, Thos. Coker. Proved before William Rugeley, J.P. in Charles Town District, by the oath of Joel Holmes, 23 July 1773. Recorded 28 Aug 1773.

G-4, 33-38: Lease & release. 27 & 28 July 1772, Michael Dorman of Charles Town, Victualer, to Jacob Valk, gentleman, for £150, 150 acres in Boonesborough Township on a branch of Long Cane called Sink Branch, adj. James Lessle. Michael Dorman (LS), Wit: Benjamin King, James

SOUTH CAROLINA DEED ABSTRACTS 1773-1778

Thompson. Proved 28 July 1772 before William Calcott, J. P. in Berkley County, by the oath of Benjamin King. Recorded 30 Aug 1773.

G-4, 39-43: Lease & release. 28 & 29 May 1773, George Mullens of Charles Town, Gentleman, to Jacob Valk of same, gentleman, for £1000 SC money, 1000 acres in Kingston Township adj. Jenkins, Waccamaw River adj. land of Alexander Skeen Esq., John Guery, Joseph Greer, William Lowery. George Mullens (LS), Wit: Dandridge Clifford, Paul Schlatter. Proved 16 June 1773 before William Colcott, Esqr., J.P., by the oath of Dandridge Clifford. Recorded 8 Sept 1773.

G-4, 43-48: Lease & release. 22 & 23 July 1773, Elizabeth Dennis, widow, to Jacob Valk of Charlestown, Gentleman, for £150 SC money, 100 acres on waters of Little Lynches Creek in Craven County, vacant on all sides, granted 1 Sept 1768. Elizabeth Dennis (mark), Wit: Dandridge Clifford, W[illiam] Sanders. Proved 27 July 1773 before William Rugeley, J.P., by the oath of Dandridge Clifford. Recorded 2 Sept 1773.

G-4, 49-50: 23 July 1773, William Burrows, Esqr., Master in Chancery at Charles Town, to John Wagner of Charles Town, merchant, whereas the said John Wagner did exhibit his bill of complaint in the Court of Chancery against Charles Carson & William Carson and the respondent William Carson by John Troup, Esqr., his Guardian, said master decreed that tract be sold, plantation of 500 acres granted 4 July 1749, on 4 July said William Burrows did sell to John Wagner, for £1050. Wit: Wm. Print, Gabriel Manigault. Proved in Charles Town District 29 July 1773 before John Troup, J. P., by the oath of William Print. Recorded 1 Sept 1773.

G-4, 50-55: Lease & release. 28 & 29 Dec 1772, Isaac McPherson of St. Pauls Parish, Colleton county, Esquire, to William Williamson of Charlestown, Esquire, for ten shillings, 500 acres in Colleton County on south west side of Saludy River; another plantation of 500 acres on waters of Saludy River adj. Thomas Watson, John Crimps, Archibald Gillison, ranted on said day to Isaac McPherson; another plantation of 500 acres in Colleton County on waters of Turkey Creek waters of Saludy, on or about a mile from the Indian line granted on said day to Isaac McPherson; also 400 acres in Craven County on waters of Reyburns Creek adj. Benjamin Elliots, Samuel Elliotts, granted on said day to Isaac McPherson; also 100 acres in craven County on waters of Little River adj. Robert Purdy, granted on said day to Isaac McPherson. Isaac McPherson (LS), Wit :Robt Ladson, Edwd Perry. Proved in Colleton County before Andrew Leitch, Esqr., J.P., by the oath of Robt. Ladson, 29 Dec 1772. Recorded 2 Sept 1773.

G-4, 55-59: Lease & release. 7 & 8 Jan 1772, Giles Chapman & Sarah his wife of Craven County, for £300 SC money, to John Jones of same, by grant 16 Dec 1766 to Giles Chapman Senr, 300 acres on Scotch Creek in the fork between Broad and Saluday River, at the time of surveying called Berkley County but now Craven County, adj. Laurance[?] Ryley, John Brooks[?]. (Plat included, being 193 acres granted by Giles Chapman to Elizabeth Teague near Rileys corner). Giles Chapman (LS) Sarah Chapman (l) (LS), Wit: Eliza Teague, Joseph Brown, Giles Chapman Junr. Proved in Craven County before Thos Wadlington, J. P., by the oath of Eliza Teague, 2 Feb 1772. Recorded 2 Sept 1773.

G-4, 60-63: Lease & release. 22 & 23 July 1772, Thomas Osborne of St. Pauls Parish, SC, Esquire, to William Williams, Esqr., of Charles Town, for ten shillings, tract of 500 in Craven County on north side Enoree River, adj. Alexander Frazier, Philip Wells. Thos Osborne Wit: Joseph Glover, Thos Hext. Acknowledged in Colleton County before Joseph Glover, J.P. Recorded 3 Sept 1773.

G-4, 63-67: Lease & release. 1 & 2 July 1773, Col. George Paddon Brown of Christ Church Parish to Jacob Read of Charles Town, for 1250 acres in Ninety Six District on Moores Creek a branch of Little Saludy River adj. George Strawder's land, Patrick Dickey, Moses Kirkland, Michael Watson, Daniel Cannon, Edward Larrymor, Daniel Hartley, John McCartney, Jane McCartney, and another plantation of 1250 acres in Ninety Six District on big creek a branch of Saludy River adj. Benjamin Garrett, Thos Cotton, Daniel Mazyck; said tracts granted on 5 May last to George Paddon Bond. George Paddon Bond (LS), Wit: John Rose, Jacob Bond Junr. Proved 13 July 1773 before James Trail, Esqr., J. P. in Charles Town District, by the oath of Jacob Bond Junr. Recorded __ Sept 1773.

SOUTH CAROLINA DEED ABSTRACTS 1773-1778

G-4, 68-69: Bond. Benjamin Guerard of Charles Town, planter, bound to George Cooke and Arthur Downes in the sum of £10,000, 29 July 1773, to insure title to land sold by lease & release 28 & 29 July 1773. Benjamin Guerard (LS), Wit: Jacob Valk. Proved in Charles Town District by the oath of Jacob Valk before Wm. Rugeley, J.P., 2 Oct 1773

G-4, 69-75: Lease & release. 27 & 28 July 1773, Philip Jacob Tyserman and Dorothy his wife of St. George Parish, Berkley County, SC, planter, to Joseph Kemmel of Charles Town, baker, for £500, 250 acres on north side Indian field swamp original grant dated in 1756; also tract of 85 acres in St. George Parish, Berkley County adj. land laid out to Philip Jacob Tyserman the original grant dated 19 March 1773; another tract of 16 acres in St. George Parish adj. land laid out to John Noah, Philip Jacob Tyserman, Rebecca Moore, Andrew Hall. Philip Jacob Tyserman (LS), Dorothy Tyserman (+) (LS), Wit: Alex Horn, Michl. Keller. Proved in Charles Town District 9 July 1773 before Hopkin Price, J. P., by the oath of Alexander Horn. Recorded 4 Sept 1773.

G-4, 75-81: Lease & release. 5 & 6 May 1773, Darby Larey of Prince Fredericks Parish, Gentleman, to Robert McCottry of same, planter, for £100 SC money, 200 acres in Craven County on the head of Black Mingo Creek adj. Blake Leay White's land. Darby Larey (LS), Wit: John Godfrey, Joseph Johnson, John Barnes. Proved 31 July 1773 before Josiah Dubordieau, J.P. for George Town District, by the oath of Joseph Johnson. Recorded 7 Sept 1773.

G-4, 81-87: Lease & release. 27 & 28 July 1773, Joseph Barnett of Berkley County, to Thomas Adams of Charles Town, merchant, for £4000 SC money, by lease & release 28 & 29 Nov 1755 between John Hamilton then of Charles Town, Esqr., to William Simpson, Esqr., and John Murray, did sell 50,000 acres above a place called Ninety Six, and by indenture of partition between William Simpson and Elizabeth his wife and said John Murray, 7 July 1758, said tract divided into equal parts, and said 25,000 acres (being the south moiety) conveyed 18,050 acres on Saludy River adj. Benjamin Walker, James Mayson, Esqr., William Murray, William Simpson, Esqr.,
Joseph Barnet (LS), Wit: John Thesson, Abraham Maddock. Proved before Hopkin Price, J. P. for Berkley County, by the oath of John Thesson, 31 July 1773. Recorded 7 Sept 1773.

G-4, 87-90: 20 July 1739, Richard Wright, Esqr., of Prov. of SC, planter, to Alexander Hext of same, for £412, 103½ acres in St. Pauls Parish, Colleton County adj. land of sd. Richard Wright, and said Alexander Hext, Thomas Elliott, being part of a tract formerly belonging to Ralph Elms. Richard Wright (LS), Mary Wright (LS), Wit: Robt Wright, John Seabrook. Proved by the oath of John Seabrook 22 Aug 1743 before Jacob Motte, J.P. (Plat included for 103 acres part of 228 acres certified 5 June 1739. Thos Witter.) Recorded 7 Sept 1773.

G-4, 90-97: Lease & release. 29 & 30 July 1773, William Alexander Brisbane and Adam Fowler Brisbane, exrs. of will of William Brisbane, late of Charles Town, Esquire, deceased, dated 7 May 1771, to Philip Tidyman, of Charles Town, Jeweller, for £4850 SC money, lot #102 in Charles Town on Stolls Alley, being two westmost of three wooden tenements adjoining each other, lately built by said William Brisbane deceased and now in the possession of William Morgan and Andrew Hewett, tenents; adj. tenements belonging to James Brisbane, James Veree, Mary Atwell. William Alexr. Brisbane (LS), Adam F. Brisbane (LS), Wit: Danl. Crokatt, Alexr. James. Proved in Charles Town District by the oath of Daniel Crokatt before William Rugeley, J.P., 7 Aug 1773. Recorded 7 Sept 1773.

G-4, 98-101: Lease & release. 20 & 21 Apr 1773, Jonah Collins of Santee, planter, to Sampson Neyle of Charles Town, Esqr., for £100 SC money, 76 acres part of 130 acres granted 1 May 1770 adj. said Jonah Collins, said Sampson Neyle. Jonas Collins (LS), Wit: Paul Douxsaint, Thos. Evance. Proved in Charles Town District 21 Apr 1773 before Jacob Motte, Esqr., J.P., by the oath of Paul Douxsaint, Esqr.

G-4, 102-104: 5 Dec 1760, Hobl. William Bull, Edward Fenwicke and Othniel Beale, Esqrs., and Isaac Mazyck, Benjamin Smith, Robt. Pringle, George Saxby, Gabriel Manigault, Thos Middleton, Esqrs., Commissioners for Building the Parish Church of St. Michael, Charles Town, to George Gardner, for £50 SC money, pew in parish church of St. Michaels, number 104. Wit: Saml. Prioleau, Saml Cordy. Assigned by George Gardner to Paul Smiser, 16 May 1763. George Gardner (LS), Wit:

SOUTH CAROLINA DEED ABSTRACTS 1773-1778

Jno Gregg, Christopher King. Proved in Georgia 21 May 1763 before David Montague, Esqr., by the oath of Christopher King, 21 May 1763. Recorded 9 Sept 1773.

G-4, 104-108: Lease & release. 10 & 11 May 1773, John Bollough, Junr, of Christ Church Parish, planter, to Hester Baldwin of same, widow, for £180 SC money, 163 acres in Christ Church Parish John Bollough Junr (LS), Wit: John White, George Ion, John Ray. Proved in Berkley County before Love Durand, J.P., by the oath of John White, 2 June 1773. Recorded 10 Sept 1773.

G-4, 108-112: 22 Sept 1731, John Bayley of Bellinaclough in county of Tipperary, Kingdom of Ireland, Esqr., son and heir of John Bayley, late of same, esqr., deceased, by Alexander French of Charles Town, merchant, attorney of said John Bayley, to William Croll and Thos. McKee of Colleton County, SC, planters, for £2000 SC money, 8000 acres part of 48,000 acres granted 16 August 1698 to John Bayly, the father, Landgrave and Cassick; John Bailey the son by his deed 9 Nov 1722 appointed Alexander French his attorney. Alexander French (LS), Wit: John Bagen, Gabriel Peyrud. Proved before Daniel Green, Esqr., by the oath of Gabriel Peyrud, 11 Dec 1731. Enrolled in the Auditors Office, 31 May 1732, Old Grant Book folio 73 by Daniel Gibson for Jas. St. John, Auditor. Recorded 10 Sept 1773.

G-4, 112-116: 27 Feb 1773, John Creighton of Parish of St. James Goose Creek, SC, Innholder, and Barbara his wife, to Daniel Tharin of Charles Town, Gentleman, for £4000 SC money, 30 acres in St. James Goose Creek on North side of Broad River from Charles Town, adj. land of John Wragg, Esqr., Daniel Legare Senior, known by the name of the old Quarter House. John Creighton (LS), Barbara Creighton (+) (LS), Wit: John Giles, James Courtonne. Proved by the oath of John Giles 11 Sept 1773 before William Rugeley, J.P. Recorded 11 Sept 1773.

G-4, 117-122: Lease & release. 14 Feb 1773, John Hatfield of Charles Town, Innkeeper, and Sarah his wife, to Jacob Valk of Charles Town, Gentleman, for £127, 200 acres in St. Marks Parish, Craven County, adj. James Lynah's land, Santee River, granted 13 Oct 1765 to said John Hatfield. John Hatfield (LS), Sarah Hatfield (LS), Wit: Benjamin King, Dandridge Clifford. Proved 10 Feb 1773 before Willins Colcott, J. P. in Charles Town District, by the oath of Dandridge Clifford. Recorded 13 Sept 1773.

G-4, 122-125: Lease & release. 19 & 20 June 1739, John McTeer of Granville Co., SC, planter, to William Croll of Colleton Co., planter, for £500 SC money, 200 acres in Colleton County. John Macteer (LS), Wit: Jas Bogs, Isabell (I) (Boggs), Saml Riggs. [check original] Recorded 13 Sept 1773.

G-4, 126-133: Lease & release. [check original] 15 & 16 Oct 1766, Henry Laurens of Charles Town, Merchant, and Eleanor his wife, to Philip Meyer of same town, Sugar Baker, for £3000 SC money, lot #315 in Charles Town, originally granted by the Lords Proprietors 28 Oct 16_6 unto Jacob Allen, and part of the square of land taken up by John Archdale called Archdales square #97, by the last will and testament of his father John Laurens, late of SC, gentleman, adj. land of John Hodsdon, Daniel Blake, Market Square. Henry Laurens (LS), Eleanor Laurens (LS), Wit: Wm. Stoutenburgh, John Hopton. Proved by the oath of John hopton 14 Sept 1773 before Wm. Rugeley, J.P. Recorded 14 Sept 1773.

G-4, 133-139: Lease & release. 19 & 20 Aug 1773, John Provost, late Serjant in his Majestys 77th Regiment of foot now of Charles Town, to George Cuhun of Charles Town, Innkeeper, for £100 SC money, 200 acres in Craven county on south side of Jeffers Creek adj. George Polks land, Thomas Oliver, William Cook, McHuges land, granted to said John Provost 6 Feb 1773. John Provost (LS), Wit: Andrew Taylor, Christian Sigwald. Proved 20 Aug 1773 before William Nisbet, J. P. in Charles Town, by the oath of Christian Sigwald. Recorded 15 Sept 1773.

G-4, 139-144: Lease & release. 29 July 1773, Roger Pinckney, Esqr., Sheriff of Charles Town District, to Fenwick Bull of Charles Town, Esqr., whereas Joseph Walker of Charles Town, Taylor was lately seized of town lot in Charleston, purchased from exrs. of the late William Hall deceased on Church St, and said Joseph Walker by his bond dated 13 Feb 1773 to Charles Atkins and Plowden Weston of Charles Town, in the sum of £992 for the payment of £461 s1 d 10, and in the court of common pleas in an action, May term 1773, sold for £1040. Roger Pinckney S. C. T. Dis.

(LS), Wit: James Lynch, Joseph Milligan. Proved by the oath of Joseph Milligan in Charles Town District 21 Aug 1773. Recorded 15 Sept 1773.

G-4, 144-148: Lease & release. 20 & 21 Nov 1769, James Cavet late of the county of Lancaster, Province of Pennsylvania, Millwright, to Joseph Dickson of Rowan County, North Carolina, Blacksmith, for £25 NC money, 100 acres in Tryon County, formerly in Mecklenburg County, North Carolina, on Mitchells Creek on the south side of fairforest creek and on north side Tyger River, first granted to Henry Forster 3 Oct 1755 then conveyed by lease and release from said Foster to Francis Beaty 20 Sept 1765 then to James Cavet from said Francis Beaty. James Cavet (LS), Wit: William McKown, John Park. Recorded 15 Sept 1773.

G-4, 148-153: Lease & release. 6 & 7 Aug 1772, John Harleston of Charles Town, Esquire, and Elizabeth his wife, to John Fulker of same, joiner, for £100,200 SC money, land in that part of Charles Town called Harleston, lot #118, on Bull Street. John Harleston (LS), Elizabeth Harleston (LS), Wit: Margaret Corbett, Thos. Corbett. Proved in Charles Town District by the oath of Thos. Corbett before J. Grimball, J. P., 24 Aug 1773. Recorded 17 Sept 1773.

G-4, 153-160: Lease & release. 15 & 16 July 1773, Mary Elliott, as well as in her own right and as guardian of Elizabeth Burnham Elliot & Henrietta Elliott, Robt. Cochran & Mary his wife, & James Darby & Margaret his wife, of Charles Town, to Jonathan Badger, late of Providence & colony of Rhode Island, but now of Charles Town, SC, for £4000 SC money; whereas Charles Burnham late of Charles Town was seized of a lot in the town of Boston purchased of one Nicholas Merick and said Charles Burnham by will 3 February 1725 did bequeath unto his six children Charles, Nicholas, Nathaniel, Jonathan, Margaret & Mary, all the residue of his estate real and personal, and the death of four of the children Charles, Nathaniel, Jonathan, and Margaret, and by the laws of the Massachusetts government descends to their mother Mary Frost formerly Mary Burnham, their brother Nicholas & their sister Mary in equal proportion that is one third of four sixths each of the whole four sixths and where Mary Frost, formerly Mary Burnham the wife of Charles Burnham, did by her will dated 8 October 1766, did give to her part of the said lot in Boston and unto her grand daughters Elizabeth Burnham Elliott & Henrietta Elliott in equal moieties, and the said Mary Frost dyed leaving her said will in full force and Nicholas Burnham by his will dated 21 July 1746 devised the residue of his estate to the nieces Mary and Margaret Elliott now Mary Cochran & Margaret Darby to be divided between them. Robt Cochran (LS), Mary Cochran (LS), Mary Elliott (LS), James Darby (LS), Margt Darby (LS). Wit: George Sheed, Saml Badger. Proved by the oath of Samuel Badger 25 Aug 1774 before John Troup, J.P. Recorded 17 Sept 1773.

G-4, 160-166: Lease & release. 1 & 2 July 1773, Christian Redlisperger of Berkley County, SC, planter, to Gasper Strobel of same, planter, for £20 SC money, 183 acres in Berkley County on four hole swamp; and also 100 acres in Berkley County adj. to said tract of 183 acres. Christian Redlisperger (LS), Elizabeth Redlisperger (+) (LS), Wit: James Linsey, Saml. Parsons. Proved 26 Aug 1773 before Thos. Caton, J.P. in Charles Town District, by the oath of James Lindsay. Recorded 20 Sept 1773.

G-4, 166-171: Lease & mortgage. 15 & 16 May 1773, James Cook of St. James Parish, Goose Creek, surveyor, to George Cook of Charles Town, merchant, for £14,000 SC money, George Cook bound to James Cook and Alexander Gillon, executors of the will of Richard Beresford late of said Town, deceased, for the payment of £7,000, tract of 400 acres in Berkley County on north west side of the eastern branch of Wando River, also 400 acres in Berkley County, and another plantation of 200 acres in Berkley Count on north side of eastern branch of Wando River. James Cook (LS), Wit: Simon Tufts, Peter Bonnetheau. Mortgage satisfied 4 Aug 1774. Geo: Cooke. Proved by the oath of Peter Bonnetheau before Thos Grimball, J.P., 24 Aug 1773. Recorded 21 Sept 1773.

G-4, 172-180: Lease & release. 9 Oct 1767, Richard Capers and Thomas Capers of Granville County, executors of will of Thomas Capers, late of Charles Town, gentleman, to Samuel Elliott, Esqr., of Charles Town, and John Harrison, Practitioner in Physick & Surgery, and Susannah his wife, for £3,550; by a grant from the Lords Proprietors 10 March 1681, lot #64 in Charles Town, to John Rose, and by his deed 20 Jan 1790 to Richd Capers of this province, but since deceased, became invested in Wm Capers late also of said province, as Eldest son & Heir at Law of said

SOUTH CAROLINA DEED ABSTRACTS 1773-1778

Richard Capers, and by his deed 7 Sept 1695, to his mother in law Mary Capers and his brothers Richard Capers and Thos Capers and sisters Mary & Elizabeth Capers, and by virtue of a partition between the survivors of Mary Capers the younger and Elizabeth Capers now Elizabeth Jenkins; 10 September 1761 by last will and testament of Thomas Capers to his two sons Richard Capers and Thomas Capers, executors. Richard Capers, Thomas Capers. Wit: John Davies, Robt Middleton. "This lease and Release is null & void. John Harrison." Recorded 22 Sept 1773.

G-4, 180-186: Lease & release. 18 & 19 Feb 1773, James Tweed of London, Great Britain, merchant, by Alexander Tweed of Black Mingo, Craven County, SC, gentleman, his attorney, to William Ancrum, George Ancrum & Joshua Hirst of Charles Town, merchants, for £3,500 SC money, 500 acres on north branch of Black River originally granted by the Lords Proprietors to Richard Wigg and by divers mesne conveyances became vested in James Tweed, and by his letter of attorney dated 20 June 1771 appointed Alexander Tweed. James Tweed by Alexander Tweed (LS), Wit: Richard Singleton, David Dickson.

G-4, 187-192: Lease & release. 31 Aug & 1 Sept 1773, Isaac Creighton of Bush River, Berkley County, Schoolmaster, to Rowland Rugeley of Charles Town, for £20 SC money, 100 acres near Bourdeaux Township & Little River in Granville County, Prince Williams Parish, granted 2 September 1767 to said Isaac Crydon. Isaac Creighton alias Isaac Crydon (LS), Wit: George Chateris, Thos Bourke. Proved 7 Sept 1773 before William Rugeley, J. P. in Berkley County, by the oath of Thomas Bourke. Recorded 23 Sept 1773.

G-4, 192-195: 3 Oct 1772, James Peart of Granville County, SC, Deputy Surveyor, to William Catterton of same, for £100 SC money, tract in Granville County, Purysburgh Township, adj. John Heyward, Ann Heyward, Col. Daniel Heyward, Joseph Lagers, Lewis Michael, Henry Pourquin, John Vickers. James Peart (LS) Wit: Wm Wells, Thos Page. Proved 16 Apr 1773 before David Giroud, J. P. in Granville County, by the oath of Thos. Page. Recorded 23 Sept 1773.

G-4, 195-199: Lease & release. 22 & 23 Jan 1772, Elias Buckingham & Margaret Buckingham his wife to Conrad Kysell for __ hundred and eighty pounds lot in Charles Town [pages in poor condition]. Elias Buckingham (LS), Margaret Buckingham (LS), Wit: Thos You, Eml. Abrahams. Proved by the oath of Emanuel Abrahams before David ___, J. P. in Berkley County, 29 Jan 1772. Recorded 22 Sept 1773. [check original of this deed]

G-4, 199-204: Lease & mortgage. 10 & 11 Sept 1773, Blake Leay White, of Charles Town, house carpenter, and wife Elizabeth, to Edward Blake of same place, merchant, for £8880 penal sum for the payment of £4440, part of a lot in Charles Town on Orange St. Blake Leay White (LS), Elizabeth White (LS). Wit: Mary Richards, John Ward. Proved in Charles Town District by the oath of <u>Joshua</u> (signed John) Ward, 11 Sept 1773, before Thos. Phepoe, J.P. Recorded 24 Sept 1773.

G-4, 204-205: John Sansum & Susanah his wife, formerly Susannah Hodgedon and formerly of Island of Bermuda but now of Charles Town, to Albert Alberson of province aforesaid, for good causes and valuable consideration, tract in St. George Parish in the Island of Bermuda, granted to the late Albert Alberson & Susannah Hodgedon by Ann Anderson, by deed of gift dated 13 Nov 1764... dated 24 Aug 1773. John Sansum (LS), Susannah Sansum (+) (LS), Wit: John White ,John Bollough, Js. Dubose. Proved by the oath of John White before John Troup, 27 Aug 1773. Recorded 24 Sept 1773.

G-4, 205-212: Lease & release. 15 & 16 Apr 1773, Peter Stevenson of Charles Town, and Mary Jones his wife, to William Hales of same, gentleman, for £1700 SC money, three lots in Charles Town 2, 12, and 13, which were of Peter Benoist, late of Charles Town, merchant, about six acres on west side of high road in Charles Town, devised to his grandson Peter Stevenson; said Peter Benoist and Abigail his wife and Mary his daughter have all departed this life. Peter Stevenson. Wit: Thos Horsey, John Gabriel Guignard. Proved in Charles Town District by the oath of John Gabriel Guignard, 16 Sept 1773, before Thos. Evance, J.P. Recorded 27 Sept 1773.

G-4, 212-217: Lease & release. 23 & 24 Nov 1767, Robt. Croft of Parish of Prince Fredericks in Craven county, SC, planter, to Childermas Croft, for £1500 SC money, 450 acres in Craven County adj. John Russes land, and another tract of 400 acres bounding to the north on the aforesaid tract. Robt. Croft (LS), Wit: Peter Croft, Roger Brown. Proved in Charles Town District before Wm. Rugeley, J.P., by the oath of Peter Croft 20 Sept 1773. Recorded 28 Sept 1773.

G-4, 218-219: Lease. 16 Aug 1773, Micajah Pickett of St. Marks Parish, to Peter Donald, Doctor of Physick of St. Matthews Parish, for £350, 50 acres adj. land of Joseph Cates, part of 250 acres granted to sd. Micajah Pickett 7 Apr 1770. Micajah Pickett (LS), Wit: Philip Henson, Ralph Smith. Proved in Charles Town District by the oath of Ralph Smith 21 Sept 1773 before William Rugeley, J.P. Recorded 28 Sept 1773.

G-4, 219-221: Release. 17 Aug 1773, Micajah Pickett of St. Marks Parish, to Peter Donald, Doctor of Physick of St. Matthews Parish, for £350, 75 acres part of 150 acres granted to Wm. Mitchel, 24 Aug 1770 conveyed by lease & release to Micajah Pickett, 2 & 3 Sept 1771. Micajah Pickett (LS), Wit: Philip Henson, Ralph Smith. Proved in Charles Town District by the oath of Ralph Smith 21 Sept 1773 before William Rugeley, J.P. Recorded 28 Sept 1773.

G-4, 221-227: Lease & release. 15 & 16 Sept 1773. Peter Horn of Charles Town to Samuel Cross of same, Innkeeper, for ten shillings, 200 acres adj. land of William Mellard, granted to sd. Peter Horn 14 Sept instant. Peter Horn (LS), Wit: Dl. Mazyck, John Young. Proved 23 Sept 1773 before John Poaug Esqr., J.P., by the oath of Daniel Mazyck. Recorded 29 Sept 1773.

G-4, 227-233: Lease & release. 4 & 5 Sept 1773, John Jacob Paul of Amelia Township, Sc, and Barbary Paul his wife, to George Barsh, for £500 SC money, 300 acres in Amelia Township, adj. land laid out to Thos Granlish, heirs of Mathews Swabb; tract granted to Jacob Winter 15 May 1753 on Santee River John Jacob Paul (LS), Barbary Paul (+) (LS), Wit: Jacob Ulmer, Francis Dufourth, Eberhard Stynwinder. Proved 10 Sept 1773 before Edmund Cossens, J. P. in Camden District, by the oath of Jacob Ulmer. Recorded 2 Oct 1773.

G-4, 233-236: Lease & release. 13 & 14 Sept 1773, John Marion of Craven County, SC, to Dalziel Hunter of Wacamaw in said province, for £1000 SC money, 300 acres granted to sd. Marion in the year 1768. John Marion. Wit: Moses Roberts, Aaron Roberts. Proved 24 Sept 1773 before Nathaniel Dwight, Esqr., by the oath of Moses Roberts. Recorded 4 Oct 1773.

G-4, 236-242: 13 May 1763, Alexander Cormack of Charles Town, Taylor, to Jonathan Badger, Carpenter & Joiner, & John Marley of same place, Gentleman; Alexander Cormack by bond to Jonathan Badger & John Marley in the penal sum of £6000 SC money, whereas by bond 2 May 1773 stand bound with Alexander Cormack unto Jacob Mott, Esqr., one of the Exors. of the will of Joseph Pickering, decd., in the penal sum of £3000, moiety of a town lot in Charles Town heretofore belonging to Thomas Elliott of Berkley County, planter, deceased, on Tradd St., adj. to heirs of Col. Brewton, Jordan Roche deceased, now belonging to Mrs. Susannah Lorimer & in the occupation of Robert Williams Junr, Esqr.... bound to Jacob Motte and James Grindlay. Alexander Cormack (LS), Wit: Joseph Bee, David Sym. Proved before James Grindlay, J. P., by the oath of Joseph Bee, 13 May 1768. Recorded 5 Oct 1773.

G-4, 242-253: Lease & release. 4 & 5 March 1762, Champernoun Williamson of Colleton County, SC, planter, Eldest son of the devisees of the last will and testament & heir at Law of Benjamin Williamson, late of said county, planter, also deceased, which Benjamin Williamson was one of the sons & Devisees of the last will & testament of John Williamson the Elder, late of Stono, planter, also deceased, to John Freer the younger, planter, for £6000 SC money, 640 acres granted 20 July 1711 under the hands of Robert Gibbes, Esqr., then Governour, and Deputy of the late Lords Proprietors, and said John Williamson executed his last will & testament 25 July 1715 and devised 640 acres to his sons John, William, Richard, Benjamin, Joseph & Hennery Williamson, to be equally divided amongst the survivors, and said Benjamin left will dated 14 Feb 1746 devised to his eldest son Champernoun Williamson, by order of the court of common pleas 3 April 1759, unto Champernoun Williamson 40 acres called Spoon, adj. land of one ___ Ferguson, said William Williamson; and a parent dated 14 Nov 1761 to William Williamson, 192 acres and said William Williamson by lease & Release 13 & 14 Dec 1761 to said Champernon Williamson, 142 acres part of said 192 acres. Champernoun Williamson, Wit: Rebecca Rivers, John Jurdine, Susannah Freer. Proved before Robert Rivers, Esqr., J.P.for Berkley County, by the oath of John Jourdine, 5 March

SOUTH CAROLINA DEED ABSTRACTS 1773-1778

1762. A memorial entered in the Audr. Office in Book L No. 11, pages 123 & 124, 18 Feb 1772. Recorded 7 Oct 1773.

G-4, 254-259: Lease & release. 7 & 8 March 1755, David Bettison of St. Helen Parish, Granville county, planter, and Elizabeth his wife, to Luke Blakely of same, scrivener, for £200 SC money, 220 acres in Colleton County on Horse shoe Savannah adj. land of John Woodward, granted 28 Apr 1733 to Joseph Dingle and said land descended to Benjamin Dingle conveyed for £80 to David Bettison. David Bettison (LS), Wit: John Hussey, John Sealy. Proved 31 May 1755 by the oath of John Hussey before Henry Hyrne, J.P. Recorded 9 Oct 1773.

G-4, 259-264: Lease & release. 29 & 30 May 1755, David Bettison of St. Helen Parish, Granville county, planter, and Elizabeth his wife, to Luke Blakely of same, scrivener, for £200 SC money, 200 acres granted 30 July 1737 to John McCaw 200 acres in Colleton County, St. Bartholomews Parish, adj. land of William Ebberson, John Cook, Mr. Bettisons land, and John McCaw conveyed to Richard Dawson, then to David Bettison. David Bettison (LS), Wit: John Hussey, John Sealy. Proved 31 May 1755 by the oath of John Hussey before Henry Hyrne, J.P. Recorded 9 Oct 1773.

G-4, 265-270: Lease & release. 25 & 26 March 1749, Riganal, James, and Henry Jackson of St. Bartholomews Parish, Colleton County, planters, to John Paycom of same, planter, for £80, 43¼ acres on the high road, adj. land of John Paycom, estate of Mr. John Peters decd. Regana1 Jackson (LS), James Jackson (LS), Henry Jackson (LS), Wit: John McPherson, Henry Mashow. Proved 28 March 1749 by the oath of John McPherson and Henry Masheow, before Culch. Golightly, J.P. Recorded 11 Oct 1773.

G-4, 270-274: Lease & release. 6 & 7 Sept 1773, John Williams of Charles Town, carpenter, to Jacob Valk of same, gentleman, by bond in the penal sum of £41,923 s1 for the payment of £2641 s10 d6, mortgage of lots in Parish of St. Philip, Charles Town, on Church Street adj. land of Nathaniel Black, and also tract of 400 acres on the marsh of the sea shore near the mouth of Santee River in Parish of St. James Santee in Craven County, granted to said John Williams 8 Nov 1757 adj. land of Robert Morrel. John Williams (LS), Wit: John Pringle, Thos Shubrick Junr. Proved by the oath of Thos Shubrick Junr before John Rutledge, J. P., 5 Oct 1773. Recorded 15 Oct 1773. Mortgage satisfied 31 Jan 1775.

G-4, 275-279: Lease & release. 4 & 5 Sept 1764, Rev. Abraham Imer and wife Ann of Purrysburgh to Champernoun Williamson of Stono, planter, for £1800 SC money, 334 acres in Parish of St. Peter, Granville County, adj. Daniel Crawford, James Bullock, Savannah Black River, granted 2 March 1763 to said Abraham Imer. Abraham Imer (LS), Ann Imer (LS), Wit: Phil. Chiffelle, William Brown, William Keith. Proved in Charles Town District by the oath of Phil. Chiffelle before Wm. Rugeley, J. P., -- Oct 1773. Recorded __ Oct 1773.

G-4, 280-284: Lease & release. 25 & 26 Oct 1771, Samuel Perdriau of Charles Town, sadler, to John Joor of St. George Parish, £1850 SC money, tract by resurvey of 29 May 1767 in St. George Parish, parts of several tracts formerly belonged to Joseph Izard, Esqr. Saml Perdriau (LS), Wit: Saml Legare, Benja. Tucker. Proved by the oath of Benjamin Tucker before John Troup, J. P.,7 Oct 1773. Recorded 17 Oct 1773.

G-4, 284-285: Sampson Neyle of Charles Town, Esqr., for five shillings, to John Williams, of same, carpenter, by bond to Revd. Alexander Garden late of St. Philips Parish, Charles Town, deceased, 17 July 1754 for the payment of £900, by virtue of lease and release 23 & 24 Oct 1758 between John Williams of St. James Parish Santee and Benjamin Garden, Sampson Neyle and Francis Bremar, recorded in Book TT, pages 369-375. Sampson Neyle (LS), Wit: Dandridge Clifford, Press Smith. Proved 5 Oct 1773 before John Rutledge, Esqr., by the oath of Dandridge Clifford. Recorded 18 Oct 1773.

G-4, 286-289: Whereas on 16 & 17 July 1750, Charles Pinckney of Charles Town, Esquire and Elizabeth his wife, to John Williams of same, joiner and carpenter, & Alexander Garden Rector of Parish of St. Philip, Charles Town, that said John Williams had agreed to purchase of said Charles Pinckney, lots of land in Charles Town, for £900... by bond dated 17 July 1753 and whereas by one indenture 13 Apr 1761 between Sampson Neyle of Charles Town, Planter, surviving executor of will of Alexander Garden and trustee for Ann Stiles then wife of Copeland Stiles and daughter of Alexander Garden & Daniel Hunt of Parish of St. Philip, Esquire, said Daniel Hunt at the request of John Williams had advanced to Sampson Neyle in trust for marriage settlement of Copeland Stiles and Ann Garden, now William Hopton of Charles Town, exr. of will of Daniel Hunt, to John Williams for £567, dated 13 Feb 1773. Wit: Dandridge Clifford, Press Smith. Proved 5 Oct 1773 before John Rutledge, Esqr., by the oath of Dandridge Clifford. Recorded 18 Oct 1773.

G-4, 289-294: Lease & release. 5 & 6 Oct 1773, James Hutchison of Berkley County, SC, to Christian Gruber of Charles Town, Inn keeper, for £180, 500 acres in Berkley County on one of the west branches of Cypress Swamp called Captain's Creek adj. James Thompson, Capt. Wm. Dewitt, granted to James Hutcheson 10 May last. James Hutcheson Wit: Dl. Mazyck, Thos Winstanley. Proved 6 Oct 1773 before Wm. Nisbet, Esqr., J.P. for Charles Town District, by the oath of Danl. Mazyck. Recorded 19 Oct 1773.

G-4, 294-297: Lease & release. 27 & 28 Sept 1773, Edmund Cossens to William Downes of Charles Town, for ten shillings, 300 acres in Craven County, St. Marks Parish, on the head branches of Sawneys Creek adj. Stephen Miller, Esquire, John Atkinson, Esqr., granted to said Edmund Cossens 5 May last. Edmund Cossens (LS), Wit: William Doughty, Arthurton Rawstorne. Proved 8 Oct 1773 by the oath of Wm. Doughty before William Nisbett, J.P.

G-4, 297-303: Lease & release. 11 & 12 Oct 1773, William Newitt Edwards and Ann his wife of St. Marks Parish, to James McGill Senr. of same, 290 acres in Fredericksburgh Township, Craven County, St. Marks Parish, adj. Robert Searight, George Saxons[?], John Williams, Wateree River, granted to sd. William Newell Edwards 15 May 1751. Wm Newitt Edwards (LS), Ann Edwards (+), Wit: Yancey Saxon, Simon Edwards. Proved 13 Oct 1773 before Richd. Winn, J.P. in Craven County, by the oath of Yancey Saxon. Recorded 20 Oct 1773.

G-4, 303-304: 13 Jan 1772, Peter Johnston of Mecklinburgh County, North Carolina, to Robert Thomas of Tryon County, North Carolina, for £20, tract in Tryon County on waters of fairforest creek adj. John Thomas, including part of the brick hill, granted to Peter Johnston 11 Nov 1778 [sic for 1768]. Peter Johnston (Seal), Wit: Thos Polk, Saml Neisbett Junr, William Byers. Recorded in Tryon County at January Term 1772. Ezekl. Polk. Recorded 20 Oct 1773.

G-4, 304-307: Lease & release. 29 & 30 Sept 1773, John Murray, of Charles Town, Esqr., to Robt. McKeown of same, gentleman, for £1 SC money, 300 acres in Craven County on Jumpers Land Creek, adj. Maurice Weaver, Michael Jumpers, John Jones land, John McMullows, granted to sd. John Murray 2 April last. John Murray (LS), Wit: Thos Winstanley, Dl. Mazyck. Proved 5 Oct 1773 before William Nisbett, J. P., by the oath of Daniel Mazyck. Recorded 21 Oct 1773.

G-4, 307-311: Lease & release. 5 & 6 July 1771, Giles Tillett and Constant his wife of Tryon County, North Carolina, to John Thomas of Craven County, SC, for £500 SC money, 300 acres on fair forest creek adj. land laid out for John Kelsey, granted to sd. Giles Tillett by Gov. William Bull 12 Oct 1770. Giles Tillett (LS), Constant Tillett (+) (LS), Wit: Robert Thomas, Saml Byrd, Martha Thomas. Proved in Berkley County, Sc, before John Ford, J.P., by the oath of Robt. Thomas, 6 July 1771. Recorded 21 Oct 1773.

G-4, 311-316: Lease & release. 10 & 11 Oct 1773, David Baty of Charles Town, to Thomas Tod of same, for £200 SC money, 250 acres in Granville County on a branch of Turkey Creek, being a half of tract of 500 acres granted to Eugene Brenan 20 Oct 1772 (plat included). David Baty (LS), Wit: James Mackie, John White. Proved 13 Oct 1773 before Wm. Rugeley, J.P., by the oath of John White. Recorded 22 Oct 1772.

G-4, 316-322: Lease & release. 16 & 17 June 1769, Stephen Drayton of Granville County, SC, Esqr., and Elizabeth, otherwise called Elizabeth Waring, only child and heir at law of Josiah Warring, late of said province, planter, deceased, to Benjamin Stead, late of Charles Town but now of London, merchant, for £1430 s10 SC money, 250 acres adj. lands late of William Wragg, Esqr., Barnard Elliott, lands now or late of Thos Ford, Benjamin Stead, which formerly belonged to Joseph Newman deceased, which 250 acres on the death of sd. Josiah Waring intestate passed by the descent to said Elizabeth Drayton as only child and heress at Law. Stephen Drayton (LS), Eliz'h

SOUTH CAROLINA DEED ABSTRACTS 1773-1778

Drayton (LS), Wit: John Bartels, William Edwards. Proved in Charles Town District before William Rugeley, by the oath of John Bartels, 23 Oct 1773. Proved 23 Oct 1773.

G-4, 322-323: Stephen Drayton of SC, Esqr., bound to Benjamin Stead, late of Charles Town, but now of City of London, merchant, in the sum of £2870, 17 June 1769, bond for performance of previous instrument. Recorded 23 Oct 1773.

G-4, 324-325: John Elliott of Berkley County, SC, planter for five shillings, to Josiah Waring, 250 acres adj. lands of William Wragg, Barnard Elliott, Thos Ioor[?], dated 20 Jan 1752. John Elliott (LS), Elizabeth Elliott (LS), Wit: Jos Brailsford, Frederick Hox. Witness for Mrs. Elliott Saml Postell, Js. Smith. Proved by the oath of James Smith 29 Sept 1774 before Wm. Rugeley, J.P. Recd. 24 February 1761 of Mr. John Durant £5 currency in full for one tract of land about 200 acres in St. Marks Parish Craven County taken up by John Hayes, decd. & Sold by me. John Waring, Exr. Recorded 24 Oct 1773.

G-4, 325-327: Joseph Davis of ninety Six, Berkley County, by bond to William Glen Senr & William Glen Junr, merchants, in the penal sum of £790 s6 d8 for the payment of £395 s3 d4 on or before 12 Nov; 150 acres in Berkley County, Ninety Six District between Broad and Saludy Rivers on a small creek called Kings Creek bounding on vacant land at time of survey but since adj. James Moore, John Perry. Joseph Davis (LS), Wit: Geo Duncan, John McCall Junr. Proved in Charles Town District by the oath of John McCall Junr before Thos Phepoe, J. P., 14 Oct 1773. Recorded 2 Nov 1773.

G-4, 327-332: Lease & release. 19 & 20 Nov 1771, James McKelvey of St. John Parish, Berkley County, planter, to Ephraim Mitchell of Orangeburgh, St. Mathews Parish, surveyor, for £5 SC money, 150 acres in St. Johns Parish, Berkley County, adj. Charles Cantey, James McKelvey, Capt. Marion, also another plantation of 150 acres in said parish adj. James Roberts, Capt. Marion, James McKelvey, Charles Cantey, Esqr. James McKelvey (LS), Wit: Ema'l. Abrahams, Thos Jolly. Proved in Charles Town District by the oath of Emanuel Abrahams, 19 Oct 1773, before William Rugeley, J.P. Recorded 4 Nov 1773.

G-4, 332-337: Lease & release. 5 & 6 Apr 1768, Henry Whetstone of Amelia Township, Berkley County,k planter, to John Mitchell of same, surveyor, for £3 SC money, lot of land of half an acre in Orangeburgh on Broughton St., adj. to Adam Jutz, it being a lot granted to his father John Wetstone 1 May 1744. Henry Whetstone (W) (LS), Wit: William Mitchell, William Ballantine. Recorded 6 Nov 1773.

G-4, 337-342: Lease & release. 29 & 30 May 1771, William Mitchell of St. James Parish, Goose Creek, planter, to John Mitchell of Orangeburg, Gentleman, son of said William Mitchell, for natural love and affection, 400 acres in Orangeburgh Township adj. Emanuel Hagleman, Ballezor Stroman, Melchior Saxweller, Jacob Pierson, Henry Wurtzer, Pon Pon River, and John Rumph, granted to said William Mitchell 19 Sept 1770. Wm. Mitchell (LS), Wit: John Pelott, William Creighton, Robt. Byers. Proved by the oath of William Creighton in Berkley County, before Wm. Mason, J.P., 22 July 1771. Recorded 6 Sept 1773.

G-4, 343-346: Lease & release. 10 & 11 Oct 1770, Hannah Mackreth of Charles Town, Mantua Maker, to John Mitchell, Gentleman, for £5, town lot in Orangeburg, #396. Hannah Mackreth (LS), Wit: Sarrah Margriller Read, Katharine Bryan. Proved 15 Feb 1771 before Andrew Cunningham, J.P. for Colleton County, by the oath of Katharine Bryan. Recorded 10 Nov 1773.

G-4, 346-350: Lease & release. 10 & 11 March 1769, Samuel Brawford of Amelia Township, St. Matthews Parish, Berkley County, planter, to John Mitchell of Orangeburgh, deputy surveyor for £66 SC money, tract granted 12 Sept 1768 to James Brawford, 400 acres in fork of Edisto, adj. William Todd, Thos Lowe, recorded in book DDD page 563. Samuel Brawford (LS), Wit: John Ogle, M. D; Casper Brown, James McCune. Proved 27 Feb 1772 by the oath of John Gole, M. D., before Wm. Thompson, J.P. in Berkley County. Recorded 11 Nov 1773.

G-4, 350-353: 17 March 1770, Henry Laurens, Esqr., of Charles Town, to John Mitchell of said town, deputy surveyor, for £665 SC money, lot on Front St., adj. John McCall. Henry Laurens (LS),

SOUTH CAROLINA DEED ABSTRACTS 1773-1778

Wit: John Corry, John Lewis Gervais. Proved in Berkley County before John Bremar, J. P., by the oath of John Lewis Gervais, 5 July 1771. Recorded 11 Nov 1773.

G-4, 353-358: Lease & release. 26 & 27 June 1769, John Simmons of Berkley County, planter, to John Mitchell of Orangeburg Township, deputy surveyor, for £20 SC money, half of lot in Orangeburg granted 26 Sept 1736 to John Simmons, deceased, father of said John Simmons, adj. to Peter Rohte. John Simmons (LS), Wit: Jo. Fisher, Henry Zon. Proved 27 June 1769 before Christopher Rowe, Esqr., J. P. in Berkley County, by the oath of John Fisher. Recorded 11 Nov 1773.

G-4, 358-362: Lease & release. 3 & 4 Oct 1768, William Tod of Charles Town, yeoman, to John mitchell, of Orangeburg, Deputy Surveyor, for £50 SC money, 100 acres in the fork of Edisto granted 12 Sept 1768 to William Tod. William Tod (LS), Wit: Emanuel Abrahams, Francis Philips. Proved 7 Dec 1768 before William Thompson, J.P. in Berkley County, by the oath of Emanuel Abrahams. Recorded 13 Nov 1773.

G-4, 362-366: Lease & release. 1 & 2 Nov 1770, David mitchell of Charles Town, yeoman, to John Mitchell of Orangeburgh, Deputy Surveyor, for £105 SC money, 100 acres in the fork of Edisto River granted to said David Mitchell 12 Sept 1768. David Mitchell (X) (LS), Wit: Thos Buttler, Benjn. Farrar. Proved 22 March 1770 before William Thompson, J.P., by the oath of Benjamin Farrar, Esqr. Recorded 15 Nov 1773.

G-4, 366-370: Lease & release. 1 & 2 Nov 1768, Thos Lowe of Charles Town, yeoman, to John Mitchell of Orangeburg, Deputy Surveyor, for £100 SC money, 100 acres in the fork of Edisto River, adj. David Mitchell, granted 12 Sept 1768 to Thos. Lowe. Thomas Lowe (LS), Wit: Thos. Buttler, Saml. Richardson, Benjn. Farrar. Proved 22 March 1770 before William Thompson, J.P., by the oath of Benjamin Farrar, Esqr. Recorded 15 Nov 1773.

G-4, 370-374: Lease & release. 27 & 28 June 1769, John Barnard Schmidt of St. Matthews Parish, Berkley County, planter, to John Mitchell of Orangeburg, Deputy Surveyor, for £20 SC money, 100 acres in Berkley County, granted 12 Sept 1768 to John Barnard Schmidt, adj. land of William Grace. John Barnard Schmidt (LS), Wit: Paul Sheier, Johannes Hock, Melchior Smith. Proved by the oath of Paul Sheier before John Colcock, J. P., in Berkley County, 6 Aug 1769. Recorded 15 Nov 1773.

G-4, 374-380: Lease & release. 7 & 8 Dec 1767, James Tilley of St. Mathews Parish, Berkley County, planter, to John Mitchell of Orangeburg, Deputy Surveyor, for £2 s10, lot of ½acre, #293, granted to his father James Tilley, 4 June 1759. James Tilley (LS), Wit: Jo Fisher, John Blitchington, Jno. Johnston. Proved 8 Dec 1767 by the oath of John Fisher before Gavin Pou, J.P. in Berkley County. Recorded 16 Nov 1773.

G-4, 381-382: 5 May 1745, George Anson, Esqr., by Benjamin Whitaker, Esqr., his attorney, to Noah Sere, Esqr., for £250 SC money, lot of one acre in Ansonborough. Benjn Whitaker (LS), Wit: George Marshall, Wm. Burrows, Christopher Gadsden, Hans William Welshing Sen. Proved by the oath of William Burrows, Esqr., before John Troup, J. P., 18 Oct 1773. Recorded 16 Nov 1773.

G-4, 382-386: Lease & release. 7 & 8 Feb 1773, Michael Hunsinger of Charles Town, Baker, to Conrad Kysell of same, inn keeper, for £100 SC money, 150 acres granted to said Michael Hunsinger 6 Feb instant on the Bounty in Orangeburg Township. Michael Hunsinger (LS), Wit: Stepn. Biddurph, Thos Keller, Francis Defour. Proved by the oath of Thos Keller before William Nisbett, J.P., 6 Oct 1773. Recorded 17 Nov 1773.

G-4, 386-392: Lease & release. 8 May 1771, Adam & Elizabeth Gutt of Craven County, to Conrad Kysell of Charles Town, for £100 sterling money of SC, 200 acres on a branch of Cedar Creek in Craven County, adj. land of Christopher Metz. Adam Gutt (+) (LS), Eliz. Gutt (&) (LS), Wit: Francis Defour, Jacob Ernst. Proved before Wm. Nisbett, Esqr., in Charles Town District by the oath of Jacob Ernst, 8 Sept 1773. Recorded 20 Nov 1773.

SOUTH CAROLINA DEED ABSTRACTS 1773-1778

G-4, 392-397: Lease & release. 20 March 1772, Jonathan & Lucy Cooper of Charles Town, to Conrad Kysell of Charles Town, for £400 SC money, 200 acres in Orangeburg Township, Berkley County, adj. land of George Preel[?]. Jonathan Cooper (LS), Lucy Cooper (+) (LS), Wit: Nicholas Fittig, Abraham Thacker. Proved in Charles Town District before Wm. Nisbett, J.P., by the oath of Nicholas Fittig, 11 Sept 1773. Recorded 21 Nov 1773.

G-4, 397-402: Lease & release. 28 Feb & 1 March 1770, George Hanersin & Barbary Hanersin of Berkly County, to Conrad Kysell of Charles Town, for £150 SC money, 150 acres on Log Creek, adj. Elizabeth Aldbright. George Henersin (LS), Barbara Henersin (X) (LS), Wit: Francis Dufour, Robert Clark, Jacob Williman. Proved in Charles Town District by the oath of Jacob Willeman before William Nisbett, J.P., 9 Sept 1773. Recorded 26 Nov 1773.

G-4, 403-408: Lease & release. 14 & 15 Oct 1770, John Beltzer of Berkley County, Butcher, to Conrad Kysell of Charles Town, for £100 SC money, 100 acres on south west side of the Congaree River near a branch called Sandy Run adj. land surveyed for Hopson Keisling, Mr. Ward, Phillip Thills. John Beltzer. Wit: Dl. Mazyck, Thos Winstanley. Proved before William Nisbett, J.P. in Charles Town District, by the oath of Daniel Mazyck, 9 Sept 1773. Recorded 19 Dec 1773.

G-4, 408-409: 2 Nov 1772, Edward Kirk of Charles Town, Gentleman, to James Fallows of same, shop keeper, for five shillings, 600 acres in Berkley County adj. land laid out to Christian Seywald. Edward Kirk. Wit: Edward Jones, William Kennedy. Recorded 31 Dec 1773.

G-4, 410-418: Power of attorney. 25 March 1772, before Isaac Mendes Belisario, Notary Publick dwelling in London by legal authority, Joseph Salvador makes power of attorney 25 September 1769, to Richard Andrews Rapley, concerning 100,000 acres. Joseph Salvador (LS), Wit: James Corren, Robt. Atkinson. Proved before William Nash, Lord Mayor of London. Recorded 3 Jan 1774.

G-4, 418-423: Power of attorney. 25 Sept 1769, Joseph Salvador makes power of attorney to Richard Andrews Rapley, concerning 100,000 acres, tracts 3 & 4 on Saludy River. Joseph Salvador (LS), Wit: Francis Salvador, Isaac Mendes Belisario. Proved by the oath of Isaac Mendes Belisario on the Pentateuch, 26 Sept 17698 before Samuel Turner, Mayor[?]. Recorded 3 Jan 1774.

G-4, 423-432: Power of attorney. 3 Feb 1773, Joseph Salvador makes power of attorney to Richard Andrews Rapley, concerning land near Long Canes Settlement, pat of tract laid out to John Hamilton, Esquire, tracts 3 & 4. Joseph Salvador (LS), Wit: Elias Burzaglo, Robt. Atkinson. Proved by the oath of Elias Burzaglo. Recorded 5 Jan 1774.

G-4, 432-436: Lease & release. 1 July 1772, George Hollingsworth, Miller, in Craven County, and Jean his wife, to John Williams of same, merchant, for £175 SC money, 155 acres, part of 350 acres on Mudlick, waters of little River, adj. land of John Caldwell, granted 14 Sept 1771. George hollingsworth (LS), Jean Hollingsworth (LS), Wit: Joseph Hollingsworth, George Hollingsworth, James Hollingsworth. Proved by the affirmation of Joseph Hollingsworth, one of the people called Quakers, before John Caldwell, J. P., 7 Aug 1773. Recorded 6 Jan 1774.

G-4, 436-439: Lease & release. 6 & 7 July 1773, Stephen Creech late of the Province of South Carolina, now of Guilford County, North Carolina, to John Williams, S. D. Merchant of District of Ninety Six, for £100 SC money, 100 acres on waters of Mudlick Creek adj. John ONeals, William ONeals, grant recorded in Book HHH, page 45. Stephen Creech (LS), Wit: John North, Martha Caldwell, Jean Caldwell. Proved in Ninety Six District before John Caldwell, J. P., by the oath of Jane Caldwell, 10 July 1773. Recorded 6 Jan 1774.

G-4, 440-444: Lease & release. 31 Dec 1772 & 1 Jan 1773, Isaac Mitchell of Colleton County, SC, and Mary his wife, to John Williams of Craven County, SC, for £838 SC money, 296 acres on a branch of Ninety Six Creek, waters of Saludy River, on a small branch being the dividing line between said Isaac Mitchell and John Williams, adj. land of Thomas Murphy, Sarah Gentry, Thomas Eustace, Cornelius Dunavan, Joseph Atkins; granted to Lachlan Mackintosh 18 May 1763, conveyed by said Lachlan Mackintosh by lease & release 5 & 6 Jan 1772 to said Isaac Mitchell.

SOUTH CAROLINA DEED ABSTRACTS 1773-1778

Isaac Mitchell (LS), Mary Mitchell (LS), Wit: Danl Bailey, John Bullock, George Forrest. Proved 1 Jan 1773 before William Anderson, J. P., by the oath of Daniel Bayley. Recorded 7 Jan 1774.

G-4, 445-450: Lease & release. 31 Dec 1772 & 1 Jan 1773, Isaac Mitchell of Colleton County, SC, & Mary his wife, to John Williams, trader, of Craven County, SC, for £200 SC money, 200 acres in Colleton County on waters of Six Miles Creek, adj. land of Thomas Murphy, Alexander Mackintosh, it being a bounty warrant granted to Thomas Eustace 1 June 1767, conveyed to John Dooley & by said John Dooley to Isaac Mitchell in the year 1766 [sic]. Isaac Mitchell (LS), Mary Mitchell (M) (LS), Wit: Danl Bailey, John Bullock, George Forrest. Proved 1 Jan 1773 before William Anderson, J. P., by the oath of Daniel Bailey. Recorded 8 Jan 1774.

G-4, 450-456: Lease & release. 31 Dec 1772 & 1 Jan 1773, Isaac Mitchell of Colleton County, SC, & Mary his wife, to John Williams, trader, of Craven County, SC, for £50 SC money, 50 acres in Colleton County on waters of Six Miles Creek, adj. land former Thomas Eustaces, Alexander McIntosh; granted to Cornelius Dunavant 1 June 1767, conveyed by Thos. Eustace to John Dooley & by said John Dooley to Isaac Mitchell. Isaac Mitchell (LS), Mary Mitchell (M) (LS), Wit: Danl Bailey, John Bullock, George Forrest. Proved 1 Jan 1773 before William Anderson, J. P., by the oath of Daniel Bailey. Recorded 12 Jan 1774.

G-4, 456-459: Lease & release. 11 & 12 Feb 1773, Matthew Motts of Craven County, SC, and Mary his wife, to John Williams, son of Daniel, merchant of county & province aforesaid, for £1150 SC money, 350 acres on Mudlick Creek, originally granted to Jonathan Motts, conveyed to the aforesaid Mathew Motts by lease & release 6 July 1768, adj. land of James Young, William Nelly, John Caldwell, and land lait out to Mary Seirs, Jacob Gray; plat recorded in Book III, page 133. Matthew Motts (M) (LS), Wit: Richd North (N), John Robinson, John Thomas. Recorded 12 Jan 1774.

G-4, 460-464: Lease & release. 9 & 10 Feb 1772, Moses Yarborough & Francis his wife of Berkley County, SC, to John Williams of 96, planter, for £800 SC money, 300 acres on a small branch of 96 Creek in Berkley County, adj. land held by John Savage of 96, one Mackintosh. Moses Yarborough (LS), Francis Yarborough (+), Wit: Hugh Mack Good, Saml Williams (S). Proved in 96 District before Champness Terry, J. P., by the oath of Mackernnas Good, 8 Feb 1773. Recorded 14 Jan 1774.

G-4, 464-467: Lease & release. 7 & 8 Sept 1772, James Lindley of Craven County, Esqr., and Mary his wife, to John Williams, merchant, of same, for £112 SC money, land granted 12 Sept 1768 to Robert Briggs, on a branch of Rabins Creek adj. land of John Turk, and said Robert Briggs did convey to Ralph Humphries, and said Ralph did on 31 Jan 1772 to James Lindley, Esqr. James Lindley (LS), Mary Lindley (LS), Wit: Thos Cohune, Randal Hennesley. Recorded 15 Jan 1774.

END OF BOOK G-4.

SOUTH CAROLINA DEED ABSTRACTS 1773-1778

H-4, 1-5: Lease & release. 16 & 17 Apr 1772, John Soulegre of Port Royal Island, SC, to Elias Robert of Prince Williams Parish, SC, surveyor, for £500 SC money, 250 acres in Prince Williams Parish, Granville County, adj. lands in dispute between John Cox and Isaac McPherson. John Soulegre (I) (LS), Wit: John Grimball, Sarah Robert Junr. Proved before Andrew Aggnew, Esqr., J. P. in Granville County by the oath of John Grimball. Recorded 31 July 1773.

H-4, 6-12: Lease & release. 9 & 10 July 1773, Elias Robert of Granville County, Sc, to Jacob Valk of Charles Town, gentleman, for £300 SC money, 250 acres in Prince Williams Parish, Granville County, about seven miles from Pocotaligo Bridge within a half mile of the main road from Pocotaligo bridge up Coosawhatchie Swamp to Mathis's bluff on Savannah River adj. lands in dispute between John Cox and Isaac McPherson. Elias Robert (LS), Wit: Henry Hall, Paul Schlatter. Proved in Charles Town District 10 July 1773 before Willins Calcot, Esqr., J.P., by the oath of Paul Schlatter. Recorded 1 Sept 1773.

H-4, 12-18: Lease & mortgage. 21 & 22 July 1773, Jacob Warley of Charles Town, Saddler, and Christianna his wife, to John Wagner of same, merchant, bound 14th of this instant in the sum of £3000, lot in Charles Town on King St., Jacob Warley. Wit: Jacob Warley Junr, William Print. Proved 26 July 1773 by the oath of William Print before William Burrows. Recorded 2 Sept 1773.

H-4, 19-23: Lease & release. 23 & 24 May 1772, Alexander Fraser, esqr., of Charlestown, to William Williamson of same, esqr., for ten shillings, 1200 acres on north side of Enoree River adj. land laid out to Robert Goodin, Benjamin Elliot's[?], granted to Alexander Fraser 20 July instant; also 3000 acres in the fork between Broad and Saludy river on a branch called Deans Creek, granted to said Alexander Fraser on same day; Alexander Fraser. Wit: Mary Jenet Boyd, Thomas Shubrick Junr. Proved in Berkley County before John Rutledge, J.P., by the oath of Thomas Shubrick Junr, 24 July 1772. Recorded 3 Sept 1773.

H-4, 23-27: Lease & release. 23 & 24 July 1772, Thomas Heyward of Charlestown, esqr., to William Williamson of same, esqr., for ten shillings, 1250 acres in the fork between Broad and Saludy River on a branch of Tigar called Beards branch, adj. Charles Wells, William Gists, granted 20 July instant to Thomas Heyward. Thomas Heyward Junr (LS), Wit: Charles Cotesworth Pinckney, Alexander Walker. Proved in Charles Town District by the oath of Alexander Walker 16 Oct 1773. Recorded 21 Oct 1773.

H-4, 27-34: Lease & release. 28 & 29 July 1773, Benjamin Guerard of Charlestown, planter, to George Cooke and Author Downs of same, merchants, for £10,000, lot on Broad St., bequeathed to Benjamin Guerard his father the late John Guerard, Esqr. Benjamin Guerard (LS), Wit: Jacob Valk, Paul Schlatter. Proved 30 July 1773 before Hopkins Price, J.P. in Charlestown, by the oath of Jacob Valk.

H-4, 34-35: At Charlestown, April 15th 17--, in consequence of continuing that street beyond Cravens Bastian, agreement between Elias Ball and John Harleston [pages in poor condition]. Wit: Robert Raper, David Brown, Ro't Brisbane[?]. Recorded 4 Sept 1773.

H-4, 35-37: Memorandum the agreement of dividing the Lott Mr. Prells point between Elias Ball & John Harleston, 7 Jan 1738. Elias Ball, John Harleston (LS), Wit: John Scott. Present when the within agreement was concluded on that Capt. Ball drew the back half lot Mrs. Ann Austin, Mrs. Eliza Vickeridg, Mr. Nicholas Harleston, Mr. Elias Ball Junr, Mr. John Ball and James Akin. Proved in Chs. Town District by the oath of Jonathan Scott before William Rugeley, J.P., 5 May 1774. Recorded 4 May.

H-4, 38-39: John Wooding of Charlestown, bound to Thomas Woodin in the sum of £428 s16 d 8 SC money, __ April 1773, to make title to two separate lands one of 150 acres and the other 632 acres in Colleton County. John Woodin (LS), Wit: Thomas Smith, m. Rhodes. Proved in Charlestown District by the oath of Wm. Rohdes[?] 31 Aug 1773 before William Rugeley, J.P. Recorded 4 Sept 1773.

H-4, 39-40: John Wooding of Parish of St. Michael, Charlestown, for £482 s16 d 8, to Thomas Woodin, 150 acres in Granville County and 632 acres taken up in the name of John Freer, Esqr., of Johns Island, 8 April 1773. John Woodin (LS), Wit: Thomas Smith, William Coats. Proved by the oath of William Coats in Charlestown District 30 August 1773 before William Rugeley, J.P. Recorded 4 Sept 1773.

H-4, 41-47: Lease & release. 26 & 27 Aug 1773, Gasper Stroble of Berkley County, planter, and Obillia his wife, to Thomas Young of Charlestown, bricklayer, for £300 SC money, 183 acres in Berkley County on four hole swamp adj. Abraham Dupoint; another tract of 100 acres in Berkley County on four hole swamp, adj. the aforesaid tract of 183 acres; another tract of 150 acres in Berkley County on a branch of four hole swamp, adj. Christian Redlisperger. Gasper Stroble (LS), Obillia Stroble (+) (LS), Wit: Alexr Keith, William Wilking. Proved by the oath of Wm Wilkins, 27 Aug 1773. Recorded 7 Sept 1773.

H-4, 47-55: Marriage settlement. 6 & 7 Apr 1773, Margret Elliott of Charleston, SC, spinster, of the first part, to James Darby late of Great Britain but now of Charleston, Gentleman, of the second part, and Mary Elliott and Anne Elliott of the same, gentlewomen, of the third part; whereas a marriage is intended between Margret Elliott and said James Darby, in trust a plantation in St. Phillips Parish on east side of the Broad Roade in Charlestown neck, 118½ acres and slaves [named], and a certain tanyard in partnership with Capt. Robert Cochan, town lot on Church St. James Darby (LS), Mary Elliot (LS), Margret Elliot (LS), Ann Elliot (LS), Wit: Henry Rivers, William Sheed. Proved by the oath of Henry Powers before William Rugeley, 3 Aug 1773. Recorded 8 Sept 1773.

H-4, 55-60: Lease & release. 7 & 8 Dec 1772, Thomas Potts of Craven County, SC, planter, to John Bouneau of same, planter, for £500 SC money, 430 acres in Craven County, adj. John Horry, granted by Gov. Robert Johnson, Esqr., to Thomas Potts, father of the party to these presents, 17 May 1734. Thos Potts (LS), Wit: Jesse Ballard, Sarah Ford, Wm. Turner. Proved by the oath of Jesse Ballard 22 July 1773, before Joseph Dubourdieu. Recorded 7 Sept 1773.

H-4, 61-66: Lease & release. 5 & 6 Aug 1773, Joseph Stanyarn of St. Pauls Parish, SC, planter, to William Holiday of Charlestown, gentleman, bound in the sum of £7760, 450 acres on Cacaw Swamp in St. Pauls Parish, adj. land of Doctor Haig, Thomas Ellis, estate of Thomas Hartley deceased, estate of Rignal[?] Smith deceased. Joseph Stanyarne. Wit: Jacob Valk, Peter LePole. Proved by the oath of Jacob Valk, 19 Aug 1773.

H-4, 67-72: Lease & release. 15 & 16 Oct 1766, Aquilla Myles of Berkley County, SC, to Thomas Sumter, merchant, for £500, 200 acres on south side Santee, granted to Aquilla Miles. Aquilla Myles (LS), Eliz'a Myles (LS), Wit: John Wilson, John Kennedy, Abner Coalman (mark). Proved by the oath of John Wilson 11 June 1773 before John Troup, J.P. Recorded 8 Sept 1773.

H-4, 73-76: Lease & release. 20 & 21 Apr 1773, Jonah Collins of Santee, planter, to Sampson Neyle of Charlestown, Esqr., for £600, 420 acres in St. James Santee, adj. William Lewis, Sampson Neyle, Jonah Collins. Jonah Collins (LS), Wit: Paul Douxsaint, Thomas Evance. Proved 21 Apr 1773 by the oath of Paul Douxsaint before Jacob Mott, J.P. Recorded 9 Sept 1773.

H-4, 76-77: Deodoris Fechtner of St. George Parish to Frederick Knobeth for £50 SC money, 150 acres whereon I now live, joining to me 100 acres that was given to said Frederick Knobeth, part of 450 acres track of bounty land granted to sd. Deodoris Fechter, to my grandson Martin Knobeth a bay horse and to my grand daughter Elizabeth Knobeth, a black sided cow branded DF, 19 July 1772. Deodoris Fetchner (mark), Wit: John Ogle, Robert Smith. Proved in Orangeburgh District before Christopher Rowe, J.P., by the oath of Robert Smith, 28 Aug 1773. Recorded 9 Sept 1773.

H-4, 78-83: Lease & release. 29 & 30 Dec 1772, Stephen miller in Parish of St. Thomas & St. Denis, SC, planter, to George Archibald Hall of same, schoolmaster, for £200 SC money, 20 acres in Berkley County adj. Beresfords Bounty, Glebe Land, John Moore. Stephen Miller (LS), Wit: Martha Glen, Archibald Thomas. Proved 30 Dec 1772 before John Syme, J.P., by the oath of Archd. Thomson. Recorded 9 Sept 1773.

H-4, 83-90: Lease & release. 11 & 12 March 1737, John Denny of Colleton County, planter, & Sarah his wife, to John Fabian Junr, Cordwinder, for £200, 187 acres in Colleton County adj. John

SOUTH CAROLINA DEED ABSTRACTS 1773-1778

Newtons, William Crowl, Bryan Kelly, John Carmichel. John Denny (I) (LS), Sarah Denny (8). Wit: John Bee Junr, Thos Sacheverell. Proved 13 Aug 1773 by the testimony of James Skirving to the handwriting of John Bee deceased, before J. Rutledge, J. P. Recorded 10 Sept 1773.

H-4, 90-93: 25 May 1748, James Vouloux of Charlestown & Louisa his wife, to Paul Smyser of same, shopkeeper, for £1000 SC money, part of a town lot on south side Broad Street in Charlestown, adj. French church. Jaques Vouloux, Louise Vouloux (LS), Wit: Ro't Remington, Mathew Vanal. Proved by the oath of John Remington, Esqr., 16 Aug 1773. Recorded 11 Sept 1773.

H-4, 94-99: Lease & release. 10 & 11 Aug 1773, John Hunt, Esqr., of St. Bartholomews Parish, SC, and wife Ann, to John McQueen, Esqr., of Charlestown, for £500 SC money, 300 acres in St. Bartholomews Parish. John Hunt (LS), Wit: John Mouatt, John Dart. Plat included stating that it was part of tract laid out to John Woodward 10 May 1707, adj. lands of the estate of John McQueen, on a public road, lands of Edward Fenwicke, Esqr. Plat certified 28 Oct 1771 by Alex's Mador Forster. Proved by the oath of John Mouatt 13 Aug 1773 before William Rugeley, J.P. Recorded 13 Sept 1773.

H-4, 99-104: Lease & release. 13 & 14 July 1773, Fredrick Glazier to Jacob Valk of Charlestown, Gentleman, £3000 SC money, 200 acres in Colleton County on the waters of Saludy River adj. Henry Foster, Morris Givins, James Norrell, plat made 23 Jan 1773. Frederick Glazier (LS), Wit: Robert Warring, Patrick Fleming. Proved 15 July 1773 before Willing Calcott, J.P., by the oath of Robert Warring. Recorded 13 Sept 1773.

H-4, 104-106: Whereas William Brisbane, late of Charlestown, deceased, by his will dated 11 May 1771, did amongst other things did order that a sum to paid to his wife Eunice Brisbane in a month after his death £7000 with lawful interest... and appointed his sons William and Adam executors.... said Eunice does quit claim to dower in said estate. Eunice Brisbane (LS), Wit: Martha Stephens, Ann Stephens. Proved by the oath of miss Martha stephens before William Rugeley, J.P., 19 Aug 1773. Recorded 13 Sept 1773.

H-4, 106-110: Lease & release. 9 & 10 Apr 1771, John Geiger of Saluda, Craven County, SC, planter, and his wife Mary, to Henery Patrick of same province, for £80, 50 acres on north side Saluda River on said River adj. land of John Wever, John Gieger [sic]; said 50 acres granted to Barbara Bomer 14 Nov 1754. John Geiger (N), Mary Geiger (X), Wit: Arthur McCracken, William Fitzpatrick. Proved 28 June 1771 before William Arthur, J. P. in Berkley County. Recorded 14 Sept 1773.

H-4, 110-115: Lease & release. 4 & 5 May 1773, Jacob Friday of Berkley County, Sc, planter, to Henery Patrick, Esqr., of same, for £20, one acre and two-fifths, part of 50 acres granted to Martain Friday 5 June 1742 in Saxegotha Township, on the main road from the Congarees to Saludy which devides the hereby bargained premises, adj. land of Joseph Kershaw & Co., and adj. to said Jacob Fridays land. Jacob Fridig, Barbara Frydig (M), Wit: Casimir Patrick, Stephen Deddurph. Proved 16 Aug 1773 by the oath of Casimir Patrick before Wm. Arther, J.P. Recorded 14 Sept 1773.

H-4, 115-119: Lease & release. 29 & 30 Sept 1766, Francis Beatey of Mecklenburg County, North Carolina, to James Cavet of Rowan County, same province, carpenter, for £25 NC money, 200 acres in Mecklenburgh County on Mitchells Creek, south side of Fairforest Creek, granted to Henry Foster 3 Oct 1755 and conveyed by Foster by lease & release to Francis Beaty 20 & 21 Sept 1765. Francis Beatey (LS), Wit: Robt Armstrong, James Beatey, Adam Meek. Proved at October Court 1766 in Mecklenburg County and recorded in the Clerks office Pr Robert Harris, C. C. Recorded 26 Sept 1773.

H-4, 119-123: Lease & release. 20 & 21 Sept 1765, Henry Foster on Catawba River, late of the County of Mecklenburgh, NC, Esquire, to Francis Beaty of Mecklenburgh County, D. Receiver of Quit Rents, for £15 NC money, 200 acres on Mitchells Creek, south side of Fairforest Creek, granted 3 Oct 1755 to said Henry Foster. Henry Foster (LS), Wit: Robt Armstrong, Francis McMeen, Hugh Beatey. Recorded in Mecklenburg County pr Robert Harris. Recorded 17 Sept 1773.

SOUTH CAROLINA DEED ABSTRACTS 1773-1778

H-4, 123-129: Lease & release. 15 & 16 Apr 1773, Peter Stevenson of Charlestown, SC, gentleman, and Mary Joans his wife, to Felix Long of same place, Innholder, for £725 about six acres on west side of the High Road on Charlestown neck, possessed by Peter Boinest, late of Charles Town, merchant, deceased, and devised to his grandson Peter Stevenson. Peter Stevenson (LS), Mary Jones Stevenson (LS), Wit: Thos Horsey, John Gabriel Guigneard. Proved in Charlestown District before William Rugeley, J.P., by the oath of Thos. Horsey 25 Aug 1773. Recorded 17 Sept 1773.

H-4, 130-136: Lease & release. 15 & 16 May 1773, Rev. Robert Smith and Alexander Gillon of Charlestown, only acting & Qualified Executors of the will of Richard Beresford, late of said town, deceased, will dated 8 July 1772, to James Cook of St. James Parish Goose Creek, for £7000, 400 acres in Berkley County on the northwest side of the eastern branch of Wando River and another tract of 400 acres on said river, and 200 acres on north side of said branch of Wando River adj. land of said Richard Beresford deceased, land now or late of David Betchelor, late of Elisa Foissin. Robert Smith (LS), Alexander Gillon (LS), Wit: John Splatt Cripps, Peter Meursot. Proved before Thomas Grimball, Junr., by the oath of John Splatt Crips, 20 Aug 1773. Recorded 8 Sept 1773.

H-4, 136-142: Lease & release. 29 & 31 Oct 1737, Cornelius DuPre of Berkley County, SC, planter, & Jane his wife, to Abraham Dupont of same, planter, for natural love and affection to his son in law Abraham Dupont, 183 acres on Four hole swamp adj. lands of said Abraham Dupont. Cornelius Dupre (LS), Jane Dupre (LS), Wit: William Smith, Francis Cordes, William Mean. Proved 19 Dec 1737 before Henry Gibbes, Esqr., J.P. in Berkley County, by the oath of William Smith. Auditor office 19th Sept 1754 ent in Book D No. 4, fol 82. Recorded 18 Sept 1773.

H-4, 142-149: Lease & release. 1 & 2 Nov 1737, Gideon Dupont of Berkley County, SC, planter, to Abraham Dupont of same, planter, for 100 acres in Berkley County upon a place commonly called Fourholes swamp, adj. lands of Cornelius Dupre, for five shillings. Gid. Dupont (LS), Wit: Fran's Corbin, Willm. Patridge, Willm. Smith. Proved 11 June 1739 by the oath of William Patridge, before Isaac Porcher. Memorial entered 10 Sept 1754 in Book D No 4, fol. 82. Recorded 21 Sept 1773.

H-4, 149-155: Lease & release. 19 & 20 Aug 1773, John Mortmer Williams of Charlestown, SC, ship carpenter, to Robert Croft of Prince Georges Parish, Craven County, for £5000, 120 acres in Christ Church Parish, Berkley County, adj. William Wissers, Andrew Quelch, Mr. Ford, and another tract of 232 acres part of tract of 300 acres lately belonging to William Wisser and John Bassnett lately deceased. John Mort Williams (LS), Wit: James Forgartice, Samuel Meverick. Proved in Charlestown District by the oath of James Forgartice, 30 Aug 1773, before William Rugeley, J. P. Recorded 21 Sept 1773.

H-4, 155-164: Lease & release. 9 & 10 Oct 1767, Richard Capers and Thomas Capers both of Granville county, Sc, executors of the last will and testament of Thomas Capers late of Charlestown, gentleman, deceased, to John Harrison of Charlestown, for £550 tract granted by Lords Proprietors 10 March 1681 to Thomas Rose then of this province but since deceased, town lot, by deed 20 Jan 1690, to Richard Capers then of this province but since also deceased, descended to Thomas Capers.. by deed 7 Sept 1695 did assign to his mother in law and his brothers Charles Capers and Thomas Capers and sisters Mary and Elizabeth Capers [deed in poor condition]... Elizabeth Jenkins widow... Thomas Capers (LS), Wit: William Print, John Perroneauf.

H-4, 164-166: South Carolina, Craven County. 3 Aug 1773, Peter Keighley of St. Davids Parish, Craven County, to John Michell of same place, merchant, for £100 SC money, 50 acres granted 17 March 1760 in Craven County on So west side of Pedee River on Marrs Bluff adj. to said River, adj. Mr. Atkins, granted to John Keighley, and said Peter Keighley as eldest son and heir of said John Keighley. Peter Keighley (LS), Wit: John Gibson, John McNeish. Proved in Craven County by the oath of John McNeish 3 Aug 1773 before Jos. Gourley. Recorded 22 Sept 1773.

H-4, 166-171: Lease & release. 13 & 14 Aug 1773, Thomas Buckle of Charlestown, merchant, and wife Mary, to Thomas Woodin of same, gentleman, for £10 SC money, 1000 acres on the big Saltcatcher Swamp in Colleton County (including 150 acres granted to Edmun Jones adj. lands of William Wournel and vacant land, and land laid out for Thomas Woodin) granted 1 December last to said Thomas Buckle. Thomas Buckle (LS), Mary Buckle (LS), Wit: Edward Trescot, Wm. Print.

Proved in Charlestown District by the oath of Edward Trescot before William Rugeley, J.P., 3 Sept 1773. Recorded 22 Sept 1773.

H-4, 171-173: 16 Sept 1773, Adrian Mager of Purysburgh in Granville County, SC, Esqr., to Melchior Fulcher of same, carpenter, for £30 sterling, 50 acres granted to John Chevillette in Purysburgh Township adj. land granted to Col. John Peter Pury, Frederick Holzendorf, Peter Abbastertier de Mon Clair. Adrian Mayer (LS), Wit: Gabriel Sausey, Christian Prising[?]. Proved by the oath of Gabriel Sausey in Granville County 16 Sept 1773 before David Geroux, J.P. Recorded 23 Sept 1773.

H-4, 173-175: 11 Aug 1773, David Huguenin of Parish of St. Philip in Georgia, planter, to Abraham Ravot of parish of St. Mathews, province aforesaid, for love and affection to his nephew and for £10, 200 acres of land nigh Purisburgh granted to Daniel Abraham David and ___, adj. John Bourquin, Ann Frank, David Giroud, and the glebe land of Purisburgh, 1000 acres granted to Melchior ___uger. David Huguenin (LS), Wit: Henery Bourquin, Clayborn Hinson. Proved in Georgia before Elisha Butler, J. P., by the oath of Henery Bourquin of St. Philips Parish, planter. Recorded 23 Sept 1773.

H-4, 175-177: 18 June 1773, Thomas Camber of purysburgh in Granville County, SC, Esqr., to Adrion Mayer of same, for £1170, 500 acres adj. David Coulier, commons of Purysburgh, Joseph Reymonds[?]. Thomas Camber. Wit: David Saussy, Jacob Strobhar. Proved by the oath of David Saussy before David Geroud, J.P. Recorded 23 Sept 1773.

H-4, 177-182: Lease & release. 10 & 11 June 1773, Thomas Keller and Eve his wife of Charlestown District, to Esther Kysell of Charlestown, Tavern Keeper, for £300, two acres and two roods part of two lots marked G and F in the general plan of George Anson, Esquire. Thos Keller (LS), Esther Keller (E) (LS), Wit: Thos Corker, Willm. Stevens. Proved by the oath of Thomas Corker before Thomas Turner, J.P., 12 June 1773. Recorded 23 Sept 1773.

H-4, 182-185: 13 Aug 1762, John Clooker and Sarah his wife of Granville County, Sc, to William Anderson of Ninety Six in Colleton County, by deed [grant?] dated 2 January 1754, 50 acres in Granville County near Savannah River adj. land of Mary Kroofin[?]. John Clooker (LS), Sarah Clooker (S), Wit: Samuel Simmons, George Rogers, John Benson. Proved in Granville County 4 Nov 1772 by the oath of Samuel Simmons before LeRoy Hammond, J.P. Recorded 24 Sept 1773.

H-4, 185-188: 14 Oct 1770, James Mayson, Esqr., of Saluday in Colleton County, SC, to William Anderson of same, on Wilsons Creek, for £200 SC money, 200 acres in Craven County on south side Enoree on a place called Warriors Creek, granted to said James Mayson 31 Oct 1769. James Mayson (LS), Ann Mayson (LS), Wit: Benj. Durborow, James Caldhun (Calhoon) (O), Joseph Freeman. Proved by the oath of Benjamin Durborow 23 Aug 1773 before Champness Terry, J.P. Recorded 24 Sept 1773.

H-4, 188-194: Lease & release. 27 & 28 May 1771, Tillman Kolb of Craven County, Sc, planter, to Joseph Dabbs of same, boat builder, for £25, 650 acres in Craven County adj.land of Samuel Martin, Pee Dee River, granted to John Kolb, Tillman Kolb Eldest son and Heir at law of said John Kolb now deceased. Tillman Kolb (LS), Wit: Jacob Kolb, Josiah Kolb. Receipt witnessed by Arthur Hart, 7 Sept 1772. Proved by the oath of Jacob Kolb in Craven County before John Alran, 21 June 1770. Recorded 25 Sept 1773.

H-4, 194-198: Lease & release. 3 & 4 Dec 1772, John White of St. Davids Parish, Craven county, Sc, planter, to John Riggs of same parish and county, for £100 SC money, 150 acres part of 200 acres on north side Jefferys Creek on a branch known by the name of Crimps branch, adj. Martha Cobbs land, William Whites land, granted to John White 22 ___ 1770. John White (LS), Wit: Thomas Oakley, Wm. White, John Dowland. Proved in Cheraw District by the oath of Thomas Oakley, 13 Sept 1773 before Joseph Gourley, J.P. Recorded 25 Sept 1773.

H-4, 198-204: Lease & release. 25 & 26 Oct 1769, Michael Branen of Craven County, Sc, planter, to William Bond, planter, for £100 SC money, 100 acres part of 200 acres on Wateree River, adj. land laid out for Jeffery Summerford, Edward Flin. William Brannam (LS), Susanna Brannam (M)

(LS), Wit: Henry Downworth, William Brannam (X). Receipt sworn before John New. Oglethorpe. Recorded 27 Sept 1773.

H-4, 204-210: Lease & release. 16 & 17 Sept 1773, David Jones of Charlestown District, cordwinder, to Oliver Wallace now of Charleston, for £500 proc. money, 100 acres on great Rockey Creek granted 25 Nov 1767. David Jones (LS), Wit: Dinham Fearis, Wm. Penny. Proved 20 Sept 1773 before William Rugeley, by the oath of William Penny. Recorded 28 Sept 1773.

H-4, 210-214: Lease & release. 16 & 17 Apr 1773, Micajah Pickett of St. Marks Parish, to Peter Donald, Doctor of Physick, for £350 SC money, 50 acres, part of 200 acres granted to sd. Micajah Pickett adj. land of Joseph Cates, granted 7 Apr 1770 and a memorial entered in Book K, No. 10, page 154, 7 May 1770. Macajah Pickett (LS), Wit: Philip Henson, Ralph Smith. Proved 25 Sept 1773 before William Rugeley, J. P., by the oath of Ralph Smith. Recorded 23 Sept 173.

H-4, 214-222: Lease & release. 9 & 10 Dec 1768, Edmund Bellinger, Esqr., of Parish of St. Andrew, SC, and Lucia his wife, to Barnard Elliott, Esqr., for £2445, tract granted 20 Dec 1702 to Landgrave Edmund Bellinger, 6000 acres on south side of Ashepoo River in Colleton County, descended to Edmund Bellinger his eldest son and Heir at law, who by his last will and testament dated 1 Feb 1739 bequeath to his sons William and John Bellinger and to his daughters Mary and Elizabeth Bellinger 977 acres, part of said 600 acres, and said Elizabeth afterwards died without leaving issue and said Edmund Bellinger as eldest brother to said Elizabeth inherited. (plat for 491 acres included in deed). Edmd Bellinger (LS), M. L. Bellinger (LS), Wit: R. P. Hatley, R. Rugeley. Proved by the oath of Rowland Rugeley 15 Dec 1774 before Jno Caldwell, J.P. Recorded 29 Sept 1773.

H-4, 222-226: Lease & release. 13 & 14 Sept 1773, Abigail Rollinson of St. Marks Parish, to William Fox of same, planter, for £25 SC money, 250 acres in the fork of Wateree & Congaree Rivers adj. land granted to said William Fox, surveyed for George Nicholas, William Rollinson, granted to said Abigail Rollinson 23 Dec 1772. Abigail Rollinson (R), Wit: John Russell, Olley Man Dodgen. Proved 15 Nov 1773 before Edmund Cossens, Esqr., J.P. in Camden District, by the oath of John Russell. Recorded 29 Sept 1773.

H-4, 226-231: Lease & release. 20 & 21 Sept 1773, James Mayson of Ninety Six, Esqr., to Charles Pinckney of Charlestown, Esqr., surviving assignee of John Benfield and Maurice Jones, merchants, for four bonds by which he is indebted to said Charles Pinckney as surviving assignee appointed for the benefit of Mr. John Nutt of London, merchant, to whom the said John Benfield and Maurice Jones are also indebted in a considerable sum, tract on waters of Ninety Six, 500 acres adj. Doctor John Murray, John Anderson, Timothy Reardon, now of Tacitus Gaillard, land now of Robert Gowdey. James Mayson (LS), Wit: john Languish, Jno Colcock. Proved in Charlestown District by the oath of John Colcock of Charlestown before Robert Williams Junr, J.P., 25 Sept 1773. Recorded 30 Sept 1773.

H-4, 232-238: Lease & release. 24 & 25 Sept 1773, Eugene Brenan of Charlestown, Tavern keeper, to David Baty of Charlestown, merchant, for £150 SC money, 250 acres on a branch of Turkey Creek, half of 500 acres granted to said. Eugene Brenan 20 Oct 1772. Eugene Brenan (LS), Wit: John White, Thos Tod. Proved 8 Sept 1773 before William Rugeley, J.P., by the oath of Thomas Todd. Recorded 30 Sept 1773.

H-4, 238-240: 8 Sept 1773, John Gaulter to Lewis Gibert now deceased, of South Carolina, planter, whereas John Gaulter did obtain a warrant for 100 acres dated 8 Jan last and that the said Gaulter "having no occation for the said warrant" for £45 paid by said Lewis Gibert, should the said warrant be Bounty warrant & Consequently free of any Charges the sum of £35 remaining to be paid shall remain in the hands of said Lewis Gibert until such time that the matter shall be publickly known in order that the sum of £20 might be employd in Chairing the said warrant of the different charges. John Gaultir (LS), Wit: John Favier, Peter Gibert. Proved 8 Sept 1773 before Lewis De St. Peair, J. P. in Ninety Six District, by the oath of John Faver and Peter Gibert. Recorded 1 Oct 1773.

H-4, 240-241: Thomas Farr, Senr, of Charlestown, planter, for natural love and affection to his son Thomas Farr of Charlestown, plantation at Stono, 600 acres where I formerly lived, and also fourteen negroes [named], dated 1 Sept 1773. Thos Farr (LS), Wit: Archibald Gamble, Thomas Biddle. Proved in Charlestown District by the oath of Thomas Biddle 30 Sept 1773 before Wm. Nisbett, J.P.

H-4, 241-248: Lease & release. 29 & 30 Sept 1773, Jonathan Badger of Charlestown, to George Flagg of same, for £7000 SC money, part of a lot in Ansonborough purchased by said Jonathan Badger from Samuel Hottow, on the broad path from Charlestown to the southward, adj. lands of Jane Wilkie, Timothy Crosby, James Reed, Esqr. Jonathan Badger (LS), Wit: George Sheed, John Hatfield. Proved in Charlestown District by the oath of George Sheed before John Troup, J.P., 1 Oct 1773. Recorded 2 Oct 1773.

H-4, 248-254: Lease & release. 24 & 25 Sept 1773, Jonathan Badger of Charlestown, Gent., to George Flagg of same, for £2800 SC money, lot in Charlestown, number 115 on Tradd Street, adj. lands of Charles Pinckney. Jonathan Badger (LS), Wit: George Sheed, John Hatfield. Proved in Charlestown District by the oath of George Sheed before John Troup, J.P., 1 Oct 1773. Recorded 4 Oct 1773.

H-4, 255: Benjamin Guerard of Charles Town, SC, planter, bound to George Cooke and Arthur Downes of same place, merchants, 29 July 1773, in the sum of £10,000, for performance of covenants, lease and release 28 & 29 July 1773. Benjamin Guerard (LS), Wit: Jacob Valk. Proved by the oath of Jacob Valk, 2 October 1773, before Wm. Rugeley, J. P. Recorded 7 Oct 1773.

H-4, 256: 19 July 1707, Thos Farr of Colleton County, SC, and William Everson of same, whereas the Lords proprietors by their grant dated 5 Nov 1704 did grant to said Thos Farr, 260 acres, now for sum of £10, sells this tract. Thomas Farr (LS), Wit: William Dun, John Williamson. A Memorial hereof entered in the Auditors Office 22 May 1733. Recorded 26 Nov 1773.

H-4, 257-258: Thomas Drayton of Berkley County, SC, to William Everson of same, for £5, 100 acres adj. lands of Henry Meshow, part of 600 acres granted to sd. Thomas Drayton on Horse Shoe Savannah; dated 13 Apr 1711. Thos Drayton (LS), Wit: William Fuller, John Williamson. A Memorial hereof entered in the Auditors Office 22 May 1733. Recorded 26 Nov 1773.

H-4, 259-265: Lease & release. 1 & 2 Nov 1773, John McQueen of Charles Town, Gentleman, to John Dart of same, attorney at law, for £8000, lot in Charles Town number 60 on south side Trad Street adj. Mrs. Townshend's land. John McQueen (LS), Wit: John Huger, Wm. Print. Proved 10 Nov 1773 before William Rugeley, J.P., by the oath of William Print. Recorded 29 Nov 1773.

H-4, 265-266: 3 Aug 1773, Jonathan Price & Mary his wife of Craven County, Sc, to James Hope of same, for £300 SC money, 150 acres between Broad River and Cataba on a branch of Allisons Creek adj. William Dickinsons. Jonathan Price (LS), Mary Price (LS), Wit: James McCord, John Hope. Proved in Camden District by the oath of James McCord before Ezekl. Polk, J.P., 18 Sept 1773 Recorded 29 Nov 1773.

H-4, 267-268: 1 July 1773, John Hope & Jean his wife of Craven County, SC, to James Hope for £300 SC money, 300 acres between Broad River and the Cataba on a branch of Allisons Creek. John Hope (LS), Jean Hope (LS), Wit: James McCord, Jacob Cooper. Proved in Camden District by the oath of James McCord before Ezekl. Polk, J.P., 2 June 1773. Recorded 29 Nov 1773.

H-4, 268-272: 24 Sept 1771, Roger Pinckney, Provost Marshall of SC, to Thomas Edwards, whereas Peter Rowlin late of Pedee was seized of 300 acres on a place called Rowlins Neck in Craven County on Pedee River adj. Thomas Edwards land, and said Peter Rowlin by bond dated 29 Oct 1765 to Joseph Brown & Co. of George Town, merchants, in the sum of £12,000 for the payment of £6000 and said Joseph Brown & Co. in the court of common pleas did implead Thomas Edwards, administrator of Peter Rowlin deceased, at August Term 1771 to levy of the goods and chattles of Peter Rowlin... Roger Pinckney Pro. Marshall (LS), Wit: Wm. Print, Hopson Pinckney. Proved in Berkley County by the oath of Hopson Pinckney 22 October 1773 before Henry Peroneau, J. P. Recorded 1 Dec 1773.

SOUTH CAROLINA DEED ABSTRACTS 1773-1778

H-4, 273: Peter Leger acknowledges possession of 50 acres pat of a tract of 150 acres of land conveyed to John Simmons 8 Nov 1757 which said 50 acres I will never call on the said John Simmons for any compensation or satisfaction. Peter Leger, Wit: John Farr, Wm. Currie. Acknowledged 22 Oct 1773 before Wood Furman, J.P. in Craven County, by Peter Leger. Recorded 1 Dec 1773.

H-4, 273-277: Lease & release. 1 & 2 May 1770, John Pickens, deputy surveyor, of Prince Williams Parish, SC, to James Liddell of said, planter, for £200 SC money, 200 acres granted to John Pickens on Penny's Creek waters of Little Pedee in the Parish of Prince William, Granville County, granted 12 ___ 1768. John Pickens Junr. (LS), Wit: Jos. Swearingham, John Cameron. Proved 2 May 1770 before Alexr. Cameron, J.P. in Granville County, by the oath of Joseph Swearingham.

H-4, 277-285: Lease & release. 16 & 17 July 1773, George King of St. Mathews Parish, Berkley County, planter, and wife Mary, to Peter Manigault of Charles Town, now occasionally being in the Kingdom of Great Britain, for £4000 SC money, 233 acres on south side Santee River in Berkley County, adj. land now or late of Tacitus Gaillard, also another tract of 400 acres on north side Santee River in Craven county adj. land now or late of said Tacitus Gaillard and on Santee River, granted by Tacitus Gaillard and Ann his wife to said George King 9 & 10 May 1765, and also another tract of 26 acres in St. Mathews Parish, adj. said George Kings land, said Tacitus Gaillard, conveyed to said King by lease & Release 4 & 5 May last past. George King (LS), Mary King (LS), Wit: Henry Mouzon Junr, Jacob Christopher Zahn. Proved in Charles Town District before John Troup, J.P., by the oath of Jacob Christopher Zahn, 22 Nov 1773. Recorded 3 Dec 1773

H-4, 285-287: Lease & release. 3 & 4 Nov 1772, Edward Kirk, of Charles Town, Gentleman, to James Fallows of same, shopkeeper, for good will and affection, 600 acres in Berkley County adj. land of Christian Sigwald, four hole swamp. Edward Kirk (LS), Wit: Edward Jones, Wm. Kennedy. Proved 25 Oct 1773 before Fenwick Bull, J.P. in Berkley County, by the oath of Edward Jones. Recorded 4 Dec 1773.

H-4, 287-292: Lease & release. 23 & 24 Oct 1772, Alexander Harvey of Charles Town, gentleman, to Nicholas Swindershine of St. Pauls Parish, planter, for £3000 SC money, 400 acres but on a resurvey found to contain 600 acres by John Tucker and Ruth his wife to John Palmer by lease &* release 29 & 30 June 1730 adj. Thos Farrs land, land formerly of John Smith, Thos Elliott & Hugh Hext, land formerly of Christopher Wilkenson, by divers conveyances since to Alexander Harvey. (plat included) Alexander Harvey (LS), Wit: J. Rutledge, John Pringle. Proved in Charles Town District before Wm. Nisbett, J.P., by the oath of John Rutledge, 23 Oct 1773. Recorded 7 Dec 1773.

H-4, 292-297: Lease & release. 22 & 23 Oct 1771, Anna Margareth Schober of Charles Town, SC, spinster, to Conrad Kysell of same, Inn keeper, for £100 SC money, 100 acres granted to the said Anna Margareth Schober 14 Sept 1771 in Berkley County in the upper part of Amelia Township on High Hill Creek. Ann Margaret Schober (+) (LS), Wit: Stephen Biddurph, Geo. Seawright. Proved 26 Oct 1773 before William Rugeley, J.P., by the oath of Stephen Biddurph. Recorded 8 Oct 1773.

H-4, 298-300: John Beard of Charles Town, bound 10 Feb 1773 to Daniel Buckmyer of same, in the of £200 for payment of £100 SC money, mortgage of lot on Boundary Street adj. lands of William Hopton. John Beard (+) (LS), Wit: Emanuel Abrahams, Solomon Proby. Proved in Berkley County before William Rugeley, J.P., by the oath of Emanuel Abrahams. Satisfied 12 Feb 1774. Recorded 9 Dec 1773.

H-4, 300-301: Daniel Buckmyer for £103 SC money to Thomas Radcliffe, assign deed of mortgage from John Beard, 27 Nov 1773. Daniel Burkmyer (LS), Wit: Charles Linning. Proved before John Troup, J.P., by the oath of Charles Linning, 27 Nov 1773. Recorded 9 Dec 1773.

H-4, 302-304: 9 March 1773, Peter Scott of Berkley County, SC, and wife Mary to John Reagon of same, by grant dated 9 April 1768 to Peter Scott, 200 acres on a branch of Saluday River known by the name of ___. Peter Scott (P) (LS), Mary Scott (+) (LS), Wit: William Skelly, Alexander McKelvey, William Aspenal (W). Proved before Wm. Hausihl, J. P., 13 March 1773 by the oath of William Aspenal. Recorded 9 Dec 1773.

SOUTH CAROLINA DEED ABSTRACTS 1773-1778

H-4, 304-310: Lease & release. 15 & 16 June 1773, Richard Muncreeff of Charles Town, and Susannah his wife, to John Pooley & John Forsyth, both of Charles Town, for £1500 SC money, lot in Charles Town, St. Philips Parish, on an alley leading from Union St. to the Bay. Richd. Muncreeff (LS), Susannah Muncreeff (LS), Wit: Saml Hrabowski, James Anderson, William Milligan. Proved 30 Oct 1773 before Wm. Rugeley, J.P., by the oath of William Milligan. Recorded 10 Dec 1773.

H-4, 311-316: Lease & release. 20 & 21 Oct 1773, John Pooley and John Forsyth, both of Charlestown, to Edward Wayman, David Batey, Edwards Oats, John Bothwell & Daniel Stevens, all of said town, for £1500 SC money, lot in St. Philips Parish on an alley leading from Union St. to the Bay. adj. land of John Scott, Richard Muncreeff. John Pooley (LS), John Forsyth (LS), Wit: James Fallows, Saml Hrabowski, William Milligan. Proved 21 Dec 1773 before Wm. Rugeley, J.P., by the oath of William Milligan. Recorded 21 Dec 1773.

H-4, 317-322: 22 Oct 1773, Edward Wayman, David Batey, Edwards Oats, John Bothwell & Daniel Stevens, all of Charles Town, to John Pooley and John Forsyth, both of Charlestown, whereas the above named parties have for some years past assembled themselves for good and charitable purposes under the name & denomination of the Marin Lodge and have contributed several sums of money to be applied towards godly and pious persons and to the relief of such poor and distrest godly persons, objects of charity, part of the money to be applied towards the purchase of a suitable house & land in Charles Town for their meeting, did agree with Richard Muncreeff, house carpenter, for the absolutely purchase and sale of a certain lot in Charles Town, convey this lot in trust. Wit: James Fallows, Saml Hrabowski, William Milligan. Proved 21 Dec 1773 before Wm. Rugeley, J.P., by the oath of William Milligan. Recorded 21 Dec 1773.

H-4, 323-325: John Pooley and John Forsyth, both of Charlestown, bound to Edward Wayman, David Batey, Edwards Oats, John Bothwell & Daniel Stevens, all of said town, in the sum of £2000 SC money, 14 June 1773, special bond concerning lot in St. Philips Parish on an alley leading from Union St. to the Bay. adj. land of John Scott, Richard Muncreeff. John Pooley (LS), John Forsyth (LS), Wit: William Milligan. Proved 21 Dec 1773 before Wm. Rugeley, J.P., by the oath of William Milligan. Recorded 21 Dec 1773.

H-4, 325-327: 4 June 1773, Joachim Heartstone and Catharine his wife of St. Peters Parish, Granville Co., SC, planter, to Jacob Holbrook of Purysbourgh in the parish aforesaid, Bricklayer, for £1000 SC money, 465½ acres, being half of tract granted to Honb'l Joseph Wragg, Esqr., 9 Apr 1736, adj. Robert Wright, Thos Owen. Joachim Hartstone (LS), Catharine Hartstone (X) (LS), Wit: Mathew McKinnie, David Saussey, Catharine Saussey. Proved in Granville County before David Giroud, J.P., by the oath of Mathew McKinnie, 18 Nov 1773. Recorded 14 Dec 1773.

H-4, 327-333: Lease & release. 7 & 8 Feb 1773, William Roth of Charles Town, Cooper, to Conrad Kysell of same, Inn keeper, for £150 SC money, 150 acres on horsepen Creek waters of Cuffy Town in colleton County granted to said William Roth 6 Feb instant. William Roth (LS), Wit: Jacob Tobias, John Harrison, Charles Gruber. Proved in Charles Town District before william Nisbett, J.P., by the oath of Jacob Tobias, 1 Nov 1773. Recorded 17 Dec 1773.

H-4, 333-341: Lease & release. 25 & 26 Oct 1773, Alexander Harvey of Charles Town, Attorney at Law, to Robert Williams (the younger) Junr of the same town, attorney at law, for £7000 SC money, lot in Charleston on south side Tradd St. (plat included showing land formerly belonging to Daniel Townsend deceased, part of lot belonging to Alexander Harvey. Alexander Harvey (LS), Wit: John Deas, Robt Livre. Proved in Charles Town District 5 Nov 1773 before Robt. Phelp, J.P., by the oath of John Deas. Recorded 18 Dec 1773.

H-4, 341-347: Lease & release. 18 & 19 Oct 1771, Jacob Coleman of South Carolina, planter, and his wife Susannah, to Conrad Kysell of Charles Town, Inn keeper, for £200, 200 acres in Berkley county in the upper part of Amelia Township on High Hill Creek, granted 14 Sept 1771 and survey certified 21 June. Jacob Coleman (LS), Susannah Coleman (+) (LS), Wit: Mickeal Lary (+), Wm. Hogarth, John Maker (---). Proved by the oath of William Hogarth before William Nisbett, J.P., 30 Oct 1773. Recorded 21 Dec 1773.

SOUTH CAROLINA DEED ABSTRACTS 1773-1778

H-4, 347-352: Lease & release. 23 & 24 Dec 1772, Samuel Marsh of Ninety Six District, SC, planter, to Arthur Simpkins, Esqr., of Ninety Six District, for £250 SC money, 250 acres in Colleton County on waters of Little Saludy, granted to said Samuel Marsh, recorded in Book EEE, folio 327. Saml Marsh (LS), Wit: James Scott, Thos Barton, Richard North (N). Proved before Moses Kirkland, J.P., by the oath of James Scott, 24 Dec 1772. Recorded 22 Dec 1773.

H-4, 352-358: Lease & release. 23 & 24 March 1773, Moses Kirkland of Ninety Six District, SC, Esqr., and Patience his wife, to Arthur Simpkins, Esqr., of Ninety Six District, for £2000 SC money, 500 acres in Colleton County, granted 22 Nov 1770 to John Tanner, on waters of Little Saludy, adj. land of Francis Sinkfeild, Patrick Thomas, now property of said Kirkland, Elizabeth Mantz, Saml Marsh; 300 acres granted to Patrick Thomas and conveyed by lease & Release from said Patrick Thomas to John Tanner 29 & 30 Sept 1770, and from said John Tanner to Moses Kirkland 23 & 24 Feb 1773, on Little Saluda adj. Elizabeth Mantz, Francis Sinkfield, lands granted to said John Tanner (excepting 50 acres laid out to Robert Davis); and 852 acres which said tract was granted to Henry Middleton Esqr., and by lease & release 4 & 5 Jan 1773 conveyed to Moses Kirkland, between Savannah River and Saluda, on a branch of Stephens Creek called Log Creek adj. Ephraim Pricketts, Arthur Simpkins, James Roberson. Moses Kirkland (LS), Patience Kirkland (LS), Wit: Wm. Daniel, Jesse Daniel. Proved before Richard Andrew Rapley, J.P. for Ninety Six District, by the oath of Jesse Daniel, 7 Aug 1773. Recorded 23 Dec 1773.

H-4, 358-362: Lease & release. 26 & 27 Oct 1773, Alexander Harvey of Charles Town, Attorney at Law, to John McQueen of same, Gentleman, for £15,000 SC money, lot number 60 on south side Tradd Street in Charleston, adj. Mr. Townshend's land, now in the occupation of Robert Williams the younger, also lot number 60 in the occupation of David Deas on south side Tradd Street adj. land of Daniel Townshend deceased. Alexander Harvey (LS), Wit: Hugh Rutledge, John Braddley. Proved in Chs. Town District before William Rugeley by the oath of John Braddley., 14 Feb 1773. Recorded 23 Dec 1773.

H-4, 363-366: Lease & release. 26 & 27 Nov 1771, Richard north of South Carolina, St. Marks Parish, and John Williams son of Daniel, of Parish & province aforesaid, for £620, 200 acres on a branch of Little River called Mudlick in Berkley County. Richard North (N) (LS), Sarah North (X) (LS), Wit: Anthony Griffin, Wm. Hamilton, John North. Proved by the oath of Wm. Hamilton before John Caldwell, J. P., 9 Dec 1771. Recorded 19 Dec 1773.

H-4, 366-370: Lease & release. 5 & 6 May 1772, William Bampfield of Charles Town, & Rebecca his wife, to John Williams, son of Daniel, of Saluda, for £800, 150 acres in Berkley County in the fork between Broad & Saludy Rivers on a small branch of Little River called Mudlick Creek, adj. land laid out to Jacob Gray, Jonathan Mott, William Nealy, granted 1 Feb 1768. Wm. Bampfield (LS) Rebecca Bampfield (LS), Wit: David George, John Owen, Oliver Dale. Proved 6 Aug 1772 before John Caldwell, J.P. in Craven County, by the oath of David George. Recorded 19 Dec 1773.

END OF BOOK H-4.

SOUTH CAROLINA DEED ABSTRACTS 1773-1778

I-4, 1-5: Lease & release. 12 & 13 Nov 1773, John Barnwell Senr. of the Town of Beaufort, planter, & Martha his wife, to Jacob Deveaux of aforesaid town, for £300 SC money, 219 acres on Gun Bluff near Archer Creek, three small islands known as sheep Islands, 20 acres. John Barnwell (LS), Martha Barnwell (LS), Wit: Andrew Deveaux, William Deveaux. Recorded 24 Feb 1774.

I-4, 5-10: Lease & release. 16 & 17 Jan 1771, Thomas Crawford of Province of Georgia, planter, to Benjamin Rees, of St. Marks Parish, SC, planter, for £300 SC money, 50 acres granted 12 Jan 1769 to said Thomas Crawford in Craven County, SC, on or near Dry Swamp, Wateree River, adj. land formerly laid out for said Thomas Crawford, James McKelvey Senr; also another tract of 150 acres granted 15 Feb 1769 to said Thomas Crawford in Craven County, St. Marks Parish, on Dry Swamp adj. land of John Hale, John Dargan. Thomas Crawford (T) (LS), Wit: Abijah Rembert, Thomas Rembert, John Perdriau Junr. Proved 21 May 1773 before Wood Furman, J.P. in Craven County, by the oath of James Rembert. (Recording date not indicated.)

I-4, 10-14: Lease & release. 7 & 8 Dec 1758, Ann Bodley of Craven County, SC, widow, to Alexander Campbell of same, taylor, £45 SC money, 200 acres in Craven County on the High Hills adj. land laid out for Josiah Cantey. Ann Bodley (&), Wit: Francis James, Henry Kerby. Proved 28 Dec 1758 by the oath of Francis James before Richard Richardson, J.P. for Craven County. Endorsed by Alexander Campbell to Capt. John Dargan, 13 Jan 1762. Recorded 17 March 1774.

I-4, 14-18: Lease & release. 13 Jan 1762, Alexander Campbell, taylor, of Craven County, Sc, to Capt. John Dargan of same, for £90 SC money, 200 acres in Craven County on high Hills adj. land surveyed for Josiah Cantey, granted to Ann Bradly [sic] 21 Sept 1756. Alexr Campbel (LS), Wit: Mathew Singleton, Timothy Dargan, Garad Kelly. Proved by the oath of Mathew Singleton 17 Dec 1773 before Wm. Rugeley, J.P. Recorded 18 March 1774.

I-4, 19-23: Lease & release. 19 & 20 Nov 1771, Benjamin Edings of Edisto Island, Colleton County, planter, and Mary his wife, to James Muray of same, planter, for £16,000 SC money, 200 acres on south side Edisto Island adj. land of John Adams, Benjamin Jenkins, Benjamin Edings. Benjamin Edings (LS), Mary Edings (LS), Wit: Joseph Jenkins, John Adams. Proved in Colleton County by the oaths of Joseph Jenkins and John Adams 5 July 1773 before Jos. Seabrook. Recorded 18 March 1774.

I-4, 24-27: Lease & release. 6 & 7 Oct 1772, Barnaby Pope of Craven County, to James Armstrong of same, for £50 SC money, 150 acres granted 16 Jan 1761 to Barnaby Pope. Barnaby Pope (LS0, Wit: James McCormick, John Cook. Proved in Camden District before John Newman Oglethorpe, J. P., by the oath of John Cook 27 Feb 1773. Recorded 18 March 1774.

I-4, 27-32: Lease & release. 26 & 27 Feb 1773, John Belton of parish of St. Marks, Craven county, Sc, to James Armstrong of same, for £205 SC money, 100 acres in Craven county on south side Wateree River on Colonel's Creek. John Belton, Wit: John Adamson, John Armstrong, Alexander Stuart. Proved in Camden District before John Newman Oglethorpe, J.P., by the oath of John Armstrong 27 Feb 1773. Recorded 19 March 1774.

I-4, 32-36: Lease & release. 10 & 11 Oct 1759, Abel Wilds of Craven County, SC, planter, to Alexr McKintosh of same, merchant, for £250 SC money, 58 acres granted 1 Aug 1758 to said Abel Wilds adj. William Killingsworth, Philip Douglass, Pedee River. Abel Wilds (LS), Wit: Philip Evans, Philip Douglass. Lease proved in Craven County by the oath of Philip Douglas before John Alvan, J. P., 25 June 1766. Release proved in Craven County by the oath of Philip Evans 12 Feb 1760 before Wm. Lard. Recorded 19 March 1774.

I-4, 37-41: Lease & release. 17 & 18 Sept 1759, Philip Douglass of Welch Neck, Craven county, SC, planter, to Alexander McKintosh of said county, merchant, for £650 SC money, 300 acres in Welch Neck granted 10 March 1743 to said Philip Douglass on Pedee River adj. Thomas Evans's land. Philip Douglass (LS), Wit: Philip Evans, Abel Wilds. (Plat included showing Alexander Mackintosh's 100 acres, Abel Wilds' land, William Killingsworth's land.) Proved in Craven County before William Lard, J.P., by the oath of Philip Evans, 12 Feb 1760. Recorded 19 March 1774.

SOUTH CAROLINA DEED ABSTRACTS 1773-1778

I-4, between pages 38 and 39: Plat, at the request of Mr. Joseph Ainger, I have resurvey tract of land granted to Edmund Bellinger and sold by said Bellinger to Thomas Butler[?] of which said Butler sold to ___ McPherson, 300 acres adj. Doctor Cuthbert, Mr. Prielow, Mr. Daniel Desaussure, dated __ Oct 1766.

I-4, 41-45: Lease & release. 26 & 27 July 1773, William Hays & Sarah his wife of Craven Co., SC, to Magnus Corgill of same, for £300 SC money, 400 acres granted 18 Jan 1743 in the Welch Tract in Craven county on Pedee River. William Hays (W) (LS), Sarah Hays (S) (LS), Wit: Matthew Griffeth, Joshua David. Proved in Craven County before Alexander Mackintosh by the oath of Joshua David 13 Sept 1773. Recorded 21 March 1774.

I-4, 46-49: 4 Oct 1766, John Wright of Parish of St. James Goose Creek, planter, to Joseph Ainger of Parish of Prince William, planter, for £2500 SC money, half of tract of 502 acres in Prince Williams Parish, Granville County, on Pocotaligo River, adj. land of Andrew Deveaux, Heires of George Cossings deceased, land of ___ McPherson, land lately belonged unto William Butler, planter, deceased, after whose death one half did descend upon the said John Wright as the only son and heir at law of Mary Wright deceased being one of the heirs of William Butler deceased, and Ann Miles deceased the other sister of said William Butler. John Wright (LS0, Wit: D. DeSaussure, Charles Dalton. Proved in Colleton County by the oath of Charles Dalton before John Hunt, J.P., 6 July 1773. Recorded 21 March 1774.

I-4, 49-50: 24 March 1762, Daniel James son & heir of Rev. Philip James deceased of the Welch Tract in the county of Craven, to John Booth of same county, for £5, 150 acres in the Welch Tract in Craven County, adj. Daniel James, land laid out to Scriven, Pedee River. Daniel James (LS), Wit: David Harry, William Luks (W). Proved 18 May 1762 by the oath of William Luks.

I-4, 51-52: 19 Nov 1753, Joseph Jolly of Welch Tract, Craven County, planter, to Daniel Devonald of same, planter, for £5 SC money, 150 acres on Pedee River adj. land laid out to William Scriven. Joseph Jolly (LS), Wit: Israel _____, Joshua Edwards. Recorded 22 March 1774.

I-4, 52-53: 18 Jan 1767, Daniel Devonald of Welch Tract, Craven Co., SC, planter, to William Furnace of same, planter, for five shillings, 150 acres on Pedee River adj. land laid out to William Screven. Daniel Devonald (LS) Wit: William Bowen, Walter Downs. Proved by the oath of Walter Downs [date obliterated]. Recorded 22 March 1774.

I-4, 53-55: 2 Aug 1769, Sarah Booth by virtue of a legacy to her made by the last will and testament of John Booth and also as executrix and Charles Booth __ of John Booth decd, both of Welch Tract, Craven County, planters, to William Furney of same county, Boat Builder, for £5 SC money, 150 acres in Welch Tract adj. Daniel James, land laid out for Wm. Screven, Pedee River. Sarah Booth (S) (LS), Charles Booth (LS), Wit: David Evans, Abel Wilds. Proved by the oath of David Evans before John Alran, J. P., 8 June 1770. Recorded 22 March 1774.

I-4, 55-60: Lease & mortgage. 14 & 15 Dec 1773, John Beard of Charles Town, Drayman, to Thomas Racliffe the younger (Junior), merchant, said John Beard by bond stands bound to said Thomas Radcliffe in the sum of £322 s8, mortgage of town lot in Charleston on Boundary St. adj. land formerly of Adam Frederick Gitsinger and now belonging to the estate of ___ Wolrich, William Hopton, Esqr., Charles Burkmire. John Beard (X) (LS), Ann Beard (X) (LS), Wit: Charles Lining. Proved by the oath of Charles Lining before John Troup, J. P., 21 Dec 1773. Recorded 22 March 1774.

I-4, 60-65: Lease & release. 8 & 9 June 1773, James Fannin of St. Marks Parish, SC, planter, to James Campble of Berkley County, weaver, ten shillings SC money, land granted 26 Oct 1767 by Gov. Tryon of NC to James Fannin, 200 acres on both sides Thickety Creek in the Parish of St. Mark. James Fannin (LS), Wit: John Fannin, William Roberts (X), Jacob Fannin. Proved in Camden District by the oath of John Fannin before Ezekiel Polk, 16 Dec 1773. Recorded 23 March 1774.

I-4, 65-70: Lease & release. 17 & 18 Feb 1773, Samuel Nelson Junr of St. Marks Parish, Gent., to James Conyers Senr of same, cooper, for ten shillings SC money, 150 acres granted 13 Aug 1762 to William Nelson in Craven County on Black River, which said 150 acres fell to sd. Samuel Nelson Junr as heir at law to said William Nelson. Samuel Nelson (LS), Wit: Hugh Gamble, John Nelson. Proved 16 Sept 1773 before John Egan, J. P., by the oath of John Nelson. Recorded 23 March 1774.

I-4, 70-73: 11 Dec 1773, William Boyd & Ann his wife of St. Marks parish, SC, yeoman, to David Boyd of same, yeoman, for £100 SC money, 144 acres on south fork of Fishing Creek in Craven county adj. land of Widow Glover, William Weers[?] land, John Workman; granted 21 July 1769 to William Boyd. Wm. Boyd (LS), Ann Boyd (LS), Wit: Hugh Whiteside, Charles Strong, Alexander Rosborough. Proved in Camden District by the oath of Hugh Whiteside before Wm. Brown, J.P., 30 Dec 1773. Recorded 24 March 1774.

I-4, 73-79: Lease & release. 23 & 24 March 1771, Thomas Doughty of Charles Town, Carpenter, and Mary his wife, to Richard Richardson of St. Marks Parish, Craven County, for £100 SC money, 800 acres between Jacks Creek & Half Way Swamp on north side Santee River now in St. Marks Parish, Craven County; also 250 acres in Amelia Township on Santee River; another tract of 100 acres in Amelia Township adj. land laid out for Thos Doughty, originally granted to Joseph Hoole and by him conveyed by lease & release to Thomas Doughty. Thos Doughty (LS), Mary Doughty (LS), Wit: Daniel Cannon, Robt. Sallens. Proved 11 Jan 1774 before Thomas Turner, J.P., by the oath of Daniel Cannon. Recorded 1 Apr 1774.

I-4, 80-82: William Luyton of Charles Town, by bond became bound to John Perkins of Prince Williams Parish, in the penal sum of £2000 for the payment of £1000, lot of land in Charles Town part of lot number 174 on Cumberland St. Wm Luyten (LS), Wit: John Forteath, Alexr Thompson. Proved by the oath of John Forteath before Saml Porcher, 26 Jan 1774. Recorded 25 Apr 1774.

I-4, 82-85: Lease & release. 27 & 28 Nov 1772, Daniel Mitchell of Granville county, planter, to Thomas Dooly of same, for £1500 SC money, 1000 acres in Granville county on Buckhalters Mill Creek adj. land of one Castleman, Michael Buckhalter, Thomas Adams, merchant at Charlestown, Phillip Goode. Daniel Mitchell (LS), Wit: John Dooly, George Dooly, David Magby (M). Proved in Granville County by the oath of George Dooly before LeRoy Hammond, J.P., 30 Nov 1772. Recorded 28 Apr 1774.

I-4, 85-89: Lease & release. 9 & 10 Dec 1771, James St. John of So Carolina, planter, and Elizabeth his wife, to Lambert Lance of Charlestown, gentleman, for £4000 SC money, lot in Charlestown on west side of Friend St. adj. land of Mr. Hern, James St. John deceased. James St. John (LS), Elizabeth St. John (LS0, Wit: Elizabeth Frier, Robt. Bruce. Proved by the oath of Robert Bruce 11 Dec 1771 before John Troup, J.P. Recorded 3 May 1774.

I-4, 90-95: Lease & release. 5 & 6 Jan 1774, Capt. Daniel Magee, late of Baltimore in the Province of Maryland, but now of Charles Town, So Carolina, to John Poaug and Laughlin Martin of Charles Town, merchants, for £20 SC money, 400 acres on a branch of Sandy Run Swamp adj. Agnes Austin, James McKelvey, Robt. McKewn, Samuel Cross. Daniel Magee (LS), Wit: John Tuke, Christian Sigwald. Proved 7 Jan 1774 before Thos. Turner, J. P., by the oath of John Tuke. Recorded 3 May 1774.

I-4, 95-99: Lease & release. 5 & 6 Oct 1768, Hannah Flint of Charles Town, to Mathew Nielson, Esqr., of St. Marks Parish, Craven County, for £10 SC money, 200 acres in Craven County on waters of Black River originally granted to said Hannah Flint 13 May 1768. Hannah Flint (LS), Wit: Eml. Abrahams, Abraham Anderson. Proved in Charles Town District by the oath of Emanuel Abrahams 19 Nov 1773 before David Rhind, J.P. Recorded 3 May 1774.

I-4, 99-102: Lease & release. 10 & 11 Oct 1768, James Summervell of Charles Town, Berkley County, SC, to Mathew Nielson of Craven County in St. Marks Parish, for £50 SC money, 100 ares in Craven County on waters of Black river adj. Joseph Canteys land, originally granted to said James Summerville 13 May 1768. James Summervelle (LS), Wit: Abraham Andrews, Emanl. Abrahams. Proved in Charles Town District 19 Nov 1773 before David Rhind, J.P. Recorded 4 May 1774.

SOUTH CAROLINA DEED ABSTRACTS 1773-1778

I-4, 103-106: Lease & release. 10 & 11 June 1771, John Rutledge of St. Philips Parish, Charles Town, Berkley County, Esqr., to Isham Clayton of St. Pauls Parish, SC, planter, for £5 SC money, 200 acres, part of 1000 acres granted to Samuel Cardy 17 Feb 1767, and by him conveyed to said John Rutledge adj. land granted to said Isham Clayton. John Rutledge (LS), Wit: Ephraim Mitchell, Wm. Mills. Proved in Berkley County before Wm. Mason, J. P., by the oath of William Mills, 23 Nov 1771. Recorded 5 May 1774.

I-4, 107-113: Lease & release. 4 & 5 Feb 1769, Elias Ball of Hyde Park in Berkley County, St. Johns Parish, SC, planter, and Catharine his wife, to Elias Ball of Kensington in said parish county & province, his unckle, for £4000 SC money, lot #49 in Charles Town adj. Mr. Rheffs land, formerly granted to Capt. John Comings at the request of Capt. John Harleston and Mr. Elias Ball, and said Elias Ball gave a part of said lot to his son John Coming Ball. Elias Ball (LS), Catharine Ball (LS), Wit: Jno Minter, Elias Ball Junr, Elias Ball of Hyde Park, Elias Ball of Kensington. Proved before Peter Simons, J.P. for George Town District by the oath of Elias Ball Junr, 9 Feb 1774. Recorded 6 May 1774.

I-4, 113-117: Lease & release. 14 & 15 Dec 1767, Esther Nivie of the Welch Tract in Craven county, Sc, to Robert Blair of same place, planter, for £1000 SC money, 300 acres in Welch Tract granted 18 Nov 1747 to John Westfield. Esther Nivie (LS), Wit: Moses Mace, Joseph Fabian. Proved in Craven County before Alexander Mackintosh, J.P., by the oath of Moses Mace 28 Oct 1769. Recorded 7 May 1774.

I-4, 117-123: Lease & release. 21 & 22 March 1742, George Hunter of Charles Town, gentleman, to Charles Pinckney of same place, esquire, for £5 SC money, by grant dated 5 March 1686, to Peter colleton, lot in Charleston containing nine acres and two Roods and twenty one perches of marsh and dry land, lot number 80, adj. lots of Thos Colleton, James Colleton, and became vested in John Colleton of Fair Lawn, Parish of St. Johns, Berkley County, and said John Colleton and his wife in 1706 for £5000 SC money did convey to said George Hunter, and said Charles Pinckney and one Thos Ellery of Charleston, Gentleman, deceased, were equally concerned with said George Hunter in said purchase... George Hunter (LS), Wit: Bethiah Beesley, Thos Pinckney. Proved in Berkley County 8 Oct 1751 by the oath of Thos Pinckney before Wm. Pinckney, J.P. Recorded 7 May 1774.

I-4, 123-129: Lease & release. 26 & 27 May 1773, Casper Koone of Craven County, SC, planter, to Thomas Taylor of same, planter, for £2000 SC money, 150 acres on waters of Broad River granted to John Geiger 10 Feb 1749, and said John Geiger by lease and release 11 & 12 Jan 1753 conveyed to Casper Faust and said Casper Faust by lease & release 1 & 2 Jan 1761 to Gasper Kuhn (alias Casper Koone); another tract granted 7 May 1767 to Gasper Kohun (alias Casper Koone), 150 acres on waters of Broad River adj. Conrad Halman; another tract granted 15 Feb 1770 to Gasper Khoone (alias Casper Koone) 100 acres on waters of road River adj. said Koone's land; and another tract granted 3 April 1772 to Casper Koone, 100 acres on waters of Broad River adj. John Taylor, said Koone. Casper Koone (LS), Wit: James Taylor, Conrad Coon. Proved 16 Feb 1774 before Thomas Turner, J. P. in Charlestown District, by the oath of James Taylor. Recorded 13 May 1774.

I-4, 129-133: Lease & release. 12 & 13 Feb 1773, Andrew Romney of Berkley County ,SC, shoemaker, to David Hay of Craven County, planter, for £100 SC money, 100 acres on north side Congaree River on Jackson Creek granted 14 May 1752 to said Andrew Romney, adj. heirs of Thomas Brown deceased, recorded in Book OO folio 74. Andrew Romney (X). Wit: Thomas Taylor, William Howell. Proved 16 Feb 1774 before Thomas Turner, J.P., by the oath of Thomas Taylor. Recorded 15 May 1774.

I-4, 133-139: Lease & release. 14 & 15 July 1773, John Scott of Charlestown, merchant, and Dorcas his wife, to Daniel Ravenell Senior, of St. Johns Parish, planter, for £5000 SC money, house & lot in village of Ansonborough on Charles town neck, letter O in the plan of said village, on George Street and Squirrel Street. John Scott. Wit: John Jeffords Junr, Thomas Ellis. Proved in Charlestown Dist 24 Feb 1774 before Wm. Parker, J.P., by the oath of Thomas Ellis. Recorded 15 May 1774.

SOUTH CAROLINA DEED ABSTRACTS 1773-1778

I-4, 139-147: Lease & release. 11 & 12 Oct 1771, Miles Brewton of Charlestown, Esquire, and Mary his wife, and Honorable Daniel Blake of same town, esquire, and Elizabeth his wife, which said Mary and Elizabeth were lately otherwise called Mary Izard and Elizabeth Izard, the only children to heiresses and devisees of Joseph Izard late of parish of St. George Dorchester, to Samuel Perdriau of Charles Town, sadler, for £4000 SC money, 1474 acres on the Cypress in St. George Parish in Berkley County (plat included made 29 May 1769 by Wm. Maine). Dl. Blake (LS) Eliz. Blake (LS), Miles Brewton (LS), Mary Brewton (LS). Wit: Elias Vanderhorst, Thos Moultrie, Thos Atkinson, Ar. Forbes. Proved in Chs. Town District before William Rugeley, J. P., by the oath of Thos Moultrie, 2 March 1774. Proved by the oath of Thomas Atkinson 23 March 1773 before James Johnston, J.P. Recorded 19 May 1774.

I-4, 147-152: Lease & mortgage. 4 & 5 Feb 1774, Donald Bruce, late of Charles Town, SC, but now of Orangeburgh in the said province, merchant, to Andrew Lord of Charles Town, merchant, bound in the penal sum of £5200 for the payment of £2100, two lotts in the town of Orangeburgh, numbers 270 and 271. Don'd Bruce (LS), Wit: George Lord, G. F. Fardo. Proved by the oath of George Lord 4 March 1774 before Wm. Nisbett, J.P. Recorded 19 May 1774. Satisfied 19 Dec 1776. Wit: Geo Sheed.

I-4, 152-160: Lease & release. 8 & 9 Sept 1766, George Ball & Esther his wife and William Outerbridge and Mary his wife, of the Island of Bermuda, mariners, which said Esther and Mary are the grandchildren and coheiresses of one Thomas Smith late of island of Bermuda, Esqr., deceased, eldest brother of Mary Basset of Charles Town, widow also deceased, to John Hodsden of Charles Town, merchant, for £4000 SC money, whereas Mary Basset late of Charles Town, widow was seized at the time of her death of a part of a town lott in Charleston, number 315, and that part of said lott descended unto Dorothy Basset only daughter of said Mary Basset deceased, and said Dorthy Basset intermarried with one John Edwards of Charles Town, merchant, and some time afterwards on 18 April 1756 departed this life without issue and said lot descended unto Esther Ball wife of said George Ball and Mary outerbridge wife of William Outerbridge, parties to this presents, as granddaughters of Thomas Smith, and eldest brother of said Mary Basset of Charles Town, widow deceased; said lot adjacent to lands of Henry Laurens, Mary Ellis. Mary Outerbridge (LS), William Outerbridge (LS), Esther Ball (LS), Geo. Ball (LS), Wit: Wm. Higgs, Thomas Pearman, Christopher Smith. Recorded 28 May 1774.

I-4, 161-162: George Ball and William Outerbridge, of Island of Bermuda, bound to John Hodsden or his certain attorney, to make title to lot in Charles Town [previous deed].

I-4, 163-167: Dedimus Potestatem and release of inheritance concerning lot in Charleston, directed to George Forbes, Jonathan Burch and Thomas Smith of Island of Bermuda, esquires, 10 Sept 1766. John Ward, attorney. Recorded 18 May 1774.

I-4, 167-173: Lease & release. 3 & 4 March 1770, Mathurin Guerin of St. Andrews Parish, Sc, Gentleman, to John Hodsden of Charles Town, gentleman, for £13,670, whereas the Lords Proprietors by grant on 19 Dec 1693 did grant to George Pawley a town lot at Charlestown, number 106, at the town angles of the market place, on the great street that leadeth from Oyster Point to the Market Place, adj. lot then of Mr. Buris[?], lot formerly belonging to Henry Hughs deceased, and said George Pawley by deed bearing date 23 Dec 1693 with Susanna Pawley his wife did convey said lot to John Flavil then of said province, mariner, who with Rebecca his wife did by deed 17 Aug 1699 convey said lot to Mathurin Guerin the father of the said Mathurin Guerin party hereto, and it descended to his eldest son. Mathurin Guerin (LS), Wit: White outerbridge, Charles King Chitty. Proved in Berkley County before Wm. Mason, J.P., by the oath of White Outerbridge, 26 June 1770. Recorded 31 May 1774.

I-4, 174-180: Lease & release. 17 & 18 Jan 1774, John Williams of Charles Town, Sc, carpenter, to John Badley of same, merchant, for £2000, lots on north side Ellery St. in St. Philips Parish, Charles Town, conveyed by Charles Pinckney, Esqr., and Elizabeth his wife to Rev. Alexander Garden on account of the said John Williams and the said Rev. Alexander Garden then Rector of St. Philips Parish, reciting that Charles Pinckney and Henry Peronneau of Charles Town, merchants, on 31 March 1747 did purchase of and from William Waties and John Coachman of Winyaw in Craven County, executors of the will of Col. William Waties late of same place, deceased, four lots in

SOUTH CAROLINA DEED ABSTRACTS 1773-1778

Charles Town numbers 201, 202, 203, and 206 on east side old Church Street, at Daniel Creek, and by indentures made 13 Feb last past between William Hopton executors of Daniel Hunt and said John Williams, and one made between Sampson Neyle Esqr. and said John Williams. John Williams (LS), Wit: G. F. Fardo, Paul Schlatter. Proved in Berkley County by the oath of Paul Schaltter, 23 Feb 1774 before Hopkin Price, J.P. Recorded 31 May 1774.

I-4, 181-187: Lease & release. 31 Dec 1773, John Davis, Esqr., of Brunswick County, North Carolina, to Parker Quince of Brunswick County, NC, for ___ SC money, lot number 1 on old church street and King Street, also lot number 3, and lot number 5, lot number 7, lot number 8. John Davis (LS), Wit: Saml. Dwight, Wm. Lord. Proved before Isaac Marion, J.P. in Craven County, by the oath of Samuel Dwight, 21 Jan 1774. Recorded 6 June 1774.

I-4, 187-202: Lease & release. 29 & 30 Dec 1773, Parker Quince, Esqr., and Susannah his wife, of Brunswick County, NC, to John Davis of same, esquire, for £10,000[?]; whereas Sarah Rhett afterwards Sarah Trott late of Charles Town, widow, was lawfully seized of sundry houses and town lots, marsh land in Charles Town, and by two certain indentures of lease & release 29 & 27 Feb 1727 between Sarah Rhett and Rev. Alexander Garden, Rector of Parish of St. Philip in Charles Town, and Jacob Wragg, merchant, did convey ten acres in Berkley County near the said Charles Town, adj. land lately belonging to Isaac Mazyck, land lately belonging to Jonathan Amory late of said province, merchant, and also ten acres near the said Charles Town, adj. land formerly belonging to John Coming, and lots 48, 305, 121, 122, 123, 209, 139; also eight acres on Cooper River adj. land of Col. William Rhett deceased, Mr. Mazyck, commonly known by the name of the Point Plantation or Rhettsberry; by indenture made between Nicholas Trott to Alexander Garden and Joseph Wragg, 7 Feb 1727, and several town lotts with the large brick mansion house Nicholas Trott and Sarah his wife, after both their deceases the intended marriage having been had between said Richard Wright and Mary Rhett, then to the heirs, and said Richard Wright and Mary his wife also being deceased, leaving an only daughter named Sarah whereby the trust estate in the said Alexander Garden and Joseph Wragg ceased, and said Sarah Wright intermarried with Mr. James Hasell... leaving Susannah Hasell and Mary Hasell and said Susannah Hasell intermarried with Parker Quincy and Mary Hasell hath intermarried with John Ancrum of the Province of North Carolina, merchant, and said Susannah having attained the age of 21 years and said Parker Quince and Susannah his wife by their petition to the Honorable Thomas Knox Gorden, Chief justice of SC, and his associates the justices of his majestys court of common pleas, setting forth that the said Susanah Quincy and Mary Ancrum being jointly seized of the said land, and Parker Quince and Susannah his wife were desirous that partition might be made. Susannah Quince (LS), Parker Quince (LS), Wit: Saml Dwight, William Lord. (Plat included showing lot numbers, marsh land adj. to Cooper River.) Proved in Craven C.county, South Carolina, before Isaac Marion, J.P., by the oath of Samuel Dwight, 21 Jan 174. Recorded 8 May 1774.

I-4, 202-208: Lease & release. 8 & 9 Dec 1773, Peter Bocquet of Charles Town, merchant, and Elizabeth his wife, to Michael Kalteison of same, gentleman, for £4500 SC money, lot on east side of King Street, number 212, lately purchased by said Peter Boquet of Peter Horlbeck and Catharine his wife, in the occupation of James Henderson and Michael Kalteisen, adj. land now of Alexander Perroneau. Peter Bocquet Junr (LS), Elizabeth Bocquet (LS), Wit: Alex'r Gillon, Henry Saltus, James Stevenson. Proved in Charlestown District by the oath of Alexander Gillon before Thos Phepoe, J.P., 8 March 1774. Recorded 11 June 1774.

I-4, 209-215: Lease & release. 23 & 24 Feb 1774, Hugh Brown of Granville County, planter, and Mary his wife, to James Henry Butler of Charles Town, Gentleman, for £___ SC money, lot on west side King Street in Charlestown, adj. land of Elizabeth Fibben, Margaret Ulrick, nd on Allen Street commonly called Dutch Church Alley, which lot belonged to Caleb Easton who by his will dated 22 Apr 1772 bequeathed to his then wife Mary Brown by the name of Mary Easton and appointed his said wife and Jacob Valk of Charles Town, exrs. Hugh Brown (LS), Mary Brown (LS), Wit: G. J. Fardo, Paul Schlatter. Proved in Berkley County by the oath of Paul Schlatter before Hopkin Price, J.P., 10 March 1774. Recorded 14 June 1774.

I-4, 215-217: Before Thomas Knox Gordon, Chief Justice of his Majesties Province of South Carolina, on 10 March 1774, Mary Brown, wife of Hugh Brown, released her inheritance in lot in Charlestown to James Henry Butler. Recorded 14 June 1774.

SOUTH CAROLINA DEED ABSTRACTS 1773-1778

I-4, 217-219: 26 Feb 1768, Theodore Gaillard of St. James Santee Parish, Craven County, SC, to John Gaillard of St. Stephens Parish, Craven County, for £10 SC money, 847 acres granted 9 Jan 1755 adj. land formerly Abraham Chinners, Peter Sinkler, Alexander Keith, lands of said John Gaillard, James Boisseau, said Theodore Gaillard; also half of tract of 585 acres granted 17 Sept 1742; another tract of 500 acres granted 17 Sept 1742 on Santee River; also tract of 500 acres granted to Richard Allen, Esqr., 6 Sept 1735, adj. land since purchased from Mary Dick widow daughter of said Allen; also part of another tract which I bought of William Gourdin, 76½ acres. Theod. Gaillard, Wit: Sam Gaillard, Michael Miers, Chas. Gaillard. Proved by the oath of Charles Gaillard before Maurice Simons, Esqr., J.P., 30 July 1771. Recorded 15 June 1774.

I-4, 219-224: Lease & release. 7 & 8 Jan 1773, John Holsinger of Craven County, SC, planter, to Martin Oatt of same, planter, for £100 SC money; whereas 200 acres granted 15 May 1750 to Thomas Hodge, in the low grounds of the Congaree River opposite to the lower part of SaxeGotha Township, said Thomas Hodge by lease & release conveyed to Jacob Snider, said Jacob Snider died intestate and 200 acres devolved on William Snider eldest son of said Jacob Snider, and said William Snider by lease & release 16 Sept 1767 conveyed 100 acres to John Holsinger, adj. land of George Powers, William Sniders, land surveyed for John George Geiger and John George Kirsh. John Holsinger (X) (LS), Wit: Simon Hirons, Thos. Morris. Acknowledged in Craven County before Philip Pearson, J. P., by John Holsinger, 8 Jan 1773. Recorded 15 June 1774.

I-4, 224-230: Lease & release. 12 & 13 Nov 1772, David McElwee of South Carolina, miller, to Andrew Williams of same, planter, for £425 SC money, 157 acres on Stephens's Creek adj. land surv'd for James Mason in Colleton County. David McElwee (LS), Wit: Samuel Gibson, Tim'y Parker. Proved 28 Apr 1773 before Richard Andrew Rapley, Esqr., by the oath of Samuel Gibson. Recorded 15 June 1774.

I-4, 230-236: Lease & release. 16 & 17 Sept 1765, Thomas Niel of Prov. of SC, and Sarah his wife, to Andrew Williamson on Stephens Creek in said province, planter, for £5 SC money, 150 acres on waters of Stephens Creek adj. land surveyed for James McCormick. Tho. Neil (T) (LS), Sarah Neil (LS), Wit: Andrew Neil, William Harris. Receipt signed by John Niel son & heir to the within named deceased Thos Neil. Proved 1 June 1772 before Alexdr. Cameron, J.P., in Granville County by the oath of Andrew Niel. Recorded 15 June 1774.

I-4, 236-241: Lease & release. 17 & 18 July 1773, William Dorres of Ninety Six District, SC, yeoman, to Andrew Williamson of same district, planter, for £300 SC money, 106 acres in Belfast Township waters of hard Labour on Stephens Creek adj. said. Andrew Williamson; also 60 acres adj. james Anderson, William Dorris, both granted to William Dorres 25 June 1771. William Dorris Wit: Tim'y Parker, John Purves. Proved in Granville County before John Purves, J.P., by the oath of Timothy Parker, 8 July 1773. Recorded 15 June 1774.

I-4, 241-247: Lease & release. 26 & 27 Sept 1759, Moses Cohen of Charles Town, Shopkeeper, and wife Dina, to Isaac DaCosta of same place, merchant, for £225, SC money tract granted to Moses Cohen 22 Jan 1759, 450 acres on Savanah Creek adj. land of William Livingston and his associates. Wit: Abr'm DaCosta, Isac Cohen Junr. Proved by the oath of Abraham DaCosta before Lionel Chalmers, J.P. for Charles Town District, 14 May 1773. Recorded 24 June 1774.

I-4, 247-253: Lease & release. 7 & 8 March 1757, Paul Trapier & Christopher Gadsden, acting Executors of the will of Thomas Hasell of George Town, Winyaw, decd., to Mary Pawley, wife of Col. George Pawley of same place, for £700 SC money, 31 acres in Prince George Winyaw parish, on Wood Street in George Town, on the Harbour, Pit Creek, adj. plantation of Paul Trapier, Esqr.; said land conveyed by John Cleland & Mary his wife 11 & 12 Sept 1753 to said Thomas Hasell, part of tract of 3996 acres granted to said John Cleland, and said Thomas Hasell by his will dated 14 July 1756 did will that his tract of land lately purchased of Dr. Fyffe should be sold to pay his debts and appointed Gabriel Manigault and said Paul Trapier and said Christopher Gadsden executors of his will, and said Gabriel Manigault refused to act. Paul Trapier (LS), Christ'r Gadsden (LS). Wit: Thos Waties, Jno Waties. Acknowledged by Paul Trapier in the presence of Wm. Shackelford and William Lupton. Proved in Craven County before Joseph Brown, J.P., by the oath of William Lupton, 8 June 1763. Recorded 22 June 1774.

SOUTH CAROLINA DEED ABSTRACTS 1773-1778

I-4, 253-255: 26 Dec 1755, Zachariah Brazier of George Town, Parish of Prince George Winyaw, and Mary Ann his wife, to George Pawley Junr of same place, planter, for £700 SC money, lot number 110 in George Town, granted to Robert Jennis, and said Robert Jennis on 19 March 1736 did make over said lot to Thomas Charnock of said place, planter, and Thomas Charnock on 10 July 1751 did sell to aforesaid Zachariah Brazier. Zachariah Brazier, Mary Ann Brazier, Wit :Jos. Brown, Wm. Fyffe. Proved in Craven County before George Pawley, Esqr., J. P., by the oath of Joseph Brown, 7 April 1756.k Recorded 21 June 1774.

I-4, 255-263: Lease & release. 21 & 22 Dec 1773, Isaac DaCosta of Charles Town, mercht., and Sarah his wife, to Major Andrew Williamson of Ninetysix District, gentleman, for £1750 SC money, two plantations containing in the whole 700 acres, one of 250 acres on a branch of Savannah River called Stephens Creek, adj. land laid out for William Leviston and his associates, granted 2 Jan 1759; the other of 450 acres on Stephens Creek adj. land of Isaac DaCosta, granted to Moses Cohen 2 Jan 1759; tract of 450 acres conveyed 26 & 27 Sept 1759 from Moses Cohen to isaac DaCosta. Isaac DaCosta, Sarah DeCosta. Wit: Richd Donavan Murray, Joseph DaCosta. Recorded 23 June 1774.

I-4, 263-267: Lease & release. 4 & 5 Feb 1774, Ann Isabella Kinlock of Charles Town, widow, to Benjamin Huger of same, esquire, for five shillings, one undivided third part of plantation of 1818 acres on Wehaw Creek in Prince George Parish, Craven county, adj. land now or lately belonging to the heirs of Anthony White, land formerly belonging to William Scriven and since to William Poole, on Black River, known by the name of Kensington Plantation. Ann Kinloch. Wit: Robert Gill, Andw Johnston, Robert Gibb. Proved in Geo Town District before Robert Heriot by the oath of Robert Gibb, 5 March 1774. Recorded 23 June 1774.

I-4, 267-272: Lease & release. 10 & 11 Feb 1774, Robert Gibb, Esquire, of Prince Georges Parish, to Benjamin Huger of Charles Town, for five shillings, one undivided third of 1818 acres on Wehaw Creek in Prince George Parish, Craven county, adj. land now or lately belonging to the heirs of Anthony White, land formerly belonging to William Scriven and since to William Poole, on Black River, known by the name of Kensington Plantation. Ann Kinloch; conveyed 5 & 6 Feb 1750 by the Honorable John Cleland of George Town to Archibald Baird and Richard Gough, gentlemen, which said third part was lately vested in Mary Esther Huger and by lease and release 8 & 9 Feb instant between Benjamin Huger and Mary Esther his wife to Robert Gibb. Robert Gibb (LS), Wit: Robert Heriot, Andw Johnston. Proved in Geo Town District before William Mason, J.P., by the oath of Robert Heriot, 10 March 1774. Recorded 24 June 1774.

I-4, 272-276: Lease & release. 8 & 9 Feb 1774, Benjamin Huger of Charles Town, Esquire & Mary his wife, to Robert Gibb of Prince George Parish, for five shillings, one undivided third of 1818 acres on Wehaw Creek in Prince George Parish, Craven county, adj. land now or lately belonging to the heirs of Anthony White, land formerly belonging to William Scriven and since to William Poole, on Black River, known by the name of Kensington Plantation. Ann Kinloch; conveyed 5 & 6 Feb 1750 by the Honorable John Cleland of George Town to Archibald Baird and Richard Gough, gentlemen, which said third part was lately vested in Mary Esther Huger. Benj. Huger (LS), Mary Esther Huger (LS), Wit: Robert Heriot, Andw Johnston. Proved in George Town District before Job Rothmahler, J. P., by the oath of Robert Heriot, 10 March 1774. Recorded 25 June 1774.

I-4, 276-280: Mary Esther, wife of Benjamin Huger, relinquished inheritance to Robert Gibb, Esquire, tract in preceding deed, 12 Feb 1774. Recorded 27 June 1774.

I-4, 280-287: Lease & release. 7 & 8 Feb 1773, Anthony Rits of St. James Parish, Goose Creek, and Itere[?] his wife, to Conrad Kysell of Charles Town, Tavern Keeper, for £100 SC money, 200 acres in Colleton County waters of Cuffy Town, granted to said Anthony Rits 6 Feb 1773. Anthony Rits (mark) (LS), Ietre Rits (LS), Wit: Hans rolla[?], John Gregg, Abraham Spidel, Eman'l Abrahams. Proved 20 March 1774 before William Rugeley, J.P., in Charles Town District by the oath of Abraham Spidel. Recorded 26 June 1774.

I-4, 287-291: Lease & release. 22 & 23 Nov 1773, Anthony Rits & Ietre Rits his wife to Hester Kysell of Chas Town, widow and Innholder, for £200 SC money, 200 acres in Craven County in the

SOUTH CAROLINA DEED ABSTRACTS 1773-1778

fork between Broad & Saludy River adj. land granted to George Risener, land granted to Jacob Hoglow, Nicholas Buntricks, land granted to Oldrick Slight, which said 200 acres was granted on the Bounty 6 Feb 17_3. Anthony Rits (mark) (LS), Ietre Rits (mark) (LS), Wit: Robert Cohen, Ema'l Abrahams. Proved 8 Feb 1774 before David Rhind, J.P., in Charles Town District by the oath of Emanuel Abrahams. Recorded 29 June 1774.

I-4, 291-298: Lease & release. 8 & 9 Nov 1773, Charles William Mackinen (McKinnen) of Savannah, Georgia, Esquire, and Hellen his wife, to Joachim Hartstone of Purrysburgh, SC, planter, for £627 Georgia money, 450 acres in Purrysburgh Township, adj. land of Captain Cobley, John Philip Merret, Hector Barringer de Beaufain, and Savannah River. Hellen Mackinen (LS), Chas Wm Mackenen (LS), Wit: John Linder (James Linder), James Robertson. Proved by the oath of John Linder, 17 March 1774 before Adrian Mayer, J.P. A memorial entered in Book M No. 12, page 475, 22 March 1774. Recorded 30 June 1774.

I-4, 298-301: 24 Aug 1754, John Cordes of South Carolina ,gentleman, to Daniel Crawford of Charles Town, merchant, the said John Cordes and Daniel Crawford are joint tenants of a certain tract in Charles Town, part of Division M of the lot number 80, John Cordes conveys his interest for £1150 SC money. adj. James Hunter, John Oram, on Charles Street. John Cordes (LS), Wit: Henry Heywood, David Crawford. Proved before Lionel Chalmers, J.P. for Berkley County, by the oath of David Crawford, 30 March 1756. Recorded 31 June 1774.

I-4, 301-306: Lease & release. 14 & 15 Oct 1770, Stephen Keisling of Berkley County, to Conrad Kysell of Charles Town, for £150 SC money, 100 acres on south side Congaree on Savannah Hunt. Stephen Keisling (LS), Wit: Francis Defour, W. Gist, Daniel Beck (X). Recorded 30 June 1774.

I-4, 307-311: Lease & release. 17 & 18 Nov 1758, William Lacey, planter, of Craven County, SC, to Mallichi Murfee of same, for £400, 400 acres on Peedee River in the Welch Tract adj. land surveyed for Saml Drake, granted 19 July 1758 to William Laccy. William Lacey (LS), Wit: Gid. Gibson, Henry Buckholds. Proved in Cheraw District by the oath of Gideon Gibson before Joseph Gourley, 10 June 1774. Recorded 30 June 1774.

I-4, 312-313: 31 July 1773, Richard Blake Senr. of Parish of St. James Santee, to his son Richard Blake Junr of same, for love and affection, 288 acres granted to John Dutarque in Parish of St. James Santee adj. land of John Mayrant decd, land now belonging to Willm. Thomas. Richard Blake (LS), Wit: Daniel Jaudon, John Blake. Proved by the oath of Daniel Jaudon 23 Feb 174. Recorded 30 June 1774.

I-4, 313-315: 3 Feb 1774, John Wagner of Charles Town, merchant, to John Bell of Congarees, whereas John Bell stands indebted to said John Wagner for £130 13, mortgage of 200 acres on north side Broad River granted to Stephen Allis in 1767 and conveyed to said Bell 2 Feb 1774. John Bell (mark) (LS), Wit: Wm. Fitzpatrick, Jonas Beard. Proved by the oath of Wm Fitzpatrick before Wm. Nother, J.P., 9 March 174. Recorded 24 June 1774.

I-4, 316-317: 1 Dec 1768, Margret Fee of Charles town, SC, to John Dooly of Ninety six, Deputy Surveyor, for five shillings, 450 acres in Boons Borough Town Ship on a small [branch] of Long Cane Creek, adj. land laid out to Serah Fee. Margret Fee (LS), Wit: Philip Goode, Daniel Horsey. Joseph Freeman.

I-4, 317-326: Lease & release. 21 & 22 March 1774, Frederick Stallings of Parish of Prince William, SC, to John Scott of same, planter, for £50, 200 acres on Savanna River granted 13 Feb 1753 to Charles Kirby. Frederick Stallings (FS) (LS), Wit: Samuel Scott, James Stallings. Proved in Charles Town District before Thomas Turner, J.P., by the oath of James Stalling, 29 March 1774. Recorded 26 June 1774.

Lease & release. 21 & 22 March 1774, Frederick Stallings of Parish of Prince William, SC, to John Scott of same, planter, for £50, 150 acres on Savanna River adj. Charles Kirby granted __ March 1757 to Elias Stallings. Frederick Stallings (FS) (LS), Wit: Samuel Scott, James Stallings. Proved in Charles Town District before Thomas Turner, J.P., by the oath of James Stalling, 29 March 1774. Recorded 26 June 1774.

SOUTH CAROLINA DEED ABSTRACTS 1773-1778

I-4, 327-332: Lease & release. 30 & 31 July 1773, John Egan of Craven County, Sc, planter, & Eleoner his wife, to Robert Willson of same, planter, for £550, land granted 7 March 1754 to William McKay and William McKay and Kathrine his wife by deed 9 April 1768 did convey to said John Egan. John Egan (LS), Eleoner Egan (mark) (LS), Wit: Moses Gordon, James Armstrong, Roger Wilson. Proved by the oath of Moses Gordon before Henry Cassels, J.P. for Craven County, 31 July 1773. Recorded 7 July 1774.

I-4, 332-337: Lease & release. 17 & 18 Jan 1774, Mary McKay of Province of SC, planter, to Robert Wilson of same, planter, for £1000 SC money, 250 acres on the east side of the north branch of Black river in St. Marks Parish, adj. land laid out for Charles McKay decd, John Ervin, Mary McKay (M) (LS), Wit: Thomas Reese, Wm Wilson, James Bradley. Proved 3 March 1774 by the oath of James Bradley before Henry Cassels, J.P. for Craven County. Recorded 3 July 1774.

I-4, 337-341: Lease & release. 17 & 18 Jan 1774, Joseph McKay of the Province of SC, planter, and Mary his wife, to Robert Wilson for £150 SC money, 150 acres in St. Marks Parish, Craven county, adj. Mary McKay, Moses Gordon, Charles McKay, Henry Cassels. Joseph McKay (mark) (LS), Mary McKay (mark) (LS). Wit: Thomas Reese, James Bradley. Proved 3 March 1774 by the oath of James Bradley before Henry Cassels, J.P. for Craven County. Recorded 3 July 1774.

I-4, 341-346: Lease & release. 12 & 13 May 1773, Joseph Debordieau, only acting executor of the will of Anthony White, late of Prince Fredericks Parish, Craven County, SC, planter, deceased, to Benjamin Trapier of same county, planter, for £150 SC money, three adjoining tracts in George Town on Wood Street, Princes Street. Joseph Dubordieau (LS), Wit: Edward Martin, Thos Wilson. Proved in George Town District before Job Rothmahler, J.P., by the oath of Thomas Wilson.

I-4, 347-349: 1 Oct 1772, Henry McMurdy of Craven county, SC, weaver, and Mary his wife, to James Paul of same, planter, £174 s10 SC money, 300 acres on Beaverdam branch or the north fork of Rocky Creek in Craven County adj. Robert Fallerton, John Ferguson, James Turner, Sarah Knox, James Bunsley, granted 3 April 1772 to Henry McMurdy. Henry McMurdy (M) (LS), Mary McMurdy (M) (LS), Wit: John Gaston, J.P., Archibald Coulter, John Kell. Proved by the oath of John Kell before John Gaston, J.P. for Camden District, 17 Feb 1774. Recorded 11 July 1774.

I-4, 349-356: Lease & release. 24 & 25 June 1773, Thomas Karwon of St. Thomas Parish, Berkley County, SC, and Mary his wife, to John Hall of same province, for £700 SC money, 230 acres in parish of St. Thomas & St. Denis which tract James Bremar purchased of Andrew Rembert 4 & 5 July 1735 also one plantation of 300 acres in Parish of St. Dennis which said James Bramer purchased of Samuel Simon 29 & 30 March 1738 which said two plantations by a certain indenture of agreement made between James Akin in right of his son James Akin a minor heir at law to his mother Sarah Akin formerly Sarah Bramer and James Marion & Mary his wife late Mary Bramer dated 13 July 1752, as heirs at law of their father James Bramer by his last will and testament, land adj. to Francis Varambo, John Pagett, Mr. Danniley, late the property of Capt. Anthony Bonneau. Thomas Karwon (LS), Mary Karwon (LS), Wit: Thomas Dearington, James Freeman. Proved 4 Apr 1774 by the oath of Thomas Dearington before John Moore, J.P. in Berkley County. Recorded 12 July 1774.

I-4, 356-362: Lease & release. 25 & 26 Jan 1774, Gavin Pou of Orangeburgh Township, Berkley County, to Robert Pou of the fork of Edisto, Berkley County, planter, for £100 SC money, 300 acres granted to Gaven Pou 29 Nov 1750, recorded in Book MM, folio 9. Gavin Pou (LS0, Wit: Thos Dicks, Jacob Wolfe, Ann Wolfe. Proved in Orangeburgh District by the oath of Jacob Wolfe Junr before Samuel Rowe, J.P., 26 Feb 1774. Recorded 13 July 1774.

I-4, 362-367: Lease & release. 29 & 30 Oct 1773, James Parsons and John Rutledge of charles Town, SC, Esquire, to Joseph Barnet of said province, for £5 SC money, 280 acres at a place called Ninety Six. James Parsons (LS), Jno Rutledge (LS0, Wit: Thos Heyward Junr, John Pringle. Proved in Chs Town District by the oath of John Pringle before Wm. Rugeley, J.P., 11 Apr 1774. Recorded 14 July 1774.

I-4, 367-373: Lease & release. 1 & 2 Jan 1774, Charles Palmer of Prince Williams Parish, planter, to William Stoutenburgh of same place, planter, for £4000... whereas Ann Palmer, mother of said

SOUTH CAROLINA DEED ABSTRACTS 1773-1778

Charles Palmer, by her last will and testament dated 6 Nov 1769 ordained that her plantation of 500 acres in the Parish aforesaid, part of 3140 acres granted to Joseph and Hugh Bryan deceased adj. land of Stephen Bull deceased, land laid out to Hill Croft and Anthony Mathewes decd, now belonging to Thomas Bowman, land of William Russell, on Pocotaligo River, should be disposed of by her executors to wit David Toomer and Archibald Calder, and Charles Palmer as highest Bidder at the sum of £3000. Charles Palmer (LS), Wit: Jacob Van Bibber, Margrett Boswood, Christian Meyers. Recorded 14 June 1774.

I-4, 373-378: Lease & release. 4 & 5 Feb 1773, Theophilus Faver of Craven County, SC, planter, and Elizabeth his wife, to William Barns of same, for £150 SC money, 400 acres granted to said Theophilus Faver in Tryon County, North Carolina, but since the continuation of the Boundary it lies in Craven County, SC, on Abittons Creek. Theophilus Faver (LS), Wit: Joseph Robinson, Moses Barns (mark). Proved in Ninety Six District by the oath of Moses Barns 4 Sept 1773 before Joseph Robinson. Recorded 15 July 1774.

I-4, 378-380: 23 March 1774, Barbary Barns of Ninety Six District, SC, to Jacob Barns also of Ninety Six District, planter, for ten shillings, 81 acres on west side Broads River. Barbara Barns (mark) (LS), Wit: William Barns, Moses Wattkins. Receipt dated 26 March 1774 witnessed by Lily Robinson. Recorded 15 July 1774.

I-4, 380-386: Lease & release. 29 & 30 Oct 1765, James Mason (Mayson) of Prov. of SC to Andrew Williamson of Stephens Creek in said province, planter, for £100, 100 acres on a branch of Stephens Creek. James Mayson (LS), Wit: John Savage, Robt Goudey, J. T. Rossel. Proved 13 Oct 1765 before Thos Bell, J. P. in Granville Co., by the oath of John Savage. Recorded 16 July 1774.

I-4, 387-392: Lease & release. 24 & 25 March 1774, Andrew Williams of Ninety Six District, planter, to John Lewis Gervais, Esquire, merchant of Charles Town, £100 SC money, 150 acres in Granville County at the place where the old path from Fork Boone to Hard Labour crosses the long Cane Creek adj. land laid out to Messrs Russell and Gervais, James Calhoun, said tract granted 25 Sept 1766 to Joseph Holmes, transferred by said Joseph Holmes by deed 5 May 1765 to Andrew Williamson. An. Williamson (LS), Wit: Wm. Coffey, Timy Parker. Proved in Ninety Six District before John Purves, J.P., by the oath of Tim Barker [sic] 26 March 1774. Recorded 18 July 1774.

I-4, 392-399: Lease & release. 7 & 8 Apr 1774, John Lewis Gervais of Charles Town, merchant, to Andrew Williamson of St. Bartholomews Parish, Colleton County, planter, for £100 SC money, tract in St. Bartholomews Parish on a small branch of Stephens Creek called Hard Labour Creek, 147 acres, adj. lands of James Parsons, John Rutledge Esquire, Henry Laurens Esqr, said John Lewis Gervais, this tract a part of 8,000 acres granted to Henry Laurens Esqr and John Lewis Gervais 8 April 1768, vested in said John Lewis Gervais by a deed of partition 11 January 1772 between said Henry Laurens Esqr. and said John Lewis Gervais. John Lewis Gervais (LS), Wit: Timy Parker, William Volentine. Proved 15 Apr 1774 before William Rugeley, Esqr., J.P. in Berkley County, by the oath of William Volentine. Recorded 18 July 1774.

I-4, 399-403: Lease & release. 16 & 17 Apr 1774, William Hest of Charles Town, SC, merchant, to Zephaniah Kinsley of Charles Town, merchant, for £900 SC money, 900 acres in Craven County on Gilkies Creek of Thicketty a branch of Broad River adj. land supposed surveyed for Zachariah Bullock, Archey Robertsons land. Wm. Hest (LS), Wit: Robert Holaday, Ezekiah Townsend. Proved in Charles Town District by the oath of Ezekieh Townsend before William Rugeley, J.P., 16 Apr 1774. Recorded 19 July 1774.

I-4, 403-410: Lease & release. 12 & 13 May 1772, John Delahow of Parish of Saint Bartholomew in Colleton County, SC, Doctor of Physic, and Ann his wife, one of the daughters and coheiresses of Thomas Walker late of Charles Town, mariner, deceased, and Edward Martin and Elizabeth his wife of Charles Town, which said Elizabeth is the other daughter of said Thomas Walker deceased, to Peter Manigault of Charles Town, barister at law, for £10,050 SC money, lot on Colleton Square in Charles Town adj. land of Thomas Ellery deceased, Hunter's Street, Charles Street, on which the said Thomas Walker built two large brick houses, and also lot of marsh land marked O on plan of Colleton Square. John de Lahowe (LS), Ann Delahowe (LS), Edwd Martin (LS), Eliz'th Martin

SOUTH CAROLINA DEED ABSTRACTS 1773-1778

(LS), Wit: Thos Evance, Isaac Lesesne. Proved in Charles Town District by the oath of isaac Lesesne before William Rugeley, J.P. Recorded 19 July 1774.

I-4, 410-416: Lease & release. 19 & 20 Apr 1774, Benjamin Wigfall of St. Thomas Parish, SC, planter, and Martha his wife, to Robert Quash of same, esquire, for £10,000 SC money, 450 acres in St. Thomas Parish, being the eastern part of a tract of 500 acres granted 1 Feb 1708/9 to one Lewis Mouzon then adj. to Anthony Boneau, Captain Linch. Martha Wigfall (LS), Benj. Wigfall (LS), Wit: Rog. Pinckney, Andw Hasell. Proved in Chas Town Dist before William Rugeley, J.P., by the oath of Roger Pinckney, 22 Apr 1774. Recorded 19 July 1774.

I-4, 416-420: Lease & release. 7 & 8 Aug 1767, John Riss of Berkley County, Sc, planter, to Christian Keyser of same, planter, for £215 SC money, 50 acres on south side Congaree River in the low ground above Beaver Creek in Berkley County adj. when surveyed to land of Barbra Tress, part of 100 acres granted to John Christopher Helterbrand 2 Jan 1754 and by him conveyed to said John Riss. John Riss (mark) (LS), Wit: Wm. Meyer, Philip Kell[?]. Proved before Henry Patrick, J.P., by the oath of Philip Kell 24 Feb 174. Recorded 23 July 1774.

I-4, 420-426: Lease & release. 11 & 12 May 1773, George Wood, Peter Boquet the younger, and Daniel Cannon of Charles Town, gentleman, executors of the last will and testament of John Marley late of said town, gentleman, to Alexander Wright of same, esquire, for £15,400 SC money, two lots in Charles Town, numbers 219 & 220, said Marley made his will 24 Apr 1772, in which he directed that his estate both real and personal be sold. George Wood (LS), Peter Bocquet (LS), Daniel Cannon (LS), Wit: George Shed, Thomas Grimball Junr. Proved 28 Apr 1774 before Richard Lambton, Esqr., J.P. in Berkley County, by the oath of Thomas Grimball Junr, Esquire. Recorded 25 July 1774.

I-4, 426-430: Lease & release. 31 March & 1 Apr 1772, Hans George Reams in Craven County, Sc, to George Ruff of same, for £125 SC money, 100 acres granted to Hans George Reams 21 Jan 1761 in the fork between broad and Saludy Rivers on the waters of Cannons [creek] in Berkley County. Hans George Ream (mark) (LS), Wit: Jacob Crommer, John Graham, George Smith. Proved in Craven County before Michael Dickert, J.P., by the oath of Jacob Crommer, 31 March 1772. Recorded 26 July 1774. A memorial entered in Book L No. 11, page 402, 30 Sept 1772.

I-4, 431-435: Lease & release. 4 & 5 Sept 1768, Samuel Hamlin of St. Georges Parish, Berkley County, SC, planter, to Henry Onsett of St. James Parish, Goose Creek, planter, for £500 SC money, 625 acres in St. James Parish Goosecreek, Berkley County, adj. land of Richard Singleton, Mr. Broughton, land of the estate of William Branford. Samuel Hamlin (LS), Mary Hamlin (LS0, Wit: Elijah Postell, William Branford, John Glaze. Memorial entered in Book M No. 12, page 481, 30 Apr 1774. Recorded 26 July 1774.

I-4, 435-442: Lease & release. 4 & 5 Apr 1774, Gavin Witherspoon and John McCauley, only acting executors of the last will and testament of James Witherspoon Junior late of Williamsburgh Township, planter, to James Blackley Junior, for £140, 550 acres in Williamsburgh Township adj. land of John Robertson, originally granted to Crafton Karwon 1 [or 5] July 1736 and by him made over to his son Thomas Karwon and by Thomas Karwon made over to said James Witherspoon Junr 14 & 15 March 1770; will of James Witherspoon Junior dated 1 July 1773 empowered the executors in case of his sons death without issue which contingency hath happened to sell a tract of land which he bought of Thomas Karwon. Gavin Witherspoon (LS), John McCauley (LS), Wit: David Witherspoon, Alexr McCrea Junr, William Heathly. Proved by the oath of William Heatly 3 May 1774 before Jas Johnston, J.P. Recorded 27 July 1774.

I-4, 442-446: Lease & release. 15 & 16 Dec 1767, Esther Nivre, daughter and heir of John Westfield of the Welch Tract in Craven County, SC, to Robert Blair of same place, planter, for £600 SC money, 300 acres in the Welch Tract granted to <u>Robert</u> Inman 4 July 1749 and <u>Thomas</u> Inman for £250 on 26 Feb 1752 did convey unto John Westfeild of same county, planter, 300 acres adj. William Evans land, John Westfields land, Peedee River. Esther Nivre (LS), Wit: Moses Mace, Joseph Fabian. Proved in Craven County before Alexander McKintosh, J.P., by the oath of Moses Mace, 28 Oct 1769. Recorded 27 July 1774.

SOUTH CAROLINA DEED ABSTRACTS 1773-1778

I-4, 447-451: 29 Jan 1774, James Montgomery son and heir to George Montgomery decd, and Margaret his wife, of St. Marks Parish, to Alexander McCrea of Craven County in Williamsburgh Township, for £1800 SC money, 250 acres part of 1000 acres formerly the property of James Akin Esqr., deceased, afterwards of one George Montgomery testator to said James Montgomery, tract in Williamsburgh Township adj. his own land, land of then Henry Montgomery but now late the property of John McElveen, land of Alexander McCrea; and tract of 114 acres in Williamsburgh Township originally granted to George Montgomery adj. land laid out for James Akin Esqr, John Holden and Thomas McCrea, William Grimes; reserving the privilege of a certain burying place containing about thirty feet square. James Montgomery (LS), Margret Montgomery (LS), Wit: John Wallace, Thomas McCrea, Alexander McCrea Junr. Proved in Berkley County 8 Jan 1774 before Richard Lambton, J.P., by the oath of Alexander McCrea. Recorded 28 July 1774.

I-4, 451-454: 12 Dec 1772, John Jenkins of Parish of St. Davids, Craven County, planter, to James Jenkins of same, for £100, 150 acres at the north end of 500 acres known as the Jacob Jenkins tract, granted 21 May 1772 to John Jinkins on SW side Peedee River adj. Wm. Blassingames land James[?] Jinkins, Thomas Lide, recorded in Book LLL page 240. John Jenkins (LS), Wit: John Westfield, William Blassengame. Proved in Charraw District before Claudius Pegues, J.P., by the oath of John Westfield, 13 Dec 1772. Recorded 28 July 1774.

I-4, 454-459: 15 March 1774, Elias Robert of Granville County, SC, planter, to Archibald Offutt, Silver Smith of same place, for £2500, two tracts in St. James Santee Parish, on south side Santee River adj. each other, 300 acres adj. Thomas Lynch's land, said Elias Roberts land, once intended to be conveyed to Sarah & Judith Robert, adj. land of Joseph Willingham; also 4550 acres in two different tracts on north side of said river in Prince Fredericks Parish opposite to said 300 acres adj. lance once Peter Robert Esqr, near John Dutarques, Francis Courage, in the whole 750 acres conveyed by Francis Kinloch to John & Elias Robert and by said John to said Elias Robert; also six other tracts adjoining each other in said St. James Santee parish, Craven County, 2095 acres adj. land of James Boyd, James Wright, and Charles Chovin on Hell Hole Swamp adj. John Mayrant, John Skrine, and the remnant of the church & town land on the back or heads of all the front or River tract of John Mayrant, Thomas Lynch, said Elias Robert, Joseph Willingham & John Skrine, said tract of 2095 acres was conveyed by said Francis Kinloch to James Robert, and by James Robert to John Robert and by John Robert to Elias Robert. Elias Robert (LS), Wit: John Grimball, Eliz'th Grimball. Proved 17 March 1774 before Charles Brown, Esqr., J.P. in Granville County, by the oath of John Grimball. Recorded 29 July 1774.

I-4, 459-465: Lease & release. 25 & 26 March 1774, Thomas Ellerbe and Sarah his wife of St. Davids Parish, Craven County, to James Reed of same parish, for £2000, 150 acres excepting 2½ acres off the south corner which is reserved for Mr. Kershaw a landing place, being a part of 650 acres in St. Davids Parish, Craven County, granted to John Ellerbee 17 March 1745 on NE side Peedee River adj. land surveyed for George Senior, and said John Ellerbe did convey 150 acres adj. land now belonging to Ely Kershaw and Alexander Gorden to Edward Ellerbe, 22 Sept 1751; said Edward Ellerbe 14 Sept 1756 did conveyed unto Thomas Ellerbe. Thomas Ellerbee (LS0, Sarah Ellerbe (LS) Wit: Catherine Hunt. Proved in Charraw District before Claudius Pegues, J.P., by the oath of Catherine Hunt, 27 March 1774. Recorded 22 July 1774.

END OF BOOK I-4.

SOUTH CAROLINA DEED ABSTRACTS 1773-1778

K-4, 1-3: 1 Feb 1774, Joseph Kershaw of Camden, SC, Esqr., to Miles Brewton of Charles Town, Esqr., for £727 s15 d7 SC money, 300 acres in Amelia Township on Santee River adj. land of James Mickie, granted to Thos Winningham 16 Sept 1738, recorded in Book FFF, page 17; Edward Winingham son and heir to said Thomas Winingham and Mary Jackson mother to said Edward Winingham did convey to John McCord 31 Aug 1754, and said John McCord 8 Dec 1761 to Joseph Kershaw. Joseph Kershaw (LS), Wit: Richd Brown, Wm. Boykin, Wm. Thompson. Proved in Berkley County before Fenwick Bull, J.P., by the oath of William Thompson, 12 Feb 1774. Recorded 30 Apr 1774.

K-4, 4-6: 26 Jan 1774, Charles Prince of Charles Town, Gentleman, and Ann his wife, bound to Jacob Valk in the sum of £2100 for payment of £1050, mortgage of lot in Tradd St., Charles Town. Ann Prince(LS), Ch's Prince (LS). Wit: Peter LePoole, John Lightwood. Proved 31 Jan 1774 before William Nisbett, J.P. in Charles Town District, by the oath of Peter Lepoole. Recorded 24 Apr 1774.

K-4, 6-11: 13 Jan 1774, Peter Slann of Charles Town, Merchant, son and heir at law of Andrew Slann, late of St. Georges Parish, Dorchester, Planter, deceased, to Samuel Wise & Jacob Valk of said province, gentlemen, for £2800, 100 acres in Welch Tract on Pedee River granted to Andrew Slann and on resurvey was found to contain 131 acres whereupon said Peter Slann obtained a second tract 31 Aug 1770, recorded in Book FFF, page 192, and said Andrew Slann obtained a rant for 200 acres but by a late resurvey was found to contain 250 acres and said Peter Slann obtained another granted 31 Aug 1770 recorded in Book FFF, page 129, and said Andrew Slann obtained another tract in Welch Tract of 100 acres which was found to contain 130 acres and said Peter Slann obtained a second grant for the same 24 Aug 1770, recorded in Book FFF, page 138. Peter Slann (LS), Wit: Rich'd Corbett, Tho's Marshall. Proved 28 Jan 1774 before Hopkin Price, J.P., by the oath of Richard Corbett. Recorded 2 May 1774.

K-4, 11-12: Lease. 26 May 1769, Richard Lang "deceased" to Daniel Williams of Hallifax County, Virginia, for ten shillings, 250 acres on a branch of Saludy River called Reedey River, originally granted to John Read 5 Nov 1755 and conveyed 1 & 2 March 1756 from John Read to said Robert Land deceased and has legally descended from said Robert deceased to his eldest son Richard Lang. Wit: Jacob Bowman, George Wright Junr, Hans Hendrick. Receipt for £60 signed by Jacob Bowman, 28 June 1770. Wit: Nimrod Williams.

K-4, 13-14: Joshua Shaw of Plimouth in the county of Plymouth, Massech. Bay in New England, for £400 to Thomas Davis and Ephraim Spooner both of Plymouth, joint partners in trace, half my lot in Craven County on Kingston Township on Little River, adj. survey of Mr. William Gould, dated 30 May 1772. Joshua Shaw (LS), Wit: Ralph Marry, William Howard. Plimouth, 21 July 1772 acknowledged by Joshua Shaw before Edward Winslow, J. P. Port of Plimouth, New England. Recorded 7 May 1774.

K-4, 15-19: Lease & release. 4 Feb 1774, Mary Handyside, widow, and her eldest surviving son William Denley, planter, of Craven County, SC, to David Hay & Howell Hay of said province, planters, for £1200 SC money, 200 acres in Craven County opposite to Saxegotha Township adj. Santee River otherwise called Congaree River adj. land of Nicholas Haines, George Satchwell now to Benjamin Farar, Esqr., Elizabeth Verditty now to David Hay, heirs of John Elders deceased, granted to Mary Hyde now Mary Handyside 12 Dec 1746. Mary Handyside (M) (LS), William Denley (LS), Wit: James Taylor, Margaret Denley (X). Proved 16 Feb 1774 before Thos Turner, J.P., by the oath of James Taylor. Recorded 11 May 1774.

K-4, 19-22: Lease & release. 7 & 8 Feb 1774, John Edwards of District of Ninety Six, SC, to Mackerness Goode of same, for £500 SC money, 500 acres in the Neighborhood of Ninety Six originally granted to hopkin Price 14 March 1757 and by him conveyed to Mary Edwards (deceased). John Edwards (LS), Wit: William Martin, David Anderson, Samuel Savage. Proved in Ninety Six District 7 Feb 1774 before James Mayson, J.P., by the oath of Samuel Savage. Recorded 12 May 1774.

K-4, 22-27: Lease & release. 9 & 10 Aug 1773, John Jackson & John Gill of Craven County, SC, planters, to Howell Hay of same county, planter, for £1300, 133 acres being the uppermost part of

300 acres granted to Elizabeth Verditty 22 Feb 1745 at a place called the Chickesaws on north side of the Congaree River opposite to Saxegotha Township adj. William Janeway, Henry Snelling, Samuel Lines, Samuel Lynes, Mary Hyde, land claimed by Edward Brown, land of George Satchwell, and Congaree River, which 304 acres was conveyed to George Haigh, Esqr., 3 & 5 Apr 1746, and he did convey 133 acres to Richard Jackson, and said Richard Jackson by deed of gift 1 Oct 1751 among other specific gifts to Henry Snelling in trust for the use of his youngest son Miles Jackson, and said Miles Jackson should die under age without lawfull issue then to John Jackson and Richard Jackson, and said Richard Jackson and Susanna his wife 29 & 30 July 1769 conveyed to John Gill all his portion. John Gill (X) (LS), John Jackson (I) (LS), Wit: James Gill (I), Richard Enlling, James Murphey. Proved by the oath of James Gill 15 Jan 1774 before William Arthur. Recorded 12 May 1774.

K-4, 28-34: Lease & release. 22 & 23 Dec 1773, Ann Wooley of Parish of Withington in the county of Gloucester, heretofore Ann Eycott spinster, but now a widow and relict of John Wooley late of same parish, gentleman, deceased, and sister & devisee of John Eycott, late of Charles Town, merchant, deceased, to Martin Campbell of Charles Town, merchant, for £300 money of Great Britain, corner lot of Ground on Broad Street & King Street with part of a timber building standing thereon and another lot with three old decayed tenements or huts standing thereon, and a lot on Charles Town Creek adj. north of the road leaving to the Quarter house. Ann Woolley (LS), Wit: Wm. Coombs, James Savery. Proved in Charles Town District by the oath of Wm. Coombs before John Coram, J.P., 2 May 1774. Recorded 15 May 1774.

James Savery of Wilthington County of Gloucester, yoeman, now of the age of sixty five years or thereabouts maketh oath that he knew & was well acquainted with John Eycott heretofore of Arencaster in County of Gloucester and the said John Eycott several years ago went over and settled as a trader in Charles Town, South Carolina, where he died, and this deponent hat known An Wooley of Parish of Withington and that she was sister of aforesaid John Eycott and that they were children of Richard Eycott by Elizabeth his wife., 18 Jan 1774. J. Hayward, Rector of Withington, In the presence of Simon Young, Church ward. Thos Collett[?] overseer, William Combes. Proved by the oath of William Combes before John Coram, J. P. 2 May 1774. Recorded 15 May 1774.

K-4, 34-36: 30 Dec 1773, John Bootwright of Craven County, SC, planter, to Thos Wade, Esqr. of Anson County, North Carolina, for £50 SC money, 200 acres granted to said John Bootwright 31 Oct 1769. John Bootwright (+) (LS), Wit: Ralph Bowman, Calep Williams (u), Jesse Botwright (I). Proved in Craven County, SC, before Arthur Hart, J. P., by the oath of Calep Williams, 3 Dec 1773. Recorded 17 May 1774.

K-4, 36-42: Lease & release. 26 & 27 Sept 1772, John Summers & Elizabeth his wife of Charles Town, to Philomon Waters of Orangeburgh District, planter, for £500 SC money, 300 acres in Craven County on NE side Pedee River adj. Daniel Blake, John Alran, Josiah Supre, Malichi Murphy, which said land was surveyed for Joshua Stroud 14 Aug 1770. John Summers (LS), Eliz'th Summers (mark) (LS), Wit: Denham Fearis, Patrick Fleming. Proved 6 March 1773 before Thos Turner, Esqr., J.P. in Charles Town District, by the oath of Denham Fearis. Recorded 18 May 1774.

K-4, 42-47: Lease & release. 2 & 3 May 1765, Rudolph Buzzard in Berkley County, SC, to Izrael Gaunt of same, planter, for £10 SC money, 200 acres on NE side Saludy River on a branch Bush Creek formerly Bush River, granted to said Rudolph Bussard 18 Jan 1765. Rudolph Bussard (LS), Wit: Hugh Creighton, John Atkins (O), Sanders Walker. Proved 1 Aug 1765 before Andrew Brown, J.P. in Berkley County, by the oath of John Atkins. Recorded 19 May 1774.

K-4, 47-51: Lease & release. 8 & 9 Nov 1766, Aaron Ayers of Craven County, St. Marks Parish, SC, Labourer, to Israel Gaunt of same place, millwright, for £25 SC money, 100 acres on a ridge between Scotch Creek and Palmetto Branch in Craven County. Aaron Ayres (LS), Wit: Joseph Kershaw, Thos Jones, Saml Boykin. Proved 15 Dec 1766 before John Newman Oglethorpe, J. P. in Craven County, by the oath of Joseph Kershaw. Recorded 19 May 1774.

K-4, 52-57: Lease & release. 24 & 25 Oct 1766, Joseph White of Berkley County, SC, to Israel Gaunt of same, for £500 SC money, 200 acres in the county aforesaid on north side Saludy River

SOUTH CAROLINA DEED ABSTRACTS 1773-1778

on a branch of Bush Creek called Youngs fork granted to said Joseph White 23 Oct 1765. Joseph White (I) (LS), Wit: Joseph Wright, James Patty, John Reagin. A Memorial entered in Book H No. 8 page 357, 30 Nov 1767. Proved in Berkley County before Jonathan Gilbert, J.P., by the oath of Jonathan Reagin, 18 Nov 1767. Recorded 25 May 1774.

K-4, 57-63: Lease & release. 21 & 22 March 1742, George Hunter of Charles Town, SC, gentleman, to Charles Pinckney of same, place, esquire, for £5 SC money, lot #80 on Cooper River adj. lots of Thomas Colleton, Esqr., James Colleton, Esqr., and Landgrave, lot run out for Capt. William Walley, Capt. James Adie, which became vested in John Colleton of fair lawn Barony in the Parish of St. Johns, Berkley County, SC, and said John Colleton and Susanah his wife 13 & 14 July 1736 conveyed for £5000 to said George Hunter and said Charles Pinckney and one Thomas Ellery late of Charles Town, deceased, were equally concerned with the said George Hunter in the said lot (plat included certified 12 Aug 1802 by Stephen Rae, annexed to a conveyance from George Charles Pinckney in Book F-4, page 58 at the request of Charles Cotesworth Pinckney, recorded on page 61). George Hunter (LS), Wit: Bethiah Beesley, Thos. Pinckney. Proved in Berkley County 8 Oct 1751 by the oath of Thomas Pinckney before Wm. Pinckney, J.P. 174 sold LM to Mr. Guignard 31 July 1745 exchagned the Lott Letter F the lott letter D August 1st. Sold the Marsh lot to James McKellis[?] who mortgaged it back to me to secure the purchase money. Recorded 25 May 1774.

K-4, 63-67: Lease & release. 14 & 15 1773, William White of Parish of St. David, Craven County, planter, to Reuben White of same parish, planter, for £300 SC money, 30 acres in Craven County on Jefferies Creek adj. Reuben Whites land, John McMuldrow, John McClendals, Riggs land, granted to said William White 4 Dec 1771. Wm. White (LS), Wit: James White, Benjn Dickinson. Proved before Joseph Gourley, J.P. for Charraw District, by the oath of James White 15 Feb 1774. Recorded 26 May 1774.

K-4, 67-71: Lease & release. 21 & 22 Jan 1774, Richard Allison of Ninety Six District, Shoemaker, to John Edwards of same, planter, for £2000 SC money, 200 acres granted to Hans George Dightel in Ninety Six District on halfway swamp creek conveyed to said Richard Allison from said Hans George Dightel 5 Aug in the 28th year of the right of George II. Richard Allison (LS), Wit: Wm. Martin, David Anderson, Saml. Savage. Proved in Ninety Six District 16 Feb 1774 by the oath of Saml Savage before James Mayson, J.P. Recorded 29 May 1774.

K-4, 71-76: Lease & release. 21 & 22 June 1773, Charles Perkins of Berkley County, Sc, to Joseph Jay of same, for £500 SC money, 196 acres on north side Saludah River adj. land of Wm. Turner, Charles Parkins, and is part of a tract formerly granted to Joseph King 4 June 1754, is part of the same that was granted to said Charles Perkins by lease & release 19 Sept 1766. Charles Parkins (LS), Patience Parkins (LS), Wit: Joseph King, David Parkins, Daniel Parkins. Proved in Ninety Six District by the oath of David Parkins before Michl. Dickert, J.P., 31 July 1773. Recorded 30 May 1774.

K-4, 76-81: Lease & release. 21 & 22 Sept 1772, Gabriel Clements of St. Peters Parish, SC, to John Bates of Berkley County, SC, for £300 SC money, 200 acres on north side Saludy River on bigg creek granted to Edward Brown 12 June 1755 and was bequeathed to the aforesaid Gabriel Clements by the last will and testament of said Edward Brown. Gabriel Clements (LS), Wit: Richard Jones, Chisby Davis. Proved in Ninety Six District before Moses Kirkland, J.P., by the oath of Richard Jones, 20 Feb 1773. Recorded 31 May 1774.

K-4, 82-87: Lease & release. 17 & 18 May 1770, Benjamin Stirk of province of Georgia, planter, and Hannah his wife, daughter and devisee of Stephen Miller late of said province deceased, to John Hodsden of province of South Carolina, merchant, for £2500, tenement now in the occupation of Henry Grainger in Union Street in Charles Town, lot number 16 adj. land late of Richard Cadwer deceased, Stephen Miller deceased, Bay of Charles Town. Benjamin Stirk (LS), Hannah Stirk (LS), Wit: John Glen, Wm. Young, Richd Churchill. Proved in Berkley County, Sc, before John Troup, J.P., by the oath of Richard Churchill, 9 Sept 1770. Recorded 3 June 1774.

K-4, 88-91: William Young and John Glen of Savannah, Province of Georgia, Esquires, by certain indenture of lease & release 18 May 1770 between Benjamin Stirk of Province of Georgia and

SOUTH CAROLINA DEED ABSTRACTS 1773-1778

Hannah his wife to John Hodsden of South Carolina, release of inheritance of lot number #16 in said deed. By writ of dedimus potestatem under the hand and seal of Honourable Robt. Pringle of, Justice of the Court of Common Pleas of South Carolina. Recorded 3 June 1774.

K-4, 91-93: 25 Jan 1755, Charles Hutto of Berkley County, SC, labourer, and Ann his wife, to Isaac Hutto and Jacob Hutto and Benjamin Hutto of same, labourers, for five shillings SC money, 300 acres in Orangeburgh Township, Berkley County, adj. land of John Role, Casper Miller, Ludwig Linder, Pon Pon River, and one town lot in Orangeburgh number 282. Charles Hutto (mark) LS) Ann Hutto (A) (LS), Wit: Christopher Rowe, David Hall, Joseph Griffeths (IG). Recorded 3 June 1774.

K-4, 93-98: Lease & release. 9 & 10 July 1770, Isaac, Jacob & Benjamin Hutto of Berkley County, Labourers, to George McMichael of same, labourer, for £100 SC money, 350 acres granted 1 March 1744 to Isaac Hutto in Berkley County adj. John Role, Casper Miller, Ludwing Linder, Pon Pon River, and one town lot in Orangeburgh number 282. Isaac Hutto (H) (LS), Anna Hutto (A) (LS), Jacob Hutto (I) (LS), Benjamin Hutto (LS), Susanna Hutto (LS), Wit: Henry Snelling, Leonard Varnado (+), Isaac Varnodo (I). Proved before Christopher Rowe, J.P. in Berkley County and Colleton County, by the oath of Isaac Varnado, 1 Feb 1771. Recorded 6 June 1774.

K-4, 98-103: Lease & release. 9 & 10 Feb 1774, George McMichael of St. Mathews Parish, Berkley County, Labourer, to William Marshall of Charles Town, merchant, for £50 SC money, 350 acres in Orangeburgh Township granted 1 March 1744 to Isaac Hutto in Berkley County adj. John Role, Casper Miller, Ludwing Linder, Pon Pon River, and one town lot in Orangeburgh number 282. George McMichael (LS), Wit: John Fisher, John Gordon (J), William Farie (E). Proved in Orangeburgh District by the oath of John Fisher before Gavin Pou, J.P., 10 Feb 1774. Recorded 8 June 1774.

K-4, 103-109: Lease & release. 1 & 2 Dec 1770, Thomas Hatcher, Shoe Maker, of berkley County, Sc, to Aunsbrey Noland of same, gentn., for £250 SC money, 250 acres between Broad & Saludie Rivers on a branch of Tiger River called Peterses Creek adj. land laid out to Capt. Saml Aubery, land said to be laid out to Isaac Fitchlin. Thomas Hatcher (LS), Welmerth Hatcher (+) (LS), Wit: Jeremiah OCain (5), Reuben Jones, John Guttrey. Proved 19 Dec 1770 by the oath of John Guttrey before Thos Gordon, J.P. Recorded 9 June 1774.

K-4, 109-115: 2 May 1768, John Smith of Savannah, Province of Georgia, Esqr., and Elizabeth his wife to Benjamin Walls of Dawfuskee Island, SC, planter, for £1500 SC money, 400 acres on Dawfuskee Island granted 13 Jan 1710 to Nathaniel Day since deceased and by his last will and testament dated 29 Nov 1711 did devi e his estate real and personal to Andrew Allen of Charles Town, Merchant, and 600 acres granted to Andrew Allen 16 March 1732 on Dawfuskee Island ad. land granted to Nathaniel Day, and said Andrew Allen by his last will and testament 29 March 1735 give to his son John allen, and soon after said John Allen by his last will and testament 5 March 1747 to devise unto his wife Ann Allen all his real estate, and said Ann Allen intermarried with John Savage of Charles Town, merchant, and jointly with him conveyed the two tracts 1 & 2 Feb 1753 to William Scott of Charles Town, merchant, which said william Scott by deeds 9 & 10 Feb 1753 conveyed the same to John Savage and said john Savage 28 & 29 Sept 1759 conveyed to Lancelot Bland, and said Lancelot Bland on 4 & 5 Jan 1762 conveyed to John Smith, one full moiety or half part of said two tracts; 500 acres on Dawfuskee Island in Granville County, SC, adj. land lately belonging to Elizabeth Varnet, Hugh Evans, Mary Martinangel and on Days Creek. John Smith (LS), Elizabeth Smith (LS), Wit: Mary Cowper, Ann Smith. Proved in Berkly County by the oath of Ann Smith now Ann McQueen before Robt Brisbane, J.P., 7 March 1774. Recorded 20 June 1774.

K-4, 115-121: Lease & release. 24 & 25 Jan 1774, Rowland Rugeley of Charles Town, merchant, to Benjamin Fuller of St. Andrews Parish, planter, for £1970 SC money, 201 acres on the north side of Ashley River in the Parish of St. Andrew, adj. land now or late of Charles Cantey, John Burford deceased, land lately belonging to Henry Wood, and William Fuller. Rowland Rugeley (LS), Wit: Danl Crokatt, George Logan. Proved in Charles Town District by the oath of Daniel Crokatt before Wm. Logan, J.P., 9 May 1774. Recorded 10 June 1774.

SOUTH CAROLINA DEED ABSTRACTS 1773-1778

K-4, 122-127: Lease & mortgage. 15 & 16 Feb 1774, Stephen Miller of Parish of St. Thomas, Esquire, and Mary his wife, to John Hodsden of Charles Town, Gentn., bound in the sum of £7002 for payment of £3501, mortgage of lot in Charles Town in front of the Markett House on Broad St., adj. land of Bryan Cape, James Laurens, William Loocock. Stephen Miller (LS), Mary Miller (LS), Wit: William Jordan, Jos. Young. Proved in Charles Town District 19 Feb 1774 before William Burrows, J.P., by the oath of Joseph Young. Recorded 10 June 1774.

K-4, 127-129: 17 July 1773, Michael Dickson, yeoman, to William Dickson, mortgage for £10,000 for tract in Boonsborough Township, 100 acres. Michael Dickson (+) (LS), Wit: Goodman Griffiths, James Seawright. Proved in Ninety Six District before Adam Crane Jones, J.P., by the oath of James Seawright, 28 Feb 1774. Recorded 13 June 1774.

K-4, 129-132: 12 Dec 1773, John Dickson, yeoman, of Ninety Six District, to Adam McKee, yeoman, of same, for natural love & affection to said Adam McKey and his wife Jenny McKey and also for the sum of £15 SC money, 200 acres in Boonsborough Township, granted 18 Feb 1763, and a memorial entered in Book A No 7, page 118, 9 July 1763, and in Secretarys Office Book XX, page 223, a Bounty. John Dickson (mark) (LS), Prudence Dickson (+) (LS), Wit: Goodman Griffiths, Margaret Dickson (mark), William Dickson. Proved in Ninety Six District by the oath of William Dickson before Adam Crain Jones, J.P., 28 Feb 1774. Recorded 14 June 1774.

K-4, 132-133: 20 Dec 1773, John and Samuel McKey of Craven County, Sc, to Robert Crawford of same, for £200 SC money, 500 acres in the Waxhaw settlement on south side of the Waxhaw Creek. John McKee (LS), Saml McKee (LS), Wit: William Massey, Charles Miller, William Correy. Proved before James Patton, J.P. for Camden District, by the oath of William Massey 20 Dec 1773. Recorded 14 June 1774.

K-4, 134-140: Lease & release. 27 & 28 Oct 1773, Honorable John Murray, Esqr., of Charles Town, to James Parsons & John Rutledge, Esquires, for £10,000 SC money, 18,050 acres above a place called Ninety Six adj. Saludy River, land of Benjamin Walker, James Mayson, Esquire, land late of William Murrey Esquire, land late of William Simpson, Esquire, part of 25,000 acres by a deed of partition dated 7 July 1758 between said William Simpson and Elizabeth his wife and John Murray of the other part, as his part of 50,000 acres granted to William Livingston 27 June 1752 and conveyed by Livingston to John Hamilton, Esqr. John Murray (LS), Wit: Amelia Ladson, Francis Ayrton, Daniel Wilson. Proved by the oath of Francis Ayrton 12 March 174 before Jno Coram. Recorded 14 June 1774.

K-4, 141-145: Lease & release. 15 & 16 Sept 1767, William Snider of Craven County, SC, sadler, to John Holsinger of same place, planter, for £100 SC money, 100 acres in the fork opposite to the Congaree part of tract of 250 acres granted to Thos Hogg 25 May 1751 and conveyed unto Jacob Snider father of said William Snider. Wm Snider (LS), Wit: Patrick Dillon, Conrad Meyer (CM). Proved in Craven County before Philip Pearson, J.P., by the oath of Conrad Myer, _ March 1773. Recorded 15 June 1774.

K-4, 145-149: 9 Oct 1770, Messor Smith of St. mathews Parish, SC, planter, to Paul Sheuer of same place, planter, for £40 SC money, 100 acres part of 300 acres granted to said Messor Smith 5 June 1770 adj. land granted to Peter Faure, Catherine Miller. (plat included dated 23 Sept 1770 by John Mitchell, D. S.) Messor Smith (LS), Wit: John Mitchell, Jno Michael Gabel, John Bernhard. Proved 14 Oct 1770 before Christopher Rowe, J.P. in Berkly County, by the oath of Michael Gabell. Recorded 16 June 1774.

K-4, 149-155: Lease & release. 3 & 4 May 1765, Doctor John Murray of province of SC, to Andrew Williamson at Stephens Creek, planter, for £100 SC money, 300 acres on a branch of Savannah River and Stephens Creek adj. land surveyed for John Hawthorn, one McCormick, David McElwee. J. Murray (LS), Wit: Ann Murray, John Ainslie. Proved 29 March 1771 before John Lewis Gervais, J. P. in Colleton County, by the oath of John Ainslie. Recorded 16 June 1774.

K-4, 155-160: Lease & release. 18 & 19 Nov 1773, William Sinquefield of District of Ninety Six, planter, to Andrew Williamson of same, for £200, 150 acres in Granville county granted to William Rogers on Savannah River adj. Casper Shirleys, said William Rogers and Mary his wife on 31 Dec

1757 conveyed to William Sinquefield. William Sinquefield (X) (LS), Wit: Francis Sinquefield, Aaron Sinquefield (A), Tim'y Parker. Proved 22 Nov 1773 before John Purves, J.P. in Ninety Six District, by the oath Timothy Parker. Recorded 17 June 1774.

K-4, 160-165: Lease & release. 12 & 13 Apr 1773, Barclay Jones of Ninety Six District, SC, Labourer, to Andrew Williamson of same, planter, for £500 SC money, 250 acres in District of Orangeburgh District on a small branch of Savanna River known as Stell Creek adj. land granted to Thomas Philport, granted to said Barclay Jones 8 Feb last. Barclay Jones (LS), Wit: Nuby Mann, Joshua Gray, John Purves. Proved in Granville County before John Purves, J.P., by the oath of Joshua Gray, 13 Apr 1773. Recorded 21 June 1774.

K-4, 165-168: 17 Apr 1759, George Pawley Junior of Prince Georges Parish, Craven County, SC, and Sarah his wife, to Elizabeth Mary Pawley, wife of Col. George Pawley, for £ 700 SC money; George Pawley Senior, William Swinton & Daniel Laroche, Esqrs., by a deed dated 5 Nov 1735 confirmed unto Robert Innis, town lot in George Town, number 110, on High Street, and said Robert Innis on 19 March 1736 did make over said lott to Thomas Charnock of same place, planter, and on 10 July 1751, said Thos Charnock did convey to Zachariah Brazier of George Town, and said Zachariah Brazier and Mary Ann his wife by their deed conveyed 26 Dec 1755 to aforesaid George Pawley Junior. George Pawley Junr (LS), Sarah Pawley (LS), Wit: Hannah Pawley, Joseph Dubourdieu. Proved in Craven County before Joseph Brown, J.P. for Craven County by the oath of Joseph Dubourdieu, 6 June 1768. Recorded 21 June 1774.

K-4, 168-170: 24 March 1774, Barbara Barns of Ninety Six District, SC, relict of Charles Barns deceased, to Jacob Barns also of Ninety Six District, planter, for £100 SC money; grant bearing date 8 Apr 1768 by Gov. William Tryon of North Carolina, granted to Charles Barns, 81 acres on Broad River on the west side in the county of Mecklenburgh then deemed a part of the province of North Carolina but now it lies in the District of Ninety Six, South Carolina. Barbara Barns (mark LS), Wit: Lily Robinson, William Barns, Moses Watkins. Proved in Ninety Six District by the oath of Lily Robinson before Joseph Robins, J.P., 2 Apr 1774. Recorded 22 June 1774.

K-4, 171-176: Lease & release. 13 & 14 May 1774, Thomas Handlen of Charles Town, Gentleman, to Alexander Tweed of Prince Georges Parish, SC, planter, for £525 SC money, 850 acres in Craven County adj. John White, Capt. Anthony White, granted 23 May 1734 to James Handlen deceased. Thos Handlen (LS), Wit: Wm. Gibson, Ezekiel Townsend. Proved 16 May 1774 before Thos Phepoe, J. P., by the oath of Ezekiel Townsend. Recorded 22 June 1774.

K-4, 176-181: Lease & release. 19 & 20 May 1774, Joseph Roper of Charles Town, Turner, to Alexander Tweed of George Town, planter, for £100 SC money, 250 acres in Craven County on Black River commonly called Black Mingo adj. John McDowel, William Fleming Esqr. deceased, Black Mingo Creek. Joseph Roper (LS), Wit: Andrew Redmon, Roger Neill, Jno Thomlinson. Proved 22 June 1774 before Thomas Turner, J.P. in Charles Town District, by the oath of Andrew Redmon.

K-4, 182-191: Lease & release. 14 & 15 Feb 1773, Ann Watson, Late of Charles Town but at present of the City of Dublin in the Kingdom of Ireland, widow, by Francis Gottier of Charles Town, Goldsmith and Jeweller, her attorney, and Isabella Gottier otherwise Blair his wife, to Samuel Jones of Charles Town, tanner, for £700 SC money, by a deed dated 29 Dec 1756 by Charles Loundes, Provost Marshall of SC, to Ann Watson of Charles Town, half of a lot in Ansonborough near Charles Town, number I adj. land belonging to Mr. Dart, Squirrel Street, William Hopton, Esquire, estate of Joseph Wragg, Esqr., and by her letter of attorney 19 Feb 1770 appointed Francis Gottier before Thomas Black, Lord Mayor of Dublin. Francis Gottier (LS) attorney for Mrs. Anne Watson. Wit: John Fox, John Gourley. Proved before John Troup, J.P. in Charles Town District, by the oath of John Gourley, 2 March 1774. Recorded 25 June 1774.

K-4, 191-193: 25 Feb 1773, Oliver Wallace of Craven County, SC, to James Woods of same, for £200 SC money, land on south fork of Fishing Creek adj. land James Hanna bought of Ephraim McClain, John Wade, his own line, by the waggon road, Benjamin Phillips corner, Samuel Rameys line, Balls line, 150 acres granted to James Hanna 28 Sept 1766. Oliver Wallace (LS), Annisbell

SOUTH CAROLINA DEED ABSTRACTS 1773-1778

Wallace (A) (LS), Wit: Sarah Woods, Benjn Phillips. Proved in Camden District by the oath of Benjamin Philips before Wm. Brown, J.P. 22 May 1773. Recorded 27 June 1774.

K-4, 193-199: Lease & release. 8 & 9 Jan 1773, Edward Teele of St.Peters Parish, Granville County, SC, and Rebecca, his wife, to John Adam Treutlen of St. Mathews Parish, Georgia, Esqr., for £55 money of Great Britain, tract in St. Peters Parish, Granville County, SC, 125 acres as the lower part of 250 acres granted to said Edward Teele. Edward Teele (LS), Rebecca Teele (/) (LS), Wit: John lynch, Charles Teele. Proved 17 March 1774 before Charles Brown, J. P. in Beaufort District by the oath of Charles Teele. Recorded 27 June 1774.

K-4, 199-205: Lease & release. 18 & 19 March 1774, John Sandiford Chinners of James Island, Berkly County, SC, planter, and Elizabeth his wife, to John Gaillard of Charles Town, Esqr., for £700 SC money, tract in St. Stephens Parish in Craven county, which belonged to Abraham Chinners late of Craven county, planter, deceased, by his last will and testament dated 16 March 1759 in which he did bequeath to his son John Sandiford Chinners, 500 acres. Jno Sandiford Chinners (LS), Elizabeth Chinners (LS), Wit: John Todd Junr, Jos. Ward. Proved by the oath of Joshua Ward in Charles Town District before James Trail, J.P., 19 March 1774. Recorded 30 June 1774.

K-4, 206-208: Tripartite indenture. 17 Oct 1772, Richard Proctor of province of SC, planter, Mary An Vinson of Charles Town, spinster, and Culcheth Gibbes and Maurice Simmons of province of SC, gentlemen; whereas a marriage is intended between Richard Proctor and Mary Ann Vinson, and said Richard Proctor is lawfully possessed of twenty negroes [named] and whereas said Mary Ann Vinson is also lawfully entitled to the sum of £4300 on a bond due payable and owing to her from James Skirving of province of SC, planter, said property in trust to Culcheth Gibbes and Maurice Simmons. Richard Proctor (LS), Culcheth Gibbs (LS), Maurice Simmons (LS), Mary Ann Vinson (LS), Wit: Mary Harvey, William Maxwell.

K-4, 209-212: 15 Feb 1749, John Vaun of Charles Town, SC, carpenter, and Judith his wife to Daniel Crawford and John Cordes of province aforesaid gentlemen, for £300, lot in Charles Town part of Division M number 80, on Pinckney Street, adj. land of James Hunter, Joseph Oram. John Vaun (LS), Judith Vaun (LS), Wit: Peter Poinsett, Robert Williams Jur, Mathew Roche. Proved by the oath of Robert Williams Junr before John Rattray, J.P. for Berkley County, 11 Apr 1750. Recorded 30 June 1774.

K-4, 212-217: Lease & release. 5 & 6 Feb 1772, Mickel Hunsinger of Charles Town, SC, to Conrad Kysell of same, for £100 SC money, 100 acres in Amelia County granted to Mickel Hunsinger 22 May 1774. Michel Hunsinger (LS), Wit: Adam Gramlick [signed in German], Casper Faust (CF). Proved 18 May 1773 before William Rugeley, J.P., by the oath of Adam Gramlick. Recorded 15 June 1774.

K-4, 217-221: An Act to incorporate the Fellowship Society. At the court of Saint James 15 June 1770 Present the Kings most Excellent Lord President Duke of Marlborough, Duke of Lancaster, Earl of Briston, Viscount Weymouth, Sir Edward Hawke. Whereas the Lt. Gov. of Province of SC in 1769 did pass an act to incorporate the fellowship society, Whereas Edward Weyman, James Brown and Robert Cripps in behalf of themselves for certain charitable purposes have subsisted these seven years last past under the name of the fellowship society... erecting a convenient infirmary or hospital for affording relief to distress persons in this province. Peter Manigault, Speaker. In the council Chamber 23 Aug 1769. Assented to by William Bull. Recorded 3 June 1774.

K-4, 221-227: Lease & release. 8 & 9 March 1774, Helen Hunter, executrix of the last will and testament of James Hunter late of Charles Town, to Samuel Cordes & James Cordes the younger of said province, esquires, for £10,000 SC money, 900 acres on north side of Santee River, said James Hunter 22 April 1769 duly made his last will and testament and provided that this tract of 90 acres by him lately purchased of James Murray called Mount Hope, did transfer to his executrix to sell; appointed his daughter Helen executrix and his friends David Rhind and William Ancrum executors, and said David Rhind and William Ancrum having refused to take upon themselves the burthen and execution of said will.... Helen Hunter (LS), Wit: Mary Swadler, James Strickland,

SOUTH CAROLINA DEED ABSTRACTS 1773-1778

Peter Fayssoux. Proved in Charles Town District 25 March 1774 by the oath of Peter Fayssoux before Thos Turner, J.P. Recorded 5 July 1774.

K-4, 227-230: 6 Dec 1768, Margaret Fee of Charles Town, SC, to John Dooly of Ninety Six, Deputy Surveyor of said province, for £13 s6 SC money, 100 acres granted 30 Aug 1765 in Boonsborough Township adj. Hugh Fee, Township line. Margret Fee (LS), Wit: Philip Goode, Joseph Freman, Daniel Horsey. Proved in Craven County before Robt. Cunningham, J.P., by the oath of Joseph Freeman, 7 Feb 1771. Recorded 5 July 1774.

K-4, 231-234: Lease & release. 21 & 22 March 1774, Frederick Stallings of Parish of Prince William, SC, to John Scott of same, planter, for £50 SC money, 50 acres granted 4 March 1757 to Elias Stallings adj. Savanna River, Charles Kerby, Thomas Kerby. Frederick Stallings (LS), Wit: Saml. Scott, James Stallings. Proved before Thomas Turner, J. P. in Charles Town District, by the oath of James Stallings, 29 March 1774. Recorded 6 July 1774.

[N. B. The page after 235 is numbered 335.]

K-4, 235-340: Lease & release. 8 & 9 Apr 1768, William McKay of Craven County, planter, and Katherine his wife, to John Egan of same, for £5 SC money, 450 acres granted to William McCay 7 March 1754. William McKay (LS), Katharine McKay (LS), Wit: Henry Cassels Junr, James Johnston, Jeane McKay. Proved 14 Apr 1768 by the oath of Henry Cassels Junr. before Henry Cassels, J.P. for Craven County. Recorded 8 July 1774.

K-4, 340-344: 11 Aug 1752, Peter Negerlie of Berkley County, Labourer, and Margaret his wife to Charles Hottow of same, for £50, 400 acres in Berkley County, Orangeburgh Township. Peter Negerlie (N) (LS), Margaret Negerlie (+) (LS), Wit: Henry Felder, Christian Roth (CR). Proved in Berkley County 15 Aug 1752 by the oath of Henry Felder before James Tilly, J.P. Recorded 8 July 1774.

K-4, 344-348: Lease & release. 17 & 18 May 1774, John McKay of Province of SC, planter, and Katharine his wife, to Robert Wilson of same, planter, for £50 SC money, 50 acres on the east of the north branch of Black River in St. Marks Parish, Craven County, adj. land of Moses Garden, Charles McKay, Mary McKay. John Mackay (LS), Cathn. Mackay (LS), Wit: Roger Wilson, Samuel Newman, David Wilson. Proved 3 March 1774 by the oath of Roger Wilson before Henry Cassels, J.P. Recorded 9 July 1774.

[N. B. The page after 347 is numbered 300.]

K-4, 300-306: Lease & release. 29 & 30 March 1774, Samuel Hopkins & Frances his wife of Charles Town, Baker, to Thomas Elfe of same, cabinet maker, for £3500 SC money, lot in Parish of St. Philips Charles Town on King Street or Broad path leading to the quarter house., adj. Patrick Kings land which said lot was lately purchased by said Samuel Hopkins of Christopher Fitzsimmons of Charles Town, Tallow Chandler, lot number 16. Saml Hopkins (LS), Frances Hopkins (X) (LS), Wit: John Love, Jas Hugh Alison. Proved by the oath of James Hugh Alison 2 Apr 1774 before William Rugeley, J.P. Recorded 11 July 1774.

K-4, 306-313: Lease & release. 19 & 20 Jan 1774, Jonathan Wood of province of SC, wheel wright, heir at law of Rebecca Wood, late of said province deceased and John Wood and Joseph Wood, Benjamin Wood and Jonathan Wood, sons of Joseph and Martha Wood, to Daniel Cannon of Charles Town, gentleman, for £400 SC money, 500 acres on Cattles Creek in Berkley County, granted to said Rebecca Wood deceased. Joseph Wood (LS), Ben'n Wood (LS), John Wood (LS), Joseph Wood (LS), Jane Wood (LS), Wit: Rachel Baker, Sarah Wood, Jas. Wood. Proved in Charles Town District before William Rugeley, J.P., 7 Apr 1774 by the oath of James Wood. Recorded 12 March 1774.

K-4, 313-320: Lease & release. 19 & 20 Jan 1774, Peter Wood deceased and Joseph Wood, or Berkley County, SC, to Daniel Cannon of Charles Town, gentleman, for £300 SC money, for the use of Joseph Woods children, 300 acres on Cattels Creek in Berkley County, adj. land laid out to one Rebecca Wood, granted 6 Nov 1751 who by a defective deed conveyed the same to said Joseph

SOUTH CAROLINA DEED ABSTRACTS 1773-1778

Wood. Joseph Wood (LS), Wit: Rachel Baker, Sarah Wood, James Wood. Proved in Charles Town District before William Rugeley, J.P., 7 Apr 1774 by the oath of James Wood. Recorded 12 July 1774.

K-4, 320-323: Lease & release. 13 & 14 Nov 1770, John Ioor of St. Georges Parish to Samuel Dwight of Parish of All Saints for £300 SC money, 184 acres. John Ioor (LS), Wit: John Glaze, Jno Dawson. Proved before Maurice Simons, Esqr., J.P. for Craven County 24 May 1774. Recorded 14 July 1774.

K-4, 323-329: Lease & release. 24 & 25 May 1765, Joseph Holmes of Province of SC, sadler, to Andrew Williamson of Stephens Creek, planter, for £30 SC money, 150 acres in Granville County at the place where the old path from Fort Boone to Hard Labour crosses the Long Cane Creek, adj. land laid out for Messrs. Russell and Gervais, James Calhoun. Joseph Holmes (+) (LS), Andrew Williamson (LS), Wit: Wm. Frewin, Robt. Ray. Proved 25 May 1765 before James Jackson, J.P. in Parish of St. Paul, by the oath of William Frewin, Esqr. Recorded 15 July 1774.

K-4, 329-333: Lease & release. 24 & 25 March 1774, Andrew Williamson of District of Ninety Six, planter, to John Lewis Gervais of Charles Town, SC, merchant, for £100 SC money, 100 acres on a branch of Stephens Creek granted 20 June 1764 to James Mayson, and by deed 30 Oct 1765 transferred to said Andrew Williamson. Andrew Williamson (LS), Wit: Wm. Coffey, Timothy Parker. Proved 26 March 1774 by the oath of Timothy Parker before John Purves, J.P. in Ninety Six District. Recorded 18 July 1774.

K-4, 333-338: Lease & release. 11 & 12 Apr 1774, John Lewis Gervais of Charles Town, SC, merchant, to Andrew Williamson of St. Bartholomews Parish, Colleton County, planter, for £100 SC money, 150 acres in St. Bartholomews Parish on a branch of Stephens Creek called Hard Labour Creek, part of 8000 acres granted to Henry Lawrence, Esqr., 8 Apr 1768, and which said tract of 150 acres became vested in John Lewis Gervais by deed of partition dated 11 Jan 1772. John Lewis Gervais (LS), Wit: Timothy Parker, William Valentine. Proved 15 Apr 1774 before William Rugeley, J.P. in Berkley County, by the oath of William Valentine. Recorded 19 July 1774.

K-4, 339-344: Lease & release. 10 & 11 Feb 1774, William Savage of Charles Town, merchant, and Martha his wife, to Thomas Latham, Daniel Latham, Jesse Hunt & Jonathan Lawrence, all of same place, distillers, for £4000 SC money, lot on Hazell Street adj. lands now or late of Admiral Frankland, Mr. Lightwood. Wm. Savage (LS), Martha Savage (LS), Wit: Francis Baker, Walter Rosewell. Proved in Charles Town District by the oath of Francis Baker before William Rugeley, J.P., 21 Apr 1774. Recorded 20 July 1774.

K-4, 344-349: Lease & release. 19 & 20 May 1773, Nicholas Highler of Berkley County, Sc, planter, to Christian Keizor of same, planter, for £250 SC money, 150 acres in the low grounds of Santee River in between Saxegotha & Amelia Townships, adj. Nicholas Federolph, Jacob Geiger, granted 18 Oct 1757 to Henry Dennis, said Hendrick Dennis by lease & release 7 & 8 May 1764, conveyed to John Wolfgang Shaley, and said John Wolfgang Shaley 7 & 8 May 1764 conveyed to Nicholas Highler. Nicholas Highler (LS), Wit: George Seawright, Geo Wactor, John Friday. Proved before Philip Pearson, J.P. for Craven County, by the oath of George Wactor, 23 Feb 1774. Recorded 21 July 1774.

K-4, 349-353: Lease & release. 15 & 16 March 1769, Edward McGraw Senr of Parish of St. Marks, planter, to William Killey Junr of same place, yeoman, for £10 SC money, 350 acres on a branch of Broad River in St. Marks Parish, granted 17 Feb 1767 to Edward McGray. Edward McGray (+) (LS), Wit: Barb'y Pope, Willm. McGraw, Joseph Harison (H). Proved before Jno. N. Oglethorpe, J.P., 31 Aug 1769 by the oath of Joseph Harrison. Recorded 21 July 1774.

K-4, 353-357: 16 Apr 1774, Jeremiah Theus of Charles Town, SC, Simner, and Eve Rosanna his wife, to Daniel Huger of same province, esqr., for £800 SC money, lot on north side of upper end of Broad Street in Charles Town, adj. lands belonging to Mr. John Wish, Rawlins Lowndes, Esqr, also the brick dwelling house thereon. Jeremiah Theus (LS), Eve Rosanna Theus (LS), Wit: David Rhind, James Theth, Simon Theus. Proved before James Simpson, J. P., by the oath of James Theth 23 Apr 1774. Recorded 23 July 1774.

SOUTH CAROLINA DEED ABSTRACTS 1773-1778

K-4, 358-360: 4 March 1774, John Fields of Craven County, SC, Parish of St. Marks, to John Pfifer of Mecklingburgh County, North Carolina, for £32 NC money, 100 acres in the Parish of St. Marks on east side of Wateree River the so side of Granies Quarter Creek, part of 200 acres granted to sd. John Fields 18 May 1771. John Fields (L). [Wit: John Smith, William Wallace]. Proved in Charles Town District before William Rugeley, Esqr., by the oath of John Smith, 27 Apr 1774. Recorded 23 July 1774.

K-4, 360-365: Lease & release. 14 & 15 Feb 1772, Silas Canaday of Colleton County, SC, and Candice his wife to Abraham Hazelwood of same, for £50 SC money, 200 acres on waters of Edisto granted to said Silas Canaday 15 May 1770. Silas Canaday (LS), Condice Canaday (+) (LS), Wit: Jno Cuningham, Abraham Hazelwood, Andrew Frederick. Proved by the oath of Andres [sic] Frederick before Christopher Rowe, 3 Aug 1772. Recorded 25 July 1774.

K-4, 365-369: Lease & release. 24 & 25 June 1765, Jacob Huffman of Craven County, SC, planter, to George Ruff of same, planter, for £100 SC money, 300 acres on Second Creek between Broad & Saluday Rivers adj. Catharine Sherly's, granted 20 June 1754 to Jacob Hoffman. Jacob Houffman (I H) (LS), Wit: George Barnard Shram, George Bongardner, Martin Wertz. Proved by the oath of George Barnard Shram before John Pearson, J.P. for Craven County, 25 June 1765. Recorded 25 July 1774.

K-4, 370-373: Richard Singelton of Berkley County, SC, Esqr., for £936 SC money, to John Flud, 234 acres on the northwest side of the western branch of Cooper River adj. lands of Honble. Col. Thomas Broughton deceased, said John Flud, and said Richard Singelton, which said tract is part of the lands which the said Richard Singelton lately purchased of John Ouldfield Senr, Esqr.; deed dated 9 Dec 1738. (Plat included certified 4 Dec 1738 by Isaac Porcher, Dept. Survr.) Richard Singelton (LS), Wit: Jno Oulfield, Isaac Lewis, Thos Dean. Proved 22 Feb 1738 by the oath of Isaac Lewis before James Kinlock. Recorded 26 July 1774.

K-4, 374-378: Lease & release. 27 & 28 March 1774, James Cain & Frances his wife to John Lewis de St. Parre, for £500 SC money, 100 acres granted to James Cain in the county of Granville, SC, 4 July 1765 adj. William Miner. James Cain (I) (LS), Frances Cain (+) (LS), Wit: Edward Keating, William Cain. Proved 29 March 1774 before Pat. Calhoun, J.P. in the District of Ninety Six by the oath of William Cain. Recorded 26 July 1774.

K-4, 378-382: Lease & release. 2 & 3 Dec 1773, Henry Winningham of Parish of St. Mathews, Berkley County, planter, and Mary his wife, to George Shular of Berkley County, planter, for £500 SC money, 250 acres in Berkley County on four hole swamp granted to Henry Winningham 16 Dec 1766 adj. said George Shular. Henry Winningham (LS), Mary Winningham (+) (LS), Wit: Peter Hill, Jno Eason. Proved 3 Dec 1773 before John Savage, J.P., by the oath of John Easom. Recorded 26 July 1774.

K-4, 383-388: Lease & release. 1 & 2 Dec 1773, Thomas Cryer of Berkley County, planter, and Elizabeth his wife, to George Shular of same, planter, for £600 SC money, 100 acres on four Holes swamp being waters of Edisto River granted to said Thomas Cryer 17 Aug 1764, also another tract of 150 acres on four Holes Swamp granted to said Thomas Cryer 21 May 1772 adj. Winninghams land and the before mentioned tract. Thos Cryer (LS), Eliz'h Cryer (LS), Wit :John Joiner, Benjamin Scott. Proved 23 Dec 1773 before John Savage, J. P. in Orangeburgh District, by the oath of Benjamin Scott. Memorial entered in Book M No. 12, page 481, 3 May 1773. Recorded 27 July 1774.

K-4, 389-393: Lease & release. 25 Feb 1752, Robert Inman of Welch Tract in Craven County, SC, planter, to John Westfield of same, blacksmith, for £250, 300 acres in Welch Tract in Craven County adj. William Evans land, John Westfield, Pedee River, granted 4 ___ 1749. Robt. Inman (LS), Wit: James Inman (mark), James Nevel. Proved in Craven County before Paul Trapier, J.P., by the oath of James Nevil, 1 Nov 1752. Recorded 27 July 1774.

K-4, 393-396: 3 May 1774, Robert Johnston of Charles Town, cooper, and Jane his wife, to Jacob Valk of same, gentleman, for £100 SC money, 100 acres in "Campden Precinct" on waters of road

River. Robert Johnson (LS), Jane Johnson (A) (LS), Wit: G. Fardo, Paul Schlatter. Proved by the oath of Paul Schlatter before John Fewtrell, 3 May 1774. Recorded 28 July 1774.

K-4, 396-398: 26 Oct 1772, Jane Jenkins of St. David Parish, Craven County, widow, and James Jenkins (Junr) of same, for £50 SC money, 100 acres on south west side Pedee River in Craven county adj. John Jenkins, Jane Jenkins, Henry Buzby, granted to said Jane Jenkins 27 Nov 1770 recorded in Book FFF page 479. Jane Jenkins (m) (LS), Wit: John Westfield, Wm. Blassingham. Proved by the oath of William Blassingham in Craven County before Claudius Pegues, J.P., 26 Oct 1772. Recorded 28 July 1774.

K-4, 398-400: 22 Nov 1771, Thomas Lide of Craven County, SC, planter, to Daniel Oquin of same, planter, for £100 SC money, tract on North east side of Peedee River about 2 Miles from said River adj. John McBrides, near Gordons land [called] Davids folly, 50 acres granted to John Crawford of North Carolina by Gov. Dobbs 20 Apr 1763, conveyed from said Crawford to James Reed 15 Nov 1763, and from said James Reed to Thos. Lide 17 July 1771. Thomas Lide (LS(), Wit: Sarah Foster (X), Saml Wise. proved in Charraw District before Claudius Pegues, J.P., by the oath of Saml. Wise, 5 apr 1773. Recorded 28 July 1774.

K-4, 400-406: Lease & release. 14 May 1772, Daniel Oquin of parish of St. Davids, SC, planter, to James Reed of same, planter, for £200 SC money, two grants 26 May 1757 and 20 Apr 1763; the first granted to John McBride, 191 acres on North east side Pedee River adj. Jacob Lipham and conveyed from John McBride to William McBride by deed of gift 13 Jan 1759 and by the death of said William McBride fell to Hugh McBride thence conveyed to Daniel Oquin by deed 31 Aug 1771; the other tract granted to John Crawford of Anson County, North Carolina, 20 Apr 1763 by Gov. Dobbs, 50 acres on NE side Pedee River adj. John McBrides, near Gordons land called Davids folly, conveyed from John Crawford to James Read 15 Nov 1763, from James Reed to thos Lide 7 July 1771, from Thos Lide to Daniel Oquin 22 Nov 1771. Daniel Oquin (LS), Wit: Claudius Pegues Junr, Claudius Pegues Senr. Proved in Craven County before Henry William Harrington, J.P., by the oath of Claudius Pegues Senr, 26 Apr 1773. Recorded 1 Aug 1774.

K-4, 406-408: 1 Jan 1774, Claudius Pegues of Craven County, SC, planter, to James Reed of same, for £550 SC money, 150 acres on North side Pee Dee River adj. said James Reeds land, granted 13 Oct 1759 to William Bell, conveyed to said Claudius Pegues 24 Nov 1768. Claudius Pegues (LS), Wit: Claudius Pegues Jun. Proved in Cheraw District before Henry William Harrington, J.P., by the oath of Claudius Pegues Junr, 19 Jan 1774. Recorded 1 Aug 1774.

K-4, 408-412: Lease & release. 25 & 26 July 1772, Antony Earnest, of Berkley County, cooper, to Christian Kinseler, planter, for £150 SC money, part of 400 acres in Craven County granted 7 June 1751 to Gilbert Gilder,and said Gilbert Gilder died intestate and it devolved on his Eldest son John Gilder the Rightfull heir at law; this tract of 50 acres on Broad River adj. John James Addey, Christian Kinseler. Antony Earnest (LS), Wit: David Fridig, Jacob Fridig, William Fost (X). Proved by the oath of William Fost 25 July 1772 before Wm. Arther, J.P. Recorded 2 Aug 1774. Memorial entered in Book M no. 12 page 483 9 May 1774.

K-4, 412-414: 25 July 1772, Harmon Kinseler of Berkley County, planter, to Christian Kinseler of same, for natural love and affection to Christian Kinseler his beloved brother and for the better maintenance, support, livelihood, and preservement, 100 acres granted to Felix Crouse 13 Feb 1753 on Broad River, adj. Gilbert Gilders land. Harmon Kinseler (LS), Wit: Mathew Hubbard. Memorandum that the Day and year first within written Harmon Kinseler the sole and absolute heir of Conrode Kinseler deceased, freeholder, died intestate whereby the Right of inheritance devolved on the said Harmon Kinseler, eldest son of said Conrad Kinseler deceased. Wit: Mathew Hubbard, William Fost (X). Proved by the oath of William Fost before Wm. Arther, J.P., 25 July 1772. Recorded 2 Aug 1774.

K-4, 415-419: Lease & release. 6 & 7 Aug 1773, Peter Simond, Esquire, of London, to Thomas Gordfrey of Georgetown, SC, planter, for £100 money of Great Britain, lot 68 in Georgetown on Prince Street, Quince Street. Peter Simond (LS), Wit: Wm. White, Maurice Simons. Proved before Fenwicke Bull, Esqr., J. P. by the oath of Maurice Simons, Esqr, 31 Dec 1773. Recorded 2 Aug 1774.

SOUTH CAROLINA DEED ABSTRACTS 1773-1778

K-4, 420-424: 4 Nov 1735, George Pawley, William Swinton & Daniel Laroche, all of Parish of Prince George, Winyaw, Craven County, Esqrs., to Robert Innis of same county, taylor, for £7 s10, lot number 110 on High Street, part of land by lease and release 14 & 15 Jan 1734 between Elisha Scriven of Parish of Prince George Winyaw to George Pawley, William Swinton and Daniel Laroche, 274½ acres at Sam Pit in parish of Prince George on George Town River adj. lands of said Elisha Screven, upon several trusts herein mentioned covering 174½ acres to be called by the name of George Town according to a plan or model of said town, said town lotts may be sold. George Pawley (LS), Wm. Swinton (LS), Danl Laroche (LS), Wit: Ed. Juislen[?], Abraham Giles. Certified that Thos Charnock of Craven County, planter, sold lot to Zachariah Brazier of George Town, lot number 110, 10 July 1751. May 19th 1735/6 Received of Thomas Charnock £450 for lot number 110. Robert Innis, Wit: Thos Bolins, John Dexter.

END OF BOOK K-4.

L-4, 1: Thomas Vaughan of Craven County, Prince Frederick Parish, for love, good will, and affection to my brother William Jones of same county and parish, planter, 100 acres in Welch Tract on SW side Pedee purchased by Evan Vaughan Dess'd and falling to me by right of inheritance, adj. William Jones, and my own land, land run out for James Omar; deed dated 3 June 1751. Thomas Vaughan (T) (LS), Wit: Benjamin Rogers, Thomas Morgan (O). Proved by the oath of Benjamin Rogers 3 June 1751 before James Gillespie, J.P. Recorded __ Aug 1774.

L-4, 2-6: Lease & release. 2 & 3 May 1774, William Jones of Parish of St. David, to Alexander Mackintosh, Esqr., for £1050 SC money, land granted 6 Dec 1744 to Evan Vaughan, tract of 100 acres in Craven County on Pee Dee River, adj. said Evan Vaughn, transferred by Thomas Vaughan son & heir of said Evan Vaughn to said William Jones by deed of gift. William Jones (LS), Wit: Thos James, Joshua Terral. Proved in Cheraw District before Henry William Harrington, J.P., by the oath of Thomas James, 3 May 1774. Recorded 2 Aug 1774.

L-4, 6-9: Lease & release. 20 & 21 Oct 1773, William Arther of Berkley County, SC, esqr., to Christian Kinseler of Craven County, planter, for £100 SC money, 200 acres in Craven County on north side on waters of Broad River adj. William Struthers, Christian Kinzelars, William Tetes. William Arthur (LS), Wit :William foost (+), Nancy Faperet (+). Proved by the oath of Nancy Faperat 26 Jan 1774 before Henry Patrick J.P. Recorded 2 Aug 1774. Memorial entered in Auditor's office Book M No. 12, page 483, 9 May 1774.

L-4, 10-16: 28 June 1773, William Burrows and Bernard Beekman, both of Charles Town, Esquires, to Michael Kalteisan, Thomas Harper, William Graham, Jacob Boomer & William Swallow of Charles Town, gentleman... by indenture 13 Apr 1761 between Jonathan Sarazin of Charles Town, Silver Smith, son and heir at law of Morreau Sarrazin of Charles Town, Silver Smith, deceased, to William Burrows, Samuel Carne, Job Milner, Barnard Beekman, Richard Park Stobo, and Robert Wilson of Charles Town, gentlemen, reciting that in the year 1752 the members of Solomans Lodge of free and accepted Masons in Charles Town being inclinable to procure a title to two pews in the new Church then about to be built in Charles Town, since called St. Michaels church, did empower two of their members to say Brothers William Henderson and Moreau Sarrazin to subscribe each £150... pew number 55... under the seal of william Bull, Fenwick and Othniel Beale Esquires and Isaac Mazyck, Benjamin Smith, Robert Pringle, George Saxby, Gabriel Manigault and Thomas Middleton, Esquires, Commissioners for building said church... title made to members of Solomans Lodge William Burrows, Samuel Carne, Job Milner, Bernard Beekman, Richard Park Stobo, Thos Stone and Robert Wilson, seven of their members, trustees to receive from the said Jonathan Sarrazin a declaration or deed in trust to the same pew, 9 Feb 1761. Wm. Burrows (LS), Bernard Beekman (LS), Michl Kalteison (LS), Thos Harper (LS), Wm Graham (LS), Jacob Bommer (LS), Wm. Swallow (LS), Wit: Wm. Knight, Thos Phepoe. Proved by the oath of Thomas Phepoe 22 July 1774 before William Rugeley, J.P. Recorded 3 Aug 1774.

SOUTH CAROLINA DEED ABSTRACTS 1773-1778

L-4, 16-20: Lease & release. 6 & 7 Apr 1770, Isaac Gourdin of Parish of Prince Frederick, SC, to John Gaillard Senior of St. Stephens Parish, planter, for £80 SC money, 150 acres part of 200 acres granted to Theodore Gourdin 20 June 1764 and by him conveyed to Isaac Gourdin 2 Oct 1766, in Parish of Prince Fredericks adj. lands of John Gaillard, Isaac Gourdin. Isaac Gourdin (LS), Wit: Rene Richbourg, Peter Gourdin. Proved in Charles Town District by the oath of Rene Richburgh before William Rugeley, J. P., 11 May 1774. Recorded 4 Aug 1774.

L-4, 21-28: Lease & release. 8 & 9 Nov 1769, Andrew Johnston of Prince Georges Parish, Craven County, planter, to Joseph Allston of All Saints Parish, Craven County, planter, for £2500 SC money, tract granted 18 July 1735 to Othniel Beale of Charles Town, two several but adjoining tracts, each 500 acres, 100 acres in the whole, in Queensborough Township in Craven County, and said Othniel Beale and ___ his wife 16 & 17 July 1756 did convey to Elisha Screven the Elder, the two plantations, and by resurvey there appeared to be a surplus of 760 acres over and above said 1000 acres and Gov. William Henry Littleton upon application did grant to said Elisha Screven 1 March 1757 this surplus, and said Elisha Screven by his last will and testament 18 Aug 1756 and by a codicil 26 Nov 1757 devised to his son Elisha Screven the younger, and by his last will and testament 21 July 1760 appointed his executors to sell, and Alexander Davidson, Joshua Screven and Rebecka Brockinton the executors did convey 17 March 1762 to Archibald Johnston 560 acres; and Gov. Thomas Broughton by grant 16 Feb 1735 did grant unto James Gordon 300 acres in Queensborough Township adj. Mrs. Moores land, Pedee River, Lynches Creek, and said James Gordon by his last will and testament 12 June 1739 did give his executors power to dispose of property and John Cleland and George Pawley, executors 15 & 16 Sept 1756 did convey to Archibald Johnston, 300 acres; said Archibald Johnston dying intestate the real estate became vested in and the property of Andrew Johnston. Andrew Johnston (LS), Wit: Charles Tighe, Charles Burnham. Proved in Craven County before Joseph Dubordieu, J. P., by the oath of Charles Burnham 9 Nov 1769. Recorded 5 Aug 1774.

L-4, 29-32: Lease & release. 7 & 8 Feb 1774, Stephen Ellis of Craven County, SC, to John Bell of same, for £100 SC money, 100 acres in Craven County on north side of Broad River on a small branch thereof, granted 17 Feb 1767 to Stephen Ellis. Stephen Ellis (S) (LS), Wit: John Alston, Martha Davis, Christopher Davis. Proved 10 Feb 1774 before Henry Patrick, J.P. for Berkley County, by the oath of John Alston. Recorded 4 Aug 1774.

L-4, 33-35: 7 Sept 1773, Ann Janeway of the Congarees in Craven County, to John Turner for £1000 SC money, 120 acres part of 400 acres on northwest side of a creek runs through the said land, granted to James St. John Esqr., 15 Feb 1735 and by him conveyed to Richard Jackson 14 May 1736, conveyed to Ann Janeway 1 May 1743. Ann Janeway (+) (LS), Wit: Ben Tarrar, Richard Jackson. Proved by the oath of Ben Farar in Charles Town District 15 May 1774 before Wm. Rugeley, J.P. Recorded 5 Aug 1774.

L-4, 35-40: Lease & release. 10 & 11 May 1774, Moses Kirkland of Ninety Six District, Esqr., to Elias Buckingham of Orangeburgh District, for £100 SC money, 94½ acres in Berkley County adj. Mr. Timsly, Michael Keller, John King, Estate of Henry Koon, Santee River, granted 7 May 1767 to said Moses Kirkland. Moses Kirkland (LS), Wit: Dl. Mazyck, Thos Corker. Proved 18 May 1774 before William Rugeley, J.P., by the oath of Thos Corker. Recorded 8 Aug 1774.

L-4, 40-45: Lease & release. 28 & 29 Nov 1772, Thomas Lide of Parish of St. David, SC, planter, to Rebeca Lide of same, spinster, for £1000 SC money, tract granted 24 May 1745 to Francis Young, on Peedee River in the Parish David, adj. Evan Vaughn, John Thompson Junior deceased; by the death of said Francis Young fell to his son Isham Young thence conveyed to Edward Homes by a deed of gift 24 Apr 1755 thence conveyed from said Homes & Rebeca his wife to Michael Alderage by deed 20 June 1763, conveyed from said Aldredge to James Pitman 14 July 1761, thence to Thos Sims by deed 21 Nov 1761, thence from sd. Sims & his wife Rebecca to Thos Lide 20 Dec 1766. Thos Lide (LS), Ann lide (A) (LS), Wit: George Hicks, Benjamin James. Proved in Charraw District before Claudius Pegues, J.P., by the oath of George Hicks, 21 Jan 1774. Recorded 9 Aug 1774.

SOUTH CAROLINA DEED ABSTRACTS 1773-1778

L-4, 45-55: Lease & release. Georgia. 15 & 16 May 1774, John Smith of Savannah, Province of Georgia, Esquire, and Elizabeth his wife, to Edward Telfair of Savannah, esquire, for £2000 Georgia money, tract granted by SC 22 Jan 1759 to John Smith, 1050 acres on Savanah River in Granville County adj. Patrick Markeys land, Charles Wright, Esquire, Richard Lambton, patent recorded in Book TT page 91, commonly called Smithfield Plantation near Savannah. John Smith (LS), Elizabeth Smith (LS), Wit: James Carsan, Geo. Walton. Proved in Charles Town District by the oath of James Carsan before William Rugeley, J. P., 25 May 1774. Recorded 10 Aug 1774.

L-4, 55-60: Lease & release. 9 & 10 Oct 1772, Robert Parsons (Person) Junr. of Bucks County, Province of Pennsylvania, to Thomas Evans of Craven County, SC, planter, for £400 SC money, 100 acres in the Welch Tract, Province of SC, on Great Peedee River adj. land of John Westfield, granted 6 Dec 1744 to Simeon Persons, recorded in Book LL, page 235, and that Wm. Persons brother and proper heir at law of said Simeon Persons did by his last will and testament 11 Sept 1749 bequeath the said tract to the above Robert Parsons Junr of Berkley County, Province of Pennsylvania, second son of Robert Parsons Senr. of the last recited county. Robert Parsons (LS), Wit: Wm. Henry Mills, Henry Chambers. Proved in Charraw District before Alexander Mackintosh, 23 Dec 1772 by the oath of Henry Chambers. Recorded 10 Aug 1774.

L-4, 60-64: Lease & release. 9 & 10 Jan 1772, George Beaird of St. Georges Parish, Berkley County, yeoman, to James McKelvey of St. Johns Parish, planter, for £100 SC money, 200 acres at a place called Wampee pond near the waters of Santee in Berkley County, adj. land laid out for George Beaird, which tract was granted to James Beaird 1 Aug 1758, recorded in Book SS, page 334. George Beaird (LS), Wit: Alexr Hamilton, Robt Hails. Proved 16 Apr 1774 before Ephraim Mitchell, J.P., by the oath of Alexr. Hamilton. Recorded 11 Aug 1774.

L-4, 65-69: Lease & release. 23 & 24 Apr 1736, Theodore Gaillard of Craven County, Sc, planter, to Thomas Lynch of Berkley County, for £550 SC money, 150 acres in Craven County on the north branch of Santee River to the westward on Bluff commonly known as Indian Landing, adj. lands of Thomas Lynch. Theodore Gaillard (LS), Wit: Bonneau Junr, John Dutarque, Joseph Russ. Proved by 31 Jan 1736/7 by the oaths of John Dutarque and Joseph Russ, before Michl. Darby. Recorded 11 Aug 1774.

L-4, 70-72: 1 Sept 1762, Sarah Johnston of Charles Town, widow, to Robert Collings of Berkley County, gentleman, one of the sons of said Sarah Johnston, whereas the said Sarah Johnston standeth seized of a certain mansion house and the part of a town lot number 71 where the said Sarah Johnston now lives on south side of Broad Street, adj. Mathews, Nicholson, for natural love and affection to her son Robert Collings said town lot and house. Sarah Johnston (LS), Wit: James Courtonne, Ann Courtonne. Proved in Charles Town District before John Troup, J.P., by the oath of James Courtone, 29 Apr 1774. Recorded 12 Aug 1774.

L-4, 73-75: 1 Sept 1762, Sarah Johnston of Charles Town, widow, to Robert Johnston of Berkley County, gentleman, one of the sons of said Sarah Johnston, whereas the said Sarah Johnston standeth seized of a certain mansion house and the part of a town lot number 71 where the said Sarah Johnston now lives on south side of Broad Street, adj. Mathews, Nicholson, for natural love and affection to her son Robert Collings said town lot and house. Sarah Johnston (LS), Wit: James Courtonne, Ann Courtonne. Proved in Charles Town District before John Troup, J.P., by the oath of James Courtone, 29 Apr 174. Recorded 12 Aug 1774.

L-4, 75-80: Lease & release. 18 Dec 1771, Benjamin Kermon of Craven County, Sc, to John Shumake of same, for £50 SC money, 100 acres where John Shumake now lives on both sides of Deer Creek granted to said Benjamin Kermon 24 Jan 1770. Benjamin Kermon (mark) (LS), Wit: Benjamin Martin, Gennins Allen (A), William Moore (+). Proved in Charraws District before Claudius Pegues, J.P., by the oath of Ginnins Allen 11 Apr 1774. Recorded 14 Aug 1774.

L-4, 80-86: Lease & release. 4 & 5 May 1774, Samuel Chollet of Charles Town, merchant, to Thomas Lord of same, for £102 SC money, tract granted for 240 acres to Jonathan Russ in 1714 and containing by resurvey 27 Apr 1773, 285 acres adj. land of Richard Beresford deceased, Edward cook, John Heskett, John Saunders. Samuel Chollet (LS), Wit: Philip Henry, Abrm. Chollet. Proved 8 May 1774 before William Rugeley, J. P., by the oath of Philip Henry. Recorded 14 Aug 1774.

SOUTH CAROLINA DEED ABSTRACTS 1773-1778

L-4, 86-92: Lease & release. 11 & 12 May 1774, James Cook of Berkely County, Surveyor, and Sarah Cook his wife, to Peter Lord and Thomas Lord of Charlestown, for £4536 SC money, 600 acres in Christ Church Parish adj. land of Henry Reaves, William Loocock, John Ward. Jas. Cook (LS), Sarah Cook (LS), Wit: Philip Henry, Thomas Atkinson. Proved 28 May 1774 before William Rugeley, J.P., by the oath of Philip Henry. Recorded 15 Aug 1774.

L-4, 92-97: Lease & release. 1 & 2 March 1774, Rachel Bronkhart of Charles Town, spinster, to George Renerson of Charles Town, Tavern keeper, for £200 SC money, 200 acres on Cattles Swamp below Orangeburgh Township in Berkley County, originally granted 22 Jan 1759 to Edward Bronkhart, father of said Rachel Bronkhart, who died intestate by which means the said Rachel Bronkhart being his only child became heiress at Law. Rachel Brunkert (LS), Wit: George Gray, Peter Horn. Proved 16 March 1774 before George Davidson, J. P. in Charlestown District, by the oath of George Gray. Recorded 26 Aug 1774.

L-4, 98-102: Lease & release. 17 & 18 Dec 1773, Aaron Steel of Granville County, SC, yeoman, to John McComb of same, blacksmith, for £375 SC money, 250 acres in Granville County on a creek that empties into the northwest fork of long Cain Creek a branch of Savannah River, granted 18 Aug 1763 to Bartholomew Crossman, adj. John Gilmer, Andrew Marison[?], conveyed 21 March 1761 to Aaron Steel. Aaron Steel (LS), Wit: Thomas Strain, John Cameron. Proved 30 Dec 1773 before Alexander Cameron, J.P. for Ninety Six District, by the oath of Thomas Strain. Recorded 17 Aug 1774.

L-4, 102-107: Lease & release. 17 & 18 Oct 1773, John Frederick Dubber of Craven County, to Michael Burkholter of Stephens Creek, waters of Savannah of Ninety Six District, for £__, 200 acres on a branch of Stephens Creek in Granville County surveyed 2 May 1758 and certified 9 Aug 1758 and granted 21 Jan 1761 recorded in Book VV, page 131. John Frederick Dubber (LS), Wit: Pott Repsommer, Beat Turnipseed. Proved by the oath of Pott Repsommer 22 Oct 1773 before Wm Arther, J. P. Recorded 17 Aug 1774.

L-4, 107-114: Lease & release. 16 & 17 Nov 1767, Thomas Duckett of Frederick County, Maryland, to Thomas Wadlington Senr late of Frederick County, Colony of Virginia, for £13 s7 Pennsylvania money, 400 acres between Broad & Saluda River near Indian Creek. Thomas Duckett (LS), Wit: David Lynn, Thos Price, Jas. Wadlington. Proved 4 Apr 1768 by the oath of James Wadlington before Joseph Curry, J.P. Proved in Maryland by the oaths of David Lynn and Thomas Price 17 Nov 1767 before John Darnall[?]. Mary Duckett, wife of Thomas Ducket, relinquished dower in Frederick County, 17 Nov 1767. Recorded 18 Aug 1774.

L-4, 114-120: Lease & release. 14 & 15 Jan 1773, Jacob Penington Junr and his younger brother Isaac Penington, planter, of Craven County, SC, to Charles King, for £300 SC money, 50 acres between Broad & Saluday Rivers on a small river of Broad River called Collinses River, tract granted to Isaac Penington for 50 acres on north side thereof, and said Isaac Penington bequeathed to his two sons Jacob and Isaac. Jacob Penington (LS), Isaac Penington (LS), Wit: James Lindsey, William Wooddall, Thomas Linsey. Proved 3 July 1773 before Michl Dickert, J.P., by the oath of James Lindsey. Recorded 19 Aug 1774.

L-4, 120-124: Lease & release. 10 & 12 Feb 1771, Jacob Penington and Mary his wife to Charles King for £1000 SC money, 350 acres granted in 1751 to Jacob Pennington on Collins River. Jacob Penington (LS), Mary Penington (LS), Wit: Thos Stark, Daniel Williams, James Hillin. Proved by the oath of Daniel Williams in Craven County before Thomas Wadlington Junr, J.P., 23 Feb 1771. Recorded 20 Aug 1774.

L-4, 124-128: Lease & release. 8 & 9 Dec 1772, John Popwell of St. Davids Parish, Craven County, SC, planter, to William Fletcher of same county and parish, planter, for £200 SC money, 250 acres on Willow Creek in craven County adj. John Purvis, granted 13 July 1762 to John Popwell. John Popwell (LS), Wit: James H. Casey, George Fletcher. Proved in Charaw District before Joseph Gourley, J. P., by the oath of James H. Casey., 2 Sept 1773. Recorded 20 Aug 1774.

L-4, 128-133: Lease & release. 10 July [September?] 1773, John Uldrick of St. Georges Parish, Berkley County, planter, to Christian Ridlesparger of same, Tavern Keeper, for L5, 50 acres, part of 100 acres granted 19 June 1772 to John Uldrick in St. Georges Parish, Berkley County, surveyed 12 Jan 1770, grant recorded in Book LL fol. 427. John Christian Uldrick (mark) (LS), Wit: Lewis Linder, William Roth, Lewis Grosman. Proved in Charles Town District before Thomas Caton, J. P., by the oath of Lewis Linder, 10 Sept 1773. Recorded 24 Aug 1774. (Plat included for 50 acres part of tract laid out to John Christian Uldrick adj. land of William Mellyard, said John Christian Uldrick, certified 7 Jan 1773.)

L-4, 133-136: Lease & release. 8 & 9 Feb 1769, Reason Nelson of St. Marks Parish, SC, to Henry Donworth of same, for £500 SC money, 200 acres on a branch called the Great Branch adj. James McCullys line, granted to said Reason Nelson for 500 acres. Reason Nelson (LS), Wit: John Plunkett, John Elkins, Nelson Dunkin. Proved before John Newman Oglethorpe, J. P., by the oath of Nelson Dunkin. Recorded 24 Aug 1774.

L-4, 137-143: Lease & release. 9 & 10 June 1774, Sarah Edwards of Charles Town, widow, to Uriah Edwards of Parish of St. George Dorchester, for £3000 SC money, 149 acres in Berkley County, St. Georges Parish, adj. land formerly belonging to Samuel Clark, the publick road from Bacons Bridge to Beach Hill, land lately belonging to Dr. Samuel Stevens, land lately belonging to Charles and Jermain Wright; also 80 acres in Berkley County on Ashley River adj. land late of Thomas Baker, Josiah Osgood, Robert Wright, Esq. Sarah Edwards (LS), Wit: John Morris, G. Fardo. Proved 10 June 1774 by the oath of George John Fardo. Recorded 25 Aug 1774.

L-4, 143-147: Lease & release. 25 & 26 Jan 1774, Robert Bailey of Ninety Six District, planter, to John Weedinman of same, planter, for £50 SC money, 100 acres granted 21 June 1765 to Ann Goin. Robert Bailey (R) (LS), Wit: George Bailey, John Foster, David Hamilton. Proved in Ninety Six District before Joseph Robinson by the oath of John Foster, 20 Feb 1774. Recorded 25 Aug 1774.

L-4, 147-151: Lease & release. 25 & 26 Jan 1774, Robert Bailey of Ninety Six District, planter, to John Weedinman of same, planter, for £100 SC money, 100 acres granted 20 Oct 1772 to Robert Bailey, surveyed 29 Oct 1768 on south side Broad River, adj. Simcock Cannon, Ann Garven. Robert Bailey (R) (LS), Wit: George Bailey, John Foster, David Hamilton. Proved in Ninety Six District before Joseph Robinson by the oath of John Foster, 20 Feb 1774. Recorded 26 Aug 1774.

L-4, 151-153: 29 Jan 1773, William Stroud of Craven County, SC, planter, and Sarah his wife, to Revd. Wm. Martin, for £750 SC money, 450 acres on east side Rockey Creek granted 9 Nov 1770 to William Stroud. William Stroud (LS), Sarah Stroud (LS), Wit: John Gaston, John Bigham, Alexander McCown. Proved in Craven County by the oath of James Bigham, J. P., by the oath of John Gaston, 1 March 1773.

L-4, 154-158: Lease & release. 10 & 11 Nov 1773, James Davis of District of Ninety Six, SC, planter, to Thomas Sanders of same, for £500 SC money, 150 acres on Savannah River granted to James Davis 25 March 1765. James Davis (LS), Wit: John Purves, Andrew Rapley. Proved 15 Nov 1773 before Benjamin Tutt, J. P., by the oath of Andrew Rapley.

L-4, 158-160: 11 June 1774, Charles McClane and Susannah his wife of Tryon County, North Carolina, to William Hall of Camden District, SC, for £525 SC money, tract on a branch of Bullocks Creek waters of Broad River granted to Robert Wood by North Carolina patent 4 Sept 1753 then deemed in Anson County, NC, adj. land of Charles McKnight, Wm. Watson, since conveyed by Robert Wood to Charles McClane by deed, 207 acres. Charles McClane (LS), Susannah McClane (LS), Wit: Ephraim McLean, Hugh Bryson, James Henry. Proved in Camden District before Ezekiel Polk, J. P., by the oath of Ephraim McClean, 11 June 1774. Recorded 7 Aug 1774.

L-4, 160-167: Lease & release. 17 & 18 June 1774, William Miller of Charles Town, gentleman, and Susannah his wife to Jacob Valk of town aforesaid, gentleman, for £615; whereas George Ferguson late of Pon Pon, planter, was in his life time seized of a tract in St. Bartholomews Parish, Colleton County, granted to said George Ferguson 1 Dec 1738 for 400 acres but upon a resurvey found to contain no more than 246 acres, sometime in the year 1757 dying intestate legally descended to his only surviving daughter Margaret Ferguson and said Margaret Ferguson intermarried with William Stead by whom she had issue Susanah Stead now Susannah Miller wife of said William Miller, about 17 Dec 1773 said Susannah intermarried with said William Miller. William Miller (LS),

SOUTH CAROLINA DEED ABSTRACTS 1773-1778

Susannah Miller (LS), Wit: G. F. Fardo, Richd Corbett. Proved in Berkley County by the oath of George John Fardo before John Fewtrell, 23 June 1774. Recorded 28 Aug 1774.

L-4, 167-171: Lease & release. 4 & 5 Nov 1772, Isaac Ramsey of Colleton County, and Sarah his wife, to Charles Boyle of same, for £95 SC money, 100 acres on Slepy Creek adj. bounty land, granted to said Isaac Ramsey 10 Apr 1771. Isaac Ramsey (LS), Sarah Ramsey (LS), Wit: Philip Zimmerman, John Clairman. Proved by the oath of Philip Zimmerman before Patrick Cunningham, J. P. for Colleton County, 8 Nov 1772. Recorded 8 Aug 1774.

L-4, 171-175: Lease & release. 8 & 9 Nov 1773, Henry Sizemore of Ninety Six District, planter, to John Hammond Senior of the same, for £200 SC money, 200 acres on waters of Savanah River in the Dist. aforesaid, granted 26 Sept 1772 to Henry Sizemore. Henry Sizemore (LS), Wit: Charles Smith, Thomas Skudder. Proved in Ninety Six District 9 Nov 1773 before LeRoy Hammond, J.P., by the oath of Charles Smith. Recorded 28 Aug 1774.

L-4, 175-177: 18 Nov 1771, William Dry of Brunswick County, North Carolina, to Jason Meadors "Juner" of Craven County, SC, for £80 proclamation money, tract in Craven county on Thompsons Creek known by the name of Jack on the ashes Camp, pat of tract granted to said William Dry 5 Oct 1751 by North Carolina before the dividing line of the said province was run, 300 acres, and when the division line was run between No and So Carolina there was the above mentioned 220 acres fell within the province of South Carolina. William Dry (LS), Wit: Thos McGere, Wm. Coleman. Proved in Craven County by the oath of Wm. Coleman before Thomas Wade, J.P., 20 Nov 1772. Recorded 28 Aug 1774.

L-4, 177-181: Lease & release. 7 May 1769, William Thomson, planter, of St. Mathews Parish, Sc, to John Satterwhite of province of North Carolina, for £210 SC money, 600 acres in Berkley County on a branch of Little River called Mudlick Creek granted to said William Thomson 2 Aug 1768. Wm. Thomson (LS), Wit: Wm. Martin, Wm. Howell, Thomas Eastland. Proved before John Caldwell, J. P., by the oath of Thomas Eastland, 10 June 1771. Recorded 29 Aug 1774.

L-4, 181-184: Lease. 14 March 1774, Elias Robert of Granville Co., SC, planter, to Archibald Offutt o same place, silver smith, for five shillings, 300 acres in St. James Santee Parish, Craven County, on south side Santee River adj. Thomas Lynch, said Elias Robert, once intended to be conveyed to Sarah & Judith Robert, Joseph Willingham; and a tract of 450 acres in Prince Fredericks Parish in two different tracts on Santee River, opposite to said 300 acres adj. Peter Robert, Esqr., John Dutarque, Francis Courage, in the whole 750 acres conveyed by Francis Kinlock to John and Elias Robert and said John to the said Elias Robert; also six other tracts in the whole 2095 acres adj. James Boyd, James Wright, Charles Chovin, John Mayrants, John Skrine, on the remnant of the church & town lands on the banks of the river tracts of said John Mayrant, Thomas Lynch, Elias Robert, John Skrine, Joseph Willingham, conveyed by said Francis Kinlock to James Robert and by said James Robert to John Robert and by said John to said Elias Robert. Elias Robert (LS), Wit: John Grimball, Elizabeth Grimball. Proved 17 March 1774 by the oath of John Grimball before Charles Browne, J. P. in Granville County. Recorded 29 Aug 1774.

L-4, 184-188: Lease & release. 25 & 26 Dec 1770, William McKinney of Parish of St. Marks, Planter, to William Taylor of same, labourer, for £45 SC money, 100 acres on Fishing Creek in Craven County. William McKinney (LS), Wit: William Wylie, John McFadden, James Ballentine. Proved by the oath of William Wylie before Jas. Patton, J.P., 3 Jan 1771. Recorded 30 Aug 1774.

L-4, 188-193: Lease & release. 6 & 7 May 1774, William Taylor of Parish of St. Mark, planter, and wife Mary, to Peter Culp of same, for £100 SC money, tract granted 7 May 1767 to William Taylor, 200 acres at Tinkers Creek, Craven county. William Taylor (LS), Mary Taylor (mark) (LS), Wit: Edwd White, Francis Campbell, William McFadden. Proved in Camden District by the oath William McFadden before James Patton, J. P., 4 June 1772. Recorded 30 Aug 1774.

L-4, 193-197: 11 Oct 1773, Edward Martin, Sheriff of the District of George Town, SC, to Joseph Allston of Waccamaw, Esquire, whereas James Hammerton late of said province deceased was in his life time seized of a tract on the east side of Waccamaw River, 1000 acres adj. Pools land, Favewells[?] land, Princes land, and whereas Robert Snead by property application did obtain administration of all the goods and chattles, rights and credits of said John Hammerton and William Wragg Esquire did impled the said Robert Snead, admrs in the court of common pleas in an action of debt and upon the proceedings the said William Wragg did recover a judgment for his debt amounting to £966... now for £585 SC money, Edward Martin, Sheriff, sells to Joseph Allston, 500 acres. Edward Martin, Sherif (LS), Wit: William Suptan, John Hall. Proved in Chas Town District before Maurice Simons, J. P., by the oath of John Hall, 15 Apr 1774. Recorded 30 Aug 1774.

L-4, 197-200: 14 Apr 1774, 14 Apr 1774, Anderson young and Elizabeth young, late Elizabeth Crain (and executrix to the last will and testament of Mark Truchet deceased of the Parish of St. Helena) to Gideon Dupont of same parish, for consideration of the year rent and covenant herein after reserved, plantation called Truchets Plantation, 200 acres on the Okaty Creek formerly in the possession of Mark Truchet, for the yearly rent of £150. Elizabeth Young (LS), Anderson Young (LS), Wit: John Bowles, John Catterton. Proved in Beaufort District before Bellamy Crawford, J. P., by the oath of John Bowles, 27 Aug 1774. Recorded 30 Aug 1774.

L-4, 200-208: Lease & release. 29 & 30 June 1774, Thomas Turner of Ansonburgh, St. Philips Parish, Charles Town, and Ann his wife, to George Flagg of Charles Town, painter[?], for £150, place on Charles Town Neck in St. Philips Parish, a moiety of half part of a lot conveyed to Jeremiah Sharp from Henry Laurens, Esq., 3 March 1770. Thomas Turner (LS), Ann Turner (LS), Wit: George Wershing, Thomas Oliver. Proved in Charles Town District 4 July 1774 before William Rugeley, J. P. Recorded 30 Aug 1774.

L-4, 208-212: Lease & release. 29 & 30 March 1774, Abner Bishop & Margret his wife of the Settlement of Enoree River, SC, to Jacob Roberts of same settlement, for £200 SC money, 50 acres which is part of 400 acres, part of 550 acres granted 7 May 1767 to James Goolsby on south side of Enoree River lying on the Warrior Creek plat recorded in Book AAA, page 439, and said Goolsby sold unto Abner Bishop 10 June 1769, and a memorial entered in Book K, No. 10, page 377. Abner Bishop (LS), Margret Bishop (LS), Wit: William Vaughn, Edward Garret. Proved in Ninety Six District by the oath of William Vaughn before John Ford, J.P., 16 June 1774. Recorded 3 Sept 1774.

L-4, 213-219: Lease & release. 7 & 8 Apr 1774, George Threadcraft and Elizabeth his wife of Prince Williams Parish to Charles Ogilvie, Esqr., of Charles Town, for £2500 current money, 323 acres in Granville County, part of a certain plantation of 500 acres granted by George II to one John Andrews 6 Apr 1733, also tract of 297 acres in Granville County part of a tract of 400 acres granted by George II to Samuel Tines 23 May 1734. Geo Threadcraft (LS), Elizabeth Threadcraft (LS), Wit: Isaac McPherson, Robert Oliver. Proved 4 July 1774 before William Rugeley, Esqr., by the oath of Robert Oliver. Recorded 5 Sept 1774.

L-4, 219-224: Lease & release. 10 & 11 Nov 1773, Arthur Brown Ross of Craven County, St. Marks Parish, SC, planter, to Charles Ogilvie, Esqr., of Charles Town, gentleman, for £250 SC money, 100 acres in Craven County the south side of Wateree River adj. land laid out for George Brown, Bryan Toland, John Richardson, John Milhous, granted to said Arthur Brown Ross 1 Feb 1771, recorded in Book GGG, page 295. Arthur Brown Ross (LS), Wit: Joseph Kershaw, Thomas Jones, William Boykin. Proved by the oath of Joseph Kershaw 11 Nov 1773 before John Newman Oglethorpe, J.P. Hannah Ross, wife of Arthur Brown Ross, relinquished dower, 11 Nov 1773 before John Newman Oglethorpe, J.P. Recorded 6 Sept 1774.

L-4, 226-229: 5 July 1774, Anthony Toomer of Charles Town, Berkley County, Bricklayer, to Archer Smith of Craven County, for ten shillings, 200 acres on a branch of Sugar Creek in Craven County. Anthy Toomer (LS), Wit: Lewis Duvall, Ralph Smith. Proved 5 July 1774 before William Rugeley, J.P., by the oath of Ralph Smith. Recorded 7 Sept 1774.

L-4, 229-234: Lease & release. 22 & 23 Apr 1771, Frederick Glazer and Mary his wife to William Banks Senr, for £500 SC money, 350 acres on a branch of Savannah River called sweet water granted 6 Feb 1773 to said Frederick Glazer. Jacob Frederick Glazer (LS), Mary Glazer (LS), Wit: Jacob Moses, Emanl. Abrahams. Proved in Berkley County, Chs. Town District, by the oath of Emanuel Abrahams before David Rhind, J.P., 29 Oct 1773. Recorded 7 Aug 1774.

SOUTH CAROLINA DEED ABSTRACTS 1773-1778

L-4, 234-239: Lease & release. 7 & 8 Apr 1756, William Fyffe of Parish of Prince George Winyaw, Chirurgeon, and Anne his wife, Margaret Morritt, to Thomas Hasell of same parish, planter, for £700 SC money, half part of a tract of 1100 acres on the ___ formerly Sameat and Parts[?] Creek, James Summers, Thomas Bonney, Henry Dauboz[?]. Willm. Fyffe (LS), Anne Fyffe (LS), Margt. Morritt (LS), Wit: Martha Walker, Richd Walker Jun. Proved 9 June 1756 before George Pawley, Esqr., J. P. in Craven County, by the oath of Richard Walker Junr. Recorded 8 Aug 1774.

L-4, 239-244: Lease & release. 6 & 7 Nov 1772, Benjamin Trapier of Prince Georges Parish, Craven County, planter, to Thomas Hasell, planter, of same, for £1000 SC money, half of 1300 acres in Prince Georges Parish, Craven County, adj. Joseph Ports land, Thomas Morrits land, William Whitesides land, William Raes land, also one full undivided moyty of ten and one half lots in George Town [numbers indicated], also one half of any lands which hath descended to Margaret Hasell wife of said Thomas Hasel and Ann Dick the sister through or by means of their father James Summers, which said moyty of said several parcels was sold by said Thomas Hasell and Margaret his wife to said Benjamin Trapier 4 & 5 november instant. Benjn Trapier (LS), Wit: Judith Trapier, Paul Trapier. Proved 27 May 1774 before Robert Heriot, Esqr., J. P., in Craven County. Recorded 18 Sept 1774.

L-4, 245-249: Lease & release. 12 & 13 Dec 1772, Lenud Summott of Berkley County, SC, carpenter, to Moses Kirkland of District of Ninety Six, for £200 SC money, 150 acres granted 16 Jan 1761 to Lemud Summott on a branch of Clouds Creek which runs into Little Salludy River, plant recorded in Book VV, folio 139. Lenud Summott (LS), Wit: Jacob Simmerly, Jonas Beard. Proved before William Arther, J.P., by the oath of Jonas Beard, 12 Dec 1772. Recorded 9 Aug 1774.

L-4, 249-251: 6 July 1774, Joseph Willingham of Charles Town, Tavernkeeper, to Dennis Egan of St. James Santee, mortgage of 650 acres in St. James Santee Parish adj. John Robbers [Rollers?], Joseph Willingham, and adj. to the other tract of 450 acres on Santee River. Joseph Willingham (LS), Mary Willingham (LS), Wit: Joseph Webb, John Young. Proved 6 June 1774 before John Egan, J.P. for Craven County, by the oath of John Young. Mortgage satisfied 2 May 1777.

L-4, 251-253: 18 Aug 1770, Henry Laurens of Charles Town, SC, Esqr., to David Maul of Charles Town, Taylor, for £300 SC money, lot in Charles Town, number 138 in Hampstead. Henry Laurens (LS), Wit: John Watson, Geo. Noddings. Proved 7 July 1774 before William Rugeley, J.P., by the oath of John Watson. Recorded 9 Sept 1774.

L-4, 253-258: Lease & release. 6 & 7 Nov 1761, John Durant of Prince Fredericks Parish, Craven County, SC, planter, and Hannah his wife, to James Bradley of same county, planter, for £125 SC money, tract in St. Marks Parish, Craven County, granted to John Hayse 1 Aug 1758, transferred to said John Durant by the executors of said John Hayse, 200 acres. John Durant (LS), Hannah Durant (LS), Wit: Robert Willson, David Willson, Grace Willson. Proved 29 March 1762 by the oath of Robert Willson before Henry Cassels, J. P. for Craven County. Recorded 10 Sept 1774.

L-4, 258-259: Elizabeth Hayes executrix & John Waring executor of the last will and testament of John Hayes decd, for £5 SC money, to John Durant of Prince Fredericks Parish, Craven County, 200 acres in St. Marks Parish, Craven County adj. David Andersons, James Bradley; dated 13 Feb 1761. Elizabeth Hayse (LS), John Waring exr. (LS), Wit: Mary Scott, Will Scott. Proved by the oath of William Scott before Jno Remington, J.P., 25 Feb 1762. Wit: Hen. Cassels, Benjn Cassels. Recorded 20 Sept 1774.

L-4, 259-264: Lease & release. 6 & 7 May 1772, Peter Mellet of Craven County, SC, and Mary his wife, to James Bradley of same, for ten shillings, 500 acres in Craven County granted to Peter Mellet 5 Oct 1753 and tract granted 10 June 1759 for 100 acres. Peter Mellet (LS), Mary Mellet (LS), Wit: John Anderson Junr, David Neilson, William Gordon. Proved 30 June 1775 by the oath of William Gordon before Henry Cassels, J. P. Recorded 11 Sept 1774.

L-4, 265-269: Lease & release. 19 Oct 1772, James McEwean of Craven County, Sc, planter, to William Coleman of same, planter, for £350 SC money, 160 acres, part of 500 acres granted 25 Apr 1767 by Gov. Tryon of Nc to James McEwean in Mecklenburg County on a branch of Fairforest and branches of Mill Creek adj. Mitchels line; said 160 acres adj. Daniel Bush corner. James McEwean (LS), Wit: Field Farer, Christopher Coleman, John Thomas. Proved by the oath of Field Farer before John Thomas, J.P. in Craven County. Recorded 12 Sept 1774.

L-4, 269-272: Lease & release. 7 & 8 July 1774, John Brodie of Charles Town, Gentleman, to David Beaty of same, for £600 SC money, 600 acres on Pacolet River at the mouth of Elex or Alex Creek in Berkley County. John Brodie (LS), Wit: John Summers, George Gray. Proved 8 July 1774 before Ephraim Mitchell, J.P. in Charles Town District, by the oath of George Gray. Recorded 12 Sept 1774.

L-4, 273-277: Lease & release. 28 & 29 June 1774, John Summers of Charles Town, Gentleman to David Baty of same, for £2500 SC money, 950 acres in Orangeburgh District at the mouth Pen Branch on North Edisto River, adj. land surveyed for John Gillard, land granted to William Murphey, this tract granted 7 May 1774; also 1500 acres in St. Johns Parish on the head of Fergusons Swamp adj. land granted to Peter Porcher, Peter Witten, Mr. McCane, Capt. William Moultrie, William Smith, and the heirs of Doctor Hardy South, granted to said john Summers 23 June 1774. John Summers (LS), Wit: John Brodie, George Gray. Proved 8 July 1774 before Ephraim Mitchell, J.P. in Charles Town District, by the oath of George Gray. Recorded 13 Sept 1774.

L-4, 277-283: Lease & release. 21 & 22 July 1774, Samuel Moores of Charles Town, Taylor, to David Baty of same, for £600 SC money, 600 acres on north side Savannah River in Granville County, land surveyed for Benjamin Ballentine by Lewis Linder, Deputy Surveyor, 4 Feb 1772, granted to said Samuel Moores 21 Apr 1774. Samuel Moores (LS), Wit: Walter Maine, Thos Tod. Proved 22 July 1774 before George Davidson, J. P. in Charles Town District, by the oath of Walter Maine. Recorded 14 Sept 1774.

L-4, 283-287: Lease & release. 7 & 8 July 1774, Daniel Agkettor of Charles Town, to Thomas Tod of same, warfinger, for £750 SC money, 750 acres in the District of Orangeburgh on Pen Branch adj. land laid out to William Tucker, granted to Daniel Agkettor 23 June 1774. Daniel Agkettor (LS), Wit: David Baty, John Fisher. Proved 9 July 1774 by the oath of John Fisher before George Davidson, J.P. in Charles Town District. Recorded 15 Sept 1774.

L-4, 287-289: 5 Dec 1771, Jane, wife of Benjamin Villepontoux of Charles Town, Gentn, relinquished dower to Andrew Lord, tract conveyed 29 & 30 Nov last, tract near Wassamasaw, 500 acres adj. land of Benjamin Villepontoux, Roger Saunders, James coachman, and a tract of 800 acres adjoining to it adj. land of Robert Johnston, Esqr., decd, James Lucas deceased, estate of Adams deceased, and also 160 acres adj. Richard Singletons land, and 500 acres in Berkley County on a part of the Four Hole Swamp commonly called Wilkinsons Swamp on Sandy Run adj. Daniel Dean. Recorded 26 Sept 1774.

L-4, 289-293: Lease & release. 7 & 8 July 1774, John Johnston of Charlestown, to Thomas Tod of same, warfinger, for £850 SC money, 850 acres in Orangeburgh District on a branch of Edisto River adj. land granted to William Murphey, John Rosewell; tract granted to John Johnston 7 June 1774. John Johnston (LS), Wit: James Hunt, Peter Hunter. Proved 9 July 1774 by the oath of Peter Hunter before George Davidson, J. P. Recorded 16 Sept 1774.

L-4, 293-299: Lease & release. 27 & 28 June 1774, John Hamilton of Charles Town, Shoemaker, to John Hamilton of same, merchant, for £350 SC money, 350 acres on a branch of Ninety Six Creek called Beaver Dam branch. John Hamilton (LS), Wit: Jona Laurence, Daniel Latham, Stephen Laurence. Proved 31 Dec 1774 before William Rugeley by the oath of Stephen Lawrence.

L-4, 299-302: Lease & release. 23 & 24 June 1774, Andrew Broughton of Charles Town, Gentleman, to Thomas Corbett of same, merchant, for £50 SC money, 36 acres exclusive of Queen Street in Charles Town, part of land granted to Cummings Esqr. adj. Broad St., granted to said Andrew Broughton 23 June 1774. Andw Broughton Sen. (LS), Wit: William Hest, Fra's. Bremar. Proved 1 July 1774 by the oath of Francis Bremar before George Davidson, J.P. Recorded 18 Sept 1774.

SOUTH CAROLINA DEED ABSTRACTS 1773-1778

L-4, 302-308: Lease & release. GEORGIA. 12 & 13 June 1765, Nathaniel Miller of province of Georgia, planter, and Elizabeth his wife, to John Steen of Province of North Carolina [lease say South Carolina], for £40 sterling, tract in Anson County, North Carolina, bought by the said Nathl Miller from Jonathan Wilkins on Thickly Creek [sic, for Thicketty] adj. William Greens. Nathl Miller (LS), Eliz'h Miller (LS), Wit: John Anderson, Don'd Fraser, Thos Trammell. Recorded 18 Sept 1774.

L-4, 308-312: Lease & release. 14 & 15 1774, Samuel Dennis on the waters of Bush Creek in Ninety Six District, SC, to Stephen Elmore of the same waters, yeoman, for £400 SC money, tract granted 31 Pct 1875 to Mathias Elmore, 200 acres on Bush Creek, adj. William Elmore, and the said Mathias Elmore by his last will & testament did bequeath unto his grandson Samuel Denis the aforesaid plantation. Samuel Dennis (LS), Mary Dennis (LS), Wit: Jacob Brooks, Joseph Thomson, John Hookey. Proved before John Caldwell, J. P., by the oath of Jacob Brook 26 Apr 1774. Recorded 21 Sept 1774.

L-4, 312-316: Lease & release. 19 & 20 1772, Daniel Tollason of Barkley County, SC, planter, and wife Sary, to Edward Coe for £82 s 10, 100 acres adj. John Warren, Daniel Shewmake and sd. Tollason, granted to said Tollason. Daniel Tollason (LS), Sary Tollason (LS), Wit: John Davis, john Warren, Thomas Blitchenden. Proved by the oath of John Warren before Thos Green, J. P., 30 Jan 1773. Recorded 21 Sept 1774.

L-4, 316-322: Lease & release. 9 & 10 Apr 1773, Micajah Williams of George Town, Craven County, Mariner, and Ann his wife, to Robert Dicks of same place, gentleman, for £1050, 450 acres on the south side of Sampit Creek, granted to Thomas Bolin and since by divers mesne conveyances became vested in said Micajah Williams. Micajah Williams (LS), Ann Williams (LS), Wit: Jacob Wm. Harvey, Wm. Mason. Proved 15 July 1773 before James Johnston, J.P., by the oath of William Mason. Recorded 23 Sept 1774.

L-4, 322-328: Lease & release. 2 & 3 June 1774, Willoughby Pough of St. Peters Parish, SC, planter, and Martha his wife, to Thomas Bradberry of St. Helena Parish, planter, for £450 SC money, 200 acres in St. Peters Parish Granville County adj. Ann Jugler, John Strober, Henry Gorman, Hartley and Gotins land. Martha Pough (LS), Willoughby Pough (LS), Wit: John Dawson, Francis Bradberry. Proved in Beaufort District before Bellamy Crawford, J.P., by the oath of John Dawson, 3 June 1774. Recorded 23 Sept 1774.

L-4, 328-329: Micajah Williams of George Town, Craven County, mariner, bound to Robert Dick of George Town, Gentleman, in the sum of £2100, 10 Apr 1773, to make title to 450 acres on South side Sampit Creek. Micajah Williams (LS), Wit: Jacob Wm. Harvey, Wm. Mason. Proved by the oath of William Mason 15 July 1774 before Jas Johnston, J.P.

L-4, 330-332: Joseph Palmenter (Parmenter) of Granville Co., planter, and wife Sarah, to Samuel Watson of same, planter, for £200 SC money, 200 acres, dated 20 July 1774. Joseph Palmenter (mark) (LS), Sarah Parmenter (LS), Wit: John Delabere, James Dunlop, Wm. Mitchell. Proved by the oath of James Dunlop before John Delabere, J.P., 20 July 1774. Recorded 23 Sept 1774.

L-4, 332-336: Lease & release. 17 & 18 June 1748, James Watson of Granville Co., SC, planter, to Dan'd Heyward of same, planter, for £550 SC money, 200 acres in Granville County on Portroyal Island adj. land of John Duball, John Hutchinson, Nisbet, on a creek out of Beaufort River which said tract was purchased by my father Saml Watson of Joseph Palmenter in 1724 and was part of 316 acres. James Watson (LS)., Wit: John Sheppard, Wm. Sealy. Proved in Granville County by the oath of William Sealy before Andrew Verdier, J. P., 26 March 1754. Recorded 24 Sept 1774.

L-4, 336-338: 1 Dec 1773, John M'Millen [McMillen] of Ninety Six District, SC, and Agnes his wife, to Francis Whelchel of same, for £240 SC money, tract on Abittons Creek in the District of Ninety Six, 200 acres, granted by Gov. William Tryon of NC to John M'Millen in 1767. John M'Millen (LS), Agnes M'Millen (LS), Wit: Francis Whelchel Junr, Joseph Robinson.

L-4, 338-339: 20 July 1770, John Fulton of Tryon County, North Carolina, to James Dewine of same for £20 current money, 100 acres on a branch of Broad River. John Fulton (LS), Wit: Robert

SOUTH CAROLINA DEED ABSTRACTS 1773-1778

McCurdy, David Porter. North Carolina, July 1770. Proved in open court and recorded in the Clerks Office. Ezekl Polk entered 21 Sept 1770.

L-4, 339-343: Lease & release. 7 & 8 June 1773, William Cattertone of SC to William Haywood of same, for £85 SC money, 100 acres in Colleton County adj. land of James Donnom, granted 1 Dec 1772 to William Catterton. William Catterton (LS), Hannah Catterton (LS), Wit: James Boyd, John Catterton. Proved before James Hamilton, J. P. for Charlestown District, Colleton County, by the oath of John Catterton, 18 Sept 1773. Recorded 20 Aug 1774.

L-4, 344-345: 25 May 1769, William Twitty of Tryon County, NC, to William Saffold of same, for £5 prock. money, 200 acres on Bullocks Creek of Thickety adj. Hugh Moors line, including the fork of Bullocks Creek. William Twitty (LS), Wit: William Saffold jurat, Reuben Saffold, Daniel Saffold (mark). July Term 1770. North Carolina, Tryon County. Proved in open court. Recorded 26 Sept 1770 in Tryon County. Recorded 26 Sept 1774.

L-4, 345-348: 2 Aug 1773, William Sims of Province of Georgia to James Fanning of Province of South Carolina, for £10 SC money, 200 acres on Gilkeys Creek granted to William Sims 25 Apr 1767 now in South Carolina but formerly in North Carolina. William Sims (LS), Wit: Zach. Bullock, Jno Nuckols, John Fannin. Proved by the oath of John Nuckols before Joseph Robinson, J.P. in Ninety Six District, 17 Nov 1773. Recorded 25 Sept 1774.

L-4, 348-350: 16 July 1774, Catharina Maclemar of Ninety Six District to William Burgess of same place, for £75 SC money, 50 acres it being laid off in the no corner and a part of the tract of 200 acres in Berkly County on waters of Cain Creek which was granted to Thomas Johnston 30 May 1768, conveyed by said Thomas Johnston to William Lithgow 6 Oct 1768, and conveyed by said William Lithgow to Catharine Cocle now Catharine Maclemar 17 & 18 Oct 1769. Catharina Maclemar (X) (LS), Wit: Thos Cargill, Jane Cunningham, George Neeley. Proved 6 July 1773 by the oath of Thomas Cargell. Recorded 27 Sept 1774.

L-4, 350-352: 1 Nov 1773, Elias Brock & Willm Crank, both of Surry County, North Carolina, to John Fanning late of Tryon County but now called Craven County, So Carolina, for £100 proc. money, 200 acres formerly in Tryon County now Craven County, SC, on No side of road River above James Fannings plantation, formerly conveyed by John Conger to Jane Crank & by her descended to Elias Brock & William Crank as her heirs. Elias Brock (LS), William Crank (LS), Wit: Edwd Hughes, James Fannin, Abraham Maginis. Proved in Craven County, SC, before Joseph Wood, J. P., by the oath of James Fannin. Recorded 27 Sept 1774.

L-4, 352-354: 23 Jan 1759, Robert Ramsey & Margret his wife of Anson County, NC, to Robert Dunlap of same, for £30 proc. money of NC, 300 acres in the County of Anson, on the north side of Cataba River on both sides of Cain Creek including a tree marked RR. Robert Ramsey (LS), Margaret Ramsey (LS), Wit: William Davis, Samuel Dunlap, William Drenen (X). April Court 1759, North Carolina, Anson County. Recorded in Anson County Book D, pages 350-352, Robert Harris, public register. Recorded 27 Sept 1774.

L-4, 355-357: 24 Jan 1774, John Stephens of George town, SC, Minister of the Gospel, to James Verree of city and county of Burlington in the Western Division of the Province of New Jersey, house carpenter, whereas Martha Stephens formerly Martha Mourey one of the daughters of Elizabeth Pearce who was daughter of George Hutcheson who formerly resided in West new Jersey, by virtue of the last will and testament of said George Hutcheson and by virtue of a quit claim and release from Anthony Morris of Philadelphia dated 17 Nov 1716 attorney to George Hutcheson of London, Peruke maker, grandson and heir at law of said George Hutcheson, became seized of a part of the estate of said George Hutcheson situate in West New Jersey, to which said Martha Stephens the said John Stephens is son and right heir at law and whereas Joseph Jacobs of the City of Philadelphia in Pennsylvania sadler did claim under the said Martha Stephens an estate in fee in a certain share of a revertion or remainder of said estate devised as aforesaid and under the claim did obtain from the Council of Proprietors of the said Western Division of New Jersey, sundry warrants directed to the surveyor general of the said Western Division requiring him or his deputy to locate for the said Joseph Jacobs sundry parcels of land and said Joseph Jacobs did obtain one warrant bearing date 3 Nov 1768 for 500 acres in the said Western Division where not before legally appropriate which warrant is marked in the margin and another warrant of the same date for 300 acres in like manner and said Joseph Jacob by a deed intended dated 3 March 1769 conveyed his rights to James Verree party hereto and whereas some doubts have arisen in respect to the validity of the said Joseph Jacobs title under the said Martha Stephens, now this indenture for £40 SC money paid by said James Verree, all his right to the said 800 acres. John Stephens (LS), Wit: Edwd Martin, Wm. Mason. Proved in George Town District before Job Rothmahler, J.P., by the oath of William Mason, Esqr., 12 July 1774. Recorded 28 Sept 1774.

L-4, 357-358: 11 July 1774, Robert Patrick of Craven County, SC, to Joshua Patrick son to Robert Patrick of same, for £5 prock. money, tract on south side of Crowders Creek adj. Alexander Osbourns corner, granted to said Robert Patrick 25 Apr 1767 by Gov. Wm. Tryon. Robert Patrick (X) (LS), Wit: Robert Patrick Juner, William Pattrick, Mary Patrick (M). Proved in Camden District 12 July 1774 by the oath of Robert Patrick Junr. Recorded 28 Sept 1774.

L-4, 359-364: Lease & release. 10 & 11 Jan 1774, Jane Elizabeth Holmes of Charles Town, widow, some time since called Jane Elizabeth Carne, to Charles Collins of Amelia Township, planter, for £500 SC money, 250 acres in Amelia township granted to Archibald Campbell 6 Apr 1753 and was conveyed to said Jane Elizabeth Carne 6 & 7 July 1758, and in the year 1767 adj. to land surveyed for Martin Peaglar, Thomas Waring. Jane Elizabeth Holmes (LS), Wit: Wm. W. Burrows, john Wagner. Recorded 29 Sept 1774.

L-4, 364-368: Lease & release. 6 & 7 July 1758, Archibald Campbell of Amelia Township, SC, planter, to Jane Elizabeth Carn of Charles Town, spinster, for £200 SC money, 250 acres. Archibald Campbell (LS), Anne Campbell (LS), Wit: Moses Thomson, Mary Heatly, Moses Thomson Junr. Jane Elizabeth Carne renounce all manner of pretensions to the this land, 3 Nov 1767, Wit: Eliza'th Carne. Recorded 29 Sept 1774.

L-4, 369-376: Lease & release. 9 & 10 March 1774, Richard Muncreef of Charles Town, Carpenter, and Susannah his wife, to Nathaniel Fuller of St. Andrews parish, planter, for £2300, several tracts of land: 220 acres, 54 acres, and 54 acres on Bear Swamp in St. Andrews Parish, Berkley County, adj. land now or late of Nathaniel Fullar, Mary Ladson, John Aigner and Francis Ladson, Thomas Drayton Esqr; also 100 acres part of a tract of 250 acres in said parish adj. Francis Ladson, Charles West, Stephen Drayton deceased, which several tracts lately belonging to James Matthewes late of parish deceased and by him devided to his wife Charlotte Matthewes and by certain indentures 21 & 22 Dec 1768 to William Bampfield, and said William Bampfield and Rebecca his wife 23 & 24 Aug 1769 to Richard Muncreef. Richd Muncreef (LS), Susannah Muncreef (LS), Wit: Thomas Bride, R. Muncreef. Recorded 1 Sept 1774.

END OF BOOK L-4.

SOUTH CAROLINA DEED ABSTRACTS 1773-1778

M-4, 1-7: 28 June 1773, William Burrows and Bernard Beekman, both of Charles Town, Esquires, to Michael Kalteisan, Thomas Harper, William Graham, Jacob Boomer & William Swallow of Charles Town, gentleman... by indenture 13 Apr 1761 between Jonathan Sarazin of Charles Town, Silver Smith, son and heir at law of Morreau Sarrazin of Charles Town, Silver Smith, deceased, to William Burrows, Samuel Carne, Job Milner, Barnard Beekman, Richard Park Stobo, and Robert Wilson of Charles Town, gentlemen, reciting that in the year 1752 the members of Solomans Lodge of free and accepted Masons in Charles Town being inclinable to procure a title to two pews in the new Church then about to be built in Charles Town, since called St. Michaels church, did empower two of their members to say Brothers William Henderson and Moreau Sarrazin to subscribe each £150... pew number 55... under the seal of william Bull, Fenwick and Othniel Beale Esquires and Isaac Mazyck, Benjamin Smith, Robert Pringle, George Saxby, Gabriel Manigault and Thomas Middleton, Esquires, Commissioners for building said church... title made to members of Solomans Lodge William Burrows, Samuel Carne, Job Milner, Bernard Beekman, Richard Park Stobo, Thos Stone and Robert Wilson, seven of their members, trustees to receive from the said Jonathan Sarrazin a declaration or deed in trust to the same pew, 9 Feb 1761. Wm. Burrows (LS), Bernard Beekman (LS), Michl Kalteison (LS), Thos Harper (LS), Wm Graham (LS), Jacob Bommer (LS), Wm. Swallow (LS), Wit: Wm. Knight, Thos Phepoe. Proved by the oath of Thomas Phepoe 22 July 1774 before William Rugeley, J.P. Recorded 3 Aug 1774.

M-4, 8-14: Lease & release. 11 & 12 May 1774, William Flud of St. Mathews Parish, Orangeburgh District, SC, to Ephraim Mitchell of Charles Town, for £500 SC money, 550 acres adj. land of Charles Conley, Esqr., on Santee River adj. 250 acres of said tract formerly conveyed to John Matthews; granted to James Flud 1 August 1758 and became vested in the said William Flud brother to the said James as heir at law. Wm. Flud (LS), Wit: John Fenwick, John Benis. Recorded 4 Aug 1774.

M-4, 14-23: Lease & release. 18 & 19 Aug 1772, Josias Allston of Waccamaw, Craven County, SC, Esquire, and his wife to Joseph Allston of same, planter, for £10,000 SC money, land granted 18 June 1711 to Robert Daniel, Esquire, part of 24,000 acres for which he obtained a patent from the Lord Proprietors, one tract of 1490 acres on Waccamaw Neck bounding on the marshes to the sea shore, Waccamaw River, lands now Archibald Johnston, Samuel Allston, taken about the year 1750 and said Robert Daniel on 19 June 1711 sold and conveyed said 1490 acres to Thomas Smith, Esquire, and Thomas Smith on 10 Sept following to Percival Pawley and said Percival Pawley by his last will and testament dated 5 June 1722 did give unto Susannah and Ann Pawley daughters of his brother Joseph Lawley 490 acres part of said 1490 acres on the southwest side of his sons land and Joseph Allen of Parish and province aforesaid intermarried with said Susannah one of the said Joseph Lawleys daughters and conceiving himself intitlted to the said 490 acres and by the demise of said Ann he with Susannah his wife on 11 & 12 March 1736 conveyed to John Allston father to Josias Allston, said John Allston finding that there was more land within the lines of the said tract of 490 acres then was specified in the conveyance caused the same to be resurveyed and obtained from Robert Johnson a grant dated 24 May 1734 for 700 acres being the said surplus with some other adjoining lands but the quantity contained within the said lines is estimated at about 300 acres more or less, by grant 28 Apr 1733 did grant to said John Allston 137 acres on the opposite side of Waccamaw River on Pawleys Creek and Allstons Creek, and by his last will and testament devised to his son Josiah Allston, but said Josias Allston finding afterwards that the said Joseph Allen and Susannah his wife had no authority to convey the reversion and inheritance but that the same was vested in and of right belonging to George Pawley, Esquire as eldest son and heir at law of the said Major Percival Pawley wherefore the said George Pawley in order to render effectual the last will and testament of his deceased father by deeds 29 & 30 Nov 1750 did sell to said Josiah Allston, now said Joseph Allston with Charlotte Allston his wife 15 & 16 June 1768 did conveyed to said Josias Allston tract of 13 3/4 acres on Waccamaw River so that said Josias Allston stands intitled unto four several pieces of land in the whole 950 3/4 acres. Ann Allston (LS), Josiah Allston (LS), Wit: Benj Young, Geo Heriot. Proved in George Town District by the oath of George Heriot 9 May 1774 before Wm. Mason, J.P. Recorded 6 Aug 1774.

M-4, 23-31: Lease & release. 13 & 14 May 1774, Ephraim Mitchell of Charles town, SC, Gentleman, to Thomas Ashby and Anthony Ashby of said province, planters, for £9,000 SC money, plantation known by the name of Pond Bluff, 700 acres on south side of Santee River in St. Johns Parish, adj. lands of Charles Cantey, Esquire, Francis Marion, also a tract of 1100 acres on north side Santee River opposite to the above said tract of 700 acres adj. land of Gabriel Marion, William Flud, Benjamin Tarar, Josiah Neilsons land, James McKelvey, John Skrine, Larkins Creek. Ephraim Mitchell (LS), Wit: Elias Horry Junr, Jo. Ward. Proved by the oath of Joshua Ward before David Deas, J.P., 14 May 1774. Recorded 9 Aug 1774.

M-4, 31-35: Lease & release. 11 & 12 June 1766, George Milligen of Charles Town, and wife Mary, to Junes Teabout, for £120 SC money, lot 54 in Beaufort Town on Port Royal Street, granted to said George Milligen 31 Oct last past. George Milligen (LS), Mary Milligen (LS), Wit: Will Theith[?], Jno Remington. Proved by the oath of John Remington, Esqr., before Peter Bonetheau, J.P., 21 May 1774. Recorded 9 Aug 1774.

M-4, 36-45: Lease & release. Georgia. 15 & 16 May 1774, John Smith of Savannah, Esquire, and Elizabeth his wife, to Basil Cowper of Savannah, gentleman, for £8400 SC money, tract which belonged to Hugh Bryan late of Province of SC, planter, 4883 acres in Granville County on Savannah River adj. Rev. William Guys land, Thomas Elliott, and after the decease of said Hugh Bryan tract came in the custody of Charles Lowndes Esquire then provost marshall, and by a writ of fieri facias from the court of common pleas it was conveyed to said John Smith 7 Feb 1757; now 1340 acres, part of said tract, in St. Peters Parish,l Granville County, SC, called Cowpers Hill Plantation at or part of the place called Black Swamp adj. lands of William Stafford, Peter Purry common called Oglethorpes Barony, adj. Thomas Gullan, John Smith. John Smith (LS), Elizabeth Smith (LS), Wit: James Carsan, Geo. Walton. Proved in Charles Town District by the oath of James Carsan 25 May 1774 before William Rugeley, J.P. Recorded 10 Aug 1774.

M-4, 45-51: Lease & release. 23 & 24 Jan 1772, James McCants, Esqr. of Prince Fredericks Parish, SC, to Thomas McCants of same; Jno Bassnett late of Williamsburgh Township, storekeeper, deceased, was possessed of 350 acres in Williamsburgh in Craven County ranted by George II unto William Turblefield 26 June 1736, and said Jno Bassnett being indebted to sundry persons which he was unable to pay, and in the court of common pleas on 27 July 1744 petitioned the court to be admitted to the benefit of the act for the benefit of insolvent debtors and said lands were assigned to Robert Pringle, Frederick Grimke & one Ribton Hutchinson now deceased in trust for themselves & the rest of the creditors, NOW for £540 SC money, transferred by James McCants to Thomas McCants. James McCants, Wit: Robert Glasco, William McElven. Proved in Craven County by the oath of Robt Glasco before Saml Nesmith, J.P., 23 Apr 1772. Recorded 11 Aug 1774.

M-4, 51-59: Lease & release. 17 & 18 Sept 1767, William Bannester of St. Johns Parish, Berkley County, planter, to James McKelvey of same place, planter, for £400 SC money, 200 acres in said parish, adj. land of Mathew Beard, granted to George Beard 11 Dec 1735 and was bequeathed by said George Beard to his son Thomas Beard, and by John Maxfield, executor of James Beard, to Josiah Brunston 23 & 24 Jan 1759, and by said Josiah Brunson by his last will and testament to said William Banester. William Banister (LS), Wit: John Mitchell, Charles Neal, Thos Powell. Proved 8 March 1768 before Josiah/Joseph Curry, J.P. in Berkley County, by the oath of Charles Neal. Recorded 12 Aug 1774.

M-4, 59-63: Lease & release. 27 & 28 Oct 1765, John Deliesseline of St. James Parish, Craven County, SC, planter, to James McKelvey of same, for £500 SC money, 250 acres in St. Marks Parish, Craven County, adj. John Skrine, Charles ONeal. John Deliesseline (LS), Wit: Thomas Hutchenson, Jacob Jenneret. Proved in Craven County before Isaac Porcher, J.P., by the oath of Thomas Hutchenson, 29 Oct 1765. Recorded 12 Aug 1774.

M-4, 63-70: Lease & release. 7 & 8 March 1774, Charles Ogilvie, late of London, Great Britain, merchant, now of Charles Town, to John Chesnut and Eli Kershaw, both of St. Marks Parish, for £2,000; three tracts in St. Marks Parish, 250 acres in Craven County on south side Wateree River adj. Noah Gless, granted to James Michie deceased July 1751; 135 acres adj. John Mackenzie; 172 acres on south side Wateree River 10 Feb 1749 to John Mackenzie, late of SC, merchant, deceased. Cha's Ogilvie (LS), Wit: Nath Russell, Robt Mackenzie Junr, Geo Ancrum Junr. Proved in Charles Town District 27 May 1774 before Wm. Rugeley, J. P., by the oath of George Ancrum Junr. Recorded 13 Aug 1774.

M-4, 71-77: Lease & release. 25 & 26 May 1774, Archibald Wilson of Granville County, SC, House Carpenter, to James Wilson Senr of same, planter, for £100 SC money, 100 acres in Granville County on waters of Stephens Creek on a branch known as Chevees Creek adj. land laid out for John Fairchild, granted to Archibald Wilson 2 March 1762 recorded in Book CCC, page 226, memorial entered Book I No. 9, page 32 6 Aug 1762. Archibel Wilson. Wit: Ann Savage, William Edwards. Proved 26 May 1774 before John Savage, J.P. in Orangeburgh District, by the oath of William Edwards. Recorded 25 Aug 1774.

M-4, 77-83: Lease & release. 1 & 2 March 1773, Rachel Bronkhart of Charles Town, spinster, to George Renerson of Charles Town, Tavern keeper, for £300 SC money, 300 acres below Orangeburgh Township in Berkley County adj. land of John Adam Eyering, granted 22 Jan 1759 to Andrew Bronkhart father of said Rachel Bronkhart who died intestate by which means the said Rachel Bronkhart (being his only child) became heiress at law. Rachel Bronkhart (LS), Wit: George Gray, Peter Horn. Proved 16 March 1774 before George Davidson, J. P. in Charles Town District, by the oath of George Gray. Recorded 25 Aug 1774.

M-4, 83-86: 4 Dec 1773, Arthur Hicklin Junr of Parish of St. Marks, SC, yeoman, to Daniel Coleson of same, yeoman, for £250 SC money, 100 acres in St. Marks Parish, adj. land of Frederick Ford, John Lenard, Benjamin Everell, granted 23 Oct 1765 to Arther Hicklin Junr. Arch'i Hicklin (LS), Wit: Gorge King (mark), Charles King (D), William Collson. Proved in Camden District by the oath of William Collson before John Gaston, J. P., 27 Apr 1774. Recorded 16 Aug 1774.

M-4, 86-88: 19 Apr 1774, William Martin, planter, of Granville Co., SC, to Samuel McMurtry and his wife Jean, for £100 SC money, 64 acres part of 200 acres granted to said William Martin 18 Aug 1763, adj. land of Josiah Martin, the part whereupon said McMurtry now dwells. William Martin (LS), Wit: Saml Watt, Henry Williams. Proved in Ninety Six District 21 May 1774 before John Bowie, J.P., by the oath of Saml Watt. Recorded 16 Aug 1774.

M-4, 88-93: Lease & release. 31 May & 1 June 1774, Christian Kincelor of St. Marks Parish, planter, to Godfrey Tryer of Saxagotha Township, planter, £216 SC money, 50 acres granted 18 Nov 1747 to Conrad Kinceler in Saxagotha Township adj. Saluda River, land of Henry Lockley, and said Conrad Kysell [sic] being deceased and his eldest son Harmon Kinceler being heir at law and afterwards did sell to the said Christian Kinceler 15 & 16 Sept 1772. Christian Kinseler (LS), Wit: Henry Fulk, Larance Mark (X). Proved by the oath of Larance Mark before Wm. Arther, J.P., 1 June 1774. Recorded 16 Aug 1774.

M-4, 93-99: Lease & release. 2 & 3 Dec 1767, Aaron Stephen (Stevens) of Frederick County, Colony of Virginia, to Thomas Wadlington Senr late of same, for £110 Va. money, 400 acres in the fork between Broad & Saludy Rivers. Adam Stephen (LS), Wit: Jacob Hite, John Hite Junr, Chs. Smith, Jas. Wadlington. Proved 4 Apr 1768 before Joseph Curry, J.P. in Berkley County, by the oath of James Wadlington. Recorded 17 Aug 1774.

M-4, 100-105: Lease & release. 16 & 17 Feb 1756, John McDugal of Charles Town, to John Pearson, Deputy Surveyor in Craven County, for £150 SC money, 150 acres in the fork between Broad and Saludy Rivers on Collins's River adj. land laid out to Bartholomew Wood by virtue of a North warrant, granted 12 Feb 1755. Jno McDugall (LS), Wit: Peter Oliver, Jane Godfrey, Adam Sheekle (+). Proved 12 Apr 1756 before James Francis, J. P. in Berkley County, by the oath of Adam Shekel. Recorded 18 Aug 1774.

M-4, 106-107: Mary Scottow of Boston, County of Suffolk, Province of Massachusetts Bay in New England, widow of joshua Scottow, late of Charles Town, SC, Taylor, deceased & daughter of Samuel Smith late of said Charles Town, Victualler, deceased, said Mary Scottow by power of attorney dated 1766 appointed Jonathan Badger of Charles Town, my attorney... by this instrument grants full power, dated 31 May 1774. Mary Scottow (X) (LS), Wit: Josiah Hatcher Junr, William Harris. Proved in Charles Town District by the oath of Josiah Hatcher before William Rugeley, J.P., 28 June 1774. Recorded 18 Aug 1774.

M-4, 107-112: Lease & release. 18 & 19 Jan 1773, Jacob Penington & Isaac Penington of Barkley County, SC, planters, to Captain Charles King, for £250 SC, 150 acres on south side of Collins's

SOUTH CAROLINA DEED ABSTRACTS 1773-1778

River adj. land laid out by a north warrant to Bartholomew Wood, for which John Pearson paid £150 to John McDugall 16 & 17 Feb 1756, said land granted to John McDugall who conveyed to Isaac Penington 24 & 25 Oct 1757, which said Isaac Pennington did bequeath unto his two sons namely Jacob Penington & Isaac Penington by his last will and testament. Jacob Penington Junr (LS), Isaac Penington (LS), Wit: James Lindsey, William Wooddall, Thos Lindsey. Proved 3 July 1773 before Michl. Dickert, J. P., by the oath of James Lindsey. Recorded 18 Aug 1774.

M-4, 113-117: Lease & release. 24 & 25 Oct 1757, John Pearson of Craven County, SC, Deputy Surveyor, to Capt. Isaac Penington of the forks of Broads River, Blacksmith, for £150, 150 acres on south side of Collins's River adj. land laid out by a north warrant to Bartholomew Wood, said land granted to John McDugall. John Pearson (LS), Wit: Jacob Pennington, Abraham Pennington, James McBurnet (+). Proved 25 Nov 1757 before James Francis, J.P., by the oath of Jacob Pennington. Recorded 20 Aug 1774.

M-4, 118-120: 29 Nov 1762, Sarah, wife of Oliver Hart of Charles Town, relinquished dower to a tract conveyed 2 & 3 Nov to Mary Atwell, spinster, and Icabod Atwell of same town, carpenter, lot #108 in Charles Town adj. formerly William Chapman decd, William Screven the younger deceased and since his death sold to one William Brisbane and lot devised by William Scriven the elder also deceased to his daughter Eleanor Screven. Recorded 20 Aug 1774.

M-4, 120-121: 22 Sept 1772, David Hunter of Craven County, farmer, to John McKewn of same, for £300 SC money, tract granted 5 Oct 1703 to David Hunter, 300 acres on a branch of Rockey Creek. David Hunter (C) (LS), Wit: Robt McFadder, Hannah McFadder, James Harper (T).

M-4, 122-125: Lease & release. 17 & 18 Jan 1774, Henry Dongworth of Craven Co., St. Marks Parish, planter, to James Kilpatrick of same, planter, for £500 SC money, 200 acres in Craven County on both sides White Oak Creek,adj. James McCulleys line, granted to Reason Neilson being part of tract of 500 acres and by said Reason Neilson the aforesaid 200 acres conveyed to Henry Dongworth 8 & 9 Feb 1769. Henry Dongworth (LS), Wit: Richd Wadeson, Thos Jones, John Wyly. Recorded 24 Aug 1774.

M-4, 126-130: Lease & mortgage. 13 & 14 June 1774, James Rowlain of Parish of St. Thomas, planter, to Susannah Latour, spinster, bond for £4200 SC money with interest for the payment of £2100 before 14 June 1775, lot on west side King Street adj. land of Blakely Whitt, Mrs. Jane Massey. James Rowlain (LS), Wit: Anthony Labbe, John Troup. Proved 25 Aug 1774 before William Rugeley in Charles Town District by the oath of Anthony Labbe. Satisfied 14 July 1778. Susanna Latour (X). Wit: Geo Sheed.

M-4, 130-133: 26 Aug 1771, James McCullock of Craven County, SC, yeoman, to John Wier of same, planter, for £50 SC money, tract granted 2 March 1768 to James McCullock, 100 acres on a small branch of Rockey Creek in Craven County. James McCulllough (LS), Wit: Wm. McCluer, Robt. Gaston. Proved by the oath of Wm. McCluer before John Gaston, J. P., 26 Aug 1771. Recorded 25 Aug 1774.

M-4, 133-136: 1 Dec 1773, Lodowick Laird of Craven county, & Elizabeth his wife, planter, to Robert Laird of same, said Lodowick Laird and Eliz'h his wife conform to a grant made to Micam Fisher in the province of North Carolina in 1752, 265 acres on both sides rockey Creek in St. marks Parish sold by said Fisher to Stephen White, blacksmith in 1759, and by said Stephen White and Agnes White his wife sold to said Lodowick Laird 24 Aug 1763[?], now said Lodowick Laird and Elizabeth his wife convey 100 acres of said tract I now live upon, adj. Thomas Gerrals lines, the creek is to be the line between the said Robert Laird my son and me. Lodowick Laird (L) (LS), Elizabeth Laird (S) (LS), Wit: John Kell, David McQuiston, George Chery. Proved in Camden District by the oath of George Chery before John Gaston, J. P., 3 Dec 1773. Recorded 25 Aug 1774.

M-4, 136-137: 3 June 1774, John Moore of Tryon County, North Carolina, to Peter Julian Senior of Craven County, in North Carolina, for £50, 125 acres on north side of Broad River in the main forks of Kings Creek, part of tract granted to Samuel Finley 4 Sept 1754 conveyed by said Samuel Finley to John Moore. John Moore (LS), Wit: Samuel McCleary, Peter Julien Junr, Ezekl. Polk. Proved by the oath of Ezekiel Polk, J.P. Recorded 26 Aug 1774.

SOUTH CAROLINA DEED ABSTRACTS 1773-1778

M-4, 138-139: 3 June 1774, John Moore of Tryon County, North Carolina, to Peter Julian Jun'r of Craven County, in South Carolina, for £50, 175 acres on north side of Broad River on both sides of Kings Creek, part of tract granted to Samuel Finley 4 Sept 1754 conveyed by said Samuel Finley to John Moore. John Moore (LS), Wit: Samuel McCleary, Peter Julien Senr, Ezekl. Polk. Proved by the oath of Ezekiel Polk, J.P. Recorded 26 Aug 1774.

M-4, 140-144: Lease & release. 24 & 25 Jan 1773, Charles Boyle and Catharine his wife of Colleton County, SC, to David Hunter of same province, for £95 SC money, 100 acres on Sleepy Creek adj. bounty land, granted 10 Apr 1771 to Isaac Ramsey, conveyed 4 & 5 Nov 1772 to Charles Boyle. Charles Boyle (mark) (LS), Catharine Boyle (LS), Wit: Robt Bryan, Wm. Perrin, Ben Hull. Proved in Ninety Six District by the oath of Robt. Bryant before Benj. Hull, J.P. Recorded 28 Aug 1774.

M-4, 144-149: Lease & release. 14 & 15 Sept 1772, Thos Vaughn of Berkley County, Sc, planter, and Agnes his wife, to Philemon Waters of Charles Town, Gentleman, for £500 SC money, 150 acres on south side Saludy River granted by George III 7 Apr 1770. Thomas Vaughn (LS), Wit: William Nichols, Thos Waters. Proved 12 Jan 1773 before John Fairchild, J. P. in Colleton County, by the oath of Thomas Waters. Recorded 29 Aug 1774.

M-4, 150: John Fifer, 500 acres Tryon on the south fork of Pacolet River above the maidens Meadow and a Little below Hutchins's Cabin adj. William Dicksons line. dated 23 Dec 1768. Wm. Tryon. Certified copy from North Carolina 19 March 1774. Recorded 30 Aug 1774.

M-4, 150-152: 2 May 1774, John Mayer of Parish of St. Thomas and St. Denis, SC, practitioner of physick, to John Huger, Esquire, of Charles Town, for love favour and affection unto his Brothers william Mayer, Thos Mayer and joseph Mayer, and for ten shillings paid by said John Huger, Esqr., tract of 50 acres in Berkley County on the east side of Lynches Creek adj. land of Moses Monier, John Deas, granted to said John Mayer 21 Feb 1772, also one acre of land commonly known by the name of the French Church, and one tract of 191 acres in Berkley County adj. land formerly laid out to Peter Monier, land formerly granted to Johnson Lynch, land formerly granted to Philemon Parmenter, said tract granted to said John Mayer 18 May 1773, likewise one silver tankard, six silver handled knives, one bay horse called the Irish Gimblet and Two Mares, to said John Hunger in trust. John Mayer (LS), Wit: Robt Wright, James Gilchrist, Richard Mayer. Proved in Charles Town District by the oath of Richard Mayer, practitioner of physic, before John Syme, 27 June 1774. Recorded 30 Aug 1774.

M-4, 152-155: Mortgage and bond. James Robertson of St. Thomas, Planter, by bond to John Imrie of Charles Town, Ship wright, in the penal sum of £700 for the payment of £350, 1 July 1774, tract of land in the Parish of St. Thomas, Berkley County, adj. land of James Aking, Esqr., and Andrew Devo formerly the property of Joseph Stone. James Robertson (LS), Wit: John Tuke, Elizabeth Henley. Proved in Charles Town District by the oath of John Tuke, 29 June 1774, before William Rugeley, J.P. Recorded 29 Aug 1774. Satisfied 3 Jan 1775.

M-4, 155-162: Lease & release. 7 & 8 June 1771, Isaac Hudson and his wife Elizabeth of Granville County, SC, planter, to Ebenezer Starns of same, planter, for £150 SC money, 150 acres in Granville County on Stephens Creek a branch of Savannah River, granted to said Isaac Hudson 5 March 1770. Isaac Hudson (LS), Elizabeth Hudson (I) (LS), Wit: Amos Richerson, John Allen, Wm. Coursey. Proved 23 June 1772 before John Purves, J. P. in Granville County, by the oath of William Coursey. Recorded 30 Aug 1774.

M-4, 162-164: 26 Oct 1773, Ezekiel Potts and George Potts, Brothers to John Potts deceased and heirs to the Land which is in this Indenture, described of the County of Tryon, North Carolina, to John Lattimore of Camden District, Craven County, South Carolina, planter, for £480 SC money, land on both sides of Charles [sic for Clarks?] Fork of Bullocks Creek granted by William Tryon, Gov. of NC, 25 Apr 1767. Ezekiel Potts (LS), George Potts (LS), Wit: George Gibson, Samuel Swann, Newbery Stockton. Proved in Camden District by the oath of Newberry Stockton, 3 Feb 1774, before Ezekiel Polk, J.P. Recorded 30 Aug 1774.

M-4, 164-166: Mortgage and bond. William Godfrey of Granville County 10 June 1774 bound to Isaac Hayne in the penal sum of £3000 SC money for the payment of £1500 tract if 400 acres adj.

SOUTH CAROLINA DEED ABSTRACTS 1773-1778

Col. Flowers [Howers?], Mr. Cobleys land, Voyers land, Rodolph, and on Savannah River. William Godfrey (LS), Wit: Wm. Hazz'd Wigg, Matthew McKennie. Proved in Beaufort District before John Bull by the oath of William Hazzard Wigg, 11 June 1774. Recorded 1 Sept 1774.

M-4, 166-169: Dedimus to Andrew Agnew, Esqr., to take renunciation of dower of Mary, wife of Daniel DeSaussure of St. Helena Parish, Granville Co., SC, merchant, respecting land conveyed 30 & 31 Dec 1771 to Jacob Vanbibber of same parish, 72 acres part of 200 acres in Granville County adj. land of Joseph Ainger, Elijah Prioleau, dated 15 July 1773. Mary Desaussure. Recorded 1 Sept 1774.

M-4, 169-170: Elias Vanderhorst in consideration of the debt due and owing to William Greenwood and William Higginson of London, Merchant, and by four several bonds, 6 oct 1770 for £5856 each with interest of five pr cent, dated 8 July 1772. Elias Vanderhorst (LS), Wit: Geo Lord, Thos Lord. Proved by the oath of Geo. Lord, 27 June 1774, before William Rugeley, J.P. Recorded 1 Sept 1774.

M-4, 170-172: Purysburgh in Granville county, South Carolina. 2 May 1774, Melchior Humbert (only son of the late David Peter Humbert of Purysburgh in the parish of St. Peters), planter, to Adrian Mayer also of Purysburgh, Esqr., for £250, tract in the township of Purysburgh adj. land granted to Robert Williams, Henry Henderly, Hugh Rose, Francis Votier and afterwards granted to William Dupius, 200 acres. Melcheor Humbert (LS), Wit: Jno Postell, Wm. Brabant. Proved by the oath of John Postell 5 May 1774 before David Giroud, J. P. Recorded 2 Sept 1774.

M-4, 172-174: Purysburgh in Granville county, South Carolina. 20 June 1774, Willoughby Pugh of Parish of St. Peters, planter, to Adrian Mayer of purysburgh, Esqr., for £102 ten shillings, tract in the township of Purysburgh adj. land granted to Frederick Holzendorf, Anthony Taton, John Jacob & Susannah Strobhar, Frances Vanai, Isaac Bonijol, 162 acres. Willoughby Pugh (LS), Wit: John OHear, William Kirk. Proved by the oath of John Ohear before David Giroud, J.P., 20 June 1774. Recorded 2 Sept 1774.

M-4, 174-178: Lease & release. 16 May 1774, John Cox and Elizabeth his wife of the Settlement of Enoree River, South Carolina, to John Gambrell of same settlement, for £50 SC money, 200 acres granted to Jno Cox in Craven County on the south side of Enoree River on a creek called the Warrior Creek. John Cox (mark) (LS), Elizabeth Cox (+) (LS), Wit: Peter Broos, William Vaughn (+). Proved in Ninety Six District by the oath of William Vaughn before John Ford, J.P., 16 June 1774. Recorded 2 Sept 1774.

M-4, 178-184: Lease & release. 14 & 15 March 1775 [sic], Joab Mitchell of District of Ninety Six, to Samuel Cobb of same, for £300 SC money, 300 acres in Ninety Six District on a branch of Enoree called Gilders Creek. Joab Mitchell (M) (LS), Wit: William Henderson, Neal McKissock, Mark Mitchell. Proved by the oath of Mark Mitchell before William Wofford, J.P., 16 March 1774. Recorded 5 Sept 1774.

M-4, 184-187: 14 May 1774, William White of Camden District, SC, planter, to Revd. Mr. John Logue of Orangeburgh District, SC, for 400 SC money, 200 acres in Craven County on the waters of Wateree River adj. land of John Roach, John Hughs, grant recorded in Book DDD, page 67, granted to John Hopkins 12 Jan 1769, conveyed by said John Hopkins and his wife Sarah 20 &* 21 Nov 1772 to William White. Wm. White (LS), Wit: Wm. Thompson, Richd Brown, John Russell. Proved 14 May 1774 before Malcom Clark, J. P. in Orangeburgh District, by the oath of col. William Thompson. Recorded 5 Sept 1774.

M-4, 187-191: Lease & release. 13 & 14 Dec 1768, William Meadleton of Craven County, planter, to Wm. Meadleton Junr of same place, planter, for £100 SC money, tract granted 4 July 1758 unto Charles Turbevell, 300 acres on north side Peede River on a prong of Tobys Creek, recorded in Book SS, page 248, said Charles Turbevell conveyed 31 Aug 1750 to James Owen, 100 acres being the west part of said tract, adj. William Chamberlains line, said William Meadleton Senr by virtue of lease and release from said James Owen 1 & 2 June 1759 has inabled him to dispose of all the sd. tract of 150 acres. William Midelton (LS), Wit: John Buxton, John Crawford. Proved before John Alvan, J. P., by the oath of Samuel Buxton 21 Dec 1768. Recorded 5 Sept 1774.

SOUTH CAROLINA DEED ABSTRACTS 1773-1778

M-4, 191-193: 26 Oct 1759, John Winn of Amelia County, Colony of Virginia, to Philip Pledger of Craven County, SC, for £500, 300 acres granted to Nathaniel Knotts 8 Aug 1753 in the Welch Tract on north side Pee Dee River, Parish of Prince George, Craven county, conveyed from said Knotts to James Jones by a power of attorney to the above named John Winn 27 May 1756. John Winn (LS), Wit: James Griffith, John Lyons (I), Anna Lyons (X). Proved in Craven County before George Hicks, J.P., by the oath of John Lyons, 8 Apr 1760. Recorded 5 Sept 1774.

M-4, 193-195: 27 May 1756, James Jones of Welch Tract, Craven County, SC, Taylor, Lawfull Attorney of Nathaniel Knotts of Onslow County, North Carolina, Carpenter, qualified before James Murray, Esqr., Justice and Secretary of the Province of North Carolina, 14 Oct 1754, to John Winn of Craven Colony, SC for £1000, 300 acres granted to Nathaniel Knotts 8 Aug 1753. James Jones (J) (LS), Wit: Philip Pledger, Jacob DeSaurencey. Proved in Craven County before John Crawford, J.P., by the oath of Jacob DeSurrency, 29 May 1756. Recorded 5 Sept 1774.

M-4, 195-202: Lease & release. 4 & 5 Nov 1772, Thomas Hasell and Margaret his wife, both of Prince Georges Parish, Craven County, to Benjamin Trapier of same place, planter, for £1000 SC money, half of tract of 1300 acres in Prince Georges Parish, adj. Joseph Ports, William Whitesides, Joseph Waters, William Raes, granted to Thomas Bouny 6 Dec 1733 and by him conveyed to James Summers father to said Margaret Hasell to whom she together with her sister now Ann Dick became coheiress of said James Summers; also half of ten and one half lotts in George Town purchased of John Cleland Esqr and Mary his wife 9 Sept 1753; Thomas Hasell (LS), Margaret Hasell (LS), Wit: Judith Trapier, Paul Trapier. Proved 27 May 1774 before Robert Heriot, J. P. in Craven County, by the oath of Paul Trapier. Recorded 8 Sept 1774.

M-4, 202-205: Thomas Karwon of St. Thomas's Parish, planter, bound to Rvd. Robert Smith of St. Philips Parish, Charles Town, in the penal sum of £5000, 3 June 1774, whereas differences have arisen between said Thomas Karwon and Robert Smith respecting the bounds of certain property in the parish of St. Thomas, bond to abide by arbitrament of Wood Furman and Joseph Purcell. Thomas Karwon (LS), Wit: Jno Darrington, Henry Purcell. Proved by the oath of Henry Purcell before Peter Bounetheau, J. P., 1 Sept 1774. Plat included by Wood Furman and J. Purcell dated 8 June 1774, Wit: John Mayer.

M-4, 206-208: John Mayer of St. Thomas Parish, planter, bound to Revd. Robert Smith of St. Philips Parish, Charles Town, in the penal sum of £3000, 1 June 1774, whereas differences have arisen between said John Mayer and Robert Smith respecting the bounds of certain property in the parish of St. Thomas, bond to abide by arbitrament of Joseph Purcell. John Mayer (LS), Wit: Sarah Purcell, John Mordeth. Proved by the oath of Sarah Purcell before Peter Bounetheau, J. P., 1 Sept 1774. Plat included by J. Purcell dated 6 June 1774, Wit: Sarah Purcell, Jacob Shubrick.

M-4, 209-213: Lease & release. 11 & 12 May 1774, James Janeway of Craven County, SC, planter, to James Taylor of same, planter, for £2000 SC money, 100 acres granted to William Janeway 12 Dec 1746 on Santee otherwise Congaree River opposite to Saxegotha Township adj. Gilbert Gibson, plat recorded in Book LL, page 315, and whereas William Janeway dyed without making any will and said James Janeway being His eldest son and heir at law. James Janeway (+) (LS), Wit: Jesse Daniell, James Gill (I). Proved in Orangeburgh District by the oath of Jesse Daniel 28 May 1774 before William Tucker, J.P. Recorded 8 Sept 1774.

M-4, 213-217: Lease & release. 21 & 22 March 1774, Moses Kirkland of Ninety Six District, Sc, Esquire, to James Daniell of Camden District, planter, for £2000 SC money, 150 acres on a branch of Clouds Creek which runs into little Salludy River, plat and grant recorded in Book VV, page 139, granted 16 Jan 1761 to Lenud Sumott, and conveyed 12 & 13 Dec 1772 to said Moses Kirkland. Moses Kirkland (LS), Wit: Jesse Daniell, Frederick Williams. Proved in Orangeburgh District before William Tucker, J.P., 28 May 1774. Recorded 9 Sept 1774.

M-4, 217-219: 5 June 1771, William Bampfield of Charles Town, Merchant, to David Maull of Charles Town, taylor, for £300 SC money, lot on Charles Town Neck, number 139, in Hampstead. Wm. Bampfield (LS), Wit: Wm. Leitz, Thos Watson. Proved by the oath of Thos Watson, 24 Jan 1772 before And. Cunningham.

SOUTH CAROLINA DEED ABSTRACTS 1773-1778

M-4, 220-223: Lease & release. 11 & 12 Dec 1772, David Anderson of Province of Georgia, planter, by virtue of a power of attorney 19 Feb 1772 from John Jones deceased, to James Bradley, of St. Marks Parish, SC, planter, for ten shillings, 60 acres in Craven County granted to John Jones 13 Apr 1750. David Anderson (LS), Wit: Edward Ball, Jonathan Searth, John Freeman. Proved in Christ Church Parish, Georgia, 14 Dec 1772 before Joseph Ottolinjke, J.P., by the oath of Edward Ball. Recorded 9 Sept 1774.

M-4, 223-228: Lease & release. 6 & 7 May 1772, Thomas Howse of Craven County, SC, planter, and Elizabeth his wife, to James Bradley of same, planter, for ten shillings, 200 acres in Craven County on north side Main Swamp of Black River adj. land of Peter Mellet, John Jones. Thomas Howse (LS), Elizabeth Howse (LS), Wit: William Gordon, Saml McKay, Martha McKay (P). Proved 30 June by the oath of William Gordon before Henry Cassels, J.P. for Camden District. Recorded 11 Sept 1774.

M-4, 228-233: Lease & release. 22 & 23 Apr 1773, Alexander Sypit of Berkley County, SC, to William Laws of same, for £250 SC money, 250 acres in Craven County Little Pedee at a place called Reedy Creek, granted to said Alexander Sypit in 1756. Alex'r Sypit (LS), Wit: Peter Sandel, John Sandel. Proved by the oath of Peter Sandel before John Troupe, J.P., 11 May 1773. Recorded 12 Sept 1774.

M-4, 233-239: Lease & release. 16 & 17 May 1774, William Murphey of Charles Town, to David Baty of Charles Town, merchant, for £750 SC money, 750 acres in the District of Orangeburgh on the North Branch of Edisto River adj. land laid out to John Summers, John Johnston, granted 7 May 1774. Wm. Murphey (LS), Wit: John Fisher, Thos Tod. Proved in Charles Town District by the oath of Thomas Tod, 11 July 1774, before William Rugeley, J.P. Recorded 12 Sept 1774.

M-4, 239-242: Lease & release. 6 & 7 July 1774, John Rosewell of Charles Town, to John Fisher of Town, cabinet maker, for £600 SC money, 600 acres in the District of Orangeburg on a branch of Edisto River adj. John Johnston, John Fisher. John Rosewell (LS), Wit: James French, Thos Tod. Proved 9 July 1774 before George Davidson, J.P. in Berkley County, by the oath of Thos Tod. Recorded 13 Sept 1774.

M-4, 243-249: Lease & release. 20 & 21 Feb 1769, Lewis Mouzon of St. Thomas Parish, SC, planter, and Susanna Elizabeth his wife, to Benjamin Wigfall of Christ Church Parish, gentleman, for £6000 SC money, 450 acres in St. Thomas Parish whereon the sd. Lewis Mouzon now Lives or Late did not thereon, adj. land of John Daniel, William Simmons, Henry Boneau, which have been lately settled by an instrument dated 16 July 1768. Lewis Mouzon (LS), Susanna Eliz'a Mouzon (LS), Wit: Jos. Maybank, Levi Durand, Henry Mouzon Junr. Recorded 27 Sept 1774.

M-4, 249-253: Lease & release. 11 & 12 March 1772, John Calhoun Senr. of the Settlement of Long Cane to William Hutton of same settlement, wheel wright, for £350 SC money, by grant dated 22 Jan 1759 to Ezekiel Cahoun, 100 acres known by the name of the Rockey Spring in the Long cane Settlement on a branch of the northwest fork of Long Cane adj. land lately laid out to James Carruth, Patrick Calhoun, James Noble. John Calhoun (LS), Wit: Alexr Noble, Joseph Calhoun. Proved 12 March 1772 by the oath of Alex'r Noble before Wm. Calhoun, J. P. Recorded 28 Sept 1774.

M-4, 253-257: 17 Feb 1774, James Higgs of St. Marks Parish, Craven County, to James Martimer Harris and Charles Haris of Charles Town, Berkley County, for £200 SC money, 400 acres in St. Marks parish on Forcau Swamp north side of Santee River in Craven County, granted by Gov. William Bull. James Higs (I) (LS), Wit: Thos Wise, John Wise, James Frazer. Proved 26 March 1774 before Ephraim Mitchell, J.P. in Berkley County, by the oath of Thos Wise. Recorded 28 Sept 1774.

M-4, 258-262: 29 Nov 1773, Joseph Bee and his wife Elizabeth of Charles Town, Berkley County, to James Mortimer Harris and Charles Harris of Charles Town, for £80 SC money, 450 acres in St. Marks Parish of Tocco Swamp a branch of Santee River in Craven County adj. land granted to James Higgs, land laid out to John Wise. Joseph Bee (LS), Elizabeth Bee (LS), Wit: Ephraim

SOUTH CAROLINA DEED ABSTRACTS 1773-1778

Mitchell, William Bee. Proved 16 July 1774 before Hopkin Price, J. P. in Berkley County, by the oath of Ephraim Mitchell, Esqr. Recorded 30 Sept 1774.

M-4, 262-266: 7 June 1774, Henry Hyrne of St. Bartholomews Parish, SC, Gentleman, to Jeremiah Miles, Josiah Miles, and Allen Miles of same province, planters, for £100 SC money, lot of land number 8 at the Publick Land Place usually called Collo. Hyrnes Landing at the head of Ashepoo River adj. land of said Henry Hyrne. Henry Hyrne (LS), Wit: Patrick Turnbull, John Ladson, Saml Shaw. Proved 7 June 1774 by the oath of all three witnesses before John Hunt, J.P. Recorded 30 Sept 1774.

M-4, 266-273: Lease & release. 2 & 3 Feb 1774, Peter Taylor of White haven, County of Cumberland, Kingdom of Great Britain, Esqr., by Thomas Smith and Benjamin Smith of Charles Town, his lawfull attorneys, to Elizabeth Ladson of St. Andrews parish, widow, for £8050 SC money, whereas Peter Taylor Esqr. late of the Parish of St. James Goose Creek deceased was possessed of lands commonly called War Hall Plantation in St. Pauls Parish, Colleton County, and by his last will and testament 1 July 1765, did bequeath all of his estate real and personal in which the said plantation was included unto his nephew Peter Taylor of Whitehaven, and by his special letter of attorney 8 Feb 1773 did appoint Thomas Smith and Benjamin Smith his attorneys. Peter Taylor by Thos Smith & Benjamin Smith, Wit: John Neufville, Wm. Henry Harvey. Proved by the oath of William Henry Harvey 20 July 1774 before Wm. Burrows. Recorded 3 Oct 1774.

M-4, 275-279: Lease & release. Elizabeth Ladson of St. Andrews Parish, to Melcher Garner of same province, planter, for £1419, tract of 260 acres part of tract granted for 500 acres to one John Pendarvis and which with divers other tracts or parts of tracts called Warhall plantation, lately sold and conveyed to said Elizabeth Ladson by Peter Taylor of Whitehaven. Elizabeth Ladson (LS), Wit: Robert Miles, Jno Calcock. Proved in Charles Town District by the oath of John Colcock before Thos Phepoe, J.P., 20 July 1774. Recorded 4 Oct 1774.

M-4, 279-282: 5 Sept 1772, Benjamin Coward & Elizabeth his wife of Craven County, SC, to John Durin of same county, for ten shillings, tract of 100 acres on Little Flat Rock Creek. Benjn Coward (LS), Eliz'th Coward (LS), Wit: James Coward, Wm. Offill, Joshua Coward. Recorded 5 Oct 1774.

M-4, 282-285: Lease & release. 1 & 2 June 1774, Michell Duvall of District of Ninety Six, planter, to Francis Salvador for £650 SC money, 300 acres above a place called Ninety Six. Michel Duval (LS), Wit: H. DeLeigler, Andrew Williamson. Proved in Ninety Six District 4 July 1774 before Alexander Cameron, J.P., by the oath of H. DeLeighler. Recorded 5 Oct 1774.

M-4, 286-290: Lease & release. 16 & 17 May 1774, Joseph Salvador of London, Great Britain, Esqr., by Richard Andrews Rapley, his attorney by letters of attorney dated 6 Oct 1773, to Francis Salvador late of Twickenham in the County of Middlesex but now of Province aforesaid, Esqr., 921 acres above Ninety Six, part of 100,000 acres granted in two tracts of 50,000 acres to William Levingstone, Esqr. Joseph Salvador (LS), Wit: Thos Sanders, John Gaw. Proved in Ninety Six District 11 June 1774 before John Bowie, J.P., by the oath of Thomas Sanders. Recorded 6 Oct 1774.

M-4, 290-292: 4 Apr 1732, the Reverend Alexander Garden, the Honourable John Fenwicke, Alexander Parrish and Eleazer Allen, Esquire, Commissioners for building and finishing the new church of St. Philip Charles Town and for erecting pews and seats therein, to Jacob Motte & Robert Austin, Churchwardens, his Excellency Robert Johnston, Esqr., the Rev. Alexander Garden, Samuel Prioleau, Benjamin DHarriette, Daniel Greene, William Yeomans, Thomas Fairchild & Gabriel Manigault, Vestry men of the second part, and Hugh Evans, Taylor, and Phillip Massey, Gunsmith, both of Charles Town, of the third part, for £30 SC money, pew number one in the gallery. Recorded 6 Oct 1774.

M-4, 292-293: Hugh Evans, Taylor, of Charles Town, for £10 SC money, to Phillip Massey, Gunsmith, half of a pew in the north gallery number one, dated 16 March 1732. Wit: Jos. Massey, John Milner. Recorded 6 Oct 1774.

SOUTH CAROLINA DEED ABSTRACTS 1773-1778

M-4, 293-294: 27 Nov 1773, Jane Massey of Charles Town, widow & Executrix of the last will and testament of Phillip Massey, Gunsmith, dated 28 July 1739, to Robert Beard, tin plate worker, for £100, pew number one. Jane Massey (LS), Wit: Elizabeth Collis, Ann Collis. Recorded 7 Oct 1774.

M-4, 294-295: 1 Jan 1774, Robert Beard of Charles Town, tin plate worker, to Henry Calwell of Charles Town, Shop keeper, for £200 SC money, pew number one in St. Philips Church. Robert Beard (LS), Wit: Will Beard, T. Falconer. Recorded 7 Oct 1774.

M-4, 295-302: Lease & release. 1 & 2 July 1772, Daniel Strobel of St. Bartholomews Parish, Colleton Co., planter, and Mary Elizabeth his wife, to Lewis Stapf of same, carpenter, for £750 SC money, 375 acres granted to Mathew Beard in Prince Williams Parish, Granville County, being one quarter of half moiety of the tract adj. Jacob Zahler, Saltcatcher River, land granted to James Ferguson. Daniel Strobel (LS), Mary Eliz'th Strobel (LS), Wit: John Brown, Thomas Patterson. Proved by the oath of Thomas Patterson, before Stephen Bull, J. P. in Granville county, 22 Aug 1772. Recorded 8 Oct 1774.

M-4, 303-308: Lease & release. 29 & 30 Aug 1768, Michael Dukes of St. Georges Parish, Berkley County, Sc, planter, to Barbary Dukes his mother of same place, gentlewoman, for £50 SC money, 100 acres in Berkley County adj. land of John Faree, land granted to William Aldridge, it being one half or moiety of 200 acres granted to Joseph Dukes the father of said michael Dukes 3 Sept 1758, recorded in Book SS, page 428 [plat included in deed]. Michael Dukes (LS), Wit: Ronald M'Donald, William M'Kenzie, George Andally. Proved 25 June 1774 before Christopher Rowe, J.P. in Orangeburgh District by the oath of George Andally. Recorded 10 Oct 1774.

M-4, 308-311: 30 Apr 1773, Joseph Nobles and Winifred Nobles his wife of Craven County, to John and William Rogers of same, for £300 SC money, 300 acres granted 19 Nov 1772 to Winifred Rogers, on high hills of Santee in Craven County, St. Marks Parish, adj. William and John Wheeler, John Michell, Jas McCormick, John James, David Laird, now Joseph Nobles and Winefred his wife who the said land was granted to in her widowhood which he has obtained by marriage. Joseph Nobles (LS), Winifred Nobles (X), (LS), Wit: Jas McCormick, Alice Pittman, William Mitchell. Proved before Wood Furman, J. P. for Craven County, by the oath of James McCormick, 19 Jan 1774. Recorded 10 Oct 1774.

M-4, 311-314: 21 Oct 1773, William Haggins and Mary his wife of Mecklingburg County, North Carolina, to William Porter of same, for £500 SC currency, tract granted to William Edday for 600 acres 18 Nov 1752 and part was by him conveyed to Mathew Gillaspy and part conveyed by Edday to Robert Barkley 10 Oct 1765, and also conveyed to William Haggins and part conveyed to Haggins from Hugh Nelson, 150 acres, part of 600 acres., on both sides Twelve Mile Creek. William Hagans (LS), Mary Hagans (LS), Wit: John Drennan, William Linn, Wm. Davies. Proved by the oath of William Davies before James Patton, J.P., 29 July 1774. Recorded 10 Oct 1774.

M-4, 314-318: 14 Sept 1764, Daniel Doyley, late Provost Marshall of South Carolina, Esqr., to James Laroach of same, planter, whereas Samuel Wincorne deceased in his life time and at the time of his death was possessed of several plantations and John Beswick, William Greenwood, and William Higgenson, in the court of common pleas did implead Benjamin Stiles, exr. of last will and testament of said Saml. Wincorne for the recovery of debt of £16,612 one shilling and d2½, Daniel Doyley did expose to public sale 30 Sept in Charlestown and sold to James Laroach for £1660 s4 SC money, 258 acres in St. Johns Parish Colleton County on Leadenwah Creek adj. land of Samuel Wincorne and Thomas Wincorne, Joseph Pheps, and a tract of 222 acres on south west part of Wadmelaw Island in Colleton County, part of tract of 1060 granted to Paul Hamilton since deceased adj. land of John Gibbons, Robert Sams, William Gibbons, and all that half part of 400 acres divided to said Samuel Wincorne by his father Thomas Wincorne by will 14 Apr 1753. Daniel Doyley (LS), Wit: Hugh Rutledge, Alexr Harvey. Proved in Chas Town District by the oath of Hugh Rutledge before William Rugeley, J.P., 3 Aug 1774. Recorded 11 Oct 1774.

M-4, 319-324: Lease & release. 18 & 19 Jan 1773, John Cole of Berkly County, Gentn, to David Mull, Taylor, for £20 SC money, 250 acres in Berkley County on NE side Edisto River granted 11 May 1772. John Cole (LS), Wit: John McLean, John Douglass. Proved 5 Aug 1774 before Thomas Turner, J. P. in Charles Town District by the oath of John McLean. Recorded 12 Oct 1774.

SOUTH CAROLINA DEED ABSTRACTS 1773-1778

M-4, 324-330: Lease & release. 26 & 27 May 1774, William Levingston of Charles Town, Merchant, Eldest son and Heir at Law of George Levingston late of same place, merchant, deceased, to James Gorden of George Town, merchant, for £3000 SC money, 1050 acres in Craven County on Northeast side Peedee adj. land of Daniel Britton, granted 16 Dec 1736 granted to Sarah Caswell and at her death descended to Thomas Sacheverall her nephew & Heir at Law who by conveyed to George Levingston. Wm. Levingston (LS), Wit: Alexr Chovin, John Smith. Proved by the oath of John Smith 5 Aug 1774 before William Rugeley, J.P. Recorded 13 Oct 1774.

M-4, 330-334: 26 June 1770, John Clarke of Tryon County, North Carolina, to Thomas Wade of Craven County, SC, Esqr., for £500 SC money, tract on north side of Great Peedee River. John Clarke (LS), Wit: George Wilson, Peter Marsales. Proved in Charaw District by the oath of George Wilson before Saml Spencer, J.P., 25 June 1774. Recorded 13 Oct 1774.

M-4, 334-338: Lease & release. 15 & 16 Aug 1758, Joseph Nelson and Mary his wife of Savannah River in Granville County, SC, planter, to Elias Hallion of said province, for £100 SC money, 100 acres in Granville County granted to James Dyer adj. Savannah River, Joseph Nelsons land, granted 9 Jan 1752. Joseph Nelson (J) (LS), Mary Nelson (X) (LS), Wit: James Bobby, Benjamin Hide (BH). Proved by the oath of James Bobby before Come't Cook, 7 Jan 1760. Recorded 14 Oct 1774.

M-4, 338-339: 14 July 1774, Thomas Wade to Samuel Wise, for £800 SC money, 400 acres on No side of Pee Dee, granted to said Thomas Wade 17 May 1766. Thos Wade (LS), Wit: Hol'n Wade, William Hardick. Proved in Charraw District by the oath of William Hardick 14 July 1774 before Claudius Pegues. Recorded 14 Oct 1774.

M-4, 340-341: 14 July 1774, Thomas Wade to Samuel Wise, for £874 SC money, 350 acres in Craven County on No side of Pee Dee, adj. Claudius Pegues, Clarks land, part of 500 acres granted to said John Clark by North Carolina 26 June 1770. Thomas Wade (LS), Wit: Hol'n Wade, William Hardik. Proved in Charraw District by the oath of William Hardick 14 July 1774 before Claudius Pegues. Recorded 14 Oct 1774.

M-4, 341-348: Lease & release. 10 & 11 Aug 1774, John Mathews of Charles Town, SC, Esqr., eldest son and heir at law of John Mathews late of said province, gentleman, deceased, to Thomas Farr the younger of the said town, gentleman, for £1100, whereas William Branford late of St. Andrews Parish, planter, deceased, and Elizabeth his wife by lease and release 30 & 31 Oct 1752, in publick registers office Book NN, page 203-211, to Anthony Mathews now deceased, and John Mathews the father of said John Mathews now also deceased, a tract of 280 acres on south side of Ashley River in Parish of St. Andrews, Berkley County, adj. Ashley Ferry Path and land late of William Miles deced, lands then of said William Branford but now of John Lloyd, Esqr., land formerly of Benjamin Stanyarn deceased, and said William Miles deceased; for the better support of Elizabeth Holmes late Smith the sister of said William Branford during her natural life and after her death then any of the children of her body, but for want of such surviving children of said ElizaBeth Holmes late Smith and said Elizabeth Holmes departed this life 20 May last leaving issue of her body and said plantation became absolutely vested in said Anthony Mathews and john Mathews and their heirs, and said John Mathews as heir at law to his late Father said John Mathews survived said Anthony Mathews. Jno Mathews (LS), Wit: Simon Tufts, Martin Miller. Proved in Chs Town District by the oath of Simon Tufts before William Rugeley, J.P., 11 Aug 1774. Recorded 18 Oct 1774.

M-4, 348-353: Lease & bond. 10 & 11 Apr 1772, John Gutzman of Charles Town, SC, victualler, to Hon. Othniel Beal of same, Esqr., bound in the sum of £4000 SC money, now for debt or said sum of £2000,lot on west side of King Street adj. land late of Edward Bullard deceased. John Gutzman (mark) (LS), Mary Gutzman (LS), Wit: John Dart, John Herman Nufer. Proved by the oath of John Herman Nufer, 29 June 1774, before Fenwick Bull, J.P. Recorded 18 Oct 1774.

M-4, 353-358: Lease & release. 31 Aug & 1 Sept 1771, James Verree of City and County of Burlington, in the western Division of the Province of New Jersey, House Carpenter, to Stephen Duvall of Charles Town, pilot, for £2800 SC money, part of a lot which said James Verree formerly purchased of William Chapman, adj. Church St., Paul Hamiltons corner. James Verree (LS), Wit: Joseph Verree, John James. Recorded 18 Oct 1774.

SOUTH CAROLINA DEED ABSTRACTS 1773-1778

M-4, 358-362: Lease & release. 24 & 25 May 1774, Joseph Salvador of London, by Richard Andrews Rapley his attorney, to Mathew Edwards of District of Ninety Six, planter, for £2270 SC money, 1480 acres above a place called Ninety Six part of 100,000 acres granted in two tracts of 50,000 acres to William Livingston, Esqr. Joseph Salvador (LS), Wit: Thomas Sanders, John Gaw. (Plat included). Proved in Ninety six District 8 July 1774 before Alexander Cameron, Esqr., by the oath of Thomas Sanders. Recorded 19 Oct 1774.

M-4, 362-366: Lease & release. 20 & 21 June 1774, Joseph Salvador of London, by Richard Andrews Rapley his attorney, to Andrew Williamson of District of Ninety Six, planter, for £2916 SC money, 1090 acres above a place called Ninety Six part of 100,000 acres granted in two tracts of 50,000 acres to William Livingston, Esqr. Joseph Salvador (LS), Wit: Thomas Sanders, John Gaw. (Plat included). Proved in Ninety Six District 8 July 1774 before Alexander Cameron, Esqr., by the oath of Thomas Sanders. Recorded 20 Oct 1774.

M-4, 366-370: Lease & release. 12 & 13 July 1774, George Rintz of Parish of St. Bartholomew, Charles Town District, late Taylor but now an over---, and his wife, to Christian Gruber of King Street, Charles Town, Tavern Keeper, eight lots in town of Jacksonburough Pon Pon [numbers included] conveyed to use in February 1773 by Lewis Stapf and Margaret his wife recorded March 1774. George Rintz (LS), Margret Rintz (X) (LS), Wit: Martin Miller, Laz'r Bryers. Proved 12 Aug 1774 before Fenwick Bull, J.P., by the oath of Martin Miller. Recorded 21 Oct 1774.

M-4, 371-373: 24 Jan 1774, John Stephens, son and heir at law of Martha Stephens late of Black Mingo in SC, Israel Jacobs of the County of Philadelphia, Pennsylvania, said Martha Stephens formerly Martha Mourey one of the daughters of Elizabeth Pierce who was a daughter of George Hutchinson, who formerly resided in West New Jersey, by virtue of the last will and testament of said George Hutcheson by virtue of a quit claim and release from Anthony Morris of philadelphia date 17 Nov 1716 as attorney to George Hutcheson of London, Peruke maker, grandson and heir at law of said George Hutcheson became seized of a part of the estate of George Hutcheson in West New Jersey, and said Martha Stephens by her deed 10 Sept 1768 did sell unto Joseph Jacobs of the County of Philadelphia merchant, brother of Israel Jacobs, and said Martha Stephens claims an undivided part of the estate of George Hutcheson by him bequeathed to the children of his daughter Elizabeth Pence... said Joseph Jacobs who is deceased sold to Israel Jacobs to James Verree of Burlington. John Stephens (LS), Wit: Edward Martin, William Mason. Proved in George Town District before Job Rothmahler, 12 July 1774, by the oath of William Mason, Esqr. Recorded 22 Oct 1774.

END OF BOOK M-4.

SOUTH CAROLINA DEED ABSTRACTS 1773-1778

N-4, 1-4: The Creek Indian Nation. 27 Aug 1772, wee the Kings head men & warriors of the Whole Creek Nation Whose names are seals are hereunto subscribed to our beloved sister Matawny Daughter to the Great Warrior of the Cowetaws called Justonogcy Micco of the same nation and her three children Judeth, George, and John, for natural love and affection, to the said Matawny and her children and future issue legitimate or natural, all our share in the rest of the lands claimed by or belonging to the Creek Indian nation, tract between Great Ogechee and Little Ogechee from the fork of said Rivers up to pen branches or pen Creek and the Eutchee path. Hed warer Lettete (LS), Sim Poffey (LS), Sallegia the Leading waror (LS), Young Leftenent (LS), Cu Se how warer (LS), Blue Salt King Cuetaws (LS), Old Ned of Cowtaws (LS), Heaed Warer of Little Town (LS), Tallafia king (LS), Chaetabea warrer (LS), Head Warrer of Para Chokters (LS), Head warer of parce choek larse[?] (LS), Cheroling King (LS), Euchees King (LS), Wit: John Miller, Thos Townsend, Benj Stedham, Stephens Forester (SF). Proved in Granville County, SC, by the oath of John Miller before John Dick, 30 Nov 1772. On 15 Feb 1773 full possession was taken of the land by the young Lieutenant and delivered over to Matawney, Judith, George and John. Young Lieutenant (mark), John Milar, Robt. Tooly, Benjamin Stedham, James McQueen, Stephen Forister (S). Wit: John Pigg interpreter, Samuel Montgomery, Patrick Carr. Proved in St. Pauls Parish, Georgia, before William Harding, J. P., by the oath of John Pigg, 9 June 1774. Recorded 7 Sept 1774.

N-4, 4-9: Lease & release. 10 & 11 July 1774, Robert Bowman and Milicen his wife of Craven County, SC, to James Hopper of same, for £2000 SC money, 400 acres in Craven County on north side Santee River & on the said river swamp adj. land of Richard Middleton. Robt. Bowman (LS), Melecen Bowman (X) (LS), Wit: Wm. Luten, James Bowman. Proved in Camden District 23 July 1774 by the oath of James Bowman before Thomas Sumpter, J.P. Recorded 7 Oct 1774.

N-4, 9-12: 3 March 1770, Henry Laurens of Charles Town, SC, Esqr., to Jeremiah Sharp of same, carpenter, for £350 SC money, lot on Charles Town Neck number 78 in Hamstead on Bull Street. Henry Laurens, Wit: Philip Hawkins, Joseph Verre, Jeremiah Sharp. Proved 1 Aug 1774 by the oath of Joseph Verree before Robt. Pringle, J. P. for Charles Town District. Recorded 10 Oct 1774.

N-4, 12-18: Lease & release. 4 & 5 Aug 1774, David Maul of Charles Town, Taylor, to Edward Shrewbury, Shipwright, for £500 SC money, 250 acres on North East side of Edisto River granted by George III 11 May 1772. David Maull (LS), Wit: James Pritchard, Eliza Ann Pritchard. Proved 5 Aug 1774 before Thomas Turner, J. P. in Charles Town District, by the oath of James Prichard. Recorded 12 Oct 1774.

N-4, 18-21: 20 Oct 1770, Jas Wilkins of Parish of St. Mark in Craven County, planter, and his wife whose name before her marriage was Elizabeth White but is now Elizabeth Wilkins, to John Morrow of same parish, for £50 100 acres granted 12 Aug 1768 to Elizabeth White in parish of St. Marks on waters of Rocky Creek in Craven County adj. Robert McCarey. James Wilkins, Elizabeth White (X), Wit: Saml Morrow, Wm. White. Proved in Camden District by the oath of Samuel Morrow before John Gaston, J. P., 3 June 1774.

N-4, 21-23: 8 Feb 1774, Abraham Wright and Margaret his wife of St. Marks Parish, Craven county, to John Bull of same, planter, for £225 SC money, 100 acres granted 2 March 1768 on the Bounty to Margret Campbell now Margaret right wife of said Abraham Wright, said 100 acres on branch of Rocky Creek in Craven county vacant on all sides. Abraham Wright (LS), Wit: Thos Morton, Wm. Moris. Proved in Camden District by the oath of Thos morton before John Gaston, J.P., 6 June 1774. Recorded 12 Oct 1774.

N-4, 23-26: 23 Feb 1774, Caleb Smith of Craven County, SC, planter, to David Nickels of same, planter, for £100 SC money, 100 acres on Rocky Creek being Ten feet wide and nine inches deep adj. Hugh Wilson, granted 26 Sept 1772 to Caleb Smith. Caleb Smith (LS), Wit: John Bell, John Kell, Arthur Scott. Proved by the oath of John Bell before John Gaston, J. P., 13 June 1774. Recorded 13 Oct 1774.

N-4, 26-28: 24 Oct 1770, Robert McCreary of Craven County, SC, planter, and Mary his wife to John Morrow Junr of same, planter, for £300 SC money, 100 acres on Rockey Creek, a branch of

SOUTH CAROLINA DEED ABSTRACTS 1773-1778

of Catawba River granted to Robert McCreary 3 May 1764. Robt McCreary (LS), Mary McCreary (LS), Wit: James Wylie, John Fortune, Peter Wylie. Proved by the oath of James Wylie before John Gaston, J. P., 3 June 1774.

N-4, 29-33: Lease & release. 11 & 12 Apr 1758, James Dyer of Savanna River, Granville County, SC, and Elizabeth his wife, to Joseph Nelson of same county, for £100 SC money, 100 acres part of a tract granted to said James Dyer on Savanna River adj. Joseph Nelsons land, granted 9 June 1752. James Dyer (LS), Elizabeth Dyer (X) (LS), Wit: Benjamin Hide (BH), Thos Loyd. Proved 17 Oct 1758 in Granville County by the oath of Benjamin Hide before Anthony Grobbs. Recorded 14 Oct 1774.

N-4, 33-38: Lease & release. 1 & 2 Jan 1774, Parker Quince of Brunswick County, North Carolina, Esqr., and Susanah his wife, to Jacob Tobias of Charles Town, esqr., for £3100 SC money, lot in Charles Town on Hasell Street which said lot was a part of a lot in a plan of a writ of partition between said Parker Quince and Susannah his wife and John Ancrum & Mary his wife dated 18 Sept 1773. Parker Quince (LS), Susanna Quince (LS), Wit: Saml Dwight, Wm. Lord. Acknowledged in the presence of James Clitherall, George Ancrum. Proved by the oath of George Ancrum, 6 Aug 1774 before John Troup, J.P. Recorded 18 Oct 1774.

N-4, 39-42: Lease & release. 3 & 4 Dec 1771, John McDonald of Craven County, planter, to Evan Pugh of same, clerk, for £60 SC money, 200 acres in Craven County granted 22 Aug 1771 to John McDonald adj. Jolly Webbs land, Evan Pugh, David Williams. John McDonald (LS), Wit: Robt Thompson, Martin Kolb, Jeremiah Briant (mark). Proved by the oath of Martin Kolb 2 July 1772 before Arthur Hart, J.P. Recorded 29 Oct 1774.

N-4, 43-48: Lease & release. 28 & 29 Aug 1773, John Hall of Charles Town, Gent., to Thomas Karwon of St. Thomas Parish, for £7000 SC money, 925 acres in St. Thomas Parish in three tracts adj. Samuel Simmons, Mrs. Bremar, land now or late of Francis Varambo, John Pagett, Mr. Danniley, Francis Pagett, Mrs. Bonneau, henry Videau, Doctor Dallas, Capt. Anthony Bonneau. John Hall (LS), Wit: George Sheed, William Sheed. Recorded 22 Oct 1774. Proved by the oath of George Sheed 6 Nov 1777 before Wm. Nisbett. Recorded 12 Nov 1777.

N-4, 48-53: Lease & release. _____ 1774, Margaret Brown the present wife of George Rentz and her husband the said George Rentz of St. Bartholomews Parish, Colleton County, planter, to George Smith of same, for £20 SC money, 100 acres on Bigg Wolf Creek adj. Mr. Sneashes land. George Rentz (LS), Margaret Rentz (LS), Wit: Samuel Youse, George Kling (X). Proved by the oath of Samuel Youse before James Stobo, J.P., 26 March 1774. Recorded 24 Oct 1774.

N-4, 53-59: Lease & release. 22 & 23 Jan 1774, James Thompson and Ann his wife of St. Bartholomews Parish, Colleton County, surveyor, to George Smith of same place, for £325 SC money, 350 acres originally granted to Richard Woodcraft the other part of 100 acres granted to said James Thompson on Hors Pen Bay. James Thompson (LS), Ann Thompson (LS), Wit: Joseph Koger, Samuel Yous, Samuel Sleigh. Proved by the oath of Samuel Yous 26 March 1774 before James Stobo, J.P. Recorded 26 Oct 1774.

N-4, 59-62: 6 Sept 1774, Mary McClinton of Prov. of SC, to Robert Crabb of Charles Town, for £115 SC money, 200 acres in Amelia Township, Berkley County, adj. Morris OHerins, Thomas Parks, George Kerleys. Mary McClinton (X) (LS), Robert Crabb. Wit: Ezekiel Townsend, Bernd. McGuckin. Proved in Berkley County by the oath of Bernard McGuckin before Thomas Phepoe, J.P., 13 Sept 1774. Recorded 28 Oct 1774.

N-4, 62-69: Lease & release. 20 & 21 March 1772, Elias Horry of Parish of St. James Santee in Craven County, SC, Esqr., to Thomas Horry of same, planter, for £5 SC money, 300 acres granted to Daniel Huger 14 Oct 1696 on Santee River on Wambaw Creek and Wattohan Creek; 160 acres granted to Daniel Huger 2 Feb 1704 adj. Daniel; 230 acres granted to Daniel Huger 14 Sept 1705 on Wambaw Creek; 500 acres granted to Daniel Huger 15 Sept 1714; all that plantation 300 acres excepted tract of 620 acres on north and south branches of Santee River known by the name of the fork Island, granted to Susanah Mayrant 7 Jan 1736 adj. Daniel Horry. Elias Horry (LS), Wit: Harriott Horry, Wm. Anderson. Proved in Craven County by the oath of William Anderson before

SOUTH CAROLINA DEED ABSTRACTS 1773-1778

Danl Horry, 22 March 1772. Recorded 29 Oct 1774. (Plats included indicating adj. land owners J. Mazick and D. Huger.)

N-4, 69-76: Lease & release. 29 & 30 May 1747, William Hancock of Berkley County, SC, Gent., eldest son and heir at law as well as one of the devisees of the last will and testament of Elias Hancock late of Charles Town, vintner, and Mary his wife, & Robert Hancock of Colleton County, Planter, to Francis Baker of Charles Town, mercht., for £605 SC money; whereas said Elias Hancock was in his life time seized of a lot in Charles Town, Number 194, and about 20 Nov 1729 make his will and bequeathed to his only daughter Deborah all the pat of a town lot, number 194, and if she should dye without issue then to be equally divided between the rest of his children, and she died without issue and likewise Elias Hancock Junr another son died without issue and Mary Hancock widow and relict are both dead, said William and Robert being the only surviving children. Will Hancock (LS), Mary Hancock (LS), Robert Hancock (LS), Mary Hancock (LS), Wit: Frederick Grimkey, Thos Lamboll. Proved in Charles Town Dist. by the oath of Frederick Grimkey before Thomas Bee, J.P., 25 Oct 174. Recorded 1 Nov 1774.

N-4, 76-79: 28 July 1774, John Hunter of Barkley County, to Joseph Burton, hatter, of same county, for £100 SC money, 100 acres in Berkly County on north side Enoree River on a small branch adj. land of Wm. Cannon, Robert Hanna, originally granted to Isaac Gray and by said Isaac Gray made over to John Hunter. John Hunter (LS), Susana Hunter (LS), Wit: George Dunrumple, James Slon, John Dunlap. Proved before Robert Cuningham, J. P., by the oath of John Dunlap, 15 Aug 1774. Recorded 1 Nov 1774.

N-4, 79-80: 5 Sept 1772, Benjamin Coward & Elizabeth his wife of Craven County, SC, to John Duren of same, for five shillings SC money, 100 acres in St. Marks Parish on Little Flat Rock Creek. Benjamin Coward (LS), Elizabeth Coward (X) (LS), Wit: James coward, William Offill, Joshua Coward (mark). Proved in Camden District before John Newman Oglethorpe, J. P., by the oath of James Coward, 20 Dec 1773. Recorded 2 Nov 1774.

N-4, 80-85: Lease & release. 2 & 3 Apr 1772, Mathew Ardis of Granville County, SC, and Christian his wife, to Valentine Linn, planter, for £100 SC money, 100 acres granted 1 Feb 1768 to Mathias Ardis near Savannah old Town in Granville County adj. Benjamin Tutt, Robert McMurdy. Mathias Ardis (MA) (LS), Christian Ardis (X) (LS) Wit: Abraham Onsel, Jacob Vies. Proved in Ninety Six District by the oath of Jacob Vies 29 Dec 1774 before John Dick, J.P. Recorded 4 Oct 1774.

N-4, 85-86, 92-94: Lease & release. 30 & 31 Dec 1773, Stephen Elmore on the waters of Bush Creek in Ninety Six District, SC, to Joseph Thompson, Tanner, of district and province aforesaid, for £700 SC money, 200 acres granted 2 Jan 1759 to Stephen Elmore in Berkley County on a branch of Bush Creek adj. land granted to Danl Campbell, grant recorded in Book TT, page 1. Stephen Elmore (LS), Sarah Elmore (LS), Wit: John Embree, John Turner, Saml Kelly. Proved in Ninety Six District by the oath of John Embree before Jonathan Downs, J. P., 14 Feb 1774. Recorded 8 Oct 1774.

N-4, 87-91: Lease & release. 30 & 31 Dec 1773, Stephen Elmore on the waters of Bush Creek in Ninety Six District, SC, to Joseph Thompson, Tanner, of district and province aforesaid, for £750 SC money, 200 acres granted 18 May 1771 to Stephen Elmore in Berkley County on a branch of Bush Creek adj. David Jenkins, Thomas Lewis[?], Cornelius Cochran, John Wilkesons, grant recorded in Book HHH, page 311. Stephen Elmore (LS), Sarah Elmore (LS), Wit: John Embree, John Turner, Saml Kelly. Proved in Ninety Six District by the oath of John Embree before Jonathan Downs, J. P., 14 Feb 1774. Recorded 7 Oct 1774.

N-4, 95-101: Lease & release. 26 & 27 Aug 1774, John Mills of Charles Town, Messinger of his Majestys Council, to William Carss of Charles Town, Master of the Free School, for five shillings, land granted 19 Nov 1774 to said John Mills, 250 acres in Colleton County on a Branch of Edisto River on Shaw Fork, adj. land surveyed for Andrew Lyme. John Mills (LS), Wit: Samuel Bansall, Robert Knox. Proved in Charles Town District before George Davidson, J. P., by the oath of Robert Knox, 27 Aug 1774. Recorded 10 Nov 1774.

SOUTH CAROLINA DEED ABSTRACTS 1773-1778

N-4, 101-105: Lease & release. 31 Aug & 1 Sept 1772, John Pittman of Barkley County, planter, to Elisha Haul of Craven County, for £100 SC money, 200 acres in Craven County on Reedy River a branch of Saluday, granted to sd. John Pittman. John Pittman (LS), Wit: John Davis, John Scudder. Proved 18 Jan 1773 before Jas. Lindley, J.P., by the oath of John Scudder. Recorded 11 Nov 1774.

N-4, 105-109: Lease & release. 3 & 4 Sept 1773, Newit Bearfoot of Craven County, SC, to John Payne of same, Blacksmith, for £300 SC money, 100 acres granted to Elizabeth Bearfoot 9 Jan 1752 then to William, Newit, and Noah Bearfoot on south side Wateree River grant recorded in Book NN folio 221, 200 acres of said tract conveyed to Jonathan Hill from William Bearfoot 11 March 1772. Newit Bearfoot (X) (LS), Wit: Thomas Jones, Richard Hoyle, Joseph Kirkland. Proved 1 Sept 1773 before John Newman Oglethorpe, J.P. in Camden District, by the oath of Richard Hoyle. Recorded 11 Nov 1774.

N-4, 110-117: Lease & release. 3 & 4 Apr 1764, James Parsons of Charles Town, SC, Esqr., and Susanna his wife, in trust to John Rutledge and Thomas Bee, Esqr., for ten shillings; James Parsons in right of the said Susanna his wife is possessed of the plantation and lott house, 745 acres in Colleton County granted 28 Apr 1733 to Jeremiah Miles the father of said Susanna adj. land formerly of Thomas Miles decd and now to John Miles, Dominy Hill, Joseph Miles, James Parsons, John Guerard, and lot in Charles Town number 71 conveyed by William Guy and Rebeca his wife 15 & 16 Jan 1734 to said Jeremiah Miles and by him his will dated 2 Feb 1736 bequeathed to said Susanna adj. to Robert Hume lately to Martha Fleming and now to the devisees under her will, lot formerly belonging to Jeremiah Miles and not to his grandson Robert Ladson. Jas Parsons (LS), John Rutledge (LS), Thomas Bee (LS), Wit: Mary Eliott Butler, Thomas Heyward, John Glen. Proved in Charles Town District by the oath of Thomas Heyward, 21 Aug 1774, before William Burrows, J.P. Recorded 14 Nov 1774.

N-4, 118-120: James Parsons and Susanah his wife by virtue of indenture 4 Apr 1764, conveyed plantation and lot, conveyed intrust to permit the said James Persons during the term of his natural life to occupy and receive the rents and profits, for the use of James O'Brien Parsons. Jas Parsons (LS), Susanna Parsons (LS), Wit: Jacob Read, Robert Ladson, Henry Nicholes. Proved in Charles Town District by the oath of Henry Nicholes before William Burrows, 23 Aug 1774. Recorded 14 Nov 1774.

N-4, 120-127: Lease & release. 20 & 21 June 1774, Isaac Mazyck and Paul Mazyck of Charles Town, Gentleman, sons and executors of the last will and testament of Isaac Mazyck late of Charles Town, decd., to Daniel Mazyck of Charles Town, Gentleman, for £2000 SC money, 450 acres in Craven County on east side Pee Dee River adj. land formerly belonging to William ____ Esqr., deceased and now belonging to Paul Mazyck, Revd. Thomas Morritt, granted from George II to Isaac Mazyck. Isaac Mazyck (LS), Paul Mazyck (LS), Wit: Christopher Holson, Robert Howard. Proved 21 Sept 1774 before William Rugeley by the oath of Robt. Howard. Recorded 15 Nov 1774.

N-4, 127-131: Lease & release. 22 & 23 June 1774, Daniel Mazyck of charles Town, Gentleman, to Paul Mazyck of Charles Town, gentleman, for £2000 SC money, 450 acres in Craven County on east side Pee Dee River adj. land formerly belonging to William Whitesides Esqr., deceased and now belonging to Paul Mazyck, Revd. Thomas Morritt, conveyed by exrs. of Isaac Mazyck. Daniel Mazyck (LS), Wit: Christopher Holson, Robert Howard. Proved 21 Sept 1774 before William Rugeley by the oath of Robt. Howard. Recorded 16 Nov 1774.

N-4, 132-136: Lease & release. 29 & 30 Sept 1769, John Rutledge of Charles Town, Esqr., and Elizabeth his wife, to James McKelvey of same province, planter, for £4000, 800 acres on north side Santee River in Craven County adj. land late of Thomas Lynch, James McKelvey; also 1000 acres in St. Johns Parish, Berkley County on Santee River, adj. said James McKelvey, said tracts conveyed by Tacitus Gaillard Esqr. and Ann his wife to said John Rutledge 22 & 23 Aug 1765. John Rutledge (LS), Elizabeth Rutledge (LS), Wit: Mary Fraser, Alexd. Fraser. Proved 27 May 1774 before Ephraim Mitchell, J. P. for Charles Town District, by the oath of ____ Fraser. Recorded 17 Nov 1774.

SOUTH CAROLINA DEED ABSTRACTS 1773-1778

N-4, 136-144: Lease & release. 28 & 29 Oct 1768, George Auston of Aston in the Parish of Shifaul in the County of Salop, Kingdom of Great Britain, by Josiah Smith the younger his attorney of Charles Town, to James McKelvey of Craven County, planter, for £1500 SC money, two tracts one on the north side and one on the south side of Santee River 200 acres adj. James Reid, Tacitus Gaillard and another 200 acres adj. Tacitus Gaillard, James McKelvey, Frenchs Barony, by power of attorney dated 26 Nov 1766 did appoint Gabriel Manigault, Robert Williams the younger and sd. Josiah Smith the younger his attorneys, recorded in Book MM page 608 in Secretarys Office. Geo Austin (LS) by Josiah Smith Junr, Wit: Wm. Banbury, Geo. Smith. Proved 27 May 1774 before Ephraim Mitchell by the oath of Wm. Banbury. Recorded 21 Nov 1774.

N-4, 144-148: Lease & release. 11 & 12 Aug 1774, Nathan Fowler of Enoree to Richard King of Turky Creek waters of Saludy River, planter, for £250 SC money, plantation now in the possession of Aaron Pinson the younger, 100 acres, on a branch of Saludy known by the name of Indian hutt branch in Berkley County. Nathan Fowler (LS), Wit: Samuel Neel, Richard Ratliff. Proved in Ninety Six District by the oath of Samuel Neal before Andrew Neel, Esqr., J.P., 20 Aug 1774. Recorded 21 Nov 1774.

N-4, 148-152: Lease & release. 5 July 1773, Benjamin Ogilvie of Craven county, planter, to Peter Pye of same, planter, for £100 SC money, 150 acres in Craven county adj. James Dozer, Peter Pye, granted 29 Feb 1772 to Benjamin Ogilvie. Benjamin Ogilvie (mark (LS), Martha Ogilvie (M) (LS), Wit: Richard Cain, John Olliver, Amos Gaskins (mark). Proved 2 Sept 1774 before Arther Hart, J. P., by the oath of Richard Cain. Recorded 22 Nov 1774.

N-4, 152-156: Lease & release. 3 & 4 Jan 1774, Patrick Morris of St. Marks Parish, planter, to John Rodgers of same, planter, for £35 SC money, 250 acres in Craven County on the branches of Sawneys Creek near a wolf pen on a path that goes from Daniel Robertson to Benjamin Simes granted to said Patrick Morris 5 May 1773. Patrick Morris (LS), Wit: William Downes, William Edwards, Simon Edwards (X). Proved 26 Sept 1774 before William Rugeley, J.P. in Charles Town District, by the oath of William Downes. Recorded 23 Nov 1774.

N-4, 156-162: Lease & release. 2 & 3 May 1774, Andrew Quelch of Christ Church Parish, planter, to William Downes of Charles Town, gentleman, for fifteen shillings, 200 acres in Berkley Count on Stono adj. Mr. Mellichamps land, Mr. Farrs land, and persons unknown, said 200 acres granted to said Andrew Quelch 21 Apr last. Andrew Quelch (LS), Wit: Thomas Winstanley, Charles Glover. Proved 2 June 1774 before Wm. Nisbett, J.P. in Charles Town District, by the oath of Thomas Winstanley. Recorded 24 nov 1774.

N-4, 162-168: Lease & release. 9 & 10 Aug 1770, John Stroble, Victualler, of Charles Town, to Michael Muckinfuse, Blacksmith, for £100 SC money, 250 acres on waters of Stephens Creek in Granville county granted to Frederick Stroble 13 Aug 1756 then bounding on all sides by vacant lands, memorial entered in book C No. 7, page 122, 14 May 1764. John Stroble (LS), Margaret Stroble (X) (LS), Wit: Denham Fearis, John Brolien. Proved 11 Aug 1770 before John Nevin, J.P. in Berkley County, by the oath of Denham Ferris. Recorded 27 Nov 1774.

N-4, 168-173: Lease & release. 7 & 8 Sept 1770, John Hume, overseer, of South Carolina to Michael Muckinfuse, Blacksmith, of Charles Town, for £27 SC money, 100 acres. John Hume (LS), Wit: Christian Gruber, Denham Fearis. Recorded 29 Nov 1774.

N-4, 173-179: Lease & release. 6 & 7 Sept 1770, Solomon Shinhur, farmer, of South Carolina to Michael Muckinfuse, Blacksmith, of Charles Town, for £45 SC money, 350 acres. Solom'n Shinhur (LS), Wit: Christian Gruber, James Starmonth. Recorded 30 Nov 1774.

N-4, 179-185: Lease & release. 7 & 8 Sept 1770, William Ekan Head, Ropemaker, to Michael Muckinfuse, Blacksmith, of Charles Town, for £70 SC money, 100 acres. Denham Fearis (LS) for William Ekan Head, Wit: John Hume. Recorded 1 Dec 1774.

N-4, 185-187: Georgia. 24 June 1768 before me personally appeared Margaret, wife of John Frentz of Savannah, relinquishes dower to a lease & release 25 & 26 Apr between John Frentz and

SOUTH CAROLINA DEED ABSTRACTS 1773-1778

Michael Muckinfuse, for tract of 200 acres in Craven county, South Carolina, before William Simpson. Recorded 2 Dec 1774.

N-4, 187-193: Lease & release. 25 & 26 Apr 1768, John Frentz, of Savannah, Province of Georgia, Peruke Maker, and his wife Margaret to Michael Muckinfuse, Blacksmith, for £14 Georgia money, 200 acres granted 21 Jan 1761 to John Frentz in the low ground of Santee River opposite Saxegotha Township, adj. land of James Randolph, John Martin, John Hills. John Frentz (LS), Marg't Frentz (LS), Wit: Leonard Badell, John Linder. Recorded 3 Dec 1774.

N-4, 194-200: Lease & release. 7 & 8 July 1772, William Catterton of Purysburg Township, Granville County, planter, to Michael Muckinfuse of Charles Town, Blacksmith, for £200 SC money, 250 acres in Granville county adj. Richard Salters, Dan Haywards, Mr. Middletons land, granted 4 Dec 1771 to Derrick Mannan and afterwards sold to Ephraim Ledbetter by sd. Mannan and lastly sold to William Catterton. William Catterton (LS), Wit: Christian Gruber. Recorded 6 Dec 1774.

N-4, 200-206: Lease & release. 25 & 26 May 1772, Ephraim Ledbetter of Granville County, Blacksmith, and Nemiah his wife, to William Catterton of same, for £250 SC money, 250 acres in Granville County adj. Richard Salters, Dan Hewards, Mr. Middletons land. Eph'm Ledbetter (LS), Wit: Alexander Wilkins, Derick Mannan. Proved 27 June 1772 before John Chisolm, J.P. in Granville County, by the oath of Derick Mannan. Recorded 8 Dec 1774.

N-4, 206-212: Lease & release. 1 & 2 Oct 1770, William Ruger of South Carolina, Shoemaker, and Christina his wife, to Michael Muckinfuse of Charles Town, Blacksmith, for £34, 350 acres in South Carolina. Wm. Ruger (LS), Christian Ruger (LS), Wit: Denham Fearis, Christian _____. Recorded 9 Dec 1774.

N-4, 212-219: Lease & release. 12 & 13 May 1774, Edward Gardner of Town of Beaufort in St. Helena Parish in Granville County, Beaufort District, cooper, & Alice his wife to John Iklar of same town, for £180 SC money, lot in Beaufort, number 150, on Scotts Street, granted to james Thomson in one grant with lot 131 on 7 Oct 1745. Edwd. Gardner (LS), Alice Gardner (X) (LS), Wit: Robert Orr, Abraham Shecut. Proved 14 May 1774 before Andrew Aggnew, J. P. in Beaufort District, by the oath of Robert Orr. Recorded 11 Dec 1774.

N-4, 219-221: Edward Gardner of Beaufort, Cooper, bound to John Iklar of same, 13 May 1774, to prevent claim of dower on lot in Beaufort. Edwd. Gardner (LS) Wit: Robert Orr, Abraham Shecut. Recorded 10 Dec 1774.

N-4, 221-226: Lease & release. 10 & 11 Sept 1774, Isaac Peace of Charles Town, only acting and qualified executor of the last will and testament of Thomas Holman, late of Ashley River, planter, deceased, to John holman of St. Andrews Parish, planter, for £13,000 SC money, 615 acres in St. Andrews Parish, Berkley County, which the said Thomas Holman by his will dated 13 January last past did order that his executors sell at publick vendue to the highest bidder all of his estate, at public vendue 8 March on which day said John Holman became the purchaser. Isaac Peace (LS), Wit: J. Fardo, Richd. Corbett. Proved by the oath of George John Fardo before John Fewtrell, J.P., 21 Sept 1774. Recorded 13 Sept 1774.

N-4, 226-231: 29 Apr 1767, Roger Pinckney, Provost Marshall of Province of SC, to Mathew Singleton of same province, planter; whereas John Dargan of Santee in Craven County, deceased, was lately possessed of several plantations: 200 acres in Craven County near the High Hills of Santee on a place called Williams old Field on a marsh and Shanks Creek granted 5 oct 1762 to John Dargan; 350 acres in Craven County adj. sd. John Dargans land, on Little River and Beach Creek granted 15 July 1765; 494 acres in Craven county adj. John Jones land, John Deas' land, Wateree River granted 13 Aug 1766 to Miles Brewton; said John Dargan by his bond 10 July 1764 bound to Miles Brewton & Thomas Loughton Smith of Charles Town, Merchants, in the penal sum of £5800 SC money for the payment of £2800, and said Miles Brewton and Thomas Loughton Smith in February term did recover a judgment to be levied of the goods and chattles which were of the said John Dargan deceased in the hands, custody, and possession of the said William Strother and Ann Dargan, executor and executrix; by writ of fieri facias, and said <u>Martha</u> Singleton being the highest and last bidder for £630 SC money. Roger Pinkney (LS), wit: Wm. Hope, H'n Pinkney. Recorded 14 Dec 1774.

N-4, 231-240: Lease & release. 22 & 23 Sept 1774, John Holman of Parish of St. Andrew, planter, & Priscilla his wife, to Peter Bacot and William Hale of Charles Town,only qualified and acting executors of the will of Lambert Lance late of Charleston, Merchant, deceased, as trustees and guardians of the person and estate of Lambert Lance, only son of aforesaid Lambert Lance deceased, now a minor about the age of sixteen years; will of said Lambert Lance dated 18 Jan 1773 did empower his executors to purchase for the use of his son a plantation and sd. executors agreed with sd. John Holman for the purchase of a plantation of 615 acres in St. Andrews Parish, for £200 SC money, 615 acres upon a resurvey adj. land of Benjamin Elliott, Thomas Elliott deceased, Wm. Brandfords estate, Jeremiah Savage, said John Holman, land of estate of Edward Miles deceased, John Lloyd Esqr. (plat included) Jno Holman (LS), Priscilla Holman (LS), Wit: G. Fardo, Richd. Corbett. Proved by the oath of George John Fardo before John Fewtrell 24 Sept 1774. Recorded 15 Dec 1774.

N-4, 240-246: Lease & release. 1 & 2 Aug 1772, Daniel Monahan of Craven County, Parish of St. David, SC, to Joshua Lucas of same, planter, for £100 SC money, 150 acres on southwest side of Pee Dee River on Neck Creek adj. land of David Harry and Philip James, Isaac Chandler, granted 14 May 1752, recorded in Book OO, page 65, granted to Daniel Monahan Senr & descended by heirship to Thomas Monahan thence by heirship unto Daniel Monahan Junr. Daniel Monahan (LS), Wit: John Bowen, John Lucas. Proved in Craven county before Charles Augustus Steward, J. P., by the oath of John Bowen, 16 Aug 1772. Recorded 17 Dec 1774.

N-4, 246-249: Lease & release. 17 Apr 1767, Daniel Devonald of Welch Neck, Craven county, Sc, to Joshua Lucas of same place, for £150 SC money, 100 acres granted to Walter Downs 2 Jan 1754 in Craven county, conveyed from Walter downs to Valentine Hollingsworth by lease & release. Dan Devonald (LS), Wit: David Evans, Wm. Edwards. Proved in Craven County, SC, before Claudius Pegues, J. P., by the oath of Wm. Edwards, 25 Apr 1771. Recorded 18 Dec 1774.

N-4, 250-253: Lease & release. 27 & 28 Sept 1774, Ephraim Mitchell of Charles Town, Surveyour, to David Baty of same, for £70 SC money, lot #21 in Charles Town, originally the property of John Mitchell brother to said Ephraim Mitchell, who dying without a will his whole estate real and personal became the property of sd. Ephraim Mitchell. Ephraim Mitchell (LS), Wit: William Downes, Martin Pfininger. Proved 9 Sept 1774 before George Davis, J. P. in Charles Town District, by the oath of William Downes. Recorded 20 Dec 1774.

N-4, 254-256: 2 Sept 1765, William Davis and Ann his wife of Waxhaws, Mecklenburgh County, North Carolina, to Roger Smith of same, yoeman, for £40, 150 acres on both sides of Campe Creek on the E side of Cataba River in the Waxhaw Settlement. Wm. Davis (LS), Wit: Joseph Barnet, Saml Thompson. July Court 1766, North Carolina, Mecklenburg County: Recorded in Register's Office 7 Dec 1760. Robert Harris, Regr. Recorded 21 Dec 1774.

N-4, 256-264: Lease & release. 8 & 9 May 1747, John Harvey of Charles Town, Gentleman, one of the sons and devisees of the last will and testament of Wm. Harvey late of the same place, gent., deceased, to Paul Townsend of same town, cooper, only son of Thomas Townsend late of same place deceased, who was only brother of John Townsend, late of the same place, cooper, decd., and heir at law to sd. John Townsend, who died without lawful issue, by lease & release 22 & 23 Feb 1743, sd. John Harvey, son of Wm. Harvey deceased, and John Townsend of same, cooper, for £1300 SC money, lots 24 & 25 in Charles Town adj. land of George Bedon decd, Story & Chapman decd, Isaac Mazyck, which said William Harvey did by his will devise to sd. John Harvey, and at the time of executing the sd. lease and release was under the age of twenty one years but has since attained his full age of twenty one years, now at the special request of Paul Townsend as heir at law to said John Townsend decd, as well as for £1100 SC money, doth convey said lots. John Harvey (LS), Wit: John Owen, Wm. Horcks. Acknowledged in Charles Town District by John Harvey before William Rugeley, J. P., 7 Oct 1774. Recorded 22 Dec 1774.

N-4, 264-266: 21 May 1772, George Dunlap of St. Marks Parish, Craven County, SC, to Gilbert Dunlap of same, for £50 SC money, 200 acres part of 350 acres on Bullocks Creek in Craven

SOUTH CAROLINA DEED ABSTRACTS 1773-1778

County adj. David Terry, granted to David Dunlap, 18 May 1763. George Dunlap (LS), Wit: Samuel Dunlap, John McDoch. Proved 21 May 1772 by the oath of Samuel Dunlap before JAmes Simpson, J.P. in Craven County. Recorded 24 Dec 1774.

N-4, 267-272: Lease & release. 21 & 22 Feb 1774, Thomas Goulden of Berkley County, SC, planter, to Jane Milhous of same, widow, for £100 SC money, 100 acres part of 200 acres on north side of Saludy River on a branch of Bush Creek called Mathews Branch granted to Thomas Golden. Thomas Goulden (X) (LS), Wit: Jno Milhous, Simon Quinn, James Daugherty. Proved 4 March 1774 before John Caldwell, Esqr., J. P. in Ninety Six District, by the oath of James Dougherty. Recorded 30 Dec 1774.

N-4, 272-274: 25 Feb 1774, Jane Milhous, widow of Robert Milhous, deceased, late of Cambden, South Carolina, to John Milhous and Samuel Milhous, Justices & guardians appointed by said John Milhous for her son Joseph Milhous, now about seven years old, for love, good will and affection, 100 acres whereon said Jane Milhous now lives part of 200 acres on north side of Saludy River on a branch of Bush Creek called Mathews Branch granted to Thomas Golden and conveyed by lease and release 22 Feb 1774 to her. Jane Milhous (LS), Wit: Samuel Kelly, Simon Quinn, James Daugherty. Proved 4 March 1774 before John Caldwell, Esqr., J. P. in Ninety Six District, by the oath of James Dougherty. Recorded 29 Dec 1774.

N-4, 275-279: Lease & release. 13 & 14 Dec 1773, Joseph Williamson of Waccamaw, Prince George Parish, Craven county, planter, to Dalziel Hunter of same parish and county, for £1200 SC money, 300 acres on Peedee River in Prince George Parish, Craven County adj. land of William Munk. Jos. Williamson (LS), Wit: George Pawley Junr, Sarah Pawley. Proved 1 Sept 1774 before Nathaniel Dwight, J.P. in Craven County, by the oath of George Pawley. Recorded 29 Dec 1774.

N-4, 279-288: Lease & release. 2 & 3 Apr 1772, Simon Tufts of Charles Town, Shop keeper, and Mary his wife, to Thomas Eveleigh of same place, merchant, for £350 SC money, 472 acres in St. Johns Parish, Berkley County, adj. land originally granted to Merchants and Colleton, lands granted to one abraham Sanders, Thomas Palmer, Charles Colleton, Thomas Cox, Doctor Repault. Simon Tufts (LS), M. Tufts (LS), Wit: Wm. Doughty, Jos. Ward. Proved by the oath of Joshua Ward 5 Oct 1775 before G. G. Powell, J.P. Recorded 31 Dec 1774. Mary Tufts, wife of Simon Tufts, relinquished dower 23 Sept 1772 before Thos. Knox Golden. Jos. Ward, attorney.

N-4, 289-291: 9 June 1774, James Simmons of Charles Town, Gentleman, and only acting executor of the last will and testament of Ebenezer Simmons late of sd. province, Esqr., deceased, to Thos Eveleigh of sd. town & Province, merchant, for yearly rents, covenants and agreements, tract which he purchased rom one Joseph Elliott now also deceased on north side Stono River in St. Andrews Parish, Berkley County, 860 acres. James Simmons (LS), Thos Eveliegh (LS), Wit: Hopkin Price, Eligah Price. Proved in Charles Town District by the oath of Hopkin Price before R. Rugeley, 31 Dec 1774. Recorded 31 Dec 1775.

N-4, 292-297: Lease & release. 15 16 Dec 1774, Isaac Weatherly of St. Helena Island, planter, to George Mathews of Charles Town, merchant, for £100 SC money, 200 acres on John Island, Colleton County adj. Robert Gibbs, Mathews, Solomon Freer, upon a creek branching out of Keywaw River adj. land of the estate of Elizabeth Cockran, which land Isaac Weatherly became entitled thereto as heir at law to his father Wm. Weatherly who died intestate. Isaac Weatherly Wit: Benjamin Mathews, Daniel Holmes. Proved in Charles Town District by the oath of Benjamin Mathews before Fenwick Bull, J. P., 16 Dec 1774. Recorded 2 Jan 1775.

N-4, 297-302: Lease & release. 15 & 17 Aug 1758, Joseph Nelson of Savannah River in Granville County, planter, and Mary his wife, to Elias Stallion, for £300 SC money, 150 acres in Granville County, adj. James Dyer, Walter Waughan, 24 Apr 1752. Joseph Nelson (mark) (LS), Mary Nelson (+) (LS), Wit: James Bobby, Benjamin Hide (BH). Proved before Cornelius Cook, J. P. for Granville County, by the oath of James Bobby, 7 Jan 1760. Recorded 4 Jan 1775.

N-4, 302-306: Lease & release. 12 & 13 Apr 1756, Richard Mader, planter, of Collony of Georgia, Elias Stallion of Granville County, SC, planter, for £20, 200 acres in Granville County granted 3 Sept 1754 adj. Savanah River, Walter Vaughan. Richd Meder (R) (LS), Wit: john Scott, James

SOUTH CAROLINA DEED ABSTRACTS 1773-1778

Dyer, Proved 13 Apr 1756 by the oath of James Dyer before Anthony Groob. Recorded 5 Jan 1775. Henry Rugeley, D. Register.

N-4, 306-313: Lease & release. 2 & 3 Aug 1773, James Hamilton & Mary his wife, John Lambright and Sarah his wife, & Jeane Beatty of St. Bartholomews Parish, widow, to Elizabeth McCollough, widow, of same, for £1048 SC money, 524 acres in St. Bartholomews Parish, Colleton County, on Welches Creek adj. Welches land, Ann Crall, Thomas Jones. James Hamilton (LS), Mary Hamilton (LS), James Lambright (LS), Sarah Lambright (LS), Jean Beatty (LS), Wit: John Freeman, Patrick Hues, David Ferguson. Proved by the oath of John Freeman 1 Sept 1773 before James Donnom, J.P. Recorded 7 Jan 1775.

N-4, 313-319: Lease & release. 9 & 10 Apr 1760, James Jones of Welch Tract, Craven county, Taylor, to Benjamin Lord of George town, leather Breaches maker, for £400 SC money, 350 acres in the Welch Tract in Craven county adj. Benjamin Watts, Robt Williams, Cornelius Reins, Isaac Hickman, conveyed to said James Jones by Thomas Harrington 5 & 6 Aug 1756. James Jones (J) (LS), Wit: Egerton Leigh, Wm. Wd. Crosthwaite. Proved by the oath of William Ward Crosthwaite before James Grindlay, J. P., 9 June 1762. Recorded 10 Jan 1775.

N-4, 319-323: Lease & release. 29 & 30 June 1774, Margaret Mann of St. Pauls Parish, Widow, daughter of Nathaniel Wickham, late of St. George Dorechester, deceased, to James Parsons of Charles Town, for £255 SC money, 255 acres in Berkley County adj. land formerly of Lawrence Sanders, Daniel Stuart, Joseph Blake, Francis Vernod, granted to said Nathaniel Wickham 10 Apr 1738, and said Nathaniel Wickham by his last will and testament dated 2 Aug 1745 gave all his real estate to his two sons Nathaniel Branchhurt Wickham and Richd Wickham, which said Rd.Wickham survived the sd. Nathaniel Branchurt Wickham who was but his brother of the half blood and afterwards died intestate and without issue and leaving sd. Margaret only sister and heir at law. Margaret Mann (LS), Wit: Michl. Meara, Henry Nicholes. Proved in Chas Town District by the oath of Henry Nicholes before John Troup, 28 Oct 1774. Recorded 10 Jan 1775.

N-4, 324-329: Lease & release. 18 & 19 March 1773, James Seawright and Elizabeth his wife, of SC, to Samuel Agnew of same, for £160 SC money, by bounty grant 17 June 1763 to James Seawright's wife Elizabeth McCullogh, 100 acres on waters of Long Cane Creek adj. Janet McCullough, Richd Brown, recorded in Book XX, folio 211. James Seawright (LS), Eliz'th Seawright (O) (LS), Wit: richd King, William Robertson. Proved in Ninety Six District 19 March 1774 before Adam Crain Jones, J.P., by the oath of William Robert[son]. Recorded 12 Jan 1775.

N-4, 329-338: Lease & release. 19 & 20 Oct 1774, Richard Waring of St. Georges Parish, Dorchester, Planter, & Ann his wife, to Elias Ball of St. James Parish, Santee, planter, for £6000 SC money; whereas John Coming Ball late of St. Johns Parish Berkley County, planter, deceased, was possessed in fee simple with Henry Laurence of sd. province, esqr., as tenant in common, of 2500 acres part of 3000 acres, as joint tenants in 500 acres being the remainder of sd. tract of 300 acres in Craven County known as Wambaw Swamp which said 3000 acres was surveyed 4 Apr 1777 [sic, for 1727?] unto John Bayley of Kingdom of Ireland son and heir at law of John Bayley of Balinaclough in sd. Kingdom, Esqr., then deceased, as part of 48,000 acres granted to him by the Lords Proprietors 16 Aug 1698, at the time of sd. survey adj. Paul Doxsaint, Isaac Legrand, and by platt of said 3000 acres certified by William Bull, Deputy Surveyor General, 4 Apr 1727, and said john Coming Ball being possessed of said lands by his last will and testament dated 28 March 1764 gave and devised unto his three daughters Elizabeth Ball (now or late the wife of Henry Smith of st. James's Goose Creek, Esqr), Catharine Ball and Ann Ball now the wife of said Richard Waring, when they should respectively marry or attain the age of 21 years, his undivided moiety or half pat of said 3000 acres, and said Henry Laurence and Henry Smith on 17 Feb 1769 applied to the justices of his Majestys Court of Common Pleas of said province for a writ of partition, and persons named in sd. writ of partition 11 March 1769 did divide the said lands, now 317 is conveyed adj. land of George Paddon Bond, described in a plat as letter C. Richd Waring (LS), Ann Waring (S), Wit: Theo Gaillard Junr, David Gaillard. Proved in Chas Town District by the oath of David Gaillard before William Nisbett, J. P., 21 Oct 1774. Recorded 15 Jan 1775.

N-4, 338-343: Lease & release. 6 & 7 June 1774, John Fields of Craven County, planter, and Sarah his wife, to Saml Milhous of same, planter, for £250 SC money, 100 acres part of 200 acres granted

SOUTH CAROLINA DEED ABSTRACTS 1773-1778

to John Fields 18 May 1771 in Craven County on east side of Wateree River on south side of Grannies Quarter Creek adj. land granted to Edward Kelley, land surveyed for William McKee, land which sd. John Fields sold to John Phifer, land surveyed for Hugh Thompson. John Fields (LS), Sarah Fields (LS), Wit: Stephen Matlock, William Matlock, Daniel McMullen. Proved 7 July 1774 before John Newman Oglethorpe, J.P. in Camden District, by the oath of Daniel McMullen. Recorded 15 Jan 1775.

N-4, 343-348: Lease & release. 2 & 3 May 1770, Eleanor Adamson of Craven County, widow, to John Dickson of same, wheelwright, for £100 SC money, 100 acres granted to sd. Eleanor Adamson 10 Nov 1761 on northeast side of Wateree River above Beaver Creek adj. land granted to William Stewart. Elinor Adamson (mark) (LS), Wit: John Adamson, Eliz'th Adamson, Henry Dongworth. Proved 13 Oct 1774 before John N. Oglethorpe, J. P. in Camden District, by the oath of Henry Dongworth. Recorded 16 Jan 1775.

N-4, 348-352: Lease & release. 23 & 24 Oct 1773, Ephraim Mitchell of Orangeburgh Township, to Robert Hails of Amelia Township, for £2000 SC money, 532 acres on the line between Amelia and Orangeburgh Townships adj. land granted to Thomas Weakley, John Thomson, George Davis, John Velstine, Cooper Springer, John Leasey; originally granted 100 acres to William Mitchell 17 Apr 1764 and 432 acres granted 25 June 1771 to Peter Gourdin. Ephraim Mitchell (LS), Wit: Jno Mouret, Jno Randolph. Recorded 26 Jan 1775.

N-4, 353-356: 8 May 1771, John Spurgin of Berkley County, SC, planter, and Elizabeth his wife to Jacob Penington of same, for £150 SC money, by grant 2 Apr 1762 to James Ronalls for 250 acres on a branch of Broad River called Indian Creek in Berkley County adj. land surveyed for Abraham Pennington, recorded in Book WW, page 11, and Memorial entered in Book F No. 6, page 97, and said James Ronalls by lease & release 7 Apr 1769 conveyed to John Spurgin. John Spurgin (LS), Eliz'th Spurgin (LS), Wit: Randolph Casey, Moses Casey, Abasel Casey. Proved by the oath of Randolph Casey before James Ford, J. P., 8 May 1771. Recorded 18 Jan 1775.

N-4, 356-360: 26 May 1769, Richard Land, Eldest son and heir at law of Robert Lang deceased, and Sarah Lang wife of Richd Lang, and Millicent Lang the relict and executrix of the last will and testament of sd. Robert Lang, for £600 SC money, to Daniel Williams of Hallifax County, Colony of Virginia, 250 acres granted to John Read 5 Nov 1755 conveyed by indenture by sd. John Read to sd. Robert Lang deceased. Richd Lang (LS), Sarah Lang (X) (LS), Mellicent Lang (R) (LS), Wit: Jacob Bowman, Geo Wright Junr, Hance Hendrick. Proved in Craven County by the oath of Hance Hendrick 12 Aug 1769. Recorded 19 Jan 1775.

N-4, 360-361: 25 May 1773, Jno McKnitt Alexander of Mecklenburg County, North Carolina, to William Walling of Craven County, SC, for £190 SC money, tract on both sides the main fork of fishing Creek granted to John McKnitt Alexander 27 Sept 1766 recorded in the Secretarys Office of North Carolina. Jno McKnitt Alexander (LS), Wit: Hugh Neeley, Edward Lee (EL). Proved by the oath of Hugh Neely before David Gordon, 15 Jan 1774. Recorded 29 Jan 1775.

N-4, 362-369: Lease & mortgage. 10 & 11 Oct 1774, James Steedman of Charles Town, carpenter, and Elizabeth his wife, to Andrew Lord of same, merchant, mortgage for ten shillings, lot on East side St. Philip Street in Charlestown. James Steedman (LS), Eliz'th Steedman (LS), Wit: James Perronneau, Jno Colcock. Proved by the oath of John Colcock 24 Oct 1774 before John Lewis Gervais, J.P. Recorded 21 Jan 1775. Satisfied 5 Aug 1778, Wit: Geo Sheed.

N-4, 369-376: Lease & mortgage. 17 & 18 Oct 1774, Benjamin Durborow of Ninety Six, SC, and Susannah his wife, to Charles Atkins and Plowden Weston of Charles Town, merchants, for £2000, 300 acres on north side Saludy River adj. James Maxfields, adj. land surveyed for Sarah Proctor, also 200 acres in Colleton County near the neighborhood of Ninety Six adj. John McFarlin; also 100 acres in Colleton County near Ninety Six adj. land late of Doctor John Murray, Roger McKinnney, Hector Dickey, Thomas Wright, James Harkins; 88 acres on the waters Ninety Six adj. land late of Thomas Brown, Daniel Micklar, Joseph Burton, and 107 acres in Colleton County adj. Daniel Mickler, Robert Gandy, Robert McCutchen, Emanuel Miller; also lot number 10 in the town of Ninety Six; also another lot in the town of Ninety Six. B. Durborow (LS), Susanna Duborow (LS),

SOUTH CAROLINA DEED ABSTRACTS 1773-1778

Wit: Wm. Ward Burrows, Joseph Jennings, John Gillbank. Proved by the oath William Ward Burrows of Charles Town, gentleman, before William Burrows, 19 Oct 1774. Recorded 28 Jan 1775.

N-4, 377-382: Lease & release. 16 & 17 Sept 1774, John Mayer of Charles town to William Swallow of same, merchant, for £650 SC money, 500 acres in Craven County, waters of Buck Creek a branch of Pacolet adj. land of Thomas Lynch, Esqr., Roger Peter Handasyde Hatley, granted to Thomas Dearington 26 Sept 1772. John Mayer (LS), Wit: Philip Henry, B. L. Marchant. Proved 28 Oct 1774 before Wm. Rugeley, J.P., by the oath of Philip Henry. Recorded 23 Jan 1775.

N-4, 382-384: William Browning of Berkley County, SC, St. Georges Parish, yeoman, for divers good causes and consideration, quit claim to James Cree of same all interest in tract of 150 acres in said parish on four hole swamp adj. Mr. Broughton, James Cummins, George Strother, by a warrant obtained dated 5 Dec 1769 entered in Auditors Office 12 July 1770 in Book KK Page 1771 [sic]. William Browning (W) (LS), Wit: Robt Black, Steph. Cater, J.P. Recorded 24 Jan 1775.

N-4, 384-389: Lease & release. 2 Nov 1769, Daniel Money of Craven County, planter, to Mallachi Murphey Junr, for £400 SC money, tract granted 29 Nov 1750 to Daniel Money, 300 acres in Craven County on Pedee River, adj. John Marden. Daniel Money (LS), Wit: John Crawford, Robert Martin. Proved 13 Sept 1771 before Jno N. Oglethorp, J. P. in Craven County, by the oath of Robert Martin. Recorded 26 Jan 1775.

N-4, 389-394: Lease & release. 31 Oct & 1 Nov 1774, John Fry of Charles Town, Gentleman, and Mary his wife, to Rebecca Minick of Colleton County, for £200 SC money, 200 acres in Colleton County, fork of Edisto, granted to sd. John Fry 30 Oct 1767. John Fry (LS), Mary Fry (LS), Wit: Joseph Wyatt, John Patrick. Proved 1 Nov 1774 before George Davidson, J. P., by the oath of Joseph Wyatt. Recorded 27 Jan 1775.

N-4, 395-399: Lease & release. 24 & 25 May 1773, Thomas Dearington of Parish of St. Thomas and St. Denis, Berkley County, SC, planter, to John Mayer of same parish, practitioner in Physic, for £1000 SC money, 500 acres on waters of Buck Creek a branch of Pacolet adj. land of Thomas Lynch, Esqr., Roger Peter Handasyde Hatley, granted to Thomas Dearington 26 Sept 1772. Thomas Dearington (LS), Wit: Peter Videau, John Dearington. Proved 1 Nov 1774 before Wm. Rugeley, J.P., by the oath of John Dearington. Recorded 28 Jan 1775.

N-4, 399-403: Lease & mortgage. 28 & 29 Oct 1774, John Allen of Ninety Six District, planter, to John Lewis Gervais of Charles Town, merchant, for better securing of payment, 100 acres in Granville County, 100 acres in Granville County, and 200 acres in Granville County. John Allen (LS), Wit: William Valentine, Lach'n Mackintosh. Proved in Charles Town District before William Nisbett, J. P., by the oath of Wm. Valentine, 3 Nov 1774. Recorded 28 Jan 1775.

N-4, 403-410: Lease & release. 29 & 30 Nov 1773, Elias Jaudon of Prince Williams Parish, Granville County, gent., to Charles Browne, Esqr., of same parish, and Thomas Hamilton of St. Georges Parish, for ten shillings, one tract in St. Helenas Parish of 650 acres granted to Robert Ogle; tract adjoining the above tract 1250 acres granted to Samuel Fickling on south west side Great Coosahacke Swamp on waters of River Pond; tract of 300 acres granted to sd. Elias jaudon on waters of sd. Coosahache known by the name of Bull Head; tract of 200 acres being the residue of 400 acres granted to sd. Elias Jaudon on Whippys Swamp waters of Great Saicahache the other being conveyed Michl. Clifton in Prince Wms. parish; tract of 654 acres on the main Salcacha Swamp where the sd. Elias Jaudon now liveth, being the remainder of an original tract of 2000 acres conveyed to him by Ann Wragg adj. John Robert; 264 acres being part of 300 acres granted to john Robert adj. sd. John Robert, James Bullock, and sd. Elias Jaudon; tract of 200 acres part of 300 acres granted to Peter Robert adj. Wm. Davis, Thos Bee, John Robert; tract of 200 acres granted to Jacob Kettle adj. Elias Jaudon, John Robert, Nathal Raymor, John Wragg, James Bullock; the five last mentioned tracts being in Prince Williams Parish and Granville County. Elias Jaudon (LS), Wit; James Robert, Peter Robert. Proved in Beaufort District before Joseph Brailsford, J. P., by the oath of Peter Robert, 3 Sept 1774. Recorded 31 Jan 1775.

N-4, 411-416: Elias Jaudon of Prince Williams Parish, Granville County, gent., to Charles Browne, Esqr., of same parish, and Thomas Hamilton of St. Georges Parish, Berkley County, bond to make

SOUTH CAROLINA DEED ABSTRACTS 1773-1778

titles to tracts in foregoing lease and release, dated 1 Dec 1773. Elias Jaudon (LS), Wit; James Robert, Peter Robert. Proved in Beaufort District before Joseph Brailsford, J. P., by the oath of Peter Robert, 3 Sept 1774. Recorded 1 Feb 1775.

N-4, 417-418: John Remington Senr. and Margaret his wife of Berkley County, for natural love and affection to our beloved daughter Ann Burton, wife of Isaac Burton, now of Charlestown, lot on the corner of Union Street and Queen Street in Parish of St. Philips in Charlestown, dated 25 Jan 1775. John Remington (LS), Mar't Remington (LS), Wit: Mary Hardy, Ab'm Alexander, Andrew wilson. Proved in Charles Town District by the oath of Miss Mary Hardy before William Nisbett, J. P., 31 Jan 1775. Recorded 1 Feb 1775.

N-4, 419-421: Martin Lloyd of Charles Town District by bond dated 8 Nov 1774 to Jacob Tobias of Charles Town District, merchant, in the penal sum of £8000 SC money for the payment of £4000, mortgage of tenement on King Street, Charles Town now in the possession of Harman Nuffer adj. lands late of the heirs of Henry Peroneau deceased, land where Ann Loyd did live. Martin Lloyd (LS), Wit: Emanuel Abrahams, Elias Evans. Proved by the oath of Elias Evans 11 Nov 1774 before William Rugeley, J.P. Recorded 2 Feb 1775.

N-4, 421-423: 20 Apr 1773, Frederick Rush of St. Marks Parish, and Barbara his wife, to Abraham Rush of same, yeoman, for £15 SC money, 100 acres granted to sd. Frederick Rush 12 Oct 1770 on a branch of Great Linches Creek. Frederick Rush (LS), Barbara Rush (LS), Wit: William Carson, Martin Oats (S), Mary Rush (O). Proved by the oath of William Carson 20 July 1774 before James Pattons, J. P. Recorded 2 Feb 1775.

N-4, 424-429: 23 Dec 1749, Humphrey Somers of Charles Town, Bricklayer, and Susanna his wife, to Hopkin Price of sd. town, tanner, for £425 SC money... whereas George II on 4 Oct 1749 did grant to sd. Humphrey Sommers a tract of marsh land and some high land, and sd. Humphrey Sommers was to make a good and sufficient Road causeway through the sd. Marsh land ten feet wide from Meeting House Street unto King Street. Susannah Sommers (LS), Humphrey Sommers (LS), Wit: Cato Ash, William Fisher. Proved by the oath of Cato Ash before Robert Williams, J.P., 9 Nov 1774. Recorded 4 Feb 1775.

N-4, 430-435: Lease & release. 1 & 2 Feb 1774, William Moultrie of Charles Town, SC, Esqr., and Elizabeth Damaris his wife, to Daniel Ravenel Junr, Esqr., of same place, for £4250 SC money, 185 acres in Parish of St. Johns Berkely County, adj. land of sd. Daniel Ravenel, sd. William Moultrie. William Moultrie (LS), Elizabeth D. Moultrie (LS), Wit: Jacob Motte, John Dart. Proved by the oath of John Sanford Dart before John Troup, J.P., 10 Nov 1774. Recorded 4 Feb 1775.

N-4, 435-439: Lease & release. 1 & 2 Aug 1769, John Palmer and Ann Palmer his wife of Parish of St. Hellena, Granville County, to Elizabeth Ball of same parish, planter, for £1375, 500 acres on Ladys Island adj. Samuel Thorpe, James Smith, John Parmer on Cusau River. Jno Palmer (LS), Ann Palmer (LS), Wit: Henry Stewart, Henry Wright. Proved 3 May 1771 before Andrew Aggnew, J. P. in Granville County, by the oath of Henry Wright. Recorded 6 Feb 1775.

N-4, 439-444: Lease & release. 9 & 10 Sept 1774, Claudius Richburg and Unity his wife of St. Marks Parish, Craven County, planter, to Moses Thompson in Rowan County, Province of North Carolina, planter, for £300 SC money, 300 acres on north side Santee River granted 9 January 1755. Cl'us Richburg (LS), Unity Richburg (LS), Wit: Joseph Fox, Peter Mellet. Proved in Camden District 21 Oct 1774 before Nathl Moore, J. P., by the oath of Peter Mellet. Recorded 8 Feb 1775.

N-4, 444-446: Robert Gray of Charles Town, Berkely County, by bond to William Williamson of Charles Town, in the penal sum of £4000 for the payment of £2000, mortgage of tract on the side of a Canal or Creek leading from old Church Street adj. land of James Towagger[?], James Fitzsimons, William Wayne, with houses erected and built for the term of seven years from 8 June 1772... dated 14 ___ 1774. Robert Gray (LS), Wit: Alexander Horn, John Turner. Recorded 8 Feb 1775.

SOUTH CAROLINA DEED ABSTRACTS 1773-1778

N-4, 446-452: Lease & release. _____ 1774, John Miolet of Charles Town, Tin Plate Worker, to Thomas Sabb of Berkley County, planter, for £500 SC money, 100 acres. John Miolet (LS), Wit: John Bush, James Courtonne. Recorded 9 Feb 1775.

N-4, 452-457: Lease & release. _____ 1774, Stephen Jeachin of Charles Town, Tin Plate Worker, to Thomas Sabb of Berkley County, planter, for £500 SC money, 100 acres. Stephen Jeachin (LS), Wit: John Bush, James Courtonne. Recorded 9 Feb 1775.

N-4, 457-461: South Carolina. 23 Nov 1773, John Black of county and province aforesaid to John McAllilley of Mclinburg County, North Carolina, for £100, 150 acres in Craven county, SC, on Buls Run between Canteburg[?] and Broad River adj. John Russells land. John Black (LS), Wit: William Martin, Alexr Wallace. Proved in Camden District 25 Aug 1774[?] by the oath of William Martin before Wm. Brown, J.P. Recorded 11 Feb 1775.

N-4, 461-466: Lease & mortgage. 15 & 16 Nov 1774, Samuel Gruber of Charles Town, cooper, to John Fisher of Charles Town, cabinet maker, bound in the penal sum of £226 for the payment of £113 SC money with interest thereof, mortgage of 350 acres on a branch of Clouds Creek called the Long Branch of West Creek being the waters of Clouds Creek adj. land of Jacob Friday. Saml Gruber (LS), Wit: David Baty, Thomas Tod. Proved in Charles Town District by the oath of Thomas Tod before William Rugeley, J.P., 8 Feb 1775. Recorded 13 Feb 1775.

END OF BOOK N-4.

O-4, 1-5: Lease & release. 9 & 10 Jan 1774, Richard Woodcraft of Colleton County, SC, planter, to James Thompson of same, for £25 SC money, 250 acres on the head of Horsepen bay. Richard Wooodcraft (LS), Wit: John Norman, Samuel Sleigh. Proved before James Stobo by the oath of John Norman, 26 March 1774. Recorded 31 Oct 1774.

O-4, 5-12: Lease & release. 14 & 16 Jan 1768, Benjamin Tutt of Colleton County, SC, merchant, and Barbara his wife, to Valentine Zinn of Township of New Windsor, Granville County, planter, for £100 SC money, 200 acres in the township of New Windsor granted to Robert Vaughan 26 June 1738, adj. land of Robt. McMurdy, Savanah River, land laid out for the use of the fort, and east on the town, on 22 Aug 1743 transferred by said Robert Vaughan and Arabela his wife to Rowland Prickett, and on 3 Jan 1743/4 transferred by James Paris and William McCartey, and on 19 Sept 1748 transferred by sd. James Parish unto his copartner Wm. McCarty and Margaret McCarty daughter oo said William McCarty being the legitimate heir unto said William McCartey and George Cornall being consumated to her by the bonds of matrimony became the propriator of same with Mary Ann his mother in law, Relict of said William McCarty, and on 13 January 1768 George Cornall and Margaret his wife and Mary Ane his mother in Law transferred to said Benjamin Tutt. Benjamin Tutt (LS), Barbra Tutt (+) (LS), Wit: Jno Gray, James Ross. Proved in Granville County before John Dick, J.P., by the oath of John Gray, 25 Jan 1768. Memorial entered in the Audr Genls Office in Book L No. 11 page 352, 15 Aug 17772. Recorded 7 Nov 1774.

O-4, 12-17: Lease & mortgage. South Carolina. 31 May 1774, Joseph Salvador of London, Esqr., to Francis Salvador, late of Twicknham, County of Middlesex, but now of said province, esqr., 5166 acres (plat included) being above a place called Ninety Six, part of 100,000 acres granted by George II to William Livingstone 27 June 1752. Joseph Salvador by his attorney Richd Andrew Rapley (LS), Wit: Thos Sanders, John Gaw. Proved in Ninety Six District 7 June 1774 before John Bowie by the oath of Thomas Sanders. Recorded 9 Nov 1774.

O-4, 17-21: Lease & release. 27 & 28 Dec 1773, Jonathan Downs, Esquire, of Ninety Six district, SC, to Joseph Thompson, Tanner, of Bush Creek, for £50 SC money, 84 acres in Craven county on a branch of Bush Creek adj. John Wilkesons, Stephen Elmores, Martha Coppick, granted 20 Jan 1773 to sd. Jonathan Downs. Jonathan Downs (LS), Sarah Downs (LS), Wit: John Embree, Stephen Elmore, Wm. Hoge. Proved by the oath of William Hoge before John Caldwell, J. P. in Ninety Six District, 26 Apr 1774. Recorded 11 Nov 1774.

SOUTH CAROLINA DEED ABSTRACTS 1773-1778

O-4, 21-28: Lease & release. 25 & 26 Aug 1774, Alexander Taylor, late of Charles Town, SC, taylor, but now Edinburgh in that part of Great Britain called Scotland, by Josiah Smith, his attorney, to Pete Bounetheau of Charles Town, for £3700, lot in Ansonborough on east side of Broad path leading from Charles Town to the new fortifications with the houses thereon lately occupied by Mr. Simpson and now or late in the possession of Mr. Elliott. Alexander Taylor by Josiah Smith Junr (LS), Wit: Mary Fogartie, Edward Darrell. Proved in Charles Town District by the oath of Edward Darrell before William Rugeley, 8 Sept 1774. Recorded 14 Nov 1774.

O-4, 28-33: Lease & release. 26 & 27 Aug 1774, Peter Bounetheau of Charles Town, SC, to Alexander Taylor, late of Charles Town, SC, taylor, but now Edinburgh in that part of Great Britain called Scotland, for debt of mortgage owing to said Alexander Taylor (same tract in preceding deed). Peter Bounetheau (LS), Wit: Edward Darrell, James Watson. Proved in Charles Town District by the oath of Edward Darrell before William Rugeley, 8 Sept 1774. Recorded 15 Nov 1774.

O-4, 34-39: Lease & release. 28 & 29 Oct 1773, Andrew Sallisbury and John Pittman of Craven County, SC, planters, to Pettegrew Sallisbury of same, for £600 SC money, 650 acres granted to William Tucker on the low grounds of Santee River in Craven County, adj. land granted to James Johnston, William Tucker, land supposed to belong to Gov. Wright or his brother. Andrew Sallisbury (LS), John Pittman (LS), Wit: Jacob Hollingsworth, Edwd. Hampton. Proved by the oath of Philip Pearson, J. P., 20 Apr 1774. Recorded 16 Nov 1774.

O-4, 39-43: Lease & mortgage. 13 & 15 March 1774, Sarah Elliott of St. Andrews Parish, widow, to Richard Park Stobo of same, esquire, for £20,000 SC money, 1972 acres in St. Bartholomews Parish conveyed by said Richard Park Stobo and Mary his wife. Sarah Elliott (LS), Wit: J. Rutledge, John Pringle. Proved in Berkley County by the oath of John Pringle 6 Apr 1774 before Robt. Pringle, J.P. Mortgage satisfied 1 Apr 1776. Richd. Park Stobo.

O-4, 44-49: Lease & release. 21 & 22 Sept 1774, George Duncan of Charles Town, Gentleman, to John Mills of Charles Town, messenger of his Majestys Council, for £500 SC money, 300 acres in Colleton County on Savannah River adj. land held by Drewry Pace, Zachariah White. George Duncan (LS), Wit: William Russell, Robt. Crabb. Proved 22 Sept 1773 before George Davidson, J.P. in Charles Town District, by the oath of Robt. Crabb. Recorded 22 Nov 1774.

O-4, 49-53: 2 Sept 1760, Job Rothmahler of Province of SC, Eldest Lawfull son and surviving acting executor of the last will and testament of Job Rothmahler, Esqr., deceased, to Joseph Ball of Charles Town, Sugar Baker, town lot of ½acre number 105, granted to William Bradley, by the will of Job Rothmahler devised to his wife and children, his wife Ann, Joseph Wragg, Esqr., Mr. Richard Lambton, merchant, and his son Job Rothmahler, exrs., dated 17 Jan 1739, duly proved, and said Ann Rothmahler during the infancy of said Job Rothmahler took upon her the administration thereof, the said Richard Lambston and Joseph Wragg having refused. Job Rothmahler (LS), Wit: James Grindlay, Thos Grimball. Proved by the oath of Thos Grimball before William Burrows, 3 Sept 1760. Recorded 23 Nov 1774.

O-4, 53-56: Lease & release. 24 & 25 Nov 1773, Frederick Kreidner, Sugar Baker, and Catharine his wife, of Charles Town, to Michael Muckinfus of same, Black smith, for £100 SC money, 450 acres in Prince Williams Parish adj. land of Spikes, Muckinfus. Frederick Kreidner (LS), Cathrine Kreidner (+) (LS), Wit: Nicholas Fittig, Emanuel Abrahams. Recorded 23 Nov 1774.

O-4, 57-60: 12 Aug 1768, Roger Pinckney, Provost Marshall of SC, to Michael Muckinfus of Charles Town, Blacksmith, whereas Robert Stewart of Amelia Township, planter, was seized of a plantation of 300 acres in the fork of Santee and Wateree Rivers, and said Robert Stewart by his bond 11 Aug 1767 bound to John Dawson & Charles Dudley, merchant, in the penal sum of £399 s16 d6 SC money, for the payment of £169 s18 d6, and said John Dawson and Charles Dudley in the court of common pleas did obtain a judgment... for £140 paid by Michael Muckinfuss, conveyed this tract of 300 acres. Roger Pinckney Pro. Mar. (LS), Wit: Robt Cochran, Wm. Pinckney.

O-4, 60-63: Lease & release. 23 & 24 Sept 1774, Peter Horry of Prince George Parish, Craven County, planter, to Elias Horry Senior of St. James Parish Santee, planter, for £5 SC money, 750 acres originally granted to Elias Horry 16 May 1745 in Prince George Parish adj. land of William Lewis, John Delesseline, ___ Gaillard, Elias Horry. Peter Horry (LS), Wit: Hendrick Sneyder, James Barns, John West. Proved by the oath of Jno West before D. Horry, 17 Nov 1774. Recorded 28 Nov 1774.

O-4, 63-67: Lease & release. _____ 1770, Mary Burn, Sempstress, to Michael Muckenfus, Blacksmith, for £21 SC money, 100 acres on a branch of Saludy River granted to Mary Burns 28 Jan 1771. Mary Burns (LS), Wit: Thos Obrien. Recorded 13 Dec 1774.

O-4, 68-78: To Thomas Knox Gordon, Esquire, Chief Justice of the Court of Common Pleas, the petition of Elias Horry Junior, Esqr., and Elizabeth his wife, one of the daughters of William Branford, late of Charles Town, deceased, sheweth that your petitioner Elizabeth's father William Branford was possessed of a tract called Old Town, about 1100 acres at or near Ashley River in St. Andrews Parish, and by his last will and testament dated 11 nov 1766 devised to his son William Branford and that the said William Branford the father on or about 1 May 1767 died leaving said will in full force and said William Branford the son on or about 31 March 1770 died intestate and without issue leaving Elizabeth wife of said Elias horry Junior and Ann wife of Thomas Horry of Charles Town a minor and that said lands divided between her and her said sister An wife of Thomas Horry, pray for a writ of partition... dated 10 August 1774. E. Horry Junr, Elizabeth Horry. Be it so. Thos Knox Gordon. Recorded 13 Dec 1774.

Partition made of tracts: 35 acres and 30 acres making 65 acres and comprehended in one grant to James Lesade 9 Sept 1696, a tract of 85 acres part of 100 acres granted to sa.d James Lesade 8 Sept 1697, and tract of 174 acres part of 240 acres granted to said James Lesade 19 Sept 1696, a tract of 119 acres part of 2845 acres granted to sd. James Lesade __ Sept 1696, a tract of 50 acres granted to William Branford 11 July 1694, tract of 41 acres granted to William Branford 5 Dec 1696, tract of __2 acres granted to William Branford 23 July 1711, tract of 10 acres granted to James Donoho 16 Dec 1676, 10 acres granted to George Canty 28 Oct 1676, tract of 19 acres part of 36 acres granted to Anthony Churne 21 Apr 1677, tract of 43¼ acres part of tract of 156 acres granted to James Bryan 9 June 1709, total 1008¼ acres adj. Ashley River lately granted to Elias Horry Junr, on Old Town Creek and marshes thereof lately granted to sd. Elias Horry, Alexander Perroneau adj. representatives of Alexander Perroneau and John Samways deceased and marshes lately granted to sd. Elias Horry Junior, lands granted to Francis Rose. dated 29 Sept 1774. Edward Lightwood (LS), Thomas Savage (LS), Edward Blake (LS), Wm. Stoutenburgh (LS), Simsor Tufts (LS). (Plat included.) Judgment signed 11 Oct 1774. James Trail, C. C. P. Recorded 13 Dec 1774.

O-4, 78-88: Lease & release. 21 & 22 Nov 1774, Thomas Horry of Charles Town, planter, to Elias Horry Junior of same, esquire, for £3000 SC money, tract of 50 acres granted to William Branford 2 Jan 1697, 150 acres granted to William Branford 11 July 1694, 41 acres granted to William Brandford 5 Dec 1796, 72 acres granted to William Branford 23 July 1711, 10 acres ranted to James Donoho 16 Dec 1676, 10 acres granted to George Cantey 28 Oct 1767, 100 acres granted to Thomas Clarke 8 July 1696, 19 acres part of 36 acres granted to Anthony Churne 21 Apr 1677, 33¼ acres part of 100 acres granted to James Lesade 8 Sept 1697, in the whole 489¼ acres. Thos Horry (LS), Ann Horry (LS), Wit: John Woodbery, Jno Bradwell. Proved in Charles Town District before Maurice Simons, J. P., by the oath of John Woodbery. Recorded 13 Dec 1774. Release from Ann, wife of Thomas Horry, Jr., before Edward Savage, Esqr., one of the justices of the Court of Common Pleas of SC. Recorded in office of common pleas Book No. 9 folio 484-488, James Trail, C. C. P.

O-4, 89-93: Lease & release. 11 & 12 Sept 1774, John Bowen, planter, of Charraw District, SC, to Joshua Lucas of same, planter, for £150 SC money, 100 acres granted to Walter Downes 2 Feb 1754 on south side of Pedee River on Hughes Creek adj. Joseph Jolleys land, land laid out to John Hughes, land since laid out to Joshua Lucas. John Bowen (LS), Wit: John Ross, Dav'd Monaghan. Proved in Cheraw District before William Henry Harington, J.P., by the oath of John Ross, 20 Dec 1774. Recorded 20 Dec 1774.

O-4, 93-97: Lease & release. 12 & 13 June 1771, James Turner of the Fork of Broad and Saluday rivers in Craven county, planter, to John Snelgrove Junr, son of Elizabeth Jenkins and supposed son of Henry Snelgrove of county and province aforesaid, for £200 SC money, 200 acres in Craven

SOUTH CAROLINA DEED ABSTRACTS 1773-1778

County between Broad & Saluday Rivers on a branch of Salludy called Bear Creek, granted to James Turner 4 Feb 1768. James Turner (T) (LS), Ann Turner (X) (LS), Wit: D'l Gartman, Bar'h Gartman, George Lufft. Proved by the oath of Daniel Gartman before Michl Dickert, J. P., 17 Aug 1771. Recorded 21 Dec 1774.

O-4, 98-103: Lease & release. 4 & 5 Oct 1774, William Loocock of Charles Town, Practitioner of Physic, to George Duncan, Wine Merchant, of Charles Town, for £200 SC money, 500 acres in the District of Ninety Six on south side of Pacolet River on a branch called Williamsons Creek, granted to sd. William Loocock 7 May 1774. (Plat included). William Loocock (LS), Wit: Charles Michie, John Gunter. Proved 6 Oct 1774 before George Davidson, J. P. in Charles Town District, by the oath of John Gunter. Recorded 22 Dec 1774.

O-4, 104-107: George Anson of Shugborough Manor in the County of Stafford, Esquire, nephew and heir at law of Thomas Anson, late of Shugborough Manor, esquire, deceased, which said Thomas Anson was brother and heir at law of the Right Honourable George Lord Anson also deceased, appoints George Roupell of Charles Town, Esqr., SC, his lawfull attorney, to take possession of all that barony of 12,000 acres and to recover all moneys, etc. G. Anson. Wit: Richard Higgins, Middle Temple London; Thomas Blackall, Shugborough Staffordshire. Recorded 23 Dec 1774.

O-4, 107-119: Lease & release in trust for marriage settlement. 24 & 25 March 1774, Alexander Wright of Charles Town, Esquire, and Elizabeth his wife (which said Elizabeth is heir at law, Devisee, legatee, and only child of John Izard, Late of said province, Esqr., deceased) to Arthur Middleton and John Izard, both of Charles Town, specially nominated in behalf of said Elizabeth, whereas said Alexander Wright and Elizabeth his wife did 9 June 1772 exhibit their original bill of complaint in the Court of Chancery against Henry Middleton and Daniel Blake, and set forth that under the will of John izard, the said Alexander Wright by his intermarriage with said Elizabeth and by his having had lawfull issue of her body, a son then living, was become intitled to the real and personal estate of said John Izard deceased, and also to that part of the estate of Paul Jenys deceased which was decreed in the manner particularly set forth in said Bill in trust. on 2 March 1774 said Alexander Wright and Elizabeth his wife did exhibit their supplemental bill in said court and did charge that the said Elizabeth did in fact attain her age of twenty one years on 23 January last ... tracts of land and negroes and slaves.... negroes [named] on Combahee Plantation and negroes on Dorchester Plantation [named], plantation in parish of St. Georges Dorchester whereon said Alexander at present resides, 1200 acres adj. John Izard, Ashley River, John Ioor deceased, lands now in the tenure of Richard Waring, Mr. Bradwell, lands formerly of Mr. Bradwell, Mr. Baker, and plantation on Combahee River in Prince Williams Parish, adj. Doctor william Rose, Ralph Izard; plantation at the Euhaws in Parish of St. Helena, 1500 acres, being one moiety of 3000 acres granted to Paul Jenys esquire, adj. William Middleton, Thomas Heyward, John Daly. Jno Izard (LS), Eliza'h Wright (LS), Alex'r Wright (LS), Arthur Middleton (LS), Wit: Chs. Cotesworth Pinckney, Chs. Pinckney Junr, Lamb't Lance. Proved before James Johnson, J. P. in Charles Town District, by the oath of Charles Cotesworth Pinckney 27 Aug 1774. Recorded 23 Dec 1774.

O-4, 120-125: Lease & release. 12 & 13 Aug 1774, James McIntosh, Late Soldier in His Majestys 42 or Royal Highland Regiment of foot, to Samuel Cross, late of Charles Town, Tavern Keeper but now of Berkley County, planter, for £50 SC money, 50 acres on his Majestys Royal Bounty in Berkley County on SW side four hole swamp on a small branch called spring branch adj. James Haley, Wiliam Mellards, Peter Harris, granted 11 Aug 1774 to said James McIntosh. James McIntosh (LS), Wit: Peter Horn, John Fry. Proved 14 Oct 1774 before Geo Davidson, J.P. in Charles Town District, by the oath of Peter Horn. Recorded 5 Jan 1775.

O-4, 125-128: Lease. 5 Sept 1774, Martin Lloyd of Charles Town, Gentlemen, to Herman Nuffer of Charles Town, Tavern Keeper, for rents and covenants hereafter reserved, lot on King St. now occupied and possessed by said Herman Nuffer and Richard Latham. Martin Lloyd (LS), Herman Nuffer (LS), Wit: Abraham Ferris, Philip Hartlung. Proved 5 Sept 1774 before Thos Turner, J. P. in Charles Town District, by the oath of Abraham Ferris. Recorded 6 Jan 1775.

O-4, 128-132: Lease & release. 28 & 29 Jan 1773, Martin Remly & Barbara his wife, carpenter, of Charles Town, to Herman Nuffer, Tavern Keeper of same, for £100 SC money, 100 acres in Craven

SOUTH CAROLINA DEED ABSTRACTS 1773-1778

County adj. land granted to Daniel Rees, granted 22 Jan 1759 to Martin Remly. Martin Remly (H) (LS), Barbary Remley (X) (LS), Wit: Leonard Martin, Mathias Wolf. Proved 18 Oct 1774 before William Nisbett, J. P. in Charles Town District, by the oath of Leonard Martin. Recorded 7 Jan 1775.

O-4, 133-140: Lease & release. 12 & 13 Aug 1774, John Hodgson of Darthdale in the Parish of Knavesdale in the County of Northumberland, Carpenter, heir at Law of John Hodgson, late of Middle Temple, London, Esquire, deceased, who was the son & heir at Law of William Hodgson next mentioned, and also heir at law of William Hodgson, Landgrave and Casique of Carolina in America deceased, to Robert Brailsford of Parish of St. Bridget, otherwise Saint Bridges London, Gentleman, and John Boss [Bass?], Leiceister, Gentleman, for £500 money of Great Britain, several tracts and baronies at or near Port Royal in South Carolina, by letter patent 11 Apr 1715 granted to said William Hodgson by Lord John Carteret Palatine and the rest of the Lords Proprietors, by virtue of instruments dated 13 Apr 1736 from Joseph Avery and William Bagshall of the Welch Copper Office, fillpot Lane, London, merchant, and Benjamin Lund of City of Bristol, county of Somerset, Merchant, in the penal sum of £10,000. John Hodgson (LS), Wit: Thos Dixon atty at Law, Joshua Hanshaw. Proved by the oath of Joshua Hanshaw of Goswell Street, Middlesex County, Book keeper to the Horse Shoe Inn. Recorded 10 Jan 1775.

O-4, 140-149: Lease & release. 19 & 20 Aug 1774, John Boss of Leicester, Gentleman, to Robert Dee of Aldersgate St. London, Inholder, for five shillings... [to do with tracts in preceding deed] said John Boss intends to sell and dispose of his aforesaid moiety but at present is not sufficient acquainted of what value the same are, the same has found it necessary and expedient to make a voyage to South Carolina and to inspect survey and take a proper admeasurement and estimate of the aforesaid lands. John Boss (LS), Wit: Wm. Herne, Thos Johnson. Proved by the oath of Thos. Johnson in London. 27 Aug 1774 before Frederick Bull, Mayor. Recorded 12 Jan 1775.

O-4, 149-155: Lease & release. 23 & 24 Aug 1774, Abel Thomas of St. Marks Parish, Craven County, SC, planter, and Mary his wife, to John Milhous of Parish of St. Bartholomew in Colleton County, Millright, for £855 SC money, 150 acres on Granies Quarter Creek in St. Marks Parish, Craven County adj. land granted to John Dobbins, David jordan, John Riddle, George Gantter, land surveyed for Charles Elliott Esqr., said tract of 150 acres granted to Daniel Mathews 1 June 1767. Abel Thomas (LS), Mary Thomas (+) (LS), Wit: Stephen Matlock, Isaac Thomas, Daniel McMullan. Proved 1 Sept 1775 before John N. Oglethorp, Esqr., J.P. in Camden District, by the oath of Stephen Matlock. Recorded 13 Jan 1775.

O-4, 155-159: Lease & release. 16 & 17 March 1773, William Elliott of Beaufort, Port Royal, Sc, Esquire, to James Parsons of Charles Town, Esquire, for ten shillings, 1000 acres between Saludy and Savannah Rivers on waters of Buckhalters Creek adj. land of John Harritons, Laurence Rambos land, John Ward, Richard Jones, Edward Kouches, John Buckhalters, said 1000 acres granted 13 March 1772 to said William Elliot. Wm. Elliott (LS), Wit: Jacob Read, Robt. Ladson.

O-4, 160-164: Lease & release. 24 & 25 June 1773, James Parsons, Esqr. of Charles Town, to George Gabriel Powell, Esqr. of Charles Town, for £1000, 1000 acres granted to William Elliott of Port Royal 13 March 1772 between Saludy and Savannah Rivers on waters of Buckhalters Creek adj. land of John Harritons, Laurence Rambos land, John Ward, Richard Jones, Edward Kouches, John Buckhalters. James Parsons (LS), Wit: Mich Meara, Henry Nichols. Proved in Berkley County by the oath of Michael Meara of Charles Town before John Troup, J.P., 25 June 1773. Recorded 19 Jan 1775.

O-4, 164-169: Lease & release. 1 & 2 Aug 1773, George Gabriel Powell, Esqr. of Charles Town, to Thomas Eveleigh of Charles Town, merchant, for £250, 1000 acres granted to William Elliott of Port Royal 13 March 1772 between Saludy and Savannah Rivers on waters of Buckhalters Creek adj. land of John Harritons, Laurence Rambos land, John Ward, Richard Jones, Edward Kouches, John Buckhalters. G. G. Powell (LS), Wit: Philip Scurlock, T. Cambridge. Proved in Charles Town District by the oath of Tobias Cambridge before Rugeley, 19 Jan 1775. Recorded 19 Jan 1775.

O-4, 169-172: Lease & release. 14 & 15 Oct 1774, Miles Brewton of Charles Town, Esquire, and Mary his wife, to Pierce Butler of same, esquire, for £1, 2000 acres on a branch of fair forest called

SOUTH CAROLINA DEED ABSTRACTS 1773-1778

Rockey Creek adj. land of Hillery Gay, William Canes, granted to said Miles Brewton 7 May in the year aforesaid. M. Brewton (LS), Mary Brewton (LS), Wit: Steph. Bull, David Grame. Proved in Charles Town District by the oath of David Grame, before Wm. Rugeley, J. P., 27 Oct 1774. Recorded 22 Jan 1775.

O-4, 173-179: Lease & release. 24 & 25 June 1774, Peter Simond of Bishop Gate Street, London, Merchant, to Robert Heriot of George Town, Winyaw, Esqr., for £70 money of Great Britain, lot number 14 in George Town and lot number 217 in George Town. Peter Simond , Wit: John Besnard, Henry Gunn. Proved in Charles Town District by the oath of Henry Gunn, 26 Oct 1774, before Geo. Davidson, J. P. Recorded 24 Jan 1775.

O-4, 179-184: Lease & release. 1 & 2 Dec 1773, Jacob Gray of Williamsburgh township, Blacksmith, and Ann his wife, to Roger Gordon of Indian Town, planter, for £600 SC money, 150 acres on a small branch of Little River of Saludy called Sandyrun, granted 20 Aug 1767. Jacob Gray (LS), Ann Gray (LS), Wit: James Ward, James Hamilton, John Edwards (X). Proved in Craven County by the oath of James Ward before Saml Nesmith, J. P., 20 Jan 1774. Recorded 25 Jan 1775.

O-4, 184-188: Lease & release. 30 & 31 Aug 1768, Alexander White of Long cane, Granville County, Sc, freeholder, to Wm. White of Lang cane, planter, for £60 SC money, 100 acres granted 21 Aug 1767 to Alexander White on waters of curltail a branch of Long Cane Creek. Alexr White (LS), Barbara White (O) (LS), Wit: Jas. Loosk, Mathew Young (+). Proved 1 Sept 1768 before Patrick Calhoun, J. P. in Granville & Colleton County, by the oath of Mathew Young. Recorded 26 Jan 1775.

O-4, 189-195: Lease & release. 6 & 7 Aug 1772, Wm Cattell of St. Andrews Parish, planter, to Thomas Horry of Charles Town, gentleman, for £1675 SC money, 67 acres in Colleton County on the Horse Shoe Savannah adj. lands belonging to the heirs or devisees of the late William Brandford deceased, of which said parcel is a part of a tract of 400 acres granted 24 May 1733 unto William Cattell deceased, the grandfather of said William Cattell party to these presents. William Cattell, Wit: Elias Horry Junr, Francis Rose. Proved in Charles Town District by the oath of William Horry Junr before William Rugeley, J. P., 3 Nov 1774. Recorded 27 Jan 1775.

O-4, 195-200: Lease & release. 18 & 19 June 1770, Henry De Mounge of South Carolina, planter, to Autoen St. John, Merchant, of same place, for £200 SC money, 200 acres on Gills Creek a branch of Santee River in Craven County adj. land granted to Benjamin Bell, granted 21 Dec 1769 to Henry De Mounge. Henry De Mounge (mark) (LS), Wit: Randolph Theus, John Leitner, Wm. Hack. Proved in Berkley County by the oath of Randolph Theus before Wm. Arther, J. P., 28 May 1772. Recorded 30 Jan 1775.

O-4, 200-204: 19 May 1743, John Chevillette of Purysburgh, Granville County, SC, to John Baptist Bourquin of same, surgeon, for £200 SC money, 450 acres in the township of Purysburgh adj. Daniel Vernezobees, James Delas. John Chevillette (LS), Wit: Peter Laffette, David Laffitte. Proved 4 June 1743 before Frederick Dezean, J. P., by the oath of Peter Laffitte. Recorded 1 Feb 1775.

O-4, 204-206: Mortgage. John Hatter of Charles Town, Berkley County, bound to John Syme, Practitioner of Physic, in the penal sum of £3500 SC money for the payment of £1750, mortgage of 100 acres on Edisto River, 500 acres with three negroes December, Juno, and Levens, forty head of cattle, forty sheep, ten hogs, and sundry articles of household furniture, 9 Aug 1773. John Hatter (LS), Wit: Thos McClellan. Proved in Charles Town District by the oath of Thos McClellan 1 Feb 1775 before Wm. Rugeley, J. P. Recorded 3 Feb 1775. Satisfied.

O-4, 207-209: Mortgage. John Hatter of Charles Town, Berkley County, bound to John Syme and Elizabeth his wife, in the penal sum of £4000 SC money for the payment of £2000, mortgage of small Island called Small Woods Island, with 2 negro men Hector and November with a boy Duck. John Hatter (LS), Wit: Mary Martimore. Proved in Charles Town District by the oath of Mary Martimore 1 Feb 1775 before Wm. Rugeley, J. P. Recorded 4 Feb 1775.

O-4, 209-210: Bond. John Hatter of Charles Town, Mariner, and wife Elizabeth, then named Elizabeth Richardson widow, bound to John Syme of Parish of St. Thomas, practitioner of physic, in trust for the separate use of Elizabeth Hatter, pursuant to a marriage agreement, 5 Dec 1773. John Hatter (LS), Wit: Clem Lemprier, James Amoss. Proved by the oath of James Amoss in Charles Town District, 1 Feb 1775 before William Rugeley, J. P. Recorded 4 Feb 1775.

O-4, 211: John Hatter of Charles Town, Mariner, bound to John Syme, Practitioner of Physic, 9 Aug 1773, in the sum of £1750 SC money. John Hatter (LS), Wit: Thos McClellan. Proved by the oath of Thos McClellan, 1 Feb 1775 before Wm. Rugeley, J.P. Principal and interest paid, July 25th 1778. John Syme. Wit: Geo Sheed.

O-4, 212-214: Mortgage. Martin Lloyd of Charles Town District, bound 8 Nov 1774 to Jacob Tobias of Charles Town District, Merchant, in the penal sum of £8000 for the payment of £4000, mortgage of tenement in the possession of Herman Nuffer on King Street in Charles Town. Martin Lloyd (LS), Wit: Eml Abrahams, Elias Evans. Proved by the oath of Elias Evans 11 Nov 1774 before William Rugeley, J.P. Recorded 4 Feb 1775.

O-4, 214-221: Lease & release. 20 & 21 Jan 1774, William Moultrie, Esqr., of Charles Town, and Elizabeth Damaris his wife, to Daniel Ravenel, Esquire of Parish of St. John in Berkly County, for £4000 SC money, 216 acres in St. John's Parish Berkley County part of a tract commonly called Northamton. William Moultrie (LS), Elizabeth D. Moultrie (LS), Wit: Jacob Motte, John S. Dart. Proved in Charles Town District 10 Nov 1774 before John Troup, J.P. Recorded 7 Feb 1775.

O-4, 221-229: Lease & mortgage. 14 & 15 July 1774, Tunes Teabout of South Carolina, Black-smith, and Sarah his wife, to Robert Philp of Charles Town, Esquire, Robert Wells of same, bookseller, and Charles Johnston and John Simpson of same place, merchants, bound in the sum of £6000, mortgage of lot #54 in Beaufort for the debt of £3000. Tunes Tebout (LS), Sarah Tebout (LS), Wit: James Trail, Jas. Johnston. Proved by the oath of James Trail 15 Nov 1774. Recorded 9 Feb 1775. Sarah, wife of Tunes Teabourt, relinquished dower before Thomas Knox Gordon.

O-4, 230-235: Lease & mortgage. 10 & 11 Nov 1774, John Kelly of Charles Town, Baker, and Mary his wife, to Thos Shirley and William Price of same, merchants, mortgage in the sum of £2491 s14 d 4 for the payment of £1245 s17 d8 SC money, mortgage of lot #261 in Charles Town. John Kelly (LS), Mary Kelly (X) (LS), Wit: Elisha Sawyer, Saml Hraboswki. Proved by the oath of Samuel Hrabowski 11 Feb 1775 before Wm. Rugeley. Recorded 13 Feb 1775. Thomas Nicholls qualified executor of the last will and testament of William Price, one of the mortgagees, and late attorney to Thomas Shirley, acknowledge that this has been fully paid, 28 Aug 1794. D. Mazyck, Register.

O-4, 236-242: Lease & release. 4 & 5 Aug 1774, Agness Stitt formerly of the Parish of Anna Kitt in the County of Down, Kingdom of Ireland, but now of Charles Town, Sister Devisee and Heir at law of William Jameson, late of Craven County, SC, planter, to Jared Nelson of St. Mathews Parish, SC, gentleman, for £6000 SC money, said William Jameson by his last will and testament dated 8 Jan 1766 did bequeath to his wife Mary since married to and now the wife of Thomas Sumpter one half of all his moveables and one half of all his personal estate with one plantation joining Mr. Neilson on Santee and devised to his said sister Agnes the remainder of his estate both real & personal... two tracts of land 400 acres and 200 acres adj. lands of Jared Neilson, Miss Hannah Ainslie a minor, land now supposed to belong to Doctor Farar and on Santee River in the Parish of St. Mark. Agness Stitt (LS), Wit: Henry Nicholes, Ellen Brown. Proved in Charles Town District by the oath of Henry Nicholes 11 Feb 1775 before Wm. Rugeley, J.P. Recorded 15 Feb 1775.

O-4, 242-249: Lease & release. 8 & 9 Sept 1774, Elijah Postell of St. George Parish Dorchester, SC, Esqr., and Susannah his wife, to Isaac McPherson, of St. Pauls Parish, Gentlemen, for £10,000 SC money, 297 acres on Horse Savannah in St. Pauls Parish, adj. land of estate of William Cattell Senr deceased, estate of Isaac Nichols, land late of James Brisbane, land now or late of Martha Miles, and partly on Samuel Wainswrights land, adj. to which said tract of 297 acres is a smaller tract of 35 acres heretofore granted to John Izard and conveyed to Isaac McPherson, and a tract of 162 acres part of 650 acres granted to one John Miles in Colleton County adj. Broad Road leading from Stono to Parkers or Fergusons Ferry, Frederick Grimkies land, by lease and release 31 March and 1 April 1767 released by said Isaac McPhersons and Elizabeth his wife to Elijah Postell. Elijah

SOUTH CAROLINA DEED ABSTRACTS 1773-1778

Postell (LS), Wit: Wit: George Smith, Thos Waring, Archer Smith. Proved by the oath of George Smith 8 Oct 1774 before Fenwick Bull, J.P. in Berkley County. Recorded 16 Feb 1775.

O-4, 249-252: Lease & release. 23 & 24 Jan 1740/41, William Waties of Parish of Prince George, SC, and Dorothy his wife, to Masters Hankins of sane, for £60 SC money, 400 acres on the head o Little River in the Parish of Prince George. Wm. Waties (LS), Dorothy Waties (LS), Wit: John Coachman, Mary Allein. Proved by the oath of Mary Dick formerly Mary Allein 11 Nov 1774 before Job Rothmahler. Recorded 17 Feb 1775.

O-4, 252-257: Lease & release. 12 & 13 May 1772, John Elvis of Craven County, Prince George Parish, SC, planter, and Mary his wife, to James Galaven of same county and province, for £100 SC money, 200 acres in Craven County, Prince George Parish, on north side Little Peedee River adj. Wm. Ramsey. John Elvis (I) (LS), Mary Elvis (C) (LS), Wit: John McDaniell, Benjn. Gause. Proved by the oath of John McDaniell 23 May 1772 before Dennis Hankins, J.P. Recorded 20 Feb 1775.

O-4, 257-262: Lease & release. 17 & 18 Sept 1772, Margaret Inabnet of Orangeburgh Township, Berkley County, SC, planter, to Samuel Rowe of same place, planter, for £100 SC money, 23½ acres adj. said Inabnets land, Samuel Rowes land, being part of 150 acres granted to Henry Wurster 17 Sept 1736 in the Township of Orangeburgh adj. John Sturtz, John Pruder[?], Ulrich Tobler, recorded in Book HH; said Henry Wurst by indenture 15 July 1752 conveyed to Margaret Inabnet tract of 150 acres for £100. Margaret Inabnet (X) (LS), Wit: Baltus Inabnit, John Inabnit, Saml Inabnit. Proved in Orangeburgh District before Christopher Rowe, J. P., by the oath of Baltuce Inabnit, 25 Sept 1773. Recorded 21 Feb 1775.

O-4, 262-269: Lease & release. 24 & 25 Nov 1774, Joseph Wyatt of Charles Town, SC, Practitioner of Physick, to William Nisbett of Charles Town, Esquire, for s15 SC money, 550 acres near Mount Parsons on Long Cane Settlement, Granville county, Ninety Six District, adj. land of James Parsons, Esquire, Ephraim Mitchell, John Craswells, land laid out to Henry McMurdy, said 550 acres granted 18 Nov instant to said Joseph Wyatt. Joseph Wyatt (LS), Wit: Thos Winstanly, R[obert] Johnston. Proved 26 Nov 1774 before Thos Skottowe, J.P., by the oath of Thomas Winstanley. Recorded 22 Feb 1775.

O-4, 269-270: 4 Oct 1774, James Brisbane of Charles Town, SC, Esqr., and Sarah his wife, to Darby Pendergrass of same town, Merchant, for £500 SC money, ten acres formerly known by the name of Stevens but now called Bacons Bridge in Berkley County, on Ashley River, adj. property formerly of Robert Wright but now said to belong to William Morgan. James Brisbane (LS), Sarah Brisbane (LS), Wit: Norman McLeod, John Greene. (Plat included).

O-4, 271-274: Lease & release. 29 & 30 Aug 1774, George Fortune, Master or commander of the Ship **Charming Sally**, to Darby Pendergrass of Charles Town, merchant, for £3000 SC money, 200 acres in Craven County, Prince George Parish, south of Waccamaw River upon Tilley Swamp adj. land laid out for Benjamin Gause, granted to said George Fortune (on Kings Bounty), 26 Aug instant. George Fortune (LS), Wit: George Thompson, Saml _____.

O-4, 275-279: Lease & release. 25 & 26 Nov 1774, Daniel Morral of Prince Georges Parish, Craven County, planter, to Darby Pendergrass of Charles Town, Merchant, for £3000 SC money, 50 acres in Prince George Parish on south side Waccamaw River adj. land of George Fortune, William Tillys land, granted to said Daniel Morral 30 Sept last. Daniel Morrall (LS), Wit: Daziel Hunter, William Cole. Proved by the oath of Daziel Hunter 20 Dec 1774 before Wm. Rugeley. Recorded 24 Feb 1775.

O-4, 279-283: Lease & release. 10 & 11 June 1773, Richard Odum of Craven County, SC, planter, to John Hawthorn of same, planter, for £150 SC money, 200 acres granted to sd. Richard Odum 10 May 1773 on eastward side of a branch of Little Peedee called the Beaver Dam. Richard Odum (O) (LS), Mary Odum (+) (LS), Wit: Henry Councel, Lott Wattson (X), Thomas Connor. Proved in Craven County before Philip Pledger, J. P., by the oath of Thomas Connor, 16 Dec 1774. Recorded 27 Feb 175.

SOUTH CAROLINA DEED ABSTRACTS 1773-1778

O-4, 283-291: Lease & release. 20 & 23 Oct 1774, Edward Harleston of St. Johns Parish, Berkley County, Esquire, only Qualified & Acting Executor of the will of John Harleston, late of Berkley County, gentleman, deceased, to Thomas Corbett of Charles Town, merchant, for £2220 SC money, said John Harleston by his will dated 21 May 1767 did give to his four sons John, Isaac, William & Edward as tenants in common, lots at Harlestonborough, and said John Harleston departed this life, probate whereof hath been granted to Edward Harleston alone, and John Harleston one of the sons and devisees of John Harleson the father dyed seized of his portion but before he departed this life on 8 Feb 1768 made his will and named Edward Harleston and John Harleston son of Nicholas to sell his real estate, and Isaac Harleston In May Term 1773 obtained from the court of common pleas a writ of partition between the said Isaac and his brothers William and Edward who then were and still are minors and on 25 Aug last past did mark partition, lots in Harleston marked in Plat A.... and Plat B. Edward Harleston (LS), Wit: John Ward, G. Manigault Junr. Proved 22 Dec 1771 by the oath of Joshua Ward before Thos Bee, J. P. in Charles Town District. Recorded 1 March 1775.

O-4, 292: [beginning of deed written and marked through]. 7 Jan 1771, Giles Chapman & Sarah his wife of Craven County, SC, yeoman, to John Johnes of same, for ten shillings, 193 acres on Scotch Creek....

O-4, 292-300: Lease & release. 20 & 21 Oct 1774, Edward Harleston of St. Johns Parish, Berkley County, Esquire, only Qualified & Acting Executor, eldest son and devisee of John Harleston, late of St. Johns Parish, gentleman, deceased, to Miss Elizabeth Harleston of Charles Town, spinster, for £2250 SC money, lots on Charleston Neck [see **Deed Book O-4, 283-291**]. Edward Harleston (LS), Wit: Isaac Harleston, William Tear. Proved 22 Dec 1774 before Thos Bee, J. P., by the oath of William Tead. Recorded 2 March 1775.

O-4, 300-306: Lease & release. 10 & 11 Oct 1772, Benjamin Screven of Craven County, SC, planter, to James Snow of same, planter, for £4000 SC money, 1000 acres in two tracts of 500 acres each in Queensborough Township, Elisha Screven Senior from Capt. Othniel Beal lawfully purchased and by a resurvey found to be within the lines of original surveys a surplus of 760 acres since granted to said Elisha Screven Senior and left to his son Elisha Screven Junior by will adj. each other on Pee Dee River adj. said James Snow's land. Benjamin Screven Wit: Francis Futhy, Wm. Moore, Francis Snow. Proved in Craven county before Saml Nesmith, J. P., by the oath of William Moore, 14 Dec 1772. Recorded 3 March 1775.

O-4, 306-311: Lease & release. 19 & 20 Dec 1774, William Green Senr of Prince Fredericks Parish, Craven County, SC, planter, to William Snow of same, planter, for £1850 SC money, 213 acres part of 450 acres granted to William Clarke deceased 8 March 1736/7 in Queensborough Township, Johnston's Island on south side of Great Pedee river adj. James Gordons land now the property of said Snow, Andrew Johnston's and David Hartees land. William Green (LS), Wit: James Snow, Richd Green Junr, John Lasey (I). Proved by the oath of James Snow before Wm. Rugeley, J.P., 21 Dec 1774. Recorded 4 March 1775.

O-4, 312-315: Lease & release. 4/14 Nov 1773, Nicholas Rodland of St. Marks Parish, planter, and Mary his wife, to Thomas Griffith of same parish, planter, for £175 SC money, 100 acres on Twenty five Mile Creek in Craven County adj. land of Samuel Wells, granted 26 Oct 1772 to Nicoliss Rodland. Nicoliss Rodland (NR) (LS), Maryan Rodland (-) (LS), Wit: John Nipper (+), John Motly (Z), James Smith (+). Proved in Camden District before John N. Oglethorpe, J. P., by the oath of John Nipper, 5 Oct 1774. Recorded 4 March 1775.

O-4, 315-319: Lease & release. 9 Oct 1770, Edward Teel and Rebekah Teel his wife of St. Peters Parish, Granville County, SC, to James Dupuis of same, £150 SC money, 250 acres formerly granted to sd. Edward Teel on Savannah River. Edward Teel (LS), Rebekah Teel (--) (LS), Wit: Richd Raines, John Teal. Proved in Granville County by the oath of John Teal before James Pace, J. P., 12 Oct 1770. Recorded 6 March 1775.

O-4, 319-321: South Carolina, Granville County. Anderson Young of St. Helena Parish bound to Adrian Mayer of Purysburgh, Esqr., in the penal sum of £422 current money for the payment of £236, 500 acres in Purysburgh Township adj. Henry Chiffelle, Anthony Goutier, Abraham Motley,

SOUTH CAROLINA DEED ABSTRACTS 1773-1778

William Coachman, David Giroud, Chs. Pury, John Buch[?], John Linder. deed dated 21 Sept 1774. Anderson Young (LS), Wit: John Linder, Gabriel Walzer. Proved in Purysburgh by the oath of John Linder 12 __ 1774 before David Giroud, J. P. Recorded 6 March 1775.

O-4, 321-322: 10 Sept 1774, Henry Meuron of Purysburgh in Granville County, planter, to Adrian Mayer, of same, esqr., for £800 SC money, 313 acres in Township of Purysburgh adj. David Humbert, Col. John Peter Pury, John Buche. Henry Meuron (LS), Wit: Wm. Holzendorff, Jacob Zimmerman. Proved by the oath of William Holzendorff 9 Sept 1774 before David Giroud, J. P. Recorded 7 March 1775.

O-4, 323-326: Lease & release. 5 & 6 June 1772, Ann Hamilton of St. Johns parish, Berkley County, and William Flud of St. Mathews Parish, to Henry Boyd of St. Marks Parish, Craven County, for £500 SC money, 200 acres in St. Marks Parish on north side Santee River opposite Saxagotha Township, adj. heirs of Henry Snellings, land granted to Samuel Synes, land of Jesse Goodwyn, land granted to Thomas Jackson, said tract of 200 acres granted to James McKelvey deceased who dyed intestate whereby said tract was hired [sic] by An Hamilton and Wm. Flud. Ann Hamilton (A) (LS), Wm. Flud (LS), Wit: Wm. Land, John Oliver, James McKelvey. Proved 29 Dec 1774 by the oath of John Oliver John Savage, J.P. Recorded 7 March 1775.

O-4, 326-329: Lease & release. 26 & 27 Dec 1774, William Walker of Long Cane Settlement, planter, and Mary his wife to James Parsons of Charles Town, Esqr., for £300 SC money, 150 acres on a small branch of Long Cane Creek in the District of Ninety Six, part of tract of 300 acres granted 10 July 1766 to said William Walker. William Walker (mark) (LS), Mary Walker (mark) (LS), Wit: Wm. Thos Caldwell, Patrick Calhoun. Proved by the oath of Patrick Calhoun of Long Cane, Esqr., before Wm. Burrows, 14 Jan 1775. Recorded 7 March 1775.

O-4, 329-335: Lease & release. 10 & 11 May 1773, Joseph Allston of Prince Georges Parish, Craven County, planter, and Charlotte his wife, to Josiah Allston of same, planter, for £13,000 SC money, 1150 acres on a neck between little River and the sea partly in said parish, county & province, and partly in the province of North Carolina, adj. land of Michael Bellune; also a tract of 330 acres in said parish adj. at the time of original survey to land to William Waites, Little River; also tract of 500 acres in the province of North Carolina, adj. Mr. Pinson, land late of William Alston; also tract of 490 acres adj. Col. Waites, little River, late of said Joseph Allston; also a tract of 884 acres in Brunswick County, North Carolina, on Little River, adj. Land formerly of William Waites, land now or lately not laid out, Jonathan Caulkings; a tract of 300 acres on northwest side of Little River in Prince Georges Parish, Craven County, and partly in North Carolina. Joseph Allston (LS), Charlotte Allston (LS), Wit: James Mackie, A. Belin Junr. Proved before Peter Simons by the oath of Allard Belin, 13 March 1774. Recorded 8 March 1775.

O-4, 335-338: 18 Jan 1773, Samuel Nealy of Parish of St. Marks, planter, to Hugh Whiteside of same, planter, for £50 SC money, 100 acres granted to Samuel Nealy 3 Apr 1772 in Craven county on east side Fishing Creek adj. Hugh Whiteside. Samuel Neely (LS), Wit: James Lusk, Saml Burnett. Proved before James Patton, J. P. in Craven County, by the oath of James Lusk 22 Jan 1773. Recorded 8 March 1775.

O-4, 338-342: Lease & release. 9 & 10 Dec 1774, Ludwick Wagerman of Colleton County, Orangeburgh District, planter, to Nathan Buzbey of Broad River in said district, planter, for £350 SC money, 200 acres granted to George Wagerman 9 Jan 1773, on south side Broad River opposite to the upper part of Saxegotha Township, recorded in Book NN page 195. Ludwick Wagerman (L) (LS), Wit: Christopher Cruser, Jacob Bower (S), Margarete Dickert (M). Proved by the oath of Jacob Bower in Ninety Six District before Michl Dickert, J. P., 16 Dec 1774. Recorded 9 March 1775.

O-4, 343-345: 1 Jan 1771, Patrick Welch to Robert Goudey of Colleton County, for £400 SC money, 350 acres granted 12 June 1761 to Patrick Welch on south side Saludie River. Patrick Welch (LS), Wit: Henry Foster, Wm. Low, Eliz'h Hearn (+). Acknowledged in Craven County before John Caldwell, J. P., by Patrick Welch. Recorded 9 March 1775.

SOUTH CAROLINA DEED ABSTRACTS 1773-1778

O-4, 345-348: 17 June 1764, William Dargan of Amelia Township, SC, planter, to Robert Gowdy of Ninety Six, Indian Trader, for £200 SC money, tract of 300 acres granted 18 March 1763 to sd. Wm. Dargan, on a branch of Ninty Six called Henleys Creek adj. land surveyed for Wm. Leveston Esqr. and his associates, sd. Robt Gowdy. Wm. Dargan (LS), Wit: Thos Catton, Daniel Kelly, Bryant Cother (+). Proved before John Hamilton, J. P. in Craven county, by the oath of Bryan Coker, 9 May 1769.

O-4, 348-352: Lease & release. 4 & 5 Dec 1773, James Jenkins of Berkley County, SC, Gent., to Thomas Taylor of Craven County, planter, for £2300 SC money, 250 acres granted 30 Apr 1748 to James Jenkins on the low grounds of Santee otherwise Congaree River opposite to the lower part of Saxegotha Township, adj. land of John Pearson, George Haig, recorded in Book MM page 1. James Jenkins (8) (LS), Wit: Wm. Rives, Philip Pearson. Proved by the oath of Philip Pearson, J. P., 27 Dec 1773. Recorded 10 March 1775.

O-4, 352-357: Lease & release. 2 & 3 Apr 1771, Alexander Sherrod of Craven County, Sc, planter, to James Megee, planter, for £1200 SC money, 616 acres in three tracts on Pedee River; one tract adj. Thos Lamb, John Daseter[?]; tract of 150 acres adj. Joshua Avant; 216 acres adj. Archabald Baird, Esqr. Alexander Sharrod (LS), Elizabeth Sharrod (LS), Wit: William Jameson, Rachael Alleison. Proved by the oath of William Jameson in Craven County, 3 Dec 1771 before Joseph Gourly. Recorded 10 March 1775.

O-4, 357-367: Lease & release. 5 & 6 Apr 1774, James Marshall of Norfolk St., Parish of St. Clemant Danes, County of Middlesex, Esquire, and Elizabeth his wife, formerly Elizabeth Walter, spinsters, afterwards the wife and since the widow & relict and sole devisee named in the last will and testament of William Haggett late of Mill Hill in said County of Middlesex, to Samuel Carne of Bartlotts Buildings in the Parish of St. Andrew Hobbow, City of London, Esquire, for £10,000, 390 acres on Southwest side of Ashley River in Berkley County, St. Georges Dorchester, South Carolina, in North America, adj. land now or late of John Walter, Samuel Wainwright, James Postell, John Wrag, William Wragg, purchased by said William Haggett, also tract called Crowfield of 1444 acres in the Parish of St. James Goose Creek in Berkly County adj. land of Mathew Baird, Andrew Allen deceased, Benjamin Marion, formerly Benjamin De----, Thomas Moore, Benjamin Gibbes, deceased, said grant of land Wiliam Middleton Esquire formerly proprietor of same built a large mansion house whereon he lived for many years which said tract was the estate of said Elizabeth Marshall at the time of her intermarriage with William Hagott deceased. James Marshall (LS), Eliz'h Marshall (LS), Wit: John Ramsden, John Palmer. Proved by the oath of John Ramsden of Margaret St. Parish of St. Mary le bone, County of Middlesex, England, before Fred. Bull, Major, 8 Apr 1774. Recorded 15 March 1775.

O-4, 367-371: Lease & release. 26 & 27 Dec 1774, Blake Leay White of Charles Town, Planter, and Elizabeth his wife, to Dalziel Hunter of same, for £1000 SC money, 384 acres on northeast end of Long Bay Waccamaw adj. William and Archibald Johnston, Josias Allston Esqr., John Weathers formerly William Allstons, William Johnston, granted 17 May 1774 to said Blake Leay White. Blake Leay White (LS), Eliz'h White (LS), Wit: Theodore Trezevant, Peter Timothy. Proved by the oath of Theodore Trezevant before Wm. Rugeley, J. P., 17 March 1775. Recorded 17 March 1775.

O-4, 371-377: Lease & release. 23 & 24 March 1768, Henry Whetstone of Amelia Township, Berkley County, planter, and Barbara his wife, to Simon Hooker of same place, planter, for £50 SC money, 300 acres in Orangeburgh Township, Berkley County, adj. land granted to John Whetstone, land granted to John Whetstone his father 6 Nov 1751. Henry Whetstone (W) (LS), Barbara Whetstone (mark) (LS), Wit: John Mitchell, Thos Colman, John Barber. Proved 4 Dec 1772 by the oath of Thos Holman before Gavin Pou, J. P. Recorded 17 March 1775.

O-4, 378-383: 21 Jan 1775, Wood Furman of St. Marks Parish, Craven County, planter, to Messrs. Edwards Fisher and Compt of Charles Town, Berkley County, merchants, bound in the sum of £8530 s10 for the payment of £4265 s5, 550 acres in St. Marks Parish, adj. land since granted to Samuel Bacot now the property of sd. Wood Furman, Wateree River Swamp, James Postell, which said 550 acres Wood Furman purchased from Barnard Beekman, also 212 acres adjoining above tract being part of 400 acres purchased from Samuel Bacot on edge of Beach Creek, adj. land laid out for George Gates and afterwards granted to William Westberry, adj. land which Wood Furman

SOUTH CAROLINA DEED ABSTRACTS 1773-1778

purchased from Tennis Tebout, also 400 acres adj. said tract which said Wood Furman purchased from Tennis Teabout adj. land which Wood Furman purchased from Saml Bacot, John Postell. Wood Furman (LS), Wit: Robt. Arrow Smith, Richd Wainwright. Proved 26 Jan 1775 before Fenwick Bull by the oath of Robt. Arrow Smith. Recorded 18 March 1775.

O-4, 383-388: Lease & release. South Carolina, Ninety Six District. 16 & 17 Jan 1775, Benjamin Eddings of district aforesaid and Elizabeth his wife to Thomas Willson of same, tract of 300 acres granted to sd. Benjamin Eddings in the name of Benjamin Edwards on a branch called Ninety Six and one called Rocky Creek surveyed 6 May 1756 for Pierce Corslie and granted to Benjamin Eddings in the name of Benjamin Edwards 12 Jan 1769. Benjamin Eddings (mark) (LS), Elizabeth Eddings (+) (LS), Wit: Rachel Anderson, Joseph Greer (mark), Peter McGrew (O). Proved 18 May 1775 before Wm. Anderson, J. P., by the oath of Rachel Anderson. Recorded 26 March 1775.

O-4, 388-393: Lease & release. 20 & 21 Jan 1775, Moses Cree of Province of SC, sole and absolute heir at law to Peter Cree deceased, as also the only exrs. of the last will and testament of Peter Cree deceased, to John Whatsman, house carpenter, of Ninety Six District, for ___, 100 acres on a branch of Little Saludee River granted 7 Aug 1764 to Peter Cree. Moses Cree (LS), wit: Benjamin Johnson (+), Nicholas Bhroad (+), Lucey Bhroad (+). Proved by the oath of Benjamin Johnston 27 Jan 1775 before John Wright, J.P.

O-4, 393-397: Lease & release. 1 & 2 Feb 1746, Elizabeth B. Elliott late widow of Edmund the Second Landgrave Bellinger of SC, to Thomas Butler of Ashepoo, planter, £1873 s5, whereas said Elizabeth Elliott is in possession of certain lands by virtue of the last will and testament of Edmund Bellinger and empowered to sell the same, tract of 837 acres on the head of Pocotaligo River adj. lands sold to Andrew Deveaux by Col. Charles Pinckney, John Bull, William Hutson. Eliz'h Elliott (LS), Wit: Henry Hyrne, Wm. Backsell. Recorded 24 March 1775.

O-4, 397-403: Lease & mortgage. 20 & 21 Jan 1775, William Mills & James Carmichael, both of Orangeburgh, SC, planters, to Ephraim Mitchell of Charles Town, surveyor, for £2500, 400 acres in Orangeburgh Township, Berkley County when granted bounded on John Rumph, Emanuel Thayler, Baltazer Stroman, Melchior Sachweiller, Jacob Pierson, Henry Wurtz, on the north fork of Edisto (also lots [numbers given] intended to be granted in mortgage). Wm. Mills (LS), James Carmichael (LS), Wit: Wm. Creighton, Wm. Mitchell. Proved by the oath of William Creighton in Chas. Town District, 22 March 1775 before William Rugeley, J.P. Recorded 22 March 1775.

O-4, 403-410: Lease & release. 15 & 16 Apr 1773, Peter Stevenson of Charles Town, Gentleman, and Mary Jones his wife, to Paul Townsend of same, merchant, for £1300 SC money, three lots on west side of high wadon in Charles Town Neck, about six acres, which Peter Benoist late of Charles Town, merchant, deceased, was in his life time possessed and by his last will and testament dated 3 March 1759 and now remaining in the Secretarys office of this province, amongst other things therein contained did give and devise unto his grandson Peter Stevenson after the death of Abigail his then wife and Mary his daughter, all that southermost pat of said parcel of land, from the School house Street, now George Street, and St. Philips Street. Peter Stevenson (LS), Mary Jones Stevenson (LS), Wit: Thos Horsey, John Guignard. Proved in Charles Town District by the oath of Thos Horsey, 31 Jan 1775, before William Rugeley, J. P. Recorded 23 March 1775.

O-4, 410-415: Lease & release. 13 Oct 1770, John Cheney of St. Lukes Parish, Granville County, and Martha his wife, to Benjamin Parmenter of same parish and county, for £600, 200 acres in St. Lukes Parish, originally granted to Capt. Charles Odingsell known by the name of Burrasus neck, and at sundry times transferred to different persons, on the marsh of Ewhaw Creek. John Cheney (LS), Martha Cheney (LS), Wit: Chs. Bealer, John Johnson, John Grimball Junr. Proved before John Sealey, J. P. in Granville County, by the oath of John Grimball Junr, 25 March 1775.

O-4, 416-420: Lease & release. 3 & 4 Dec 1773, John Hill of District of Ninety Six, planter, to James Brewer of same, blacksmith, for £262 SC money, tract granted to John Hill 15 May 1772, in the district aforesaid, 350 acres adj. land of Peter Day. John Hill (LS), Wit: David Thweatt, Richd Kirkland, James Thomas. Proved 17 Jan 1774 by the oath of David Thweatt before LeRoy Hammond, J.P. Recorded 25 March 1775.

SOUTH CAROLINA DEED ABSTRACTS 1773-1778

O-4, 420-421: 3 Oct 1772, John Dickinson of Augusta County, Colony of Virginia, to Robert Looney, of Craven County, SC, tract on land on south side of Broad River on Gilkeys Creek at the upper cane brake, granted to Samuel Gilkey 11 May 1753 and transferred by him to Adam Dickinson of Augusta County in Virginia, and now fell to me of the subscriber by heirship. John Dickinson (LS), Wit: David Looney, Richd. Humphreys, Saml Givens. Proved in Craven County by the oath of David Looney before Joseph Brown, J. P. 20 Nov 1772. A Memorial entered in Book M No. 12, page 13, 19 July 1774. Recorded 27 March 1775.

O-4, 422-423: 22 Sept 1774, Zachariah Bullock of Ninety Six District, SC, to Nathaniel Jeffreys of same place, for £250 SC money, 300 acres adj. Looneys line. Zachariah Bullock (LS), Wit: Francis Carlisle, Vardry McBee, Robt. Looney. Acknowledged by Zachariah Bullock before Jno Nuckols, J. P., 26 Sept 1774. Recorded 27 March 1775.

O-4, 423-429: Lease & release. 20 & 21 March 1773, Jacob Abenor of Craven County, SC, planter, and Catharine his wife, to Benedick Nonemacker of Craven County, for £500 SC money, 400 acres granted to George Abenor 7 June 1751 on southwest side Broad River, Jacob Abenor as heir at law to George Abenor. Jacob Abenor (LS), Catharine Abenor (X) (LS), Wit: George Swighard, James Kennerley, Jacob Busar. Proved by the oath of George Swykard before Wm. Ather, J. P., 9 Apr 1773. Recorded 27 March 1775.

O-4, 429-433: Lease & release. 4 & 5 July 1772, William Bates of Craven county, Sc, planter, to John Cooke of same, planter, for £200 SC money, 200 acres granted 11 June 1772 to William Bates on Great Saluda River. Wm. Bates (LS), Wit: Ephraim Puckett, William Penuce. Proved in Craven County before Philip Pearson by the oath of Ephraim Puckett 9 Sept 1772. Recorded 28 March 1775.

O-4, 433-436: Lease & release. 14 Oct 1772, Philip Goode of Craven County, SC, to Jeremiah White of Dinwidde County, Colony of Virginia, for £980 SC money, 300 acres granted to James Noloboy on Stephens Creek in Granville County. Philip Goode (LS), Wit: George Rodgers, Charles Smith, Solomon Newman. Proved 14 Oct 1772 in Granville County by the oath of Solomon Newman before LeRoy Hammond, J.P. Recorded 29 March 1775.

O-4, 436-442: Lease & mortgage. 24 Sept 1774, Peter Belin of South Carolina, planter, to Lachlan McKintosh of Charles Town, Esquire, bound in the sum of £2400 to be paid on or before 1 Feb 1776 for the payment of £1200, mortgage of 334 acres in St. Pauls Parish, Colleton County, adj. land of George Livingston Senr, John James and Isaac Girardeau, now or late the property of Benjamin Stead Esqr.; also 700 acres in Prince George's Parish at Waccamaw adj. land of John Syme, Theodore Trezevant, Francis Withers, granted 22 Nov 1771 to said John Syme. (plats included). Peter Belin (LS), Wit: Frances Charlotta Troup, John Troup. Proved by the oath of John Troup 29 March 1775 before Wm. Rugeley, J.P. Recorded 29 March 1775.

O-4, 443-449: Lease & release. 24 & 25 June 1774, John James of St. Marks Parish, Craven County, SC, to John Rodgers of same, for £800 SC money, 200 acres in Craven County granted to Nicholas Broadway 1 Aug 1758, adj. land of William Harris deceased, conveyed by Nicholas Broadway 9 Feb 1759 to John James. John James (LS), Wit: John Williams, Daniel Hart, Wm. Gilliam. Proved 26 June 1770 before Nathaniel Moore, J. P. in Camden District, by the oath of Daniel Hart. Sarah James, wife of John James, relinquished dower before Nathaniel Moore, J.P. Recorded 31 March 1775.

O-4, 450-457: Lease & release. 1 & 2 Feb 1775, Alexander Rose of Charles Town, merchant, to Miles Brewton of same, esqr., for bond in the penalty of £675, in trust for R. Mayne and Company of London, Great Britain, merchants, for payment of a debt of £337 s10, 795 acres in Christ Church Parish, Berkley County, on Wacondaw Creek adj. land of Andrew Quelch, late of Jacob Bond, Capt. Clement Lempriere, Sandford Dart, Esqr., marshal party on land late of John Cooper, merchant, but now of Peter Sanders, which said plantation is commonly known by the name of the Distillery. Alex'r Rose (LS), Wit: Thos Atkinson, Geo. Ogilvie. Proved before William Nisbett, Esqr., by the oath of Thomas Atkinson, 10 Feb 1775. Recorded 3 Apr 1775.

END OF BOOK O-4.

SOUTH CAROLINA DEED ABSTRACTS 1773-1778

P-4, 1-3: Lease & release. 5 & 6 March 1773, Rudolph Buzard (Boshart) and Britta his wife on Broad River in Berkley County, adj. land of John Putatt, to Joseph Fish for £1761, 100 acres granted to Britta Sleighen, 21 Jan 1761. Rudolph Boshart (LS), Britta Boshart (M) (LS), Wit: Jams. Lindsey, Charles Coates, George Smith. Proved 15 Dec 1773 before John Johnston, J. P., by the oath of Jams. Lindsay. Recorded 13 Feb 1775.

P-4, 4-6: Lease & release. 2 Aug 1774, James Mckleroy and Dinah his wife of Craven County, SC to Herman Kolb of Boonsborough Township, for £100 SC money, 100 acres granted to Sarah Fee 13 Aug 1765, in Boonsborough Township adj. land laid out to Hugh Fee. James McElroy (--) (LS), Dinah McElroy (X) (LS), Wit: John Blasingham, Willm Ross, Willm. Bracher. Proved 15 Oct 1774 by the oath of William Ross before John Bowie, J.P. Recorded 14 Feb 1775. Rowl. Rugeley, Regr.

P-4, 7-11: Lease & release. 31 Dec 1774 & 1 Jan 1774 [sic], Sarah McNichol formerly Sarah Seawright of Craven County, SC, to Thomas Bradley, David Nelson, John Gordon, Henry Cassels, and John Armstrong, of Craven County, St. Marks Parish, for £250 SC money, 200 acres in Craven County, on the north branch of Black River and known by the name of Salem on Black River, adj. Henry Cassels, Samuel Bradley, with the assistance of other well disposed Christian Protestants did agree to build upon said tract for the use of a Presbyterian minister, congregation known as Salem on Black River. Sarah McNichol (LS), Wit: Robt Carter, Francies Brezina, Joseph McKay. Proved 1 Jan 1774 [sic] by the oath of Francis Brezina before John Savage, J. P. Recorded 16 Feb 1775.

P-4, 11-14: Lease & release. 1 & 2 Sept 1763, Hang Jurg Bower of Berkley, planter, to Joseph Curry of Craven County, Esqr., for £20 sterling money of Great Britain, 100 acres granted to said Hans Jurg Bower in Craven County on the branch of Wateree commonly called Sawny Creek on the part where the old Cataba path crosses said creek. Hans Jurg Bower (X) (LS), Wit: Benj. Clements, Hannah Rutledge. Proved by the oath of Hannah Rutledge 23 May 1774 before William Arther, J. P. Recorded 27 Feb 1775.

P-4, 15-17: Lease & release. 18 & 19 Sept 1766, Joseph Curry, Esqr., of Craven County, to Thomas Connerly of same, for £175, 100 acres on Sawneys Creek on the part where the old Cataba path crosses said creek, originally granted to Hans Jurg Bower. Joseph Curry (LS), Wit: Francis Jones, Ralph Humphreys. Proved 6 Jan 1767 by the oath of Francis Jones before William Tucker, J. P. for Craven County. Recorded 18 Feb 1775.

P-4, 18-21: Lease & release. 30 & 31 May 1774, Thomas Connerly of Charles Town, Chairmaker, to John Armstrong of Camden District, planter, for £150, 100 acres on Sawneys Creek on the part where the old Cataba path crosses said creek, originally granted to Hans Jurg Bower, transferred to Joseph Curry 2 Sept 1766. Thom's Connely (LS), Wit: Jeduthan Gibson, John Witherspoon, Joseph Mickle. Proved 9 July 1774 by the oath of John Witherspoon before Thomas Charlton, J. P. in Camden District. Recorded 18 Feb 1775.

P-4, 22-24: Lease & release. 23 & 24 Feb 1774, John Weedingman of Ninety Six District, SC, planter, and Barbara his wife, to John Cunningham of same, planter, for £167 s10 SC money, 200 acres on south side Broad River in Mecklenburg County, then deemed a part of North Carolina, but now since the continuation of the Boundary line in Ninety Six District, between Broad and Pacolet River, granted to John Weedingman by North Carolina 28 Apr 1768. Johannes Weedinman (LS), Barbara Weedingman (N) (LS), Wit: John Foster, Joseph Robinson, John Hendrick. Proved in Ninety Six District by the oath of John Foster 2 March 1774 before Joseph Robinson, J.P. Recorded 27 Feb 1774.

P-4, 25-27: Lease & release. 23 & 24 Feb 1774, John Weedingman of Ninety Six District, SC, planter, and Barbara his wife, to John Cunningham of same, planter, for £167 s10 SC money, 200 acres between Broad and Pacolet River in Craven County, granted to Daniel Thomas 30 Oct 1772. Johannes Weedinman (LS), Barbara Weedingman (N) (LS), Wit: John Foster, Joseph Robinson, John Kendrick. Proved in Ninety Six District by the oath of John Foster 2 March 1774 before Joseph Robinson, J.P. Recorded 27 Feb 1774.

P-4, 28-31: Lease & release. 18 & 19 May 1774, William Pawley of Prince George Parish, Craven county, planter, and Mary his wife, to Thomas Butler of same, for £10 SC money, tract of land being part of two or more tracts on Waccamaw Neck in Prince George Parish, adj. Thomas Butler, lands formerly belonging to Colonel George Pawley but now of Anthony Pawley, 280 acres (plat included). Wm. Pawley (LS), Mary Pawley (LS), Wit: Dalziel Hunter, Anthony Pawley. Proved in Craven County before Peter Simons, J. P., by the oath of Anthony Pawley, 29 Oct 1774. Recorded 28 Feb 1775.

P-4, 32-35: Lease & release. 31 May & 1 June 1774, Godfrey Dreher of Saxe Gotha Township, Berkley County, to Christian Kinceler of Craven County, Parish of St. Marks, for £50 SC money, 5 3/4 acres, part of 100 acres granted 22 Feb 1743 to Henry Lockley in Saxe Gotha Township adj. Conrad Kuntzler, Santee River, conveyed by Henry Lockley to Godfrey Drehr 1 & 2 Feb 1749. (plat included dated 3 May 1774 by R. Humphreys, opposite to the widow Weaver's ferry.) Gottfird Drehr (LS), Wit: Henry Fulk, Lorance Mark (X). Proved by the oath of Lornce Mark before Wm. Arther, 1 June 1774. Recorded 3 March 1775.

P-4, 36-38: 17 Aug 1774, Charles Hutto of Orangeburgh District, planter, to John Fisher of same, esquire, for £200 SC money, 400 acres on the Pon Pon River. Charles Huto (K) (LS), Wit: Don'd Bruce, Geo: Purvis, George Hesse (X). Proved 23 Nov 1774 by the oath of Don'd Bruce before Ephraim Mitchell, J.P. Recorded 3 March 1775.

P-4, 38-40: (plat included). 26 Jan 1773, Zachariah Harrell & Martha his wife of Craven County, SC, shoemaker, to Robert Moses of same, planter, for £100 SC money, 175 acres, part of 350 acres granted to said Harrell granted 3 Apr 1772 (surveyed for him 4 Sept 1770) in Craven County on east side Wateree River both sides of Bum Swamp, adj. Robt Moses, Barbara Remley, Thomas Crawford. Zachariah Harrell (LS), Martha Harrell (X) (LS), Wit: Samuel Morrison, Arthur Richardson. Proved in Camden District 24 June 1774 by the oath of Arthur Richardson before Nathl. Moore, J.P. Recorded 6 March 1775.

P-4, 41-42: 23 Nov 1774, Robert Speer of Craven County ,Ninety Six District, planter, to John Turner of same, planter, for £240 SC money, 100 acres on north side Saludy River on a small branch known as Ramptons branch adj. John Turner, granted to Robert Speer 12 Sept 1768. Robert Speer (LS), Ann Speer (mark), Wit: Edward Turner, John Fox, George Cox. Proved in Charles Town District by the oath of Edward Turner before William Rugeley, J.P., 14 Dec 1774. Recorded 6 March 1775.

P-4, 43-44: 2 Nov 1770, William Miles of St. Andrews Parish, Berkley County, planter, to John Fisher of Orangeburgh, for £5 SC money, 300 acres in Colleton County granted to William Miles 12 Oct 1770 on south branch of Edisto River, land granted to William Kidd[?] and George Farquahr, land granted to Sarah Rutledge. William Miles (S), Wit: John James Haig, John Goldie. Proved 26 Apr 1774 by the oath of John James Haig before William Tucker, J.P. Recorded 6 March 1775.

P-4, 43-47: Lease & release. 28 & 29 Dec 1774, Edward Miskelly of Camden, SC, Cooper, to Samuel Milhous of Craven county, planter, for £100 SC money, 100 acres granted to Edward Miskelly 13 May 1768 on a branch of Granny's Quarter Creek called Cedar Branch. Edward Miskelly (LS), Wit: John Chesnut, Stephen Matlock, John Wyly. Proved 2 Jan 1775 before Thomas Charlton, Esqr., in Camden District by the oath of John Chesnut. Recorded 13 March 1775.

P-4, 48-50: 15 Apr 1774, William Gibbes, Esqr., of Charles Town, Berkley County, to Wood Furman of St. Marks Parish, Craven county, Esqr., for and in consideration of a certain covenant dated 15 Sept 1770, one half of a warrant, 1000 acres in Granville County on Coosahatchie Swamp, a tract recommended by said Wood Furman to be taken up by said William Gibbs and granted 12 Oct 1770, adj. Mr. Snipes. Willm Gibbes (LS), Wit: George Jenkins, Thomas Yates. Recorded 13 March 1775.

P-4, 50-52: 5 June 1772, Thomas Evance of Charles Town, Berkley County, and Margaret his wife, to Wood Furman of St. Marks Parish, Craven County, planter, for £100, half of 1000 acres on great branch of Black River bounded to the land of Alexander Ball, granted 21 May 1772 to said Thomas Evance. Thos Evance (LS), Wit: Thos Jones, Stolberg Adler. Proved in Charles Town District by the oath of Thomas Jones 18 Jan 1775 before William Rugeley, J. P. Recorded 14 March 1775.

SOUTH CAROLINA DEED ABSTRACTS 1773-1778

P-4, 52-59: Lease & release. 8 & 9 Jan 1771, Elias Horry Senr. of St. James Parish Santee, Craven County, Esqr., to James Horry son of said Elias Horry, of Prince Georges Parish, Craven County, planter, for natural love and affection, whereas John Bell Sr., late of Craven County, planter, deceased, being seized of 500 acres in Craven County on Santee River adj. land of John Bell, also 500 acres adj. Capt. Gaillard, and by lease and release 9 & 10 Dec 1720 did convey the same unto Elias horry of Craven County, planter, father of said Elias Horry, party hereto, and said Elias Horry the father now deceased on 19 Sept 1736 by his last will and testament did devise all his real estate (except a tract of 700 acres) unto his executors appointed to wit Daniel Huger Esquire and his two sons Daniel and Elias Horry, and said Daniel Huger and Daniel Horry on 1 & 2 June 1739 did convey said 50 acres on orth side of Santee River adj. Elias Horry, John Harry, Wabbecaw Creek, Tacitus Gaillard; and the Lords Proprietors did on 14 Feb 1714 did grant unto Bartholomew Gaillard deceased, two tracts of land 300 acres each adj. each other on north west side of santee River in Craven County, which said Bartholomew Gaillard devised to his three sons Theodore, Alimus, and Tacitus to be equally divided, and they being of full age at the of their father's death divided the same by deed of partition wherein their Eldest Brother Frederick joined in order to confirm their title by reason of some defect in their father;s will, purchased by John Bell and vested in Elias Horry party hereto, who by deed 28 & 29 March 1745 conveyed to Elias Horry; and George II on 29 Nov 1735 did grant to said Elias Horry, tract of 222 acres in Craven county on Santee River, Horse Creek, adj. land of Wm. Izard. Elias Horry (LS), Wit: Peter Belin, Peter horry, Hugh Horry. Proved in Craven County by the oath of Hugh Horry before Paul Trapier, 25 apr 1771. Recorded 29 March 1775.

P-4, 59-60: South Carolina, Berkley County. Isaac Utsey, planter, by bond for £524 s8 SC money, to Barbara Shuler of same, planter, to sell 400 acres on Stevenses swamp within two miles of the saw mills, dated 1 Jan 1775. Isaac Utsey (LS), Wit: Adam Snell, Adam Ullmer. Proved in Charles Town District 19 Jan 1775 before William Rugeley, J. P. Recorded 30 March 1775.

P-4, 59-60: 6 Dec 1774, Thomas Grimball Junr, Esqr., Sheriff of Charlestown District, to Isaac Peace of Charlestown, Gentleman, for £3060; whereas Alexander Peronneau the younger late of province aforesaid deceased was at his death seized of a plantation of 424 acres in St. Andrews Parish, Berkly County, adj. land of Sarah Lining, Francis Rose, late of Thomas Godfrey deceased, land late of Nathaniel Brown deceased, land late of William Branford deceased, and John Webb of Charles Town, merchant, in the court of common pleas in 1774 did obtain a judgment for the sum of £455 s8 d7 SC money, to be levied of the goods and chattles, of the aforesaid Alexander Peronneau deceased in the hands of John Edwards, executor of his last will and testament. T. Grimball Junr Shff. C. D. Wit: Benja Villepontoux, Joseph Milligen. Proved 20 Jan 1775 by the oath of Joseph Milligen before Thomas Turner, J.P. Recorded 21 Apr 1775.

P-4, 64-70: Lease & release. 14 & 15 Jan 1775, William Snow and Margaret his wife, to William Britton, all of Craven County, SC, whereas by grant 12 Aug 1737 to William Clark, a tract of 450 acres in Craven County in Queensborough Township on Pee Dee River adj. David Hartee, James Gordon, and said William Clark by deed 16 Apr 1742 did sell to Edward Clark the above mentioned plantation, and said Edward clark did convey 1 Sept 1755 to John & Francis Avant, and Francis Avant by deed 11 Nov 1748 did sell to William Green his moiety of half part of said tract, the upper part, and said William Green by his deed 19 Dec 1774 did convey to William Snow, the above 225 acres, now for £653 SC money to William Britton. William Snow (LS), Margaret Snow (LS), Wit: Joseph Britton, Francis Goddard. Proved in George Town District before Francis Britton, J. P., by the oath of Joseph Britton, 10 Feb 1775. Recorded 21 Apr 1775.

P-4, 71-76: Lease & release. 8 & 9 March 1758, Anna Margaret Reinger, late of Charles Town, Labourer, to Abraham Beakes of Berkly County, yeoman, for £200 SC money, 100 acres on a branch of Broad River known by the name of Tyger River otherways a creek and includes three small islands. Anna Margaret Ranger (LS), Wit: John Assey (I), Michael Gromer, Edwd. Musgrove. Proved 9 March 1758 by the oath of Edward Musgrove before Peter Crim, J. P. A Memorial entered in Book L. No. 11, page 96[?], 3 Dec 1771.

P-4, 76-79: Lease & release. 2 March 1775, George Smith of Craven County, planter, to Darby Pendergrass of Charles Town, merchant, for £8 SC money, 100 acres granted to said George Smith 6 Jan last. George Smith (LS), Wit: Alexander Craig, Constantine Neptown (mark). Proved in

SOUTH CAROLINA DEED ABSTRACTS 1773-1778

Charles Town District by the oath of Alexander Craig before Wm. Rugeley, J. P. 14 Apr 1775. Recorded 26 May 1775.

P-4, 79-86: Lease & release. 27 & 28 March 1775, Thomas Lenoir of St. Marks Parish, Craven County, planter, to Isaac Lenoir of same, for £1000 SC money, 200 acres granted to me in hundred acre tracts, 1 June 1767 adj. Philip Payne, John Shivers, John Bradley, and the other 100 acres adj. John Bradley, sd. Thomas Lenoir, part of 200 acres granted to John Spyer 12 July 1771 adj. England land, Joseph Paynes land, land laid out for Jacob Braswell, in Fredericksburg Township. Thos Lenoir (LS), Wit: Wm. Caldwell, Saml Wier. Acknowledged by Thomas Lenoir before Wood Furman, J. P., 29 March 1775. Also a schedule of goods and chattles, a negro woman Sarah, 42 head of neat cattle, 1 gelding, 2 mears, a feather bed and furniture, 6 sheet, cooper and carpenter tools, household furniture, saddles, bridles, etc, all wheels, cats, ploughs, loom. Recorded 27 May 1775.

P-4, 86-89: Lease & release. 2 & 3 Sept 1774, Thomas Curtis of St. Mathews Parish, planter, to William Lucas of same, planter, for love and affection for his daughter Precillah wife of Alexr Wilson, carpenter, and for five shillings paid by William Lucas, 100 acres in Berkley County, granted 23 Oct 1765. Thomas Curtis (LS), Wit: Wm. Thompson, Volantine Shoemake (+), Martin Beagler. Proved 7 Sept 1775 before John Savage, J.P. for Orangeburgh District, by the oath of William Thompson. Recorded 30 May 1775.

P-4, 90-96: Lease & release. 20 & 21 Apr 1773, John Gough of St. Bartholomews Parish, Colleton County, planter, to Thomas Jones of same, planter, for £8000 SC money, 436 acres originally granted to Thos Elliott 8 Apr 1733 and a tract of 578 acres granted to Ann Elliott in 1735, adj. land of Thomas Elliott, Roger Sanders. John Gough (LS), Wit: Alexr Kerr, John Barker. Proved 19 June 1773 before Philip Smith, J. P. in Colleton County the oath of John Barker. Recorded 30 May 1775.

P-4, 96-100: Lease & release. 17 Sept 1755, Thomas Loyd & wife Patience of Granville County, SC, to John Manor of same, for £350 SC money, 350 acres in Granville County on Stephens Creek granted 6 Oct 1752. Thos Loyd (LS), Patience Loyd (P) (LS), Wit: John Royall, Henry Bedingfield, Wm. Miner. Proved in Granville County 18 May 1756 before Richd. Wallace, J. P., by the oath of John Royall. Recorded 31 May 1775.

P-4, 100-104: Lease & release. 10 & 11 May 1765, Tacitus Gaillard of Berkley County, planter, and Ann his wife, to George King, for £1000 SC money, two tracts totalling 633 acres, in Berkley County, 233 acres on south side Santee River and 400 acres on north side of Santee River. Tacitus Gaillard (LS), Ann Gaillard (LS), Wit: John Wright, Isaac Gaillard. [Plats included, indicating 300 acres granted to Samuel Hudson and land adj. Peter Manigault.] Proved 3 Aug 1772 by the oath of Isaac Gaillard before John Savage, J. P. in Colleton County. Recorded 1 June 1775.

P-4, 105-108: Lease & release. 1 & 2 May 1768, Ralph Izard, Esqr., of Parish of St. James goose Creek, Berkley County, SC, to Peter Manigault of Charles Town, for £300 SC money, 64 acres part of a plantation of 210 acres on the Broad Road near the Quarter house, also a tract of 90 acres formerly sold by John Bulloch to Ralph Izard, Esqr., ancestor of the sd. Ralph Izard. R. Izard (LS), Wit: John Mackenzie, Joseph Levy.

P-4, 108-112: Lease & release. 11 & 12 June 1771, Tacitus Gaillard of Parish of St. Mathew, Berkley County, to Peter Manigault of Charles Town, Barrister at Law, for £3000 SC money, 200 acres being an island between Congree and wateree River called Pearsons Island, also tract of 100 acres between Santee & Wateree River in Craven county opposite to Pearsons Island, adj. land laid out for Henry Laurens and granted to Egerton Leigh, on Santee River, also 230 acres in St. Marks Parish, Craven county, adj. land laid out to Henry Laurens but granted to Egerton Leigh, Tacitus Gaillard, Esqr., also 175 acres being half of a tract which did contain 350 acres in Amelia Township, also one half of a town lot number 117. Tacitus Galliard (LS), Wit: Benjn Farrar, George Rilhover. Proved by the oath of George Rilhover 3 Apr 1773 before John Poaug, J.P. Recorded 2 June 1775.

P-4, 113-115: 26 May 1774, George Fickling of St. Johns Colleton County, SC, planter, to Hugh Montgomery of Williams Burgh Township, Craven County, for £436 SC money, 350 acres in Wmburgh Township granted to John Holden Junr deceased and now the said George Fickling Junr as heir. Geo. Fickling Junr (LS), Wit: John McFadden, Thos. Paisley. John McFadden Junr. Proved by the oath of John McFadden Junr before Saml Nesmith, J. P., 1 June 1774. Recorded 3 June 1775.

P-4, 115-118: Lease & release. 22 & 23 Dec 1774, Michl. Lourigh of Orangeburg District, planter, to Wm. Ballentine of same, for £131 SC money, land granted 27 Aug 1751 to Andrew Emmerck, 50 acres between Saluda & Broad River on a branch of Crims Creek. Michl Lourigh (LS), Wit: John Ewing, Wm. Warner. Recorded 3 June 1775.

P-4, 118-121: 2 June 1762, John Jacob Fridig of Saxegotha Township, planter, to David Fridig of same, planter, for natural love and affection to David Fridig, his beloved brother, as also for the better maintenance, support, livelihood, and preferment, 100 acres originally granted to John Matthews 16 Sept 1738 on Santee River adj. John Coleman, adj. common & part on the glebe land. Jacob Fridig (LS), Wit: Henry Hartley, John Fridig. Jacob Fridig, the sole heir of Martin Fridig late of Saxegotha deceased, free holder, died intestate whereby the right of inheritance devolved on John Jacob Fridige eldest son of Martin Fridig. Proved by the oath of Henry Hartley 2 June 1762. Memorial entered in Book C, N 7 page 60, 11 Apr 1763. Recorded 3 June 1775.

P-4, 121-124: Mortgage. 26 Apr 1775, Joseph Willingham of St. James Santee, SC, planter, to Dennis Egan of same, planter, whereas Joseph Willingham is indebted to sd. Dennis Egan in several sums of money amounting to £3200 SC money, one bond payable 2 Apr 1777 the other 26 March 1778, one negro man Quacon and man named Anthony and one negro boy Jack, one tract of land granted to John Francis Gignillett, 200 acres, granted by Hon. Robert Daniell, Sept. Govr. Mary Easter Gaillard, 226 acres and another plantation granted to John Francis Gignillett 200 acres, another tract granted to Isaac Debous 100 acres, another tract of 100 acres, and a tract of 200 acres, on Santee River adj. Mr. Thos Lynches land, adj. land now the property of John Egan Esqr. Joseph Willingham (LS), Wit: John Blake, Andw Barrett, George Powell (X). Proved in Camden District 28 Apr 1775 by the oath of Andw Barrett before John Egan, J. P. Recorded 9 June 1775. Mortgage satisfied 2 May 1777.

P-4, 124-126: 4 February 1758, Benjamin Rogers of the Welch Tract, Craven County, planter, to David Harry, planter, for £100 SC money, 400 acres in the Welch Tract adj. land of Wm. Huges, Wm. Smith, John Lukes[?], granted to 4 July 1759 to Benjamin Rogers. Benjn Rogers (BR) (LS), Wit: Daniel Luke, William James. Proved in Craven county before Alexr Mackintosh, J. P., by the oath of Danl Luke, 14 July 1764. Recorded 9 June 1775.

P-4, 126-131: Lease & release. 13 & 14 May 1774, Thos Evans of Charraw District, planter, to Charles Irby of same, for £100 SC money, 100 acres granted 6 Dec 1754 to Simon Parsons, on Peedee River adj. John Westfield, recorded in Book LL, page 235 8 Dec 1744; after the death of sd. Simon Parsons became the property of Wm. Parsons brother and lawful heir of said Simon Parsons and said William by his last will and testament did give said 100 acres to Robert Parsons Junr of Bucks County, Pennsylvania, second son of Robert Parsons Senr, and transferred by sd. Robert Parsons Senr to the use of Thos Evans, 9 & 10 Oct 1772. Thos Evans (LS), Wit: John Heustess, Isaac Wishart. Proved before Henry Wm. Harrington, J. P., by the oath of James Wishart, 30 July 1774. Recorded 12 June 1775.

P-4, 131-135: Lease & release. 1 & 2 May 1775, Joseph Bee and Hester his wife of St. Paul Parish, Colleton County, planter, to Benjn. Huger of Chas Town, Gentleman, for £5000 SC money, one acre in Ansonborough, Letter U in the General Plat of the Lands of George Anson Esqr., on George St. Joseph Bee (LS), Esther Bee (LS), Wit: Sarah Ferguson, James L. Richards.

P-4, 135-140: Lease & mortgage. 22 & 23 Feb 1775, James Gilchrest Simpson of St. Pauls Parish Colleton County, and Sarah his wife, to Isaac Lesesne of Charles Town, for the penal sum of £7246 SC money, for payment of a debt of £3623, 281 acres near a certain ferry on Stono River in St. Pauls Colleton County, adj. certain glebe lands commonly called Copuis heretofore belonging to the late Thos Farr deceased, lands now or late of Thomas Fuller, lands now or late of Mathew Seller, also 200 acres in the District of Sapola in the Province of Georgia adj. land now or late of Captain James McRay, now or late of White Outerbridge. James Gelchrest Simpson (LS), Sarah

SOUTH CAROLINA DEED ABSTRACTS 1773-1778

Simpson (LS), Wit: Robert Williams Junr, John Postell Junr. Proved in Charles Town District by the oath of James Postell Junr before Wm. Rugeley, 17 May 1775. Recorded 13 June 1775.

P-4, 141-143: 2 Feb 1773, Gabriel Pickens of Prince Williams Parish, SC, planter, and Saphiah his wife, to James Ponder, planter, of same, for £475 SC money, 200 acres on east side Great Rocky Creek in Granville County. Gabriel Pickins (LS), Zaruviah Pickens (Z) (LS), Wit: Robert Anderson, John Woods. Proved 26 May 1774 by the oath of John Woods before Robert Anderson, J.P. in Ninety Six District. Recorded 14 June 1775.

P-4, 143-145: 11 Apr 1775, Thomas Egan of St. James Santee Parish, Craven County, planter, to Dennis Egan of same, whereas Francis Kinlock, late of Craven County deceased was seized of 200 acres in the parish of St. James Santee, which is part of a moiety of two tracks of 200 acres each granted by the Lords Proprietors to Francis Gignilliat, on Santee River adj. land purchased by Archld. Offutt in 1774, John Roberts, part of sd. 500 acres, adj. land purchased by Jno Marion from John Skrene by him sold to John Jaudon who conveyed the same to Joseph Winningham, conveyed by Francis Kinloch to John Roberts of Granville County, Gunsmith, & Elias Robert his brother, and said John Roberts conveyed his moiety to James Gillard and said Gaillard conveyed the same to Bejn. Cumming who conveyed the same to Joseph Willingham, now said Dennis Egan and John Egan Junr his son for ten shillings paid by Thos Egan, this said 200 acres. Dennis Egan (LS), John Egan (LS), Wit: Jno Blake, Daniel Jaudon. Proved 6 May 1775 before Paul Douxsaint in Charles Town District by the oath of Daniel Jaudon. Recorded 14 June 1775.

P-4, 146-151: Lease & release. 7 & 8 Oct 1772, The Rev. Robert Smith and Alexander Gillon of Charles Town, only acting and qualified executors of the will of Richard Beresford, late of Charles Town, deceased, to Susannah Mann of Prince George Parish, for £810 SC money, lot number 43 in George Town, owned by sd. Richd. Beresford, and by his will dated 8 July 1772 appointed his wife Sarah Beresford during her widowhood executrix and sd. Robert Smith and Alexr Gillon with Christopher Gadsden, Thomas Smith of Broad St. and his son when the[y?] respectively should attain the age of 21 years, exrs. Robert Smith (LS), Alex Gillon (LS), Wit: Florian Charles Mey, George Nixon, Proved in Charlestown District by the oath of Florian Charles Mey, 15 June 1775, before William Rugeley, J.P.

P-4, 151-157: 19 Sept 1772, Robert Mackenzie, Edward Blake, Wm. Gibbes,and George Kincaid of Charles Town, tenants in common, to Samuel Legan of same town, merchant, for £10,000 SC money, nine acres or thereabouts in the south part of Charles Town contiguous to two town lots in Charles Town numbers 283 and 284 adj. Mr. Garden, said lots were purchased as tenants in common from Wm. Burrows Esqr., as Master in Chancery, also lot #78 on Ashley River, purchased from Edward Lightwood Junr, also half a quarter of an acre of marsh land above lot #311. Robert Mackenzie (LS), Edward Blake (LS), Willm. Gibbes (LS), Geo. Kincaid (LS), Wit: John Berwick, Chas. Johnston. Proved 4 Apr 1775 before John Mitchell, J.P. for Colleton County, by the oath of John Berwick. Recorded 15 June 1775. (plats included)

P-4, 157-162: Lease & release. 18 & 19 May 1775, George Nodings of Charles Town, ship carpenter, to Dalziel Hunter of same, for £1400 SC money, lots in Charles Town Neck number 136 and 137 described in the general plan of the lands of Henry Laurens. Geo. Noddings (LS), Wit: Chas Ramadge, E. Brenan. Proved 16 May 1775 before Thos Turner, J. P. in Charles Town District, by the oath of Eugene Brenan. Recorded 17 June 1775.

P-4, 163-169: Lease & release. 20 & 21 July 1774, William Ward of District of Ninety Six, planter, to Wm. Hutchinson of same, miller, for £2000 SC money, 400 acres in Granville County on a branch of Savannah River called north west fork of Long Cane Creek adj. Wm. Calhouns, Hugh Calhoun, Mathew Patton, Saml Clark, granted 6 Aug 1766 to Edwd. Dickey, transferred by Edward Dickey 4 Oct 1771 to Wm. Ward. Wm. Ward (LS), Wit: Andrew Williamson, Timy. Parker. Proved in Ninety Six District 26 July 1774 before John Bowie, J.P., by the oath of Timy. Parker. Elizabeth, wife of William Ward, relinquished dower before John Caldwell, Champneys Ferry, and Robert Dillon, 18 July 1774. Recorded 19 June 1775.

P-4, 169-173: Lease & release. 5 & 6 Sept 1773, James Miscampbell of District of Ninety Six, planter, to Arthur Patton & John Huges of same, planters, for £500 SC money, 250 acres granted

SOUTH CAROLINA DEED ABSTRACTS 1773-1778

to James Miscampbell 13 Apr 1767, in Belfast Township, Granville County, adj. Eliz'h Kirkwood, Robert Read. Jam's Miscampbell (LS), Wit: Robert Taylor, Thos Clark. Proved 6 Sept 1773 before Lewis de St. Pierre, J. P., by the oath of Robert Taylor and Thomas Clark. Recorded 20 June 1775.

P-4, 173-176: Lease & release. 4 & 5 May 1775, Adam Tappley of St. Marks Parish, planter, to Elizabeth Dansby of same, for £600 SC money, 150 acres granted 10 Apr 1771 to Jacob Dansby on High Hills of Santee, St. Marks Parish, adj. land granted to Thos Prestwood. Adam Tapley (LS), Edna Tapley (X) (LS), Wit: Wm. Denkins, Mary Tapley (X), Benj. Arnold (or Arendell). Proved 16 May 1775 before Nathl. Moore, J. P., by the oath of Benjn. Arnold. Recorded 21 June 1775.

P-4, 177-182: Lease & release. 23 & 24 Aug 1773, Wm. Simmons of Charles Town, to Wm. Lee of same, butcher, for £17 SC money, 100 acres on north side Saluda River adj. Robert Cunningham, granted on Bounty 12 Sept 1768. Wm. Simmons (LS), Wit: Abraham Pearce, Eleanor Pearce. Proved 17 May 1775 before Geo. Davidson, J.P. in Charles Town District, by the oath of Abraham Pearce. Recorded 22 June 1775.

P-4, 182-185: Lease & release. 22 & 23 Dec 1774, Arthur Patton & John Hughes of Ninety Six District, to Andrew Williamson of same, for £100 SC money, 100 acres in Belfast Township granted 30 Oct 1772 to James Miscampbell, adj. said Miscampbells land, Michael Lemer[?], transferred by James Miscampbell to Arthur Patton and John Hughes, 5 & 6 Sept 1773. Arthur Patton (LS), John Hughes (I) (LS), Wit: James McBride, Timy Parker. Proved in Ninety Six District 31 Dec 1774 by the oath of Timy Parker before John Bowie, J.P.

P-4, 185-187: Thomas Boone of Parish of Saint Ann Soho, County of Middlesex, whereas Richard Stevens late of South Carolina, Esquire, is sometime since dead having made his last will and testament and appointed Lewis Reeves and Thomas Middleton of South carolina, executors of his will and guardian of his daughter Margarett Stevens, late of South Carolina, but now of the Parish of Saint George Hanover Square, County of Middlesex, Spinster, and said Thomas Middleton afterwards died and said Lewis Reeves survived him and is since dead having made his will and appointed Robert Gibbs, James Carsons, and John Barnwell Junr, all of South Carolina, executors, and themselves took the burthen of the execution and said Margaret Stevens by certain deedpole bearing even date with these presents hath appointed said Thomas Boone to be her guardian, and in consideration of the good opinion which he hath of John Barnwell the younger and John Joyner of the same place, appointed them his lawful attornies to settle all accounts, 18 March 1775. Tho Boone (LS), Wit: M. Meggot, Ralph Izard Junr. Proved 20 June 1775 before Richard Lambton by the oath of Ralph Izard Junr.

P-4, 188-191: Lease & release. 14 & 15 Oct 1774, Samuel Esler of District of Ninety Six, planter, to Andrew Williamson of same, for £100 SC money, 300 acres in Belfast Township on a branch of Stephens Creek called Rocky Creek granted 9 Feb 1773 to Samuel Esler. Samuel Esler (LS), Wit: Thomas Edwards, Timy. Parker. Proved 22 Oct 1774 by the oath of Timothy Parker before john Bowie, J. P.

P-4, 191-194: 29 Oct 1774, David Lemmon in Williams Burgh Township, planter, to George McConnell of said township, planter, for £27 SC money, 150 acres part of 300 acres granted to John Lemon 11 Nov 1743. David Lemmon (LS), Wit: David Ihons (Jones), John Burrows, William Hanna. Proved 9 Jan 1775 before Samuel Nesmith, J. P. in Craven County, by the oath of William Hannah.

P-4, 194-198: Lease & release. 19 & 20 May 1775, Ephraim Mitchell, Deputy Surveyor, to James Parsons of Charlestown, Esqr., for £50 SC money, 414 acres adj. land of James Parsons, William Walker, Giles Williams, John Craswell, granted 4 May 1775 to sd. Ephraim Mitchell. Ephraim Mitchell (LS), Wit: Edwd Darrell, Jams. Smith, John C. Colhoun. Proved in Berkley County by the oath of John C. Calhoun, 26 May 1775 before William Rugeley, J. P. Recorded 29 June 1775.

P-4, 198-200: 15 Feb 1775, John Hamer of Anson County, No Carolina, to Claudius Pegues of St. Davids Parish, SC, for £300 current money, 240 acres being the upper part of a tract of 640 acres granted to John Hicks by George II under the Great Seal of North Carolina 22 May 1741, on north east side of Pedee River, which said John Hicks conveyed to John Hamer Senior late of No

SOUTH CAROLINA DEED ABSTRACTS 1773-1778

Carolina 17 June 1743. John Hamer (LS), Wit: William Pegues, William Hicks. Proved 20 Feb 1775 before Henry William Harington, J. P. in Cheraw District, by the oath of William Pegues. Recorded 30 June 1775.

P-4, 200-203: Lease & release. 16 & 17 Dec 1774, Lewis Linder of Orangeburgh District, Deputy Surveyor of Land, to John Rowand Forrester of Charles Town, Gentleman, for £300 SC money, 150 acres in Berkly County in Amelia Township, adj. John Bungardner & John Morrow, Thomas Morrow, Elizabeth Ribols, Robert Morrow, also 250 acres in Colleton County adj. land surveyed for David and John Deas, Bells land, which said tracts were granted to said Lewis Linder 9 Dec 1774. Lewis Linder (LS), Wit: William Catterton, Peter Bremar. Proved 27 Feb 1775 before john Troup, Esqr., by the oath of Peter Bremar. Recorded 1 July 1775.

P-4, 203-207: Lease & release. 24 & 25 June 1775, Josias Allston of Waccamaw, SC, planter, to Plowden Weston of Charles Town, merchant, for £1575 SC money, 700 acres in Craven County near Sochorsta Creek adj. Joseph Princes land, Mr. Marions land. Josiah Allston (LS), Wit: Patk. Simons, George Croft. Proved by the oath of George Croft 18 May 1775 before Hopkin Price, J. P. Recorded 1 July 1775.

P-4, 208-212: Lease & release. 5 & 6 Oct 1774, Charles Harison of 96 District, Constable, to Plowden Weston of Charles Town, for £350 SC money, 250 acres near West Creek adj. land of John Hall, William Norris, Goodridge Hughes, John Caldwell, granted 5 May 1773 to Charles Harrison. Charles Harrison (LS), Wit: George Powell, Sivility Powell (X), Patience Powell. Proved 6 Oct 1774 before John Fairchild, J. P. in Orangeburgh District, by the oath of George Powell. Recorded 17 July 1775.

P-4, 213-220: Lease & release (marriage settlement). 28 & 29 Nov 1766, William Wragg of Charles Town, Esquire, to John Mathews of Charles Town, Esqr., and Robert Gibbes and John Wragg of the third part, where as marriage is shortly to be solemnized between John Mathews and Mary Wragg, daughter of said William Wragg... 1082 acres, part of Ashley Barony, on south side of Ashley River. William Wragg (LS), John Mathews (LS), John Wragg (LS), Wit: Isaac Godin, Charles Martyn. Bond for £500. Proved before Rowland Rugeley, Esqr., J.P. for Charles Town District, by the oath of Isaac Godin. Recorded 18 July 1775.

William Wragg has granted to John Wragg, Esqr., for ten shillings, tract of land from Jacob Creek Bridge along the high road as far as a Cross Ditch lately dug to a Gall on the east side of a place where I formerly made Bricks, dated 3 May 1771. W. Wragg. Wit: John Walker, Hector Creswell. Proved by the oath of John Walker before William Nisbett, J.P. in Charles Town District, 13 July 1775. Recorded 18 July 1775.

P-4, 220-223: Lease & release. 26 & 27 Oct 1772, Edmond Egan of Berkley County, Brewer, to John Milhouse of Colleton County, Mill wright, for £20 SC money, 100 acres granted to Edmund Egan 21 May 1772 in Colleton County on the north for of the Saltcatchers River called Lemons Swamp adj. land laid out to Thos Ferguson, Esqr., Chas Elliott, John Milhous, grant recorded in Book LLLL, page 179. Edm'd Egan (LS), Wit: Elisha Hodghison, James Morgan, John Cole. Proved before William Swinton, J.P. for Colleton County, by the oath of John Cole, 3 Nov 1772. Recorded 27 July 1772.

P-4, 224-226: Lease & release. 1 & 2 Feb 1775, William Coats of Charles Town, SC, Esqr., to Wm. Donaldson of same, merchant, for £490 SC money, 650 acres in Berkley County on Poke Swamp adj. land laid out for Thomas Smith. William Coats (LS), Wit: Alex. Macbeth, Robt. Rose. Proved by the oath of Alexander Macbeth before Thomas Phepoe, J. P. for Charles Town District, 15 May 1775. Recorded 1 Aug 1775.

P-4, 226-229: 13 June 1774, Robert Stark, Sheriff of the District of Ninety Six, to James Parsons, Esqr., of Charles Town, whereas Robert Dillon the Debtor of the District and province aforesaid, was seized of a tract of land of 1603 acres in the district of Ninety Six, and whereas Martin Campbell, James Parsons, and William Guerin in the court of common pleas at February Term 1763 recovered a judgment for the sum of £19,938 s14 current money, and for £2330 current money paid by James Parsons, tract of 1603 acres in Ninety Six District adj. land late of John Murray

SOUTH CAROLINA DEED ABSTRACTS 1773-1778

deceased now of said James Parsons & John Rutledge Esqr., land of James Mayson Esqr., on Saludy River, land of Alexander Cameron, Stephen Anderson, William Anderson, heir and devisee of Thomas Bell deceased, William Davis, John Savage, Ben. Durborows land. Robert Stark (LS), Sheriff. Wit: Henry Nichols, James Smith. Proved in Charles Town District by the oath of Henry Nicholes before John Troup, J. P., 2 May 1775. Recorded 28 Aug 1775.

P-4, 229-231: 2 Feb 1770, Roger Pinckney, Provost Marshall of South Carolina, to John Wagner of Charles Town, whereas John Fremouth was sized of a tract of 100 acres in Saxe Gotha Township adj. land of David Webb, Henry Weaver, George Haig, Henry Gallman, John Geiger, and also a town lott in Saxe Gotha number 132, and whereas William Scott in the Court of Common Pleas at Charles Town at August term 1769 did obtain against said John Fremouth and Hannah his wife a judgment for the sum of £1106 s15 d 8 SC money... sold for £51 SC money.... Roger Pinckney, Wit: Hopson Pinckney, John Martin. Recorded 23 Aug 1775.

P-4, 232-236: Lease & mortgage. 27 & 28 May 1774, Robert Dick of George Town, SC, gentleman, to Micajah Williams of same, mariner, by bond of £3180 SC money, and bond in the penal sum of £16,000 for the payment of £8000, tract on south side Sampit Creek 450 acres on George Town River common known by the name of Sampit Creek adj. Abraham Bond, Robert Stuart, Henry Bossard. Robert Dick (LS), Anne Dick (LS), Wit: Jacob Wm. Harvey, Wm. Mason. Proved 11 July 1774 by the oath of Wm. Mason before Jas. Johnston, J. P. Recorded 30 Aug 1775.

P-4, 236-238: 15 June 1775, Wilson Cooke of St. Bartholomews Parish, planter, to Jacob Valk of Charles Town, gentleman, bond in the penal sum of £1432 s 12 d 8 SC money, for the payment of £716 s6 d8 like money, 500 acres in Craven County on a branch of Little River the waters of Saludy River, adj. land surveyed for Robert McCleland. Willson Cooke (LS), Wit: Paul Schlatter, Geo Jno Fardo. Proved in Berkley County by the oath of Paul Schlatter 16 June 1775 before Hopkin Price, J.P. Recorded 30 Aug 1775.

P-4, 238-243: Lease & release. 13 & 14 Sept 1771, Peter McGuire of settlement of Long Cane in Granville County, Tobacco Spiner, to Donald Bruce of Charles Town, for £101 s 11 SC money, 150 acres in Long Cane settlement, adj. Hugh Simpson, sd. Peter McGuire, the tract being granted on Bounty to Terence[?] McGuire deceased father of said Peter McGuire, 2 Oct 1767. Peter McGuire (LS), Alexr Noble, James Noble, John Calhoun. Proved 14 Sept 1771 before Patrick Calhoun, J.P. in Granville County by the oath of Alexander Noble. Recorded 30 Aug 1775.

P-4, 243-246: 22 Apr 1775, George Harkness of Charles Town, SC, to James Mortimer Harris of Charles Town, for £50 SC money, 500 acres on Cross Swamp in St. Bartholomews Parish adj. land of Lazerous Brown, Mr. Boatwright. George Harkness (LS), Wit: Wm. Miller, Willm. Hartley. Proved by the oath of William Hartley 17 June 1775 before Wm. Nisbett, J. P. Recorded 4 Sept 1775.

P-4, 246-250: Lease & release. 30 & 31 May 1775, Gabriel Marion of St. Stephens Parish, to Plowden Weston of Charles Town, for £8000 SC money, 200 acres by resurvey 730 acres on Waccamaw River in Craven County, adj. land formerly belonging to John Lloyd, Col. William Waties, conveyed for 500 acres 20 & 21 June 1751 between Paul Trapier of George Town, merchant, to Gabriel Marion of Prince Georges Parish. Gab'l Marion (LS), Wit: Job Marion, Richd Mason. Proved before John Troup in Charles Town district by the oath of Richard Mason, 27 June 1775. Recorded 5 Sept 1775.

P-4, 250-254: Lease & release. 5 & 6 Nov 1774, Alexander Caddell of Parish of St. Philip, Charles Town, Breeches Maker, to William Arthur of the Congarees, Saxagotha Township, planter, for £30, 95 acres in Berkley County, Saxagotha Township, Congarees, adj. land of William Arthur, Doctor Farrar, Henry Gallman. Alexander Caddell (LS), Wit: John Wagner, John Freymouth. Proved 26 June 1775 before Rowland Rugeley, J. P., by the oath of John Freymouth. Recorded 8 Sept 1775.

P-4, 254-259: Lease & release. 19 & 20 Dec 1774, Samuel Warnock of Charles Town, Bricklayer, to Jonathan Sarrazin of Charles Town, Jeweller, for the debt or sum of £1900 owing to said Jonathan Sarrazin, lot in St. Philips Parish, Charles Town, on the north side of a new street lately laid out & called Hasell Street, part of lands lately sold by Parker Quince & susannah his wife to

SOUTH CAROLINA DEED ABSTRACTS 1773-1778

said Jonathan Sarrazin. Samuel Warnock (LS), Wit: John Newton Hartley, John Webb. Proved before John Troup, J.P., by the oath of John Newton Hartley, 3 July 1775. Recorded 11 Sept 1775.

P-4, 259-263: Lease & release. 7 & 8 July 1775, Haswell Miles of Amelia Township, Berkley County, Blacksmith, and Sarah his wife, to Martin Beagler of Amelia Township, Planter, for £200 SC money, 222 acres in Amelia Township, St. Mathews Parish, Berkley County, adj. Herman Rush, James Brown, Ezekiel Cox, Daniel Williams, granted 19 June 1772. Haswell Miles (LS), Sarah Miles (X) (LS), Wit: Ann Savage, Henry Beagler. Proved 8 July 1775 by the oath of Henry Beagler before John Savage, J.P. in Orangeburgh District. Recorded 18 Sept 1775.

P-4, 263-268: Lease & release. 16 & 17 Nov 1774, Charles Palmer of Granville County, planter, & Elizabeth his wife, late Elizabeth Jones widow and formerly Elizabeth St. John, one of the daughters and devisees of James St. John, planter, deceased, to Archibald Calder of Edisto Island, planter, for £3000 SC money, 883 acres part of a larger tract granted to said James St. John in Black Swamp adj. land of William Williamson, George Brown, Alexander Fitzgerald. Charles Palmer (LS), Eliz'th Palmer (LS), Wit: John Giles, Othn'l Giles. Proved before John Coram, J. P. in Charles Town District, by the oath of John Giles, 21 July 1775. Renunciation of dower by Elizabeth Palmer before John Fewtrell. Recorded 19 Sept 1775.

P-4, 268-270: 3 Aug 1775, William Wilson of Prince Fredericks Parish, Craven County, planter, to Joseph Johnson of St. Davids Parish, for twenty shillings, 250 acres in St. Davids Parish on both sides of Hills Creek adj. Mathew Golding[?], Richard Deas, Joseph Hancock. William Wilson (LS), Wit: Richd Brooks, Randolph Theus. Proved in George Town Dist. by the oath of Richard Brooks before W. Mason, J.P., 3 Aug 1775. Recorded 21 Sept 1775.

P-4, 270-271: 2 May 1775, Paul Couturier of St. Stephens Parish, Craven County, to James Lynah of same, physician, for £800 SC money, 100 acres in St. Stephens Parish granted 1 Aug 1758 to Paul Couturier. Paul Couturier (LS), Wit: David Dubose, David Gaillard, Is. Dubose. Proved 13 July 1775 before John Frierson, J. P. for Charles Town District, by the oath of Isaac Dubose. Recorded 21 July 1775.

P-4, 271-276: Lease & release. 2 & 3 May 1775, Arnoldus Vanderhorst of Charles Town, SC, and Elizabeth his wife, only child & heiress at Law of William Raven late of said province, esqr., deceased, to Samuel Legare of said town, merchant, for £5000 SC money, lot in Charles Town number 5, the southernmost part of which is occupied by Mary Stevens widow, the same where the Coffee House is now kept and was heretofore that is to say at the time of the Great Fire in Charles Town in the possession of Messrs. Stead, Evans & Company, and sometime before in the possession of one George Smith deceased... except that part thereof where the piece of land formerly of Mary Besset daughter of said George Smith deceased is taken out of it... Arnoldus Vanderhorst (LS), Elizabeth Vanderhorst (LS), Wit: George Petrie, Mary Collins. Proved by the oath of George Petrie in Charles Town District before R. Rugeley, 10 Aug 1775. Dower relinquished before Charles Mathew Cosslett. Recorded 21 Sept 1775.

P-4, 276-279: Lease & release. 4 & 5 May 1775, Samuel Legare of Charles Town, SC, and to Arnoldus Vanderhorst of said town, for £5000 SC money, lot in Charles Town number 5, the southernmost part of which is occupied by Mary Stevens widow, and the same where the Coffee House is now kept and was heretofore that is to say at the time of the Great Fire in Charles Town in the possession of Messrs. Stead, Evans & Company, and sometime before in the possession of one George Smith deceased... except that part thereof where the piece of land formerly of Mary Besset daughter of said George Smith deceased is taken out of it... Samuel Legare (LS), Wit: Willm. Savage Junr, Jas. Ward. Proved in charles Town District by the oath of William Savage Junr before R. Rugeley, 18 Aug 1775. Recorded 22 Sept 1775.

P-4, 280-282: Lease & release. 29 March 1775, George hope of Ninety Six Dist., to Henry McCollum of Craven County, Camden District, for £100, 100 acres on Sandy River of Broad River adj. Edmund Franklins line. Geo. Hope (M) (LS), Jude Hope (G) (LS), Wit: Thomas Ferney, James Thomas, Robert Coles (X). Proved in Ninety Six District by the oath of Thos Ferney before Elias Hollingsworth, 29 March 1775. Recorded 12 Oct 1775.

SOUTH CAROLINA DEED ABSTRACTS 1773-1778

P-4, 282-285: Lease & release. 16 & 17 May 1775, Lewis Ogier of Charles Town, merchant, and Catherine his wife, to Philip Henry of same place, for £50 SC money, two tracts of 250 acres in Granville county on Russells Creek waters of Savannah River, part of 500 acres granted to John Swint and by said John Swint conveyed to Lewis Ogier. Lewis Ogier (LS), Catharine Ogier (LS), Wit: Shad Windsor, Isaac Dacosta. Proved by the oath of Shad Windsor 26 Aug 1775 before Wm. Nisbett, J. P. Recorded 12 Oct 1775.

P-4, 285-288: Lease & release. 22 Jan 1770, George Haig of Colleton County, Gentleman, to David Hay of Craven County, planter, for £1000 SC money, 304 acres in Craven County adj. land of William Janeway, Henry Snelling, Samuel Lynes, George Satchwell, granted 22 Feb 1745 to Elizabeth Verditty[?], grant recorded in Book LL folio 290, conveyed by said Elizabeth 1 & 2 Apr 1746 to George Haig, Esqr., deceased, whereas the said George Haig died intestate and said George Haig Junior inherited the north east part of said tract, 174 acres. Geo Haig (LS), Wit: Edward Legge Junr, Willm. Benet. Proved before Robert Goodwyn, J. P. in Craven county by the oath of Edward Legge Junr, 15 Dec 1772. Recorded 23 Oct 1775.

P-4, 288-293: Lease & release. 3 & 4 March 1775, Thomas Hasell & Robert Dick of Prince George's Parish, Craven County, planter, to Roger Smith, George Heriot, and Daniel Tucker of same province, merchants, for £2605 SC money, town lott on the north east side of Front St. in George Town, number 24. Thomas Hasell (LS), Robert Dick (LS), Wit: John Brown, Henry Harvey. Proved before Robert HerioT, J. P. in Craven County, by the oath of John Brown, 21 Aug 1775. Recorded 13 Oct 1775.

P-4, 293-298: Lease & release. 20 & 21 June 1751, Paul Trapier of George Town, Craven county, Merchant, to Gabriel Marion of Prince George Parish, planter, for £758 s10 SC money, 500 acres in Craven County on Waccamaw River adj. land formerly belonging to Mr. John Lloyd but once in the possession of Mr. William Allston Senr, Col. William Waties, by deed between William Allston Senior and said Col. William Waites & was purchased of the said Col. William Waties by said William Alston Senior and by William Allston for natural love and affection to isaac Marion his son in law 5 June 1742, and by said Isaac Marion first mortgaged 23 Feb 1750 conveyed to said Paul Trapier. Paul Trapier (LS), Wit: John Lesesne, John Stuart. Acknowledged in George Town District before Benjamin Young, J.P., by Paul Trapier, 19 Dec 1774. Recorded 16 Oct 1775.

P-4, 298-299: 5 July 1775, William Godfrey of St. Peters Parish, planter, to James Peart, Dept Surveyor, for £50 current money, tract on waters of Coosawhatchie and Stoney Run adj. land granted to Thomas Searson, Stephen McDaniel, John Grimbal, granted 4 May to contain 1250 acres. William Godfrey (LS), Wit: Henry Thippy (H), Arnold Harvey. Proved in
Purysburgh in Granville County by the oath of Arnold Harvey before David Geroud, J. P., 5 july 1775.

P-4, 299-300: _____ 1775, John Pelot of St. Peter's Parish, planter, to James Peart, surveyor of land, for £100 SC money, tract of land on a branch of the north west branch of Long Cane called Penny's Creek adj. lands of Michael Dorman, James Liddle, Robert Black, Jemson Hatcher, David Hunter, Michael Blair, John Johnston, granted ____ 1775. John Pelot (LS), Wit: Susannah Thomas, George Allison. Proved by the oath of George Allison 10 Aug 1775 before Adrian Mayer. Recorded 26 Oct 1775.

P-4, 301-302: Before Robt. Pringle, Esqr., J. P. in the court of Common Pleas, on 27 Oct 1769, appeared Susanah Hume, wife of John Hume of Charles Town, relinquished dower to tract conveyed by lease and release 1 & 2 Oct 1769 by John Hume to Henry Laurens, lot in Charles Town, number 159, on north side of an Alley leading from Church St. to old Church St. John Troup, Attorney.

P-4, 302-305: Lease & release. 6 & 7 Jan 1775, Thomas Wade of Anson County, North Carolina, Esqr., to Richard Middleton of Craven County, SC, planter, for £300 SC money 200 acres granted 31 Oct 1769 to Jno Boatwright on both sides of Buflow Creek a branch of Great Lynches Creek, recorded in Book DDD page 485. Thos Wade (LS), Wit: Jas Kelly (N), William Jones (W), Neilson Kelly (N). Proved in Camden District 7 Aug 1775 before John N. Oglethorpe by the oath of William Jones. Recorded 6 Nov 1775.

SOUTH CAROLINA DEED ABSTRACTS 1773-1778

P-4, 305-306: Robert Gray of Craven County, SC, by bond to John Balfour in the sum of £15,000 before 1 Jan 1781 for the payment of £7500, 150 acres in Cheraw District adj. Pedee River; 300 acres adj. Godfrey Jones, John Westfield; 350 acres in the Welch Tract adj. Hardy Counsel, William Evans, Pedee River. Robert Gray (LS), Wit: William Simpson, John Moncrieffe. Proved in Cheraws District before Alexander Mackintosh, J. P., by the oath of William Simpson, 16 oct 1775. Recorded 10 Nov 1775. Mortgage satisfied 12 aug 1778. Wit: Geo Sheed.

P-4, 307-309: Lease & release. 1 & 2 Dec 1774, Darby Larey of George Town, SC, to Thomas Phepoe of Charles Town, Esquire, for £150 SC money, 250 acres on Muddy Creek near Lynch's Creek adj. land of George Sno, Mrs. McIvor, Thomas Snow. Darby Larey (LS), Wit: Thomas Pratt, Danl Tucker. Proved 1 Dec 1774 before Robert Heriot, J.P., by the oath of Doctor Thomas Pratt. Recorded 22 Nov 1775.

P-4, 309-310: John Asbill of St. Georges Parish, Berkley County, Orangeburgh District, planter, to my loving son Isaac Asbill of same, 250 acres in St. Georges Parish, Berkley County, Orangeburgh District... dated 6 Dec 1774. John Asbill (LS), Wit: William Spires (X), Lewis Linder. Proved in Charles Town District by the oath of William Spires before R. Rugeley, 21 Nov 175. Recorded 11 Dec 1775.

P-4, 310-315: Lease & mortgage. 8 & 9 June 1775, Zachariah Gibbs of Fair Forest, late in Tryon County, Province of North Carolina, but now in the province of South Carolina, to Rowland Rugeley at Richmond near Charles Town, SC, merchant, by bond in the penal sum of £472 SC money, to the payment of £236 like money, tract of land lately in Tryon County, Nc, but ow in South carolina on the south side of Fair Forest on both sides of the lick branch about a mile below Millers Waggon Road adj. Giles Tillets land, granted to Thomas Bullion 16 Dec 1769 by william Tryon [Governor of NC]. Zachariah Gibbs (LS), Wit: Thom's Bourke, Arch'd Carsan. Proved in Charles Town District by the oath of Thomas Bourke before John Coram, 17 Jan 1776. Recorded 18 Jan 1776.

P-4, 315-321: Lease & mortgage. 26 & 27 Feb 1773, Jacob Jones of St. Marks Parish, planter, and Rachael his wife, to Henry Rugeley of London, Great Britain and Rowland Rugeley of charles Town, merchants, by bond dated 27 Feb 1773 in the penal sum of £1556 s15 d8, for the debt of £528 s7 d10, 250 acres, part of 350 acres originally granted to Charles Harvey 18 May 1771 and conveyed to said Jacob Jones, on a branch of Little River adj. land of Moses Caldwell, Elizabeth Caldwell. Jacob Jones (l) (LS), Wit: Alexr Moultrie, John Hall. Proved before John Troup, J. P., by the oath of Alex: Moultrie. [Dower relinquishment only partially filled out]. Recorded 19 Jan 1776.

P-4, 321-327: Lease & mortgage. 25 & 26 Aug 1772, Philemon Waters of Charles Town, and Mary his wife, to Henry and Rowland Rugeley of same town, merchants, said Philemon Waters by his bond is obligated to said Henry Rugeley and Rowland Rugeley in the sum of £1400 SC money, 200 acres on south side of Saludy River in Berkley County and a tract of 250 acres in the township of Purysburgh, Granville County, and a tract of 250 ares surveyed 20 March 1768 for James Couch on Enoree River on the north side thereof. P. Waters (LS), Mary Waters (LS), Wit: George Chateris, Edward Sewell. Proved in Charles Town District before John Troup, J.P., by the oath of George Chateris, 16 Apr 1776. Recorded 16 Apr 1776.

P-4, 328-331: Lease & release. 15 & 16 Nov 1776, James Smith and Elizabeth his wife of Craven County, farmer, to Thomas Tod of said county, for £500 SC money, 400 acres in Craven County on Tyger River granted to Robert Irwin by the Governor of North Carolina 4 May 1769, and since purchased by the said James Smith, which said land by the continuation of the boundary line between this Province and North Carolina now falls within the limits of this government, above his former survey, plat annexed to a grant by the said Lt. Gov. of SC to James Smith dated 9 Sept 1774. James Smith (T) (LS), Eliz'th Smith (mark) (LS), Wit: Jos. Wofford, James Oliphant. Proved in Charlestown District before George Sheed, J.P., by the oath of James Oliphant, 3 March 1777. Recorded 8 March 1777.

P-4, 331-334: Lease & release. 26 & 27 Nov 1776, Edmund Bearden and Ann his wife of Craven county, farmer, to James Spears of same, house carpenter, for £350 SC money, 350 acres granted

SOUTH CAROLINA DEED ABSTRACTS 1773-1778

to the said Edmund Bearden 11 Aug 1774 on south side of Tyger River adj. said river, John Spurgen. Edmund Bearden (LS), Ann Bearden (X), Wit: John Clayton, Thos Tod. Proved before Ralph Smith, J.P. in Craven County, by the oath of Thomas Tod, 4 Dec 1776. Recorded 15 March 1777.

P-4, 335-337: Lease & release. 10 & 11 Dec 1776, Thomas Tod of Craven county, farmer, to James Oliphant of Charlestown, jeweller, for £500 SC money, all the undivided half of a tract known by the name of Bell Mont, it being a moiety of two tracts of land granted to Samuel Bell containing in all 450 acres, the first of which was granted 2 June 1769, 200 acres on the head of French Mans Creek waters of Enoree River in Craven County; the second granted 11 Aug 1774, 250 acres adj. to aforesaid tract, which two tracts were purchased from Samuel Bell in May last past by the aforesaid James Oliphant and Thomas Tod jointly. Thos Tod (LS), Wit: Wilm Templeton, Jas. Spears. Proved before David Hopkins, J. P. in Craven County, by the oath of William Templeton, 23 Dec 1776. Recorded 15 March 1777.

P-4, 338: South Carolina, Beaufort. Daniel Stevens of Parish of St. Helena, Granville County, for love, good will and affection to my loving brother Cotton Mather Stevens of Portsmouth in Piscatigua, New England, Taylor, all that parcel of land in new England which fell to me by right of my mother Katharine Stevens, dated 8 January 1777. Daniel Stevens (LS), Wit: James Sharp, Tho. Fell. Proved in Charlestown District before George Sheed, J. P. by the oath of James Sharp, 8 March 1777. Recorded 13 March 1777.

P-4, 338-341: Lease & release. 14 & 15 Dec 1773, Lewis Golson, Esqr., of St. Mathews Parish, SC, to Adam Bowers of province aforesaid, planter, for £100 SC money, tract granted 6 Oct 1752 to Lewis Golson, 50 acres on north side of Congaree River adj. John George Kersh, Philip Raiford, George Bowers, Michael Snider. Lewis Golson (LS), Wit: George Bowers (X), Peter Staley, John Golson. Proved in Camden District by the oath of George Bowers before Philip Pearson, J. P., 30 July 1774. Recorded 15 March 1777.

P-4, 341-344: Lease & release. 20 & 21 May 1775, Wm. Meyer of the Congarees, planter, to Jacob Meyers of same place, planter, for £600 SC money, tract granted 1 Jan 1767 to Wm. Meyer, 150 acres on north side Santee River adj. when surveyed by lands surveyed for Rudolph Meyer, land surveyed for Mathias Fender, land surveyed for John Hamilton, land surveyed for Jacob Hanisance. Wm. Meyer (LS), Wit: John Marshal, Hubert Rowell. Proved 4 Nov --- by the oath of Hubert Rowell before Robert Goodwyn, J.P. for Camden District. Recorded 15 March 1777.

P-4, 344-347: Lease & release. 21 & 22 Jan 1777, Adam Bauers of Camden District, SC, planter, to Jacob Myers of same, for £265 SC money, land granted 6 Oct 1752 to Lewis Golsan, 50 acres on north side Congaree River adj. John George Kirsh, Philip Raiford, George Bowers, Michael Snider. Adam Bowers (B) (LS), Wit: Jacob Sayler, Godfrey Pringel, Jacob Lohner[?]. Proved in Charlestown District before George Sheed, J. P., by the oath of Jacob Sayler, 23 Feb 1777. Recorded 22 March 177.

P-4, 347-350: Lease & release. 16 & 17 Feb 1777, Daniel Helterbrand of Orangeburg District, planter, to Adam Bowers of Camden District, for £10 SC money, part of a tract granted 2 Jan 1754 to John Christopher Helterbrand, 100 acres on south side of Congaree River in Berkley County adj. Barbra Tresses; half of said 100 acres, being 50 acres. Daniel Helterbrand (DH) (LS), Wit: Jacob Myers, Conrod Jumper (X), George Corly (X). Proved in Charlestown District by the oath of Jacob Myers before Geo. Sheed, 28 Feb 1777. Recorded 22 March 1777.

P-4, 350-353: Lease & release. 4 & 5 Feb 1777, Richard Brooks of George Town, Craven County, Taylor, to Abraham Cohen of same, merchant, whereas the said Richard Brooks by his bond dated 13 Oct 1776 in the penal sum of £1600 SC money, for the debt or sum of £800 SC money, town lot in George Town on High Street, number 125. Richard Brooks (LS), Wit: J. Bedgegood, Jno Glegg. Proved 18 Feb 1777 before Job Rothmahler, J.P. for Georgetown District, by the oath of John Bedggood. Recorded 22 March 1777.

P-4, 354-358: Lease & release. 1 & 2 Feb 1775, Archibald Brown of Charlestown, merchant, to Aaron Loocock of same town, merchant, for £11,000 SC money, 800 acres in Parish of St. James

SOUTH CAROLINA DEED ABSTRACTS 1773-1778

Goosecreek in Berkley County adj. land of John Deas, Esqr., Heires of Joseph Norman deceased, John Dutarque, esqr., col. Benjamin Singellton, Alexander Mazyck, Esqr., which said tract was originally granted to James Williams, Surgeon, deceased, and also tract of 90 acres in parish of St. James Goose Creek formerly purchased by Roger Moore from Col. James moore deceased, and is part and parcel of a plantation thereon the said James Moore then dwelt, adj. land formerly of Robert Stevens, now or late of John Lloyd, and above mentioned tract of 800 acres. Archd. Brown (LS), Wit: William Boykin, Geo. Redhead. Proved 10 march 1777 before George Sheed, J. P. in Charlestown District, by the oath of William Boykin. Recorded 22 March 1777.

P-4, 358-361: Lease & release. 19 & 20 Oct 1775, George Flag of Charlestown, & Mary Magdalen his wife, to John Gaborial of same place, carpenter, for £1700 SC money, lot in Ansonborough on the Broad road leading from Charlestown to the southward adj. land of Jane Wilkie, Timothy Crosby, James Reid. George Flagg (LS), Wit: Jos Badger, George Rout. Proved by the oath of Joseph Badger before John Troup, J. P., 13 March 1777. Recorded 22 March 1777.

P-4, 363-365: Lease & release. 13 & 14 Apr 1776, William Gamble of Parish of Prince Fredericks, SC, shoemaker, to Robert Hutchison of same parish, planter, for £1200 SC money, 400 acres granted to James Gamble 13 March 1752 in Craven County adj. James Agnews land (it is also aserted that the above 400 acres of land cometh to me William Gamble as being Heir at law to my Grandfather James Gamble). William Gamble (LS), Wit: James Boyd, William Gamble, Robert Gamble. Proved by the oath of William Gamble 4 March 1777 before John Troup, J. P. Recorded 29 March 1777.

P-4, 365-366: Received by the hands of Paul Trapier from Messrs. Thos Lynch,l Elias horry Junr, Geo. Gab. Powell, Saml Wrag, Thomas Godfrey, Joseph Allston & the said Paul Trapier, Commissioners appointed for building a Court House & Public Goal in Geo. Town... full considering for all my right, title, interest, and claim in two lots of land in George Town, number 155 and 156, for £100... dated 6 Aug 1770. Henry Dexter (LS), Wit: Hugh Swinton. Proved by the oath of William Vaux who swore that he has frequently seen Hugh Swinton (the evidence to the within instrument of writing who is since deceased) sign his name and that this is his handwriting, 31 Jan 1777. Recorded 27 March 1777.

P-4, 366-369: Lease & release. 3 & 4 Oct 1775, William Smith of Parish of St. Mark, SC, boutcher, and Martha his wife, to Robert Hutchison of Parish of Prince Frederick, planter, for ten shillings, 150 acres granted to William Smith 25 Apr 1774 on Black River Swamp, Parish of st. Mark, Craven County. Will. Smith (LS), Martha Smith (+) (LS), Wit: William Cookson, John Rowan. Proved by the oath of William Cookson 13 Nov 1775 before James Fleming, J.P. in Craven County. Recorded 29 March 1777.

P-4, 369-372: Lease & release. 27 Apr 1768, John Lee, Breeches Maker of Prov. of SC, to Ezekiel Williams of same, for £100 SC money, 100 acres granted to John Lee 2 March 1774 in Granville County on Savannah River. John Lee (LS), Wit: Samuel Alexander, James Turner, James Cayson (J). Proved by the oath of Samuel Alexander before John Dick, J.P. in Granville County, 11 May 1770. Recorded 29 March 1777.

P-4, 372-377: Lease & release. 14 & 15 June 1775, William Pinckney, Esqr., of Colleton County, Planter, & Deborah his wife, to John Turner of Granville County, mercht., for £300 SC money, 200 acres in Granville county on Savannah River near the mouth of New Three Runs, known by the name of Point Comfort, granted to said William Pinckney. Willm. Pinckney (LS), Deborah Pinckney (LS), Wit: James Willson, Robert Caborn. Proved 17 June 1775 before And. Cunningham, J. P. Recorded 29 March 1777.

P-4, 377-378: Robert Goodwyn of Camden District, Esquire, for £5 Sc money, to Elizabeth Hay of same state and district, widow, 300 acres, that is to say 200 acres granted to John Fairchild 4 July 1749 and 100 acres granted to said John Fairchild 5 Sept 1750, adj. each other, in Craven County on Raifords Creek waters of the Congaree River... dated 16 Dec 1776. Robert Goodwyn (LS), Wit: Solomon Peters, Hardy Hay, Gilbert Gibson. Proved in Chas. Town District before John Colcock, J. P., by the oath of Hardy Hay, 20 March 1777. Recorded 12 Apr 1777.

SOUTH CAROLINA DEED ABSTRACTS 1773-1778

P-4, 378-382: Lease & release. 3 & 4 May 1776, Philip Raiford of Camden District, SC, planter, to Adam Summers Junr of Ninety Six Dist., planter, for £950 SC money, 150 acres part of 450 acres granted 13 March 1752 to Charles Hill on north side Broads River, property transferred by the said Charles Hill to Philip Raiford father of the above named Philip Raiford, and before his death said Philip Raiford made a will dated 18 Jan 1760 and remaining on record in the Secretary's Office of this province 27 July 1761 wherein there being 150 acres of the land of the above mentioned 450 acres made over to the said Philip Raiford son of before mentioned Philip Raiford decd. Philip Raiford (LS), Wit: William Manning, Gasper Byerley (B), Michael Dickert [signed in German]. Proved in Ninety Six Dist by the oath of William Mannen before Michl. Dickert, J.P., 23 Sept 1776. Recorded 12 Apr 1777.

P-4, 382-385: Lease & release. 6 & 7 Nov 1776, William Orr, planter, to John Johnson, Esqr., for £170 SC money, 100 acres on a branch of Tyger River called the Beaver Dam Creek adj. land laid out to John Gordon, land laid out to Tarance Carrel, granted [surveyed] 19 May 1772 by Enoch Pearson D. S., granted to said William Orr 20 Oct 1772. William Orr (O) (LS), Wit: Daniel McKee, David Dickson, Samuel Otterson. Proved 30 Nov 1776 before John Caldwell, magistrate for Ninety Six District, by the oath of Samuel Otterson. Recorded 12 Apr 1777.

P-4, 385-387: Lease & release. 10 & 11 Sept 1773, Moses Britton of Craven County, SC, planter, to Henry Price of same, planter, for £150 SC money, tract in Prince Fredericks Parish, Craven County, on Muddy Creek on the west prong of said creek adj. land of George Snow, Mr. Mays, 150 acres. Moses Britton (LS), Wit: Thos Snow, Stephen Britton, James McDanel. Proved in Craven County by the oath of Thomas Snow before Saml Nesmith, J.P., 15 Jan 1774. Recorded 12 Apr 1777.

P-4, 387-390: Lease & release. 21 & 22 March 1777, William Floyd of Craven County, SC, cooper, to Patrick Fagen of same, planter, for £200 SC money, 150 acres in Craven County on Newmans branch adj. sd. Patrick Fagen. William Floyd (W) (LS), Alleys Floyd (X) (LS), Wit: Jno McFadden, Jas. Conyers Senr (+), Evan Benbow. Proved in Charlestown District before John Troup, J. P., by the oath of Jno. McFadden, 26 March 1777. Recorded 12 Apr 1777.

P-4, 390-393: Lease & release. 1 & 2 May 1768, Robert Howell and Mary his wife of Craven County, Sc, planter, to Francis Goodwin of same, planter, for £500 SC money, 100 acres granted to William Hart 15 May 1751 in the low ground on the north side of Congaree River adj. land laid out to Arthur Howell, Hugh Butler, Thos howell, Raifords Creek; also 100 acres granted to James Weston 8 Aug 1753 on Congaree River adj. land of Vincent Simmons. Robt Howell (LS), Mary Howell (LS), Wit: Charles Russell, John Howell, Rachel Lloyd. Proved in Orangeburgh Dist before Ralph Humphries, J.P., by the oath of John Howell, 13 March 1777. Recorded 12 Apr 1777.

P-4, 394-397: Lease & release. 17 Nov 1772, William Dargan & Sarah his wife and Jeremiah Dargan of St. Mathews Parish, Berkley County, to James Henry of same, for £150 SC money, 250 acres in two tracts of land originally granted to Timothy Dargan in 1759 in Amelia township, Berkley County, adj. Robert Wright, 250 acres granted to William Dargan 16 Jan 1772 adj. Jane Newton, Timothy Dargan, Wm. Adams, John Murdey. Jeremiah Dargan (LS), Wm. Dargan (LS), Sarah Dargan (LS), Wit: Chas. Heatly, Joshua Lawrence, Charles Waddell. Proved 8 March 1777 before John Caldwell, J. P., by the oath of Chas. Heatly. Recorded 12 Apr 1777.

P-4, 397-400: Lease & release. 10 & 11 March 1777, James Henry & Ann his wife of Amelia Township, Berkley County, planter, to Francis Roche of same, planter, for £180 SC money, two tracts, one of 250 acres but by resurvey contains 325 acres, one of 100 acres granted 1759 to Timothy Dargan adj. land of Robert Wright, Esqr.; the other tract granted to William Dargan 16 Jan 1772. James Henry (LS), Ann Henry (X) (LS), Wit: William Heatly Junr, John Whilden, John Williams. Proved 18 March 1777 before John Caldwell, J.P., by the oath of J. Whilden. Recorded 12 Apr 1777.

P-4, 401-406: Lease & release. 15 & 16 March 1777, Peter Bounetheau of Charlestown, to John Fisher of same, gentleman, for £1800 SC money, tract of land (lately belonging to Vincent Francis deceased, 100 acres in Christ Church Parish, adj. land of Daniel Legare, Mitheringham, south on the Broad Road, on Wakendau Creek. Pet: Bounetheau (LS), Wit: John Wagner, Christian Sigwald.

SOUTH CAROLINA DEED ABSTRACTS 1773-1778

Proved in Chas. Town District before George Sheed, J. P., by the oath of John Wagner, 3 Apr 1777. Peter Bounetheau and William Banbury of Charlestown, bound to John Fisher of same, in the sum of £1800 on 26 March 1777. Pet Bounetheau (LS), William Banbury (LS), Wit: John Calvert. Proved 5 Apr 1777. Recorded 12 Apr 1777.

P-4, 406-410: Lease & mortgage. 25 & 25 Feb 1777, John Vivian of Prince Georges Parish, Craven County, to Paul Trapier, Esqr., of same parish, for debt of £1000 SC money to be paid 21 Feb next, half part of 500 acres in Prince Georges Parish Winyaw about three miles rom George Town, known by the name of Anthonys Bluff, adj. land known by the name of Musgrove, land supposed to belong to Andrew Johnston, Sampit River, formerly belonging to Landgrave Thomas Smith, and sold by him to his brother Capt. George Smith as P a memorial registered 26 June 1732. John Vivian (LS), Wit: Pet. Lesesne, J. Bidggood. Proved in George Town District before Job Rothmahler by the oath of Peter Lesesne, 17 March 1777. Recorded 12 Apr 1777.

P-4, 410-413: 8 March 1777, John Kesson of Charlestown, in the body of the state, to Cassimer Boutel and Elisabeth his wife, for £200 SC money, 1000 acres on Wasmasaw, Berkley County adj. Col. Thomas Smith, Mr. Ragan. John Kesson Wit: Jno Nevin, Daniel McCoy. Proved 2 Apr 1777 before John Troup, J. P., by the oath of John Nevin. Recorded 19 Apr 1777.

P-4, 413-416: Lease & release. 27 & 28 Nov 1764, Daniel DeSaussure and Mary his wife of Prince William Parish, Granville County, SC, to Thomas Camber of St. Peters Parish, for £800 SC money, whereas Doctor Daniel Brabant by virtue of a warrant from his Excellency Robert Johnson, Gov. of SC, had laid out to him 500 acres in the township of Purrysbourgh in Granville County adj. land of Henry Bourquin, the town common, Loudovick Keills, David Coutier, and said Doctor Daniel Brabant died intestate by means of which his son Isaac Brabant became possessed of said 500 acres as heir at law, and said Isaac Brabant by lease and release 21 & 22 June 1763 for £100 to Daniel DeSaussure. D. DeSaussure (LS), Mary DeSaussure (LS), Wit: T. Desaussure, John Keating. Proved at Purysburgh by the oath of Thomas DeSaussure, 27 July 1775 before Adrian Mayer, J.P. Recorded 26 Apr 1777.

P-4, 416-418: 1 July 1774, William Holzendorf of Puresburgh and Mary his wife to John Frederick Holzendorf of same place, Tavern Keeper, for £10, one seventh part of 200 acres granted to late Capt. John Frederick Holzendorf in the Township of Purisburgh adj. lands granted to late Col. John Peter Pury, John Wunderly, Peter Ganet Vanderheiden, Peter Albateslur De Mon Clair, and land granted to late Col. John Chevilette, and also one undivided seventh part of another tract granted to sd. John Frederick Holzendorf in the township of Purisburgh of 250 acres. Wm. Holzendorff (LS), Mary Holzendorff (LS), Wit: John C. Postell, David Trushet. Proved 5 July 1774 before John Lewis Bourquin, J.P. in Granville County, by the oath of David Trushet. Recorded 26 Apr 1777.

P-4, 418-419: 1 July 1774, John Postell of Purisburgh and Rosina his wife to John Frederick Holzendorf of same place, tavern keeper, for £10, one seventh as yet undivided part of a tract of 200 acres granted to late Capt. John Frederick Holzendorf in the township of Purisburgh adj. land granted to late Col. John Peter Pury, John Wunderly, Peter Ganet Vanderheiden, Peter Albasteslier de Mond Clair, Col. John Chevillette, also one seventh part of another tract granted to sd John Frederick Holzendorf, 250 acres adj. Mary Bourquin. Jno Postell (LS), Rosina Postell (LS), Wit: William Holzendorff, David Trushett. Proved 5 July 1774 before John Lewis Bourquin, J.P. in Granville County, by the oath of David Trushet. Recorded 26 Apr 1777.

P-4, 419-421: 18 July 1774, John Russell in Prince William Parish, Beaufort District, and Elizabeth his wife to John Frederick Holzendorf of Purisburgh, tavern keeper, for £10, one seventh as yet undivided part of a tract of 200 acres granted to late Capt. John Frederick Holzendorf in the township of Purisburgh adj. land granted to late Col. John Peter Pury, John Wunderly, Peter Ganet Vanderheiden, Peter Albateslier de Mon Clair, Col. John Chevillette, also one seventh part of another tract granted to sd John Frederick Holzendorf, 250 acres adj. Mary Bourquin. John Russell (LS), Elizabeth Russell (LS), Wit: Jno Postell, David Trushett. Proved 5 July 1774 before David Giroud, J.P. in Granville County, by the oath of David Trushett. Recorded 26 Apr 1777.

P-4, 421-422: 12 May 1775, Willoughby Pugh of St. Peters Parish, planter, to Adrian Mayer of Purysburgh, parish aforesaid, Esqr., for £350 SC money, 350 acres originally granted to Thomas

SOUTH CAROLINA DEED ABSTRACTS 1773-1778

Page in Granville County adj. land granted to Henry Bourquin, and also tract of 220 acres granted to William Wells in County of Granville adj. land of Joachim Hardstone, Henry Gindras, Thomas Page, Paul Porcher. Willoughby Pugh (LS), Wit: Joseph Gernett, Charles Trushett. Proved in Purisburgh by the oath of Charles Trushett before David Giroud, J. P., 13 May 1775. Recorded 26 Apr 1777.

P-4, 422-424: 21 June 1775, John F. Holzendorf of Purisburgh in Granville County, Tavern Keeper, to Adrian Mayer of same, esqr., for £250 SC money, the six seventh sa yet undivided part of 200 acres granted to the late Capt. John Frederick Holzendorf adj. land granted to late John Peter Pury, land granted to John Wunderly, land granted to Peter Ganet Vanderkeyden, late Col. John Chevilette, and one seventh part of another tract of 250 acres ranted to sd. Capt. John Frederick Holzendorf adj. land granted to Mary Bourquin. John Holzendorf (LS), Wit: Jno Linder Junr, Joshua Brown. Proved in Purisburgh by the oath of John Linder Junr 12 July 1775 before David Giroud, J. P. Recorded 26 Apr 1777.

P-4, 424-425: 2 Aug 1775, Theodore Gauthier of Savannah, Georgia, Taylor, to Adrian Mayer of Purrysburgh, merchant, for £150 SC money, 300 acres in the Township of Purysburgh, Parish of St. Peter, adj. land of John Vauchier, land granted to Rev. Henry Chiffelle, John Long, Leonard Reinauer, granted 28 June 1767 to John Baptiste Gauthier. Theodore Goteare (LS), Wit: Richard Price, Jo'n Bostick. Proved by the oath of Richard Price 3 Aug 1775 before David Giroud, J. P. Recorded 26 Apr 1777.

P-4, 425-427: 9 Aug 1775, James Peart, D. Surveyor of Land, to Adrian Mayer of Purrysburgh, Esqr., for £900 SC money, 1000 acres on waters of Coosawhatchie and Stoney Run adj. land granted to Thomas Searson, Stephen McDaniel, and a moiety of land containing 300 acres being part of 800 acre tract granted to Thomas Searson which parcel is butting on the remaining part of said 800 acre tract now Thomas Searsons land, Stephen McDaniel, land granted to William Godfrey, adj. part of a barony called John Wraggs, land granted to William Godfrey. James Peart (LS), Wit: Joseph Garnett, Richard Price. Proved by the oath of Joseph Garnett 11 Aug 1775 before David Giroud, J. P. Recorded 26 Apr 1777.

P-4, 427-428: 9 Aug 1775, James Peart, Dep. Surveyor of Land, to Adrian Mayer of Purrysburgh, Esqr., for £1000 SC money, land granted to Josiah Pendarvis for 2000 acres on the Cherokee line at head of a branch of Savannah River called Johnstons Creek, near to the old Togoloo Trading Path, plat dated 4 May of the above date. James Peart (LS), Wit: Joseph Garnett, Aquila Miles. Proved by the oath of Joseph Garnett 11 Aug 1775 before David Giroud, J. P. Recorded 26 Apr 1777.

P-4, 428-429: 13 Sept 1775, Gabriel Watser of Purysburgh Township, to Adrian Mayer of same, Esqr., for £300 SC money, 150 acres in Purysburgh Township granted to the late Peter Harkey, adj. land of Henry Gasman, and also tract of 250 acres in said township granted to Ana[?] Mary Agnice adj. land of Daniel Pillet, Major James Richard, Sebastian Zuberbuhler, Frederick Holzendorf, Mary Bourquin, Benedict Bourquin, Henry Megerhoffer. Gabriel Watser (LS), Wit: Richard Price, Abraham Benenger. Proved by the oath of Richard Price 15 Sept 1775 before David Giroud, J. P. Recorded 26 Apr 1777.

P-4, 430-431: 23 Dec 1775, James Peart, Deputy Surveyor, to Adrian Mayer of Purrysburgh, Esqr., for £700 SC money, 1000 acres in Granville County on waters of Savanna River on a branch called Rockey River adj. land granted to William Burrows, Esqr., land now the property of Francis Bremar, Esqr., Willoughby Pugh, land granted to Katherine Keall, Cherokee land. James Peart, Wit: Thomas Bussey, Willoughby Pugh. Proved by the oath of Willoughby Pugh 23 Dec 1775 before David Giroud, J. P. Recorded 26 Apr 1777.

P-4, 431-432: 8 Dec 1775, Doctor Frederick Rehm and Catharine Keall his wife, to Adrian Mayer, Esqr., for £100 SC money, 200 acres in Granville County adj. lands granted on Rockey River to Willoughby Pugh, Cherokee Indian land, land granted to James Peart. Frederick Rehm (LS), Catharine Reall now Rehm (LS), Wit: John Francis Greniere, Willoughby Pugh. Proved by the oath of John Francis Greniere 14 Dec 1775 before David Giroud, J. P. Recorded 26 Apr 1777.

SOUTH CAROLINA DEED ABSTRACTS 1773-1778

P-4, 432-434: 11 Dec 1775, Willoughby Pugh of Purysburgh, planter, to Adrian Mayer, of same, Esqr., for £150 SC money, 450 acres in Granville County adj. land laid out to Wm Campbell, Cherokee Indian land, land granted to Catharine Keall, Gamaliel Hays. Willoughby Pugh (LS), Wit: Thomas Bussey, James Peart. Proved by the oath of James Peart 23 Dec 1775 before David Giroud, J. P. Recorded 26 Apr 1777.

P-4, 434-435: 27 Aug 1776, James Peart, Dep. Surveyor, to Adrian Mayer of Purrysburgh, Esqr., for £2350 SC money, 3200 acres on a branch of the northwest branch of Long Cane called Johnstons Creek adj. land laid out to Josiah Pendarvis 3 Apr 1775 now the property of sd. Adrian Mayer, Esqr., also all that moiety of a tract of 450 acres part of 2050 acres granted to John Pelot 1 June 1775 and said John Pelot conveyed to said James Peart 12 July 1775, adj. Capt. David Hunter, James Liddle, John Johnston, Michael Blanes, on the waters of Long Cane and a branch called Pennys Creek in Ninety Six District. James Peart (LS), Wit: Richard Sweney, John Forbes. Proved in Purysburgh by the oath of John Forbes 3 March 1777 before David Giroud, J. P. Recorded 26 Apr 1777.

P-4, 435-439: Lease & release. 7 & 8 Jan 1776, Isham Moore of St. Marks Parish, to John Gabriel Guignard of same, for £1500 SC money, 338 acres on the High Hills of Santee on north east side of Wateree River in Craven County granted to Samuel Hopkins 18 Aug 1763, and by him conveyed to said Isham Moore 6 & 7 Feb 1771. Isham Moore (LS), Wit: Wm. Richardson, Mattw. Singleton. Proved by the oath of William Richardson 3 Apr 1777 before Jno Colcock, J. P. Recorded 26 Apr 1777.

P-4, 439-443: Lease & release. 4 & 5 March 1777, Ann Clark, widow and executrix of Samuel Clark deceased, and William McConnico, executor, both of St. Marks Parish, SC, to John Gabriel Guignard of same, for £1500 SC money, 150 acres on the High Hills of Santee in St. Marks parish, Craven County adj. land granted to Arthur Richardson, John Beekman, John McIntosh, Philip Pettypool, land granted to Samuel Hopkins. Ann Clarke (LS), Wm. McConnico (LS), Wit: Robert Singleton, Richard Singleton. Proved 4 March 1777 before Nathaniel Moore, J. P., by the oath of Robert Singleton. Recorded 26 Apr 1777.

P-4, 444-449: Lease & release. 1 & 2 June 1775, Samuel Chollet of Charlestown, merchant, to James Oliphant of same, jeweller and Silver smith, for £50 SC money, 150 acres in Craven county on a branch of Tyger River called Fergusons Creek, waters of Broad River, and 200 acres on a fork of Sugar Creek a branch of Fairforest waters of Santee River adj. land of James Ainsworth, Jacob Womack; 250 acres on the north side of Tyger River adj. Philip Mulkeys; 300 acres on waters of Fairforest adj. land of James McIlwean, Zachariah Bullock; 300 acres in Craven County between the forks of Broad and Saludy River on a branch of Enoree River called Beaver Dam Branch adj. land of Barlet Brown, Robert Hannah, Giles Tillett, Isaac Gray; last five plantations total 1200 acres granted to Thomas Elliott and by him conveyed 23 & 24 Jan 1775 to John Bremar, Esqr., and by him to said Samuel Chollet; also 1000 acres in Craven County on south west side of Pedee River adj. Thomas Hudson, William Fletcher, John Popwell, Aaron Baker, William Green, Mary Blackland; 200 acres 200 acres on Swifts Creek waters of Pedee which said last plantations were granted to John McQueen, Esqr., and conveyed to John Bremar, and by him to Samuel Chollet; also 100 acres on South side Wateree River on Peech Tree and Bee Tree branches, 200 acres on the Twenty five Mile Creek, south side of Wateree River adj. land of Isaac Ross, Henry Dongworth, which said plantations were granted to Paul Townsend and by him conveyed to John Bremar and by him to Samuel Chollet; also 100 acres in Craven county on the head of Toby's Creek waters of Pee Dee River adj. William Herons, Doctor John Murray, Charles Turbeville, granted to Reuben White and by him conveyed to John Bremar and by him conveyed to Samuel Chollet; also 350 acres in Amelia Township adj. land surveyed for Robert Gosling, land belonging to Barnard Elliott Esquire, John McWilliams, Col. William Thompsons, granted to Philip Henry and by him conveyed to Samuel Chollet; also 400 acres in Ninety Six District between the south fork of Long Cane adj. land of James McGaw, John McGaw, widow Clark; 300 acres in St. Matthews Parish, Berkley County on a branch of Four Hole Swamp adj. land of John Goodbee, George Brown, granted to Samuel Chollet; Samuel Chollet (LS), Wit: A. Chollet, James Clitherall. Proved in Charlestown District before George Sheed, J.P., by the oath of Abraham Chollet, 12 Apr 1777. Recorded 3 May 1777.

SOUTH CAROLINA DEED ABSTRACTS 1773-1778

P-4, 449-454: Lease & release. 21 & 22 March 1777, Alexander Gillon of Charlestown, merchant, and Mary his wife, to Francis Goodwin of Congarees in SC, planter, for £8790 SC money, 400 acres in Craven County on the low grounds of Congaree River bounded at the time of the original grant 22 Jan 1759 to James Randolph, on said river and on vacant land, recorded in Book TT, page 15; conveyed by James Randolph and Jane his wife to John Cook and by him to said Alexander gillon, also 186 acres in Craven County on north side of Congaree River granted to Elizabeth Ricker adj. Robert Goodwin. Alexander Gillon (LS), Mary Gillon (LS), Wit: Florian Charles Mey, Peter Meurset. Proved in Charlestown District before George Sheed, J.P., by the oath of Peter Meurset, 15 Apr 1777. Recorded 3 May 1777

P-4, 454-455: 4 Nov 1776, Zachariah Bell of Craven County, Camden District, SC, to James Bell of same, for £500 SC money, 166 acres on Bells Creek granted to sd. Zachariah Bell, being one third part of tract of 500 acres granted 8 July 1774. Zachariah Bell (LS), Wit: William Bell, John McCool. Proved in Charlestown District before George Sheed by the oath of William Bell 15 Apr 1777. Recorded 3 May 1777.

P-4, 455-456: 5 Aug 1776, Mary Waight of St. Johns Parish, Colleton County, widow, to Benjamin Waight of same, for natural love and affection to said Benjamin Waight her son, 100 acres on waters of Twenty Five Mile Creek in Craven County adj. lands of John Waight Senr., John Waight Junr. Mary Waight (LS), Wit: Abrahm Waight Senr, Abram Waight Junr, Mary Waight. Proved in Charlestown District before George Sheed by the oath of Abraham Waight Junr. 15 Apr 1777. Recorded 3 May 1777.

P-4, 457-461: Lease & release. 11 & 12 Apr 1777, John Fyfe of Charlestown, Cabinet maker, and Sarah his wife, to Charles Desel of same, cabinet maker, for £800 SC money, lot in Charlestown in Colleton Square, adj. land of Thomas Eveleigh, Jacob Valk, Church St. John Fyfe (LS), Sarah Fyfe (LS), Wit: N. W. Hutchings, John Troup. Proved 17 Apr 1777 before George Sheed by the oath of John Troupe, Esqr. Recorded 3 May 1777.

P-4, 461-464: Lease & release. 29 & 30 Apr 1771, John Savage of Ninety Six, Storekeeper, to Tacitus Gaillard of Parish of St. Matthew, planter, for £300 SC money, 400 acres on Ninety Six Mile Creek in Colaton County formerly called Berkley County, granted 3 Apr 1754 to Andrew Carthey, conveyed by William Carthey heir at law to said Andrew Carthey 28 Jan 1768 to John Savage. Jno Savage (LS), Wit: D. Cunningham, Joseph Freeman, John Walker. Proved 4 May 1771 before John Lewis Gervais, J. P., in Colleton County, by the oath of David Cunningham. Recorded 3 May 1777.

P-4, 464-467: Lease & release. 10 & 11 Feb 1773, Peter Manigault of Charlestown, SC, Barister at Law, to Tacitus Gaillard of Parish of St. Mathew, planter, for £300 SC money, 500 acres in St. Pauls Parish, Horse Pen Branch between Ninety Six and the Ridge adj. John Bruce, Thomas Fletcher, Henry Schuckall, and also a tract of 450 acres on a branch called Mountain branch near Ninety Six adj. James Jamerson, William Winn, Henry Borington, John Thomerson, Jamerson, William Laurel. P. Manigault (LS), Wit: Thos Farr Junr, Gabriel Manigault Junr. Proved by the oath of Thomas Farr Junior, Esqr., 1 Apr 1773 before John Troup, J.P. Recorded 3 May 1777.

P-4, 467-469: Lease & release. 15 & 16 Nov 1774, Benjamin Farar of Saxagotha Township, Berkley County, to Tacitus Gaillard of Parish of St. Mathew, for £10 SC money, 200 acres at Ninety Six on Ninety Six Creek granted to Thomas Brown 8 Dec 1744 and by the last wills of said Thomas Brown and Patrick Brown the said land descended to Richard Brown who by deed conveyed the same 22 May 1770 to said Benjamin Farar. Benjn. Farar (LS), Wit: Herman Gallman, Robert Martin. Proved by the oath of Robert Martain, 4 Dec 1774 before William Arthur, J.P. Recorded 3 May 1777.

P-4, 469-473: Lease & release. 9 & 10 Sept 1776, John Savage of Parish of St. Mathew, planter, to Tacitus Gaillard and Isaac Gaillard, planters, for £3000 SC money, tract at Ninety Six in Colleton County containing originally 300 acres but now supposed 390 acres, allowing ten acres more or less out of the original conveyance for the town lots, streets & public lands whereon the Court House and Goal now standeth... adj. Robert Boudey, John Murray Esqr., conveyed by said John Murray to said John Savage 22 July 1767. John Savage (LS), Wit: Jacob Christopher Zahn, Isaac

SOUTH CAROLINA DEED ABSTRACTS 1773-1778

Deliesseline, Robert Lithgow. Proved 10 Apr 1777 before John Caldwell, J. P. for Orangeburgh District by the oath of Jacob Christopher Zahn. Recorded 20 May 1777.

P-4, 473-476: Lease & release. 13 & 14 Apr 1774, Sarah Elliott of Charles Town, Widdow, and Thomas Elliott of same place, merchant, for £100 SC money, 300 acres being a moiety of half part of 600 acres in Berkley County on the south side of Four Hole Swamp adj. land of Edward Perry, Thomas Clark, also tract of 897 acres being the westernmost moiety of half part of tract of 1794 acres adj. John Moore, Abraham moore, Henry Woods, Mr. Dunklin, George Evans, Edward Perry, originally granted 18 May last to said Sarah Elliott. Sarah Elliott (LS), Wit: Martha Rees, John Bush. Proved in Charlestown District before George Sheed, J. P., by the oath of John Bush 29 March 1777. Recorded 10 May 1777. Plats included: By the desire of Mr. Thomas Elliott I have equally divided and set of from a certain tract belonging to Miss Sarah Elliott, 300 acres, being one half of 600 acre tract for which Sarah Eliott obtained a grant 18 May 1773... dated 10 March 1774, Benjn. Cook, D.S.; by the desire of Mr. Thomas Elliott I have equally divided and set of from a certain tract belonging to Miss Sarah Elliott, 897 acres, being one half of 1794 acre tract for which Sarah Eliott obtained a grant 27 Apr 1773... dated 10 March 1774, Benjn. Cook, D.S.

P-4, 476-479: Lease & release. 3 & 4 Apr 1775, William Elliott to Thomas Elliott of Charlestown, merchant, for £10 SC money, eight tracts of land: three in Berkley County, that is to say one tract of 147 acres adj. Henry Wood, Mr. Elliott, John Moore; one of 200 acres on waters of Bush River adj. George Derumple, Lewis Jones, James Young; one tract of 853 acres in St. Georges Parish; two tracts in Craven County, 300 acres on a fork of Raeburns Creek called Browns fork a branch of Saluda River, one tract of 300 acres adj. Ralph Humphreys; three in Granville County one tract of 1000 acres on head of Three Runs on Tinkers Creek adj. Richard Hall; 1000 acres on head of Three Runs on Tinkers Creek adj. William Elliott; one other tract of 1000 acres on head of Three Runs adj. Benjamin Farrar, William Elliott. Wm. Elliott (LS), Wit: Geo Chateris, John Bush. Proved 29 March 1777 before George Sheed, J. P. in Charlestown District, by the oath of John Bush. Recorded 10 May 1777.

P-4, 479-481: Lease & release. 20 & 21 June 1775, John Vaughan of St. Marks parish, Camden District, to Thomas Elliott of Charlestown, merchant, for £10 SC money, 350 acres in Craven County adj. Yeats, John Baitman, granted to said John Vaughan 4 June 1759. [plat included showing 350 acres on waters of Watree River]. John Vaughan (X) (LS), Wit: John Bush, Daniel Wilson. Proved 29 March 1777 before George Sheed, J. P. in Charlestown District, by the oath of John Bush. Recorded 10 May 1777.

P-4, 481-483: Lease & release. 20 & 21 June 1775, John Vaughan of St. Marks parish, Camden District, to Thomas Elliott of Charlestown, merchant, for £10 SC money, 50 acres in Craven County on east side Wateree River, adj. William Helton, John Baitman, John Vaughan, granted to said John Vaughan 16 Jan 1772. [plat included]. John Vaughan (X) (LS), Wit: John Bush, Daniel Wilson. Proved 29 March 1777 before George Sheed, J. P. in Charlestown District, by the oath of John Bush. Recorded 10 May 1777.

P-4, 483-486: Lease & release. 22 & 23 Feb 1777, Casper Foust of Craven County to Richard Strother for £100 SC money, 200 acres on east side Broad River adj. Herman Geiger, George Hiles, land granted to Casper Foust Senr decd 7 May 1762. Casper Foust (LS), Wit: Francis Strother, Jeane Strother (+). Proved 17 Apr 1777 before James Kennerly, J.P., by the oath of Francis Strother. Recorded 20 May 1777.

P-4, 486-490: Lease & release. 9 & 10 March 1775, John Witherspoon of Craven county, Parish of St. Mark, planter, to John Adamson of same, vintner, for £3000 SC money, 400 acres in Craven county in Fredericksburgh Township on north side Wateree River adj. said river, granted to Samuel Neilson 28 Nov 1748 recorded in Book EE, page 325, conveyed to John Witherspoon., 28 (29 May 1753. John Witherspoon. Wit: Henry Sanders, John Savage, Richd. Wadeson. Proved in Camden District 18 April 1777 before Jno. N. Oglethorpe, J. P., by the oath of Richard Wadeson. Recorded 10 May 1777.

P-4, 490-492: 9 Nov 1774, Joseph Kershaw, John Chesnut, Ely Kershaw, William Ancrum and Aaron Loocock, province of SC, merchants, to John Adams of Camden, Tavernkeeper, for £750, lots in

SOUTH CAROLINA DEED ABSTRACTS 1773-1778

town of Camden, numbers 30 and 31. Joseph Kershaw (LS), Jno. Chesnut (LS), Ely Kershaw (LS), Wm. Ancrum (LS), Aaron Loocock (LS), Wit: John Wyly, William Rea. Proved in Camden District 18 Apr 1777 before Jno. N. Oglethorpe by the oath of Wm. Rea. Recorded 10 May 1777.

P-4, 492-494: 16 Apr 1777, Joseph Kershaw of Camden in Craven County, merchant, to John Adamson of Camden, inholder, for £6000 SC money, lots 56, 57, 58, 59, 60, 61, 76, 77, 78, 79, 80. Joseph Kershaw (LS), Wit: Thomas Jones, William Rea. Proved in Camden District 18 Apr 1777 before Jno. N. Oglethorpe by the oath of Wm. Rea. Recorded 12 May 1777.

P-4, 494-497: Lease & release. 16 & 17 Dec 1756, William James, Esqr. of the Welch Tract, in Craven County, planter, to Thomas Harry of same, planter, for £300 SC money, 200 acres in the Welch Tract granted to sd. William James 6 Oct 1752. Wm. James (LS), Wit: David Harry, Benjamin James. Proved in Craven County before Alexr. Mackintosh, J. P., by the oath of David Harry, 13 March 1765. Recorded 31 May 1777.

P-4, 497-500: Lease & release. 25 & 26 Apr 1774, John Mikell and Ann his wife of Craven County, planter, to Abel Kolp of same, planter, for £300 SC money, 100 acres granted to John Still 13 July 1762 on Great Pee Dee River adj. Joshua Edwards, William Hughes, Daniel Monohan, conveyed by John Still to John Mikell 24 & 25 Aug 1770. John Mikell (LS), Ann Mikell (LS), Wit: Jethro Moore, Wm. Dewitt. Proved in Cheraw District before Alexr. Mackintosh, J.P., by the oath of William Dewitt, 1 Dec 1774. Recorded 31 May 1777.

P-4, 500-504: Lease & release. 13 & 14 May 1774, Samuel Cross of St. Georges Parish, planter, and Susanna his wife, to Richard Jackson of Chesterfield County, Colony of Virginia, for £450 SC money, 150 acres in St. Georges Parish, Berkley County adj. Dupont, land surveyed for James Haley. Saml Cross (LS), Susanna Cross (LS), Wit: John Remington Junr, Thos Fell, William Mellard, Elisha Mellard. Proved in Chas. Town District 14 May 1774 before Geo Davidson, J.P., by the oath of William Mellard. Recorded 31 May 1777.

P-4, 504-508: Lease & release. 4 & 5 July 1774, Michael Hunsinger to Christina Stamburger for £100 SC money, 150 acres in Orangeburgh Township on a branch of Edisto River adj. sd. Michael Hunsinger and land granted to George Breehl. Michael Hunsinger [German signature] (LS), Wit: Philipp Henrich, William Lawss. Proved 6 July 1774 before Hopkin Price, J. P. in District of Chas. Town, by the oath of Philip Henrich and William Lawss. Recorded 31 May 1777.

P-4, 508-513: Lease & release. 24 & 25 March 1777, Col. Tacitus Gaillard of SC, and Ann his wife, to William Bull the younger of Charles Town, for £11,500 SC money, 614 acres of River Swamp land part of an Island on south side of Santee River in St. Matthews Parish, Berkley County; also 492 acres part of a larger tract of 592 acres on the south side of Santee River in St. Matthews Parish adj. land now of Henry Laurens, Esqr., and 100 acres reserved by said Tacitus Gaillard, adj. John McWilliams, estate of John McNichols [plat included]. Tacit's Gaillard (LS), Ann Gaillard (LS), Wit: Paul Turquand, John Monk. Proved 10 Apr 1777 before John Caldwell, J. P. for Orangeburgh District, by the oath of Paul Turquand. Recorded 31 May 1777.

P-4, 513-515: Lease & release. 10 & 11 May 1775, John Bean of Amelia Township, Berkely County, to James Wages of same, for 50 acres part of a tract of 250 acres granted to Martin Stoutenmire on the Bounty 9 Jan 1752 in Amelia township adj. land of Thomas Smith Senior, John Mitchell, Jacob Powell, George Rowe [Roye?]. John Bean (X) (LS), Wit: Henry Hutto, John Cooke (X), Thomas Smith (X). Proved in Charlestown District before George Sheed by the oath of Thomas Smith, 1 May 1777. Recorded 31 May 1777.

P-4, 515-519: Lease & release. 14 & 15 Feb 1777, John Heard of Charlestown, Gentleman, to John Fisher of same, cabinet maker, by bond in the penal sum of £1000 SC money, for debt of £500, tract of 1000 acres on north side of Waccamaw River in Craven county originally granted 17 March 1775 to James Greenwood adj. land of Arthur Baxter, McDugle, David Jordan, and persons unknown. Jno Heard (LS), Wit: John Forteath, Wm. Print. Proved in Charlestown District before George Sheed by the oath of William Print, 3 May 1777. Recorded 31 May 1777.

SOUTH CAROLINA DEED ABSTRACTS 1773-1778

P-4, 519-524: Lease & release. 5 & 6 Nov 1775, William Drayton & Alexander Rose, acting exors of the will of John Drayton Junr deceased of Charlestown, to Thomas Rose of Parish of St. Andrews, planter, whereas John Drayton Junior by his will dated 24 Oct 1773 did direct that his plantation at Wappoo in St. Andrews Parish be sold by his exors, now for £5798 SC money, 446 acres being pat of the plantation at Wappoo adj. land of Sarah Lining, Thomas Rose, Elizabeth Rivers, William Harvey, on the road from James Island to Ashley River. [plat included] Wm. Drayton (LS), Alex Rose (LS), Wit: James Penman, George Mellard, Edward Fenwick, Thos Fenwick. [last two witnesses to Alexr Rose's signing]. Proved in Charlestown District by the oath of Thomas Fenwick before Geo: Sheed, 9 May 1777. Recorded 31 May 1777.

P-4, 524-528: Lease & release. 6 & 7 Apr 1777, Susannah Vergereau of Charlestown, widdow, William Tennent of same place, clerk and, Susannah Tennent his wife, to Lewis Pintard of the Citty of New York, merchant, for £1600 current money of New York, all that dwelling house and lot of ground in the City of New York in the east ward of said city, in the street commonly called Smiths Valley formerly the property of Peter Vergereau, Goldsmith, of the said city, and sd. Peter Vergereau conveyed to his son Peter Vergereau and confirmed unto his mother Susannah Vergereau 12 Jan 1765. Susana Vergereau (mark), Wm. Tennent (LS), Susanna Tennent (LS), Wit: Sarah Parker, Willm. Parker, John Hiet. Proved by the oath of Willm. Parker before William Gibbes, J.P., 30 Apr 1777. Recorded 31 May 1777.

P-4, 528-529: This is to certifye that for love and good will which I have for my son Willm. Coachman at his arriving to the age of 21 years, I have given him all the lands I bought of Anthony White upon Pedee River, 650 acres adj. lands of John Palmer, to him the said William Poole Coachman. James Coachman (LS), Wit: Thomas Labruce, Stephen Clyatt, Catharen Clyatt. Proved in George Town District before Francis Britton, J. p., by the oath of Stephen Clyatt, 3 Dec 1776. Recorded 31 May 1777.

P-4, 529-532: Lease & release. 20 & 21 Oct 1775, Peter & Thomas Lord of Charlestown to Hugh Swinton of same place, for £3200 SC money, 400 acres in the parish of Christ Church in Berkley County adj. land now or late belonging to Henry Reeves, marsh land now or late belonging to James Cook on Wando River, land of William Loocock and John Ward. Peter Lord (LS), Thomas Lord (LS), Wit: Wm. Rudnall, Anthony McHugo. Proved 21 Oct 1776 before Maurice Simons, J. P., by the oath of Wm. Rudhall. Recorded 5 July 1777.

P-4, 533-536: Lease & release. 9 & 10 Sept 1774, Claudius Richbourgh and Unity his wife of St. Marks Parish, Craven County, planter, to Moses Thompson of Rowan County, North Carolina, for £300 SC money, tract on north side Santee River 300 acres by plat and grant dated 9 Jan 1755. Claudius Richbourg (LS), Unity Richbourg (LS), Wit: Joseph Fox, Peter Mellet. Proved in Camden District before Nathl. Moore, J.P., by the oath of Peter Mellet, 21 Oct 1774. Recorded 5 July 1777.

P-4, 536-540: Lease & release. 1 Sept 1775, John Langford of Province of Georgia, and Ann his wife, to Peter Mellet of St. Marks Parish, SC, planter, for £300 SC money, 300 acres near the Wateree River in Craven County adj. land of James Michie, Thomas Jones, granted 6 June 1757 to Alexander Shepheard who died intestate by which means the said tract of land become vested in the said Ann only child of said Alexander Sheppard who has since intermarried with said John Langford. Jno Langford (LS), Ann Langford (LS), Wit: John Durst, John Hamilton, Francis Allen. Proved in Charlestown District before George Sheed by the oath of Francis Allen, 19 March 1777. Recorded 5 July 1777.

P-4, 541-545: Lease & release. 5 & 6 Dec 1769, John James Soulegre of Colleton County, Sc, planter, to William Greaves of Charlestown, merchant, for £200 SC money, 250 acres on the south side of Edisto River granted by George II 4 March 1760 to sd. John James Soulegre. John James Soulegre (J) (LS), Wit: Jno Dooly, Joel Poinsett. Proved 19 Dec 1769 before Jacob Motte, J. P. in Berkley County, by the oath of Joel Poinsett. Recorded 5 July 1777.

P-4, 546: Joseph Stone of Charlestown, carpenter, for natural affection to my brother Benjn Stone of Parish of St. James Santee, taylor, tract in Parish of St. Thomas & Denis on east side Cooper River adj. Jeremiah Russell, Francis Pagets, dated 27 Dec 1776. Joseph Stone (LS), Wit: Abraham

SOUTH CAROLINA DEED ABSTRACTS 1773-1778

Sutliff, John White. Proved in Chs. Town District before D. Horry, by the oath of Abraham Sutliff, 5 Apr 1777. Recorded 5 July 1777.

P-4, 546-550: Lease & release. 5 & 6 July 1773, James Smith and Sarah Smith is wife of Craven County, SC, planter, to Timothy Dargan of same, planter, for £400 SC money, 300 acres in Craven County on Bluff head a branch of Black River adj. land ranted to one Pinckney. James Smith (LS), Sarah Smith (2) (LS), Wit: John Newton, Jas. McCormick, William Griffen. Proved 7 March 1775 before Wood Furman, J.P. for Craven County, by the oath of James McCormick. Recorded 5 July 1777.

P-4, 550-553: Lease & release. 24 & 25 Apr 1775, William Young and Mary his wife of Prince Fredericks Parish, Craven County, planter, to James Frierson Senr of St. Marks Parish, planter, for £180 SC money, 108 acres on Mount Hope Swamp in Craven County, part of tract formerly belonged to Sarah West adj. Richard Tier, sd. Young. Willm. Young (LS), Mary Young (LS), Wit: John Cantey, John Cossens, Robert Henderson. Proved in Camden District by the oath of John Cantey before J. M. Harris, J. P., 25 March 1777. Recorded 5 July 1777.

P-4, 554-564: 13 June 1775, Stephen Miller of Berkley County, Esquire, and Mary his wife to Brian Cape of Charlestown, merchant, whereas Mary Darby the daughter and devisee of Joseph Warnock heretofore of the Parish of St. Thomas in her life time and at the time of her death was seized of by virtue of the will of her father said Joseph Warnock in a tract about 500 acres common called the Cowpen above Cainhoy in said Parish and upon the death of said Mary Darby the said plantation of 500 acres did descend to and upon Joseph Darby son and heir at law of said Mary Darby his mother and said Joseph Darby the son after the death of his mother entered into and upon the said plantation and said Joseph Darby departed this life about the month of February in the year 1739 a minor and without issue and said 500 acres did come to and upon his three sisters Anna, Maria alias Mary and Margaret as his Coheiresses, and the said Margaret afterwards departed this life an infant and without issue whereupon the inheritance and fee simple of said plantation became wholly vested in the said two surviving sisters Anna and Mary as copartners, and said Anna Darby afterward intermarried with Benjamin Singletary of the parish aforesaid, planter, and said Mary with Elias Bonneau of same parish, planter, and at his Majestys' Court of Common Pleas holden at Charlestown in November term 1747 upon application a writ of partition was issued and divided said tract in equal moieties, one part thereof containing two fifth parts of the whole (being tho less in Quantity yet equal in value) adj. Garrens Creek on Stephen millers land, Mr. Lesesnes, Elias Bonneau and Mary his wife by lease and release 9 & 10 March 1748 released to said Stephen miller all that parcel of 216 acres, and the late Lords Proprietors by deed or grant 14 April 1709 did grant to William North then of said province, tract in Berkley County, 500 acres, and said William North on 21 Nov 1711 with consent of Elizabeth North his wife, did convey to John Westcot 100 acres, and said John Westcot and Elizabeth his wife conveyed 12 Aug 1712 to Vincent Guerin, and Vincent Guerin by lease and release 23 & 24 Apr 1740 did sell to Isaac Guerin said 100 acres, and by indenture 6 & 7 July 1750 made between Isaac Guerin and Martha his wife to Joseph Heskett of same parish, and Joseph Heskett at the time of his death was seized of said tract and died intestate without issue of his body whereby the same descended unto George Heskett of Berkley County, Chair maker, as eldest surviving brother and heir at law, and said George Heskett to Mary Heskett, widow of Charlestown, by lease and release 8 & 9 Feb 1750 sold 100 acres part of 500 acres in the Parish of St. Thomas adj. Stephen Miller, and Mary Heskett 1 & 2 July 1775 did convey to Stephen Miller. Stephen Miller (LS), Wit: Jas. Forgartie, Stephen Fogartie, Lewis Fogartie. Proved in Charlestown District before George Sheed, J.P., by the oath of James Fogartie, 5 July 1777. Recorded 12 July 1777.

END OF BOOK P-4.

SOUTH CAROLINA DEED ABSTRACTS 1773-1778

Q-4, 1-5: Lease & release. 19 & 20 May 1774, Samuel Minear of Black Swamp, Beaufort District, SC, planter, and Mary his wife, to James Cane of Savannah River in 96 District, planter, for £350 SC money, 150 acres on north east side of Savannah River in Granville County, Ninety Six District, adj. William Bedingfield. Samuel Maner (LS), Mary Maner (LS), Wit: John Stafford, James Rattrey. Proved 20 May 1774 before John Chisolm, J.P. in Beaufort District. Recorded 13 Feb 1775.

Q-4, 5-9: Lease & release. 8 & 9 June 1773, William McMahan and Jane his wife of Prov. of SC, to David Cahoon of North Carolina, for £150 SC money, 150 acres granted 26 Oct 1767 by William Tryon, Gov. of NC, to Wm. McMahan at that time in Mecklenburg County on the north fork of Tyger River but the late province line being run it is fallen into South Carolina adj. land of Francis Williams. Wm McMahan (LS), Jane McMahan (O) (LS), Wit: John Ward, Harman Dildene (+), John Vines. Proved in Ninety Six District by the oath of John Ward 9 June 1773 before John Ward, J.P. Recorded 14 Feb 1774 [sic for 1775].

Q-4, 9-11: 10 July 1774, Thomas Conner of Cheraw District, SC, planter, to Henry Council of same, blacksmith, for £460 SC money, 150 acres being a moiety or half part of a tract granted to Joseph Laws called the Mealy[?] Spott, 15 Dec 1753. Thomas Conner (LS), Wit: Luke Munkey, Lewis Conner. Proved in Cheraw District before Philip Pledger, J. P., by the oath of <u>James</u> Conner, 3 Nov 1774. Recorded 14 Feb 1775.

Q-4, 11-13: 16 Feb 1771, Henry Hancock and Sarah his wife of Craven County, SC, to John Potts of same, planter, for £300 SC money, 250 acres on the southwest side of Peedee River adj. Robert Finley. Henry Hancock (H) (LS), Sarah Hancock (LS), Wit: Dickerson Green, Samson Baker. Proved in Craven County by the oath of Sampson Baker before Jos. Gourly, 9 Nov 1773. Recorded 15 Feb 1774.

Q-4, 14-18: 4 May 1772, Katharine Finley Senior & Katharine Finley Junr of Charles Town, to Thomas Potts of Craven County, SC, planter, for £250 SC money, tract of 500 acres in Craven County, on south side Peedee River which said tract by the last will of Robert Finlay deceased dated 13 Jan 1742 was left to his wife Katharine Finley Senr and Katharine Finlay Junr his Eldest daughter jointly, said tract granted 6 Feb 1735 and a memorial entered in Book L. No. 11, page 217 on 6 May 1772. Katharine Finlay Senr (LS), Katharine Finlay Junr (LS), Wit: John Wragg, John Cross. Proved 5 May 1772 before John Poaug, J. P., by the oath of John Wragg. Recorded 15 Feb 1775.

Q-4, 18-22: 2 Nov 1773, Thomas Burton & Elizabeth his wife of Craven County, Sc, planter, to Thomas Potts of Craven County, planter, for £300 SC money, 500 acres in Craven County which by the will of Thomas Burton Senr deceased dated 22 Jan 1756 was left to his grandson Thomas Burton. Thos Burton (LS), Eliz'th Burton (B) (LS), Wit: Isaac Neavel, Jesse Stephens (J). Proved 8 Jan 1774 before Joseph Gourley, J. P., by the oath of Isaac Nevill. Recorded 16 Feb 1775.

Q-4, 22-26: 23 Dec 1765, John Mayer of Craven County, SC, planter, to Henry Hancock of same, for £50 SC money, 250 acres in Craven County on great Peedee River in the township of Queensborough adj. land of Mr. Robert Finlay. John Myers (M) (LS), Mary Myers (C) (LS), Wit: Simon Malphrus Junr (+), Elias Taylor. Proved in Craven County 17 Jan 1766 before David Fulton, J.P., by the oath of Simon Nolphes Junr. Recorded 17 Feb 1775.

Q-4, 26-28: South Carolina, Craven County. Whereas a tract of land granted to Col. William Waties in 1736 on Wacamaw River sold by sd. Waties to my father Nicholas Frink now deceased and by the will of my father bequeathed to me and my brother Ephraim Frank equally to be divided and now 3 Dec 1767, Jabesh Frink of Parish of Allsaints, Craven County, with the consent of Nathan Frink & Ephraim Frink my Elder Brothers and with the approbation of my nephew John Frink son of my deceased brother John Frink, to David Hewitt of same parish, for £20 SC money, half of the above tract bequeathed to me by my father the whole content being 400 acres, 300 acres and the northermost part of the same, bounding on the province line my aforesaid brother Ephraim Frink sold over unto Edward Wingate Senr by sale 4 Aug 1750. Jabesh Frink (LS), Nathan Fraink (LS), Jon Frink. Wit: Martha Frink, Thomas Frink. Proved in George Town District before Dennis Hankins by the oath of Thomas Frink, 2 Nov 1774. Recorded 17 Feb 1775.

SOUTH CAROLINA DEED ABSTRACTS 1773-1778

Q-4, 28-32: Lease & release. 5 & 6 Apr 1773, Charles Spears and Sarah Spears his wife of St. Marks Parish, to Warner Tucker of same, for £100 SC money, 100 acres granted to said Charles Spears on a branch of Twenty five mile creek called Bells Branch on west side of Water Ree River granted 31 March 1761, recorded in Book NN, page 23. Charles Spears (LS), Sarah Spears (LS), Wit: Isaac Ross, Jeremiah Pierson, Anthony Seal (+). Proved by the oath of Jeremiah Pearson before Jno. N. Oglethorp, J.P., 29 Apr 1773. Recorded 18 Feb 1775.

Q-4, 32-36: Lease & release. 21 & 22 Nov 1770, Jacob Johns and Patience his wife of St. Marks Parish, to Warner Tucker of same, for £100 SC money, 100 acres granted 3 Nov 1762 to Benjamin Wells in St. Marks Parish, Craven County, on Bell Branch another branch of Twenty five Mile Creek. Jacob Johns (mark) (LS), Patience Johns (mark) (LS), Wit: William Stribling, Vinuas Turner. Proved 22 Nov 1770 by the oath of Vinuas Turner before John Winn, J.P. Recorded 20 Feb 1775.

Q-4, 37-38: 12 March 1773, John Cox of Granville County, SC, planter, to Mathew Long of same, planter, for £50 SC money, 150 acres granted to sd. John Cox 6 Apr 1768. John Cox (LS), Wit: Patrick Roach, Samuel Black. Proved 21 Sept 1774 in Granville County before Robert Anderson, J.P., by the oath of Samuel Black. Recorded 21 Feb 1775.

Q-4, 39-44: Lease & release. 1 & 2 Dec 1774, Michael Thompson of Craven County, Sc, planter, to Joseph Burch of same, planter, for £10 SC money, 200 acres on north east side of Peedee River in Watree[?] Neck adj. Secheverals land, Burches land. Michael Thompson (LS), Wit: Peter Lord, Stephen Prosser. Proved 1 Dec 1774 before Fenwick Bull, J.P., by the oath of Stephen Prosser. Recorded 22 Feb 1775.

Q-4, 44-48: Lease & release. 25 & 26 Nov 1774, Wm. Nisbett of Charles Town, Esqr., to James Parsons of same, esqr., for ten shillings, 50 acres near Mount Parsons in the Long Canes settlement, Granville County, Ninety Six District adj. sd. James Parsons, Ephraim Michael, Henry McMurdy, Alexander Robertson. Wm. Nisbett (LS), Wit: Henry Nichols, James Smith. Proved in Berkley County by the oath of Henry Nicholes, Gentleman, 20 Dec 1774 before John Troup, J. P. Recorded 22 Feb 1775.

Q-4, 48-50: 2 Sept 1774, Thomas Platt of St. Matthews Parish, Berkley County, planter, to John Fisher of Orangeburgh, Merchant, for £50 SC money, 500 acres in Colleton County granted 2 Apr 1773 to Thos Platt, land adj. to John Fisher, Edisto River, Peter Nuggelie, Anthony Robertson. Thomas Platt (LS), Wit: William Simpson, David Dickson. Proved 2 Sept 1774 in Orangeburgh District before John Savage, J.P. Recorded 22 Feb 1775.

Q-4, 51-53: 12 Dec 1772, Thomas Bass, cordwinder, of Granville County, to Robert Lowery, planter, of Craven County, for £300 SC money, 300 acres on Jeffers Creek on Alligator Branch in Craven County granted 16 Dec 1766 to Thomas Bass. Thomas Bass (T) (LS), Wit: Lucy Nettles, Thomas Bass Junr. Proved in Cheraw District by the oath of Thomas Bass Junr before Joseph Gourley, 4 Oct 1773. Recorded 22 Feb 1775.

Q-4, 53-57: Lease & release. 26 & 27 July 1774, Benjamin Cooke to Darby Pendergrass of Charles Town, merchant, for £3000 SC money, 1000 acres in Prince Georges Parish, Craven County, on Waccamaw River adj. land of Charles Gause, William Porter, John Marions land, granted to Benjamin Cooke 7 June last. Benjn Cook (LS), Wit: Simeon Theus, William Long. [No proving data] Recorded 23 Feb 1775.

Q-4, 57-60: Lease & release. 3 & 4 Nov 1774, Joseph Tilly of Craven County, planter, eldest surviving brother and heir at law to Wm. Tilly, late of same place, planter, deceased, to Darby Pendergrass of Charles Town, merchant, for £1000 SC money, 100 acres in Craven county,k Prince Georges Parish, on south east side of Waccamaw River on Tilley Swamp, granted to William Tilly who died intestate. Joseph Tilly (LS), Wit: Dalziel Hunter, Alexander Craig. Proved in Charles Town District 20 Nov 1774 before William Rugeley. Recorded 23 Feb 1775.

Q-4, 61-65: Lease & release. 9 & 10 Nov 1774, Alexander Craig of Prince George Parish, Craven County, Schoolmaster, to Darby Pendergrass of Charles Town, merchant, for £1000 SC money, 100 acres in Craven County, Prince Georges Parish, on north side of Waccamaw on Maple Swamp, adj. Constantine Newtons land, granted to sd. Alexander Craig 30 Sept last. Alexr. Craig (LS), Wit: Dalziel Hunter, Moses Roberts. Proved in Chs. Town District by the oath of Dalziel Hunter before William Rugeley, 20 Dec 1774. Recorded 23 Feb 1775.

Q-4, 65-69: Lease & release. 6 & 7 Oct 1774, William Hort of Charles Town, merchant, and Alice his wife, to William Downes of same, sawyer, for £300 SC money, 1250 acres on the head branch of Beaver Dam a branch of Thickette Creek waters of Broad River in Craven County adj land of persons unknown, sd. William Hort, granted to sd. William Hort 17 Feb 1773. Wm. Hort (LS), Alice Hort (LS), Wit: Press Smith, Daniel Caine. [No proving data] Recorded 24 Feb 1775.

Q-4, 69-75: Lease & release. 12 & 13 Aug 1774, John Brandon of Charles Town, gentleman, to John Hatfield of same, Inn keeper, for £5 SC money, 100 acres on Private[?] branch of Black River in Craven County, St. Marks Parish, granted to sd. John Brandon 11 Aug 1774. John Brandon (LS), Wit: Alexr. Walker, Peter Horn. Proved 17 Dec 1774 before Thomas Turner, J. P. in Charles Town District, by the oath of Peter Horn. Recorded 25 Feb 1775.

Q-4, 75-81: Lease & release. 29 & 39 Sept 1775, Peter Sanders of Christ Church, Planter, to John Hatfield of Charles Town, Inn keeper, for £25 SC money, 500 acres in Craven County adj. John Hatfields land, Benjamin McKennys land, granted 23 June last to sd. Peter Sanders. Peter Sanders (LS), Wit: D'l Mazyck, John Young. Proved 20 Dec 1774 before William Nesbitt, J.P. in Charles Town District, by the oath of Daniel Mazyck. Recorded 27 Feb 1775.

Q-4, 81-89: Lease & release. 21 & 22 Nov 1773, Edward Harleston of St. Johns Parish, Berkley County, Esqr., the only qualified and acting Executor, Eldest son and devisee, of the will of John Harleston, late of St. Johns parish, Esqr., deceased, to Thomas Corbett of Charles Town, merchant, for £1000 SC money, lots number 48 and 37 on Charles Town Neck in Harleston; sd. John Harleston by his will dated 21 May 1767 did give lots to his sons John, Isaac, William, and Edward and named sd. Edward Harleston, Nicholas Harleston and Benjamin Smith of Goose Creek, executors, but before sd. John Harleston the father died, he on 8 Feb 1768 empowered his executors Edward harleston and John Harleston son of Nicholas to sell the rest of the estate... in May term in 1773 from the court of common pleas at Charles Town obtained a writ of Partition. Edward Harleston (LS), Wit: Isaac Harleston, William Tread. (Wit. to lease: Jos. Ward, Gabriel Manigault Junr.) Proved 22 Dec 1774 before Thomas Bee, J.P. in Charles Town District, by the oath of William Tead. Recorded 7 March 1775.

Q-4, 89-92: 20 Dec 1738, Francis Burch to Abraham Ehrhard of Purysburgh, for £250 SC money, to 200 acres in Township of Purysburgh, Granville County, on Savannah River adj. Peter Maille, J. Redorfgrand. Francis Burch (T) (LS), Wit: Paul Brineau, Augustus Laurence, Isaac Mazyck. Proved in Berkley County by the oath of Isaac Mazyck 19 Feb 1747 before Jacob Mott. Recorded 7 March 1775.

Q-4, 92-96: Lease & release. 19 & 20 Dec 1774, Joseph McCleskey of Long Cane Settlement, planter, and Agnes his wife, to James Parsons, Esqr., of Charles Town, for £145 SC money, 150 acres in Granville County adj. Alexander Robenson, granted 2 March 1768 to sd. Joseph McCleksey. Joseph McCleskey (LS), Agnes McCleskey (mark) (LS), Wit: James Noble, Joseph Calhoun, Alex. Noble, Patk. Calhoun. Proved in Berkley County by the oath of Patrick Calhoun 14 Jan 1775 before Wm. Burrows. Recorded 7 March 1775.

Q-4, 96-100: Lease & release. 22 Sept 1774, Thomas Heyward Senr of Charles Town, Esqr., to Mary Stevens of same, vintner, for twenty shillings, 500 acres surveyed for James Smith 12 Sept 1772 on Thicketty Creek adj. land of William McGowens, land supposed to be the property of Thomas Wade, James Campbell, granted 25 Apr 1774. Thomas Heyward Senr (LS), Wit: Philip Henry , J. L. Peyer im Hoff. Proved in Charles Town District by the oath of Philip Henry before Wm. Nisbett, 3 Jan 1775. Recorded 8 March 1775.

Q-4, 100-106: Lease & release. 25 & 26 Aug 1772, William Dodgeon late of Craven County, Sc, planter, to William Burton of same, for £100 SC money, 300 acres granted 12 Apr 1771 to William Dodgeon on Little River and waters thereof adj. David Emery, Hameton Murdock, Robert Goudey,

SOUTH CAROLINA DEED ABSTRACTS 1773-1778

Thomas Green, William Burton. William Dodgeon (LS), Wit: Anthonoy Preston (mark), Thescilla Preston, Isaiah Preston, Josiah Burton. Proved before John Caldwell, J. P. in Ninety Six District, by the oath of Anthony Preston 30 March 1773. Recorded 8 March 1775.

Q-4, 106-110: Lease & release. 6 Sept 1773, Arthur Patton & John Huse of the District of Ninety Six, planter, to James Miscombell of same, for £600 SC money, tract granted to Arthur Patton 23 Jan 1759 in Belfast Township, 500 acres. Arthur Patton (LS), John Huse (I) (LS), Wit: Robert Taylor, Thomas Clark. Proved 9 Sept 1773 before Ldw. Pierce, J.P., by the oath of Robert Taylor & Wm. Clark. Recorded 9 March 1775.

Q-4, 110-112: Thomas North of Craven County, by bond in the penal sum of £6000 for the payment £3000, to be paid on or before 1 Jan 1779, 275 acres granted to Col. William Rhett upon Black River adj. lands of James Fowler, Alexander Davidson deceased... dated 26 July 1774. Thomas North (LS), Wit: William Paulding, William McIver. Proved in Georgetown District 8 Sept 1774 before William Wilson. Recorded 9 March 1775.

Q-4, 113-115: 2 Oct 1772, John Fairchild of Colleton County, SC, Esqr., to John Hamilton of Craven County, planter, for £300 SC money, 300 acres granted 5 Oct 1753 to John Fairchild on north side Santee River adj. land of Philip Raiford Senr. John Fairchild (LS), Wit: Gersham Kelly, John Humphries. Proved 3 Jan 1774 before Edward Cossens, J. P. in Camden District, by the oath of Gersham Kelly. Recorded 9 March 1775.

Q-4, 115-120: Lease & release. 13 & 14 Nov 1772, William Wayne of Charles Town, Gentleman, to William Simpson of same place, gentleman, for £1900 SC money, lot on east side of old Church Street in Charles Town, adj. land of Christopher Fitsimmons. William Wayne (LS), Wit: Geo Sheed, James Simpson. Proved in Charles Town District by the oath of James Simpson before William Rugeley, J.P., 12 Jan 1775. Recorded 10 March 1775.

Q-4, 120-124: Lease & release. 3 & 4 Apr 1772, David Jackson of Craven County, SC, planter, to James Brent of same, planter, for ten shillings, 150 acres in Craven county on north side Broad River adj. land held by John Hunt. David Jackson (D) (LS), Wit: John Joyner, Joseph Joyner, William Downes. Proved 6 Apr 1772 before William Thompson, J. P. in Berkley County,k by the oath of William Downes. Recorded 10 March 1775.

Q-4, 124-125: Lease. 9 Dec 1774, Jesse Deloach of St. Peters Parish, planter, to Michael Deloach of same, planter, for ten shillings, 100 acres in said parish on dry near. Jesse Deloche (LS), Wit: James Thompson, Abel Goodwin. Proved in Beaufort District by the oath of James Thompson, J.P, 10 Dec 1774. Recorded 20 March 1775. [For release, see Q-4, pages 168-170.]

Q-4, 126-130: Lease & release. 1 & 2 Nov 1774, William Williams of Craven County, District of Camden, to Capt. Charles King of District of Ninety Six, for £150 SC money, 100 acres in the fork between Broad & Saludy Rivers granted to David Williams 5 Dec 1761, on south fork of Kings Creek adj. Wm. Hamilton, Mathew Hall... said plantation assended to sd. William Williams by the decease of his father David Williams. William Williams (LS), Wit: Thomas Lindsay, Joseph Brown, James Lindsay. Proved 1 Dec 1774 before John Johnston, J. P. in Ninety Six District, by the oath of Thos. Lindsay. Recorded 11 March 1775.

Q-4, 130-134: Lease & release. 27 & 28 Dec 1774, Charles King of Craven County, District of Ninety Six, and Charity his wife, to William Hamilton of same, for £200 SC money, 100 acres in the fork between Broad & Saludy Rivers granted to David Williams 5 Dec 1761, on a fork of Kings Creek adj. Wm. Hamilton, Mathew Hall... conveyed by William Williams heir to David Williams decd, 2 Nov last 1774. Charles King (LS), Charity King (LS), Wit: Thomas Lindsay, Jeremiah Stark, Abel Anderson. Proved 3 Jan 1775 before John Johnston, J. P. in Ninety Six District, by the oath of Abel Anderson. Recorded 13 March 1775.

Q-4, 134-138: Lease & release. __ Jan 1775, Dalziel Hunter of Prince Georges Parish, Craven County, to Peter LePoole of Charles Town, merchant, for £500 SC money, 600 acres on Waccamaw River adj. Othaniel Beal Esqr., Adam Stewart, Nathaniel Row, Shingelton, granted to sd. Dalziel Hunter 19 June 1772. Dalziel Hunter (LS), Wit: David Kauffman, Richard Corbett. Proved by the

SOUTH CAROLINA DEED ABSTRACTS 1773-1778

oath of David Kauffman in Charles Town District before Wm. Rugeley, J. P., 14 March 1775. Recorded 14 March 1775.

Q-4, 138-139, 160-3: Lease & Release. 27 March 1765, Henry Whetstone and Barbara his wife of Amelia Township, Berkley County, SC, wheelwright, to Simon Hooker of same place, planter, for £125 SC money, 250 acres in Orangeburg Township on Ox Creek of Santee River granted adj. land granted to Freeman Snellgrove. Henry Whetstone (W) (LS), Barbary Whetstone (LS), Wit: John Mitchel, William Mitchel. Proved 4 Oct 1768 before Wm. Thompson, Esqr., by the oath of John Mitchell. Recorded 14 & 17 March 1775.

Q-4, 140-143: Lease & release. 5 & 6 Jan 1775, Dalziel Hunter of Prince Georges Parish, Craven County, to Peter LePoole of Charles Town, merchant, for £500 SC money, 250 acres on Long Bay Waccamaw adj. land of Peter Lesesne, land laid out for John Lesesne but now belonging to Samuel Rice, granted to Dalziel Hunter 19 June 1772. Dalziel Hunter (LS), Wit: David Kauffman, Richard Corbett. Proved by the oath of David Kauffman in Charles Town District before Wm. Rugeley, J. P., 14 March 1775. Recorded 14 March 1775.

Q-4, 143-146: Lease & release. 17 & 18 Oct 1774, Dalziel Hunter of Craven County, to Peter LePoole of Charles Town, merchant, for £100 SC money, 100 acres in Long Cane Settlement in Granville County, adj. land of John Murray, Michael Dorman. Dalziel Hunter (LS), Wit: John Hamilton, David Kauffman. Proved by the oath of David Kauffman in Charles Town District before Wm. Rugeley, J. P., 14 March 1775. Recorded 15 March 1775.

Q-4, 146-149: Lease & release. 5 & 6 Jan 1775, Dalziel Hunter of Prince Georges Parish, Craven County, to Peter LePoole of Charles Town, merchant, for £500 SC money, 300 acres in Craven County on Buck Creek, surveyed by Nathan Franks in 1753 and granted to sd. Dalziel Hunter 5 May 1773. Dalziel Hunter (LS), Wit: David Kauffman, Richard Corbett. Proved by the oath of David Kauffman in Charles Town District before Wm. Rugeley, J. P., 14 March 1775. Recorded 15 March 1775.

Q-4, 150-153: Lease & release. 12 & 13 Oct 1774, Dalziel Hunter of Prince Georges Parish, Craven County, to Peter LePoole of Charles Town, merchant, for £500 SC money, 500 acres in Craven County on Buck Creek a branch of Waccamaw River, granted to sd. Dalziel Hunter 23 Jan 1773. Dalziel Hunter (LS), Wit: John Hamilton, David Kauffman. Proved by the oath of David Kauffman in Charles Town District before Wm. Rugeley, J. P., 14 March 1775. Recorded 15 March 1775.

Q-4, 153-156: Lease & release. 5 & 6 Jan 1775, Dalziel Hunter of Prince Georges Parish, Craven County, to Peter LePoole of Charles Town, merchant, for £500 SC money, 378 acres on Waccamaw River, granted to George Pawley 15 Feb 1770, adj. land of Mr. Hameston, Mr. John Lessessne, Mr. Sinkler. Dalziel Hunter (LS), Wit: David Kauffman, Richard Corbet. Proved by the oath of David Kauffman in Charles Town District before Wm. Rugeley, J. P., 14 March 1775. Recorded 16 March 1775.

Q-4, 156-159: Lease & release. 5 & 6 Jan 1775, Dalziel Hunter of Prince Georges Parish, Craven County, to Peter LePoole of Charles Town, merchant, for £500 SC money, 384 acres on Waccamaw Neck, granted to Blake Leay White 7 May 1774, adj. land of Wm. and Archibald Johnston, Josiah Allston Esqr, John Weathers, William Allston, William Johnston. Dalziel Hunter (LS), Wit: David Kauffman, Richard Corbet. Proved by the oath of David Kauffman in Charles Town District before Wm. Rugeley, J. P., 14 March 1775.

Q-4, 160-163: [see above lease & release, pages 138-139]

Q-4, 163-169: Lease & release. 19 & 20 July 1774, Blake Leay White of Charlestown, planter, & Elizabeth his wife, to Samuel Chollet of same, merchant, for £4000 SC money, lot in Charles Town on Orange Street in the Parish of St. Michaels, adj. land of Frederick Gimkey[?], John Stevenson, said Blake Leay White. Blake Leay White (LS), Eliz'a White (LS), Wit: Philip Henry, A. Chollet. Proved 25 Jan 1775 before William Rugeley, Esqr., J.P. in Charles Town District, by the oath of Philip Henry. Recorded 18 March 1775.

SOUTH CAROLINA DEED ABSTRACTS 1773-1778

Q-4, 169-174: Lease & release. 5 & 6 Jan 1775, Henry Ephraim Schultz of Prov. of SC, Baker, to John Speissiger of Chas Town, organ Maker, for £100 SC money, 200 acres in District of Orangeburgh, Colleton County. Hen'y Eph'm Schultz (LS), Wit: Conrad Shlapper, Chas Roberts. Proved 6 Jan 1775 before Robt. Pringle, J.P., by the oath of Conrad Shlapper. Recorded 18 March 1775.

Q-4, 175-179: Lease & release. 12 & 13 Apr 1773, Thomas Gordon of Craven County, Wheel Right, and Elizabeth his wife, to William Gordon of same, for £300 SC money, 300 acres on the north side of Enoree River adj. the plantation where Mrs. Ruth Anderson now lives granted 23 Feb 1754 to John Gordon Snr. by North Carolina, and Thomas Gordon, son and heir at law of sd. John Gordon Senr, deceased, conveyed by John Gordon decd. 20 Nov 1756. Thos Gordon (LS), Eliz Gordon (O) (LS), Wit: James Caldwell, John Orr, Govin Gordon. Proved before John Johnston, J. P. for Craven County, by the oath of James Caldwell, 13 Apr 1773. Recorded 20 March 1775.

Q-4, 179-184: 13 Apr 1773, Thomas Gordon of Craven County, Wheel Right, and Elizabeth his wife, to William Gordon of same, planter, for £50 SC money, 200 acres on a branch of Enoree River, adj. land of Isaac Pitchline[?], a memorial entered in Book No 9, Page 319, granted 22 March 1769. Thos Gordon (LS), Elizabeth Gordon (O) (LS), Wit: James Caldwell, John Orr, Govin Gordon. Proved before John Johnston, J. P. for Craven County, by the oath of James Caldwell, 13 Apr 1773. Recorded 21 March 1775.

Q-4, 184-188: 25 Oct 1774, Thos Grimball Junr, Esqr., Sheriff of Charles Town District or Precinct, to Jacob Valk of Charles Town, Doctor, whereas John Williams of Charles Town, was lately seized of a tract of land with marsh of the sea shore near the mouth of Santee River on Parish of St. James Santee, 400 acres adj. land of Robert Morrel, and said John Williams by bond dated 6 Sept 1773 bound to sd. Jacob Valk in the penal sum of £4923 one shilling for the payment of £2461 ten shillings six pence, said Jacob Valk in the court of common pleas in 1774 obtained judgment, now for £600. Thos Grimball Junr Shff. C. T. Dist. (LS), Wit: John Cordes, Joseph Milligan. Proved by the oath of Joseph Milligan 21 March 1775 before Wm. Rugeley, J. P. Recorded 21 March 1775.

Q-4, 188-193: Lease & release. 30 & 31 Jan 1775, Jacob Valk of Charles Town, Gentleman, to Robert Walker of Parish of St. James Santee, for £500 SC money, tract of land with marsh of the sea shore near the mouth of Santee River on Parish of St. James Santee, 400 acres adj. land of Robert Morrel. Jacob Valk (LS), Wit: Geo. Jno. Fardo, Paul Schlatter. Proved in Chas Town District 31 Jan 1775 by the oath of Paul Schlatter before Hopkin Price, J.P. Recorded 23 March 1775.

Q-4, 193-201: Lease & release. 28 & 29 Jan 1775, Alexander Taylor, late of Charles Town, Taylor, but now of Edinburgh in the pat of Great Britain called Scotland, by Josiah Smith his attorney, of Charlestown, merchant, to Paul Townsend, for £600 SC money, tract of sundry houses and lots in Ansonborough adj. land now or late of Mrs. Elliott. Alexr Taylor by Josiah Smith his attorney (LS), Wit: Edwd Darrell, Thomas Horsey. Proved by the oath of Edwd Darrell before William Burrow, 9 March 1774. Recorded 23 March 1775.

Q-4, 201-204: 25 Jan 1775, Thomas Farrell and Jean his wife of St. Marks Parish, Craven County, to William Patton of Berkley County, for £550 SC money, 550 acres granted to Thos Farrell 31 March 1753 by North Carolina, land on south fork of Cataba River in the Waxhaws now in the province of South Carolina. Thomas Farrel (LS), Jane Farrel (8) (LS), Wit: William Simpson, Thomas Creighton, Andrew McIlwain. Proved 26 Jan 1775 by the oath of William Simpson before James Patton, J.P. in Camden District. Recorded 23 March 1775.

Q-4, 205-208: Lease & release. 15 Aug 1774, Thomas Shockley of Craven County, SC, and Prudence his wife, to John Sartor of same, for £175 SC money, 350 acres on south side Broad River on Fish Dam Creek granted 28 Aug 1767 to Thomas Shockley. Thomas Shockly (T) (LS), Prudence Shockley (LS), Wit: John Rixey, Thomas Hollingsworth, Isaac Hollingsworth. Proved in Ninety Six Dist. by the oath of John Rixey before Thomas Fletchall, 22 Aug 1774. Recorded 24 March 1775.

Q-4, 209-213: Lease & release. 13 & 41 March 1770, Hezekia Rose of St. Lukes Parish, Granville County, SC, planter, to John Cherry of same, planter, for £400 SC money, 200 acres originally granted to Dingrel Karwon[?] by the name of Burrows Neck transferred to sundry different persons. Hezekia Rose (LS), Wit: Thomas Dawson, Rachel Brackley. Proved in Granville County by the oath of Thomas Dawson 30 Jan 1774 before John Sealy, J.P. Recorded 24 March 1775.

Q-4, 214-217: Lease & release. 26 & 27 Apr 1767, Robert Miller of Granville Co., gent., to John Pickens of same, planter, for £40 SC money, 100 acres on waters of Long Canes on Norens Creek granted 23 Oct 1765 to Robert Miller. Robert Miller (LS), Jane Miller (LS), Wit: John Bowie, William Anderson. Proved by the oath of Wm Anderson 12 Nov 1767 before John Pickens, J.P. Recorded 25 March 1775.

Q-4, 218-223: Lease & release. 28 & 29 Apr 1767, Jeremiah Strother and Cath'ne his wife to Elias Daniel for £200 SC money, 300 acres granted to Jeremiah Strother 2 Aug 1757. Jeremiah Strother (LS), Catharine Strother (LS), Wit: Simon Hirons, John Strother. Proved 10 March 1770 by the oath of Simon Hirons before Philip Pearson, J.P. Recorded 27 March 1775.

Q-4, 223-227: Lease & release. 14 Dec 1767, John Atkins of Craven County, St. Marks Parish, and wife Sarah to David Jinkins of same, for £100 SC money, 200 acres, part of 400 acres granted to John Atkins 16 Dec 1766 on the head of Scotch Creek adj. land laid out for Aaron Ayrs, recorded i Book AAA page 199. John Atkins (I) (LS), Sarah Atkins (J) (LS), Wit: Francis Atkins, Israel Gant. Proved in Craven County before Michael Dickert, J.P., 23 Nov 1770. Recorded 27 March 1775.

Q-4, 227-230: 4 Jan 1775, Samuel Maverick of Charles Town, carpenter, to Eliza Johnston of same, widow, by bond 2 Jan 1775 in the penal sum of £3000 for the payment of £1500, tract in Christ Church Parish on Wando River adj. lands laid out for a school, Stephen Townsend, 200 acres. Samuel Maverick (LS), Wit: George Sheeds, Peter Bounetheau. Proved in Berkly County by the oath of Peter Bouneatheau before Hopkin Price, J. P., 9 Feb 1775. Recorded 27 March 1775.

Q-4, 230-235: Lease & release. 21 & 22 Sept 1772, Richard Bell of Craven County, planter, to John Cook of same, planter, for £50 SC money, 300 acres on north side of Congaree River adj. land of Jos. Cooke, granted to Richard Bell 5 June 1770. Richard Bell (LS), Wit: Ephraim Prickett, Edward Penrice, Philip Pearson. Acknowledged by Richard Bell before Philip Pearson, J.P., 22 Sept 1772. Recorded 28 March 1775.

Q-4, 235-239: Lease & release. 13 & 14 Dec 1768, Thomas Cochran of Long Cane Settlement, SC, carpenter, to Wm. Gray of same, planter, for £50 SC money, 100 acres granted 6 Dec 1768 to Thomas Cochran, in the long cane Settlement adj. land of John Andrews, Arthur Reid, Arther Gray, Wm. Deall. Thomas Cochran (LS), Wit: William McClellon, Arthur Gray. Proved 19 Dec 1769 by the oath of Arthur Gray before Patk. Calhoun, J.P. Recorded 29 March 1775.

Q-4, 239-243: Lease & release. 19 & 20 May 1771, William Lamar and Penelopey his wife of Prov. of SC, to Philip Goode, for £230 SC money, 150 acres on Stephens Creek granted to James Nollsbey 4 Sept 1750. Wm. Lamar (LS), Wit: Wm. Coursey, Hezekiah Bussey. Proved 25 Sept 1771 before John Purves, J. P., by the oath of William Coursey. Recorded 29 March 1775.

Q-4, 243-247: Lease & release. 12 Nov 1774, Michal Taylor of Berkly County, Orangeburg District, SC, to George Strother of same, for £100 SC money, 50 acres on south side Seludy River adj. land of Michal Taylor, granted 8 March 1755 to John Daniel Maltz with ten acres between the fifty acres and the mouth of Rocky Creek part of tract granted to Mickel Taylor deceased now my property. Mical Taylor (MT) (LS), Wit: John Kincsler, Addam Gordon (AG), Benjamin Durant. Proved in Ninety Six District before Jonathan Downes, J.P., by the oath of John Kinslar, 17 Nov 1774. Recorded 30 March 1775.

Q-4, 248-254: Lease & release. 6 & 7 Jan 1774, Joseph Kershaw of Camden, in Craven County, Parish of St. Marks, Merchant, to John Rogers of county aforesaid, Inholder, for £500 SC money, 100 acres in the High Hills of Santee adj. land of John Hope, Wm. Hariss, Roger Rees, granted to Alexander Campbell 3 June 1755 recorded in Book YY, page 515, and conveyed to Joseph Kershaw by deed 20 & 21 Oct 1757. Joseph Kershaw (LS), Sarah Kershaw (LS), Wit: Jos. Cary, John Wyly,

SOUTH CAROLINA DEED ABSTRACTS 1773-1778

Thomas Jones. Sarah Kershaw, wife of Joseph, relinquished dower. Proved 7 Jan 1774 in Craven County before Jno N. Oglethorp by the oath of Thos Jones. Recorded 30 March 1775.

Q-4, 254-260: Lease & release. 8 & 9 Dec 1774, Elizabeth Ladson of St. Andrews parish, widow, to William Bowler of St. Bartholomews Parish, planter, for £3500, 391 acres adj. Robert Ladsons land formerly James Ladsons, part of 1124 acres in Colleton County, St. Bartholomews parish, adj. John Godfrey, Henry ____, granted 28 Apr 1733 to Robert Ladson and sd. Elizabeth Ladson is daughter and Heir at Law of Robert Ladson Junr who was one of the sons of sd. Robt Ladson, hath for fifteen years last past been in the actual possession of 319 acres being the southermost third part of said 1124 acres the other two third parts in the possession of Robert Ladson and Thomas Ladson, grandsons of sd. Robert the grantee (plat included showing adj. land owners Richard Perry decd, Mr. Thomas Collier, Mr. Francis Young). Eliz. Ladson (LS), Wit: Henry Nicholes, James Smith. Proved in Chs. Town District by the oath of James Smith before Wm. Rugeley, J.P., 31 March 1775. Recorded 1 Apr 1775.

Q-4, 260-264: Lease & release. 3 & 4 Jan 1774, John George Ressinger of Ninety Six District, planter, to Fight Resssinger of same, planter, for £100 SC money, 125 acres originally granted to sd. John George Ressinger 8 March 1755, it being the half part of said 250 acres in the fork between Broad and Saludy River adj. Ulrick Sleys, estate of Hermond Geiger deceased. John George Ressinger (LS), Rachel Ressinger (LS), Wit: John Buchanan, William Hutchison, Giles Tinley. Proved in Ninety Six District by the oath of John Buckanan 8 Feb 1774 before Michl. Dickert, J.P. Recorded 3 Apr 1775.

Q-4, 264-267: 3 Jan 1775, Alexr Gordon and his wife Mary and son Robert Gordon of St. Davids Parish, Craven County, SC, to Thomas Lide of same place, planter, for £3500 SC money, 546½ acres: one tract of land containing 300 acres on northeast side Peedee adj. lands now possessed by John Husbands on a creek commonly known by the name of Hainers or Husbands Creek and also that plantation on which I now live on north east side of Peedee River 246½ acres 100 acres of which adj. land now belonging to Francis Gillespie willed to Elizabeth Gordon & Conveyed to me by Robert Gordon 50 acres formerly granted to John Ellerbe conveyed to me by Edward Ellerbe adj. the lands mentioned tract 96½ acres conveyed to me by Wm. Black. Alexr Gordon (LS), Mary Gordon (/) (LS), Robert Gordon (LS), Wit: Calvin Spencer, Sarah Foster (+). Proved in Cheraw Dist. before Charles Augustus Steward, J.P., by the oath of Calvin Spencer, 4 Jan 1775. Recorded 3 Apr 1775.

Q-4, 267-270: 5 July 1774, Robert Tindall of Craven County, SC, Cord Winder, and Mary his wife, to William Gaston of same, planter, for £500 SC money, 150 acres granted 15 May 1771 to Robert Tindall on James Kirkpatricks branch of Turkey Creek in Craven County adj. James Kirkpatrick, James Love. Robert Tindall (LS), Mary Tindall (LS), Wit: Andrew Woode, James Fannin, Frame Woode. Proved in Camden District by the oath of Andrew Woode before John Gaston, J. P., 10 Sept 1774. Recorded 4 Apr 1775.

Q-4, 270-273: 27 Aug 1774, David Eakins of Craven County, SC, planter, and Margaret Eakins his wife, but formerly before marriage Margaret Boden, to William Gaston of same, planter, 100 acres granted 12 Aug 1768 to Margaret Boden on Little Turkey Creek on north side of Broad River. David Eakins (LS), Margt. Eakins (X) (LS), Wit: Alexander Gaston, Andrew Woode. Proved in Camden Dist. by the oath of Andrew Woods 10 Sept 1774 before John Gaston, J. P. Recorded 4 Apr 1775.

Q-4, 273-279: Lease & release. 18 & 19 Oct 1774, Nathl. Jones of Charles Town, carpenter, and Ann Jones his wife, to Saml. Hrabowski, trader, for £300 SC money, 150 acres in St. Mathews parish, land surveyed for Elizth. Jones, Benjamin Campbell, Sam. Hrabowski, granted 25 May 1774 on the Bounty. Nathl. Jones (LS), Ann Jones (LS), Wit: Arthur Phips, George Forbes. Proved 5 Apr 1775 before Wm. Rugeley, in Charles Town District, by the oath of George Forbes. Recorded 6 Apr 1775.

Q-4, 279-285: Lease & mortgage. 6 & 7 Feb 1775, Thomas Singleton and Wm. Strother of Charles Town, to Charles Augustus Steward of St. Davids Parish, in the penal sum of £10,400 for the payment of £5200, 1500 acres in St. Davids Parish on south west side Thompsons Creek adj. land

SOUTH CAROLINA DEED ABSTRACTS 1773-1778

of Wm. Ancrum, Benjn Rogers, now or late the property of Heirs of Wm. Godfrey deceased.... also negro slaves (named). Thos Singleton (LS), Wm. Strother (LS), Wit: Is. M. Harris, Philip Henry. Proved in Chs. Town District by the oath of Philip Henry before wm. Rugeley, J. P., 14 Feb 1775. Recorded 5 Apr 1775. Mortgage satisfied 11 Jan 1779 by George Gabriel Powell, attorney of Charles Augustus Steward. Proved 24 May 1786.

Q-4, 285-289: Lease & release. 6 & 7 July 1772, William Cockran of Colleton County, SC, to Thomas M'Ginnis of same, planter, for £50 SC money, 100 acres in St. Pauls Parish on Loy[?] Creek adj. land granted to Thomas M'Ginnis granted 22 Nov 1771 to William Cockran. Wm Cockran (W) (LS), Wit: Robert Wallace, John Stewart. Proved in Granville County by the oath of John Stewart 22 Aug 1772 before John Purves, J.P. Recorded 6 Apr 1775.

Q-4, 289-296: Lease & release. 21 & 22 Jan 1774, Alexander Perroneau of Charles Town, Gentleman, and Margaret his wife, to John Webb of same, merchant, for £8750 SC money, lot in Charles Town on corner of Old Church and Moore Streets, adj. land of Peter and John Horlbeck. Alex'r Peronneau (LS), Margt. Perronneau (LS), Wit: Daniel Cannon, William Trusler. Proved in Chs. Town District 29 Jan 1774 before Peter Bounetheau, J.P., by the oath of Daniel Cannon. Recorded 7 Apr 1775.

Q-4, 296-305: Lease & release. 2 & 3 Jan 1775, Joseph Joyner of Amelia Township, planter, and Catherine his wife, to Thomas Elfe of Charles Town, Cabinet Maker, for £2000 SC money, 956 acres in Amelia Township, Berkley County, composed of several smaller tracts. (plat included showing land adj. Morgan Sabb, Mr. Mazyck, Edward Mortimer, made at the request of William Elfe 9 Jany 1775 by Malcom Clarke, D.S.) Joseph Joyner (LS), Catherine Joyner (O) (LS), Wit: Wm. Thomson, Charles Heatley. Proved 28 Jan 1775 before Malcom Clarke, J. P. in Orangeburgh District, by the oath of Wm. Thomson. Recorded 8 Apr 1775. Dower relinquishment of Catharine Joyner taken by dedimus directed to William Thomson and Charles Heatly of Amelia Township. Recorded 10 Apr 1775.

Q-4, 305-306: James Willson Senr. of Ninety Six District, Colleton County, for natural love, good will and affection to my daughter Mary Cockerham, wife of Bryan Cockerham and her son James Cockerham, 100 acres part of 350 acres originally granted to sd. James Willson on a small branch of Cuffy Town Creek waters of Savannah River adj. Blakleys line. James Wilson (M) (LS), Wit: James Jones (X), Robert Wallace. Proved 13 Jan 1775 before Benj. Tutt, J. P., by the oath of Robert Wallace. Recorded 10 Apr 1775.

Q-4, 306-310: Lease & release. 13 & 14 July 1748, Wm. Belin and Allard Belin of Prince George Winyaw Parish, Craven county, Sc, planter, to Theodore Gaillard of St. James Santee, for £160, 450 acres in the parish of St. James Santee by virtue of a warrant and grant dated 8 March 1743 to sd. William Belin. Wm. Belin (LS), Allard Belin (LS), Wit: Elias Horry, Tacitus Gaillard, Isaac LeGrand Danl. Proved in Berkley County before Robert Austin, J.P., by the oath of Tacitus Gaillard. Recorded 11 Apr 1775.

Q-4, 310-314: Lease & release. 27 & 28 Feb 1754, Lewis Gourdin of Parish of St. James Santee, Craven County, to Theodore Gaillard of same, planter, for £250 SC money, 365 acres granted to him 9 Oct 1752 on Santee River Swamp on Murrys Creek adj. Theodore Gaillards land, Porchers land. Marian Gourdin (lll) (LS), Lewis Gourdin (LS), Wit: Peter Robert, James Davis, Peter Gourdin. Proved in Chas. Town District by the oath of Josiah Robert who testified to the handwriting of Peter Robert his father, 18 Feb 1775. Recorded 12 Apr 1775.

Q-4, 314-318: Lease & release. 11 & 12 Nov 1757, William Gourdin of St. Stephens Parish, Craven County, planter, to Theodore Gaillard of St. James Santee Parish, Craven County, planter, for £750 SC money, 263 acres part of a tract ranted to Elizth. Ward 600 acres on Santee River, St. Stephens parish, adj. land of Peter Gourdin, Joseph Porcher, Theodore Gaillard (plat included dated 19 Apr 1756 by Isaac Porcher, D.S., showing the portion of the land of William Gourdin being his part of land devised unto him by his father.) William Gourdin (LS), Wit: Peter Gourdin, Bath. Gaillard, John Gaillard. Proved 15 Feb 1775 by the oath of John Gaillard before Thos Turner, J.P. Recorded 12 Apr 1775.

SOUTH CAROLINA DEED ABSTRACTS 1773-1778

Q-4, 319-323: Lease & release. 1 & 2 Feb 1774, John Hopkins of the Congarees, SC, executor of the will of George Strother deceased, to Andrew Frederick of Orangeburgh, for £200 SC money, 200 acres in Berkly County on the low ground of Edisto River adj. Peter Taylor, land granted to Solomon Peters, land surveyed for John Simmons, tract granted to Chs. Strother 22 Oct 1768, which George Strother purchased from his brother Charles Strother 2 & 3 June 1769. John Hopkins (LS), Wit: Adam Gromleish, George Ryly (+), John Golson. Proved before Lewis Golson, J.P. in Orangeburgh District, by the oath of Adam Gromleish. Recorded 13 Apr 1775.

Q-4, 323-329: Lease & release. 1 & 2 Jan 1775, Samuel Waddingham of Prince Fredericks Parish, SC, planter, to Josiah Smith, exr. of the will of George Austin deceased, by obligation in the penal sum of £16,265 s10 d4 for payment of £8,132 s15 d2, tract of 5192 acres adj. lands of Alexr Pawderdussen, John Oldfield, Robert Herriott, Peter Creek, Wm Willson, Wm. Hill, Mr. Man, two other tracts of 1100 acres on south side Black River one granted to Edward Bullard now belonging to sd. Waddingham adj. Artur Foster, and 200 acres also since purchased by sd. Waddingham adj. Mr. Laroch, Mr. Johnston. Saml Waddinghan (LS), Wit: Mary Fogartie Junr, Edwd. Darrel. Proved in Chs. Town Dist., by the oath of Edward Darrel before Wm. Rugeley, 21 Feb 1775. Recorded 15 Apr 1775.

Q-4, 329-334: Lease & release. 23 & 24 Dec 1774, John Swint of Charles Town, Doctor of Medicine, to Jacob William, Butcher, for £750 SC money, 500 acres in Orangeburgh Township in Berkley County adj. Henry Hurgers, Henry Snells. John Swint (LS), Wit: Benjn Godfrey, Peter Bounetheau. Proved 4 Dec 1774 in Chs. Town by the oath of Peter Bouneatheau before John Coram, J.P. Recorded 18 Apr 1775.

Q-4, 334-338: Lease & release. 2 & 3 May 1774, Percivell Pawley, George Pawley & Wm. Pawley, Exors of the will of Col. George Pawley, deceased, to Joseph Allston, planter, for £1500 SC money, 500 acres in Craven County on Peedee River adj. land of Joseph Yates, on a pleasant lake. William Pawley (LS), Geor. Pawley (LS), Per'l Pawley (LS), Wit: Thos Butler, Edwd Drake. Prove din George Town Dist. by the oath of Edward Drake before Josias Allston, J. P., 17 June 1774. Recorded 28 Apr 1775.

Q-4, 338-345: Lease & release. 5 & 6 May 1774, Wm. Allston Senr of George Town, Craven County, planter, and Sabenah his wife, to Joseph Allston of Waccamaw in Craven County, planter, for £1400 SC money, three tracts adjoining each other, one of 200 acres on north side Great Peedee River adj. Col. George Harleys land known by the name of Red Bluff granted 20 May 1757 to John Malden; 100 acres on north east side of sd. river adj .land granted to John Malden late Thomas Burtons granted 29 Oct 1766 to Reuben Windham; 40 acres on north east side sd. river adj. land granted to John Malden late Thos Burtons adj. Col. George Pawleys land granted 27 Nov 1770 to James Mikell[?]. Wm. Allston (LS), Sabina Allston (LS), Wit: George Croft, John Allston. Proved in Geo Town District before Benjn. Young, J.P., by the oath of George Croft, 6 May 1774. Recorded 20 Apr 1775.

Q-4, 345-349: Lease & release. 30 Aug 1774, George Eiland of St. Davids Parish, Georgia, planter, to Absalom Eiland of South Carolina, Colleton County, planter, for £500, 350 acres in Granville County, by warrant dated 4 Oct 1749 and renewed 7 May 1754 to George Eiland, at the mouth of Seder Creek & Nobles Creek. George Eiland (LS), Wit: Abner Eiland, Saml Williford, Jacob Sims (I). Proved in St. Mathews Parish, Georgia, by the oath of Jacob Sims before Benjn. Lanner[?]. Recorded 21 Apr 1775.

Q-4, 349-353: Lease & release. 3 & 4 Oct 1774, Absalom Eiland of South Carolina, Colleton County, planter, to John Rainsford, for £500 SC money, 350 acres in Granville County, by warrant dated 4 Oct 1749 and renewed 7 May 1754 to George Eiland, at the mouth of Seder Creek & Nobles Creek, on waters of Savanah River. Absalom Eiland (LS), Wit: Basil Lamar, Frans. Sinquefield. Proved in Ninety Six District 15 oct 1774 before Wm. Anderson, J. P., by the oath of Francis Sinquefield. Recorded 21 Apr 1775.

Q-4, 353-358: Lease & release. 18 & 19 Jan 1775, Ephraim Mitchell of Charles Town, SC, surveyor, to Wm. Mills and James Carmichael, both of Orangeburgh, planters, for £2500 SC money, 400 acres in Orangeburgh Township in Berkley County and when granted bounded by land of John Rumph,

SOUTH CAROLINA DEED ABSTRACTS 1773-1778

Emanuel Kaygleman, Baltzager Stroman, John Rumph, Melchior Sachweiler, Jacob Pierons, Henry Wurtzers, north fork of Edisto or Pon Pon River, formerly granted to Wm. Mitchell brother of sd. Ephraim Mitchell, excepting out of sd. premises lots [numbers given]. Ephraim Mitchell (LS), Wit: Wm. Crighton, William Mitchell. Proved in Chas Town District before John Troup, J.P., by the oath of William Creighton. Recorded 22 Apr 1775.

Q-4, 358-362: Lease & release. 14 & 15 Dec 1773, William Palmer atty for Robert Palmer of Parish of St. Thomas, North Carolina, to John May Senr of Craven County, St. Davids Parish, for £50 SC money, 200 acres in parish of St. David, SC, on Thomsons Creek above where the Catawba Path crosses the sd. creek. Wm. Palmer (LS), Wit: Robt Lowry, Mary Palmer, Jane Gurria. Proved in Camden District before John N. Oglethorpe, J.P., by the oath of Robert Lowry. Recorded 24 Apr 1775.

Q-4, 363-365: 14 Jan 1774, Thos Wade of Anson County, North Carolina, Esq., to Francis Bettis of Craven County, SC, planter, for £600 SC money, tract in Craven County, South Carolina, but at the time of the grant in Anson County, North Carolina, 600 acres on north side of Lynches Creek south fork, granted to John Crawford 30 March 1751 and by his last will and testament sold by his executor Thomas Crawford to Thomas Wade by deed 27 Dec 1773. Thos Ward (LS), Wit: Ensunt Bettis, Robert Anderson, John Clark. Proved in Cheraw District before Charles Augustus Steward, J.P., 21 July 1774, by the oath of Ensunt Bettis. Recorded 24 Apr 1775.

Q-4, 365-369: Lease & release. 24 & 25 Feb 1775, Arthur Rows of Granville County, planter, to Jacob Buxton of same, planter, for £500 SC money, 116 acres in Granville County, adj. land of Christian Bours[?], Wm. Gamble, Savannah River. Arthur Rows (X) (LS), Wit: Mildred Hitchcock (H), James Thomson. Proved by the oath of James Thomson, J.P. for Beaufort District, 25 Jan 1775. Recorded 25 Apr 1775.

Q-4, 369-371: 20 Feb 1775, John Harvey of Granville County, SC, planter, to James Thompson of same, for £50 SC money, 100 acres adj. Mark Thorntons land, granted 2 Apr 1773. John Harvey (LS), Wit: Elijah Oglesbee, Anthony Buckholds (A). Proved by the oath of Anthony Buckholts before John Chisolm, J. P. in Beaufort District, 27 Feb 1775. Recorded 25 Apr 1775.

Q-4, 371-373: 25 Feb 1775, James Thomson of Granville county, SC, planter, to Jacob Buxton of same, planter, for £100 SC money, land conveyed by deed 20 Feb 1775 from John Harvey to sd. James Thomson, 100 acres adj. Mark Thorntons land, granted 2 Apr 1773. James Thomson (LS), Wit: John Chisolm, Robert Stafford. Proved by the oath of John Chisolm, J.P., 24 Feb 1775. Recorded 25 Apr 1775.

Q-4, 373-374: 28 Feb 1775, Jacob Buxton of Granville county, planter, to Wm. Wise of same, planter, for £100 SC money, 100 acres near Briar Creek adj. Andrew Irvin, Esqr., Daniel Blake, Wm. Calvert, grant dated 23 June 1774. Jacob Buxton (LS), Wit: Wm. Hitchcock, Gilles Kelly (K). Proved before John Chisolm, J.P. in Beaufort District, by the oath of wm. Hitchcock. Recorded 26 Apr 1775.

Q-4, 375-380: Lease & mortgage. 22 & 23 Feb 1775, James Johnston of Charles Town, late Baker, to Joseph Allston of Prince George Parish, Esqr., by obligation in the penal sum of £2000 for the payment of £1000, two lots in Charles Town, numbers 24 and 25. James Johnston (LS), Wit: Wm. Rudhall, John Auldje. Proved in Chas. Town District by the oath of Wm. Rudall, 24 Feb 1775, before George Davidson. Recorded 26 Apr 1775.

Q-4, 381-387: Lease & release. 9 & 10 Dec 1772, Alexander Michie of Charles Town, merchant, & Henrietta his wife to the Rev. Alex'r Hewat of same place, for £100 SC money, 500 acres on ranches of Little River called Lick Creek and Morgans branch near line of John Winn Esqr., granted to Alexr Michie 14 Aug 1772. Alexr Michie (LS), Henrietta Michie (LS), Wit: Robert Robertson, Alex Petrie. Proved 7 March 1775 before Wm. Rugeley, J. P., by the oath of Robert Robertson. Recorded 27 Apr 1775.

Q-4, 387-393: Lease & release. 6 Jan 1774, Christopher Rogers of Charles Town, taylor, and Eliz'th his wife, to Dennis Egan, Tavern Keeper, for £600 SC money, a lot of ground up the path in St.

Philips Parish, lot #8. Chris'er Rogers (LS), Eliz'th Rogers (LS), Dennis Egan (LS), Wit: Wm. Kelsey, Thomas Russ. Proved 6 Jan 1774 before Thomas Turner, J. P. in Charles town District by the oath of Wm. Kelsey. Recorded 28 Apr 1775.

Q-4, 393-397: Lease & release. 10 & 11 Feb 1775, Dennis Egan of Charles Town District, to Rowland Rugeley of same district, for £1300 SC money, lot #90 up the path in St. Philips Parish on Broad Road from Charles town. Dennis Egan (LS), Wit: John Egan, Thomas Phepoe. Proved in Charles Town District by the oat of Thos Phepoe before William Rugeley, J.P., 7 June 1775. Recorded 29 Apr 1775.

Q-4, 397-406: Lease & mortgage. 6 & 7 Jan 1775, Wm. Morgan of Berkley County, planter, and Mary his wife, to Andrew Thomson, merchant, by bond for £12,600 for the payment of £6300 with 8% interest, 500 acres in Prince Georges Parish on Waccamaw River and also tract of 500 acres in St. Bartholomews Parish, Colleton County on Edisto River, also 300 acres in St. Georges Parish adj. David Hoy, and 500 acres in Williamsburgh Township on Black River adj. James Polard, and lot 108 in Williamsburg. William Morgan (LS), Mary Morgan (LS), Wit: Susannah Green, James Simpson. Proved in Charles Town District before Wm. Nisbett, J. P., 10 Feb 1775 by the oath of James Simpson. Recorded 1 May 1775.

Q-4, 406-414: Lease & release. 1 & 2 Sept 1774, Alexander Wright of Chas. Town, Esqr., and Elizabeth his wife, to John Webb of same, merchant, for £6725 SC money, lot on Broad Street which belonged to Paul Jenys deceased at the time of his death, adj. land of John Paul Grimke, Wm Logan and also a lot on Church St. adj. land of Gabriel Manigault, Thomas Smith, and Paul Jenys by his will dated 16 March 1752 devised to his brother George Jenys and to his cousins Walter Thomson, Thomas Izard, and John Izard; George Jenys has since departed this life without issue and before he reached the age of 21 years and said Thomas Izard also departed this life intestate and without issue; John Izard only son and heir at law of Walter Izard who was eldest brother and heir at law of Thomas Izard and by writ of partition between him and Elizabeth Wright then Elizabeth Izard, only daughter of John Izard deceased, and writ directed to Isaac Mazyck, Gabriel Manigault, John Savage, Thomas Smith of Broad Street and Daniel Cannon... (plat included). Alex Wright (LS), Eliz'th Wright (LS), Wit: Daniel Cannon, Elisha Poinsett, Peter Bocquet. Proved by the oath of Daniel Cannon 1 May 1775, before William Rugeley, J.P. Recorded 1 May 1775.

Q-4, 415-422: Lease & release. 3 & 4 May 1773, Alexander Gillon of Charles Town, and Mary his wife, to George Hanhbaum, for £3300 SC money, lots 281 and 282 in Charles Town. Alex Gillon (LS), Mary Gillon (LS), Wit: John Splatt Cripps, Peter Meuratt. Proved in Charlestown District by the oath of John Splatt Cripps before Wm. Rugeley, J. P., 7 March 1775. Recorded 3 May 1775. Mary Gillon relinquished dower 7 May 1773.

Q-4, 422-432: Lease & release. 26 & 27 Oct 1773, James St. John and wife Elizabeth, planter, to Thomas Handlin, House Carpenter, for £2000 SC money, part of town lot adj. land of Rawlins Lowndes, Esquire, on Friend St., estate of James St. John late deceased, grandfather to sd. James St. John. James St. John (LS), Elizabeth St. John (LS), Wit: John Troup, Thos Phepoe. Proved in Chs. Town District by the oath of John Troup 11 May 1775 before William Rugeley, J. P. Elizabeth St. John relinquished dower 27 Oct 1773. Recorded 11 May 1775.

Q-4, 433-437: Lease & release. 2 & 3 Jan 1775, Paul Trapier of Prince George Parish, Craven county, planter, and Elizabeth his wife, to Daniel Morrall of Prince Georges Parish, planter, for £600 SC money, 400 acres in Prince Georges Parish on the south branch of Little River adj. land of James Elks, Mr. Finks, Thomas Blith, which land was granted to Judith Lewis 30 Sept 1736. Paul Trapier (LS), Eliz. Trapier (LS), Wit: Benjn Trapier, Jos. Wragg. Proved in Chs. Town District by the oath of Jos. Wragg ___ 1775. Recorded 13 May 1775.

Q-4, 437-439: 17 Nov 1774, William Kirk of Savannah, Georgia, Junior Shopkeeper, to Adrian Mayer of Purrysburgh, Granville County, SC, for £126 current money, 250 acres in the Township of Purrysburgh granted to George Telebach late of Charlestown, Masson, adj. land of John Jamblers[?] alias Hramblers land, adj. land granted to Peter Ganet Vanderheiden, land granted to Ann Villard, Daniel Choupart, John Strother, John Ulrich Hougard[?], Michael Gambra alias

SOUTH CAROLINA DEED ABSTRACTS 1773-1778

Gampert. Will Kirk Junr. (LS) Wit: William Holzendorff, John Farnum. Proved in Purysburgh by the oath of William Holzendorf before David Giroud, 20 __ 1774. Recorded 15 May 1775.

Q-4, 440-446: Lease & release. 23 & 24 Sept 1774, Samuel Dubois of St. Johns Parish, Berkly County, SC, planter, and Susannah his wife to Peter Marion of St. Stephens Parish, planter, for £6000 SC money, 500 acres in St. Johns Berkley County part of 1200 acres granted to Saml Dubois 16 Feb 1773, one other tract of 300 acres on north side Santee River adj. land of Edward Newman, John Michell, Robert Irvin, and a tract of 200 acres adj. Scots Old field, John Hays, Chas. Cantey, Santee River. Saml Dubois. Susan Dubois. Wit: Peter Couturier, Isaac Couturier. Proved 27 Sept 1774 before John Frierson by the oath of Peter Couturier Junr. Recorded 18 May 1775.

Q-4, 447-452: Lease & release. 22 & 23 Sept 1773, Jacob Eagner and Mary his wife of Saxegotha Township, Berkly County, SC, planter, to Henry Patrick, Esqr., of Saxegotha Township, Berkley County, merchant, for £2000 SC money, 250 acres granted 7 Nov 1758 to Eliz'th Mercer on south west side of Santee River in Saxegotha Township adj. estate of George Haig deceased, land surveyed for Wm. Baker, and sd. Eliz'th Mercer intermarried with David Webb by which means the sd. David Webb became entitled to said plantation and David Webb and Elizth Webb his wife conveyed to said Jacob Eagner 12 & 13 Dec 1768. Jacob Eagner (LS), Mary Eagner (+) (LS), Wit: Andrew Kagler, Jacob Taylor. Proved 24 March 1774 by the oath of Jacob Taylor before Wm. Tucker, J. P. Recorded 19 May 1775.

Q-4, 452-454: 18 Nov 1774, Saml. Harrison of St. Davids Parish, Craven county, planter, to John Frierson of Williamsburg, Craven County, planter, for £50 currency, 200 acres in St. Davids Parish, Craven County, on fork Creek. Saml Harrison (LS), Wit: Chas Evans, Joshua Frierson. Proved 20 March 1775 before Henry Cassell, J. P. for Camden District, by the oath of Joshua Frierson. Recorded 19 May 1775.

Q-4, 454-459: Lease & release. 2 & 3 Nov 1774, Isham Clayton of St. Pauls Parish, Colleton county, Esqr., to John Curtis of St. Bartholomews Parish, Colleton County, for £300 SC money, 200 acres granted to Wm. Glover of St. Bartholomews Parish 16 July 1765 on freshes of Edisto River, recorded in Book LL, page 162, said William Glover deceased conveyed tract of John Liddle of St. Bartholomews Parish, Colleton County, 2 Jan 1774, and sd. John Little conveyed to Isham Clayton of St. Pauls Parish. Isham Clayton (LS), Wit: John Clayton, Henry Wood, John Gilbert. Proved in Chs. Town District by the oath of John Gilbert before Geo. Davidson, J.P., 27 March 1775. Recorded 20 May 1775.

Q-4, 459-461: 5 Apr 1773, Richd. Gough of Chas. Town, gent., to Rachl. Caw of same place, widow, for love and affection, 500 acres in St. Johns Parish in Berkley County, heretofore consisted of three smaller tracts and was formerly seized and possessed by Col. George Pawley and by him conveyed to Richd. Gough deceased, the father of the sd. Richd Gough. Richd. Gough (LS), Wit: Edward Simons, Keat'g Simons. Proved before Peter Simons, J. P., by the oath of Keating Simons, 16 Feb 1775. Recorded 23 May 1775.

Q-4, 461-468: Lease & release. 30 & 31 March 1775, Barnard Elliott of Charles Town, Esqr., to Benjamin Dart of same, for £4500 SC money, 169 acres on north side Ashley River commonly called Accabee in St. Andrews Parish, Berkley County, with the marsh land opposite, adj. land late of William Elliott, on the High Road from Chas. Town to Ashley Ferry, land of Roger Smith, which is part of tract of 227½ acres formerly belonging to sd. Wm. Elliott who by a deed 8 Sept 1749 conveyed to his brother Barnard Elliott, the father of sd. Barnard Elliot who by his will dated 16 May 1758 devised the same unto his son sd. Barnard Elliott. Barn'd Elliott (LS), Wit: Walter Dick, Jacob Edmonson. Proved in Chas. Town District before Henry Peronneau, J. P., by the oath of Walter Dick, 3 Apr 1775. Recorded 23 May 1775.

Q-4, 468-470: Release. 10 Dec 1774, Jesse Deloach of Parish of St. Peters, SC, planter, to michl. Deloach of same, planter, for £200 SC money, 200 acres on the head of Dry Branch near Savannah River in St. Peters Parish, granted 20 Jan 1773 to Jesse Deloach. Jesse Deloch (LS), Wit: James Thomson, Abel Goodwin. Proved in Beaufort District by James Thomson, J.P., 10 Jan 1774. Recorded 5 Oct 1775. [For lease, see Q-4, pages 124-125.]
END OF BOOK Q-4.

SOUTH CAROLINA DEED ABSTRACTS 1773-1778

R-4, 1-4: Lease & release. 5 & 6 Dec 1772, John Land of Craven County, SC, to John Yarborough Senr, of same, for £300 SC money, 200 acres on Rocky Creek, Craven County adj. land laid out for William Clehoin, part of 250 acres granted 16 July 1765 to John Land. John Land (LS), Wit: Thomas Dye, Lewis Yarborough. Proved by the oath of Thomas Dye before James Patton and John Gaston, J. P., _____ 1773. Recorded 25 March 1775.

R-4, 4-8: Lease & release. 1 & 2 Nov 1772, William Hay of Craven County, SC, to Dortch Hay of same, for £100 SC money, 400 acres granted to Richard Jackson 5 June 1750 near the Congaree and said Richard Jackson conveyed to William Hay and the northermost part of this tract adj. William Howell, heirs of James May deceased, line made between Dortch Hay and Hardy Hay, 100 acres. William Hay (LS), Wit: David Hay, Zachariah Aughtry. Proved 19 March 1774 by the oath of David Hay before Wm. Tucker, J.P. Recorded 4 Apr 1775.

R-4, 8-11: Lease & release. 10 & 11 May 1773, John White of St. Davids Parish, Craven County, to Thos. Williams of same, for £500 SC money, 100 acres on north side of Pedee River on head of one of the branches of Beverdam Creek, granted to John White 21 May 1772. John White (LS), Wit: John Downs, John Rigs (I). Proved in Cheraw District before Philip Pledger, J.P., 13 Jan 1773. Recorded 5 Apr 1775.

R-4, 12-17: Lease & release. 26 & 27 Sept 1774, George Forbes and Hannah his wife of Charles Town District, to Samuel Hrabowsky of same, for £250 SC money, 250 acres in St. Mathews Parish, Berkly County, adj. land run for Mordicai McFarlin now George Kings, land run for Alexr Tate Junr, Richd. Balducks. George Forbes (LS), Hannah Forbes (LS), Wit: J[ames] Purcell, Chs. Michie. Proved 6 Apr 1775 before William Rugeley, J. P., by the oath of Chs. Michie. Recorded 6 Apr 1775.

R-4, 18-20: 16 Jan 1775, Archibald Clark of St. Marks Parish, planter, & Jean his wife, to John Latta of same, planter, for £700 SC money, 345 acres granted 17 May 1754 by Mathew Rowan, President of North Carolina, to John Kelsey, on Waxhaw Creek, Parish of St. Mark, Province of SC since the boundary line was run, conveyed by John Kelsey to Samuel Thompson by deed 18 Feb 1756 a memorial entered in the Registers Office in Meclingburg by Robert Harris and by the death of sd. Samuel Thompson the said tract devolved to John Thompson and said John Thompson made said tract of 345 acres to Archibald Clark by deed 21 Feb 1774. Archibald Clark (LS), Jean Clarke (I) (LS), Wit: John Thompson, Henry Foster, James Patton. Proved 17 Jan 1775 before James Patton by the oath of Robt. Patton. Recorded 7 Apr 1775.

R-4, 21: John Arnel Pender and George Grier, both of St. Marks Parish, bound to John Latta of same in the sum of £2400 SC money, to keep clear of any incumbrances hindrance for the tract which John Latta purchased from Archibald Clark. George Grier (LS), John Arnel Pender (mark) (LS), Wit: Robt. Patton, Henry Foster. Recorded 7 Apr 1775.

R-4, 21-27: Lease & release. 14 & 15 Oct 1774, Benjamin Lord of Charles Town, Sc, Schoolmaster, and Ann his wife, to David Williams of Pedee, planter, for £700 SC money, 350 acres in the Welch Tract in Craven County adj. land of Benjamin Walls, Robert Williams, Cornelius Reins, Isaac _____. Benjn Lord (LS), Anne Lord (LS), Wit: Rebecca Mace, John Cross, J. Gilbank. Proved by the oath of John Gilbank before John Troup, J. P., 15 Oct 1774. Recorded 11 Apr 1775.

R-4, 28-31: Lease & release. 28 & 29 Jan 1754, Lewis Gourdin and Mary Ann his wife of Parish of St. James Santee, Craven County, to Theodore Gaillard of same, planter, for £300 SC money, 58 acres on the High Road adj. Joseph Porcher, sd. Gourdin taken out of the 600 acres said Gourdin now lives on. Lewis Gourdin (LS), Mariane Gourdin (m) (LS), Wit: Peter Robert, James Davis, Peter gourdin. Proved in Chs. Town District by the oath of Jonah Robert who testified to the handwriting of Peter Robert his father, 19 Feb 1775, before William Rugeley, J. P. Recorded 12 Apr 1775.

R-4, 31-32: 11 Apr 1768, Hugh White of Macklenburgh County, North Carolina, to Thomas McCullock of same, for £11 NC money, 41 acres in the county of Macklinburgh on the east side of Fishing Creek adj. said Hugh White. Hugh White (LS), Wit: G. Gill, John Davis. Proved April term 1768 in Mecklinburgh County, NC, before Robert Harris, C. C.

R-4, 33-35: 3 Feb 1774, John Nealy of Parish of St. Marks, SC, yeoman, and Elizabeth his wife, to Thomas McCullock of same, carpenter, for £100 lawful money, 150 acres, part of 300 acres granted 24 Sept 1754 to Thomas Nealy, in the County of Anson, North Carolina, but now in Craven County, South Carolina, on west side Fishing Creek, said Nealy died intestate and having no issue said John Nealy, elder brother to the deceased, possessed the premises. John Nealy (I) (LS). N. B. The above named Eliz'th Nealy was deceased before the sealing & delivery of these presents. Wit: Hugh Whiteside, Thos Gill, Robt. Gill. Proved by the oath of Hugh Whiteside before Wm. Brown, 31 Dec 1774.

R-4, 36-38: 5 May 1768, James Waughup of Mecklenburgh County, North Carolina, planter, to Robert Crawford of Craven County, SC, for £723 SC money, 250 acres granted to sd. James Wahub by Gov. Arthur Dobbs of North Carolina, 28 March 1755 on the river bank on McCowans corner. James Waughup (LS), Wit: Robt. Crockett, James Paxton. Proved by the oath of Robert Crockett before Wm. Rugeley, J. P., 11 Feb 1775. Recorded 15 Apr 1775.

R-4, 38-41: Lease & release. 12 Feb 1775, James Williams of Ninety Six District, SC, planter, to Thomas Young of same, planter, for £10 SC money, 400 acres in Ninety Six District on Little Stephen Creek where the Long Cane Rode crosses the sd. Creek, granted 12 Oct 1770 by James Williams. James Williams (+) (LS), Mary Williams (M) (LS), Wit: Nicholas ____, Moses Williams, Aron Bluler (X). Recorded 15 Apr 1775.

R-4, 41-47: Lease & release. 30 & 31 May 1774, James Hamilton and Mary his wife of Colleton County, planters, to Gavin Witherspoon of Craven County, planter, for £262 s10 SC money, 350 acres in Williamsburgh Township adj. land laid out to Daniel Money, John Robertson, Black River, part of 400 acres granted to Mary McElroy 16 Apr 1736. James Hamilton (LS), Mary Hamilton (LS), Wit: John Lambright, Wm. Lambright, Wm. Murray. Proved 22 Nov 1774 before John Wragg, J. P. in Berkly County, by the oath of Wm. Lambright. Recorded 20 Apr 1775.

R-4, 47-53: Lease & release. 20 & 21 Jan 1775, William Snow of Craven County, and Margaret his wife, to William Britton of same, planters, for £3000 SC money, 400 acres granted to James Gordon 16 Feb 1735, by resurvey of Hugh Giles found to contain 840 acres in Queensborough Township on Pedee River adj. land of James Abercromby Esqr., Mr. Clarks, and said James Gordon legally conveyed said tract to Josiah Garnia Dupree and Daniel Doyley provost Marshall by execution conveyed to Francis Gotteer 10 Sept 1772, and said Francis Gotteer and Isabella his wife 1 Dec 1774 conveyed to William Snow. William Snow (LS), Margaret Snow (LS), Wit: Joseph Britton, Francis Goddard. Proved before Francis Britton, J. P. in G. Town District, by the oath of Joseph Britton, 10 Feb 1775. Recorded 21 Apr 1775.

R-4, 54-57: Lease & release. 14 Jan 1773, Josiah Cantey of Craven County, SC, to David Brunson of same, for £150 SC money, 100 acres granted 15 July 1768 to Josiah Cantey, on Lynches Creek adj. land of Robert Twist[?]. Josiah Cantey (LS), Wit: Arthur Graham, Wm. Brunson. Proved 6 June 1775 by the oath of William Brunson before Henry Cassels, J. P. for Craven county. Recorded 21 Apr 1775.

R-4, 57-63: Lease & release. 12 & 13 Oct 1774, Susannah Durand of Parish of Christ Church, widow, formerly Susannah Hext widow of Hugh Hext late of Colleton County, deceased, to Robert Wells of Charles Town, Bookseller, for £5250 SC money, the easternmost part of lot on south side of Tradd Street in Charles Town, number 6. Susannah Durand (LS), Wit: Mary White, Peter Croft, John Mort. Williams. Proved before Rowland Rugeley, J. P. for Charles Town District, by the oath of Peter Croft, 10 Jan 1775. Recorded 25 Apr 1775.

R-4, 63-67: 13 Nov 1750, Humphrey Sommers of Charles Town, Bricklayer, and Susannah his wife, to Hopkin Price of said town, Tanner, for £400 SC money, lot on west side of old Church Street otherwise called Meeting house Street, remainder of marshal or land already conveyed by sd. Sommers to Hopkin Price and the lot of land late of Robert Stell deceased. Humphrey Sommers (LS), Susannah Sommers (LS), Wit: Samman Jones, Thos Lamboll. Proved in Berkley County before Wm. Rugeley, 3 March 1775 by the oath of Mrs. Lambel Thomas who swore to the handwriting of Thomas Lamboll decd. Recorded 27 Apr 1775.

SOUTH CAROLINA DEED ABSTRACTS 1773-1778

R-4, 67-68: Hamlet, 20 May 1774. A small tract of 32 acres about one mile from Charles Town bequeathed by our father Barnard Elliott decd. by his last will and testament to his daughters Elizabeth Baker, Mary Guerin, Amerinthea Elliott & Catharine Elliott after the death of our mother which happen'd about the year 1768 near six years ago and one of the daughters Elizabeth Elliott Baker dying & leaving lawful issue the other three joining with Robt. Baker husband to the decd. Elizabeth Baker in agreement to divide by lot four ballots were according made and put in to a hat & Robert Baker for his wife Elizabeth [page torn]. Richd Bohun Baker (LS), Mary Guerin (LS), Amerintha Elliott (LS), Catharine Elliott), Wit: Richard Bohun Baker Junr, Barnard Elliott Junr. Proved in Chs. Town District by the oath of Richard Bohun Baker Junr before Wm. Rugeley, 4 March 1775.

R-4, 68-69: Bond. Susannah Duran of Christ Church Parish, widow, late Susannah Hext, widow of Hugh Hext late of Colleton County, planter, and Levi Durand of Christ Church Parish, for £___, 12 Oct 1774, bond to make title to Robert Wells of a town lot on south side Tradd St. Susannah Durant (LS), Levi Durand (LS), Wit: Peter Croft. Proved before Rowland Rugeley, J. P., by the oath of Peter Croft, 10 Jan 1775. Recorded 27 Apr 1775.

R-4, 70-73: Lease & release. 8 & 9 Oct 1771, Rawlins Lowndes, Esqr., to Christopher Rogers of Charles Town, for £350 SC Money, lot up the path in St. Philips Parish fronting on the Broad Road, number 9, adj. Mary Laney lot 8. Rawlins Lowndes (LS), Wit: Benjn Wish, Wm. Kelsey. Proved 6 Jan 1774 before Thomas Turner, J.P. in Charles Town District, by the oath of William Kelsey. Recorded 28 Apr 1775.

R-4, 74-78: Lease & release. 7 March 1775, Rowland Rugeley of Charles Town, SC, Esqr., to Dalziel Hunter of same, for £1000 SC money, lot up the path in St. Philips Parish on the Broad Road, adj. land of Rawlins Lowndes, Esqr, known as lot number 9, adj. Mary Laney lot 8. Rowland Rugeley (LS), Wit: Thos Burke, Danl Tharin. Proved 29 Apr 1775 before William Rugeley, J.P. in Charles Town District, by the oath of Thomas Burke. Recorded 29 Apr 1775.

R-4, 78-82: Lease & release. 12 & 13 Aug 1774, Peter Keighley of St. Davids Parish, Craven County, SC, planter, to James Callcote of same, planter, for £200 SC money, 194 acres on NE side Pedee River adj. John Walkers, Moses Bass, said Peter Keighley, Mr. LaRush, granted to William Green and conveyed by him to said Peter Keighley. Peter Keighley (LS), Wit: William Cade, Gid. Gibson Junr. Proved in George Town District by the oath of William Cade before Joseph Gourly, 23 Aug 1774. Recorded 1 Apr [sic, for May] 1775.

R-4, 82-86: Lease & release. 12 & 13 Aug 1774, Peter Keighley of St. Davids Parish, Craven County, SC, planter, to James Callcote of same, planter, for £300 SC money, 200 acres on Pedee River granted 5 Sept 1755 to John Sanders adj. Messrs Daniel and Thomas Laroche, conveyed by John Sanders 15 & 16 Apr 1749 to John Alran and said John Alran 12 & 13 May 1760 to Wade Blair, and said Wade Blair to John Simpson 10 Dec 1761, and said John Simpson to Peter Keighley 30 & 31 Jan 1769. Peter Keighley (LS), Wit: William Cade, Gid. Gibson Junr. Proved in George Town District by the oath of William Cade before Joseph Gourly, 23 Aug 1774. Recorded 1 May 1775.

R-4, 86-92: Lease & release. 12 & 13 Aug 1774, Peter Keighley of St. Davids Parish, Craven County, SC, planter, to James Callcote of same, planter, for £300 SC money, 900 acres on Pedee River granted 16 Dec 1736 to Abraham Satur since deceased in Craven County adj. land of Mr. Soloman Middleton, said Abraham Satur, since the death of said Abraham Satur and by virtue of sundry wills and conveyances, said land became vested in Edward Jerman Esquire, who conveyed 29 March 1771 to Gideon Gibson who conveyed 29 March 1773 to Peter Keighley.... 225 acres platted by John Loveless, adj. Solomon Middleton, James Sanders. Peter Keighley (LS), Wit: William Cade, Gid. Gibson Junr. Proved in George Town District by the oath of William Cade before Joseph Gourly, 23 Aug 1774. Recorded 3 May 1775.

R-4, 92-100: Lease & release. 1 & 2 March 1775, James Postell of St. Pauls Parish, Colleton County, SC, planter, and Susannah his wife, to John Sommers of same, planter, for £4000 SC money, 594½ acres on east side South Edisto River in Colleton County, ad. land of Thomas Deston, Melcher Garner, James Parsons, John Summers, William Carter, Edward Wilkinson. James Postell (LS), Susannah Postell (LS), Wit: Beulah Rivers, G. J. Fardo. Proved in Chs. Town District by the oath of G. J. Fardo before Wm. Rugeley, J. P., 7 March 1775. Recorded 4 May 1775. Susannah Postell relinquished dower before Thomas Knox Gordon, 3 March 1775.

R-4, 101-103: James Marshall of Norfolk Street in the Parish of St. Clement Danes, County of Middlesex, Esquire, and Elizabeth his wife, formerly Elizabeth Walter, spinster, afterwards the wife and since the widow relict and sole devisee named in the will of William Haggett, late of Mill hill in County of Middlesex, deceased, exrs. of the last will of William Haggatt, appointed John McCall the younger of Charles Town, South Carolina, gentleman, and John Walter of same place, esquire, our true and lawfull attorneys, we now annul this letter of attorney, and appoint Samuel Carne of Bartletts Buildings, Parish of St. Andrews, Holborn in the City of London, our attorney, 19 April 1774. James Marshall (LS), Eliza Marshall (LS), Wit: John Ramsden, Jackson Browne. Proved before Frederick Bull, Lord Mayor of London, by the oath of John Ramsden, 22 Apr 1774. Recorded 5 May 1775.

R-4, 104-110: Lease & release. 9 & 10 Jan 1775, Thomas Lynch of Charles Town, SC, esqr., to Phillip Britton of St. Marks Parish, pedee, for £3500 SC money, 400 acres in Queensborough Township, Craven County on South side Pede River, adj. lands of James Abercromby, also 400 acres on south side Pedee River adj. Abraham Stapler, James Abercromby, total of 800 acres. Thos Lynch (LS), Wit: Benjn Huger, Robt. Gibb. Proved in G. Town District before Francis Britton, J.P., by the oath of Robert Gibb, 18 Jan 1775. Recorded 5 May 1775.

R-4, 110-114: Lease & release. 20 & 21 June 1766, Robt. Dorrill Senr of Parish of Christ Church, Berkley County, planter, to Thomas Wells of Kain Hoy in St. Thomas Parish, for £1000 SC money, 330 acres English measure in the Parish of St. James Santee, adj.land of John Baker, William Townsand, William Benison, and the sea marsh. Robt Dorrill Senior (LS), Wit: Wm. Cook, Thos Barton, Eliza. Dorrill (+). Proved 2 Jan 1769 before Andrew Hibben, J.P. in Berkley County, by the oath of Thomas Barton. Memorial entered Book H No. 8, page 422, 19 Apr 1768. Recorded 8 May 1775.

R-4, 114-116: 4 Jan 1770, Stephen Townsend, exr. to the estate of William Townsend deceased, of St. Michaels parish, Charles Town, cabinet maker, to Thomas Wells of parish of St. James Santee, Craven County, planter, for £34 SC money, tract in St. James Parish, Santee, Craven County, 1000 acres granted to my brother William Townsend. Stephen Townsend (LS), Wit: Benjamin Wheeler, J[ames] Gottier Eden. Proved in Berkley County before William Mason, J.P., by the oath of Benjamin Wheeler.

R-4, 116-120: Lease & release. 14 Dec 1774, Valentine Cranich of Berkley County, and Marian his wife, to John Bear of same county, for £86 s8 SC money, 200 acres in Berkley County on Pen Swamp waters of four holes adj. Mathew Egils. Valentine Cranick (LS), Maryann Cranick (m) (LS), Wit: Nicholas Hunter, Bostian Smith, Philip Arrant. Proved in Orangeburgh District before Henry Felder, J. P., by the oath of Nicholas Hunter, 24 Dec 1774. Recorded 9 May 1775.

R-4, 120-123: Mathew Drake, late of Waccamaw, Parish of George Town, Craven county, but now of city of Exeter, County of Devon, England, merchant, Gilbert Neyle of said city of Exeter, merchant, Robert Collier of Jopsham in County of Devon merchant, and James Collins of the city of Exeter, appoint Sampson Neyle of Charles Town, South Carolina, merchant, and Edward Drake of Winyaw, our lawful attorneys, to take possession of two tracts called Canteys containing 552 acres in Prince Fredericks Parish, Craven County, on north side of Santee River on Canteys Creek adj. land of Master John Tunis (Junes?), and negroes and slaves men, women, and children, 3 August 1770. Mathew Drake (LS), Gilbert Neyle (LS), Robt Collier (LS), James Collins (LS), Wit: John Triggs Junr of St. Thomas the Apostle in County of Devon, Gent. Thos Dodge, Mayor of the City of Exeter. Recorded 10 May 1775.

R-4, 123-127: Lease & release. 24 & 25 Feb 1775, John Lyon of Charles Town, to James Weir of same, for £50 SC money, 450 acres in Orangeburgh District on Cedar Pond Branch waters of Edisto River adj. land granted to James Mitchell, Henry Mouzon Junr, grant dated 3 Feb 1775. John Lyon (LS), Wit: William Creighton, James Mitchell. Proved 25 Feb 1775 before Ephraim Mitchell, J.P., 25 Feb 1775. Recorded 10 May 1775.

SOUTH CAROLINA DEED ABSTRACTS 1773-1778

R-4, 127-129: 7 Oct 1771, Joseph Neal of Broad River, Tryon County, North Carolina, to William Smith of Broad River, county and province aforesaid, for £30 proclamation money, tract in County of Tryon, on both sides of a branch of Broad River known as Kings Creek, 100 acres granted to said James Neal 5 May 1769. Joseph Neal (Seal), Wit: Jacob Handall, G. Julian. North Carolina, Tryon County. The within deed and clarks certificate duly entered in the publick register of said county 3 March 1772. Thos Neel, Register. Recorded 10 May 1775.

R-4, 129-136: Lease & release. 24 & 25 May 1774, Peter Bocquet Junr of Charles Town, merchant, and Elizabeth his wife, to Isaac Chanler of same, Doctor of Physick, for £4400 SC money, 350 acres in Parish of St. George Dorchester in Berkley County, adj. Ralph Izard, ____ Walkers Barrony, on the road from Dorchester to Goose Creek. Peter Bocquet (LS), Eliz'h Bocquet (LS, Wit: Peter Fayssoux, John Agner. Proved in Chs. Town District by the oath of John Wagner before Wm. Rugeley, J. P., 11 May 1775. Recorded 11 May 1775. Elizabeth Bocquet relinquished dower 26 May 1774.

R-4, 137-141: Tripartite deed. 25 June 1774, Thomas Booth of Iwamlow, County of Chester, Esquire, surviving devisee named in and executor of the will of Thomas Lowndes, late of said County of Chester, deceased, of the first part, Richard Wilbrahan Booth of Latham in County Palatine of Lancaster, Esquire, only son and heir and executor of Randle Wilbrahan, late of Lincolns Town, County of Middlesex, deceased, who was the other devisee of said Thomas Lowndes, and Edward Lowndes, late in the service of the Honorable East India Company but now of Grase Inn, County of Middlesex, Mariner, nephew of said Thomas Lowndes, whereas said Thomas Lowndes made his will dated 6 May 1748, in which amongst other things (with his interest or estate in any Barony or Tracts of Land in Carolina) devised the same to his heirs in trust to be sold to pay to each of his executors £100 lawful money of Great Britain, and said Thomas Lowndes son afterwards died and said Randle Wilbraham and Thomas Booth proved his will in the prerogative court of the Archbishop of Canterbury, and said Randle Wilbraham died in the year 1770 having made his will and appointed said Richard Wilbraham Boothe his son, sole executor, said Thomas Booth and Richd. Wilbraham Boothe are willing to relinquish said legacies or sums of £100 and to vest all such estate in Carolina in the aforesaid Edward Lowndes for his own use, now for ten shillings money of Great Britain. Thos Booth (LS), Richd Wilbraham Boothe (LS), Wit: Chas. Clowes of Lincolns Town, Robt Grice. Proved before Frederick Bull, Lord Mayor of London by the oath of Robert Grice, 28 June 1774. Recorded 12 May 1775.

R-4, 141-142: Robert Dee, late of London, Great Britain, but now of Charles Town, south carolina, gentleman, appoint Henry Houseman, late of Great Britain, but now of Charles Town, my lawful attorney, to take possession of my baronies, plantations, and tracts of land in said province, 4 March 1775. Robert Dee (LS), Wit: Wm. Nisbett, John Sturgeon. Proved in Chs. Town District by the oath of William Nisbett before William Rugeley, J.P. Recorded 12 March [sic] 1775.

R-4, 143-148: Lease & release. 6 & 7 Oct 1772, David Giroud Senr. of St. Peters Parish, planter, to Daniel DeSaussure of St. Helena Parish, merchant, for £2000 SC money, 200 acres in St. Peters Parish, Purysburgh Township, adj. lands of Samuel Montague, Esqr., land granted to John Grancer, Henry Lewis DuPont, also one other tract adj. the other, 200 acres, adj. Jeremiah Remond, Christr. Rink, John Grancer. David Giroud (LS), Wit: Lewis DeSaussure, Jno. Postell. Proved in Beaufort District 14 March 1775 before Andrew Aggnew by the oath of Lewis DeSaussure. Recorded 13 May 1775.

R-4, 148-152: Lease & release. 2 & 3 Jan 1775, Paul Trapier of Prince Georges Parish, Craven County, and Elizabeth his wife, to Daniel Morall of same, for £500 SC money, 230 acres in Prince Georges Parish on the south branch of Little River adj. a salt marsh belonging to James Elks, Mr. Frinks[?] land, Thomas Bliths, granted to Judith Lewis 30 Sept 1736 [release states granted to Mary Smith 30 Sept 1736]. Eliz. Trapier (LS), Paul Trapier (LS), Wit: Benjn. Trapier, Jos. Wragg. Proved in Chs. Town District by the oath of Jos. Wragg before ____, ____ 1775. Recorded 13 May 1775.

R-4, 152-157: Lease & mortgage. 14 & 15 Nov 1774, Thomas Cochran of Charles Town, merchant, to John Dorsius of same, by bond in the sum of £6300 s10 SC money, for the payment of £3150 s15 like money, 348 acres in St. Thomas Parish being part of land lately belonging to the estate of

SOUTH CAROLINA DEED ABSTRACTS 1773-1778

Richard Beresford deceased and sold by his executors to Leonard Askew, adj. land of James Rolain, land late of said Leonard Askew (now David Maull's), John Moore's land, on a creek of Cooper River, by deed of conveyance from Thomas Grimball Esquire, Sheriff of Charles Town District to said Thomas Cochran. Thomas Cochran (LS), Wit: John Dart, Charles Warham Junr. Proved in Berkley County by the oath of John Dart before David Deas, J.P. Recorded 15 May 1775.

R-4, 157-159: 2 March 1775, James Akin of St. Thomas Parish, Berkley County, planter, and Ann his wife, to Charles Harris of Charles Town, for £5 SC money, 500 acres on south west side of Little Pedee River in Craven County, adj. land of Mr. Adams, granted 7 May last to James Akin. James Akin (LS), Ann Akin (LS), Wit: Jos. Russell, John Brian. Proved 6 March 1775 before Hopkin Price, J.P., by the oath of John Brian. Recorded 16 May 1775.

R-4, 160-161: Esther Wrand of Charles Town, for five shillings, to William Wrand, all my interest and claim lot #19 in Charles Town, on Unity Alley, adj. the other part of said lot conveyed by James Crockatt unto James Amos, part of lot conveyed by James Crokatt to Darby Pendergrass... conveyed to William Wrand in trust for his daughters Hester Wrand and Sarah Wrand, 21 Dec 1770. Esther Wrand (R) (LS), Wit: Philip Williams, James Brockinton. Proved before John Coram by the oath of James Brockinton in Charles Town District, 28 March 1775. Recorded 16 May 1775.

R-4, 161-162: Esther Wrand of Charles Town, for five shillings, to Margaret Gough, wife of John Gough of Charles Town, all my interest and claim lot #115 in Charles Town, by lease and release 28 August 1753 between Robert Hawkes to me... dated 21 Dec 1770. Esther Wrand (R) (LS), Wit: Philip Williams, James Brockinton. Proved before John Coram by the oath of James Brockinton in Charles Town District, 28 March 1775. Recorded 16 May 1775.

R-4, 163-164: Esther Wrand of Charles Town, for five shillings, to William Wrand of Charles Town, all my interest and claim lot #17 in Charles Town, by lease and release 22 March 1759 between William Glen and Margaret his wife to me... dated 21 Dec 1770. Esther Wrand (R) (LS), Wit: Philip Williams, James Brockinton. Proved before John Coram by the oath of James Brockinton in Charles Town District, 28 March 1775. Recorded 16 May 1775.

R-4, 164-168: 6 Dec 1774, William Scott of St. Marks Parish, planter, and Mary his wife, to Miles Brewton, for £750 SC money, 50 acres in St. Marks Parish adj. lands of sd. Miles Brewton, which said William Scott bought of Joseph Curry and whereon said William Scott now resides. William Scott (LS), Mary Scott (+) (LS), Wit: Wm. Thompson, Isaac Rivers. Proved 22 Feb 1775 before Malcom Clark, J. P. in Orangeburgh District. Recorded 17 May 1775.

R-4, 168-171: Lease & release. 16 & 17 Feb 1775, Henry Seastrunk of Craven County, Camden District, to Henry Patrick, Esqr., of Berkley County, Saxegotha Township, for £100 SC money, 100 acres in Craven County on Congaree River granted to Henry Ceasetrunk deceased, in 1749, adj. land granted to Henry Felkland. Henry Seastrunk (+) (LS), M. Magdalen Seastrunk (+) (LS), Wit: Andrew Heren, Ralph Humphreys. Proved by the oath of Ralph Humphreys 18 Feb 1775. Recorded 17 May 1775.

R-4, 172-176: Lease & release. 15 & 16 Sept 1774, Caspar Suestrunk of Orangeburgh District, to Henry Patrick, Esqr., of the Congarees, for £1000 SC money, 300 acres on north side Santee River other Congaree River opposite Saxegotha Township, granted 10 Feb 1749 to Henry Fulkhard, adj. land granted to Henry Sistrunck, Casper Fust. Felix Smith, and said Henry Fulkard conveyed to Henry Suestrunk Senr, all said tract of land, and after the decease of said Henry Suestrunk Senr. became the property of Henry Suestrunk his son as heir by law, and by said Henry Sustrunk Junr. conveyed 150 acres 8 & 9 1773 to Casper Sustrunk. Gospar Sustrunk (LS), Wit: Peter Staley, John Golsan, Ulrick Ott. Proved by the oath of Peter Staley before Lewis Golsan, J. P. in Orangeburgh District, 19 Sept 1774. Recorded 19 May 1775.

R-4, 176-183: Lease & release. 2 & 3 Aug 1771, Susannah Hall & George Sheed of Charles Town, executrix and executor of the will of William Hall, late of Charles Town, carpenter, deceased, to Thomas Hall Junr., of same, gent., for £2500 SC money, whereas William Hall by his will dated 1 Apr 1768 did impower his executors to convey lands on New Church Street in Charles Town, lot number 37, now in the occupation of William Glenn, adj. land of Thomas Bee Esqr., attorney at

SOUTH CAROLINA DEED ABSTRACTS 1773-1778

law, and gateway on south side of said lot next to the west end of the house of tenement lately built by John Cooper and Mary his wife (now the property of said Thomas Bee)... so that the window shutters will not be obstructed from opening or shutting or that the light may not be stopped. Susannah Hall (LS), George Sheed (LS), Wit: Mark Morris, Chs. Feulon[?]. Proved 31 March 1775 before Thomas Turner, J. P., by the oath of Mark Morris. Recorded 20 May 1775.

R-4, 183-189: 15 Feb 1775, William Ancrum, George Ancrum, and William Hale, exrs. of the will of David Linn, late of Wandower in the Province of South Carolina, to Alexander McNilage of Christ Church Parish, SC, for £1410 SC money, 372 acres in Christ Church Parish on Wackindaw Creek adj. lands formerly belonging to Mr. Wilkes deceased but now or lately belonging to John Rose, John Rassnett but now Robert Wilson & Alexr. Chisolm, lands formerly belonging to Edward Croft deceased but now to John Mortimer Williams, Combraw Creek adj. lands formerly belonging to Peter Benoist or Paul Townshend, tract by lease and release 22 & 23 March 1759 conveyed by Robert Brewton of Charles Town to said David Linn, said David Linn by his will dated 29 Sept 1774 did direct his estate to be sold. George Ancrum (LS), Wm. Hale (LS), Wm. Ancrum (LS), Wit: Wm. Roach, Henry Troup. Proved by the oath of Henry Troup 1 Apr 1775 before John Troup, J.P. Recorded 22 May 1775.

R-4, 189-194: Lease & release. 23 & 24 March 1760, The Honourable John Cleland, Esqr., of Craven County, SC, to Archibald Baird of same place, esquire, for £150 SC money, 282 acres adj. on land of said John Cleland called Wehaw, adj. land granted to Anthony White, lands now William Shackelford, and sd. Archibald Baird, part of a larger tract granted to sd. John Cleland 17 Jan 1750 (plat included dated 9 Jan 1760 by Thomas Blythe, Dept. Surv.). John Cleland (LS), Wit: Robert Heriot, Wm. Simpson. Proved before Charles Fyffe, J. P. for Craven County, by the oath of Robert Heriot, 4 May 1767.

R-4, 194-201: Lease & release. 8 & 9 Feb 1775, Francis Yonge of St. Pauls Parish, Colleton County, planter, and Susannah his wife, to James Gilchrist Simpson of same parish, planter, for £5500 SC money, 281 acres near a certain ferry on Stono River in St. Pauls Parish, Colleton County, adj. Glebe lands commonly called Capers, adj. land belonging to the last Thomas Farr Esqr., deceased, Thomas fuller, Mathias Seller, which land formerly belonged to sd. Mathias Seller and conveyed 5 & 6 March 1770 to Francis Young. Francis Yonge (LS), Susannah Yonge (LS), Wit: Robert Williams Junr, John Postell. Proved in Chs. Town District by the oath of Robert Williams Junr. before William Rugeley, J. P., 14 Feb 1775. Recorded 24 May 1775.

R-4, 201-206: Lease & release. 28 & 29 Oct 1748, James Taylor in English Santee, Prince Fredericks Parish, Craven County, planter, and his wife Mary, to James Witherspoon of Williamsburgh Township, for £70 SC money, 150 acres adj. Roger Gibsons land. James Taylor (T) (LS), Mary Taylor (LS), Wit: Anthony Williams, David Witherspoon. Proved before Roger Gibson, J. P. in Craven County by the oath of David Witherspoon, 15 Jan 1756. Recorded 24 May 1775.

R-4, 206-207, 215-218: Lease & release. 4 & 5 Apr 1774, Gaspar Faust and his wife of Craven County, planter, to Henry Patrick, Esqr., of Saxegotha Township, Berkley County, merchant, for £80 SC money, 100 acres within the limits of Saxegotha Township adj. Santee or Congaree River, land laid out to Robert Lang, John Sandricur, said tract granted to Solomernier Aberlain who married one Daniel Ellis and by him conveyed to John Parson, and seized by Roger Pinckney then provost marshall of SC, and conveyed to Casper Faust, 30 Oct 1764. Gasper Foust (CT) (LS), wit: Harman Geiger, Joseph Haubigh. Proved 20 March 1775 by the oath of Harmon Giger before William Tucker, J.P. Recorded 24 May 1775.

R-4, 208-214: Lease & release. 15 & 16 March 1775, Alexander Burn of Charles Town, Shop keeper, to William Risk oat present of the same place, gent., for £3200 SC money, 300 acres on Edisto River in Colleton County adj. land laid out to John Robertson, Jane Jesseret, Christopher Dixon, Col. Jackson Smith, also a tract of 300 acres on waters of Saltcatchers, Colleton County, adj. Daniel Blake, Esqr., Joseph Perry, land laid out to James Berrie, John Irvin, Thomas Bee, Esqr., and tract of 500 acres on south side of Saltcatchers, and between Eleven and twelve miles form Edisto River in St. Bartholomews Parish, Colleton County, also 500 acres on waters of Saltcatcher in Colleton County, adj. Thos Bee, Esqr., John Roberts, James Atkins, and a lot in Parish of St. Philip, Charles Town, on east side of Broad path leading from Charles Town on Burns Alley, adj.

other parts of said lot formerly sold by Alexander Burn to Robert Hewie and Godfrey Bohner, adj. land of William Hopton, Esqr., Charles Burkmyer. Alexr Burn (LS), Wit: Andrew Thompson, Thos Gibbson. Proved in Chs. Town District by the oath of Andrew Thompson before Wm. Rugeley, J.P., 24 May 1775. Recorded 24 May 1775.

R-4, 218-224: Lease & release. 31 March & 1 Apr 1775, Thomas Hall Junr. of Charles Town, gentleman, to Mary Abel Allen Cripps of same, widow, for £3500 SC money, lot on east side of New Church Street in Charles Town, number 37. Thomas Hall Junr. (LS), Wit: Geo. Sheed, Saml. Gordon. Proved 1 Apr 1775 by the oath of George Sheed before Thomas Turner, J.P. Recorded 27 May 1775.

R-4, 224-229: Lease & release. 3 & 4 March 1775, James Reid of Charles Town, Esqr., to Darby Pendergrass of same, for £5000 SC money, lot on eastern side of the High Road on Charles Town Neck in the Village of Ansonborough, Parish of St. Philip, adj. lot conveyed by Jonathan Badger unto Timothy Crosby, which lot was sold by said Jonathan Badger and Mary his wife. James Reid (LS), Wit: John Walker, Thos. Winstanley. Proved in Chs. Town District by the oath of Thos. Winstanley 27 May 1775 before William Rugeley, J.P. Recorded 29 May 1775.

R-4, 230-233: Lease & release. 25 & 26 Apr 1773, Joseph Milligan of St. Mathews Parish ,planter, to Edmund Godfrey Cossens of St. Marks Parish, planter, for £1500 SC money, 300 acres on southwest side of Santee granted 16 Dec 1738 adj. land laid out to William Loe, Christian Gottlieb Gruber, Freeman Snellgrove, Miles Jackson. Joseph Milligan Wit: George Gossling, Charles McCord. Proved 18 May 1774 before Malcom Clarke, J.P. in Orangeburgh District, by the oath of George Gossling. Recorded 30 May 1775.

R-4, 234-239: 14 March 1775, Mathew Drake, late of Waccamaw in Craven county, but now or late of the City of Exeter in England, Gilbert Neyle of said city of Exeter, merchant, Robert Collier of Jopsham in County of Devon merchant, and James Collins of the city of Exeter, by Sampson Neyle of Charles Town, South Carolina, merchant, their attorney, for £2000 SC money, land known as Canteys containing 552 acres in Prince Fredericks Parish, Craven County, on north side of Santee River on Canteys Creek adj. land of Master John Tunis (Junes?), which consists of two tracts one of 352 acres granted to Elizabeth Palmer and 200 acres granted & sold by Landgrave Thomas Smith to William Waites. Mathew Drake (LS), Gilbert Neyle (LS), Robt Collier (LS), James Collins (LS) by Sampson Neyle. Wit: Christ'r Gadsden, Chs. Pinckney. Proved before Wm. Maxwell, Esqr., J. P. for Chas. Town District by the oath of Chris. Gadsden, 11 Apr 1775. Recorded 31 May 1775.

R-4, 239-243: Lease & release. 14 & 15 Dec 1767, Isaac Godin of Parish of St. James Goose Creek, Berkley County, SC, Esqr., to Peter Manigault of Charles Town, Barrister at Law, for £500 SC money, tract in Parish of St. James Goose Creek, 101 acres, adj. land formerly of John Sanders but now of Alexander Fraser, land on a creek which leads out of Goose Creek, adj. part of same tract formerly sold by Isaac Godin to Peter Manigault. Isaac Godin (LS), Wit: John Parker, John Cross. Proved in Chs. Town District 29 Apr 1775 before Wm. Rugeley by the oath of John Parker. Recorded 1 June 1775.

R-4, 244-249: Lease & release. 5 & 6 Nov 1767, William Drayton of Parish of St. Andrew, Berkley County, SC, Esquire, to Peter Manigault of Charles Town, esquire, for £318 SC money, 106 acres on north side Ashley River in Berkley County adj.lands heretofore of George Cantey and William Cantey his son, James Dunnoha, James Flacks, John Cantey, Thomas Barker[?], Capt. James Cantey. Wm. Drayton (LS), Wit: John Huger, Chs. Motte. Proved 12 Nov 1767 before Jacob Mote, J. P., by the oath of Charles Motte. Recorded 1 June 1775.

R-4, 250-253: Lease & release. 23 & 24 March 1758, William Bee of James Island, planter, and Rachel his wife, to Peter Manigault of Charles Town, Barrister at Law, for £200 SC money, part of lot number 166 in Charles Town upon the street that lads from the new church, adj. land purchased by Peter Manigault of David Brown, land purchased by said Peter Manigault of said William Bell and Mary Bell his sister. Wm. Bee (LS), Rachel Bee (LS), Wit: Hugh Anderson, Wm. Jeanes Salmon, Ann Anderson. Proved in Chs. Town District before Peter Bounetheau, J. P., by the oath of Ann Bounetheau, the last subscribing witness to the within deed by her maiden name Ann Anderson, 11 Apr 1775.

SOUTH CAROLINA DEED ABSTRACTS 1773-1778

R-4, 254-260: Lease & release. 5 & 6 March 1775, Richard Hutson of Charles Town, Esqr., Alexander Wright of same place, esqr., for £50,000 SC money, 1935 acres on Combahee adj. land land of col. Daniel Heyward, John Gibbes, granted 15 Sept 1705 to John Palmer and these tracts became vested in Mary Hutson (now deceased) late Mary Chardin and heretofore Mary Woodward daughter and devisee of Richard Woodward deceased, and on the death of Mary Hutson descended to Richard Hutson. Rich'd Hutson (LS), Wit: Joseph Cox, Martha Morris, John Tucker. Proved 17 Apr 1774 before Richard Lambton, Esqr., by the oath of Joseph Cox. Recorded 3 June 1775.

R-4, 261-264: Lease & release. 16 & 17 Dec 1774, Jacob Fulmore of Orangeburgh District, planter, to William Ballantine of same, hatter, for £30 SC money, 100 acres granted 25 May 1774 to Jacob Fulmore, on waters of Broad River in Craven County adj. Michael Lowrick. Jacob Fulmore (LS), Wit: John Ewing, Wm Currie. Recorded 6 June 1775.

R-4, 265-269: Lease & release. 13 Sept 1748, Patrick Brown of SC, gent., to Martin Fridig of Saxegotha Township, for £200 SC money, 100 acres in the limits of Saxegotha Township in Berkley County on Santee River adj. land laid out to John Coleman, Hans Sporg, adj. common and part of the glebe land. Patrick Brown (LS), Wit: John McCord, Edmund Poythress. Charles McCord son of John McCord made oath to the hand writing of said John McCord, 4 March 1773, before John Savage, J.P. Recorded 9 June 1775.

R-4, 270-273: Lease & release. 19 & 20 Feb 1775, Thomas Port of Prince Fredericks Parish, planter, to Ebenezer Dunnam of Prince Georges Parish, planter, for £20 SC money, 36 acres on north side Pedee river in Queensborough Township, granted to Thomas Port 20 Dec 1762 adj. land of sd. Thomas Port, John Goodwin, Archibald Johnston. Thos Port (LS), Wit: Hugh Giles, Sarah Giles, Ann Mikell. Recorded 9 June 1775.

R-4, 274-275: 20 May 1771, Thomas McManus of St. Davids Parish, Craven County, planter, to Peter Arand of same, for £250 SC money, 466 acres on north side Lynches Creek surveyed to Capt. James McManus, 100 acres of said tract. Thomas McManus (LS), Wit: Peter Beller, John Mulcaster. Proved by the oath of Peter Beller 3 Oct 1771 before Thomas Wade, J.P.

R-4, 276-277: 6 June 1774, Peter Arand of St. Davids Parish, to Robert Anderson of same, for £400 SC money, 466 acres on north side Lynches Creek surveyed to Capt. James McManus, 100 acres of said tract. Peter Arran (LS), Wit: Edward Crawford, James Rich. Proved in Cheraw District by the oath of Edward Crawford 21 Oct 1774 before Chs. Augs. Steward. Recorded 10 June 1775.

R-4, 277-278: Lease. 15 Oct 1774, 15 Oct 1774, Edward Crawford of St. Davids Parish in Craven County, planter, to John Mitchell of same, for ten shillings, 100 acres on north side Linches Creek, part of a tract of land surveyed for Capt. James McManus for 466 acres. Edward Crawford (LS), Wit; Alexander Crawford, John Shumake. Proved in Cheraw District before Charles Augt. Steward by the oath of Alexander Crawford, 21 Oct 1774. Recorded 10 June 1775.

R-4, 279-282: Lease & release. 16 & 17 March 1764, John Ragnous of Berkley County, planter, to Jacob Terrick of same, planter, for £25 SC money, 75 acres, part of tract granted to John Ragnous 8 March 1763 on High Hill Creek one of the northern branches of Saludy River adj. Thomas Smith. John Ragnous (LS), Wit: John Terrick (O). Recorded 10 June 1775.

R-4, 283-292: Lease & mortgage. 20 & 21 May 1773, John Burn of Charles Town, merchant, but now of London, to John Mayne, of London, merchant, whereas this day John Mayne and John Burn have settled accounts, for securing the Repayment of £3000, lot on the Bay at Charles Town with two wharfs at Charles Town being nearly opposite to said tenement and storehouse, were heretofore of the estate of Charles Mayne deceased which the said John Burn purchased after the deceased of the said Charles Mayne. John Burn (LS), Wit: Daniel Sill, Henry Jackson. Proved before John Wilkes, Lord Mayor of the City of London, by the oath of Daniel Sill, 9 March 1775. Recorded 12 June 1775.

R-4, 292-298: Lease & release. 3 & 4 May 1775, William Brown of Granville County on or near Savannah River, SC, planter, to Elias Robert of same, planter, for £80 SC money, 350 acres adj. Brailsford, William Hext, Edward Wilkinson, Stephen Bull Esqr. William Brown (LS), Wit: Bartlett

Brown, John Audebert, Robt. Stafford. Proved before John Chisolm, J.P. in Granville County, by the oath of John Audebert, 5 May 1775. Recorded 14 June 1775.

R-4, 298-302: 29 Jan 1774, Hugh Thompson of Craven County, SC, planter, to Thomas Lide of same, planter, for £300 SC money, 150 acres in Craven County on northeast side of Pee Dee River adj. William Bell. Hugh Thompson (LS), Wit: Eliz'h Waring, Sarah Foster (X). Proved before Charles Augt. Steward by the oath of Elizabeth Waring 23 March 1775. Recorded 14 June 1775.

R-4, 302-306: 20 Jan 1774, Peter Pye of Charles Town, planter, to Hugh Thompson of Craven County, planter, for £20 SC money, 150 acres in Craven County on northeast side of Pee Dee River adj. William Bell. Peter Pye (LS), Wit: Peter Kolb, Robert Thompson. Proved in Chs. Town District by the oath of Peter Kolb before Arthur Hart, J. P., 23 March 1774. Recorded 16 June 1775.

R-4, 306-310: 19 Sept 1772, Samuel Legare of Charles Town, Gent., to William Gibbes of same, for £2000 SC money, lot on the White Point in Charles Town part of the lands lately walled & filled in jointly by Robt McKenzie, Edward Blake, George Kincade, and said William Gibbes (as tenants in common), on Ashley River on South Bay Street. Saml Legare (LS), Wit: John Berwick, Chs. Johnston. Proved 4 Apr 1775 before John Mitchell, J.P., by the oath of John Berwick. Recorded 17 June 1775.

R-4, 311-315: Lease & release. 27 & 28 Sept 1771, James Ferrell and Mary [one place states Margaret] his wife of SC to John Spann of same province, for £200 SC money, 200 acres in Colleton County on Redbank Creek granted 5 March 1770 to Mary Ferral, and said Mary Ferral did inter into an estate of Holy Matrimony with above James Ferrall. James Ferrel (LS), Mary Ferel (LS), Wit: Wm. Spann, Daniel Burnet, John Burnet. Proved in Colleton County before john Fairchild, J.P., by the oath of William Spann, 6 April 1772. Recorded 17 June 1775.

R-4, 315-319: Lease & release. 13 & 14 Aug 1772, James Robinson and Hannah his wife of Long Cane Settlement, SC, to Jaston Hatcher of same settlement, for £100 SC money, 100 acres in the Long Canes Settlement near Piney Creek a branch of the northwest fork of Long Canes adj. Wm. Alexander, granted 15 March 1771 to James Robinson. James Robinson (LS), Hanah Robinson (H), Wit: Moses Edmondeston, Chs. Hay. Proved 17 Aug 1772 before Alexander Cameron, J.P. in Granville County, by the oath of Moses Edmondeston. Recorded 17 June 1775.

R-4, 319-323: Lease & release. 3 & 4 June 1772, Joseph Turner of Parish of St. Bartholomew, Yeoman, to John Bowie of same, esquire, for £20 SC money, 100 acres in St. Pauls Parish on Saludy River granted 2 March 1768 to John Turner. Joseph Turner (LS), Wit: Joseph Coil, Henry Weems. Proved 20 Dec 1774 before Andrew Rapley, J. P., in Ninety Six District by the oath of Henry Weems. Recorded 26 June 1775.

R-4, 324-327: Lease & release. 13 & 14 Sept 1774, Elias Gibson of Ninety Six District to Andrew Williamson of same, for £225 SC money, 100 acres in Granville County on waters of Hard Labour Creek adj. Samuel Gibson, John Bell, granted 21 May 1772 to Elias Gibson. Elias Gibson (LS), Wit: Tim Parker, William Coffey. Proved in Ninety Six District 22 Oct 1774 by the oath of Tim Parker before John Bowie, J.P. Recorded 27 June 1775.

R-4, 327-333: Lease & release. 8 & 9 May 1775, Abraham Shecutt of Town of Beaufort in Beaufort District, SC, Bricklayer, and Mary his wife, to Thos Brooks of same town, ship carpenter, for £300 SC money, tow lot in Beaufort granted to Jonathan Bryan 4 May 1745, conveyed 25 & 26 Aug 1773 to Daniel Desaussure, and Daniel Desaussure 29 & 30 Aug 1773 to Abraham Shecutt. Abrah'm Shecutt (LS), Mary Shecutt (LS), Wit: John Iklar, Ann Iten. Proved 16 May 1775 before Andrew Aggnew, J.P. in Beaufort District, by the oath of John Iklar. Recorded 28 June 1775.

R-4, 333-340: Lease & release. 9 & 10 March 1775, Francis Goddard of Prince Fredericks Parish, Craven County, planter, to Plowden Weston of Charles Town, merchant, for £1200 SC money, 450 acres on east side Waccamaw River in Parish of Prince George Winyaw, known by the name of Lorill Hill adj. land of Capt. John Murell, on the old road to the Sand Hills, land late of Isaac Marion but now of Gabriel Marion, to a barony of Gabriel Marion called Rice Hope; one other tract 250 acres with a small island called Dwights Island, being a tract of swamp land on west side

SOUTH CAROLINA DEED ABSTRACTS 1773-1778

Waccamaw adj. Mr. Broughtons, Wm. Vereens Senr and Junr, when the whole was in the possession of James Coachman, given in a deed of gift by James Coachman to Wm. Vereen Junr, above Capt. Murrells house. Francis Goddard (LS), Wit: John Lord, Jos. Ward. Proved by the oath of Joshua Ward 10 March 1775 before Robert Philp, J.P. Recorded 3 July 1775.

R-4, 340-348: Lease & mortgage. 4 & 5 Apr 1775, Henry Clark and Jonah Clark of Craven county, SC, planters, to Joseph Allston of sd. province, esqr., by bond in the penal sum of £10,000 SC money, 500 acres in Craven County on Peedee River adj. land of Joseph Yates, on Red Bluff, granted 20 May 1747 to John Malden, also tract of 100 acres on northeast side of Santee River adj. land granted to John Malden, granted 20 Oct 1766, and 47 acres, [adj. land?] granted to John Malden late Thomas Burton, Col. George Pawleys, granted 27 Nov 1770 to James Mikell. Henry Clark (LS), Jonah Clark (LS), Wit: Thos Labruce, William Waties. Proved in Geo Town District before Saml Dwight, J.P., 9 May 1775 by the oath of Thos. Labruce. Recorded 6 July 1775.

R-4, 349-353: Lease & release. 9 & 10 Nov 1774, Goodridge Hughs of Colleton County, St. Pauls Parish, Ninety Six District, to Plowden Weston of Charles Town, merchant, for £500 SC money, 150 acres granted to Goodridge Hughes 26 Oct 1769 on West Creek. Goodridge Hughs (LS), Wit: William Norris, John Frederick, John Johnston. Proved in Ninety Six District before John Fairchild, J.P., 24 Dec 1774 by the oath of Wm. Norris. Recorded 8 July 1775.

R-4, 354-358: Lease & release. 6 June 1770, Wm. West and Mary his wife, to Wm. Norris, both parties of Little Saluda & the branches thereof, for £200 SC money, tract granted 13 Oct 1759 to Wm. West, 250 acres in Berkley County on a branch of Little Saluda River near joyning to land then held by Conrad Kincler. Wm. West (LS), Mary West (X) (LS), Wit: Nathan Melton, Jean Carson, Richard Williams. Proved in Colleton County before John Fairchild by the oath of Richd. Williams, 30 Nov 1770. Recorded 9 July 1775.

R-4, 358-365: Lease & release. 8 & 9 Feb 1775, James Gilchrist Simpson of St. Pauls Parish, Colleton County, planter, and Sarah his wife, to Francis Young of same, planter, for £5500 SC money, 400 acres on west side of Wadmalaw River in Colleton County, St. Pauls Parish, part of larger tract of 640 acres granted 13 Aug 1695 to Thoms. Smith, adj. land of Isaac Lesesne. (plat included) James Gilchrist Simpson (LS), Sarah Simpson (LS), Wit: Robert Williams Junr, John Postell. Proved in Chas. Town District before William Rugeley, J. p., 14 Feb 1775 by the oath of Robert Williams Junr. Recorded 15 July 1775.

R-4, 365-372: Lease & release. 13 & 14 March 1775, Christian Ridlesparger of Parish of St. Georges, SC, planter, and Elizabeth his wife, to Thomas Young of Charles Town, Bricklayer, for £575 SC money, 250 acres a half part of tract of 500 acres granted to Abraham Dupont in St. Georges Parish adj. land of Thomas Young, also 140 acres adj. said 250 acres. (plat included, being a resurvey showing adj. land owners Gasper Strouble, Thomas Young, Abraham Dupont, Gideon Dupont, certified 28 Feb 1775.) Christian Riddlesparger (CR) (LS), Elizabeth Ridlesparger (LS), Wit: John Frank, John Fullerton. Proved in Chas. Town District before William Rugeley, J. p., by the oath of John Fullerton. Recorded 18 July 1775.

R-4, 372-376: Lease & release. 15 & 16 Oct 1772, John Ward of Berkly County, SC, merchant, to John Milhous of same, for £10 SC money, 500 acres in Colleton County on a branch of Saltcatcher Swamp called Lemon's Swamp, granted 15 May 1772 to John Ward, adj. land of Thos Ferguson, Charles Elliott. John Ward (LS), Wit: Anudn. St. John, Mary St. John, John Cole. Proved before Will Swinton, J. P. for Colleton County, by the oath of John Cole, 3 Nov 1772. Recorded 27 July 1775.

R-4, 377-381: 10 May 1774, John Potts of Craven County, Sc, planter, to Thomas Potts of same, planter, for £1500 SC money, 250 acres in Craven County on south side Peedee River in township of Queensborough, adj. land of Robert Findley, Thomas Potts, also a tract of 200 acres in Craven county on north east side Peedee River adj. lands set apart for the use of the Township of Queensborough adj. Peedee River, Catfish Creek, lands of William Dewitts, said Thomas Potts. John Potts (LS), Wit; Alexander Swinton, Sampson Baker. Proved 2 Sept 1774 before Francis Britton, J.P. for Craven County, by the oath of Alexander Swinton. Recorded 28 July 1775.

SOUTH CAROLINA DEED ABSTRACTS 1773-1778

R-4, 381-386: Lease & release. 6 & 7 Nov 1774, David Melson and wife Annar of Granville County, Sc, to John Pussell of same, planter, for £200 SC money, 400 acres in Granville County granted to David Melson 28 Nov 1771 on Horns Creek adj. land of Thomas Roberts Junr, William Stringer, Thomas Roberts Senr, John Pursell, Andrew Mock. David Melson (X) (LS), Wit: Anner Melson (+) (LS), Wit: Lott Warren, Thomas Roberts. Proved in Ninety Six District 4 Feb 1775 before LeRoy Hammond, J.P., by the oath of Lott Warren. Recorded 2 Aug 1775.

R-4, 387-389: John Eberly of Charlestown, SC, cordwainer, bound to Philip Meyer of Charles Town, Sugar Baker, in the penal sum of £3000, said John Eberly by bond 1 March 1774 bound to Mary Ellis of Charlestown, widow, in the sum of £3000 for the payment of £1500, mortgage of lot in Charlestown, #207, on Cross Street, adj. land formerly of Joseph Ward now of Mary Lochon, land formerly belonging to the heirs of Sarah Trott but now to __ Ancrum, Guignards Street. John Eberly (LS), Wit: Wm. Rugeley, Richd Hutson, Abraham Becu. Proved in Charles Town District by the oath of Abraham Becu before Row'd Rugeley, 4 Aug 1775. Recorded 5 Aug 1775. Mortgage satisfied 3 Dec 1777.

R-4, 390-394: 2 Nov 1774, Thomas Eustace & his wife to James Mortimer Harris and Charles Harris of Charles Town, for £37 s13 d 9 SC money, 200 acres in St. Marks Parish, adj. land granted to James Higgs, land survd. for Charles Harris, granted 30 Sept 1774. Thos Eustace (LS), Susannah Eustace (+) (LS), Wit: Dn. Mazyck, Elias Evans. Proved 3 June 1775 before Ephraim Mitchell, J.P., by the oath of Elias Evans. Recorded 9 Aug 1775.

R-4, 394-397: 5 May 1772, the Rev. James Edmonds of Prov. of SC, Clerk, and Sarah his wife, to David Maull of Charles Town, Taylor, for £1500 SC money, house and part of a town lot in Charles Town, adj. land heretofore of George Heskett deceased heirs or devisees, land lately of one John Rattray deceased. James Edmonds (LS), Sarah Edmonds (LS), Wit: John Scott, john Scott Junr. Proved in Charles Town District by the oath of John Scot Senior before Geo. Davidson, J. P., 9 June 1775. Recorded 11 Aug 1775.

R-4, 398-400: Thomas Douglass of Township of Salisbury, County of Lancaster, Province of Pennsylvania, being seized of two sundry tracts at Pinetree, County of Craven, Colony of South Carolina, one of them 300 acres the other 150 acres, now appoints Simon Berwick and John Berwick, both of Charles Town, my lawful attorney, to lease or demise the said tracts... 8 April 1775. Thos Douglass (LS), Wit: Wm. Having, George Oliver. Proved in Charles Town District by the oath of George Oliver, 2 May 1775, before Fenwicke Bull, J.P. Recorded 12 Aug 1775.

R-4, 400-404: South Carolina. 15 Dec 1774, Julian Gilbert of Province aforesaid, spinster, to Elizabeth Sness, late the widow of Conrad Snees, of province aforesaid, for £100 SC money, 100 acres in the fork of Saltcatchers in Colleton County adj. land laid out to Ann Gilbert, granted on his Majesties Bounty to said Julian Gilbert. Julian Gilbert (X) (LS), Wit: Em'a Abrahams, Samuel Jones. Proved by the oath of Emanuel Abrahams after the manner of his professed religion in Charles Town District 19 Dec 1774 before Thomas Turner, J.P. Recorded 17 Aug 1775.

R-4, 404-406: Lease & release. 6 & 7 Nov 1763, Wm. Alexander of Mecklenburgh County, North Carolina, to Richard Robinson of same, for £20 SC money, 200 acres in Granville County on the waters of Northwest Fork of Long Cane Creek waters of Savannah River. William Alexander (LS), Rebeckah Alexander (R) (LS). Made over before me, James Wyly, J.P. Recorded 17 Aug 1775.

R-4, 407-408: 17 Feb 1775, William Jackson of Province of Georgia, Parish of St. Paul, to David Thweatt of Province of South Carolina, Ninety Six District, for £100 SC money, 200 acres granted John Perkins on Stephens Creek in Granville County, SC, adj. Nolloboys, said 200 acres conveyed by John Perkins to John Lamar and by said Lamar to George Rodgers, and by sd. Rodgers to said William Jackson. William Jackson (LS), Wit: Jno Walton, William Glascock, Thomas Glascock. Proved in Ninety Six District 7 Apr 1775 before Leroy Hammond, J. P., by the oath of William Glascock. Recorded 22 Aug 1775.

R-4, 409-410: 15 Oct 1772, George Rodgers of Granville County, SC, planter, to William Jackson of County of Amelia, Colony of Virginia, for £700 SC money, 200 acres granted John Perkins on Stephens Creek in Granville County, SC, James adj. Nolloboys, said 200 acres conveyed by John

SOUTH CAROLINA DEED ABSTRACTS 1773-1778

Perkins to John Lamar and by said Lamar to George Rodgers. George Rodgers (LS), Wit: Jere White, Charles Smith, Solomon Newsum. Proved in Granville County 15 Oct 1772 before Leroy Hammond, J. P., by the oath of Solomon Newsum. Recorded 23 Aug 1775.

R-4, 411-414: Lease & release. 19 & 20 May 1775, Thomas Landtrip of District of Ninety Six, & Hannah his wife, to Thomas Holden, for £70 SC money, 100 acres granted to Thomas Landtrip 9 Sept 1775 on north side Tyger River in said district adj. land of William Curry, Aron Fincher, David Farmer. Thomas Landtrip (X) (LS), Wit: Ralph Smith, Thos Compton. Proved in Ninety Six District by the oath of Thomas Compton before Ralph Smith, J.P., 6 June 1775. Recorded 24 Aug 1775.

R-4, 415-419: Lease & release. 15 & 16 Feb 1774, Drury Spillock and Comfort his wife, of Craven County, SC, to Robert Bowman of same, for £300 SC money, 250 acres in Craven County on Sammy's[?] Branch of Black River. Drury Spillock (D) (LS), Comfort Spillock (C) (LS), Wit: Robert Spullock, James Bowman. Proved in Craven County by the oath of James bowman before J. M. Harris, J. P. Recorded 29 Aug 1775.

R-4, 419-422: 9 Nov 1769, Roger Pinckney, Provost Marshall of SC, to Gersham Kelley, whereas Vincent Hurlock of St. Mathews Parish, planter, was seized of a tract of 150 acres on Santee River adj. Martin, Wm. Killingsworth, and said Hurloch by bond to John Caldwell, merchant, 13 June[?] 1765, in the sum of £165 for the payment of £132 s 10 with interest, and said John Caldwell in the court of common pleas did implead and recovered judgment... sold for £96 currency. Roger Pinckney Prs. Mar. (LS), Wit: Hopson Pinckney, John Martin.

R-4, 423-429: Lease & release. 1 & 2 Jan 1774, Parker Quince, Esqr., and Susannah his wife, of Brunswick County, North Carolina, to Mr. Philotheos Chifelle of Charles Town, merchant, for £20,500 SC money, lot in Charles Town on old Church Street, adj. lands now belonging to John Ancrum & Mary his wife, adj. part of sd. lot lately sold by Parker Quince and Susannah his wife to Jonathan Sarazin, by deed of partition between Parker Quince and Susannah his wife and John Ancrum and Mary his wife, lot number 2; also lot in Charles Town number 6 in Charles Town. Parker Quince (LS), Susannah Quince (LS), Wit: Saml Dwight, Wm. Lord. Proved in Chs. Town District before John Troup, J. P., by the oath of Saml. Dwight, 2 June 1775. Recorded 4 Sept 1775.

R-4, 430-438: Letter of attorney. By lease and release 23 Feb 1774, Joseph Salvador late of Lime Street, London, but then of Parish of St. James Westminster in the County of Middlesex, Esqr., said Rebecca Mendes Da Costa of second part, and David Grame of Chas. Town in American, Esqr., and John Lewis Jervis of Charles Town, of the third part, now appoint Francis Salvador of "Cornacre" in said Province, planter, attorney, and in his death or absence said David Grame. Rebecca Mendes DaCosta (LS), Wit: Ephraim de Agiular, Jona'n Thompson. Proved by the oath of Jonathan Thompson of Broad Street, Gentleman, 14 March 1775 at Gildhall before John Wilkes, Mayor. Recorded 6 Sept 1775.

R-4, 438-443: Lease & release. 28 & 29 Jan 1774, Josiah Murdaugh of Georgia, planter, to Miles Reiley of Prince Wms. Parish, SC, for £___ SC money, 1000 acres on waters of Saltcatcher adj. land surveyed of John Miller. Josiah Murdaugh (LS), Wit; Wm. Creek, Gid'n Allen. Proved 23 June 1775 before Isham Clayton, J. P. for the District of Orangeburgh by the oath of Wm. Creek. Recorded 9 Sept 1775.

R-4, 443-448: 27 June 1775, Clement Lempriere of Wandow, SC, planter, to Wm. Ancrum, Wm. Hale, and George Ancrum, executors of the will of David Linn, late of same place, by bond bearing even date with these presents, in the penal sum of £200 SC money for the payment of £11,000 like money, tract of 50 acres on north side of Wackindaw Creek in Christ Church Parish, adj. land formerly belonging to Edward Crofts but now belonging to John Mortimer Williams, A
Andrew Quelch but now the estate of sd. David Linn, land formerly belonging to Wm. Vier[?] but now to John Mortimer Williams and partly on marsh, also tract of 50 acres adj. the other tract on north side Wackindaw Creek on Wando River. Clement Lempriere (LS), Wit: Henry Troup, Wm. Roach. Proved by the oath of Henry Troup before John Troup, 27 June 1775. Recorded 11 Sept 1775.

SOUTH CAROLINA DEED ABSTRACTS 1773-1778

R-4, 448-450: Edward Barnard of St. Pauls Parish, Province of Georgia, bound to George Galphin, Esqr., of South Carolina, in the penal sum of £1200 SC money for the payment of £600 before 1 June 1769, tract of £250 acres on Savanah River opposite Augusta, originally granted to Jas. Fraser decd. as also tract of land of 250 acres granted to John Shakespear adj. said tract, and 100 acres granted Webber adj. the above second tract and land granted to James Parsons... dated 25 June 1769. Edward Barnard (LS), Wit: Henry Young, Wm. Barnard. Proved by the oath of Henry Younge Junr, before John Sinkler, 25 March 1769. Recorded 12 Sept 1775.

R-4, 450-456: Lease & release. 20 & 21 Sept 1773, Rev. Robert Smith and Alexr. Gillon of Charles Town, executors of the will of Richd. Beresford, late of sd. town, deceased, to Henry Reeves of same, merchant, for £7500 SC money, whereas Richd Beresford was seized of tracts of 530 acres, 100 acres, and 180 acres in Berkley County in Christ Church Parish, band 8 July 1772 made his will in which he appointed his wife Sarah, Robert Smith and Alexr. Gillon with Christopher Gadsden, Thomas Smith of Broad Street, and his sons when they attained the age of 21 years, exrs. Robert Smith (LS), Alexr. Gillon (LS), Wit: Peter Butler, Peter Mettrsel. Recorded 14 Sept 1775.

R-4, 456-458: 26 May 1775, Andrew Leitch, Esqr., of Parish of St. Paul, planter, to Catharine Spooler of same, by an act of General Assembly 25 Oct 1762 impowered nine commissioners Robert Williams, James Stanyard, Charles Elliott, Benjn Shingleton, Saml Elliot, Francis younge, Archd. Stanyarne, Thos Hartly & Thomas Ferguson, to sell pews in the new church in St. Pauls Parish, Colleton County, and for £80 did sell to Andrew Leitch, Esqr., pew number 38, now for £100 SC money to Catherine Spooler. Andw. Leitch (LS), Wit: Philip Spooler, Margaret Spooler, Henry Bursell. Proved by the oath of Phillip Spooler and Henry Bursell before Robt. Williams, J. P., 25 June 1775. Recorded 14 Sept 1775.

R-4, 458-459: 26 May 1775, Mrs. Catharine Spooler, planter, of Parish of St. Paul, planter, to Andrew Leitch of same, by an act of General Assembly 25 Oct 1762 impowered nine commissioners Robert Williams, James Stanyard, Charles Elliott, Benjn Shingleton, Saml Elliot, Francis younge, Archd. Stanyarne, Thos Hartly & Thomas Ferguson, to sell pews in the new church in St. Pauls Parish, Colleton County, and for £80 did sell to Andrew Leitch, Esqr., pew number 47, now for £100 SC money to Catherine Spooler. Catharine Spooler (CS) (LS), Wit: Philip Spooler, Margaret Spooler, Henry Bursell. Proved by the oath of Phillip Spooler and Henry Bursell before Robt. Williams, J. P., 23 June 1775. Recorded 15 Sept 1775.

R-4, 460-464: Lease & mortgage. 21 & 22 June 1775, Thos Roberts of Jacksonburgh, Parish of St. Bartholomews, SC, and Isabella his wife, to John Logan exor. to the estate of George Logan, decd., said Thos Roberts by bond in the sum of £1866 SC money for the payment of £933, tract in St. Bartholomews Parish on west side of Pon Pon River by a late survey 500 acres adj. Dedcott, Joseph Kelly. Thos Roberts (LS), Wit: Thos Shepheard, Saml Riley. Proved in Chs. Town District by the oath of Charles Shepheard before William Rugeley, J.P., 8 July 1775. Recorded 19 Sept 1775.

R-4, 464-466: Lease & release. South Carolina. 25 & 26 May 1775, David Raymond of province aforesaid, to John OHear of St. Peters Parish, for £80 SC money, lot in town of Purisburgh, St. Peters Parish, number 43 granted to Mr. Joseph Raymond 2 Feb 1735 adj. John Rodolph Netmons, Abraham Meurons lott. David Raymond (LS), Wit: Denham Faris, Peter Francis Greneire, Constantyne Bambasine. Proved by the oath of Constantyne Bambozine in Granville County 26 May 1775 before David Ramond, J.P. Recorded 19 Sept 1775.

R-4, 466-472: Lease & release. 12 & 13 July 1775, John Kelly of Charles Town, and Mary his wife, to Thos Shirley and william Price of same, merchant, for £350 SC money, lot on west side of King St. adj. land of Harris, Richard Beresford Esqr., decd. John Kelly (LS), Mary Kelly (/) (LS), Wit: Elisha Sawyer, Saml Hrabowsky. Proved before Fenwicke Bull, J.P., by the oath of Elisha Sawyer 14 Sept 1775. Recorded 22 Sept 1775.

R-4, 472-473: Thos James of Cheraw District, planter, bond to make title to 250 acres on north east side Little River, Colhons Creek, survey by Robt Edwards in 1758, the refusal shall pay the sum of £2000 SC money, 27 Jan 1774, to be paid to Joseph Johnson. Thomas James (LS), Wit: Richard Brooks, Joseph Allen. Proved in Geo. Town District by the oath of Richd. Brooks before Wm. Mayson, J. P., 25 March 1775. Recorded 23 Sept 1775.

SOUTH CAROLINA DEED ABSTRACTS 1773-1778

R-4, 475-477: Lease & release. 13 & 14 Feb 1775, Michl. Bouyer alias Pyer of Orangeburg District, planter, to William Currie & Evan McLaurin of same, merchants, for £100 SC money, 50 acres, part of 150 acres in the fork of Broad & Saluda River in Craven County on so side of Broad River on a branch of the wateree Creek granted to Michl. Pyer, adj. Christian Rauster. Mich Buyer alias Pyer (MB) (LS), Wit: Peter Coon, John Ewing, John Prent. Proved in Orangeburgh District by the oath of John Ewing before William Houseal, 1 Aug 1775. Recorded 25 Sept 1775.

R-4, 477-480: Lease & release. 15 & 16 May 1775, James Simpson of Charles Town, Esqr., to James Mayson of Ninety Six District, esqr., for £20 SC money, 100 acres in Craven county on a branch of Wms. Creek bounded east by Bounty land, adj. land called Gestas land, granted to Daniel Heyward and conveyed to James Simpson. Jams. Simpson (LS), Wit: Philip Henry, Thos Gibbson. Proved in Chs. Town District by the oath of Philip Henry 14 Aug 1775 before Rowland Rugeley. Recorded 25 Sept 1775.

R-4, 480-485: Lease & release. 26 & 27 May 1775, Allen Miles of St. Pauls Parish, Colleton County, to Richard Walter of St. Georges Parish, for £1770 SC money, 120 acres on a swamp called the Cypress Swamp in St. Georges Parish, Berkley County, adj. Daniel Blake, Edward Perry, John Glaze, Benjamin Coachman, David Kittleband. Allen Miles (LS), Wit: Edward Perry, Robert Miles. Proved 27 May 1775 before John Matthews by the oath of Edward Perry. Recorded 27 Sept 1775.

R-4, 485-491: Lease & release. 5 & 6 Apr 1772, James Petigrew, House Carpenter, and Elizabeth his wife, of Colleton County, to George Forest, planter, of same, for £400 SC money, two tracts of land each out of a 350 acre grant to Robert McCutchen; a tract of 250 acres on a small branch known as Beaver Creek which runs into Ninety Six miles Creek granted to Robert McCutchen 13 July 1762 and 100 acres of sd. land being sold by lease and release to Heard 26 Apr 1768 by Robert Maccutchen adj. land of Wm. Robinson, robert McCutchen, also 100 acres sold out of the above 350 acres grant to sd. McCutchin to sd. Thos Heard 24 Dec 1768 adj. Mary Smith. James Petigrew (LS), Elizth Petigrew (LS), Wit: Daniel Bailey, John Wms. S. D., Joseph Linsey. Proved 4 Aug 1772 before Robt. Cunningham, J. P. in Ninety Six District by the oath of John Williams. Recorded 2 Oct 1775.

R-4, 492-497: Lease & release. 29 & 30 May 1775, James Mayson of Ninety Six District, Esqr., to Philip Henry of Charles Town, for £660 SC money, 100 acres in Craven county on a branch of Wms. Creek bounded east by Bounty land, adj. land called Gestas land, granted to Daniel Heyward and conveyed to James Simpson and then to James Mayson; also 400 acres in the fork of Tyger River, on the middle fork and south fork adj. land of Wm. Sharp, granted to James Mayson. James Mayson (LS), Wit: Lewis Ogier, James Wakefield. Proved 5 Aug 1775 by the oath of James Wakefield before William Nisbett, J.P. Recorded 7 Oct 1775.

R-4, 498-503: Lease & release. 24 & 25 Apr 1775, Thomas Warburton Powell and Elizabeth his wife of Charles Town, to Philip Henry of same, for £1000 SC money, 1000 acres on Big Beaver Creek in Orangeburgh District granted to sd. Thomas Warburton Powell 21 Apr 1775. Thos Warburton Powell (LS), Eliz'th Powell (LS), Wit: A. Cholet, G. H. Hartley. Proved 23 Aug 1775 before Rowland Rugeley, J. P., by the oath of Abra'm Chollet. Recorded 11 Oct 1775.

R-4, 503-509: Lease & release. 7 & 8 March 1775, Benjamin Young, of Waccamaw in Craven County, SC, planter, and Martha his wife, and Peter Simons of same place, planter, and Eleanor his wife, only surviving daughters and coheiresses of John Weston late of province aforesaid, deceased, who was eldest son and devisee under the will of John Allston of the Parish of Prince George, county aforesaid, planter, deceased, to Josias Allston, planter, for £10 SC money, 700 acres near Sochasta adj. land of John Allston Senr, Sochasta Creek, Joseph Prince, Mr. Marion. Benjn Young (LS), Martha Young (LS), Peter Simons (LS), Eleanor Simons (LS), Wit: Robert Heriot, Thos. Mitchell. Proved in Georgetown District before Paul Trapier, J. P., by the oath of Robert Heriot, 26 June 1775. Recorded 17 Oct 1775.

R-4, 509-514: Lease & release. 25 & 26 July 1775, Miles Reiley of Prince Wms. Parish, Sc, planter, to John Cox of same, planter, for £1000 SC money, 1000 acres on waters of Saltcatcher adj. land of John Miller, granted 8 March 1765 to Charles Odingsell. Miles Reily (MR) (Seal), Wit: John

McTeer, Arthur Keef, Nathaniel Salmon. Proved by the oath of John Macteer, 19 Aug 1775, before Wm. Maine. Recorded 20 Oct 1775.

R-4, 514-516: _____ 1775, Josiah Pendarvis of St. Helena Parish, planter, to James Peart, Dept. Surv. of land, for £100 SC money, 300 acres on a branch of north branch of Long Canes called Peneys Creek. Josiah Pendarvis (LS), Wit: George Allison, John Kerr. Proved by the oath of George Allison 10 Aug 1775 before Adrian Mayer. Recorded 25 Oct 1775.

R-4, 516-519: Lease & release. 21 & 22 Aug 1775, Mary Stevens of Charles Town, widow, to Jervis Henry Stevens of same, gentleman, for £10 SC money, 600 acres in Craven county on Lynches Creek adj. James Parsons, Esqr., granted to sd. Mary Stevens by George III. Mary Stevens (LS), Wit: Philip Henry, Wm. Henderson. Proved in Charles Town District by the oath of Philip Henry 6 Sept 1775 before Fenwicke Bull, J. P. Recorded 26 Oct 1775.

R-4, 519-525: South Carolina. 8 Feb 1775, John Moultrie, Esqr., Lt. Gov. of East Florida, Wm. Moultrie, Esqr., of Charles Town, Sc, Thos. Moultrie, & Alexr. Moultrie, Esqr., of same place, devisees and residuary legatees under the will of John Moultrie, physician, deceased, to Wm. Gickie, late a mariner but now of the Parish of St. James Goose Creek, Berkley County, Gentleman, for £5030 SC money, tract supposed to contain 750 acres, conveyed by one Wm. Steed to Wm. Saunders, Esqr., late of same province, deceased, and Wm. Sanders finding upon resurvey that tract contained 822 acres, conveyed the same to John Moultrie, and John Moultrier on 7 March 1750 finding it to contain 832 acres and marsh land adj. to it, sixty one acres. John Moultrier (LS), Wm. Moultrie (LS), Thos. Moultrie (LS), Alexr Moultrie (LS), Wit: David Yeats, Alexr Skinner, James Wallace. Proved by the oath of James Wallace 19 Feb [1775] before John Troup, J.P.

R-4, 525-529: Lease & release. 20 & 21 Sept 1775, Laughlin Martin of Charles Town, Shopkeeper, and Eleanor his wife, to Wm. Downes of same, gentleman, for £20 SC money, 500 acres in raven County in Camden District on a branch of Black River called home Swamp, adj. James Carey, granted 15 Sept 1775 to sd. Laughlin Martin. Laughlin Martin (LS), Eleanor Martin (LS), Wit: John Allen, Thos Winstanley. Proved in Charles Town District before Rowland Rugeley by the oath of Thos Winstanley, 6 Oct 1775. Recorded 3 Nov 1775.

R-4, 530-533: Lease & release. 25 & 26 Feb 1770, Wm. Beard of Parish of St. Marks, SC, planter, to James Adams of same, for £50 SC money, 250 acres on north side of Broad River on a branch of Broad River, Wilkersons Creek granted 2 June 1769 to Wm. Beard. Wm. Beard (LS), Wit: Thos McElhenny, Pattk. McGee. Proved before John Newman Oglethorpe, 26 Feb 1770, by the oath of Patk. McGee. Recorded 6 Nov 1775.

R-4, 534-537: Lease & release. 27 & 28 Sept 1775, Wm. Miller of ____ County, SC, to Richd. Morgan of ____ County, same province, for £___, 100 acres on west side of Timothy Creek in Berkley County adj. land of Doctor Simpson. Wm. Miller (LS), Wit: James Crandon, David Middleton. Proved in Charles Town District by the oath of James Crandon 28 Sept 1775 before R. Rugeley. Recorded 8 Nov 1775.

R-4, 537-543: Lease & release. 14 Apr 1775, Chas. Elliott of St. Pauls Parish, Sc, & Ann his wife, to Benjn Elliott of St. Andrews parish, gentleman, for £12,000 SC money, lot in Charles Town number 240 which Wm. Livingston, formerly of Charles Town, clerk deceased, was in his lifetime seized, and bequeathed to his son George Livingston and sd. George Livingston by deed 20 & 21 Dec 1736 conveyed sd. lot to James Stobo and said James Stobo by deed 24 & 25 Feb 1763 conveyed to James Skirving, and sd. James Skirving by deed 20 & 21 Apr 1764 conveyed sd. lot to Charles Elliott. Chas. Elliott (LS), Ann Elliott (LS), Wit: Andrew Johnston, R. Parker Saunders. Proved by the oath of R. Parker Sanders in Charles Town District, 10 Nov 1775, before R. Rugeley. Recorded 20 Nov 1775.

R-4, 543-544: Isaac Underwood of Charaws District, Planter, bound to John Balfour of same, in the sum of £10,000 SC money, 28 Aug 1775, to execute to sd. John Balfour by 1 Jan 1779 titles to a tract of 250 acres adj. land of John Hustess, Thos. James. Isaac Underwood (LS), Wit: Robert Gray. Recorded 11 Nov 1775.

SOUTH CAROLINA DEED ABSTRACTS 1773-1778

R-4, 544-545: Robert Clary of Craven County, Cheraws District, SC, planter, bound to John Balfour of same, bound in the sum of £40,000 SC money, 20 Dec 1774, whereas sd. John Balfour did on 17th inst. buy of sd. Robert Clary, 300 acres granted to Anthy. White 17 Feb 1767 adj .Francis Young, John Lloyd, Wm. Rhodes, Jas. Henry[?], Thos Bowen, Daniel Desurney, also so much of a tract of 384 acres granted to Saml. Desurney 22 Jan 1747 adj. land of James Jones, Peedee River, ont he high road from Long Bluff to the Cheraw hill, per line run by Jas. Knight Junr 17th instant. Robert Clary (R) (LS), Wit: Robert Gray, Wm. Dewitt. Recorded 11 Nov 1775.

R-4, 545-552: South Carolina. Lease & release. 15 & 16 Jan 1771, George Gabriel Powell of Prov. aforesaid, Esqr., to Benjamin Elliott of same, esquire, for £27,000 SC money, 1312½ acres in Craven County on south side Peedee River consisting of several smaller parcels of land, one of 800 acres which George Seaman late of Charles Town, merchant, deceased, by deed 22 & 23 Apr 1751 conveyed to sd. George Gabriel Powell, another tract of 250 acres (being surplus land within the lines of the part of the said last mentioned tract) for which the George Gabriel Powell obtained a grant 1 Dec 1769 and a tract of 262½ acres which Thomas Lynch to Andrew Johnston by lease & Release 8 & 9 July 175- conveyed to George Gabriel Powell; also 50 acres on Peedee River adj. land of John Stanyarne deceased conveyed by Henry Farewell and Mary his wife, 1766 to said George Gabriel Powell.... said 1312½ acres called Weymouth (plat included). George Gabriel Powell (LS), Wit: Thomas Lide, Jno. Colcock. Proved by the oath of John Colcock, 18 Nov 1775, before Benj. Young.

END OF BOOK R-4.

S-4, 1-6: Lease & release. 20 & 21 Sept 1774, Samuel Dubois and Susannah his wife of Parish of St. Johns Berkley County, to Peter Marion of St. Stephens Parish, planter, for ten shillings, 350 acres in parish of St. Johns Berkly, adj. land of Charles Cantey Esqr., Gabriel Marion, John Matthews, John McKelvy, granted 4 May 1771 to said Samuel Dubois. Samuel Dubois, Susannah Dubois. Wit: Peter Couturier Junr, Isaac Couturier Junr, Joseph Palmer. Proved 27 Sept 1774 before John Frierson, J. P. in Charlestown District, by the oath of Peter Couturier Junior. Recorded 26 May 1775.

S-4, 6-10: 19 Dec 1774, Adam McCole of Craven County, SC, Cambden District, yeoman, to Joseph McCole of same, 600 acres in Anson County, North Province, on north side Broad River known by the name of Round about and opposite to Thomas Hughs land granted 3 Sept 1753 by Gov. of North Carolina recorded in the Secretarys and Adjunt Genls offices of sd. North Province and likewise in South carolina. Adam McCole (LS), Wit: James Johnston, William McCluney, Jno McDonald. Proved in Camden District by the oath of William McCluney before Joseph Brown, J.P., 21 March 1775. Recorded 26 May 1775.

S-4, 10-16: 25 Oct 1765, Roger Pinckney, Provost Marshall of SC, to Hugh Thompson of St. Bartholomews Parish, planter, whereas Isham Andrews of colleton County, St. Bartholomews Parish, was seized of 400 acres in St. Bartholomews Parish part of 600 acres adj. lands of Thomas Boone, Esqr., Mr. Newton, land now or lately sold by said Thomas boone to Sarah Saunders, relict of Laurence Saunders decd, Mr. Woodcrafts lands, Richard Bailey, Mrs. Oswald and Mrs. Whitsetts, and by indentures 2 & 3 March 1763 under the hands of Thomas Boone and Charles Boone, and said Isham Andrews by bond 2 March 1762 bound to Daniel Legare junr and Moses Darquier, merchants, in the penal sum of £1848 s10 d6 SC money for payment of £924 s5 d3, and said Daniel Legare Junior and Moses Darquir in the court of common pleas did implead the said Isham Andrews in an action of debt, tract sold to Hugh Thompson for £60 SC money. Rog'r Pinckney Pro. Mar. Wit: John Martin, Hopson Pinckney. Proved in Chas. Town District before Wm. Rugeley, J. P., by the oath of Hopson Pinckney, 5 Apr 1775. Recorded 27 May 1775.

SOUTH CAROLINA DEED ABSTRACTS 1773-1778

S-4, 16-22: Lease & release. 30 & 31 March 1775, The Honourable Barnard Elliott, Esqr., and Benjamin Elliott, and William Scott, executors of the will of Sarah Elliott, late of St. Andrews Parish, widow, deceased, to Josiah Smith of charles Town, for £5865 SC money, lot of land late of Sarah Elliott deceased in Parish of St. Michael in Charles Town, on Tradd St., adj. land of Charles Elliott, Mary Stobo. (plat by Benja. Lord, D. S., dated 31 March 1775, showing land of Richd. Park Stobo.) Barnard Elliott, William Scott, Benja. Elliott. Wit: Richard Park Stobo, Benjamin Smith. Proved in Charles Town District by the oath of Benjamin Smith, 6 apr, before William Rugeley, J.P. Recorded 27 May 1775.

S-4, 23-26: 16 Dec 1774, Francis Jenkins of Camden District, SC, planter, to John Price of same, planter, for £96 __ shillings and nine pence SC money, tract on Sandy Creek granted to George Miller 20 Aug 1767, 100 acres sold by said George Miller to William Sanders, and sold by William Sanders to Francis Jenkins. Francis Jenkins (LS), Wit: Nicholas Bishop, Samuel Whary. Proved in Camden District by the oath of Samuel Whary before Wm. Brown, J.P., 16 Oct 1775. Recorded 29 May 1775.

S-4, 26-32: Lease & release. 25 & 26 Oct 1773, William Thompson of St. Matthews parish, to Edmund Godfrey Cossens of St. Marks Parish, for £900 SC money, 500 acres in Amelia Township on southwest side of Santee River granted to Miles Jackson 16 Sept 1738, recorded in Book FFF, fol. 12, said Miles Jackson dying intestate the above tract was inherited by his eldest son Joseph Jackson as heir at law, and conveyed to William Thompson 5 & 6 Nov 1766. Wm. Thomson (LS), Wit: Ebenezer McAnair, Richd. Buckloe. Proved 6 Nov 1773 before John Fairchild, J. P., by the oath of Richard Burkloe. Recorded 30 May 1775.

S-4, 32-37: Lease & release. South Carolina. 23 & 24 June 1773, James Cook of sd. province, to Edmund Godfrey Cossens of the same, for £120 SC money, 250 acres in Berkly County in Amelia Township on the head of Peigulars branch adj. Lt. Gov. Bull's land, Isaac Hugers land, Wm. Wallings land, Chas. Collins land, Jacob Hornes land, granted 14 Aug 1772 to said James Cook. Jas. Cook (LS), Wit: Atherton Rawston, James Anderson. Proved 23 June 1773 before John Troup, J. P., by the oath of Atherton Rawstone. Recorded 31 May 1775.

S-4, 38-45: Lease & release. 22 & 23 Jan 1770, John Maner of Granville County, Sc, and Mary Ann Maner his wife, to Edward Keating of Augusta, Georgia, for £1500 SC money, 350 acres granted to Patrick March 6 Oct 1752 in Granville County. John Maner. Mary Ann Maner. Wit: Wm. Maner, Job Brooks. Proved 23 Jan 1770 before John Purves, J.P., by the oath of William Maner. Mary Ann Maner relinquished dower before John Purves, J.P., 23 Jan 1770. Recorded 1 June 1775.

S-4, 45-51: Lease & release. 17 & 18 March 1775, Hardy Williams of St. Matthews Parish, Orangeburgh District, SC, planter, to Christian Redlesparger of St. Georges Parish, Chas. Town District, planter, for £300 SC money, 150 acres in Berkly County adj. lands of Mr. Patrick and Peter Shuman, land formerly laid out to Mr. Lewis Lormiere, granted 10 Nov 1761 to William Blackman. Hardy Williams (LS), Grace Williams (LS), Wit: Lewis Linder, Jacob Linder, Jo'h Uldrick. Proved by the oath of John Uldrick 18 March 1775 before Lewis Linder, J. P. Recorded 2 June 1775.

S-4, 51-57: Lease & release. 19 & 20 Jan 1775, Thomas clark of Charles Town District, to Christian Ridlesparger, Tavern keeper of same, for £50 SC money, 100 acres on southwest side of Four Hole Swamp adj. Felix Brown, sd. Christian Ridlesparger. Thos Clark (LS), Sarah Clark (O) (LS), Wit: Simon Irons. Acknowledged before me Thos. Caton, J. P., 20 Jan 1775. Proved by the oath of Simon Irons 20 Jan 1775 before Thos. Caton. Recorded 3 June 1775.

S-4, 57-60: 28 Feb 1774, Thomas Elders of St. Marks Parish, Craven county, to William Denby of same, for £1800 SC money, 200 acres in parish aforesaid, adj. land granted to Mary Hide, land granted to James Lasley now belonging to Gabl Gerrill, land granted to Samuel Lyons now belonging to John Boyd, on Santee River commonly called Congaree River, granted to Thomas McFersion 19 July 1748., became the property of John Elders and by him expressly given and bequeathed in his will to his son Thomas Elders, said will dated 13 Oct 1770. Thomas Elders (X) (LS), Wit: Benj. Farar, Eliz. Farar. Proved by the oath of Benjamin Farar before Robert Goodwyn, J. P., 3 Dec 1774. Recorded 5 June 1775.

SOUTH CAROLINA DEED ABSTRACTS 1773-1778

S-4, 60-67: Lease & release. 20 & 21 Apr 1775, Jacob Hanizance of the Congarees, SC, planter, to Jacob Meyers of Craven County, planter, for £200 SC money, 200 acres granted to Jacob Hanizance on north side of Santee River opposite to Saxagotha Township adj. land of George Haig, sd. Jacob Hanizance heir at law to the deceased Hanisance, Jacob Meyers. Jacob Hanisance (LS), Wit: John Lowerman (I), Wm. Meyer. Proved 24 Apr 1775 by the oath of William Meyer before Robert Goodwyn, J.P. Recorded 6 June 1775.

S-4, 67-75: Lease & release. 30 June 1753, Barnard Lindsey and Eleanor his wife of Amelia township, planter, to John Fouquet of same, for £200 SC money, 350 acres in Amelia Township. Barnard Lindsey (S) Eleanor Lindsey (T). Wit: Henry Hamond, John Bonnett. Proved 12 Oct 1754 before John Chevillett, J. P. in Berkly & Colleton Countys, by the oath of Henry Hammond. Recorded 9 June 1775.

S-4, 75-82: Lease & release. 27 & 28 March 1740, John Mathews of Saxe Gotha Township, Berkly County, Labourer, to Thomas Brown of same place, Indian Trader, for £70 SC money, 100 acres granted 16 Sept 1738 to John Matthews in the Township of Congres now called Saxe Gotha in Berkly County on Santee River, adj. land of John Coleman, on the common and the glebe land. John Matthews (X), Wit: Christian Mote, Thos Corker. Proved before George Haig, J. P., by the oath of Christian Mote, 4 Apr 1740. Recorded 10 June 1775.

S-4, 82-90: Lease & release. 1 & 2 Feb 1774, Eliza Johnson of Charles Town, widow, to John Gough of Charles Town, for £1200 SC money, lot in Colleton Square in Charlestown adj. land of Alexander Taylor, on a half brick house. Eliza Johnson (LS), Wit: Richd Corbett, G. J. Fardo. Proved before Hopkin Price, J. P., 4 Feb 1774, by the oath of Richard Corbett. Recorded 12 June 1775.

S-4, 90-99: Lease & release. 24 & 25 Aug 1772, Samuel Prioleau the younger of Charles Town, SC, Vendue Master, and Catharine his wife, to John Gough of christ Church Parish, for £3000 SC money, the easternmost part of lot in Colleton Square in Charles Town, lot number 5, adj. land of Hopkin Price, Guignard Street. Samuel Prioleau Junr (LS), Catherine Prioleau (LS), Wit: T. Grimball Junr, Alexander Keith. Proved in Berkly County by the oath of Thomas Grimball Junr 13 June 1775. Catharine Prioleau relinquished dower 27 Aug 1772 before Thomas Knox Gordon, Chief Justice of SC.

S-4, 100-109: Lease & release. 12 & 13 May 1775, Samuel Carne of City of London, now in Charles Town, SC, to Samuel Wainwright of same, gentleman, for £5000 SC money, 1300 acres part of 2700 acres adj. land of William Wragg, Esqr., Ashley River, land of William Morgan, James Postell deceased, sd. Samuel Wainwright, which lately belonged to William Wragg Esqr., who conveyed 16 & 17 Oct 1770 to William Haggart and said William Haggatt by his will 18 May 1773 devised to his wife Elizabeth Haggatt and said Elizabeth having shortly afterwards intermarried with James Marshall Esqr. and they conveyed 4 & 5 Apr 1774 and said Elizabeth on 7 April relinquished dower before William Lord Mansfield, Chief Justice of Kings Bench at Westminster, to Samuel Carne. Samuel Carne (LS), Wit: Anthy Toomer, Archar Smith. Proved in Charles Town District by the oath of Archer Smith 13 May 1775 before Wm. Rugeley, J. P. Recorded 14 June 1775.

S-4, 109-112: Lease & release. __ Feb 1775, Jabez Evans of Berkly County, Sc, to Samuel Jackson of Craven County, SC, for £140 prock. money of NC, tract on north fork of Paclet river joining and between the lines of Elizabeth Clark & Alexander Kill Patrick including some Beaver Dams on a small creek, 250 acres, granted to James Howard 26 Oct 1767 by North Carolina, adj. conveyed to Thomas Wade 17 May 1770 and from him to Jebus Evans 29 May 1773. Jabez Evans (LS), Wit: William Howe, Joseph Blyth, John McLean. Proved in Ninety Six District 13 Feb 1775 by the oath of William Howe before Thomas Neel, J.P. Recorded 19 June 1775.

S-4, 112-116: 28 March 1775, Edward Henderson of St. Marks Parish, SC, yeoman, to Hugh Morton of same, for £400 SC money, 200 acres granted 15 May 1772 to Edward Henderson, in Craven County on a small branch of Rocky Creek called Hunters Creek. Edward Henderson (LS), Wit: Joseph Gaston, Francis Campbell, Matthew Johnson (mark). Proved by the oath of Joseph Gaston before John Gaston, J.P., 14 Apr 1775. Recorded 20 June 175.

SOUTH CAROLINA DEED ABSTRACTS 1773-1778

S-4, 116-121: Lease & release. 5 & 6 Sept 1773, James Misscampbell of District of Ninety Six, Sc, to Arthur Patton & John Hughs of same, for £100 SC money, 100 acres in Belfast Township, Craven County, granted 1 Sept 1773 to James Miscampbell adj. Michael Lomen, Thomas Wates[?]. James Miscampbell (LS), Wit: Robert Taylor, Thos Clark. Proved 6 Sept 1773 by the oaths of Robt Taylor & Thomas Clark before Lewis de St. Pierre, J.P. Recorded 22 June 1775.

S-4, 121-126: Lease & release. 26 & 27 Dec 1774, Patrick Gibson of Ninety Six District, planter, to Andrew Williamson of same, planter, for £250 SC money, 110 acres in Granville County on Hard Labour Creek, part of 400 acres on Stephens Creek adj. land of William Gibson, Samuel Gibson. (plat included dated 2 Dec 1774 by Dd. Cunningham, D.S.), granted 17 Feb 1767 to Patrick Gibson. Patrick Gibson (LS), Wit: Elias Gibson, Timy Parker. Proved in Ninety Six District 31 Dec 1774 before John Bowie, J. P., by the oath of Tim. Parker. Recorded 23 June 1775.

S-4, 126-131: Lease & release. 22 & 23 Dec 1774, Arthur Patton & John Hughes of Ninety Six District, to Andrew Williamson of same, planter, for £250 SC money, 250 acres granted to James Miscampbell 22 Sept 1767 adj. lands laid out for Eliz'th Kirkwood, Robert Read, conveyed 5 Sept 1773 by James Miscampbell to Arthur Patton & John Hughes. Arthur Patton (LS), John Hughs (I) (LS), Wit: James McBride, Tim Parker. Proved 31 Dec 1774 before John Bowie, J. P., by the oath of Tim Parker. Recorded 24 June 1775.

S-4, 131-135: Lease & release. 22 & 23 Aug 1774, John Wright of Ninety Six District, planter, to Andrew Williamson of same, for £200 SC money, 200 acres on the head of a fork of Carans Branch near Belfast Township, Granville County adj. John Crawfords, granted 6 Apr 1768 to John Wright. John Wright (LS), Wit: Adm. Jones, Wm. Calhoun. Proved in Ninety Six District 23 Aug 1774 before John Bowie, J. P., by the oath of Adam Crain Jones, Esqr. Recorded 26 June 1775.

S-4, 135-140: Lease & release. 20 & 21 Oct 1774, Christopher Humble of Ninety Six district, planter, to Andrew Williamson of same, for £100 SC money, 100 acres on Sleepey Creek on waters of Savannah River granted to John Frederick Beckman 30 Aug 1765, conveyed by Michael Beckman to said Christopher Humble 16 & 17 Nov 1773. Christoph Hummel [German signature] (LS), Wit: Wm. Cofey, Timy Parker. Proved in Ninety Six District 22 Oct 1774 before John Bowie, J.P., by the oath of Timy. Parker. Recorded 27 June 1775.

S-4, 140-144: 24 Apr 1770, Henry Laurens of Charles Town, SC, to Barnard Leitz of St. Thomas Parish, SC, for £300 SC money, lot number 135 in Charles Town on the Broad Road. Henry Laurens (LS), Wit: Saml. Cardie, Edmd. Egan. Proved by the oath of Samuel Cardy 15 June 1770 before John Troup, J. P. Recorded 27 June 1775.

S-4, 145-153: Lease & release. 11 & 12 March 1772, William Barefoot & Millie his wife of Craven County, SC, to Jonathan Hill of same, for £800 SC money, 200 acres part of a tract of 300 acres granted to William Newitt and Noah Barefoutt adj. land surveyed for Newell Giles on Wateree River. William Barefoot (B) (LS), Melia Barefoot (M) (LS), Wit: Joseph Kershaw, John Chesnut, Richard Sutton. Proved 18 Feb 1775 before John Newman Oglethorpe by the oath of John Chesnut. Newet Barefoot of Parish of St. Mark, Craven county, yeoman, acknowledge that i have no right to a tract of 200 acres to be conveyed to Jonathan Hill, 12 March 1772. Newit Baarfoot (+) (LS), Wit: Jonathan Hill, John Pain. Recorded 28 June 1775.

S-4, 153-158: Lease & release. 13 & 14 Nov 1774, Jonathan Gregory of Oringburgh District, planter, to Isaac Arledge, both of Prov. of SC, for £300 SC money, 278 acres on south side of Wateree River granted to Richard Gregory and said Richard Gregory died without a will and said Jonathan Gregory, oldest son of said Richard Gregory, is the heir at law. Jonathan Gregory (LS), Wit: Isabell Fairchild, John Thos Fairchild, Abraham Fairchild. Proved in Orangeburgh District before John Fairchild, J. P., by the oath of John Thos. Fairchild, 14 Nov 1774. Recorded 28 June 1775.

S-4, 158-165: Lease & mortgage. 8 & 9 May 1775, Cornelius Dewees of Charles Town, planter, and Sarah his wife, to John Savage, of same, merchant, by bond in the amount of £14,000 SC money for the payment of £7000 before 9 Sept 1775, sd. Cornelius Dewees Island or plantation anciently known by the Indian name of Timicau now Dewees Island in Berkley County 810 acres. Cornelius

SOUTH CAROLINA DEED ABSTRACTS 1773-1778

Dewees (LS), Sarah Dewees (LS), Wit: Jas. McCall, Jos. Ward. Proved by the oath of Joshua Ward 13 May 1775 before David Deas, J. P. Recorded 25 July 1775.

S-4, 166-171: Lease & release. 28 & 29 Aug 1772, Carl Ludwig Uckerman [Ackerman?] of Berkley County, SC, planter, to Conrad Kysell of Charles Town, Tavern Keeper, for £50 SC money, 100 acres in Amelia Township, Berkley County, adj. land of Jacob Resor, Thos Sabb Senr, granted to sd. Carl Ludwig Ackerman, 19 June 1772. Carl Ludwig Uckerman (LS), Wit: John L. Uckerman, George Gardner. Proved by the oath of Francois Defour before Wm. Rugeley, 8 June 1775. Recorded 17 July 1775.

S-4, 171-176: Lease & release. 22 & 23 Apr 1773, Alexander Syfritt of Berkley County, SC, to Wm. Laws of same, for £250 SC money, 250 acres in Craven County on Little Peedee at a place called Reedy Creek, granted to in 1756 to sd. Alexar Syfrit. Alexr Syfritt (LS), Wit: Peter Sandel, John Sandel. Proved before John Troup, J. P., by the oath of Peter Sandel 11 May 1773. Recorded 18 July 1775.

S-4, 177-183: Lease & release. 29 & 30 Sept 1774, William Norris of Ninety Six District, planter, to Plowden Weston of Charles Town, merchant, for £540 SC money, tract of 100 acres in Berkely County on Little Saludy River, part of 250 acres adj. land surveyed for Conrad Kinsler, granted 13 Oct 1759 to Wm. West and conveyed by Wm. West and Mary his wife to Wm. Norris, 6 June 1770. Wm. Norris (LS), Wit: William Day, Dl. Mazyck. Proved 7 Oct 1774 before Fenwicke Bull, J. P., by the oath of Wm. Day. Recorded 21 July 1775.

S-4, 184-191: Lease & release. 1 & 2 March 1770, Henry Talbird of Parish of St. Helena in Granville County, SC, planter, to Ann Bowman of same, widow, for £200 SC money, town lot in Beaufort number 126 granted 2 Aug 1757 to Henry Talbird adj. land granted to Thomas Bowman [Powman?], James Thomson, Major Wm. Pinckney. Hen'y Talbird (LS), Wit: Jno Rhodes, Mary Nelson. Proved 21 Apr 1775 before Andrew Aggnew, J. P. in Beaufort District by the oath of Mary Nelson. Recorded 24 July 1775.

S-4, 192-198: Lease & release. 6 & 17 Jan 1775, James Cane Junr of ninety Six District, Granville County, SC, planter, and Bathsheba his wife, to Elijah Baker of same, planter, for £60 SC money, 150 acres on north east side of Long Cane Creek below Hillsborough Township at the mouth of little Buffaloe Creek granted 3 Apr 1772 to sd. James Cane. Jams Cain Junr (LS), Barshaba Caine (+) (LS), Wit: Elisha Baker, Robert Guthrie. Proved 4 March 1775 before Patk. Calhoun, J.P., by the oath of Elisha Baker.

S-4, 198-200: 25 Dec 1772, John Fondren of Craven County, SC, to John Dover of same, for £200 "south money," land on east side of Broad River on both sides of the High Sole a branch of Kings Creek adj. line of James Fannings late survey, 300 acres, near Stephen Philips path. John Fondren (LS), Wit: William Britton, Jacob Gardner. Proved in Craven County by the oath of Jacob Gardner before John Brown, 2 Jan 1773. Recorded 29 July 1775.

S-4, 200-206: Lease & release. 13 & 14 July 1761, Wm. Kerbey & Dorthy his wife of Craven county, SC, to Wm. Ragan of same, for £300 SC money, 150 acres on north side Santee River in Craven county near the Cypress Swamp adj. laid out for Thomas Maples, granted to Wm. Leonard 29 Nov 1750. Wm. Kerbey (LS), Wit: T. Prestwood, Betty Prestwood. Proved in Craven County by the oath of Thos Prestwood 9 May 1767 before Andw. Alison. Recorded 3 Aug 1775.

S-4, 207-209: 22 Oct 1771, Thomas Bullion of Tryon County, North Carolina, to Zach'h Gibes of fairforest in the same county and province, for £25 proclamation money of NC, 200 acres on both sides of Buffelo Lick Creek in Tryon County, granted 16 Dec 1769. Thomas Bullion (LS), Wit: Richard Price, Essix Capshaw. Proved October Court 1771 in Tryon County. Thos Neel, Register.

S-4, 209-214: Lease & release. 1 & 2 May 1775, William Fox of Camden District, SC, planter, to Capt. John Russell of same, for £200 SC money, 100 acres part of 250 acres granted to a Abegal Rollinson 23 Dec 1771 in the fork of Wateree and Congaree Rivers adj. land granted to Wm. Fox, land surveyed for George Nickles, Wm. Bollison, John Russell, and said Obigal Rollison conveyed

SOUTH CAROLINA DEED ABSTRACTS 1773-1778

13 & 14 Sept 1773 to Wm. Fox. Wm. Fox (WF) (LS), Wit: John McCord, Wm. Tucker (+). Proved 25 May 1775 before Richd. Brown, J. P., by the oath of John McCord. Recorded 7 Aug 1775.

S-4, 214-221: South Carolina. Lease & release. 26 & 27 Dec 1772, John and George Ioor, executors of John Ioor deceased, for £1000 SC money, to Richard Saltus of same province, planter, tract of land to the southward of the Altamaha River on a branch of a large inland swamp commonly called the Buffaloe Swamp, on the freshes of Turtle River, adj. land surveyed for Philip Smith, land surveyed for David Jeffreys in the Province of Georgia, 100 acres granted to John Ioor deceased 3 June 1763. John Ioor (LS), George Ioor (LS), Wit: Richd Walker, John Glaze. Proved 1 June 1775 before Charles Cantey, J. P. in Charles Town District, by the oath of Richard Walker. Recorded 9 Aug 1775.

S-4, 221-244: Joseph Salvador of the City of London, Mercht, whereas by deed poll or Publick Instrument of procuration 25 Sept 1769 reciting therein that sd. Joseph Salvador stood at that time invested with the legal property of 100,000 acres within the line of the plats No. 3 & 4 in South Carolina on Saluda River near Long Canes settement adj. land granted to John Hamilton, in order to make a legal recovery of all rent or arrears of rent then due did appoint Richd Andrews Rapley of City of London, Gentleman, then on his departure into foreign parts to be his lawful attorney, and also to sell or dispose of 5050 acres over and above 5000 acres, and another instrument of procution dated 26 March 1772, to sell or dispose of 10,000 acres, and by another deed poll dated 2 Feb 1773, granted to his sd. attorney Richard Andw Rapley further powers, and by another deed poll dated September 1773, did grant further powers to sell and dispose of land, now willing to enlarge and five further powers to dispose of 20,000 acres of land over and above previous powers... dated 1 March 1775. Joseph Salvador (LS), Wit: R. Collett Junr, Thos Lake. Proved by the oath of Richd. Collett the younger in Parish of St. Andrew Holborn, London, Gent., 1 March 1775 before Fred. Bull, Locum Tenes Mayor. Recorded 19 Aug 1775.

S-4, 244-249: Lease & release. 28 & 29 Jan 1773, Wm. Moseley and Sarah his wife, of Granville County, SC, to James Adams, late of Virginia, now of same county, for £250 SC money, 300 acres in Granville County on south side of Noble Creek adj. land granted to John Plowman White, Laurence Rambo, plat and grant recorded in Book LLL, page 198, granted 21 May 1772 to Wm. Moseley. Wm. Moseley (+) (LS), Sarah Moseley (M) (LS), Wit: Chrimas Ray, Thomas Adams, Isaac Ray (+). Proved in Ninety Six District 3 July 1773 before LeRoy Hammond, J.P., by the oath of Thos Adams. Recorded 24 Aug 1775.

S-4, 250-254: 15 Dec 1774, Ann Gilbert of Charles Town District, to Elizth. Snees, late the widow of Conrad Snees, deceased, for £100 SC money, 100 acres in the fork of Salt Catchers in Colleton County adj. land laid out to Julian Gilbert, granted to sd. Ann Gilbert on his Majestys Bounty. Ann Gilbert (+) (LS), Wit: Ema. Abrahams, Abraham Andrews. Proved in Charles Town District by the oath of Emanuel Abrahams 19 Dec 1774 before Thomas Turner, J.P. Recorded 23 Aug 1775.

S-4, 254-258: 2 Feb 1770, Roger Pinckney, Provost Marshall of SC, to John Wagner, merchant of Charles Town, whereas James Hopkins of province aforesaid deceased was in his life time seized of tract of 150 acres in Saxagotha Township and by his will recorded in the Secretarys office at Charles Town bequeathed said tract to Hannah Hopkins his wife and after her death to his child or children by his said wife, and should she died before he she or they came of age, then to revert to his next heir at law, and said Hannah Hopkins after the death of her sd. husband James did intermarry with John Freymouth of sd. province who then became possessed of the tract and Wm. Scott in his majestys court of common pleas at August Term in 1769 did recover against sd. John Freymouth and Hannah his wife the sum of £1100 s15, now by a writ of fiere facias, public sale on 1 February sold for £437 SC money. Roger Pinckney Pm. (LS), Wit: Hopson Pinckney, John Martin. John Wagner for £437 currency assigned unto Wm. Arthur of Saxagotha Township all my right, title and interest, 10 February 1774[?]. Wit: Nicolas Fittig, Michael Muckenfuss.

S-4, 259-264: Lease & release. 19 & 20 May 1775, Ephraim Mitchell, Deputy Surveyor, to Patrick Calhoun of Long Cane settlement, Granville County, for £20 SC money, 55 acres in Granville county in the Long Cane Settlement, Ninety Six District, adj. land of Hugh Calhoun, Wm. Ward, Alexr Clark, Samuel Patton, Jane Totton, granted 4 May 1775 granted to sd. Ephm. Mitchell.

SOUTH CAROLINA DEED ABSTRACTS 1773-1778

Ephm. Mitchell (LS), Wit: Edwd Darrell, James Smith, John E. Colhoun. Proved in Berkley county by the oath of John E. Colhoun before William Rugeley, J.P. Recorded 25 Aug 1775.

S-4, 264-271: Lease & release. 9 & 10 Feb 1774, John Wagner of Charles Town, merchant, to Wm. Arther of Saxagotha Township, planter, for £437, 100 acres in Saxagotha Township adj. David Wells, Henry Weaver, George Haig, Henry Gallman, John Geiger. John Wagner (LS), Wit: Nicolas Tiffit, Michael Muckinfuss. Proved 19 June 1775 before R. Rugeley, J. P., by the oath of Michael Muckenfuss. Recorded 29 June 1775.

END OF BOOK S-4.

T-4, 1-29: Lease & mortgage. 2 Feb 1775, Joseph Salvador late of Lime Street, London, now of Parish of St. James Westminster, County of Middlesex, Esquire, to Rebecca Mondes DaCosta of Broad Street Buildings, London, Widow, by bond to secure the payment of £680, by two grants each dated 27 June 1752, tracts number 3 and number 4, granted to William Livingstone and by lease and release 12 & 13 June 1753 to John Hamilton, and by him conveyed to Joseph Salvador 27 & 28 Nov 1755.... by letters of attorney Richard Andrews Rapley conveyed to Abraham Pado of Twitenham in the county of Middlesex, about 2700 acres. Joseph Salvador (LS), Rebecca Mendes DaCosta (LS), Wit: Jona. Thompson, James Tierney. Proved before John Wilkes, Esqr., Lord Mayor of London, by the oath of James Tierney, 14 March 1775. Recorded 31 July 1775.

T-4, 30-32: Lease & release. 1 & 2 July 1773, Capt. Charles King of Province of SC, and Charity his wife, to William Calmess of Frederick County, Colony and Dominion of Virginia, for £1422 s 20 SC money, 350 acres in Craven County on Collins River granted in 1752 to Jacob Penington, and Jacob Penington and Mary his wife conveyed 11 & 12 Feb 1771 to Charles King for £1000 currency. Charles King (LS), Charitey King (LS), Wit: John Lindsey Junr., Jams. Lindsey. Proved by the oath of Jam. Lindsey before Michl. Dickert, J.P., 3 July 1773. Recorded 2 Aug 1775.

T-4, 33-35: Lease & release. 1 & 2 July 1773, Capt. Charles King of Craven County, SC, and Charity his wife, to William Calmess of Frederick County, Colony and Dominion of Virginia, for £200 SC money, 50 acres granted 5 Nov 1755 to Isaac Penington, in the fork of Broad and Saluda Rivers adj. land belonging to Jacob Penington, and the said Isaac Penington did bequeath to his two sons Jacob Penington and Isaac Penington by his will, land on Collins River called by the name of the Enoree, and said Jacob Penington Jr. and Isaac Penington conveyed 14 & 15 Jan 1773 to Charles King for £300 currency. Charles King (LS), Charitey King (LS), Wit: John Lindsey Junr., Jams. Lindsey. Proved by the oath of James Lindsey before Michl. Dickert, J.P., 3 July 1773. Recorded 2 Aug 1775.

T-4, 36-37: 23 June 1772, Charles Harvey of Craven County, carpenter, to William McAteer of same, for £200 SC money, 100 acres being part of 340 acres granted to said Charles Harvey 18 May 1771. Charles Harvey (O) (LS), Wit: John Davison, John Cargill Junr, John Harvey. Proved before John Caldwell, J.P. in Ninety Six District, by the oath of John Davison 18 Jan 1773. Recorded 5 Aug 1775.

T-4, 37-41: Lease & release. 25 & 26 May 1775, Edward Perry of St. Pauls Parish, and Mary his wife, to John Glaze of St. George Parish, Berkley County, for £1950 SC money, 134 acres in St. Georges Parish, Berkley County, adj. said John Glaze, Allen Miles, Benjamin Coachman, William Henry Drayton, Cypress Swamp. Edward Perry (LS), Mary Perry (LS), Wit: Robert Miles, Allen Miles. Proved 27 May 1775 before Andrew Leitch by the oath of Robert Miles. Recorded 5 Aug 1775.

T-4, 42-46: Lease & release. 11 & 12 Jan 1775, Elias Horry Junior of Charles Town, SC, esquire, to Thomas Horry of same place, esquire, for £10 SC money, tract on Santee River granted 4 Feb 1714/5 to Bartholomew Gaillard for 300 acres adj. land of John Bell and also tract granted the last day above mentioned to sd. Bartholomew Gaillard for 300 acres. Elias Horry Junr (LS), Wit: Thos Farr Junr, Benj. Dickinson. Proved by the oath of Thoms. Farr Junr, Esqr., before D. Horry, 2 Aug 1775. Recorded 15 Aug 1775.

SOUTH CAROLINA DEED ABSTRACTS 1773-1778

T-4, 46-50: Lease & release. 2 & 3 May 1775, Thomas Horry of Charles Town, Esqr., to Elias Horry Junior of same place, esqr., for £10 SC money, whereas tract granted 4 Feb 1714 to Bartholomew Gaillard for 300 acres adj. land of John Bell, and tract of 300 acres on Santee River adj. said tract, and said Elias Horry Jnr is seized of a plantation originally granted to Elias horry father of said Elias and at the time of the grant called Elias Horry Junr 29 Nov 1735 for 272 acres and upon resurvey found to contain 450 ares and said Elias did on 21 April 1775 obtain a new grant for said 450 acres adj. Wadbecan Creek formerly called the northeast branch of Santee River on Wild horse Creek and Mr. Izard's land, and part of said 450 acres is contained within the lines of two tracts mentioned, now Thomas Horry conveys to Elias Horry all such part of said two tracts heretofore conveyed to him by said Elias as contained with those lines. Thomas Horry (Seal), Wit: Thoms. Farr Junr, Benj. Dickinson. Proved before Thomas Evance, J. P., by the oath of thoms. Farr Junr, 3 Aug 1775. Recorded 21 Aug 1775.

T-4, 50-53: 20 May 1774, Thomas Grimball Junr, Sheriff of Charles Town District or Precinct, SC, to William Miller of said province, planter, whereas James Clatworthy of St. George's Parish, Berkley County, was seized of a tract of 100 acres on west side of Timothy's Creek in Berkeley County adj. lands of Doctr. Lupton, and said James Clatworthy by his bond 14 May 1770 bound to John Dawson & Richard Walter, merchants, in the penal sum of £3517 s7 SC money, for the payment of £1750 s13 d9 and also said James Clatworthy was bound 14 Aug 1773 to said John Dawson & Richard Walter in the penal sum of £1455 s20 d8 for payment for £727 s15 d8 with interest, and said John Dawson & Richard Walter obtain a judgment in the court of common pleas in August Term 1773, and by writ, sheriff sold for £35 SC money, tract of 200 acres. T. Grimball (LS), Wit: Alex Keith, Joseph Mulligan. Proved before Rowland Rugeley by the oath of Alexander Keith, ____ 1775. Recorded 2 Sept 1775.

T-4, 53-59:(plat on page opposite page 53 shows land belonging to the estate of Isaac Nicholes on Stono River, St. Pauls Parish, "Old Barn Tract" "New Barn Tract" dated 27 June 1775.)

19 Aug 1775, James Nichols of St. Pauls Parish, Colleton County, planter, to Henry Nicholas of same parish, planter, whereas Isaac Nicholes late of St. Pauls Parish deceased, father of the said James Nichols and Henry Nichols, was seized of considerable real estate and the said Isaac Nicholes by his will dated 5 March 1759 did devise unto his beloved sons, said James and Henry, all his lands to be equally divided between them when they arrived to the age of 21 years, and the said Isaac Nichols some short time after the executing of his said will died seized of a tract of 2660 acres on the north branch of Stono River adj. lands of Isaac McPherson, Charles Elliott Esquire, William Cattell Esquire, estate of Silas Miles deceased, Robert Miles, Arthur Middleton Esquire, Barnard Elliott, Algernon Wilson deceased, and said James Nicholas and Henry Nicholes have attained the age of twenty one years and have enjoyed the tract as tenants in common and being desirous of occupying and enjoying their shares and proportions did appoint James Lytten Richards with John Fenwicke, gentleman, to partition said land. James Nicholes (LS), Henry Nicholes (LS), Wit: Dennan McPherson, Wm. Print. Proved in Chs. Town District by the oath of Wm. Print 19 Sept 1775 before Jno Coram. Recorded 4 Oct 1775.

T-4, 60-63: Lease & release. 15 & 16 Nov 1774, Robert Blair of Cheraw District, SC, planter, to Robert Gray of same, planter, for £3500 SC money, 350 acres granted 18 Nov 1747 to John Westfield by SC, and Esther Nivie for £1000 14 & 15 Dec 1767 did convey to Robert Blair said 350 acres adj. William Evans, Hardy Counsell, Pedee River. Robert Blair (LS), Wit: George Manderson, Jonathan John. Proved by the oath of George Manderson before Alexr. Mackintosh in Cheraw District. Recorded 12 Oct 1775.

T-4, 63-69: Lease & release. 5 Dec 1766, Sir William Baker, Knight and one of the Aldermen of the City of London, Great Britain, & Nicholas Linwood & Brice Fisher of the parish of St. Martin in the Fields, County of Middlesex, in said Kingdom, by Paul Trapier of George Town in Craven county, SC, gentleman, their attorney, to Robert Heriott of Craven County, planter, for £7700 SC money, 1200 acres English measure known as Hobcaw Point on the Hobcaw Barony on Waccamaw River in Parish of Prince Georges in Craven county, granted by the late Lords Proprietors unto John late Earl of Granville. Brice Fisher by Paul Trapier, Nicholas Linwood by Paul Trapier, William Baker by Paul Trapier (LS), Wit: Thos Mitchell, Anthy Bonneau. (plat included)

SOUTH CAROLINA DEED ABSTRACTS 1773-1778

T-4, 70-73: Lease & release. 14 & 15 Jan 1772, Benjamin Huger of Charles Town, Esqr., to Robert Heriot of George Town, esqr., for £11,000 SC money, 1711 acres in Prince George's Parish, Craven County, adj. land of said Robert Heriot, Waccamaw River, Sir William Baker, Nicholas Linwood & Brian Fisher of Great Britain, which said tract of 1711 acres is part of a barony of 12,000 acres known as the Hobcaw Barony, conveyed 1 & 2 Jan 1747 by Paul Trapier of George Town as attorney of Sir William Baker, Nicholas Linwood & Brian Fisher. Benjn. Huger (LS), Wit: Thomas Bee, John Raven Mathewes. Proved in Berkley County by the oath of John Raven Mathewes 20 Jan 1772. Recorded 20 Oct 1775.

T-4, 73-76: 27 Feb 1734, George Pawley, William Swinton & Daniel Laroche, all of Parish of Prince George, Winyaw in Craven County, Esqrs., to Othniel Beal of Charles Town, merchant, for £7 s10 SC money, tract conveyed 14 & 15 Jan 1734 from Elisha Screven of Parish of Prince George Winyaw, Gent., and Hanah[?] his wife to said George Pawley, William Swinton & Daniel Laroche, 274½ acres in said parish, on George Town River, adj. lands of said Elisha Screven, a town to be called George Town. George Pawley (LS), Wm. Swinton (LS), Dan Laroche (LS), Wit: William Cripps, Stephen Hartley, James Atkins. Othniel Beale for sum of £500 to Robert Heriot, all right title & intrest in lot in George Town, number 13, dated 3 May 1771. Othniel Beale (LS), Wit: A. W. Carr, Robert Mylne. Proved in Berkeley County before John Troup, J. P., by the oath of Robert Mylne, 30 Aug 1771. Recorded 21 Oct 1775.

T-4, 77-80: Lease & release. 9 & 10 June 1772, John Croft of Prince Georges Parish, Craven County, SC, shipwright, to Robert Heriot of same, planter, for £275 SC money, tract on a neck of land fronting George Town, opposite to Lot 224 on Kings Street, Sampit Creek or Georgetown River. John Croft (LS), Wit: Willm Shackleford, George Croft. Proved 10 June 1772 before Job Rothmahler, J. P., by the oath of George Croft. Recorded 23 Oct 1775.

T-4, 80-82: Lease & release. 23 & 24 Oct 1775, William Sanders & An his wife of SC, to Henry Purcell of Charles Town, for £10 SC money, 500 acres in Craven County on waters of Beaver Creek of Little River adj. land of Benjamin Mazyck, granted by George III to said William Sanders. William Sanders (LS), Ann Sanders (LS), Wit: Phillip Henry, Jas Sanders. Proved in Charles Town District by the oath of Phillip Henry, 1 Nov 1775. Recorded 3 Nov 1775.

T-4, 82-85: Lease & mortgage. 13 & 14 Jan 1775, James Williams of Little River, Parish of St. Marks, merchant, to Rowland Rugeley, of Charlestown, merchant, by bond in the penal sum of £9400 SC money for the payment of £4700, tract whereon the said James Williams now lives and lately purchased by him of John Caldwell, 1250 acres on both sides Little River of Saludy adj. land of John Williams, William Neale, James Johnson, and by land lately purchased by said James Williams of Peter Krozer[?], also another tract lately purchased by said James Williams of Peter Strozer[?] 200 acres adj. land belonging to George Neal. James Williams (LS), Wit: Thomas Bourke. Proved by the oath of Thomas Bourke in Chas. Town District, 17 Jan 1776 before Jno Coram. Recorded 18 Jan 1776.

T-4, 85-88: Lease & release. 3 & 4 Sept 1773, John McKoy, late of Granville County, SC, now of Georgia, to James Harris of Granville County, for £5 SC money, 100 acres on a branch of Stephens Creek, grant recorded in Secretaries office in Book TTT, page 189, memorial entered in Book L No.11, page 53 20 Sept 1771. John Macoy (LS), Wit: Danl Ellis, Joseph Vann, James Robson. Proved in 96 District before Moses Kirkland, Esqr., by the oath of James Robertson, 2 apr 1774. Recorded 5 Dec 1775.

T-4, 88-95: Lease & release. 28 & 29 Apr 1774, John Boss, late of Leicester but now residing in London, gentleman, to William Sandys of Petty France Westminster, County of Middlesex, Confectioner, for £250 money of Great Britain, several tracts of land near Port Royal in SC, granted by Lords Proprietors 11 Apr 1715 granted to William Hodgson, also one fourth share in one undivided moiety of half part of dwelling houses, store houses, etc., also one fourth part of a moiety which by lease and release dated 25 & 26 Feb 1772, conveyed by John Hodgson of Darkdale, Parish of Ruaresdale, County of Northumberland, carpenter, to Robert Brailsford of Parish of St. Bridget otherwise Saint Brides London, and the said John Boss as tenants in common. John Boss (LS), Wit: Fenwick Lyddal, William Leighton. Proved by the oath of William Leighton 25 Oct 1775 in London before John Wilkes, Mayor. Recorded 27 Feb 1776.

SOUTH CAROLINA DEED ABSTRACTS 1773-1778

T-4, 95-108: Lease & release. 29 & 30 Sept 1775, John Boss of Parish of St. Martin in the Fields, County of Middlesex, Gentleman, to William Whayman of Southampton Buildings Parish of St. Andrews Holborn in County of Middlesex, Gentleman, for £500 lawful money of Great Britain... whereas by lease and release 12 & 13 Aug 1774 between John Hodgson of Darkdale, Parish of Horarsdale, County of Northumberland, Carpenter, heir at Law of John Hodgson, late of Middle Temple, London, Esquire, deceased, who was the son and heir at law of William Hodgson next mentioned, and also heir at law of William Hodgson Landgrave and Cassique of South Carolina, deceased, to Robert Brailsford of Parish of St. Bridget otherwise St. Brides, London, Gentleman, to said John Boss, tracts of land at or near Port Royal in South Carolina, granted 11 Apr 1715 to said William Hodgson... having excepted out of the grant unto Joseph Avery of Inverness in North Brittain, Esquire, tracts of land conveyed by indenture of William Hodgson and Joseph Avery 30 Apr 1736 and by bond of said Joseph Avery and William Bayshall all of the Welch Cooper Office, Philpot Lane, London Merchant, and Benjamin Lunn of City of Bristol, Merchant, in the penal sum of £10,000. John Boss. Wit: John Mathews, Joseph Wells Liversedge, Southampton Building Holvorn. Acknowledged by John Boss before Sir William DeGrey Knight Chief Justice of Court of Common Pleas at Westminster at my house at Englefield Green near Egham in the County of Surry.

William Whayman of Southampton Buildings, Parish of St. Andrew, appoint Joseph Hodge of Parish of St. Margeret Westminster, County of Middlesex, Gentleman, & Stephen Bull of Charles Town, attorneys, 30 Sept 1775. William Whayman (LS), Wit: John Mathews, Joseph Wells Liversedge. Proved by the oath of Joseph Wells Liversedge 25 Oct 1775 before John Wilkes, Mayor. Recorded 27 Feb 1776.

T-4, 108-111: Lease & release. 12 & 13 June 1775, William Smith of Charles Town, to Thomas Tod of same, Wharfinger, for £150 SC money, 1000 acres in Granville County on waters of Beaver Dam Creek a branch of Stephens Creek waters of Savannah River adj. land surveyed by John Purves, Esqr., John Logan's land, Nathl Johnston's land, Thomas Boone's land, John Mason's land, widow Minter's land, Thomas Goode's land, Bartley Jones's land, John Murpheys land, granted to said William Smith 9 June curr't. William Smith (LS), Wit:John Fisher, John Forteath. Proved in Charles Town District before John Troup, J. P., by the oath of John Fisher, 15 Dec 1775.

T-4, 111-115: Lease & release. 1 & 2 Feb 1776, Elias Horry the younger of Charles Town, Sc, esquire, and Elizabeth his wife, to Thomas Horry of same, esquire, for £15,000 SC money, 209 acres part of 4500 acres granted 28 Apr 1733 to Col. Thomas Lynch, late of said Coloney, deceased, also another tract of 250 acres part of tract originally granted 26 June 1736 to sd. Col. Thomas lynch deceased, for 500 acres by resurvey by said Elias Horry found to contain 558 acres for which said Elias Horry obtained a grant 21 Apr 1775, and also a small piece of land of 14 acres part of tract of 500 acres granted to sd. Col. Thomas Lynch deceased, 26 June 1736. total 770 acres in Prince George Parish, Craven County, on Bluff Beech Creek adj. lands of Thomas Shubrick Esquire. (plat included, dated 11 April 1776). Elias Horry Junr, Elizabeth Horry (LS), Wit: Elizabeth Branford, John Witter. Proved by the oath of John Witter 8 Apr 1776 before Jeremiah Savage. Recorded 11 Apr 1776.

T-4, 115-119: Lease & release. 18 & 19 March 1776, Rawlins Lowndes, Esqr., to Rowland Rugeley of same, for £2700 SC money, 16 acres on Charles Town Neck in Berkley County adj. said Rowland Rugeley, Daniel Cannon, Bernard Elliott Esqr., lands formerly belonging to ___ Hunter deceased, and sundry lots sold by said Rawlins Lowndes to sundry persons. Raws. Lowndes (LS), Wit: Archd. Carson, Rezon Nelson (R). Recorded 11 Apr 1776.

T-4, 119-124: Lease & release. 12 & 13 Sept 1775, Andrew Reynolds of Long Canes in Granville County, SC, to Henry Rugeley of Charles Town, merchant, for £600 SC money, 300 acres on a fork of Bakers Creek which is an eastern branch of the western fork of Long Cane adj. land of Hugh Horn, granted to sd. Andrew Reynolds 22 Sept 1767. Andw Reynolds (LS), Wit: Archd Darson, Jas. Crandon.

T-4, 125-131: Lease & release. 1 & 2 Jan 1770, John Robert of Granville County, Sc, planter, to Elias Robert of same, surveyor, for £500... whereas James Robert made a purchase of Francis Kinloch of Craven County of six several tracts or part of tracts in the Parish of St. James Santee,

179

two tracts one of 600 acres adj. lands of Charles Chovin, Hell Hole Swamp, the other 700 acres adj. west side of former and on Hell Hole Swamp, granted to John Guilles decd, also two tracts one of 250 acres one of 226 acres granted to Mary Esther Gaillard in her widowhood, also one half of 200 acres adj. lands of James Wright, Esqr., Gov. of Georgia, granted to Moses Carion decd, also 219 acres on north side of last mentioned tract of 200 acres adj. James Boyd, on the church or town lands, John Mayrants land being part of 360 acres granted to the inhabitants for a town, church & etc., and sold to said John Gaillard who with his widow after his deceased were sole owners of all tracts and by their wills became the property of said Francis Kinloch, 2095 acres in one body adj. lands of James Boyd, James Wright, Charles Chovin, Hell Hole Swamp, John Maynard, John Skrine, Joseph Willingham, and said James Robert hath sold to John Robert. (plat included). John Robert (LS), Wit: Elias Jaudon, John Grimball. Proved 17 March 1774 before Charles Brown, J. P., by the oath of John Grimball. Recorded 5 July 1777.

T-4, 131-137: Lease & release. 3 & 4 Sept 1764, James Robert of Granville county, Sc, Gent., to John Robert of same, gunsmith, for £2095 SC money [same tracts in previous deed]. Ja. Robert (LS), Wit: John Connors, James Roux, James Barr. Proved in Granville County before Elijah Prioleau 15 June 1767 by the oath of John Conyers. Recorded 5 July 1777.

T-4, 137-140: Lease & release. 10 & 11 Feb 1777, Abraham Warnock of st. Marks Parish, SC, and Ann his wife, to John Flinn of same, for ten shillings, 150 acres granted to Charles Warnock and transferred to sd. Abraham Warnock on Douglass's Swamp south side of Lynches Creek, Craven County. Abraham Warnock (LS), Ann Warnock (X) (LS), Wit: Jemima Dubose, Fredk. Bell, John Willson. Proved 8 May 1777 by the oath of Frederick Bell before Hen: Cassels. Recorded 5 July 1777.

T-4, 140-144: Lease & release. 30 June & 1 July 1774, Hester Wrand of Charles Town, Shopkeeper, to George Virgent of same, for £1500 SC money, lot in Charlestown on north side of Unity Alley, number 19, adj. lot belonging to Hester Wrand, Darby Pendergrass, Moses Mitchell (plat included). Hester Wrand (R), Wit: Fras. Bremar, Peter Bremar. Proved by the oath of Peter Bremar 10 Sept 1774 before J. Bremar, J.P. Recorded 5 July 1777.

T-4, 144-149: Lease & release. 11 & 12 Feb 1777, Jesse Hunt of Charles Town, mariner, to Jonathan Lawrence of same, merchant, for £6000 SC money, lot in Ansonborough in Charlestown being part of the lands commonly called Lynches Pasture on south side Hasell St., adj. lot late of Mr. Bushell, Admiral Frankland. Jesse Hunt (LS), Wit: Daniel Latham, Stephen Lawrence. Proved by the oath of Stephen Lawrence 14 May 1777 before Geo: Sheed. Recorded 5 July 1777.

T-4, 149-151: South Carolina. Whereas the late Lords Proprietors of this Province 11 Apr 1715 granted to William Hodgson the title of Landgrave and Casique with Four Barronys, and John Hodgson being the heir at law of said William Hodgson having conveyed to Robert Brailsford and John Boss the whole of the above named Barronys and also 5000 acres purchased and all lands , erections, etc., first to William Sandys 1/4 part of said Bosses half & one eighth of the whole 29 Apr 1774, secondly to Robert Dee, one quarter part of said half 10 Aug 1774, and lastly the remaining half to William Whayman being one half of his share and one fourth of the whole 30 Sept 1775... said purchasers shall pay expenses which may arise, dated 14 Feb 1776. Robert Brailsford (LS), Wm. Sandys (LS), Robert Dee (LS), Joseph Hodge for William Whayman (LS), Wit: Henry Houseman, Wm. Nisbett. Proved in Charles Town District by the oath of Henry Houseman and William Nisbett 21 June 1777 before Jno Colcock, J.P. Recorded 5 July 1777.

T-4, 151-158: Lease & release. State of South Carolina. 18 & 19 Apr 1777, Josiah Smith the younger, George Croft and William Cole, Gentleman, only qualified executors of the will of Samuel Waddingham, late of Craven County, planter, deceased, to Press Smith of state aforesaid, gentleman, for £16,824 SC money.. whereas said Samuel Waddingham was seized of a tract of 592 acres partly in Parish of Prince George and partly in the parish of Prince Frederick, in 1773 did make his will and did bequeath all the rest, residue and remainder of his estate both real and personal unto his daughter Sarah Waddingham when she should arrive to the age of eighteen years but in default of issue of his said daughter, to sell and dispose of said estate and the monies arising from such sale (after his executors had kept and retained so much as would be sufficient to pay unto his Father and mother the annuity in his said will mentioned) appointed his wife Rebekah

SOUTH CAROLINA DEED ABSTRACTS 1773-1778

Waddingham executrix as long as she remained his widow and his cousin sd. William Cole and his friends Thomas Hutchinson and Josiah Smith, Edward Darrel of Charlestown, merchant, and sd. George Croft and George Smith of Winyaw, executors and in some short time after making his will said Samuel Waddingham died, and sd. Josiah Smith, George Croft and William Cole alone have proved the said will and taken the burthen of the execution, the testators daughter the said Sarah Waddingham departed this life without issue and sd. executors did advertise the said track to be sold at publick vendue at George Town 20 Feb last past.. .said tract of 592 acres adj. land granted to Col. Alexander Venderdusen deceased, land of Robert Heriot Esquire, Peters Creek, land of Samuel Wragg, land of William Wilson, Isaac Bates, Susannah Moor[?], William Stitts, Col. Pawley and persons unknown. (plat of resurvey included, dated 7 March 1777 by Alex's M. Forster.) Josiah Smith Junr (LS), George Croft (LS), William Cole (LS), Wit: Jno. Glegg, Jno. H. Green. Proved in George town District by John Glegg 1 May 1777 before Job Rothmahler. Recorded 12 July 1777.

T-4, 159-162: Lease & release. 28 & 29 March 1777, Samuel Benoist & Margaret his wife, to Thomas Giles, for £3500 SC money, 400 acres, part of 800 acres granted to thomas Palmer 1 June 1709, in Berkley County, St. Johns Parish. Samuel Benoist (LS), Margaret Benoist (LS), Wit: Lightfoot H. Davis. Proved 29 March 1777 by the oath of Lightfoot Harrison Davis before John Frierson, J. P. for Berkley County. Recorded 12 July 1777.

T-4, 163-166: Lease & release. 9 & 10 Apr 1767, John James Senr. of Craven County, SC, to Mattw. Singleton of same, for £100 SC money, 150 acres on north side Watree River adj. land laid out for John Huggins, said land granted to John James Senr, 10 Sept 1765. John James Senr. (LS), Wit: Thos. Prestwood, Saml. Clarke. Proved in Camden District 11 July 1775 before Nathl Moore, J.P., by the oath of Samuel Clarke. Recorded 13 Sept 1777.

T-4, 166-170: Lease & release. 3 & 4 Oct 1771, John Huggins of Craven county, Sc, planter, to Matthew Singleton of same, for £200 SC money, 100 acres in Craven county on Sandy Creek a branch of Santee River. John Huggins (LS), Wit: Isham Moore, Joseph Hill, john Foster. Proved 13 March 1775 before Malcom Clark in Camden District by the oath of Isham Moore. Recorded 13 Sept 1777.

T-4, 170-174: Lease & release. 14 & 15 June 1775, Hugh Rees of Craven County, SC, planter, to Isham Moore of same, for £500 SC money, 150 acres on Santee River Swamp, St. Marks Parish, Craven County, granted to Hugh Rees 10 Feb "the year above mentioned" adj. land of James Sincklear, Edward Richardson, James Lyner, John Hatfield of Charlestown. Hugh Rees (LS), Wit: John James, Robt. Moses. Proved 15 June 1775 before Nathl. Moore, J. P., by the oath of John James. Recorded 13 Sept 1777.

T-4, 174-179: Lease & release. 18 & 19 Aug 1777, Martin Lloyd, late of Colleton County, SC, planter, and Elizabeth his wife, for £1000 SC money, to John Guiness of state aforesaid, trader, 574½ acres in Colleton County, being the one full fourth part or moiety of tract belonging to Doctr. Jacob Martin deceased & Grandfather to said Martin Lloyd which said tract of 2298 acres sd. Jacob Martin by his will did bequeath to his grandson Martin Lloyd. Martin Lloyd (LS), Elisabeth Lloyd (LS), Wit: Ema. Abrahams, Robt. Conaway. Proved 22 Aug 1777 before George Sheed, J. P. in Berkley County, by the oath of Emanuel Abrahams. Recorded 13 Sept 1777.

T-4, 179-183: Lease & release. 21 & 22 July 1777, William Bull the younger of Charlestown, to Rev. Robert Smith of same, for £7610 SC money, 360 acres in the parish of St. Thomas lately called Parsons Point, now Point Hope, on Wando River, on Watboe now Beresford Creek, adj. St. Martins now Cooks Creek, also 460 acres in St. Thomas Parish on Beresford Creek on Hobshaw now Addisons Creek adj. land lately belonging to Rachel Hemele now Paul Pritchard, John St. Martin now Cook, total 820 acres. Will: Bull Junr (LS), Wit: Jacob Valk, Wm. Blacklock. Proved in Charlestown District before George Sheed, J.P., by the oath of William Blacklock 7 Sept 1777. Recorded 13 Sept 1777.

T-4, 183-190: Lease & release. 30 & 31 Dec 1776, Thomas Fuller of St. Andrews Parish, Berkley County, Esquire, and Catharine his wife, to Nathaniel Fuller of same parish, esquire, for £6000 SC money, 550 acres on south side Ashley River in St. Andrews Parish composed partly on the northernmost part of a tract of 1030 acres originally granted to William Fuller deceased and partly of a tract of 200 acres granted to Abraham Smith deceased and became vested in Thomas Fuller, with Lydia his wife, 22 & 28 Jan 1758 conveyed to Sarah Simpson of Charlestown, and said Sarah Simpson 11 & 12 July 1764 conveyed to Daniel Legare the younger of Charlestown, merchant, who with Elizabeth his wife 22 & 24 Jan 1767 conveyed to Benjamin Guerard of Charlestown, Esquire, who with Sarah his wife 17 & 18 March 1768 conveyed to sd. Thomas Fuller. Thos Fuller (LS), Katherine Fuller (LS), Wit: Edw Darrell, Wm. Print. Proved in Charlestown District before George Sheed, J.P., by the oath of William Print, 29 Aug 1777. Recorded 20 Sept 1777.

T-4, 190-193: Lease & release. 28 & 29 Aug 1764, William Mazyck, of Charlestown, Gentleman, to Benjamin Farar, of parish of St. John Berkley County, for £10 SC money, 900 acres in Craven county adj. land granted to Benjamin Sims, John Hamilton Esqr., Mary Catharine Spitzen, ___ Rolison, John Everet, Jesse Goodwyn, Rebeca Mack, estate of Thomas Howell, heirs of ___ Myrick, said tract originally granted to sd. William Mazyck 29 June 1764. William Mazyck (LS), Wit: Paul Mazyck, Daniel Mazyck. Proved in Berkley County before William Thomson, J. P., by the oath of Daniel Mazyck. Recorded 29 Sept 1777.

T-4, 194-197: Lease & release. 2 & 3 Apr 1772, Samuel Parsons of Parish of St. George, planter and Tavern Keeper, and Anna his wife, to Thomas Pendarvis of same, planter, for £200 SC money, 100 acres in Berkley County on waters of Indian Field Swamp adj. land of William Blackman, Nicholas Noes, granted to Samuel Parsons 4 Dec 1771. Samuel Parsons (LS), Anna Parsons (X) (LS), Wit: Simon Irons, John Archbould, Jno Pendarvis. Proved 25 July 1777 before John Fullerton, J.P., by the oath of Simon Irons. Recorded 20 Sept 1777.

T-4, 197-201: Lease & release. 9 & 10 Jan 1776, Thomas Pendarvis of Parish of St. George, SC, planter, and Elizabeth his wife, to Christian Riddlespurger of same parish, planter and Tavern keeper, for £300 SC money, 100 acres in Berkley County on waters of Indian Field Swamp adj. land of William Blackman, Nicholas Noes, granted to Samuel Parsons 4 Dec 1771 conveyed by Samuel Parsons and Anna his wife to Thomas Pendarivs. 2 & 3 Apr 1772. Thom's Pendarvis (LS), Elizabeth Pendarvis (X) (LS), Wit: Simon Irons, John Archbould, Thomas Pendarvis. Proved 25 July 1777 before John Fullerton, J.P., by the oath of Simon Irons. Recorded 20 Sept 1777.

T-4, 202-203: Edmund Cossens of St. Bartholomews Parish, gentleman, bound to Thomas Ferguson of st. Pauls Parish, in the sum of £10,000 SC money, 13 April 1776; whereas said Edmund Cossens in right of Rachel his wife is possessed of tract of 1000 acres on the eastern branch of Salcacha River in Colleton County adj. land formerly of David Hext afterwards Samuel Prioleau, land formerly of Benjamin Deharriette but now of Thomas Ferguson, also 600 acres adj. to it, which said Edmund Cossens and his said wife Rachel (when she shall arrive to the age of 21) agree to convey to said Thomas Ferguson. Edmd Cossens (LS), Wit: Alex Macbeth. Proved by the oath of Alexr. Macbeth, 13 Sept 1777. Recorded 20 Sept 1777.

T-4, 203-207: Lease & release. 9 & 10 Dec 1776, Jacob Hickman of Camden District, Sc, planter, to Isaac DaCosta Junr of same, planter, for £550 SC money, 100 acres granted to sd. Jacob Hickman 23 Oct 1765 on Flatt Rock Creek, Craven County. . Jacob Hickman (X) (LS), Rachel Hickman (R) (LS), Wit: John Drakeford, James Denman, Reason Nellson Junr. Proved in Charlestown district before George Sheed, J.P., by the oath of Reason Nellson Jr., 29 Aug 17777. Recorded 20 Sept 1777.

T-4, 207-211: Lease & release. 30 & 31 Oct 1776, John Keenan of Colleton County, planter, to William Gibson of same, for £2550 SC money, 300 acres on north side of Saltcatcher Swamp in Colleton County adj. Colonel Lucas's land. Jno Keenen (LS), Wit: John Hughs, John B. Cockeran, Arthur Keeffs. Proved 16 Aug 1777 before Philip Smith, J. P. in Charlestown District, by the oath of John Hughes. Recorded 20 Sept 1777.

T-4, 211-215: Lease & release. 22 & 23 Aug 1777, George Noddings of Charlestown, Ship Carpenter, to John Torrans of same, for £900 SC money, lot on north bay in Charlestown, number 5, adj. land of said John Torrans. Geo Noddings (LS), Wit: J. Poaug, Thos Phepoe. Proved 4 Sept 1777 before Joseph Glover, J.P. in Berkly County, by the oath of John Poaug of Charlestown. Recorded 20 Sept 1777.

SOUTH CAROLINA DEED ABSTRACTS 1773-1778

T-4, 215-216: Lachlan Martin of Charlestown, Gentleman, for good will and affection to my beloved friend Mordecai McFarlan of St. Mathews Parish, Berkley County, Land surveyor, and for five shillings, tract of 82 acres in St. Georges Parish, Berkley County, adj. land of Ralph Izard, Doctor Dubar, Daniel Blake, dated 11 June 1774. Laughlin Martin (LS), Wit: John Cross, Sarah Cross.

I do hereby give all right & Title I have to the land within mentioned to Mrs. Mary Clatworthy. Mordecai McFarlan. Wit: John Audebert, Michael Muckenfuss. June 12, 1774.

I do hereby give all right & Title to my son James Clatworthy, 16 Aug 1777. Mary Murphy. Wit: William Fletcher, John Burke. Deed from Laughlin Martin proved before George Sheed by the oath of John Cross, 1 Sept 1777. Charlestown District. Deed from Mordecai McFarland proved by the oath of Michael Muckenfuss 29 Aug 1777 before Geo. Sheed. Deed from Mary Murphy to Jas. Clatworthy proved by the oath of William Fletcher before Geo: Sheed, 12 Sept 1777. Recorded 27 Sept 1777.

T-4, 216-220: Lease & release. 20 & 21 Aug 1777, James Clatworthy of Parish of St. George, Gentleman, to Henry Metscar of Dorchester in same parish, for £500 SC money, eight acres adj. land of Thomas Dunbarr, Ralph Izard, Henry Metscarr. James Clatworthy (LS), Wit: David Duncan, John Troup. Proved 29 Aug 1777 before George Sheed, J.P. in Charlestown District, by the oath of John Troup, Esqr. Recorded 27 Sept 1777.

T-4, 220-225: Lease & release. 6 & 7 May 1777, Moses Curtis, late of Webbs Creek in St. Mathews Parish, Berkley County, Shoemaker, to William Greaves of Charlestown, merchant, for £53 SC money, 300 acres in St. Mathews Parish, Berkley County, granted 5 June 1770 to said Moses Curtis. Moses Curtis (LS), Wit: Thos Fletchall, John Fletchall. Proved 20 May 1777 before John Thomas Junr, J.P. in Ninety Six District, by the oath of John Fletchall. Recorded 27 Sept 1777.

T-4, 225-229: Lease & release. 12 & 13 May 1777, William Savage of Charlestown, and Martha Savage his wife, to James Holmes of ninety six District, planter, for £300 SC money, 300 acres in Granville County on a branch of the northwest fork of Long Canes called Hogskin Creek adj. land laid out for said James Holmes, original survey for one William Stevenson which said 300 acres was on 29 July 1769 granted to sd. William Savage. William Savage (LS), Martha Savage (LS), Wit: Susannah Lloyd, James Pritcher. Proved 13 May 1777 before George Sheed, J.P. in Charles Town District, by the oath of James Pritchard. Recorded 27 Sept 1777.

T-4, 230-234: Lease & release. 12 & 13 May 1777, Tacitus Gaillard and Isaac Gaillard of St. Matthews Parish, Ninety Six District, planters, to James Holmes of ninety Six in district aforesaid, planter, for £2700 SC money, tract of land at Ninety Six in Colleton County in the first division from the great Survey, number 1, formerly run out for John Hamilton, Esquire, 400 acres but now supposed to contain 290 acres allowing ten acres for the division for the Town Lotts, streets, and public land whereon the court house and goal now stand, adj. land of Robert Goudey now deceased, formerly property of John Murray, Esquire, conveyed by John Hamilton to said John Murry who by deeds 21 & 22 July 1767 conveyed to John Savage of Ninety Six and sd. John Savage 9 & 10 Sept 1776 conveyed to sd. Tacitus Gaillard and Isaac Gaillard. Tacit's Gaillard (LS), Isaac Gaillard (LS), Wit: Jacob Read, James Pritchard, Hugh Turpin. Recorded 27 Sept 1777.

T-4, 234-240: Lease & mortgage. 23 & 24 May 1777, James Holmes of Ninety Six District, SC, planter, and Ann his wife, to Jacob Read of Charlestown, esquire, 390 acres at Ninety Six [same property as in preceding deed], mortgage in the penal sum of £3000 SC money for payment of £1500. James Holmes (IH) (LS), Ann Holmes (X) (LS), Wit: James Pritchard, Wm. Freeman. Proved 24 May 1777 before Edward Wilkinson, J. P. in SC, by the oath of James Pritchard. Recorded 27 Sept 1777. Mortgaged satisfied 2 July 1778.

T-4, 240-244: Lease & release. 1 & 2 June 1776, Robert Hutchinson of Parish of Prince Fredericks, SC, planter, and Mary his wife, to William Croskry of same, planter, for ten shillings, 150 acres granted to William Smith 24 Apr 1774 on Black River Swamp, St. Marks Parish, Craven County, conveyed from William Smith and Martha his wife 3 & 4 Oct 1775 to said Robert Hutchinson. Robt. Hutchinson (LS), Mary Hutchinson (LS), Wit: John Scott, Michael Haywood, John Hawkins.

SOUTH CAROLINA DEED ABSTRACTS 1773-1778

Proved before Gavin Witherspoon, J.P. for George Town District, by the oath of John Scott, 1 Sept 1777. Recorded 27 Sept 1777.

T-4, 244-248: Lease & release. 1 & 2 June 1776, Robert Hutchinson of Parish of Prince Fredericks, SC, planter, and Mary his wife, to William Croskry of same, planter, for ten shillings, 250 acres granted to Mary Brown 21 Apr 1775 on Black River, St. Marks Parish, Craven County, adj. land of Derrick Mannin. Robt. Hutchinson (LS), Mary Hutchinson (LS), Wit: John Scott, Michael Haywood, John Hawkins. Proved before Gavin Witherspoon, J.P. for George Town District, by the oath of John Scott, 1 Sept 1777. Recorded 27 Sept 1777.

T-4, 248-250: John Hubert of Saxe Gotha Township, SC, Taylor, and Jacob Spear of same, laborer, for £52 SC money, to Thomas Brown of Craven County, Indian Trader, 50 acres in Saxe Gotha Township on South west side of Santee River in Berkley County adj. land laid out to John Weldrick Miller now belonging to Hannah Miller widdow, Jacob Spear, and land reserved for a town in said township, the front half of 50 acres laid out for John Hubert and Jacob Spear... dated 2 May 1738. John Hubert (mark) (LS), Johan Jacob Spear [German signature] (LS), Wit: Stephen Maret, Charles ONeal. Proved before George Haig, J. P. in Berkley County, by the oath of Stephen Moret, 3 May 1738. I do resign my full intentions concerning with within instrument of writing to Jacob Spear, 17 Dec 1746 .Thos Brown. Wit: John Kelly, Henrich Galmon. Proved by the oath of Captn. John Gallman who swore to the name and signing of his deceased father Henry Gallman, 14 Aug 1777, before Henry Patrick,J.P. Recorded 4 Oct 1777.

T-4, 250-252: 10 Apr 1777, Stephen Tomkings and Thomas Tomkings of the County of Anson, State of North Carolina, to William Pegues of the County Craven, South Carolina, for £670 SC money, 130 acres on north side of Great Pedee River on Marks's Creek adj. John Bones lower corner, part of 300 acres granted to Samuel Goodman 17 June 1745. Stephen Tomkins (LS), Thomas Tomkins (LS), Wit: Carney Wright, Francis Tomkins. Proved in Cheraw District before Claudius Pegues, J. P., by the oath of Carney Wright 26 May 1777. Recorded 4 Oct 1777.

T-4, 252-260: Lease & release. 26 & 27 May 1777, Benjamin Farrar of the Congarees, planter, and Elizabeth his wife, to Gabriel Manigault of Charles Town, Esquire, for £70,650 SC money, 5000 acres on south side Santee River in St. Matthews Parish, Berkley County, District of Orangeburgh, adj. lands of ___ Holman, heirs or assigns of William Sabb, of John Rice, of George Eyrick, of one Bates, of one Berline, and of John Caldwell, Esqr, lands of William Adams, George King, James Lynah, sd. Williams, John Mark; said land composed of one tract of 150 acres granted to Col. Moses Thompson deceased, 450 acres granted to John Cook, tract of 450 acres and another of 1000 acres ranted to Andrew Broughton, one tract of 700 acres granted to John Rutledge Esqr which were severally conveyed to said Benjamin Farar, and also 300 acres granted to Benjamin Spurlock which was conveyed to sd. Benjamin Farar by John Rutledge, and 60 acres part of 550 acres purchased by sd. Benjamin Farar of one John Ray to whom the same was originally granted, and 1400 acres part of 2000 acres granted to Honble. Robert Wright, Esqr., deceased, and conveyed to sd. Benjamin Farar in three tracts one of 600 another of 400 acres by sd. Col. Moses Thompson and the other of 400 acres by John Rutledge , also another tract of 180 acres on east side of Congaree River in Craven County in the district of Camden adj. lands of one McGrew, Benjamin Farrar, Audeon St. John, James Gill, Thomas Taylor and James Taylor, Peter Foust, and Congaree River, composed of several small tracts, one of 250 acres granted to one James St. John who sold to Thomas Brown, 150 acres ranted to sd. Thomas Brown from whom the said three tracts descended be became vested in one Richard Brown who conveyed the same to sd. Benjamin Farar; and one tract of 445 acres granted to sd. Benjamin Farar, one tract of 350 acres granted to one Sarah Hodge who conveyed to Benjamin Averet who conveyed to Benjamin Farar, and 342 acres part of 1000 acres granted to Theodore Gourdin who conveyed to sd. Benjamin Farar; also 8500 acres in the great Savannah in St. Marks Parish in the district of Camden adj. land of James Reid Esquire, land granted to William Osborn, and late now or late of Thomas Sumter, Jared Neilson, Thomas Cook, James Bowman, Matthew Bowman, heirs or assigns of ___ Allen, heirs or assigns of ___ Scott, and heirs or assigns of Peter Manigault Esqr., decd, granted to John Mayrant decd, lands of Philip and John Frierson, William Fludd, heirs or assigns of John Ainslie, heirs or assigns of William Jamison deceased, tract of Col. Richardson, tract of one William Wood, and tract of 8500 acres composed of smaller tracts one of 1957 acres granted to Benjamin Mazyck, one tract of 2000 acres ranted to Thomas Cooper, tract of 150 acres granted to Henry Richbourg, tract of 100 acres granted to

SOUTH CAROLINA DEED ABSTRACTS 1773-1778

William Sims, tract of 900 acres part of 1000 acres granted to Mary Munck, and 130 acres part of 250 acres granted to Elias Ball Junr, tract of 90 acres granted to Martin Witts, by which said Benjamin Mazyck, Thomas Cooper, Henry Richburg, William Sims, Mary Munck, Elias Ball Junr, and Martin Witts conveyed to sd. Benjamin Farar; also tract of 629 acres granted to sd. Benjamin Farar. (Plats included made at the request of William Thompson & Benjamin Farar, for two tracts 5000 acres, dated at St. Mathews, April 12, 1777, by Malcom Clarke, D. S., and James Bunyie.) Benj. Farar (LS), Eliz. Farar (LS), Wit: James Bunyie, Jno Colcock. Proved in Charlestown District before John Troup, J.P., by the oath of James Bunyie 5 June 1777. Recorded 4 Oct 1777.

T-4, 260-264: Lease & release. 17 & 18 Aug 1777, William Allston the younger of Prince Georges Parish, Craven County, and Rachel his wife, to Plowden Weston of state aforesaid, merchant, for £500 SC money, 142 acres part of tract of about 700 acres formerly sold to sd. William Allston by Joseph Allston Esquire, adj. land of said William Alston, Plowden Weston, Mrs. Lesesne. (plat included). Wm. Allston Junr (LS), Rachel Allston (LS), Wit: Benja. Young, Anthy. Mitchell. Proved in Charlestown District before George Sheed, J.P., by the oath of Benjamin Young, Esqr., 21 Aug 1777. Recorded 4 Oct 1777. Agreement between Plowden Weston of Charlestown and Marian his wife, by indenture dated 11 Feb 1777, and William Allston the younger, tract of record in Book A, page 449-453, 20 Sept 1777. Plowden Weston (LS), Wm. Allston Junr (LS), Wit: John Todd, Jos. Ward. Proved in Charlestown District by the oath of Joshua Ward, Esqr., before George Sheed, 23 Sept 1777. Recorded __ Oct 1777.

T-4, 265-269: Lease & release. 10 & 11 Sept 1777, John Crawford of Prince Fredericks Parish, Craven County, to Mordecai Myers of George Town, for £250 SC money, 500 acres in Craven County on Pee Dee River adj. James Futhys land, Thomas Ellery, originally granted 13 May 1735. John Crawford (LS), Wit: Abr'h Cohen, Christo. Taylor, J. Bidggood. Proved in George Town District before Job Rothmahler, J. P., by the oath of John Bidggood, 12 Sept 1777. Recorded __ Oct 1777.

T-4, 269-273: Lease & release. 1 Aug 1770, Edward Martin and Ann Delahowe, exrs. of the will of Thomas Walker late of Berkley County, deceased, to Daniel Kaylor of same, for £450 SC money, 530 acres on east side of Cooper River on Simons Creek adj. Free School Lands in St. Thomas Parish, Peter Johnsons land, formerly Lewis Dutarques land, land formerly Richard Griffins. Edward Martin (LS), Ann Delahowe (LS), Wit: Wm. Keith Junr, Charles Tighe, John Mills, John Troup. Proved in Charlestown District 22 Aug 1777 before George Sheed, J. P., by the oath of Doctr. William Keith Junr. Recorded 4 Oct 1777.

T-4, 273-278: Lease & release. 26 & 27 June 1775, Samuel Blenco of Colleton County near Ashepoo, planter, to John Audebert of St. Helenah's Parish, Granville County, gentleman, for £5 SC money, 500 acres granted 6 Sept 1775 to said Samuel Blenco, on Cain Gall Branch waters of Coosawhatchie, adj. John Garvin, Elias Jaudon. Samll. Blenco (LS), Wit: Sarah Butler (mark), Elias Robert. Proved before Henry Gindrat, J.P. for Beaufort District, by the oath of Elias Robert, 3 July 1777. Recorded 4 Oct 1777.

T-4, 279-280: Purrysburgh in Granville County. Sth Carolina. 24 July 1777, John Audebert of St. Peters Parish, Granville County, planter, to Adrian Mayer of Purysburgh, Esqr., for £2000 SC money, 500 acres on the head of a branch of Cyprus Creek called Can Gall branch, waters of Coosawhatchie River, granted to John hughes and by him conveyed to sd. John Audibert, also tract of 500 acres on Cane Gall Branch waters of Coosawhatchie adj. John Garvin, Elias Jaudon, granted to Samuel Blinco and conveyed to sd. John Audebert. John Audebert (LS), Wit: Willoughby Pugh, John Holzendorf. Proved in Purysburgh by the oath of John Holzendorf before Bellamy Crawford, J.P., 18 Aug 1777. Recorded 4 Oct 1777.

T-4, 281-283: Lease & release. 24 & 25 Feb 1777, Richard Waring of St. Georges Parish, SC, esquire, and Ann his wife, to George Smith of state aforesaid, gentleman, for £10,000 SC money, 428 acres on Sandy Island in Prince Georges Parish, adj. lands of John Postell, Benjamin Waring, on a thoroughfare. Richd Waring (LS), Ann Waring (LS), Wit: B. Waring, John Douglass. Proved 26 June 1777 before Hopkin Price, J.P. in Berkley County, by the oath of Benj. Waring. Recorded 11 Oct 1777.

SOUTH CAROLINA DEED ABSTRACTS 1773-1778

T-4, 283-285: Lease & release. South Carolina. 1 & 2 March 1777, Benjamin Waring of state aforesaid to George Smith of same, for £600 SC money, 300 acres part of 1000 acres granted to sd. Benjamin Waring in 1771 in Craven county on Waccamaw Neck adj. land granted to Edwd. Thomas, land of Willm. Allston Senr. Bn. Waring (LS), Wit: Maurice Lee, John Douglass. Proved 22 March 1777 before William Morgan, J.P. in Berkley County, by the oath of Maurice Lee. Recorded 11 Oct 1777.

T-4, 286-290: Lease & release. 26 & 27 Sept 1777, Christopher Shetts of Charlestown, shopkeeper, and ___ his wife, to Jacob Valk of same, gentleman, for £7620 SC money, lot on west side of Old Church Street commonly called Meeting Street in Charles Town, adj. land of the public whereon the armory now stands, and adj. land of Matheruin Guerin, Paul Smiser, land formerly of John McKensie Esquire deceased, conveyed by sd. McKensie to Christopher Shetts 30 & 31 Jan 1769. Christopher Sheets (LS), Susannah Schitz [German signature], Wit: James Culliatt, Paul Schlatter. Proved 30 Sept 1777 before George Sheed, J.P., by the oath of Paul Schlatter. Recorded 11 Oct 1777.

T-4, 290-293: Lease & release. South Carolina, 96 District. 18 July 1777, Thomas Edghill Senr, planter of district aforesaid, to William Goggins Junr, planter, of same, for £100 SC money, 100 acres in Berkley County on a small branch of Little River call'd Sandy Run adj. land of Robert Johnston, granted 1 Feb 1768, Book BBB, page 436. Thos Edghill (LS), Sarah Edghill (LS), Wit: T. Edghill Junr., Richd. Edghill, Fredrick Jones (X). Proved before James Williams, J.P. in Ninety Six District, by the oath of Thomas Edghill Junr, 13 Sept 1777. Recorded 11 Oct 1777.

T-4, 294-297: 26 March 1772, Roger Pinckney, Provost Marshall of SC, to Samuel Grove of Beaufort, St. Helena Parish, Granville County, merchant, whereas Francis Stuart of province aforesaid, merchant, was seized of lots in Town of Beaufort, #34 on Port Royal Street, lot #9 and a low water in the Town of Beaufort; Thomas Shubrick and Richard Shubrick in the court of common pleas at February Term 1772 obtained a judgment for the sum of £21473 s15 SC money, also £92 s7 d8 expenses, against sd. Francis Stuart deceased, at the time of his death in the hands of Henry Stuart and Lewis Reeve admrs. and James Carson and Ann his wife lately otherwise called Ann Stuart admx. of said Francis Stuart; now Roger Pinckney for £3880 SC money to Samuel Grove. Roger Pinckney (LS), Wit: Hopson Pinckney, Joseph Milligan. Proved before George Sheed by the oath of Joseph Milligan, 1 oct 1777. Recorded 11 Oct 1777.

T-4, 297-300: Lease & release. 23 & 24 Sept 1777, John Giles of Charlestown and Jean his wife, to John Philips of same, for £3900 SC money, lot #136 conveyed to said John Giles and Jean his wife by Daniel Monroe, on King Street, adj. lands of the estate of Michael Boomer, land belonging to a negro named Free Matt, parsonage lands, land known by the name of the Crown Inn. John Giles (LS), Jean Giles (LS), Wit: Michl. Kalteison, William Lowe. Proved in Charles Town District by the oath of William Love 25 Sept 1777 before Wm. Nisbett, J. P. Recorded 11 Oct 1777.

T-4, 300-303: Lease & release. 7 & 8 June 1776, Joseph Kershaw of Camden, Craven County, merchant, to John Payne of same, blacksmith, for £500 SC money, 41½ acres on north east side of Wateree River on Pine Tree Creek adj. land of said John Payne and Joseph Kershaw. Joseph Kershaw (LS), Wit: Thomas Jones, Jno Chesnut, James Murphew. (Plat included for 41½ acres in Fredericksburgh Township part of 350 acres laid out for William Gray, granted 3 Apr 1754 to said Wm. Gray. Plat certified 7 June 1776, John Belton, D. S.) Proved by the oath of Thomas Jones in Camden District 8 June 1776. Recorded 11 Oct 1777.

T-4, 303-306: Lease & release. South Carolina, Ninety Six District. 15 & 16 Apr 1777, John Moore of district aforesaid, shoemaker, to David Neilson Henderson of same, planter, for £100 SC money, 200 acres granted to John Moore 15 Oct 1774 on NW fork of Long Cane, waters of Savannah River, adj. Archibald Hamiltons land, recorded in Book TTT, page 283. John Moore (LS), Susannah Moore (mark) (LS), Wit: Samuel Crockett, Gabriel Pickens. Proved 16 Apr 1777 before Robert Anderson, J. P. in Ninety Six District, by the oath of Samuel Crockett. Recorded 11 Oct 1777.

T-4, 306-311: Lease & release. 5 & 6 Aug 1777, Thomas Smith and Isaac Motte of Charlestown, only qualified acting and surviving executors of the will of Benjamin Smith, late of Charlestown, esquire, deceased, to Jonathan Lawrence of same, for £10,150 SC money, said Benjamin Smith in his lifetime was possessed of a certain brick tenement on the Bay of Charles Town and said Benjamin Smith executed his will dated 15 Feb 1768 by which he gave to his wife Mrs. Mary Smith the use of the said brick tenement during the term of her widowhood only and afterwards to his son Benjamin Wragg Smith at the expiration of his mother's the said Mary Smith's widowhood by death or marriage, and if said Benjamin Wragg Smith died before he attained the age of 21 years the said tenement should be sold by his said executors and appointed his brother Thomas Smith and his son in law Isaac Motte (together with his eldest son Thomas Loughton Smith and Miles Brewton of Charlestown Esquires since deceased) executors... said Benjamin smith departed this life leaving said will in full force ... the events in the said will mentioned have taken place by the death of said Mary Smith and by the death of said Benjamin Wragg Smith who departed this life since under the age of 21.... Thos Smith (LS), Isaac Motte (LS), Wit: Aaron Loocock, Benja. Smith. Proved in Charlestown District before George Sheed, J. P., by the oath of Aaron Loocock, Esqr., 4 Oct 1777. Recorded 11 Oct 1777.

T-4, 311-314: Lease & release. 8 & 9 June 1770, John Bell and ___ his wife of Craven County, Sc, weaver, to John Murray of same, planter, for £300 SC money, 250 acres in Craven County on a branch of little River called Neds branch adj. Earismans land, granted 13 May 1768 to sd. John Bell. John Bell (LS), Wit: Bryan Rylie (X), John Kelly (K), Winie Kelly (X). Proved 31 Aug 1772 before John Winn, J.P. in Craven County, by the oath of Bryan Rylie. Recorded 11 Oct 1777.

T-4, 314-317: Lease & release. 16 & 17 Apr 1762, Joseph Spencer of Santee in Craven County, planter, to Mark Huggins of Santee, planter, for £150 SC money, 400 acres in Prince George Parish, commonly known by the name of Newfoundland, adj. land of John Gough, George Smith, which tract was granted to John Steel. Joseph Spencer (LS), Wit: Wm. Mathews, Paul Furquand, Duke Bell. Proved before John Mayrant, Esqr., J.P. in Craven County by the oath of Duke Bell, 4 May 1762. Recorded 18 Oct 1777.

T-4, 317-322: Lease & release. 3 & 4 Sept 1777, John Paul Grimkie of Charleston, esquire, and Mary his wife, to Edward Hare of Charlestown, gentleman, for £8500 SC money, town lott number 14 in Charlestown on north side of Broad Street, adj. land of William Hopton, John Heskett, Union Street. John Paul Grimkie (LS), Mary Grimkie (LS), Wit: James Wright, John Mills. Proved in Charles Town District by the oath of John Mills 9 Oct 1777 before Wm. Nisbett, J.P. Recorded 18 Oct 1777.

T-4, 322-327: Lease & release. 26 & 27 Sept 1777, Lachlan McKintosh of Charles Town, Gentleman, and Elizabeth his wife, to Thomas Evance of same, esquire, for £2000 SC money, 1000 acres on Potatoe Creek in St. Marks Parish, Craven County, granted 17 Feb 1773 to sd. Lachlan McKintosh adj. Robert Hamilton, Thomas Sumpter, grant recorded in Book OOO, page 123; also a plantation of 250 acres on Potatoe Creek a north branch of Santee adj. land of Robert hamilton. [plat included 250 acres to Thomas Potts on Santee on Potatoe Creek (surveyed for sd. Thomas Potts 20 Jan 1759) dated 6 Nov 1759 and plat for 1000 acres]. Lach. Mackintosh (LS), Eliz'th McIntosh (LS), Wit: James Culliatt, Paul Schlatter. Proved before George Sheed by the oath of James Culliatt, 10 oct 1777. Recorded 18 Oct 1777.

T-4, 327-328: Agreement between Thomas Loughton Smith of Charlestown and Doctor James Clitherall of same place, said Thomas Loughton Smith sells the brick house at the corner of Church and Broad Streets where he now resides for £500 currency. Thos Ltn. Smith (LS), James Clitherall (LS), Wit: John Farquharson. Proved by the oath of John Farquharson 16 July 1777 before
John Troup. Recorded 18 Oct 1777. Received of Mr. James Clitherall 1 Aug 17771 one bond for £4000 one bond for £5000 one bond for £6000 & John Giles & John Creighton's Joint bond for £2000. Wit: Sam Chollet. John Farquharson testified to the handwriting of Saml Chollet, 16 July 1777. Recorded 18 Oct 1777.

T-4, 328-330: 7 Apr 1777, John McNeese of Ninety Six District, SC, to Samuel Laird of same, for £3000 SC money, 150 acres on a branch of Duncans Creek, granted to sd. John McNeese 24 Nov 1774. John McNees (LS), Wit: Robert Hanna, Robt. Mortin, Lodwick Lard (U). Proved by the oath of Robert Martin in Charlestown District before Geo: Sheed, 13 Oct 1777. Recorded 18 Oct 1777.

SOUTH CAROLINA DEED ABSTRACTS 1773-1778

T-4, 330-334: Lease & release. 8 & 9 Oct 1777, Daniel Bourdeaux of Charlestown, SC, merchant, and Martha his wife, to James Bowman of state aforesaid, planter, for £500 SC money, 320 acres in St. Marks Parish, Craven County. Danl Bourdeaux (LS), Martha Bourdeaux (LS), Wit: Nathl Bourdeaux, Anthony Bourdeaux. Proved 9 Oct 1777 before John Troup, J.P., by the oath of Anthony Bourdeaux. Recorded 18 Oct 1777.

T-4, 334-338: Lease & release. 25 & 26 June 1777, Thomas Grimball the younger of Charlestown, SC, Esqr., and Mary Magdalen his wife, to John Chambers of said state, merchant, for £5100 SC money, lot in Charlestown, number 6, on south side Tradd Street, adj. land of Robert Wells, David Grame Esqr., Samuel Prioleau, Esq. T. Grimball Junr (LS), Mary Mag'le Grimball (LS), Wit: Joseph Milligan, John Gregg. Proved in Chas. Town District by the oath of Joseph Milligan before Pet: Bounetheau, 1 Oct 1777. Recorded 18 Oct 1777.

T-4, 338-340: 7 Apr 1772, Thomas Fulton of Craven County, SC, to John Patton of County of Augusta, Colony of Virginia, for £50 lawful money, 450 acres granted 28 Aug 1772 on Fishing Creek in Craven County adj. land of John Smith, Patrick, McKenney, William Taylor, Henry Culp, Wm. Smith. Thomas Fulton (LS), Wit: William Fulton, John Patton, John Walker. Proved in Camden District by the oath of John Patton, __ May 1773. Recorded 18 Oct 1777.

T-4, 340-342: 17 Feb 1773, Robert McFadden of Craven County, SC, to John Patton of County of Augusta, Colony of Virginia, for five shillings, 50 acres part of 150 acres granted 14 Aug 1772 to Robert McFadden adj. land granted to Henry Culp, Thos. Fulton. Robt. McFadden, Wit: William Fulton, Edward McFadden, Isaac McFadden. Proved in Camden District by the oath of William Fulton before Ezekl. Polk, J.P., 27 Apr 1773. Recorded 18 Oct 1777.

T-4, 342-343: James Willson Senr of Ninety Six District, planter, for love, goodwill, and affection to my loving son John Willson of same, 100 acres in Granville County on Cheeves Creek granted to Archd. Wilson 2 March 1768, Book CCC, page 286, and memorial entered in Book I No. 9, page 31 on 6 Aug 1768 and by sd. Archibald Wilson transferred to sd. James Willson 25 & 26 May 1774 recorded in the Public Registers Office Book M No. 4, page 71.... dated 18 July 1777. James Willson (mark) (LS), Wit: Robert McConn, James Rowan. Proved in Ninety Six District 19 July 1777 before John Purves by the oath of James Rowan. Recorded 25 Oct 1777.

T-4, 343-349: Lease & release. South Carolina. 15 & 16 Sept 1777, Robert Dick of Prince George Parish, Craven County, SC, planter, and Ann his wife, to Ann Fyffe, widow of William Fyffe, late of George Town, phisician, deceased, for £500 SC money, tract which the Rev. Thomas Morrit late of county and state aforesaid deceased, by the death of himself and his only son Thomas Morrit a minor, the said tracts of land became vested in his two daughters Alice Morrit and Ann Moritt as coheiresses, and Ann first intermarried with James Summers and afterwards with the above named William Fyffe, and said Ann Fyffe by her deed dated ____ 1772 conveyed to Robert Dickson undivided full moiety of half part of tracts, in the whole 2100 acres...now conveys 250 acres on south side of Black River in Craven County adj. land of Samuel Miller, Richard Briers, said tract granted to Richard Briers in the year 1709 and from said Richard Briers by divers deeds to above named Thomas Morrit, also one half part of a tract of 240 acres on Black River which tract was granted to Thomas Morrit 19 July 1738, also one half part of 1000 acres on Six Mile Swamp adj. Captain Beauchamp, granted to sd. Thomas Morrit in 1739. Robert Dick (LS), Anne Dick (LS), Wit: William Luptan, William Withers. Proved in Geo Town District before Job Rothmahler, J.P. in George Town District, by the oath of William Luptan 11 Oct 1777. Recorded 25 Oct 1777.

T-4, 349-353: Lease & release. 2 & 3 Oct 1777, James Clitherall of Charlestown, practitioner of Physick, and Elizabeth his wife, to Roger Smith, Esquire, for £17,500 SC money, two lot on south side of Broad Street and west sid e of old Church Street in Charlestown adj. land of William Smith, John Boomer, being that lot bought by Benjamin Smith from ____ Wattson which said lot was in the possession of Thomas Loughton Smith late of charlestown, Esquire, deceased, and sold to said James Clitheral, adj. land of Benjamin Smith but now of his son William Smith. James Clitherall (LS), Eliza Clitherall (LS), Wit: Wm. Ancrum, George Ancrum. Proved in Charlestown District before John Troup, J.P., by the oath of Geo: Ancrum, 9 oct 1777. Recorded 25 Oct 1777.

SOUTH CAROLINA DEED ABSTRACTS 1773-1778

T-4, 354-357: 20 Oct 1777, Robert Stark, Sheriff of the District of Ninety Six, to the Honourable William Henry Drayton, Esquire, for £1000 SC money ...whereas Alexander Cameron late of the province of SC now State of SC and District of Ninety Six was seized of three tracts adjoining each other called Lockabor, 2350 acres, and John Ward and Peter Leger, merchants of Charlestown, in the court of Common Pleas at February term 1777 did obtain a judgment for £35,865 s18 d8 SC money... Robert Stark sheriff (LS), Wit: John Huger, Wm. Mason. Proved by the oath of John Huger and William Mason 22 oct 1777 before John Syme, J.P. Recorded 25 Oct 1777. (Plat included "Pursuant to a warrant... dated 5 Nov 1765 I have admeasured and laid out unto Alexander cameron a plantation or tract of vacant land on the Kings Bounty containing 2000 acres on a small branch of the northwest fork of Long Cane Creek bounded north part on vacant land & part on land laid out to Henry Hays, S. Eastwardly on lands laid out to James Brimmingham, John Robeson, Edward Giles & William Edmonston...." Certified 1st May 1765. Pat Calhoun, D.S.)

T-4, 357-360: Lease & release. South Carolina. 27 & 28 May 1777, Benjamin Farar of Saxagotha Township, Esquire, and Elizabeth his wife, to William Ancrum of state aforesaid, for £37,500 SC money, tracts of land a total of 3000 acres adj. to each other in Craven County at the Congarees adj. lands of Col. Charles Pinckney, said Benjamin Farar, Andrew Lord. Benja. Farar (LS), Eliz. Farar (LS), Wit: Robert Lithgow, James Bunyie, Ralph Humphreys. Proved in Charles Town District before John Troup, J.P., by the oath of James Bunyie 5 June 1777. Recorded 25 Oct 1777. (Plat included).

T-4, 360-364: Lease & release. 14 & 15 May 1777, John White of Craven County, yeoman, and Elizabeth his wife, to David Smith of Cecil County in Maryland, Gentleman, for £1200 SC money, as it passeth between merchant and merchant, 450 acres in Craven County on north side of Fishing Creek. John White (LS), Elisabeth White (LS), Wit: George Gibson, Thomas Clendinen, Patrick McGoraty (W). Proved in Craven County 13 Sept 1777 by the oath of Thos Clandenin before Wm. Bratton, J.P., 13 Sept 1777. Recorded 25 Oct 1777.

T-4, 364-368: Lease & release. 5 & 6 June 1777, Martin Fryer of Granville County, Orangeburgh District, planter, and Mary his wife, to John Ingles of Savannah, Georgia, esquire, for £100 Georgia money, 100 acres in Granville County on Savannah River at the time of the original grant to the said Martin Fryer 12 Oct 1770 on land granted to Francis Stringer, land granted to Alexander Nielson, on Bounty Land. Martin Fryer (LS), Mary Fryer (X) (LS), Wit: Jesse Cruise, Robert Hankison. Proved in Orangeburgh District by the oath of Robert Hankinson 5 July 1777 before Wm. Robison, J. P. Recorded 1 Nov 1777.

T-4, 369-373: Lease & release. 6 & 7 June 1777, Thomas Castillow of Granville County, Orangeburgh District, SC, planter, and Mary his wife, to John Inglis of Savannah, Georgia, Esquire, for £50 Georgia money, 124 acres, part of 500 acres granted to sd. Thomas Castillow 16 Sept 1774 adj. land of Ralph Wilson, John Bush. (Plat included for 124 acres in Cracker Neck, certified 25 Apr 1775 by Isaac Perry, D.S.) Thos Castellaw (LS), Mary Castellaw (LS), Wit: Isaac Bush, Robert Hankinson. Proved in Orangeburgh District by the oath of Robert Hankinson 5 July 1777 before Wm. Robison, J. P. Recorded 1 Nov 1777.

T-4, 373-378: Lease & release. 25 & 26 July 1777, Francis Stringer of Burks County, Halifax District, Georgia, & Lucresa his wife, to John Inglies of Savannah, Georgia, Esquire, for £220 Georgia money, 200 acres in Granville County on Savannah River, SC, bounded at the time of the original grant to sd. Francis Stringer 3 June 1765 by land granted to Jacob Hurr, ____ Smith, Martin Fryer. Francis Stringer (LS), Lucretia Stringer (LS), Wit: Robert Hankinson, Joseph Miller. Proved in Orangeburgh District by the oath of Robert Hankinson 1 Aug 1777 before Wm. Robison, J. P. Recorded 1 Nov 1777.

T-4, 378-383: Lease & release. 17 & 18 Jan 1772, David Williams of Charles Town, Berkley County, Sc, planter, to Edmund Botsford of same, clerk, for £35,000 SC money, seventeen plantations called the Brotherhood Plantations, 100 acres granted in the name of William Deloach 22 Jan 1757, 200 acres (part of 250 acres) granted in the name of Edward Boykin 22 Jan 1757, 250 acres granted in the name of Jacob Buckholts 22 March 1745, 100 acres granted to Robert William 12 Feb 1755, 200 ares granted to Robert Williams 24 Nov 1764, 200 acres granted to Robert Williams 24 Nov 1764, 400 acres granted to James Baber 12 Apr 1748, 100 acres granted to Robert Williams 29 Nov 1751,

SOUTH CAROLINA DEED ABSTRACTS 1773-1778

150 acres granted to Samuel Wiggin 20 May 1747, 150 acres granted to Henry Roach 4 Sept 1749, 50 acres granted to Robert Williams 14 May 1752, 300 acres granted to Robert Williams 20 May 1747, 100 acres granted to John Evans 6 Dec 1744, 100 acres granted to Robert Williams 30 Apr 1748, 200 acres granted to Cornelius Reine 20 May 1744, 100 acres granted to John Newbury 6 De 1744, 250 acres granted to William James 12 June 1756, 175 acres granted to William Screven 7 June 1751, total 3025 acres on Pedee River in St. Davids Parish, Craven County. (Plat included). David Williams (LS), Wit: Ichd. Attwell, George Harris, Oliver Hart Junr. Proved 27 Oct 1777 before George Sheed, J. P., by the oath of Oliver Hart Junr. Recorded 1 Nov 1777.

T-4, 383-387: Lease & release. 10 & 11 Sept 1772, Edmund Botsford of Charlestown, Berkly County, Clerk, to David Williams of same place, planter, for £35,050 SC money, 3025 acres in seventeen plantations called the Brotherhood plantations. Edmund Botsford (LS), Wit: Thos Rivers, John Beddeley, Thos Young Junr. Proved 27 Oct 1777 before George Sheed, J.P., by the oath of Thomas Rivers. Recorded 1 Nov 1777.

T-4, 387-390: Lease & release. 23 & 24 June 1773, George DeFrance, Taylor, of new Bourdeaux, Hillsborough Township, SC, Prince Williams Parish, to Peter Moragne of same township, planter, for £20 SC money, tract called Vyniard Lott in Hillsborough Township four acres, lot number 67, adj. vinyard Lott of Stephen Thomas, Maria Cayrel Bayles, Peter Moragne, granted 5[?] March 1770 to said George DeFrance. G: Defrance (LS), Wit: [German signature, apparently Mari Weber]. Proved 20 June 1773 before Lewis de St. Pierre, J.P. in Ninety Six District, by the oath of Bartolemy Rilliette who also so Mary Webber signed her name as witness. Recorded 15 Nov 1777.

T-4, 390-394: Lease & release. 25 & 26 July 1775, John Bonneau of Goose Creek to Francis Bremar of Charlestown, gentleman, for £1500 SC money, 3000 acres on waters of Savannah River on a branch called Rockey River, in the angle of land laid out and land now the property of James Peart, said 3000 acres ranted to sd. John Bonneau of Goose Creek 21 july 1775. John Bonneau (X) (LS), Wit: James Greenwood, Dl. Mazyck. Proved 27 July 1775 before David Hopkins, J.P. in Camden District. Recorded 15 Nov 1777.

T-4, 394-396: 12 May 1777, Francis Bremar of Charlestown, Esqr., to Adrian Mayer of Purysburgh, Esqr., for £500 SC money, 3000 acres in the upper district, commonly called Ninety Six District, in Granville County, adj. land granted to William Nisbett, land granted to James Peart, land granted to William Burrows, and the present Cherokee boundary line, originally granted to Charles Webb and by him conveyed to said Francis Bremar, also tract of 3000 acres in the district aforesaid granted to John Bonneau and by him conveyed to Francis Bremar, adj. land granted to John Sturgeon, land granted to Josiah Pendarvis, on a branch of Savannah River called Rocky River. F. Bremar (LS), Wit: Frederick Rehm, John Forbes. Proved in Purysburgh by the oath of Doctor Frederick Rehm, 14 May 1777. Recorded 15 Nov 1777.

T-4, 396-398: Lease & release. 21 Aug 1777, Hezekiah Rose, planter, of St. Helena Parish, to Hannah Catterton, widow of same, for £25 SC money, 500 acres in Granville County on waters of Coosawhatchie, on Beaver Dam branch adj. land of Adrian Mayer Esqr., land supposed to be Derry Gillisons, plat certified by John Bremar 7 Feb 1775 and granted 4 May 1775, recorded in Book XXX page 333. Hezekiah Rose (LS), Wit: Joseph Wells, James Hogg. Proved in Purysburg by the oath of Joseph Wells before David Keatt, J.P., 29 Sept 1777. Recorded 15 Nov 1777.

T-4, 398-399: 29 Sept 1777, Hannah, relict of the late William Catterton of St. Helena Parish, to Adrian Mayer of Purysburgh, Esqr., for £300 SC money, 500 acres in Granville County on waters of Coosawhatchie, on Beaver Dam branch adj. land of Adrian Mayer Esqr., land supposed to be Derry Gillisons, granted 4 May 1775 to Hezekiah Rose and by him conveyed to Hannah Catterton, 21 Aug current. Hannah Catterton (LS), Wit: Joachim Harston, John Linder. Proved in Purysburg by the oath of John Linder Senr before David Keatt, J.P., 11 Oct 1777. Recorded 15 Nov 1777.

T-4, 400-402: 3 March 1770, Henry Laurens of Charlestown, SC, esquire, to Joseph Verree of same, carpenter, for £350 SC money, lot number 67 on Charlestown neck called Hamstead on Front Street, Drake Street. Henry Laurens (LS), Wit: Geo: Kincaid, David Williams. Proved in Charlestown District by the oath of George Kincaid 1 Nov 1777 before Geo: Sheed. Recorded 15 Nov 1777.

SOUTH CAROLINA DEED ABSTRACTS 1773-1778

T-4, 402-406: Lease & release. State of South Carolina. 30 & 31 Oct 1777, George Barksdale and Solomon Milner of Christ Church Parish, and Ann his wife, to Samuel Sorsby of State of North Carolina, for £1000 SC money, 350 acres on the Wateree River near the entrance of Wateree Creek adj. land laid out to Richard Gregory, Joseph Cates. George Barksdale Junr (LS), Solomon Milner (LS), Ann Milner (LS), Wit: Nathan Legare, Duncan McGuirman. Proved by the oath of Duncan McGuiriman before John Troup, 31 Oct 1777. Recorded 15 Nov 1777.

T-4, 406-412: Lease & release. 4 Nov 1777, Fenwick Bull of Charlestown, SC, gentleman, to Mary Haley of same, widow, for £900 SC money, lot on Charles Town Neck, number 73, now called Hampstead, on Drake Street and Front Street. Fenwicke Bull (LS), Wit: Robt. Johnston, Alexr. Forrester. Proved in Charlestown District before George Sheed, J.P., by the oath of Robert Johnston, 5 Nov 1777. Bond of Fenwicke Bull to Mary Haly in the sum of £3500 SC money to secure title from claim of John Bull now or late of Charlestown, carpenter, and Thomas Bull now or late of same place, 5 Nov 1777. Recorded 15 Nov 1777.

T-4, 412-416: Lease & release. 1 & 2 March 1774, Mary Ellis of Charles Town, widow, to John Eberly of same, for £1500 SC money, part of town lot number 207 adj. land formerly of Joseph Ward but now of Mary Lochon, land formerly belonging to heirs of Sarah Trott but now to ___ Ancrum, on Guignard Street. Mary Ellis (LS), Wit: Mark Moris, Wm. Hopkins. Proved in Charlestown District before George Sheed by the oath of Mark Morris, 6 Nov 1777. Recorded 15 Nov 1777.

T-4, 416-419: 1 Nov 1777, John Cross of Charlestown, SC, to William Thompson Junr and Sarah Ann Thompson of Pedee, for £5 SC money, 500 acres part of 1000 acres granted to sd. John Cross in craven County on north east side of Pedee River adj. land of William Thomson, Catfish Creek, land of William Herring, Rev. Hector Allison, Charles Dueits land. John Cross (LS), Wit: Will. Blamyer, James Sinkler Junr. Proved 5 Nov 1777 before George Sheed by the oath of James Sinkler Junr. Recorded 15 Nov 1777.

T-4, 419-422: Lease & release. 2 & 3 May 1774, Jean Dupuy of Hills Borough Township, SC, planter, to William Goodwin of same, planter, for £73 s10 SC money, 100 acres in Hills Borough Township granted 30 Aug 1764 to Jean Dupuy adj. land laid out to Matthias Beraud, Reuben Roberts, Jams. MacColough. Jean Dupuy (LS), Wit: David Warham, Lucas Florin. Proved before John Lewis Gervais by the oath of Lucas Florin, 13 Nov 1777. Recorded 29 Nov 1777.

T-4, 422-423: Agreement. St. Helena, 13th January 1775, Mr. Isaac Wetherly and Cornelius McCarty agree for the sum of £8000, that said Wetherly hath bargained and sould a tract of land on St. Helena 447 acres... to make good titles. Isaac Weatherley. Jacob Stobo, Gen., made oath to the hand writing of said Isaac Weatherley, 18 Nov 1777, before Jas. Parsons, J.P. Recorded 19 Nov 1777.

T-4, 423-427: Lease & release. 5 & 6 Nov 1777. Jacob Valk of Charlestown, gentleman, to Thomas Waring of same, gentleman, for £8000 SC money, lot on west side of old Church Street commonly called Meeting Street adj. land of Paul Smiser, land formerly of John McKensie Esqr., deceased, conveyed by John McKensie to Christopher Shetts 20 & 31 Jan 1769, and conveyed by Christopher Shetts to said Jacob Valk 26 & 27 Sept 1777. Jacob Valk (LS), Wit: James Culliatt, Paul Schlatter. Proved in Chas. Town District before George Sheed, J.p., by the oath of Paul Schlatter, 15 Nov 1777. Recorded 29 Nov 1777.

T-4, 427-430: Lease & release. 24 & 25 Apr 1773, John Wragg of SC, Esqr., to John Audibert of Granville County, merchant, for £700 SC money, 10½ acres part of a Barony of 12,000 acres belonging to sd. John Wragg at Coosahache in Granville County, adj. Isaac Deederys, on the Broad Road from Coosahache Bridge to Bees Creek, Messrs. Drayton and Fullers lots, lot of John Grimball, and sd. John Wragg. John Wragg (LS), Wit: Laughlin Martin, Elanor Martin. Proved in Charles Town District before George Sheed by the oath of Laughlin Martin, 12 Nov 1777. Recorded 29 Nov 1777.

T-4, 430-434: Lease & release. 16 & 17 Oct 1777, John Audibert of St. Peters Parish, Granville County, SC, planter, and Judith his wife, to Thomas Adamson of St. Helenas Parish, same county,

SOUTH CAROLINA DEED ABSTRACTS 1773-1778

10½ acres [same land as preceding deed]. (Plat included, dated 16 Oct 1777 by Elias Robert, D. Surveyor.) John Audibert (LS), Judith Audibert (LS), Wit: Elias Robert, John Rowell. Proved before Henry Gindratt, J.P. in Beaufort District, by the oath of Elias Robert, 17 Oct 1777. Recorded 29 Nov 1777.

T-4, 434-436: Lease & release. 27 & 28 Feb 1775, William Gibbes, Esqr., to John Rutledge, for £5 SC money, 850 acres granted to said William Gibbes 3 Feb instant in purysburgh Township, Granville County adj. land of Col. Samuel Mountague, Hector Berenger de Beaufain, David Gender, John Lowes Shiffell. Willm. Gibbes (LS), Wit: Henry Peronneau Junr, Thomas Yates. Proved before George Sheed by the oath of Henry Peronneau Junr., 21 Nov 1777. Recorded 28 Nov 1777.

T-4, 436-438: 28 Oct 1777, Richard Morgan of Charlestown, Shoemaker, to Joseph Atkinson of same, merchant, by indenture between Thomas Harvey and said Richard Morgan, Thomas Harvey is to sell to Richard Morgan a lot in the Parish of St. Philip in Charlestown, number 14, on Commings Street, now for £1000 SC money, said Richard Morgan sells to Joseph Atkinson. Richd. Morgan (LS), Wit: E. Rutledge, John Parker Junr. Proved in Charlestown District before George Sheed by the oath of John Parker Junr., 18 Nov 1777. Recorded 29 Nov 1777.

T-4, 438-441: Lease & release. 12 & 31 March 1777, Samuel Lynes of St. James Parish, Berkley County, to John Boyd of St. Marks parish, Craven county, for £50 SC money, 50 acres granted to said Samuel Lynes near the Congarees north side of Santee River adj. land laid out to Elizabeth Verdilly, Richard Jackson, Henry Snelling, James McKelvey, part of 200 acres ranted to sd. Samuel Lynes. Saml Lynes (LS), Wit: Philip Coutrier, Henry Boyd. Proved 13 March 1777 before Job Marion, J.P. in Berkly County, by the oath of Henry Boyd. Recorded 6 Dec 1777.

T-4, 441-446: Lease & release. South Carolina. 9 & 10 Oct 1777, George Ford Junior and Sarah his wife, lately otherwise called Sarah Singleton, daughter and Heiress at law of William Singleton, late of state aforesaid, deceased, to Isaac Hayne of St. Bartholomews Parish, Esquire, trustee for Samuel Singleton, a minor son and heir at law and devisees of Samuel Singleton late of St. Bartholomews Parish, planter, deceased, for £2250 SC money.... whereas William Singleton, late of the state aforesaid by his will did devise to his four sons Richard, William, Daniel, and Samuel Singleton, a tract of 822 acres granted to sd. William Singellton 24 May 1734, bounded at the time of original survey on lands of Thomas Golding, and they were all (except the eldest son Richard) only tenants for life, and the said Richard as eldest son and heir at law of his father the said William was seized in fee of his fourth part of said land immediately on his fathers death.. said Richard Singellton son and heir at law of said did die in his minority and without issue by which his brother the said William Singellton as heir at law to him the said Richard became seized of Richards fourth part, and said William Singellton afterwards married and died leaving his wife and child, which was afterwards born and proved to be a daughter to wit the Sarah Ford wife of said George Ford Junior... said Daniel and Samuel have since died by which the said Sarah hath become entitled to the whole of said tract of land... now bounded on land of Joseph Dobbins, William Harvey, John Singellton, and Samuel Singellton. George Ford Junr (LS), Sarah Ford (LS), Wit: Jno. Singellton, William Oswald. Proved by the oath of William Oswald, 12 Nov 1777 before Andrew Cunningham, J. P.

These are to certify that my son George Ford is several days past the age of twenty one years, being born the fifth day of October 1756.... 11 Oct 1777. George Ford Senr. Test: Jno Singellton, William Oswald. Recorded 6 Dec 1777.

T-4, 447-450: 21 Oct 1777, Thomas Shirley, late of Charlestown, SC, merchant, but now of Kingdom of Great Britain, by William Price of Charlestown in SC, merchant, his attorney, and Ann his wife, for £4200 SC money, to Philip Nesser of Charlestown, whereas said Thomas Shirley and William Price as seized as tenants in common of a lot on west side of King Street and was sold to them Thomas Shirley and William Price by John Kelly of Charlestown, baker, and Mary his wife, 13 July 1772. Thomas Shirley (LS), by his atty Wm. Price. Wm. Price (LS), Ann Price (LS), Wit: Daniel Smith, Nich. Langford. Proved in Charlestown District before George Sheed by the oath of Nicholas Langford, 15 Nov 1777. Recorded 6 Dec 1777.

SOUTH CAROLINA DEED ABSTRACTS 1773-1778

T-4, 450-454: Lease & release. 7 & 8 Oct 1777, James Bowman of Parish of St. Mark, Craven County, to Gabriel Manigault of Charlestown, Esqr., for £1500 SC money, 200 acres in Craven County near Pearse's Swamp on north side Santee River originally granted to sd. James Bowman, also 100 ares in Craven county on Pearses Swamp waters of Santee originally granted to one John Bowman, conveyed by Robert Bowman (eldest son and heir at Law of said John Bowman deceased) and Amey his wife to the said James Bowman (plat included). James Bowman (LS), Wit: Elizabeth Hasell, William Banbury. Proved before George Sheed by the oath of William Banbury, 6 Nov 1777. Recorded 6 Dec 1777.

T-4, 454-460: Lease & release. 21 & 22 Dec 1768, Elizabeth Petrie, extx. and James Laurens, Robert Philp and Robert Brisbane, exrs. of the will of Alexander Petrie of Charlestown, gentleman, deceased, to Alexander Rigg of same place, gentleman, for £1966 SC money, two lots in Charlestown, numbers 229 and 178, known by the name of the Orange Garden, on Broad Street and Tradd Street, which on 6 & 7 Oct 1767 conveyed by Samuel Carne of London, merchant, by John Rose of Charles Town, gentleman, and Robert Willson of same place, practitioner in Physick, his attornies, to said Alexander Petrie, lots adj. to john Burn esqr. in rust for a free negro woman named Amey, and land belonging to the heirs of ___ Watson (plat included). Eliz. Petrie (LS), Ro Brisbane (LS), Robert Philp (LS), James Laurens (LS), Wit: George Thomson, John Bremar. Proved before George Sheed by the oath of George Thomson, 22 Nov 1777. Recorded 6 Dec 1777.

T-4, 460-464: Lease & release. 1 & 2 July 1777, Darius Dalton of the Parish of Prince William, Beaufort District, SC, planter, and Mary his wife, to Benjamin Toomer of Parish of St. Helena, same district, planter, for £4000 SC money, 520 acres on the road leading to and from Port Royal Island, adj. land of heirs of William Bowery deceased, land of Cornelius Dupont, on the marshes of Husper Creek. Darius Dalton (LS), Mary Dalton (LS), Wit: Thos Taylor, Jacob Neal, Evan Evans. Proved 16 July 1777 before Andrew Agnew, J.P. in Beaufort District, by the oath of Thomas Taylor. Recorded 6 Dec 1777.

T-4, 464-467: 3 March 1770, Henry Laurens of Charlestown, SC, esquire, to Philip Hawkins of same town, merchant, for £900 SC money, lot in Charlestown, number 115 in Hamstead, on Hanover Street, Columbus Street, also lot number 115 on Hanover and Nassau Street, also lot number 5 on a piece of ground laid out for a square, also lot number 7 on said square. Henry Laurens (LS), Wit: Geo Kincaid, David Williams. Proved in Berkley County 10 Oct 1771 before William Burrows, J.P., by the oath of David Williams. Recorded 13 Dec 1777.

T-4, 467-471: Lease & release. 25 & 26 Nov 1776, Rachel Elfe of Charlestown, SC, widow, qualified and acting executrix, and Thomas Hutchinson & Benjamin Baker of same, exrs. of will of Thomas Elfe, late of Charlestown, cabinet maker, deceased, to Philip Hawkins of Charlestown, merchant, £461 s5 SC money, land granted 17 Dec 1772 to Thomas Elfe, 900 acres in Craven County on Raibourn Creek, and by his will dated 7 July 1775 mentioned that this land should be put to sale. Rachel Elfe (LS), Thos: Hutchinson (LS), Benjamin Baker (LS), Wit: Christ'r Hart, John Wagner. Proved by the oath of Christopher Hart before John Troup, J. P., 8 March 1777. Recorded 13 Dec 1777.

T-4, 471-474: Lease & release. 27 & 28 May 1777, George Haig of State of South Carolina, Esquire, and Susanna his wife, to Benjamin Farar, of Saxagotha Township, for £4400 SC money, 300 acres in Saxagotha Township adj. land granted to John Miller, Henry Weber, land adj. to the heirs of James Hopkins deceased, on Congaree River, granted 15 July 1736. Geo. Haig (LS), Susannah Haig (LS), Wit: Lambert Lance, Matthias Libecap. Proved by the oath of Mathias Libecap 30 May 1777 before Andw. Leitch, J.P. Recorded 13 Dec 1777.

T-4, 474-477: Lease & release. 17 & 18 May 1777, Benjamin Farar of Saxagotha Township, SC, esquire, and Elizabeth, his wife, to Philip Hawkins of Charlestown, merchant, for £20,000 SC money, tracts adj. each other in Saxagotha Township on south side Congaree River, total 3832 acres, adj. land of John Shillins, Jacob Geiger, John Stroup, John Chesnut, Jacob Friday, David Friday, William Arthur, Laurence Charles, Moses Kirkland. (Plat included indicated tracts of Henry Weaver, Edward Southwell, Job Marion, dated 17 July 1777 by Ralph Humphreys, D. Surveyor., wit. by Jno Colcock, Noah Stevenson.) Benj. Farar (LS), Eliz. Farar (LS), Wit: Robert Lithgow,

SOUTH CAROLINA DEED ABSTRACTS 1773-1778

James Bunyie, Ralph Humphreys. Proved before John Troup by the oath of James Bunyie, 5 June 1777. Recorded 13 Dec 1777.

T-4, 477-480: 10 Apr 1776, Thomas Egan of St. John's Parish, SC, overseer, to Dennis Egan of St. James Parish, Santee, for and John Egan Junior, his son, for £2000 SC money, 200 acres in said Parish of Santee, half of two tracts of 200 acres each granted by the late Lord Proprietor to Francis Gignilliat, adj. land purchased by Archibald Offut in 1774, John Roberts, land purchased by John Marion from John Skreene, and by him sold to John Jaudon who conveyed the same to Joseph Winningham and by him to Dennis Egan.... by virtue of a bargain dated 11 Apr 1775, 200 acres commonly called Lenneaus Ferry in the Parish of St. James Santee, on Santee River adj. lands purchased by Archibald Offut, and adj. two tracts before mentioned. Denis Egan (LS), Wit: Jno Blake, Thos Jones, Robt. Jessup. Proved before William Davis, J.P., by the oath of Robert Jessup, 8 Oct 1777. Recorded 13 Dec 1777.

T-4, 480-482: Lease & release. 1 & 2 Dec 1777, Abner Casey of Ninety Six District, planter, to Levi Casey, planter, of same, for £900 SC money, 200 acres in the fork between Broad and Saluda River granted 10 July 1766 to John Carsey [sic] the reputed father of the aforesaid Abner whereof the said Abner is the proper "hair," on a branch of Enoree River called Duncans Creek, recorded in Book AAA, page 22, audited in Book H No. 8, page 66, 1 Nov 1765. Abner Casey (LS), Wit: Josias Duckett, Joseph Duckett, James Bogan. Proved before John Johnston, J.P. by the oath of James Bogan, 2 Dec 1777. Recorded 13 Dec 1777.

T-4, 482-486: Lease & release. South Carolina. 18 & 19 June 1777, Robert Hails of State aforesaid, planter, to William Bull the younger of same, esquire, for £5375 SC money, land in Berkley County on south side Santee River, 200 acres, adj. said river, granted to Thomas Hails __ June 1759, recorded in Book YY, page 157, also tract of 250 acres in Berkley County on south side of Santee River granted to Robert Witten adj. land of Thomas Hails, granted 20 Dec 1762 recorded in Book WW, page 212, bequeathed by said Robert Witten in his will to George and Robert Hails. Robert Hails (LS), Wit: Sarah McNichol, John Bonnea, John Westcott. Proved in Charlestown District before George Sheed by the oath of John Bonnea, 25 Nov 1777. Recorded 13 Dec 1777.

T-4, 486-490: Lease & release. South Carolina. 4 & 5 Apr 1770, Joseph Pack of province aforesaid, to Philemon Waters of same, for £500 SC money, 350 acres in Craven County on a branch of Tyger River called Rockey branch, granted to sd. Joseph Pack by Gov. Montague. Joseph Pack (LS), Wit: George Beasley, William Ruger. Proved 27 Nov 1777 before Paul Townsend, J.P. in Chas. Town District, by the oath of Wm. Ruger. Recorded 17 Jan 1778.

T-4, 490-496: Lease & release. 28 & 29 Nov 1755, John Hamilton of Parish of St. George Hanover Square, County of Middlesex, but now of Charlestown, SC, to William Simpson of Charlestown, and John Murray of same place, physician, £8000 money of Great Britain, 50,000 acres part of 200,000 acres granted by four grants to William Livingston, which William Livingston conveyed to said John Hamilton (plat included). j. Hamilton (LS), Wit: James Grindlay, John Little. Proved in Charlestown District by Isaac DaCosta, merchant, who testified to the handwriting of John Hamilton, 3 Dec 1777. Recorded 17 Jan 1778.

T-4, 496-501: Deed of Partition. 7 July 1758, William Simpson of Charlestown, Esqr., and Elizabeth his wife, and John Murray of same, physician, whereas the two parties stand seized in joint tenancy of 50,000 acres, part of 200,000 acres granted to William Livingston, and conveyed to John Hamilton, now by agreement, and for £10 SC money, paid by said John Murray, confirm unto John Murray 25,000 acres the southeast half of said 50,000 acres above a place called Ninety Six on a branch of Santee River called Saludy adj. tract laid out to Benjamin Walker, marked A on plat (included in deed). William Simpson (LS), Elizabeth Simpson (LS), Wit: John Murray, Wm. Murray, James Grindlay. Proved by Joshua Ward who testified to the handwriting of Wm. Simpson, 3 Dec 1777, before George Sheed. Recorded 17 Jan 1778.

T-4, 502-505: 17 Jan 1771, Roger Pinckney, Provost Marshall of SC, to James Parsons and John Rutledge of Charles Town, Esquires, for £6350 SC money... whereas John Hamilton was seized of 50,000 acres above a place called Ninety Six granted 25 June 1752 to William Livingston and his associations and bounded by another tract of 50,000 acres granted to said William livingston, and

SOUTH CAROLINA DEED ABSTRACTS 1773-1778

said John Hamilton by his bond 26 Feb 1750 bound to George Hunter of Charleston, Gentleman, in the sum of £600 money of Great Britain for the payment of £300 like money, and Robert Brisbane admr. with the will annexed of George Hunter deceased, left unadministered by William Woodrop, exrs., in the court of common pleas did implead John Murray and Thomas Adams, admrs. of sd. John Hamilton, at November Term 1770 and did obtain a judgment.... Roger Pinckney Pro. Mar. (LS), Wit: Jacob Read, Robt. Ladson. Proved in Berkley County by the oath of Robert Ladson 29 Aug 1771 before John Troup, J.P. Recorded 17 Jan 1778.

T-4, 505-507: Lease & release. 25 & 26 Nov 1777, Michael Martz of Orangeburgh District, SC, yeoman, to Hezekiah Mayam and John James Haig, Esquires, for £1500 SC money, 200 acres in Saxagotha Township, Orangeburgh District, on south side Santee River granted to Johannes Martz 18 Oct 1757 adj. land laid out to Frederick Reys, ___ Auger, land granted to Andrew Wawsaw, and Michael Martz being eldest son & heir at law to said Johannes Martz. Michael Martz (X) (LS), Wit: Philip Benoist, Matthias Fender (X), Danl. Tateman. Proved 1 Dec 1777 by the oath of Daniel Tateman before William Tucker, J.P. Recorded 17 Jan 1778.

T-4, 508-509: 27 Dec 1773, Thomas Crawford of Wake County, No Carolina, to Thomas Wade of Anson County, NC, for £400 SC money, 600 acres in Craven County now but at the time it was ranted in Anson County, NC, on both sides Lynches Creek South fork, granted to John Crawford 30 March 1751 and by his will left to be sold by his executor the sd. Thomas Crawford for the payment of his debts. Thomas Crawford (LS), Wit: John White, John Wade, Fra. Moseley. Proved in Cheraw District by the oath of John White before Saml Spencer, J.P., 27 Dec 1773. A Memorial entered in Auditors Office in Book M. No. 12, page 464 12 Feb 1774. Recorded 17 Jan 1778.

T-4, 509-512: Lease & release. 24 & 25 Apr 1775, Garret Doyle of SC, planter, to Thomas Chadwick of same province, weaver, for £2000 SC money, 550 acres granted to Patrick Doyle 12 Sept 1757 and surveyed by John Wade 15 March 1757. Garret Doyle (O) (LS), Wit: Jno Morse, Thomas Bourk. Proved in Ninety Six District before David Zubly, J.P., by the oath of Thomas Bourk, 27 Apr 1775, "at my house in New Windsor." Recorded 17 Jan 1778.

T-4, 513-515: 28 Oct 1777, Thomas Holden of District of Ninety Six, planter, and Margaret, his wife, to David Adam of same, storekeeper, for £266 s13 d4 SC money, 100 acres in Craven County on north side Tyger River adj. David Farmer, William Curry, Aaron Fincher. Thomas Holden (LS), Margaret Holden (LS), Wit: Jno Nevin, John Pearson, Abraham Adams (A). Proved by the oath of John Nevin before Wm. Kennedy, J.P., 4 Dec 1777. Recorded 17 Jan 1778.

T-4, 515-518: Lease & release. 3 & 4 May 1776, William Montgomery of St. Marks Parish, Craven County, planter, and Margaret his wife, to Henry Montgomery, of same, for twenty shillings SC money, 600 acres, part of tract granted to sd. Wm Montgomery on north side Santee River in Craven County adj. land of Jno Cantey. William Montgomery (LS), Martha Montgomery (LS), Wit: Saml Bennet, Judith Wilbun, Jno Parrock. Proved in Camden District by the oath of Samuel Bennet before J. M. Harris, J. P., 30 Jan 1777. Recorded 17 Jan 1778.

T-4, 518-519: Christopher Singleton of the County of King William, Colony of Virginia, planter, appoint my son Robert Singleton of same, but shortly intending to make a journey to the Province of South Carolina, constitute him my attorney, to sell a tract of land whereof I am seized, 300 acres on the High Hills of Santee, Craven County, SC, granted to me 8 May 1758... dated 6 June 177. Christopher Singleton (LS), Wit: John Wingfield, Jos. Oliver, Mordecai Booth. Proved 6 June 1777 before Robert Brook, one of the Justices of the Commonwealth of Virginia in King William County, by John Wingfield, Joseph Oliver, and Mordecai Booth. Recorded 17 Jan 1778.

T-4, 519-522: Lease & release. 15 July 1777, Christopher Singleton in the State of Virginia, to Isham Moore of Craven County, SC, for £2500 SC money, 300 acres at the High Hills of Wateree River adj. land laid out for Peter Porcher, Mathias Singleton. Christopher Singleton (LS), Wit: Mattw. Singleton, Thos. Moffett, Mary Singleton. Proved in Camden District by the oath Matthew Singleton 1 Dec 1777 before John James Junr. Recorded 17 Jan 1778.

T-4, 522-524: Lease & release. 5 & 6 Nov 1777, Robert Morriss and Richard Stratford of Craven county, St. Marks Parish, SC, ship carpenters, to Isham Moore of same county and parish, planter,

SOUTH CAROLINA DEED ABSTRACTS 1773-1778

for £300 SC money, 150 acres at the high hills of Santee granted 23 Feb 1768 to Thomas Prestwood recorded in Book Three C's Page 58 and a memorial entered in Book H No. 8, page 436 and said Thomas Prestwood conveyed tract to Robert Morris and Richard Stratford, 28 & 29 June 1769. Robo't Morris (LS), Richard Stratford (LS), Wit: Matthw. Singleton, W[illiam] Bracey, Miles Gilliam. Proved in Camden District by the oath of Matthew Singleton, 1 Dec 1777 before John James Jur. Recorded 17 Jan 1778.

T-4, 524-526: Lease & release. 5 & 6 Nov 1777, Robert Morriss and Richard Stratford of Craven county, St. Marks Parish, SC, ship carpenters, to Isham Moore of same county and parish, planter, for £200 SC money, 100 acres at the high hills of Santee granted 12 Sept 1768 to William Brown recorded in Book DDD Page 537 and a memorial entered in Book I No. 9, page 537 and said William Brown conveyed tract to Robert Morris and Richard Stratford, 12 & 13 May 1769. Robo't Morris (LS), Richard Stratford (LS), Wit: Matthw. Singleton, W[illiam] Bracey, Miles Gilliam. Proved in Camden District by the oath of Matthew Singleton, 1 Dec 1777 before John James Jur. Recorded 17 Jan 1778.

T-4, 527-530: Lease & release. 21 & 22 Feb 1775, Joel Tapley of Craven County, SC, to Isham Moore of same, for £200 SC money, 133 acres on a branch of Black River called Tupelo Head granted to Joel Tapley 8 Dec 1774, recorded in Book III page 654. Joel Tapley (LS), Wit: James Mason, Robert Paslay, Thos Moffett. Proved 13 March 1775 before Malcom Clarke, J.P. in Camden District, by the oath of Thomas Moffett. Recorded 17 Jan 1778.

T-4, 531-533: Lease & release. 1 & 2 June 1774, Reuben Gilder of Ninety Six District, SC, planter, to William Smith of Camden District, overseer, for £100 SC money, 100 acres granted 12 Dec 1768 to Reuben Gilder, on a branch of Enoree River called Abners Creek between Broad and Saludy Rivers. Reuben Gilder (LS), Wit: James Daniell, Jese Daniell, George Slappey. Proved before Henry Patrick, J.P., by the oath of George Slappey, 12 Feb 1777. Recorded 17 Jan 1778.

T-4, 533-534: 23 Oct 1777, Hugh McClelland of Craven County, SC, to James Tate of Mecklenburgh County, North Carolina, for £400 South currency, 100 acres in Craven County on the stoney fork of Fishing Creek adj. the tract of land sd. Hugh McClelland lives on, the same granted to John Macknitt Alexander 27 Sept 1766, and number 474, recorded in the public registers office 22 Jan 1775, Book F-4, page 165. Hugh McCleland (LS), Wit: Samuel Lusk, Elizbeth Lusk (X). Proved in Camden District before Michael Dickson, J.P., 28 Oct 1777 by the oath of Samuel Law. Recorded 17 Jan 1778.

T-4, 535-536: 23 Oct 1777, Hugh McClelland of Craven County, SC, to James Tate of Mecklenburgh County, North Carolina, for £880 South currency, 300 acres in Craven County on the stoney fork of Fishing Creek adj. William Smith, Thomas Neely, Samuel Lusk, on the muddy branch, Mary Smith, granted to Hugh McClelland by a north patent 30 Oct 1765, number 98, a memorial entered Book M No. 12, page 468 22 Feb 1774. Hugh McCleland (LS), Wit: Samuel Lusk, Elizbeth Lusk (X). Proved in Camden District before Michael Dickson, J.P., 28 Oct 1777 by the oath of Samuel Lusk. Recorded 17 Jan 1778.

T-4, 536-537: 14 Jan 1775, John Barkly of St. Marks Parish, SC, planter, and Agnes his wife, to John Latta of same, for £300 SC money, 200 acres granted to John Thompson 13 Aug 1766 in the "Wexhaws" and said tract was made to Archibald Clark by deed 21 Feb 1774, and a memorial entered and from sd. Archibald Clark to George Grier 21 Nov 1774 and from said George Grier to John Barkley 14 Jan 1775. John Barkley (LS), Agness Barkley (O) (LS), Wit: Wm. Simpson, Robert Barkley, Joseph Barnet. Proved 16 Jan 1775 before James Patton, J.P. in Camden District, by the oath of Wm. Simpson.

T-4, 538-542: Lease & release. 17 & 18 July 1771, Edward Harleston of St. Johns Parish, Berkley County, SC, executor of the will of John Harleston, Esqr., deceased, to James Fogarthie of Charlestown, carpenter, for £1200 SC money, 36 acres on Charlestown Neck, part of the land formerly called Cummings Point but now named by the name of Harleston, by will 24 May 1767, who did devise to his son John Harleston and to each of his three daughters, and appointed said Edward Harleston with Nicholas Harleston and Benjamin Smith of Goose Creek, exrs.... Edward

SOUTH CAROLINA DEED ABSTRACTS 1773-1778

Harleston (LS), Wit: John Dart, Wm. Print. Proved in Charlestown District before George Sheed by the oath of William Print, 22 Dec 1777. Recorded 22 Jan 1778.

T-4, 542-546: Lease & release. 2 & 3 May 1777, James Graves of Charlestown, Bricklayer, and Massey his wife, to John Dill and John Witter of James Island, planter, for £____ SC money, 224 acres at Wappoo in St. Andrews Parish, adj. marsh lands of Thomas Tucker, lands of Jeremiah Savage and of Jacob Hincle, Stono River, which land was conveyed by Richard Godfrey and Rebecca his wife 12 & 13 Jan 1756 to Thomas Graves deceased who devised the same to James Graves his son. James Graves (LS), Massey Graves (LS), Wit: Jno Colcock, Richard Mason. Proved in Charlestown District before George Sheed by the oath of John Colcock, Esqr., 2 Jan 1778. Recorded 22 Jan 1778.

T-4, 546-550: Lease & release. 4 & 5 Dec 1777, Aaron Loocock of Charlestown, merchant, and Mary his wife, to Bryan Foskey of same, pilot, for £500 SC money, lot on the corner of Union Street and Rapers Alley in Charlestown, adj. to the south on a brick house formerly belonging to one James Withers. Aaron Loocock (LS), Mary Loocock (LS), Wit: F. Saunders, Carolina Harrison. Proved in Charlestown District by the oath of Francis Saunders before Geo Sheed, 5 Jan 1778. Recorded 22 Jan 1778.

T-4, 550-552: Lease & release. 5 & 6 Feb 1776, John Huggins of Craven County, SC, planter, to Joseph Frizer Sr. of Christ Church Parish, for ten shillings, 192 acres in Christ Church Parish. John Huggins (LS), Wit: Samuel White, Jacob Bonhorste, John English. Proved before John Syme, J.P., by the oath of John English, 20 Dec 1777. Recorded 22 Jan 1778.

T-4, 552-556: Lease & release. 23 & 24 March 1775, George Bland of Beaufort District, SC, Shoemaker, to Elizabeth Read of same, for £300 SC money, lot number 141 in Town of Beaufort, adj. public square, Carteret Street. George Bland (LS), Wit: Danl John Greene, John Guinn, Edward Gardner. Proved 28 Aug 1775 before Andrew Agnew, J.P. in Beaufort District, by the oath of Daniel John Greene. Recorded 22 Jan 1778.

T-4, 556-559: Lease & release. 5 & 6 Jan 1778, Robert Dee, late of Goswell Street in the City of London, but now of Charleston, SC, gentleman, to William Glenn and George Duncan, merchants, for £3625 SC money, 500 acres in Granville County which is pat of a Barony granted to Landgrave William Hodgson of the Six Clerks Office, County of Middlesex, Kingdom of Great Britain, number 22, adj. land of Thomas Rivers, William Sandys deceased, James Peart, Robert Brailsford. (Plat included, certified by John Linder, D.S.) Robert Dee (LS), Wit: Robt. Johnston, Alexr. Forrester. Proved in Charlestown Dist., by the oath of Robert Johnston 6 Jan 1778 before Geo: Sheed. Recorded 22 Jan 1778.

END OF BOOK T-4.

V-4, 1-5: Lease and release. 4 & 5 June 1772, Philoman Waters of Charles Town, Gentleman, and Mary his wife, to Willoughby Pugh of Prince Williams Parish, Granville County, for £500 SC money, 250 acres in Purrysburgh Township granted 10 Sept 1768, made to sd. Philoman by George Lasman son & heir of John Martin Lasman deceased. P. Waters (LS), Mary Waters (LS), Wit: Saml Cross, Jacob Ham. Proved 5 June 1772 before William Mason, J.P. in Berkly County, by the oath of Jacob Ham. Recorded 4 Sept 1775.

V-4, 6-11: Lease and release. 7 June 1775, William Godfrey & Jane his wife of Parish of St. Peter to Isaac Hayne of Colleton County, St. Bartholomews Parish, planter, for £3372 SC money, 400 acres in Granville County adj. at time of original grant to Col. Flower, Mr. Colley, Vovers land, Rodolph, and Savannah River, granted __ March 1735 to David Gautier in the Township of Purrysburgh, and descended on the death of said David Gotier to Mary Gautier his only Child and heiress, afterwards the wife of Chas. Christopher Peter, and on 1 & 2 June 1761 sd. Charles Christopher Peter with Mary Gautier then Mary Peter, did sell unto Mary Hayne said tract, and said Mary Hayne died some years after without issue & intestate whereupon the said land came by descent to Isaac Hayne who on 9 & 10 June conveyed to Wm. Godfrey. William Godfrey (LS), Jane Godfrey (LS), Wit: Wm. Harr. Wigg, Anthony Godfrey. Proved in Beaufort District by the oath of William Harr. Wigg 9 June 1775 before Bellamy Crawford. Recorded 6 Sept 1775.

SOUTH CAROLINA DEED ABSTRACTS 1773-1778

V-4, 11-17: Lease and release. 16 & 17 Sept 1772, James Screven of Georgia, planter, and Anthony Toomer of Charles Town, SC, Bricklayer, executors of the will of Charles Odingsell, late of Georgia, deceased, to Josiah Murdaugh, of the province of Georgia, planter, for £400 SC money, 1000 acres on the waters of Saltcatcher adj. land surveyed for John Miller, originally granted to said Charles Odingsell 8 March 1765. Anth'y Toomer (LS), James Screven (LS), Wit: Geo: Davidson, Dalziel Hunter. Proved 17 Sept 1772 before James Johnston, J. P. in Berkly County, by the oath of George Davidson. Proved 22 Apr 1774 before Parmenas Way, J. P. in Parish of St. John, Province of Georgia, by the oath of Charles Odingsell. Recorded 8 Sept 1775.

V-4, 17-22: 16 Apr 1774, John Wyly, Sheriff of the district of Camden, to William Gibson of same, planter, whereas Isaac Laney of Bullocks Creek in the district of Camden, planter, was seized of a tract of land in Craven County, before the division line between this province and North Carolina, supposed to be in Tryon County in North Carolina on both sides of Bells Mill Creek adj. Bell, McDaws, 200 acres part of 240 acres granted to William Bell 14 Nov 1771 memorial entered in the Auditor Generals Office of South Carolina Book M No. 12, page 31, 10 Dec 1772, and Isaac Laney by bond dated 30 July 1767 bound to Zachariah Bell in the sum of £200 for the payment of £100, and said Zachariah Bell in the court of common pleas obtained a judgment in February Term 1774... sold for £200 s5 SC money. John Wyly sheriff (LS), Wit: Thomas Jones, Richd. Hoyle, William Kershaw. Proved 30 Aug 1774 before Jno Newman Oglethorpe, J.P., by the oath of Thomas Jones.

V-4, 22-28: Lease and release. 26 & 27 June 1775, John Hatter of Charles Town, mariner, and Elizabeth his wife, to James Fallows of same, shopkeeper, for £1113 SC money, 483 acres on north side Edisto River and a tract of 1000 acres on the north side of Edisto River in Berkly County adj. land of sd. John Hatter. John Hatter (LS), Elizabeth Hatter (LS), Wit: Jno Mackie, Hy. Gerdes. Proved on Chs. Town District before John Coram, J.P., by the oath of Henry Gerdes. Recorded 14 Sept 1775.

V-4, 28-29: Sarah Beresford of Charles Town, widow, relict of Richard Beresford, late of said town, deceased, for five shillings, relinquish dower by Susannah Mann of Prince Georges Parish, Winyaw, widow, her third right and title of dower to lot in George Town, number 43, dated 8 Oct 1772. Sa. Beresford (LS), Wit: Peter Meursett, George Nixon. Recorded 19 Sept 1775.

V-4, 29-30: Francis Fincher of Ninety Six District, SC, bound to Thomas Holden of same, in the sum of £5000 SC money, to make title to 100 acres on Tyger River formerly granted to James Pickett, dated 11 March 1775. Francis Fincher (LS), Wit: Jesse Fincher, John Pearson, John Townsend (T). Proved in Ninety Six District before Thos. Gordon, J.P., by the oath of John Pearson, 4 July 1775. Recorded 19 Sept 1775.

V-4, 30-31: John Boss, Gentleman, do give unto my sister Ann Boss 1000 acres, dated 22 Feb 1775. Jno Boss (LS), Wit: Jane Stewart, Samuel Brewer, [Ann Stewart]. Proved by the oath of Mrs. Jane Stewart 29 July 1775 before John Troup, J.P. Recorded 19 Sept 1775.

V-4, 31-38: Lease and release. 30 & 31 Dec 1772, Hugh Brown of Charles Town, Cabinet Maker, and Mary his wife, to John Kelly of same, baker, for £2430 SC money, lot on west side King Street adj. land of George Blake, lot lately sold to George Gitsinger, land of harris, and land now or late belonging to Richard Beresford, Esquire, deceased, which said lot belonged to Caleb Easton in his life time and at the time of his decease, and by his will 22 April last past did bequeath to his then wife Mary Brown by the name of Mary Easton, and appointed his said wife with Jacob Valk of Charles Town, executors. Hugh Brown (LS), Mary Brown (LS), Wit: John Dart, Thos Stewart. Proved in Berkley County before David Deas, J.P., by the oath of John Dart, 15 July 1775. Recorded 20 Sept 1775.

V-4, 39-41: 28 March 1775, Ebenezer Dunnam of Prince Georges Parish, SC, planter, to Joseph Johnson of St. Davids Parish, Sadler, for £40 SC money, 600 acres granted to Ebenezer Dunnam 8 July 1774 in Granville County on Horse Creek. Ebenz'r Dunnam (LS), Wit: Eben Dunnam Junr, Jacob Dunnam, John Dunnam. Proved by the oath of John Dunnam 21 March 1775 before Francis Britton, J.P. Recorded 25 Sept 1775.

SOUTH CAROLINA DEED ABSTRACTS 1773-1778

V-4, 41-42: 22 March 1775, Zachariah Bell of Craven County, Camden District, SC, to William Bell of same, for £50 SC money, tract on north side of Broad River on a branch of Bullocks Creek called Bells Creek being one third part of 500 acres granted to sd. Zachariah Bell for 500 acres, 166 acres on Zachariah Bells old line, granted to sd. Bell 8 July 1774. Zachariah Bell (LS), Wit: Samuel Barkley, Jean Rodgers (M). Proved in Camden District by Jane Rogers before Joseph brown, J.P., 30 July 1775. Recorded 25 Sept 1775.

V-4, 43-47: Lease and release. 15 & 20 Apr 1774, Charles Cantey of St. Stephens Parish, Craven County, to Richard Walter of St. Georges Parish, Berkly County, for £5 SC money, 400 acres granted 19 Nov 1772 in St. Georges Parish, adj. land of Ralph Izard, John Izard, Richard Saltus, Peter Bocquett Junior. Cha's Cantey (LS), Wit: James Sinkler, Thomas Cooper. Proved 8 May 1775 before Maurice Simons, J.P., by the oath of James Sinkler. Recorded 27 Sept 1775.

V-4, 48-51: Lease and release. 24 & 25 May 1775, Philip Henry of Charles Town, and Sarah Maria Henry his wife, to Lewis Ogier of same place, for £20 SC money, four tracts of land (1) 250 acres on waters of Little River adj. land surveyed for Wm. Griffin Senior (2) 250 acres in the Forks of Tyger Rivers adj. land of Daniel Mooring (3) 250 acres in Berkly County on waters of Bush Creek adj. land of Susanah Kersey and Peter Hawkins (4) 250 acres in Craven county on north east side of Reedy River on Reybournes Creek adj. land laid out to Mary Richie, a total of 1000 acres. Philip Henry (LS), S. M. Henry (LS), Wit: John Heard, Anthony Cooper. Proved in Charles Town District by the oath of John Heard 17 Aug 1775. Recorded 27 Sept 1775.

V-4, 51-53: Joseph Barnet of Ninety Six District bound to Lionel Chalmers of Charles Town, physician, in the penal sum of £3000 for the payment of £1500 on or before 26 July to make title to 250 acres in Granville County on a small branch of Long Cane Creek called Sandy Run adj. Henry Downs, also 50 acres at a place called Thompson's Ford on the north west fork of Long cane Creek adj. land of Robt. Turnbull, 200 acres about twenty miles southwest of Boonsborough Township on the dividing ground between the waters of northwest fork of Long Cane and Savannah River on Sanes Creek, dated 26 July 1775. Jos. Barnett (LS), Wit: Robert Buchanan, Jos. Waring. Proved in Charles Town District 31 July 1775 by the oath of Joseph Waring before Wm. Nisbett, J.P. Recorded 2 Oct 1775.

V-4, 53-58: Lease and release. __ March 1775, Andrew Broughton Senior of Charles Town, to Philip Henry of same place, for £1000 SC money, 300 acres in Ninety Six District on north east side of Saludy River on a branch called Wallnut Creek adj. William Arthur, land laid out on the Bounty, and vacant land; 200 acres in the fork of Broad and Saludy Rivers on the long branch waters of Saludy adj. land of John Rall, Moses Kirkland; 150 acres on waters of little River adj. land surveyed for William Griffin Senior; 250 acres in the forks of Tyger River adj. land of Daniel Mooring; 20\59 acres in Berkeley County on waters of Bush Creek adj. land of Susannah Kersey and Peter Hawkins; 250 ares in Craven county on north east side of Reedy River on Reybourns creek adj. land of Mary Riche; total 1500 acres. Andw Broughton (LS), Wit: William Hext, Francis Bremar. Proved 22 Aug 1775 before Rowland Rugeley, J.P., by the oath of Francis Bremar. Recorded 7 Oct 1775.

V-4, 58-61: Lease and release. 9 & 10 May 1775, Samuel Chollet of Charles Town, to Philip Henry of same, for £50 SC money, two tracts of land (1) 1000 acres in Craven county on branches of Little Cherokee Creek waters of road River three miles below George Blanton, Esquires, adj. land of R. P. H. Hatley, Esqr. (2) 450 acres in Craven County on a branch called Linshes Branch waters of Enoree River adj. land of William Sims, Richard Winnes, Pierce Butler, John Hall, Thomas Farr Senior, Esqr. Samuel Chollet (LS), Wit: James Clitherall, A. Chollet. Proved in Charles Town District by the oath of Abraham Chollet 23 Aug 1775 before R. Rugeley, J.P.

V-4, 61-62: Purrysburgh in Granville County. 8 July 1774, John Audibert of St. Helena Parish, Tavern Keeper, to Mary Ann Vaigneur of St. Peters Parish, for £50 SC money, 100 acres Bounty granted to said John Audibert 6 Feb 1773 in St. Peters Parish, adj. land granted to Henry Gindrat, said Mary Ann Vaigneur. John Audebert (LS), Wit: James Peart, John L. Vaigneur. Proved in Purysburgh by the oath of James Peart 18 July 1775 before Adrian Meyer. Recorded 18 Oct 1775.

SOUTH CAROLINA DEED ABSTRACTS 1773-1778

V-4, 63-64: 1 June 1775, Josiah Pendarvis of St. Helena Parish, planter, to James Peart, Dep. Surveyor of lands, for £300 SC money, 3000 acres on waters of Savannah River on a branch of Long Cane called Johnstons Creek adj. land laid out to said Josiah Pendarvis 3 Apr 1775, granted 4 May 1775. Jos. Pendarvis (LS), Wit: Eliza. Bryan, Thos Rivers. Proved in Charles Town District by the oath of Thomas Rivers before Fra's Bremar, J.P. Recorded 18 Oct 1775.

V-4, 64-65: 15 June 1775, Josiah Pendarvis of St. Helena Parish, planter, to James Peart, Dep. Surveyor of lands, for £150 SC money, 2000 acres on the Cherokee Line adj. land laid out to B--- Wilkinsons, granted 4 May. Jos. Pendarvis (LS), Wit: Eliza. Bryan, Thos Rivers. Proved in Charles Town District by the oath of Thomas Rivers before Fra's Bremar, J.P., 28 Aug 1775 Recorded 19 Oct 1775.

V-4, 66-67: 29 Aug 1775, Josiah Pendarvis of St. Helena Parish, planter, to James Peart, Dep. Surveyor of lands, for £10 SC money, 50 acres on waters of New River and branch of the great swamp adj. land granted to Ann Catterton now Joseph Willcox, land laid out to Willm. Catterton now Michael Peter's. Jos. Pendarvis (LS), Wit: George Allison, John Kerr. Proved by the oath of Charles Allison before Adrian Meyer, J.P., 10 Aug 1775 Recorded 19 Oct 1775.

V-4, 67-69: 13 June 1775, William Godfrey, planter, of St. Helena Parish, Granville County, to James Peart, D. Sur. of Land, for £50 SC money, 750 acres on waters of New River and branch of the great Swamp granted 3 Apr 1775. Wm Godfrey (LS, Wit: George Allison, Anthony Godfrey. Proved by the oath of George Allison 10 Aug 1775 before Adrian Mayer. Recorded 24 Oct 1775.

V-4, 69-70: Colleton County, Carolina. John Jackson for £5 s6 to Henry Jackson of province of Carolina, 100 acres English measure granted by the Lords Proprietors 10 May 1701... dated 12 Apr 1706. John Jackson, Wit: William Wosbery, Thomas Peter, Sarah Hendrick.

V-4, 70-71: 3 March 1774, John Ladson of St. Bartholomews Parish, planter, to Margaret Ladson of same, widow [no consideration mentioned], 461 acres in parish aforesaid adj. lands of Richd. Timmons, Thomas Timmons Junr, Joseph Perry, Daniel Blake, Esqr., Arthur Middleton, Esqr. John Ladson (LS), Margarett Ladson (LS), Wit: John Barron, Wm. Hull, Patrick Turnbull. Proved before John Troup, J.P., by the oath of William Hull, 16 Sept 1775. Recorded 26 Oct 1775.

V-4, 71-76: Lease and mortgage. 15 & 16 Sept 1775, John Ladson of St. Bartholomews Parish, Colleton County, planter, to Peter Leger and William Greenwood of Charles Town, merchants, whereas Robert Ladson, late of St. Bartholomews Parish, Colleton County, planter, deceased, was seized of tract in parish aforesaid and by his will bequeathed said tract to said John Ladson, now by his bond to sd. Peter Leger and William Greenwood in the sum of £1938 SC money, 483 acres adj. land of Thomas Timmons, Daniel Blake, Arthur Middleton, ___ Bery, Richard Timmons but now of Thomas Racliffe. Jno. Ladson (LS), Wit: Jos Ward, John Walters Gibbs. Proved by the oath of John Walters Gibbs, 18 Sept 1775 before John Coram. Recorded 27 Oct 1775.

V-4, 76-79: Lease and release. 4 & 5 Aug 1775, John Remington Junior of Charles Town, esquire, and Sarah his wife, to Wm. Downes of same, gentleman, for £20 SC money, 350 acres in Craven County, St. Marks Parish, on the south fork of Dutchmans Creek adj. land of James Hardridge, ranted 7 May 1774 to said John Remington Junr. John Remington Jnr. (LS), Sarah Remington (LS), Wit: James Donovan, Isaac Donavan. Proved in Chs. Town District before John Coram by the oath of James Donavan, 23 Sept 1775. Recorded 1 Nov 1775.

V-4, 79-82: Lease and release. 20 & 21 Sept 1775, James Wright of Charles Town, Gentleman, and Rebecca his wife, to William Downes of same, gentleman, for £20 SC money, 350 acres in Ninety Six District, on the west side of Bush River on branches thereof adj. land of Patrick Blain, Thomas Johnson, Patrick Blain, James Dalrymple, Charles ONeal, also 150 acres in Ninety Six District, Craven County on east side of Saludy River on Beaverdam Creek adj. land of Peter Scott, one Murphy, John Wright, granted to said James Wright 15 of this instant September. James Wright (LS) Rebecca Wright (LS), Wit: Wm. Davie, John Rushurt[?]. Proved in Chs. Town District before R. Rugeley by the oath of William Davie, 9 Oct 1775. Recorded 2 Nov 1775.

SOUTH CAROLINA DEED ABSTRACTS 1773-1778

V-4, 82-85: Lease and release. 1 & 2 March 1775, Ephraim Mitchell of Town of Orangeburgh, Esquire, to Wm. Downes of Charles Town, for £5 SC money, lot of half an acre in Town of Orangeburgh, number 395. Ephraim Mitchell (LS), Wit: Fra's Bremar, Peter Bremar. (Plat included). Proved by the oath of John Bremar 24 Oct 1775 before R. Rugeley, J.P. Recorded 3 Nov 1775.

V-4, 85-88: Lease and release. 24 & 25 Aug 1775, John Deas, Esqr., of Charles Town, and Elizabeth his wife, to Charles Graville Montague, former Governor of the said Province of SC, for £5 s13 SC money, 500 acres on Savannah River in the District of Ninety Six adj. land of Ezekiel Harlin, land of Ward, land of Bedingfield, granted 13 Sept last past by said John Deas. John Deas (LS), Wit: Jams. Smith, J. Ewing Colhoun.

V-4, 88-91: Lease and release. 29 & 30 Aug 1774, George Fortune, Master or Commander of the Ship Charming Sally, to Darby Pendergrass of Charles Town, mercht., for £3000 SC money, 200 acres in Craven County, Prince Georges Parish, south of Waccamaw River upon Tiley Swamp adj. land of Benjn Gause, granted to sd. George Fortune (on the Kings Bounty) 26 Aug instant. George Fortune (LS), Wit: George Thompson, Saml Prioleau Junr.

V-4, 91-94: Lease and release. 28 & 29 July 1775, Joshua Loper of Beaufort District, SC, planter, to Robt. Marlow of same, for £75 SC money, 250 acres granted to Joshua Loper 15 Sept 1771 on Savannah River adj. land of David Graham, Esqr., land of Danl Blake, Esqr. Joshua Loper (LS), Wit: James Thompson, Peter Banner, Wm. Thompson. Proved in Beaufort District by the oath of James Thompson 29 July 1775. Recorded 9 Nov 1775.

V-4, 94-96: Lease and release. 11 & 12 June 1775, James Pritchard, Esqr., of Ninety Six, SC, to James McKelvey of St. Johns Parish, Berkley County, planter, for £10 SC money, 500 acres in the parish of St. Johns Berkley adj. land granted to Francis Kinloch, James McKelvey, Isaac Huger & Wm. Locock, James & George Beird, Gabriel Marion, Josiah Brunson. James Prichard (LS), Wit: Ephraim Mitchell, John Mort. Williams. Recorded 4 Nov 1775.

V-4, 96-101: Lease and release. 13 & 14 Sept 1770, James Thomson of Craven County, SC, and Elizabeth his wife, to Aaron Baker of same, planter, for £350 SC money, 250 acres, part of 860 acres granted to Mary Cofer otherwise called Mrs. Mary Raven in Craven County on Pedee River adj. Francis Wood, part of said tract now William Clarks land. James Thomson (LS), Wit: Joseph Burch (IB), Joshua Baker. Proved in Craven County by the oath of Joseph Burch 3 Nov 1772 before Joseph Gourly. Recorded 17 Nov 1775.

V-4, 101-107: Lease and release. 18 & 19 Oct 1775, James Cook of Christ Church Parish, SC, Surveyor, and Sarah his wife, to John Syme of St. Thomas Parish, Practitioner of Physick, whereas Richard Beresford late of Charles Town was possessed of a tract of 500 acres English measure granted 17 Aug 1700 to Elias Foissin in Berkly County on Wandoe River, and on 8 July 1772 made his will and named his wife ____ Beresford executrix during her widowhood and Robt. Smith and Alexander Gillon with Christopher Gadsden, Thomas Smith of Broad Street, and his sons when they attained the age of 21 years, executors, and said Robert Smith and Alexr. Gillon executors conveyed 25 & 26 May 1773 sold to said James Cook, this tract, now for £250 SC money, convey said 400 acre tract.... they will suffer John Hatter of Charles Town, mariner, and Elizabeth his wife, during their lives to live on said plantation. Jas. Cook (LS), Sarah Cook (LS), Wit: Jos. Ward, Jno Heard. Proved 21 Oct 1775 before Thomas Turner, J. P. in Charlestown District, by the oath of Jno Heard. Recorded 18 Nov 1775.

V-4, 107-111: Lease and release. 20 & 21 Nov 1775, Rawlins Lowndes of Charles Town, esquire, to Rowland Rugeley of same, for £513 SC money, lot near the Town Gates of Charles Town upon the Broad Road leading to and from Charles Town all the way down the road which divides the lands of Daniel Canon from the lands of said Rawlins Lowndes, on the line of a tract lately sold by said Rawlins Lowndes to said Rowland Rugeley. Raw's Lowndes (LS), Wit: Esther West, Raws Lowndes Junr.

V-4, 111-113: Lease and release. 21 & 22 Nov 1772, John Vernon and Mary his wife of Granville County, to Lacon Ryan of same, for £500 SC money, 300 acres in Granville County on waters of

SOUTH CAROLINA DEED ABSTRACTS 1773-1778

Stevens Creek adj. Benjn. Ryans, David Lockhart, Walker. John Vernon (LS), Mary Varnon (X) (LS), Wit: Barton Harriss, Benj. Ryan. Proved in Ninety Six District 26 Aug 1775 by the oath of Benja. Ryan before LeRoy Hammond, J. P. Recorded 4 Dec 1775.

V-4, 114-117: Lease and release. 21 & 22 Sept 1774, James Harris of Granville County, SC, planter, to Joseph Rees of same, planter, for £400 SC money, 100 acres granted to John McKoy 22 Aug 1771 on a branch of Stephens Creek near the hand of sd. branch, grant recorded in Book TT, page 189... memorial entered in Book L. No. 11, page __ 20 ___ 1771, conveyed by said John McKoy to said James Harris. James Harris (H) (LS), Elizabeth Harris (LS), Wit: Thos Hagens, Moses Haris, Thomas Oden. Proved in Ninety Six District before Moses Kirkland, J.P., by the oath of Moses Harris., 24 Sept 1774. Recorded 5 Dec 1775.

V-4, 117-121: Lease and release. 26 & 27 May 1773, Thomas Hoddy of Prov. of SC, planter, to Alexander Anderson of same, both of parish of Prince George Winyaw, Craven County, for £500 SC money, 300 acres on north side of George Town Creek in parish of Prince George adj. Mr. Ports, Mr. Wilks, Mr. Smith, granted 6 Aug 1735 to John Hoddy deceased, and said Thomas Hoddy & Elizabeth his wife legal and sole heir unto said John Hoddy deceased... Thomas Hoddy (X) (LS), Elizabeth Hoddy (R) (LS), Wit: Thomas Durant, Thomas Martyn Sanders, Vallintine Butler. Proved in Geo. Town Dist., before Benjamin Young, J.P., by the oath of Thos. Martyn Sanders, 17 Dec 1774. Recorded 8 Dec 1775.

V-4, 121-125: Lease and release. 10 & 11 Oct 1775, James Doharty of Beaufort District, planter, to Henry Talbird Senr of same, for £1000 SC money, 100 acres on Hilton Head in St. Helena Parish, Beaufort District, adj. Mr. Ward, on a branch of the River May, Scull Creek, adj. said Henry Talbird formerly the property of Phillip Delegall, which was conveyed by Denham Feares & Mary his wife 7 Sept 1770 to James Doharty. Jas. Doharty (LS), Wit: Richard Yeadon, Willm. Smith. Proved in Charles Town District, 6 Nov 1775 by the oath of Richard yeadon before Thomas Turner, J.P. Recorded 13 Dec 1775.

V-4, 126-129: 2 May 1775, Thomas Grimball Junr, Sheriff of Charles Town District, SC, to Thomas Shirley & William Price of Charles Town, merchants, whereas John Gossman, late of Charles Town, Tavern Keeper, deceased, was seized of lot on west side of King Street in Charles Town, and by his bond 10 Apr 172 to Othniel Beale, Esqr., of Charles Town, for £4000 SC money, and John Beal, exr. of the will of Othneil Beale, obtained a judgment against Philip Harting and Mary his wife late Mary Gossman, extx. of the will of John Gossman deceased... lot on west side of Kings Street adj. land late of Edward Bullard deceased, land of Martha Clifford. T. Grimball Junr (LS), Shff Wit: Phil Prioleau, Joseph Gaultier. Proved in the Public Register Office by the oath of Philip Prioleau 20 March 1776 before Fenwicke Bull, J.P. Recorded 20 March 1776

V-4, 130-132: Lease and release. 28 & 29 Jan 1775, John Thomson of Parish of St. Marks, Craven county, planter, to Willm McKee of same, for £100 SC money, 100 acres on south side Beaver Creek a branch of Wateree River in Parish of St. Marks, adj. Jeduthan Gibson, Willm. McKee, Jonathan Alexander, granted 28 Jan 1775 to John Thomson. John Thomson (O), Molly Thomson (X), Wit: William Mccullough, Adm. Tomson. Proved in Camden District by the oath of Adam Thomson, 26 July 1775 before R. Rugeley. Recorded 15 Dec 1775.

V-4, 132-135: Lease and release. 3 & 4 March 1773, James Williams of Parish of St. Marks, Craven County, planter, to Thomas Creighton of same, for £230, 100 acres on Beaver Creek part of 200 acres held by the said James williams and part of tract granted to him adj. James Miller, James Douglass. James Williams (LS), Wit: John Simmons, Stephen Irons, Willm. Coward, Alexr. Tomb. Proved in Camden District before R. Rugeley 26 July 1775. Recorded 18 Dec 1775.

V-4, 132-135: Lease and release. 6 & 7 Sept 1769, William Milbank of Charles Town, to Michael Muckenfuss, Tavern Keeper, for £25 SC money, 200 acres. Wm. Millbank (LS), Wit: Denham Fearis, Christian Gruber. Proved in Charles Town District by the oath of Christian Gruber before R. Rugeley, 26 Nov 1775. Recorded 3 Jan 1776.

V-4, 140-146: Lease and release. 4 & 5 Dec 1772, Rawlins Lowndes of Charles Town, Esquire, to Rowland Rugeley of same, gentleman, for £350 SC money, 14 acres on Charles Town Neck in

SOUTH CAROLINA DEED ABSTRACTS 1773-1778

Berkley County adj. lands of sd. Rawlins Lowndes, intersecting the Broad Road which divides the land of Daniel Cannon from said Rawlins Lowndes adj. Col. John Smith deceased. Raw's Lowndes (LS), Wit: Jere'h Theus, Thos Shubrick Junr. Recorded 9 Jan 1776.

V-4, 146-152: Lease and release. 9 & 10 Jan 1775, Joseph Burton of District of Ninety Six, planter, to Rowland Rugeley of Charles Town, merchant, by bond for £1600 for the payment of £800, 400 acres granted to Emanuel Miller 18 Aug 1763 and conveyed by said Miler to Robt. Mitchell 222 & 23 Dec 1773 which said Robert Mitchell conveyed to Joseph Burton 14 & 15 Feb 1774. Joseph Burton (LS), Wit: Arch'd Carsan, Henry Rugeley. Proved in Chas. Town District before John Troup, J.P., by the oath of Archibald Carsan, 17 Apr 1776. Recorded 17 Apr 1776.

V-4, 153-157: Lease and release. 21 Dec 1774, Darby Pendergrass of Charles Town, merchant, to Rowland Rugeley of same, for £1000 SC money, lot in Charles Town, number 331 which has been divided into seventeen small lots. Darby Pendergrass (LS), Wit: Henry Rugeley, Thom's Bourke. Proved in Chas. Town District 17 Apr 1776 before John Troup by the oath of Henry Rugeley. Recorded 17 Apr 1776.

V-4, 158-161: Lease and release. 17 & 18 March 1775, Richard Adams of Craven County, SC, planter, to William Tucker of same, planter, for £150 SC money, 150 acres in the fork of the Congaree and Wateree Rivers granted 15 March 1771 to Richard Adams. Richard Adams (LS), Wit: John Russell, John Edward (J). Proved 13 June 1775 before Richard Brown by the oath of John Russell. Recorded 17 July 1777.

V-4, 161-163: 1 Apr 1774, Robert Crafford and Jane his wife of Craven County, to William Massey of same, for £1000 SC money, 280 acres granted to William McKee and conveyed by John McKee, William McKees heirs, on south side Waxhaw Creek (plat included). Robert Crawford (LS), Jane Crawford (LS), Wit: Andw Foster, Isabella Hellena Foster (O), James Barnet. Proved in Camden District by the oath of Andrew Foster, 1 Apr 1774 before James Patton. Recorded 12 July 1777.

V-4, 164-167: Lease and release. 17 Oct 1754, James Finley of the Welch Tract, Craven County, SC, planter, to James James of same, planter, for £250 SC money, 200 acres in the Welch Tract, on northwest side Pedee River adj. land of Wm. Screven, Abrm. Staples, Wm. James, Owen David, granted 19 Nov 1750 to sd. James Finley. James Finley (LS), Wit: Valentine Hollingsworth, James Rogers. Proved in Craven County before Alexr. McKintosh by the oath of James Rodgers 17 May 1763. Recorded 12 July 1777.

V-4, 167-171: Lease and release. 6 & 7 Feb 1761, Thomas Jones of Welch Tract, Craven County, SC, planter, to Abel Edwards of same county, planter, for £200 SC money, 150 acres granted 29 Nov 1750 to sd. Thomas Jones. Thomas Jones (LS), Wit: Edward Jones, Lewis Gardner. Proved before John Alran by the oath of Edward Jones, 8 June 1767. Recorded 12 July 1777.

V-4, 171-175: Lease and release. 3 & 4 Sept 1765, James James of Welch Tract, Craven County, planter, to Abel Edwards of same county, for £250 SC money, 200 acres in Craven County in the Welch Tract granted 29 Nov 1750 to James Finley, and conveyed to James James 17 & 18 Oct 1754. James James (J) (LS), Wit: Edward Jones, William Bevill. Proved before John Alran, J. P., by the oath of William Bevil, 4 May 1767. Recorded 12 July 1777.

V-4, 175-177: South Carolina, Craven County. 25 Jan 1777, Joseph Port of Prince George Parish, planter, to Frances Port, widdow, for £3000 SC money, three tracts in Queensborough Township on Great PeDee River adj. each other, the one of 3000 acres purchased by Thomas Port from George More 31 Oct & 1 Nov 1763, the other two tracts of 250 acres on north side and the other on the south side of Great PeDee River purchased by Thomas Port from George Saxby 2 & 3 June 1762, which three tracts being purchased by the above said Thomas Port have since the death of Thomas Port descended to the above said Joseph Port by heirship. Joseph Port (LS), Wit: Saml Tyler, Benjamin Port, William Bellune. Proved in Geo. Town District before Francis Britton, J. P., by the oath of William Bellune, 5 July 1777. Recorded 12 July 1777.

V-4, 177-180: South Carolina, Craven County. 1 March 1777, Joseph Port of Prince George Parish, planter, to Frances Port, widdow, for £1000 SC money, 500 acres in Queensborough Township on south east side of PeDee River granted to John Hammerton adj. land of 20,00 acres and land laid out to Samuel Baker and purchased by Edward Martin, Esqr., High Sheriff of George Town District by Thomas Port 27 Apr 1774, which descended to Joseph Port by heirship. Joseph Port (LS), Wit: Saml Tyler, William Bellune, John Bellune. Proved in Geo. Town District before Francis Britton, J. P., by the oath of William Bellune, 5 July 1777. Recorded 12 July 1777.

V-4, 180-184: 27 Sept 1776, Samuel Perdriau of Charlestown, SC, sadler, to John Perdriau of the Parish of St. George, planter, for £3000 SC money, 737 acres on the Cypress in St. Georges Parish in Berkley County, the north east moiety or half past and division of 1474 acres formerly the property and in possession of Joseph Izard deceased, and lately by Miles Brewton and Mary his wife and Daniel Blake and Elizabeth his wife (which said Mary and Elizabeth were the only children and devisees of Joseph Izard deceased) and conveyed to said Samuel Perdriau (plat included showing house). Samuel Perdriau (LS), Wit: M. Hutchinson, Archd. McDowell. Proved by the oath of Archd. McDowell 24 July 1777 before John Troup, J.P. Recorded 19 July 1777.

V-4, 184-185: Agreement. John Crofts and John Skrine to continue for the term of seven years 1 Dec 1771, only on provision John Crofts should at any time be desirous to settle himself on the place or tenement where the ferry is kept that then said Skrine will deliver up to him, having a convenient notice, as far as the lowermost line of Mr. Johnston, the line of his tract that divides his land from Nathaniel Wickhams land and the remainder of that tract... to pay to said John Croft £100 per annum. John Croft (Seal), John Skrine (Seal), Wit: Thos Jones. Proved before Job Rothmahler, J.P., by the oath of Thomas Jones, 17 May 1777. Recorded 18 July 1777.

V-4, 185-190: Lease and release. 2 & 3 June 1777, Henry Laurens of Charles Town, SC, esquire, to Thomas Broughton of St. John's Parish, Berkley County, planter, for £500 SC money, tract of high land lately surveyed and partitioned off from Mepkin High Land in the Parish of St. John, 600 acres adj. Elias Ball of Kensington or Chilsbury estate, adj. 120 acres of Swamp land lately or now the property of said Thomas Broughton by him sold to said Henry Laurens (plat included). Henry Laurens (LS), Wit: Owens, John Wells Junior. Proved 18 June 1777 before Thomas Walter, J.P., by the oath of John Owen. Recorded 19 July 1777.

V-4, 190-195: Lease and release. 2 & 3 June 1777, Thomas Broughton of St. John's Parish, Berkley County, planter, and Elizabeth his wife, to Henry Laurens of Charles Town, esquire, for £5 SC money, tract of high land lately surveyed and partitioned off from Mepkin High Land in the Parish of St. John, 120 acres of swamp land in St. Johns Parish on Cooper River (plat included). Thos Broughton Junr (LS), Elizabeth Broughton (LS), Wit: Sarah Parker, Wm. Scott Junr. Proved 6 June 1777 before John Colcock, J.P., by the oath of William Scott Junr. Recorded 19 July 1777.

V-4, 195-200: Lease and release. 26 & 27 May 1777, Benjamin Farar of Berkley County, SC, Esquire, and Elizabeth his wife, to John Pamor of Craven County, Esqr., for £10,000 SC money, 1000 acres in St. Marks Parish, Craven County, on the low ground of Santee River adj. land of Theodore Gaillard Junior, William Fludd, estate of Robert Ervine, Izzard, and John Cook, Daniel Ravenell, Henry Ravenell and Job Marion, granted to sd. Benjamin Farar 2 May 1770, also another tract of 155 acres adj. said ___ Izzard, Benjamin Farar, land surveyed by John Mitchell now owned by William Fludd, Robert Ervine, Santee River, granted to sd. Benjamin Farar 13 July 1770. Benj. Farar (LS), Eliz. Farar (LS), Wit: R[obert] Hails, James Bunyie, Ralph Humphreys. Proved 5 June 1777 before Samuel Dwight, J.P., by the oath of James Bunyie. Recorded 19 July 1777.

V-4, 201-205: Lease and release. 26 & 27 March 1777, Benjamin Trapier of Prince Georges Parish, Craven County, planter, to Thomas Hasell of same, planter, for £1000 SC money, one full undivided moiety of half part of 1300 acres in Prince Georges Parish, Craven county adj. Joseph Ports land, Thomas Morrils, William Whitesides, Joseph Waters, William Raes land; also a half part of lot and a half in George Town #239 and 242. Benjn. Trapier (LS), Wit: Pet'r Foissin, John Waties Junr. Proved before Paul Trapier, J.P., by the oath of John Waites Junr, 27 March 1777. Recorded 19 July 1777.

V-4, 206-209: Lease and release. 23 & 25 March 1771, Alard Belin of Craven County, SC, Gentleman, to Thomas Horry, Peter Horry, Hugh Horry & Jonah Horry of same, for affection which said Alard Belin beareth to his wife Margaret and to his children Sarah, Mary, James &

Margaret and also for ten shillings, paid by Thomas Horry, Peter Horry, Hugh Horry and Jonah Horry, lots in New Town, numbers 45, 47, and 17 also 35 heard of Black Cattle branded AB also fifteen horses, seven branded E, one branded I one E one D and five MB also five negro slaves Watchman, Milas, Greenwick, Lerette & Will, all household furniture, plantation tools, etc. Allard Belin (LS), Wit: Fran's Withers, James Horry. Proved in Craven County before Danl Horry, J.P., by the oath of James Horry 1 Apr 1771. Recorded 19 July 1771.

V-4, 210-213: Lease and release. 5 & 6 Nov 1776, Jacob Christopher Zahn of St. Matthews Parish, Berkly County, SC, planter, to Isaac Gaillard of same, planter, for £300 SC money, 27 acres in St. Matthews Parish adj. lands of said Zahn, Elizabeth McNichols, Santee River, part of 200 acres granted 21 Dec 17__ to Isaac Porcher, Esqr. (plat included). Jacob Christopher Zahn (LS), Wit: John Thompson Deliesseline, John McCullogh. Recorded 19 July 1777.

V-4, 214-218: Lease and release. 29 & 30 Sept 1775, Henry Liebenhent of Parish of St. Paul, Colleton County, planter, to David Grame of Charlestown, Esquire, by bond for £7000 SC money, for the payment of £3500, lot in Charlestown, part of four town lots numbers 256, 257, 258 & 259 belonging to Richard Beresford, Esqr. Henry Liebenhent (LS), Wit: John Hogg. Proved by the oath of John Hogg 3 June 1777. Recorded 26 July 1777.

V-4, 219-221: 29 Jan 1776, Joseph Woods of Parish of St. Marks, planter, to Frame Woods of same, for ten shillings, 200 acres in Craven County on east side Broad River on Dry Creek adj. land of James Fanin, David Hamilton, granted 8 Dec 1774 to Joseph Woods. Joseph Woods (LS), Isable Woods (O) (LS), Wit: Archib'd Scott, George Black, Alexander Hamilton. Proved in Camden District by the oath of Alexander Hamilton before Joseph Brown, J. P., 17 June 1776. Recorded 26 July 1777.

V-4, 221-226: Lease and release. 30 & 31 May 1777, Daniel Huger, now of the Island of New Providence, but late of Charelstown, SC, Esquire, by John Huger, Thomas Bee & James Keith, all of Charlestown, SC, gentleman, his attornies, to William Nesbitt of Charlestown, Esquire, for £11,500 SC money, lot #274 on north side Broad Street in Charlestown, by letter of attorney dated 1 Feb 1776. Wit: John Mills, Joseph Scott Cray. Proved in Chas. Town District by the oath of John Mills before Geo: Sheed, 2 July 1777. Recorded 26 July 1777.

V-4, 227-230: Lease and release. 2 & 3 June 1777, William Nisbett of Charles Town, Esquire, to John Huger of same, Esquire, for £500 SC money, lot on north side of upper end of Broad Street in Charles Town, number 274. Wm. Nisbet (LS), Wit: Joseph Scott Cray, John Mills. Proved in Chas. Town District by the oath of John Mills before Geo: Sheed, 2 July 1777. Recorded 26 July 1777.

V-4, 230-235: Lease and release. 11 & 12 July 1777, Elisha Tamplett of St. Stephens Parish, Planter, to Thomas Phepoe of Charlestown, Attorney at Law, for £1000 SC money, 1500 acres in Craven County adj. land of William Meshow, land said to be Simons (plat included). Elisha Tamplett (LS), Wit: Alexr Forrester, Robt. Johnston. Proved in Charlestown District before George Sheed, J.P., by the oath of Robert Johnston, 12 July 1777. Recorded 26 July 1777.

V-4, 235-239: Lease and release. 11 & 12 July 1777, Thomas Hendlen of Charlestown, SC, Carpenter, to Audeon St. John of same state, merchant, town lot in Charlestown adj. land of James St. John, Estate of Lambert Lance, Land of Rawlins Lowndes. Thos Hendlen (LS), Wit: Lambert Lance, William Fraser. Proved in Charlestown District before George Sheed by the oath of William Fraser 12 July 1777. Recorded 26 July 1777.

V-4, 240-244: Lease and release. South Carolina. 18 & 19 June 1770, Henry DeMounge of said province, to Audeon St. John of same, merchant, for £200 SC money, 200 acres on Gills Creek a branch of Santee River in Craven county adj. land granted to benjamin Bell, granted 21 Dec 1769 to Henry DeMounge. Henry DeMounge (mark) (LS), Wit: John Leitner, Wm. Stack, Randolph Theus. Proved in Berkley County by the oath of Randolph Theus before Wm. Arthur, J. P., 28 May 1772. Recorded 26 July 1777.

SOUTH CAROLINA DEED ABSTRACTS 1773-1778

V-4, 244-246: 4 May 1775, James Peart, Dept. Surveyor, to Stephen McDaniel, Planter, of St. Helena Parish, for £50 SC money, 200 acres, part of 1250 acres granted to William Godfrey 4 May of the present year adj. John Grimball but now John Audibert, John Wraggs barony, land granted to sd. Stephen McDaniel (plat included). James Peart (LS), Wit: James Eggerton, George Allison. Proved by the oath of George Allison 10 Aug 1775 before Adrian Mayer. Recorded 26 July 1777.

V-4, 246-247: 27 Apr 1777, James Bullock of Savannah, Georgia, Esqr., to Adrian Mayer of Purysburgh, Esqr., mortgage for £1750 SC money, to be paid 1 Jan 1778, 500 acres adj. the common of the Town of Purysburg granted to Doctor Daniel Brabant. James Bulloch (LS), Wit: Lawrence Mertz, David Giroud. Proved in Charlestown District before George Sheed by the oath of Lawrence Mertz, 10 July 1777. Recorded 26 July 1777.

V-4, 247-253: Lease and release. 1 & 2 July 1777, Stephen McDaniel of Stony Run in St. Helena's Parish, Granville County, SC, planter, to John Audebert of St. Peters Parish of Black Smith Settlement, county and state aforesaid, for £400 SC money, part of 1250 acres granted conveyed by James Peart 4 May 1775 on Stony Run waters of Coosawhatchie adj. land then thought to be John Grimballs since granted to John Audebert, John Wraggs barony, granted to Stephen McDaniel. Stephen McDaniel (LS), Wit: John Rowell, Elias Robert. Proved before Henry Gindrat, J.P. for Beaufort District, by the oath of Elias Robert, 3 July 1777. Recorded 26 July 1777.

V-4, 253-254: 3 July 1777, John Audebert of St. Peters Parish, Granville County, Sc, planter, to Adrian Mayer of Purysburgh, Esqr., for £1200 SC money, 200 acres, being the easterly part of 1250 acres granted to Wm. Godfrey, adj. land granted to John Audibert, Stephen McDaniel, John Wraggs barony. John Audebert (LS), Wit: Willoughby Pugh, David Trushet. Proved in Granville County by the oath of David Trushet 4 July 1777 before David Keatt[?], J.P. Recorded 2 Aug 1777.

V-4, 255-260: Lease and release. 17 & 18 March 1777, Charles Elliott, Esqr., of St. Pauls Parish, Colleton County, to James Nicholes of said parish, planter, for £2000 SC money, 190 acres in St. Pauls Parish adj. land of said James Nicholes, Henry Nicholes, Charles Elliott, on the public road leading to Stono Bridge (plat included dated 1 March 1777 by John Fenwick, Survr.). Charles Elliott (LS), Wit: James Ferguson, Francis Guerin. Proved in Charlestown District 23 May 1777 before John Troup by the oath of James Ferguson. Recorded 2 Aug 1777.

V-4, 260-266: Lease and release. 27 & 28 Apr 1777, John Belton, Surveyor, and Mary his wife, of Craven County, St. Marks Parish, SC, to Pere Wikoff and Isaac Wikoff of City of Philadelphia, merchants, for £1600 SC money, two adj. tracts of land 750 acres on south prong of Lynches Creek waters of Peedee, Craven county, one tract of 600 acres granted to john Belton Senr 1 Feb 1758 and the said John Belton Senr. having departed this life said tract by legal descent became the property of John Belton and the other tract of 150 acres granted to sd. John Belton 31 Oct 1765. John Belton (LS), Mary Belton (LS), Wit: Thomas Jones, Wm. Belton, Henry Houseman. Proved 29 Apr 1777 before John N. Oglethorpe, J.P. in Craven County, by the oath of Thomas Jones. Recorded 31 July 1777.

V-4, 266-270: Lease and release. 12 & 13 July 1774, Robert Bowman of St. Marks Parish, Craven County, planter, to Jas. Bowman Senr of same, planter, for £100 SC money, 100 acres in Craven county on Pearses Swamp granted to Doctor John Bowman 7 Oct 1752. Robert Bowman (LS), Amely Bowman (X) (LS), Wit: James Bowman, Mary Bowman (+). Proved in Camden District by the oath of James Bowman Junr., 22 Feb 1777 before Wm. brown, J. P. Recorded 2 Aug 1777.

V-4, 271-275: Lease and release. 7 & 8 Dec 1775, John Sullivan of Craven County, SC, to Robert Bowman of same, for £20 SC money, 50 acres on Santee River adj. John Shorters land, John Sullivans land, land laid out for Thomas Sumter. John Sullivan (LS), Wit: Will Luton, Sarah Bliss (X). Proved in Camden District by the oath of William Luton before Wm. Brown, J.P., 25 Feb 1777. Recorded 2 Aug 1777.

V-4, 275-278: Lease and release. 9 & 10 June 1775, John Egan, Esqr., of St. James Santee, Craven county, to Samuel Commander of St. Marks Parish, planter, for £1000 SC money, 450 acres on south side Lynches Creek in Craven County adj. John Conners land. John Egan (LS), Wit: John

SOUTH CAROLINA DEED ABSTRACTS 1773-1778

Gibson, John Shaw. Proved 10 June 1775 by the oath of John Gibson before Hen. Cassels, J.P. for Craven County. Recorded 2 Aug 1777.

V-4, 278-282: Lease and release. 14 & 15 March 1777, John Robinson of Louisa County, Province of Virginia, planter, to Robert Blair of Cheraw District, planter, for £66 SC money, 66 acres in the Welch Tract in Craven County granted 19 Sept 1758 to John Robinson. John Robinson (I) (LS), Wit: Richd Estridge, Peter Chambliss. Proved in Cheraws District before Able Kolb, J.P., by the oath of Peter Chambliss, 3 May 1777. Recorded 2 Aug 1777.

V-4, 282-287: Lease and release. 6 & 7 March 1772, Andrew Burn of Charlestown, Cabinet maker, and Hannah his wife, to David Rhind of same, esquire, by bond for £6000 SC money for the payment of £3000, lot on Church Street in Charles Town adj. land of Doctor Fotheringham, Daniel Blake, Lambert Lance. Andrew Burn (LS), Hannah Burn (LS), Wit: John Troup. Proved in Charlestown District before George Sheed 9 July 1777 by the oath of John Troup. Recorded 2 Aug 1777.

V-4, 287-291: Lease and release. 3 & 4 May 1773, Rebecca Holmes, executrix, and Thomas Bee, executor of the will of Isaac Holmes Junr., late of Charlestown, merchant, deceased, who was the only surviving executor of the will of Isaac Holmes the elder, of Charlestown, deceased, to William Savage of same, merchant, for £9000 SC money, lot in Broad Street in Charlestown adj. land of the heirs of Daniel Bourgett decd, Arthur Peroneau, heirs of said Isaac Holmes Junior deceased, and by will dated 9 July 1751 of Isaac Holmes the elder bequeathed to his wife Elizabeth Holmes (lately deceased) and appointed his two brothers in law Henry Peronneau deceased and Alexander Peronneau executors and his son Isaac Holmes who survived. Rebekah Holmes (LS), Thos Bee (LS), Wit: Jno Raven Mathewes, John Simmons. Proved in Charlestown District before George Sheed by the oath of John Raven Mathewes, 9 July 1777. Recorded 9 Aug 1777.

V-4, 292-297: Lease and release. 26 & 27 July 1777, Mary Watson, late of Charlestown, SC, widow, by the Rev. Robert Smith of Charlestown her attorney, to Frances Susannah Pinckney of Charlestown, for £9040 SC money, widow, lot on west side of Church Street in Charlestown, part of lot number 43, and said Mary Watson by deed pool 23 Sept 1776 did appoint said Robert Smith her attorney. Mary Watson by her attorney Robert Smith (LS), Wit: David Warham, Jos. Ward. Proved by the oath of Joshua Ward 17 July 1777 before W. Poaug, J.P. Recorded 9 Aug 1777.

V-4, 298-303: Lease and release. 8 & 9 June 1774, James Thomson of Charlestown to Samuel Cross of St. Georges Parish, Berkly County, planter, for £1000 SC money, 1000 acres on Mill Creek in St. Mathews Parish, Berkly County, adj. land granted to Benjamin Campbell, land surveyed for William Greaves, Mordecai McFarlanes, Peter Burns, Thomas Compton, Tacitus Gaillard, granted 7 June 1774. James Thomson (LS), Wit: John Brown, Samuel Burn. Proved 8 Aug 1774 before George Davidson, J.P., by the oath of John Brown. Recorded 9 Aug 1777.

V-4, 303-306: Lease and release. 10 & 12 Apr 1777, William Finley and Ann Finley his wife, of Richmond County, State of Georgia, planter, to Humphrey Hubbard of same, for £90 SC money, 150 acres in Township of New Windsor, SC, on Savannah River. William Finley (LS), Ann Finley (A) (LS), Wit: Pryde Williams, John Bruton. Proved in Ninety Six District 6 July 1777 before LeRoy Hammond, by the oath of Pryde Williams. Recorded 9 Aug 1777.

V-4, 306-308: 19 June 1773, David Giroud of Purysburgh, Granville County, SC, Esquire, to John Vouchar of same, shoemaker, for £5 SC money, 450 acres in Parish of St. Peters, Granville County. David Giroud (LS), Wit: John Niess, Lewis Mrgill [Morgan in proof]. Proved by the oath of John Niess 21 June 1773 before Adrian Mayer. Recorded 9 Aug 1777.

V-4, 308-310: Purysburgh in Granville County, So Carolina. 1 Apr 1775, John Bull of Parish of St. Helena, to Adrian Mayer, Esqr., of St. Peters Parish, for £10 SC money, 100 acres on waters of Coosawhatchie on Beaver Dam Branch, adj. land laid out to Adrian Mayer, land granted to James Peart now Hugh Burns, land granted to William Godfrey now James Peart. John Bull (LS), Wit: Henry Jeannerett, William Catterton. Proved in Purysburgh by the oath of Henry Jeanneret 25 Oct 1776 before Bellamy Crawford, J.P. Recorded 9 Aug 1777.

SOUTH CAROLINA DEED ABSTRACTS 1773-1778

V-4, 310-311: South Carolina, Granville County. 19 Aug 1775, John Buche of Purrysburgh, Granville County, Post Master, to Adrian Mayer also of said place, merchant, for £100 SC money, 550 acres in the Township of Purysburgh adj. land of John Vauchiers, Abraham Bininger, John Linder, Anderson Young, James Sturly, Nicholas Rigen. John Buche (LS), Wit: Jno Postell, John Holzendorf. Proved in Purysburgh by the oath of John Postell 28 March 1777 before David Giroud, J.P. Recorded 9 Aug 1777.

V-4, 312-313: 1 Apr 1777, John Vachier of Purysburgh, St. Peters Parish, Granville County, Shoemaker, to Adrian Mayer, also of Purysburgh, Esqr., for £100 sterling, 450 acres in Parish of St. Peter. John Vauchier (LS), Wit: Willoughby Pugh, John Forbes. Proved in Purysburgh by the oath of Willoughby Pugh 6 May 1777 before David Giroud. Recorded 9 Aug 1777.

V-4, 313-316: 11 Feb 1767, Isaac Knighten of St. Marks Parish, Craven County, yeoman, and Margaret his wife, to Moses Green of same county, carpenter, for £300 SC money, 400 acres granted to Isaac Knighten 11 Feb 1762 adj. John James. Isaac Knighton (LS), Margreat Knight (LS), Wit: Thomas Knighton, John Green. Proved by the oath of John Green 11 Oct 1767 before Moses Thomson. Recorded 9 Aug 1777.

V-4, 316-319: 21 July 1773, Moses Green of Craven County, carpenter, and Comfort his wife, to Henry Haynsworth of same, for £1000 SC money, 400 acres on the high hills of Santee granted to Isaac Nighton adj. John James and conveyed by him. Moses Green (LS), Comfort Green (LS), Wit: Jos. Cantey Robert Green. Proved in Camden District before Thos. Sumter, J.P., by the oath of Joseph Cantey 2 Feb 1774. Recorded 9 Aug 1777.

V-4, 320-322: 5 July 1777, William Luton of St. Marks Parish, Craven County, to Henry Hainsworth of same parish, planter, for £1500 SC money, 300 acres on north side Santee in St. Marks Parish adj. land of Jared Neilson, said Henry Haynsworth, Benjamin Farar. Will Luton (LS), Wit: Mary Bosher, William Knighton. Proved 19 July 177 before Nathl. Moore, J.P., by the oath of William Knighten. Recorded 9 Aug 1777.

V-4, 322-327: Lease and release. 4 & 5 June 1764, Robert Clemons & Clement Lamprier, Exors of the will of James Allen, late of Christ Church Parish, planter, and Ann Lampriere, wife of said Clement, to Samuel Hopkins of Charlestown, for £1500 SC money, lot on Tradd Street, part of lot number 223 and King Street, belonging to the devisees of James Allen deceased. Clem't Lempriere (LS), Ro't Clemmons (LS), Ann Lampriere (LS), Wit: Alexa Chisolme, Moses Joy. Proved in Charlestown District before William Gibbes, Esquire, by the oath of Moses Joy, 6 Aug 1777. Recorded 9 Aug 1777.

V-4, 327-331: Lease and release. 21 & 22 Apr 1777, Benjamin Villepontoux of Charlestown, Gentleman, and Jane his wife, to John McIlraith of St. Georges Parish, four Holes, for £350 SC money, 550 acres on north side Four Hole Swamp in Berkley County granted to James Coachman and by divers conveyances descended to said Benjamin Villepontoux. Benja. Villepontoux (LS), Jane Villepontoux (LS), Wit: Wm. Mason, John Bee Holmes. Proved by the oath of William Mason 17 Aug 1777 before Wm. Nisbett, J.P. Recorded 10 Aug 1777.

V-4, 332-335: 1 Sept 1775, William Burrows, Esquire, Master of his Majesty';s Court of Chancery, and Benjamin Garden, Esquire (heir at Law of the Rev. Alexander Garden, clerk, late Rector of the Parish of St. Philip, Charlestown, who was the surviving trustee named in deeds by way of trust between Nicholas Trott and Sarah his wife to said Alexander Garden and Joseph Wragg 12 & 13 March 1734 in pursuance of the order from the court of Chancery 28 April last past) to William Downes of Charlestown, whereas Sir Thomas Frankland of Middlesex, Great Britain, Baronet, did exhibit his bill of complaint in his Majesty's Court of Chancery against Thomas Smith and Sarah his wife, Edward Harleston, John Harleston (a minor), Benjamin Garden, James Laurens, Rebeccah Bampfield, and Margaret Naylor, which decreed that they should be barr'd of all right, title, and interest in the land in Charlestown mortgaged to said Sir Thomas Frankland by Eleazer Allen & Sarah his wife... sixteen lots of land on Trotts Point commonly called Admiral Franklands land, now for £380 to William Downes lot on Trotts Point in Charlestown. Wm. Burrows (LS), B'n Garden (LS), Wit: Willm Rea, James Philips, Michael Muckenfuss, Fredk. Grunsweig. Proved 3 July 1777 before George Sheed by the oath of Michael Muckenfuss. Recorded 10 Aug 1777.

SOUTH CAROLINA DEED ABSTRACTS 1773-1778

V-4, 335-336: 11 Apr 1771, Thomas Panting, rector, Thomas Fuller, Benjamin Fuller, William Scott and Isaac Ladson, Vestry men, and William Cattell, Church Warden of Parish of St. Andrews, to Francis Rose, for £130 SC money, pew number 22 in said parish church. Thos Panting rector (LS), Thos Fuller (LS), Benj. Fuller (LS), William Scott (LS), William Cattell, Church Warden (LS), Wit: Saml Legare, Jno Man. Proved by the oath of Samuel Legare 23 June 1777 before Wm. Nisbet. Recorded 10 Aug 1777.

V-4, 337-338: 29 Apr 1777, Francis Rose of St. Andrews Parish, to Elias Horry the younger of Charlestown, for £190 SC money, pew number 22 in St. Andrews Parish Church. Franc's Rose (LS), Wit: John Macklin. Proved by the oath of John Macklin before Richard Park Stobo, 3 July 1777. Recorded 16 Aug 1777.

V-4, 338-340: 24 Sept 1764, Hob'le John Drayton, Esqr., John Cattle, Isaac Ladson, Thomas Fuller, John Miles, Vestry Men, and Owen Roberts and William Drayton, Church Wardens of the Parish of St. Andrew, to William Branford of said parish, for £300 SC money, pew number 13 in parish church. Jno Drayton (LS), Thos Fuller (LS), W. Drayton (LS), Isaac Ladson (LS), John Miles (LS), John Cattell (LS), Ow Roberts (LS), Wit: Joseph Williams, Jno Man. Proved by the oath of Benjamin Fuller who attested to the handwriting of the signatures (several of whom are now dead) and with the witness;s (who are dead) 27 June 1777 before Wm. Mason, J.P. Recorded 16 Aug 1777.

V-4, 340-341: 6 Nov 1760, William Bull, Edward Fenwicke, Othniel Beale, Isaac Mazyck, Benjamin Smith, Robert Pringle, George Saxby, Gabriel Manigault, and Thomas Middleton, Commissioners for building the Parish Church of St. Michael, Charlestown, to William Branford, for £350 SC money, pew number 35 in parish church. W. Bull (LS), Rt. Pringle (LS), Ed. Fenwicke (LS), Geo Saxby (LS), Othniel Beale (LS), Gabriel Manigault (LS), Isaac Mazyck (LS), Tho Middleton (LS), Bn. Smith (LS), Wit: Saml Prioleau, Saml Cardy Arch't. Proved by the oath of Samuel Prioleau before William Mason, J.P. Recorded 16 Aug 1777.

V-4, 341-348: Lease and release. 21 & 22 July 1777, Henry Reeves of State of SC, and Charlotte his wife, to Samuel Jones of same, for £3600 SC money, whereas Mary Frost of Charles Town, widow, in her will dated 8 Oct 1766 devised to her grand daughter the above named Charlotte Reeves, two lots in Charles Town. Henry Reeves (LS), Charlotte Reeves (LS), Wit: Lambert Lance, William Fraser. Proved before George Sheed by the oath of Lambert Lance 22 July 1777. Recorded 16 Aug 1777.

V-4, 348-353: Lease and release. 2 & 3 June 1777, Peter Bocquet of Charlestown, exr. of will of Sarah Edes, late of Charles Town, spinster, deceased, to William Glen of said town, merchant, for £2000 SC money, by the will of Sarah Edes dated 7 Nov 1765 did authorize her executors to sell a lot on Union Street. Peter Bocquet (LS), Wit: Christian Sigwald, Charles Gruber, John Shutterling. Proved before George Sheed by the oath of Charles Gruber, 30 July 1777. Recorded 16 Aug 1777.

V-4, 353-358: Lease and release. 3 & 4 Apr 1769, Mary Smith of St. James Goose Creek, Berkley County, widow and relict of Langrave Thomas Smith, late of Goose Creek aforesaid, deceased, and executrix of his will, to Thomas Smith of same parish, gentleman, for £100 SC money, tracts of high land, swamp land, and marsh land remaining of the Thomas Smith barony in Prince George Winyaw Parish, Craven County. Mary Smith (LS), Wit: Elizabeth Dixon, Ann Ball. Proved in Berkley County before Henry smith, J.P., by the oath of Ann Ball, 4 Apr 1769. Recorded 16 Aug 1777.

V-4, 358-361: Lease and release. 27 & 28 July 1777, Ephraim Mitchell of Charlestown, Esquire, to William Downs of same, gentleman, for £600 SC money, lot in Hampstead known by number 61 on Drake Street, Reed Street. Ephraim Mitchell (LS), Wit: James Lynch, David Milling. Proved before George Sheed by the oath of James Lynch, 2 Aug 1777. Recorded 23 Aug 1777.

V-4, 362-367: Lease and release. 26 & 27 July 1771, Isaac Porcher of Charlestown, planter, to Tacitus Gaillard of St. Matthews Parish, Planter, for five shillings, two tracts of land: (1) 200 acres in Berkley County on a branch of Mudlick called Pages Creek adj. land of Benjamin Farar granted to me 10 May 1770 (2) 200 acres in St. Matthews Parish on Santee River adj. William McNickols,

SOUTH CAROLINA DEED ABSTRACTS 1773-1778

Bryan White, Christopher Hutson, Peter Manigault, granted 10 Dec 1769 to me. Isaac Porcher (LS), Wit: Wm Ancrum, George Ancrum. Proved 29 Oct 1771 before Samuel Porcher by the oath of George Ancrum. Recorded 23 aug 1777.

V-4, 367-368: Thomas Lennon bound to Tacitus Gaillard in the sum of £1000,13 Dec 1771, to make title to tract of 350 acres in Amelia Township granted to Barnard Lindsay and conveyed to John Fouquet. Thoms Lennon (LS), Wit: George Ancrum. Proved by the oath of George Ancrum 27 July 1777 before John Troup, J.P. Recorded 23 Aug 1777.

V-4, 368-372: Lease and release. 19 & 20 Jan 1772, Benjamin Moore, late of Craven County, SC, planter, to Tacitus Gilyard (Gaillard) of same, for £200 SC money, 200 acres granted to Benjamin Moore 3 Nov 1770 on waters of Saluda on a small branch called Cain Creek adj. land of William Purse, Mary Edwards. Benjamin Moore (LS), Wit: Richard Golding, Jane Caldwell, John Donaho (N). Proved before John Caldwell, J.P. in Craven County, by the oath of John Donaho 27 Jan 1772. Recorded 23 Aug 1777.

V-4, 372-376: Lease and release. 29 & 30 Dec 1773, Charles Cantey of Parish of St. Stephen, planter, to Isaac Gaillard of St. Matthews Parish, for £50 SC money, 1000 acres granted to sd. Charles Cantey 15 May 1772 in the fork of Savannah and Rockey Rivers in Granville County adj. land of James Crawford, James Cowan, John Pickens, John Middleton, Henry Mann. Chas Cantey (LS), Wit: Willm. Sharpe, Ezekiel Backler. Proved 17 July 1775 before John Frierson, J.P. for Charlestown District, by the oath of Ezekiel Backler Junr. Recorded 23 Aug 1777.

V-4, 376-382: Lease and release. 8 & 9 Apr 1777, William Moore of Craven County, planter, and Barbary his wife, to James Sanders, Esquire, for £4250 SC money, 250 acres in Craven county on the high hills of Santee adj. at the time of the original grant to Nathaniel Moore, John James, John Green, one Ferguson, David Holladay, which by deed 25 & 26 July 1775 conveyed by Nathaniel Moore and Frankey his wife to William Moore; also a tract of 200 acres part of 350 acres on waters of Santee granted to one James Miles, conveyed from James Freeman and Ann his wife to said William Moore, conveyed by said James Miller to sd. James Freeman; also 150 acres on north side of Wateree River adj. John James, James Miles, William Holtons[?], Thomas Knighton, Francis James, granted to Nathaniel Dodd and conveyed from Nathaniel Dodd and Margaret his wife 25 & 26 July 1775 to William Moore. William Moore (LS), Barbara Moore (LS), Wit: Benjamin Holladay, Saml Willison. Proved in Chas. Town District before John Colcock, J.P., by the oath of Samuel Willison, 24 May 1777. Recorded 23 Aug 1777.

V-4, 382-386: 14 June 1774, Thomas Grimball Junr, Sheriff of Charlestown District, to William Hort of Charlestown, Factor, for £2560, whereas Samuel Hopkins of Charlestown, was seized of a lot in Charlestown, number 223, on Tradd Street, King Street, adj. land of John Cattell, and the devisees of James Allen deceased, and said Samuel Hopkins by bond 8 Oct 1772 to William Hort in the sum of £39,600... said William hort obtained a judgment in the court of common pleas in February term 1774. T. Grimball Junr, Shff (LS), Wit: Hext Prioleau, Joseph Milligan. Proved before George Sheed by the oath of Hext Prioleau, 15 Aug 1777. Recorded 23 Aug 1777.

V-4, 386-390: 1 Sept 1775, William Burrows, Esquire, Master of the Court of Chancery, to and Benjamin Garden, heir at law of Rev. Alexander Garden, Clerk, late Rector of the Parish of St. Philip, Charleston, who was surviving trustee named in deeds of trust between Nicholas Trott & Sarah his wife and said Alexander Garden and Joseph Wragg 12 & 13 March 1734 and in pursuance of the order of the court of chancery made 28 Apr last past, whereas Sir Thomas Frankland of Middlesex, Great Britain, Baronet, did exhibit his bill of complaint in his Majesty's Court of Chancery against Thomas Smith and Sarah his wife, Edward Harleston, John Harleston (a minor), Benjamin Garden, James Laurens, Rebeccah Bampfield, and Margaret Naylor, which decreed that they should be barr'd of all right, title, and interest in the land in Charlestown mortgaged to said Sir Thomas Frankland by Eleazer Allen & Sarah his wife... lot of land on Trotts Point commonly called Admiral Franklands land, now for £3420 to George Flagg lot on Trotts Point in Charlestown, A number 8, 9 and 10. Wm. Burrows (LS), B'n Garden (LS), Wit: Willm Rea, James Phillips, Michael Muckenfuss, Fredk. Grunsweig. Proved 16 Aug 1777 before George Sheed by the oath of James Phillips. Recorded 30 Aug 1777.

SOUTH CAROLINA DEED ABSTRACTS 1773-1778

V-4, 390-392: 30 June 1772, Henry Clark of Craven County, SC, to John Nuckols of same, for £35 Proc. money of America, 150 acres on Thicketty Creek being the land said Clark purchased of Stephen Jones part of tract granted to Stephen Jones by patent whereon the said Clarke now lives. Henry Clark (LS), Wit: William Sims, George hide (+). Proved in Craven County by the oath of George Hide, 7 July 1772 before Jo. Brown. Recorded 25 Aug 1777.

V-4, 392-394: ___ July 1775, James Hurlick and Sarah Huney his wife and Charity Huney Sizzer, all of Amelia Township, SC, to Sarah Reese, wife of Evans Reese of township aforesaid, and grandmother to the said Sarah Huney Hurlick, Charity Huney Sizzer and grandmother in law to said James Hurlock, for natural love and affection to said Sarah Reese our grandmother, 200 acres granted to Thomas Allison by George II in Amelia Township and said Thomas Allison died intestate and having no other lawful heir the right of inheritance devolved unto Sarah Allison then widow of said Thomas and heir at law to his Real and personal estate, and said Sarah Allison (now Sarah Reese after the name of her present husband) did by deed of gift conveyed said 200 acres to Sarah Huney Sizzer and Charity Huney Sizzer both granddaughters to the then Sarah Allison and now Sarah Reese, recorded in Book PP page 361. James Hairlock (X) (LS), Sarah Hairlock (LS), Charity Sizer (XX) (LS), Wit: Wm. Simpson, Thomas Colman. Proved in Orangeburgh District by the oath of Thomas Colman 14 Sept 1776 before Lewis Golsan, J.P. Recorded 30 Aug 1777.

V-4, 394-400: Lease and release. 16 & 17 Feb 1777, Richard Wise and Mary Wise of St. Marks Parish, Camden District, to John Wise of same, for twenty shillings, 100 acres, part of 300 acres on ___ Savannah, north of Santee River in Camden District, being a square tract originally taken up between Richard, Thomas, & John Wise. Richard Wise (LS), Mary Wise (LS), Wit: John Leighton, Thos Wise, Shadk. Mathewes. Proved 17 Feb 1777 before Mortimer Harris, J.P. in Camden District, by the oath of John Leighton. Recorded 30 Aug 1777.

V-4, 400-403: Lease and release. 10 & 11 Feb 1776, George Fraweek (Traweek) to James Brown, both planters in Craven County, for £60 SC money, 100 acres, the north end corner of 1000 acres granted to William Pouncey excepting so much as may be overflowed by a mill pond. George Fraweek (LS), Leditha Fraweek (LS), Wit: Lewis Blalock, William Brown (X). Proved before George Hicks, j.P., by the oath of William Brown, 12 March 1776. Recorded 30 Aug 1777

V-4, 404-409: Lease and release. 7 & 8 May 1777, the Rev. Robert Smith and Alexander Gillon of Charlestown, extrs. of the will of Richard Beresford, late of Charlestown, deceased, to William Bull the younger, esquire, the £7710 SC money, two tracts in the whole 820 acres which said Richard Beresford died seized of and in his will 8 July 1772 appointed his wife Sarah Beresford during her widowhood executrix and said Robert Smith and Alexander Gillon with Christopher Gadsden, Thomas Smith of Broad Street, and his sons when they should respectively attain the age of 21 years, executors, now convey tract in Parish of St. Thomas called Parsons Point, 360 acres on Wando River, Watco's Creek, St. Martins Creek, and also tract adj. to it of 460 acres on Hobshaw Creek adj. land lately belonging to Jonathan Russ now to Rachel Himeli, John St. Martins land, both granted 23 July 1711 to Richard Beresford, father of said Richard Beresford deceased. Robert Smith (LS), Alexander Gillon (LS), Wit: John Splatt Cripps, Florian Charles Mey. Proved 6 Aug 1777 before Geo: Sheed by the oath of John Splatt Crips. Recorded 30 Aug 1777.

V-4, 409-410: 13 Dec 1773, John Burchfield and Lucrecy his wife of Craven County,Sc, to George Blanton of same, for £3000 SC money, 400 acres on Thicketty Creek granted by North Carolina ___ Nov 1771 being the land whereon Vardry McBee now lives. John Burchfield (I) (LS), Lucrecy Burchfield (+) (LS), Wit: William Tate, Jesse Tate (T), John Park (l). Proved in Ninety Six District before John Tagert, J.P., by the oath of Jesse Tate, 31 Oct 1775. Recorded 30 Aug 1777.

V-4, 410-414: Lease and release. 5 & 6 Apr 1776, George Blanton of Tryon County, North Carolina, and Susannah his wife, to John Young of Ninety Six District, South Carolina, planter, for £313 SC money, 400 acres on Thicketty Creek granted ___ Nov 1771 to John Burchfield then in the county of Tryon but since in the province of South Carolina, conveyed by John Burchfield and Lucrecy his wife to George Blanton, Esqr. George Blanton (LS), Susannah Blanton (J) (LS), Wit: James Wood, John McCrackin, Blarwell Blanton (X). Proved by the oath of James Wood, Esqr., in Ninety Six District, 3 July 1776 before W. Wofford. Recorded 30 Aug 1777.

SOUTH CAROLINA DEED ABSTRACTS 1773-1778

V-4, 414 [pages 415 and 416 appear to be bound after page 431 in this book]: 22 June 1776, John Timmons of Ninety Six District, SC, to Francis Howell of same, son in law of said John Timmons, for natural love and affection, 160 acres, part of 1000 acres on both sides north fork of Tyger River adj. Samuel Timmons. Jno Timmons (I) (LS), Wit: Thomas Prince, Tho Bennett, Thos Hathway. Proved by the oath of Thomas Prince in Ninety Six District 15 June 1776 before James Wood, J.P. Recorded 30 Aug 1777.

[the following instruments follow that from John Timmons to Francis Howell]

Lease & release. 22 June 1776, John Timmons of Ninety Six District, SC, to Thomas Timmons of same, son of said John Timmons, for natural love and affection, 160 acres, pat of 1000 acres on both sides north fork of Tyger River adj. Samuel Timmons. Jno Timmons (I) (LS), Wit: Thomas Prince, Tho Bennett, Thos Hathway. Proved by the oath of Thomas Prince in Ninety Six District 15 June 1776 before James Wood, J.P. Recorded 30 Aug 1777.

Lease & release. 20 & 21 Apr 1742, John Fenwicke of Charlestown, SC, Esquire, to Robert Gibbes of Johns Island in Colleton County, for £1000 SC money, 201 acres by deed of grant 23 Apr 1735 in Colleton County adj Mr. Ravens, Mr. Ladson, Abraham Waits, said John Fenwicke Esquire. Jno Fenwicke (LS), Wit: Jno Gibbes, Andw Rutledge. Proved before John Rutledge, J.P. for Berkley County, by the oath of Andrew Rutledge, Esqr, 11 March 1744/5. Recorded 30 Aug 1777.

V-4, 418-420 [pages 421-422 indicated as missing or blank]: Lease and release. 4 & 5 Aug 1777, William Price of Charlestown, SC, merchant, and Thomas Price late of Charles Town, but now of Kingdom of Great Britain, merchant, by said William Price his attorney, to Israel Joseph of Charlestown, shopkeeper, for £2500 SC money, lot in Charlestown on west side of King Street adj. lands now or late of Martha Clifford, said Thomas Price appointed William Price with John Smyth and Joshua Ward his attorneys, but John Smyth and Joshua Ward have declined to act. Wm. Price (LS), Thos Shirley by Wm. Price his atty (LS), Wit: Edw. Darrell, John Joulee. Recorded 6 Sept 1777. Proved in Charlestown District before Thomas Bee, J.P., by the oath of Edw. Darrell. [completion of this deed on pages 447-449]

V-4, 423-427: Lease and release. 15 & 16 Oct 1776, Zachariah Bullock of Ninety Six District, Sc, to John Thomas of same, for "a certain sum paid," 250 acres granted 9 Sept 1774 to Zach. Bullock, adj. Robt. Thomas's line, John Thomas's Senrs line, John Gibbs's line. Zach. Bullock (LS), Wit: James Jordan, John Pearson, Duncan McCreevan. Proved in Ninety Six District __ Aug 1777 by the oath of Duncan McCreevan before James Wood, J.P., 4 Aug 1777. Recorded 6 Sept 1777.

V-4, 427-430: Lease and release. 3 & 4 Oct 1775, James Carruth of Rowan County, North Carolina, to Patrick Calhoun of District of Ninety Six, SC, Esqr., for £108 SC money, 150 acres in Granville County on a branch of Calhoun's Creek, granted to said James Carruth 16 Dec 1766. James Carruth (LS), Wit: John Harris, Matthew Robinson (S), John Braly. Proved 12 Aug 1775 before William Calhoun, J.P., by the oath of John Harris. Recorded 6 Sept 1777.

V-4, 430-436: Lease and release. 1 & 2 Apr 1777, Hugh Calhoun of Long Cane Settlement in Ninety Six District, SC, yeoman, and Jannet his wife, to John Ewing Calhoun of same, studt. at law, for £700 SC money, 200 acres whereon the said Hugh Calhoun now liveth in Ninety Six district on a branch of the NW Fork of Long Canes, called Calhoun's Creek, adj. Edward Dicke, James Noble, John Huster, granted to Hugh Calhoun in separate tracts of 100 acres each one granted 20 Feb 1760 and the other 23 Feb 1768. Hugh Calhoun (LS), Jannet Calhoun (I) (LS), Wit: Arthur Gray, William Bain. Proved 3 Apr 1777 before Pat. Calhoun, J. P. in Ninety Six district by the oath of William Bain. Recorded 6 Sept 1777.

V-4, 436-440: Lease and release. 22 & 23 July 1777, John Long of Ninety Six District, planter, to John Ewing Calhoun of same, for £800 SC money, 400 acres in Granville County, Ninety Six District, above Long Cane Settlement, on a small branch of Savannah River called Rosses Creek, adj. land whereon Samuel Morrow now liveth, granted to Mathew Long deceased 10 Sept 1765. John Long (LS), Wit: Martha Calhoun, William Bain. Proved 24 July 1777 before Patrick Calhoun, J.P., by the oath of William Bain. Recorded 6 Sept 1777.

SOUTH CAROLINA DEED ABSTRACTS 1773-1778

V-4, 440-443 [the last part of this deed is found following page 416]: Lease & Release. 1 & 2 July 1774, Stephen Drayton of Sunbury, Province of Georgia, Esquire, and Elizabeth his wife, to the Honorable John Drayton, of Charlestown, SC, for £13,000 SC money, the undivided moiety of half part of 400 acres in Granville County, SC, being part of 4000 acres granted to Ann Drayton adj. land of Thomas Fuller, late of Thomas Drayton, Esquire deceased, plat dated 10 June 1754 certified by James McPherson; also an undivided moiety or half part of 1442 acres, part of 3000 acres in Granville County granted to sd. Thomas Drayton 6 Apr 1733, per plat 20 June 1772 certified by Alexius Mader Forster, which lands were allotted to John Drayton Esquire,s son of said Thomas Drayton, pursuant to his will and upon the death of said John became and are now vested in said Stephen and his brother Thomas as tenants in common. (plats included) Stephen Drayton (LS), Elizabeth Drayton (LS), Wit: Hugh Rutledge, Benj. Huger, R[oger] Kelsall, Job Colcock. The signature of Stephen Drayton proved by the oath of Hugh Rutledge, Esqr., 10 July 1777 before Wm. Mason, J.P. The signature of Elizabeth Drayton proved by the oath of Job Colcock, 22 July 1777 before Wm. Mason, J.P. Recorded 6 Sept 1777. Whereas according to the directions of the will of Honble Thomas Drayton, Esqr., deceased, William Drayton & Stephen Drayton, two of the executors did make a general division of a tract commonly called the Cowpen tract and one other small tract contiguous thereto... Mary Ainslie extx of the will of the deceased. dated __ Apr 1773. Mary Ainslie, Jno Drayton, Wm. Drayton. (plat included)

V-4, 447-449: [see pages 418-420]

V-4, 449-452: Lease & release. 10 & 11 Dec 1773, Robert Cunningham to William Abney, both of District of Ninety Six, SC, for £300 SC money, 200 acres granted 11 Feb 1773 to Robert Cunningham on a small branch called the upper Tarrapen waters of Saludy River in Colleton County. Robt. Cunningham (LS), Wit: John Thomas, Oliver Fowler, Jno Norris. Proved before John Caldwell, J.P., 19 Jan 1774, by the oath of John Thomas. Recorded 6 Sept 1777.

V-4, 453-455: 8 Feb 1776, Margaret Man, widow of Henry Mann, late of St. Bartholomews Parish, SC, deceased, to Mary Speitz, Martha Carpenter, and Sarah Mann, three daughters of the above named Margaret Mann, for natural love and affection, 1400 acres on waters of Waccamaw River in Craven County, to be equally divided between them, it being a tract of land formerly of my father Nathaniel Wickham now deceased, and I the said Margret Mann, now being the only surviving issue. Margaret Mann (LS), Wit: Jas Stewart, Robert Crockett. Proved by the oath of Robert Crockett in Charlestown District before Thos Phepoe, J.P., 1 March 1776. Recorded 13 Sept 1777.

V-4, 455-456: Margaret Mann, relict of Henry Mann, and only heir in law to Nathaniel Wickham deceased, for natural love and affection to my only son Henry Wickham Mann, tract formerly the property of my said father Nathaniel Wickham, on Winyaw Bay in craven County, known by the name of Wickhams Land, and another survey on Santee River known by the name of the Weektee Lake. Margaret Mann (LS), Wit: Jas Stewart, Robert Crockett. Proved by the oath of Robert Crockett in Charlestown District before Thos Phepoe, J.P., a March 1776. Recorded 13 Sept 1777.

V-4, 456-458: 18 Apr 1775, George Grierson and Katharine his wife of St. Marks Parish, Craven County, to William Hudson of same, for £400 SC money, tract granted 21 June 1765 to George Grierson, 200 acres on waters Fishing Creek between said creek and Catawba River. George Grierson (LS), Katharine Grierson (O) (LS), Wit: John Davies, Archibald Clark, John Doby. Proved 19 Apr 1775 by the oath of John Doby before James Simpson, J.P. in Camden District. Recorded 13 Sept 1777.

END OF BOOK V-4.

SOUTH CAROLINA DEED ABSTRACTS 1773-1778

W-4, 1-5: Lease and release. 15 & 16 Nov 1774, Robert Blair of Cheraw District, SC, to Robert Gray of same, planter, for £3000 SC money, 300 acres in the Welch Tract in Craven county granted 4 July 1749 to Robert Inman and by lease and release 25 & 26 Feb 1752 conveyed to John Westfield, planter, adj. Wm. Evans, John Westfield, on Peedee River, and Esther Nivie conveyed for £600 15 & 16 Dec 1767 to Robert Blair. Robt Blair (LS), Wit: George Manderson, Jonathan John. Proved in Ch. District before Alexander Mackintosh, J.P., by the oath of George Manderson, 17 Apr 1775. Recorded 14 Oct 1775.

W-4, 5-9: Lease and release. 15 & 16 Nov 1774, Robert Blair of Cheraw District, SC, to Robert Gray of same, planter, for £1000 SC money, 150 acres on Peedee River adj. Godfrey Jones, granted 29 Nov 1750 to John Westfield, conveyed by Allan Brown and Esther[?] his wife 1 & 2 Dec 1769 for £150 to Robt Blair. Robt Blair (LS), Wit: George Manderson, Jonathan John. Proved in Ch. District before Alexander Mackintosh, J.P., by the oath of George Manderson, 17 Apr 1775.

W-4, 9-17: Lease and release. 1 & 2 Jan 1767, Sir William Baker, Knight and one of the Aldermen of the City of London, Great Britain, Nicholas Linwood and Brice Fisher of Parish of St. Martin in the fields, County of Middlesex, by Paul Trapier of George Town, gentleman, their attorney, to Benjamin Huger of Craven County, SC, planter, for £6300, 1000 acres on Waccamaw River granted by the Lords Proprietors to John, late Earle Granville. Wit: Peter Horry, Jno. Skrine. Proved in Craven County before John Troup by the oath of John Skrine, 15 Jan 1772.

W-4, 17-21: Lease and mortgage. 29 & 30 Aug 1775, John Anderson (near the ridge) of Colleton County, SC, Tavern Keeper, to Rowland Rugeley, of Charles Town, merchant, mortgage in the penal sum of £400 for the payment of £200 before 20 __ 1776, tract of 100 acres in Colleton County called the sedge pond granted 28 Aug 1724 to John Anderson. John Anderson (LS), Wit: Thomas Bourke, Jas. Crandon .Proved by the oath of Thomas Bourke in Chas. Town District 17 Jan 1776 before John Coram. Recorded 20 Feb 1776.

W-4, 21-25: Lease and mortgage. 19 May 1775, Samuel Swann of Bullock's Creek, planter, [and heir at law?] to Robert Swann, late of Bullocks Creek, deceased, to Henry Rugeley [amounts left blank], 500 acres called the Big Meadow in Berkely County;, granted to said Robert Swann 31 Aug 1770 adj. land of Hugh Quin. Saml Swann (LS), Wit: Thos Bourke, Arch: Carsan. Proved in Chs. Town District by the oath of Thomas Bourke 17 Jan 1776 before Jno Coram.

W-4, 26-28: Lease and release. 30 Jan 1770, William Maner of SC, planter, to Edward Keaton (Keeting) of Augusta, Georgia, for £254 SC money, 50 acres in Granville County on north side Great Stephens Creek that Thomas Maner purchased of John Scott, adj. Patrick Marches, John Martin. W. Maner (LS), Wit: William Harvey, Jeremiah Lamar. Proved in Granville county before John De La Howe, J.P., by the oath of Wm.Harvey, 6 Jan 1775. Recorded 21 Feb 1776.

W-4, 29-31: Lease and release. 10 March 1775, Thomas Landtrip and Hannah his wife of Ninety Six District, planter, to Jesse Fincher of same, for £100 SC money, 100 acres in Craven county on north side of Tyger River adj. Wm. Curry, Aaron Fincher, granted to Thomas Landtrip __ Sept 1774. Thos Landtrip (P) (LS), Hannah Landtrip (X) (LS), Wit: Wm. Young, Sarah Gist, Owen Swillevin. Proved in Ninety Six District by the oath of William Young 30 Oct 1775 before Wm. Gist, J.P. Recorded 21 Feb 1776.

W-4, 31-32: James Cook of Christ Church Parish, SC, surveyor, and Sarah his wife, bound to John Syme of St. Thomas Parish, __ Oct 177-, to make title to 500 acres in Berkly County on north side Wandoe River. Jas. Cook (LS), Wit: __ Ward, __ Heard.

W-4, 33-34: Lease and release. 6 & 7 March 1772, Thomas Murray of St. Mathews parish, planter, to George Hails of same, planter, for £130 SC money, 60 acres granted to sd. Thos Murray 14 Aug 1770 adj. land of sd. George Hails. Thomas Murray (LS), Wit: Henry Wheeler, Jno. Easom. Proved 16 Aug 1775 before Malcom Clarke, J.P., by the oath of John Easom.

W-4, 34-36: Lease and release. 16 & 17 March 1773, Wm. Elliott, Esqr., of Beaufort, Pot Royal, to James Parsons, Esqr., of Charlestown, for ten shillings, 1000 acres on Buckhalters Creek adj. John

SOUTH CAROLINA DEED ABSTRACTS 1773-1778

Harritons, Laurence Rambo, Richard Jones, Edward Houck, granted 30 March 1772 to Wm. Elliott. Wm. Elliott (LS), Wit: Jacob Read, Robt. Ladson. Recorded 25 Feb 1776.

W-4, 36-38: Lease and release. 15 & 16 May 1775, Benjamin Deason Senr of Craven County, SC, and Tereser his wife, to Conrad Arrant of same, for £410 SC money, 100 acres, part of 200 acres granted to Mary Gibson on Flat Creek, transferred to Thomas Waid 15 May 1760, then from Thomas Waid to John Bratton 21 May 1763, then to Cronamus Zinn 1 March 1769, then to Thomas Childre 23 March 1771, then to Benjn. Deason. Benjamin Deason (X) (LS), Tereser Deason (X) (LS), Wit: Gail Frizell (G), John Metheny (X). Proved in Camden District by the oath of Gale Grisel 24 July 1775. Recorded 26 Feb 1776.

W-4, 38-42: Lease and release. 21 & 22 Nov 1769, Judith Brown of Parish of St. Marks, SC, planter, to John Cook of same, planter, for £120 SC money, 250 acres granted 10 nov 1761 to Judith Brown in Craven County on waters of Wateree River near Granys Quarters. Judith Brown (+) (LS), Wit: John Drakeford, John McWatty, Richard Brown (RB), Walter Rowe (M). Proved in Camden District by the oath of John Drakeford 18 Feb 1776 before Jno. N. Oglethorpe, J.P. Recorded 26 Feb 1776.

W-4, 42-44: 1 March 1747, Abraham Colson of SC, planter, to John Cook for £___ SC money, land known by the name of the Alligator Pond granted to Capt. William Sanders, 300 acres. Abr. Colson (LS), Wit: William Deloatch, Tob:s Ford, Robert Moor. Proved by the oath of William Deloatch 2 March 1747 before Jas. Gillespie. Recorded 26 Feb 1776.

W-4, 45-49: Lease and release. 4 & 5 Sept 1764, Rev. Abraham Imer of Purysbourgh, SC, and Ann his wife, to Chanpn. Williamson of Stono, SC, planter, for £1800 SC money, 330 acres in St. Peter's Parish, Granville County adj. Daniel Crawford, on Savannah Back River originally granted 2 March 1764 to sd. Abraham Imer. Abr. Imer V. D. M. (LS), Ann Imer. Wit: Phil. Chifelle, ___ Brown, Will. Keith. Proved in Chas. Town District by the oath of Phil. Chifelle 16 Oct 1774 before William Rugeley. Recorded 26 Feb 1776.

W-4, 49-51: Robt. Gray of Charles Town bound to William Williamson of Charles Town, Esqr., in the penal sum of £4000 SC money for the payment of £2000, to make title to tract on the south side of a canal or creek from old Church Street into Meeting Street adj. land of James Towsigger, James Fitzsimons including buildings thereon from 8 June 1772.... dated 14 __ 1774. Robt. Gray (LS), Wit: Alexr. Horn, John Turner. Recorded 26 Feb 1776.

W-4, 51-53: 16 May 1775, Benjamin Deason Senr. of Craven County, SC, to Conrad Arrant of same, for £410 SC money, 100 acres on Flatt Creek being part of 200 acres granted to Mary Gibson transferred to Thomas Waid 15 May 1760 from said Thomas to John Bratton 21 May 1763 to Cronamus Zinn 1 March 1769 then to Thos Childre 22 March 1771, then to Benj. Deason. Benjamin Deason (X) (LS), Tereser Deason (+) (LS), Wit: Gail Frisel (G), John Metheny (+). Proved in Camden District by the oath of Gale Frisell 24 July 1775 before R. Rugeley. Recorded 26 Feb 1776.

W-4, 53-56: 1 Nov 1766, John Bratton, Blacksmith of Mecklinburgh County, North Carolina, and Mary his wife, to Conrad Arrant, planter, of Craven County, SC, for £220 SC money, 100 acres part of 200 acres granted sd. John Bratton to Cronimus Zinn on Flat Creek a south branch of the north prong of Lynches Creek, granted to Mary Gibson [chain of title unclear, but appears to be same property as in preceding deed]. John Bratton (LS), Mary Bratton (M) (LS), Wit: Michael Miars, John Meloney (I). Proved in Craven County before Claudius Pegues, J.P., by the oath of Michael Miars, 13 Dec 1776. Recorded 1 March 1776.

W-4, 57-60: Lease and release. 24 & 25 May 1773, Thomas Dearington of Parish of St. Thomas and St. Dennis, Berkley County, SC, planter, to John Mayer of same, practitioner in Physick, £1200 SC money, 500 acres in Craven County adj. Thos lynch Esqr., P. H. Hatley, granted 6 Sept 1772 to Thomas Dearington. Thos Dearington (LS), Wit: Peter Videau, Jno Dearington, Laurence Mayer. Proved 1 Nov 1774 before R. Rugeley, J.P., by the oath of John Dearington. Recorded 1 March 1776.

SOUTH CAROLINA DEED ABSTRACTS 1773-1778

W-4, 61-65: Lease and mortgage. 11 & 12 Dec 1777, John Goff of George Town, Craven County, to Paul Trapier the elder, of George Town, Esquire, for debt of £1500, town lot in George Town on north east side of Front Street, number 241. John Goff (LS), Wit: Eliza Trapier, John Heath. Proved in George Town District before Job Rothmahler, J.P., by the oath of John Heath, 17 Dec 1777. Recorded 24 Jan 1778.

W-4, 65-67: Lease and release. 19 & 20 Dec 1777, Gilbert Gibson of Camden District, SC, planter, to Howel Hay of same, planter, for £800 SC money, 31 acres in Camden District on north side of Congaree River on a large Lake commonly called Handysides Lake, part of tract granted to James Lesley for 300 acres. Gilbert Gibson (LS), Wit: William Goodwyn, Casper Slappey. Proved in Orangeburgh District before Ralph Humphreys, J.P., by the oath of William Goodwyn, 20 Dec 1777. (plat included, dated 17 Dec 1777, shows adj. land owner Andrew Lord and Howell Hay). Recorded 24 Jan 1778.

W-4, 67-71: Lease and release. 16 May 1774, John Brodie of Charlestown, to David Baty of same, for £600 SC money, 600 acres on Pacolet River in Berkley County granted 7 May 1774. John Brodie (LS), Wit: Walter Main, Thos. Tod. Proved 15 Dec 1777 before Hopkin H. Price, J.P., by the oath of Walter Main. Recorded 24 Jan 1778.

W-4, 71-73: Lease and release. 8 & 9 Dec 1777, David Baty of Charlestown, to Thomas Tod of Craven County, for £600, 600 acres on the mouth of Alexr Creek of South Pacolet River, granted to John Brodie 7 May 1774. David Baty (LS), Wit: W. Livington, Archd. Carson. Proved 22 Dec 1777 before Hopkin Price by the oath of Archd. Carson. Recorded 24 Jan 1778.

W-4, 73-75: Lease and release. 6 & 7 Jan 1778, Mary Abel Allyne Cripps, sole heir and executrix of the estate of the deceased Robert Cripps, late of Charlestown, taylor, to Thomas Tod of Craven County, SC, farmer, for £500 SC money, 500 acres on south side South Pacolet River granted to Robert Cripps 7 June 1774. Mary Abl. All. Cripps (LS), Wit: John Fyfe, David Baty. Proved 7 Jan 1778 before Hopkin Price by the oath of David Baty. Recorded 24 Jan 1778.

W-4, 76-78: Lease and release. 7 & 8 Sept 1773, James Wood of Lawsons Fork, planter, to William Wood Junior of ____ Fork, for £200 SC money, 300 acres on Lawsons fork of Pacolet River below Thomas Williamsons land, granted 22 May 1772 in Tryon County, North Carolina, since has fell in the province of South Carolina. James Wood (LS), Wit: Thomas Hathaway, Henry Woolf. Proved in Ninety Six District before James wood, J.P., by the oath of Thomas Hathaway, 23 Jan 1774. Recorded 24 Jan 1774 [sic].

W-4, 78-79: 29 Dec 1777, Thomas Hathaway of District of Ninety Six, SC, to Israel Morris of same, for £400 SC money, tract in Tryon County, North Carolina, now in State of South Carolina, 500 acres on both sides of Fawn Branch of Lawsons fork of Pacolate River granted to said Thomas Hathaway 23 May 1772. Thomas Hathaway (LS), Wit: James Rice, John Leech, Obadiah Roberts. Proved in Ninety Six District by the oath of James Rice 30 Dec 1777 before James Wood, J.P. Recorded 24 Jan 1778.

W-4, 80-84: Lease and release. 8 & 9 Jan 1778, hopkin Price of Charles Town, Esquire, to John McDougall, Second Lieutenant of the Continental Frigate Randolph, for £4000 SC money, lot on north side of Tradd Street in Charlestown, number 39. Hopkin Price (LS), Wit: Wm. Print, John Keill. Proved before George Sheed by the oath of William Print, 9 Jan 1778. Recorded 24 Jan 1778.

W-4, 84-90: Lease and release. __ March 1777, Mary Swadler of St. Bartholoomews Parish, Colleton County, widow, to John Postell the younger of same, planter, for £5400 SC money, two tracts: (1) 286 acres formerly belonging to Doctor James Skirving who conveyed it to Abraham Swadler whose will devised it to his son George Swadler who also by will devised it to Mary Swadler adj. William Mitchell, Philip Hext, Rawlins Lowndes, Esqr., and land formerly of John Cook deceased, and Horse Shoe Creek; (2) 69 acres originally granted to Doctr. James Skirving adj. William Mitchell, Daniel Legare. Mary Swadler (LS), Wit: Robt. Beard, Thomas Collis. Proved before George Sheed by the oath of Robert Beard, 9 Jan 1778. Recorded 24 Jan 1778.

SOUTH CAROLINA DEED ABSTRACTS 1773-1778

W-4, 90-91: James Ervin of Williamsburgh Township, Craven County, bound to Robert Ervin, son and heir to John Ervin, late of Williamsburgh Township, deceased, in the sum of £20,000 SC money, 14 May 1773, to make title to three tracts of land, two known by Pudding Swamp Tracts in Craven County one of 400 acres the other of 50 acres, the third tract of 300 acres on a branch of Santee (or Saludy) River called Turkey Creek. James Ervin (LS), Wit: Saml James, John Scott. Proved before Gavin Witherspoon, J.P., by the oath of John Scott, 1 Sept 1777. Recorded 29 Jan 1778.

W-4, 91-92: James Ervin of Prince Fredericks Parish, bound to John Ervin Junr., son and heir to John Ervin Sr., late of Williamsburgh Township, deceased, in the sum of £25,000 SC money, 14 May 1773, to make title to three tracts of land, one of 400 acres on Santee River Swamp adj. Wm. Whitesides, Richard Bacon, James Nowell, John Williams, another tract of 100 acres on Santee River Swamp adj. William Whitesides, Joseph Cantey, David Daniels, the third tract of 100 acres in St. Marks Parish on north side Santee River on Great Pond adj. Joseph Cantey, Watson, Davies. James Ervin (LS), Wit: Saml James, John Scott. Proved before Gavin Witherspoon, J.P., by the oath of John Scott, 1 Sept 1777. Recorded 29 Jan 1778.

W-4, 92-95: Lease and release. 9 & 10 Apr 1777, George Roye of South Carolina, planter, to Lenard Samet of same, planter, for £500 SC money, 150 acres granted 30 Oct 1772 to George Roye in Amelia Township, on a branch of Lions Creek in Berkley County adj. Barnard Lindsay, Edward Brady, John Mitchell, Jacob Powel, Martin Stoutenmire, William Jackson. George Roye (+) (LS), Wit: John Isaacs, Andrew Rumley (+), Nicholas Meigler [German signature]. Proved 10 May 1777 before Henry Patrick, J.P., by the oath of Andrew Rumley. Recorded 29 Jan 1778.

W-4, 95-98: Lease and release. 9 & 10 Apr 1777, George Roye of South Carolina, planter, to Lenard Samet of same, planter, for £500 SC money, 150 acres, part of 250 acres in Amelia Township adj. John Cambel, Thomas Allison, granted 9 Jan 1752 to Martin Stoutenmire, conveyed by Martin Stoutenmier to Robert Bean, then Robert Bean conveyed 150 acres to said George Roye. George Roye (+) (LS), Wit: Geo Seawright, Adm. McKachey, Martin Weighter (X). Proved 10 May 1777 before Henry Patrick, J.P., by the oath of Martin Weighter. Recorded 29 Jan 1778.

W-4, 98-101: Lease and release. 24 & 25 Oct 1776, John McClure of Craven County, Parish of St. Mark, Camden District, weaver, to Thomas Camron of same, weaver, for £240 SC money, 250 acres on Rockey Creek on So Fork Road that goes to Charlestown in Craven County adj. Michael Dickson, granted 13 May 1768 to John McClure. John McClure (T), Wit: John Combest, John Brown. Proved by the oath of John Brown before Michael Dickson, J.:P., 3 Apr 1777. Recorded 29 Jan 1778.

W-4, 101-103: 29 Sept 1777, Francis Gillan of Mecklenburgh County, North Carolina, to Isaac Barr of Craven County, SC, for £79 s10, 250 acres on Hanahs Creek a branch of Catawba River adj. Isaac Barr, granted 21 March 1768. Francis Gillan (B) (LS), Wit: Abm. Caslick, John Phillips. Proved in Camden District by the oath of John Philips before James Simpson, 27 Dec 1777. Recorded 29 Jan 1778.

W-4, 103-104: 12 Apr 1777, Robert Carnahan of St. Marks Parish, Craven county, SC, to John McClenehan of same, for £35 SC money, 250 acres granted 26 July 1775 to Robert Carnahan in Camden District on Beaver Dam adj. James Pursley, adj. an Irish survey, John Gaston. Robert Carnihan (O) (LS), Wit: Amos Tims, Michael Dickson, Robt. Patton. Proved in Camden District by the oath of Robert Patton before John Gaston, J. P., 25 Nov 1777. Recorded 28 Jan 1778.

W-4, 104-108: Lease and release. 22 & 23 Apr 1774, Terrence Carrel of Ninety Six District, to William Hill of the Colony of Virginia, for £800 SC money, 100 acres in Ninety Six District on a small branch of Broad River called Tyger river granted 21 Apr 1774 to Terrence Carrel. Ter'ce OCarrol (T) (LS), Anne OCarrol (-) (LS), Wit: Robt Wilson, William Mays, John Doyle. Proved before Thos Gordon, J.P. for Ninety Six District, by the oath of William Mayes. Recorded 5 Feb 1778.

W-4, 108-111: Lease and release. 30 & 31 May 1775, Thomas James of Cheraws District, SC, to Charles Irby of same, for £1000 SC money, 50 acres granted 29 Oct 1756 to howel James in the Welch Tract on north east side Pee Dee adj. John Westfield, Simon Persons, and on 1 Oct 1774 conveyed by William Henry Mills, Sheriff of Cheraws District to said Thomas James by virtue of a writ of fieri facias to be levied on the goods and chattles of said Howel James, deceased, at the suit of Joseph Allston. Thomas James (LS), Wit: John Hustess, Edward Feagin. Proved before William Pegues, J.P., by the oath of Edwd. Feagin, 28 Oct 1775. Recorded 5 Feb 1778.

W-4, 111-114: Lease and release. 22 & 23 Apr 1776, William Downes of Charles Town, Gentleman, to David Reynolds of St. Marks Parish, Craven County, for £20 SC money, one half of 800 acres on north side of Broad River on Flat Rock and Bartins Run adj. land now or late of James Ogelbay, John Long, John Newell, William Richardson, Thomas Owens. Wm. Downes, Wit: George Rout, Wm. Nisbett, Proved by the oath of William Nisbet before Geo. Sheed, 21 Jan 1778. Recorded 5 Feb 1778.

W-4, 114-117: Lease and release. 8 & 9 May 1775, Richard Rideout of Amelia Township, Sc, to Evan Reese of same, for £45 SC money, 50 acres part of tract of 300 acres ranted to sd. Richd. Rideout 13 Oct 1772 adj. John Wooten. Richard Rideout (LS), Wit: Moses Duesto, John Wootan, James Wages (ll). Proved in Orangeburgh District before John Caldwell, J.P., by the oath of Moses Duesto, 1 Sept 1777. Recorded 5 Feb 1778.

W-4, 117-122: Lease and release. 11 & 12 Nov 1768, Joseph Dubourdieu of George Town, Craven County, SC, merchant, and Mary his wife, to Josias Allston of All Saints parish, same county, planter, for £250 SC money, whereas John White of said county deceased by his will dated 24 Feb 1758 devised to his executors full power to dispose of certain lands and Anthony White and Joseph White, executors, by deed 18 Oct 1768 did sell to said Joseph Dubourdieu, lot in said town, number 93 on Prince Street and Prince Street. J. Dubourdieu (LS), M. Dubourdieu(LS), Wit: Robert Heriot, Benjn. Trapier. Proved in Craven County by the oath of Benjamin Trapier 19 Dec 1768 before Benja. Young. Recorded 5 Feb 1778.

W-4, 122-126: Lease and release. __ Apr 1777, Benjamin Young of Prince George's Parish, Craven county, planter, and Martha his wife, to Francis Allston of same parish and county, sea shore plantation on Waccamaw Neck adj. lands of Peter Simons lately deceased, Joseph allston, on Old Cape Fear Road, 492 acres (plat included). Benj. Young (LS), Martha Young (LS), Wit: Thos Mitchell, Edward Mitchell. Proved by the oath of Thomas mitchell before Job Rothmahler 1 May 1777. Recorded 5 Feb 1778.

W-4, 126-130: Lease and release. 17 & 18 Sept 1777, Henry Ravenel of St. John's Parish, Berkley County, SC, Esquire, and Mary his wife, to John Pamor of St. Stephens Parish, SC, for £10,000... whereas Paul De. St. Julian, late of St. Johns Parish, Gentleman, deceased, was possessed of three several plantations each of 500 acres, which said three tracts of land on south side Santee River in Craven County and by his will 6 Apr 1741 did devise to his daughters Mary De. St. Julian now wife of Henry Ravenell and Elizabeth De. St. Julien, the late wife of Job Marian of Charlestown, Esquire, all those lands, and each daughter should have 750 acres. Henry Ravenel (LS), Mary Ravenel (LS), Wit: John Palmer Junr., Job Marion, Henry Ravenel Junr. Proved before John Frierson by the oath of John Palmer Junr, 3 Oct 1777. Recorded 5 Feb 1778.

W-4, 131-133: Lease and release. 28 & 29 Aug 1777, William Ballantine of Orangeburgh District, hatter, and Mary his wife, to William Currie of same, merchant, for £1000 SC money, 150 acres in Craven County on Broad River adj. said river, __ Ellis, David Edwards, granted 3 Apr 1762 to William Ballantine, recorded in Book HHH, folio 522. William Ballantine (LS), Mary Ballantine (+) (LS), Wit: George Dawkins Junr., John Ewing. Proved in Ninety Six District by the oath of John Ewing 27 Nov 1777 before Michl. Dickert, J. P. Recorded 5 Feb 1778.

W-4, 134-137: Lease and release. 14 & 15 March 1775, John Soverance of Parish of Christ Church, planter, to Andrew Quelch of same, planter, for fifteen shillings, 300 acres in Craven County, St. Marks Parish, about twenty miles above Camden adj. land of Richard Kirkland, Wateree River, granted to said John Soverance 3 Feb last. John Soverance (LS), Wit: Elizabeth Quelch, John Wingood, Willm. Roya. Proved 23 March 1775 before John Sandfort Dart, J.P. in Charlestown District, by the oath of John Wingood. Recorded 5 Feb 1778.

SOUTH CAROLINA DEED ABSTRACTS 1773-1778

W-4, 137-141: Lease and release. 4 & 5 March 1776, William Raines of Coosawhatchie in Prince Williams parish, Granville County, planter, to John Grimball of same, planter, for £1000 SC money, 550 acres granted to William Raines 12 March 1773 adj. lands of Joseph Grimball (now said John Grimball), Acquilla Miles, surveyed for said William Raines 15 May 1763 and certified 5 Jan 1773. Wm. Raines (LS), Wit: James Thomson, Hen'y Gindrat. Proved in Beaufort District by the oath of James Thomson, J.P., 16 March 1776. Recorded 12 Feb 1778.

W-4, 142-145: Lease and release. 16 & 17 Dec 1776, John Higdon of Little Saludy in Ninety Six District, SC, planter, to Elias Robert of St. Peters Parish, Beaufort District, surveyor, for £30 SC money, 400 acres in Prince Williams Parish granted to John Higdon 15 June 1771 recorded in Book III, page 4, land on a large branch of the Great coosawhatchie Swamp known by the name of McPhersons branch adj. James Smith. John Higdon (l) (LS), Wit: John Audebert, Drury Mims. Proved by the oath of John Audebert before Henry Gindrat, J.P. in Beaufort District, 18 Sept 1777. Recorded 12 Feb 1778.

W-4, 145-149: Lease and release. 27 Jan 1778, Samuel Butler of Charlestown, yeoman, to Darby Larey of same, yeoman, for £3050 SC money, 100 acres on south side Lynches Creek in Craven county granted 17 Jan 1777 to Samuel Ratcliffe who built a dwelling house whereon he lived for several years and at the time of his death by will 29 July 1772 gave the same to Samuel Butler his grandson. Samuel Butler (LS), Wit: Peter Johnson, Rueben Minor, Benja. Cowar. Proved 27 Jan 1778 before George Sheed by the oath of Peter Johnson. Recorded 12 Feb 1778.

W-4, 149-151: 16 Dec 1776, Elisha Parker of Craven County, SC, to Thomas Tomkins of same, for £250 SC money, 130 acres on northeast side Great Pedee River on Marks' Creek, adj. John Bones, persimmon branch, Elisha Parker's line, part of 300 acres granted to Samuel Goodman 17 June 1765. Elisha Parker (P) (LS), Wit: William Johnson (W), Elisha Harris Parker. Proved in Cheraw District before William Pegues by the oath of Elisha Harrison Parker, 24 Dec 1776. Recorded 12 Feb 1778.

W-4, 151-152: 5 Dec 1777, John McCants of State of South Carolina, planter, to William Pegues of St. Davids Parish, for £1000 SC money, two tracts of 250 acres each on south west side Pedee River adj. land formerly the property of Claudius Pegues, John Murfee, granted to John McCants 1 Aug 1758. John McCants (LS), Wit: John Lefevre, Henry Willm Harrington. Proved before Claudius Pegues by the oath of Henry William Harrington 7 Dec 1777. Recorded 12 Feb 1778.

W-4, 152-153: 25 May 1777, George Hancock Junr to Thomas Woodward, for £500, mortgage of 2300 acres between waters of Broad and Catawba River on Jacksons Creek... Richard Winn and Priscilla his wife... George Hancock (LS), Wit: Thos Harbert, Mary Raiford. Proved in Camden District before Barnaby Pope by the oath of Thomas Harbert, 17 Jan 1778. Recorded 12 Feb 1778.

W-4, 154-156: Lease and release. 23 & 24 Jan 1775, Samuel Elliott of Charlestown, Esquire, to Benjamin Elliott and Wm. Scott of same, executors of the will of Sarah Elliott, late of St. Andrews parish, Widow, deceased, whereas Thomas Elliott, late of St. Andrews parish, planter, deceased, in 1751 purchased of said Samuel Elliot, and by his will said Thomas Elliott bequeathed said real estate to his wife Sarah Elliott, 48 acres adj. Benjamin Elliott, Sarah Elliott (plat included for 248 acres the property of Thomas Jones and sold by him to Thomas Elliott deceased). Benja. Elliott (LS), William Scott (LS), Wit: Joseph Verree, Chs. Motte. Proved by the oath of Joseph Veree 20 Jan 1778 before Geo: Sheed. Recorded 12 Feb 1778.

[Here pages are in poor condition and some may be out of sequence.]

W-4, 156-157: 21 July 1775, Benjamin Elliott and William Scott, executors of Sarah Elliott, late of st. Andrews Parish, widow, to Barnard Elliott and Thos. Elliott of Charlestown, for £250 SC money, whereas Thomas Elliott was possessed of 48½ acres and in his will.... on Stono River adj. Lambert Lance [deed in very poor condition]. Benja. Elliott (LS), William Scott (LS), Proved by the oath of Joseph Veree 26 Jan 1778 before Geo: Sheed. Recorded 12 Feb 1778.

W-4, 158-160: Lease and release. 21 & 22 Dec 1773, Hermon Geiger of Berkley County, and wife Margaret, to John Buckhannon, late of same, for £1150 SC money, 450 acres on Broad River

SOUTH CAROLINA DEED ABSTRACTS 1773-1778

granted 7 June 1751 to Hermon Geiger. Hermon Geiger (LS), Margaret Geiger (X) (LS), Wit: Jacob Geiger [German signature], Jacob Gibson, William Geiger. Proved in Ninety Six District by the oath of Jacob Gibson 22 Aug 1774 before Michael Dickert, J.P. Recorded 12 Feb 1778.

W-4, 161-165: Lease and release. 15 & 16 Sept 1776, Barnard Elliott of Charlestown, Esquire, and Susannah his wife, to Thomas Elliott of same, gentleman, for £4300 SC money, tract purchased 21 ___ 1775 from Benjamin Elliott and William Scott, two tracts adj. each other, 1218 acres in St. Andrews Parish. Barnard Elliott (LS), Susannah Elliott (LS), Wit: John Bush, Benja. Elliott. Proved in Charlestown District by the oath of Benjamin Elliott before Geo Sheed, 7 Jan 1778. Recorded 12 Feb 1778 (plat included).

W-4, 165-170: Lease and release. 4 & 5 July 1770, Mark Oliver of Christ Church Parish, SC, planter, and Rachel his wife, to George Hugins of same parish, planter, for £140 SC money, 192 acres in Christ Church Parish adj. Richard Joy, land which formerly belonged to Mark Oliver grandfather to Mark Oliver to whom the same descended as only ___. Mark Oliver (LS), Rachel Oliver (X) (LS), Wit: John White Junr, Richard Blake Junr, Gabl. Capers. Proved in Charlestown District by the oath of Gabriel Capers, Esqr., before Geo Sheed, 22 Jan 1778. Recorded 19 Feb 1778.

W-4, 171-173: Lease and release. 19 & 20 Dec 1777, Philip Person and Collin Person of Brunswick County, State of Virginia, Gent., to William Burrows of Charlestown, Esquire, for £2500 SC money, whereas by letter patent 9 Jan 1752 to John Lloyd 350 acres in the fork between Congaree and Wateree Rivers, SC, and said John Lloyd 17 & 18 Jan 1764 to John Person, and said John Person by his will did bequeath to his sons Philip Person and Collins Person. Phillip Person (LS), Collin Person (LS), Wit: William Thomson, Malcom Clarke. Proved by the oath of William Thomson before John Troup, J.P., __ Jan 1778. Recorded 19 Feb 1778.

W-4, 173-176: Lease and release. 19 & 20 Dec 1777, Philip Person and Collin Person of Brunswick County, State of Virginia, Gent., to William Burrows of Charlestown, Esquire, for £1500 SC money, 200 acres, part of 250 acres granted to Christopher Reyquart on Toms Creek, adj. John Lloyd. Phillip Person (LS), Collin Person (LS), Wit: William Thomson, Malcom Clarke. Proved by the oath of William Thomson before John Troup, J.P., __ Jan 1778. Recorded 19 Feb 1778.

W-4, 177-182: Lease and release. 8 & 9 Dec 1777, George Croft of George Town, SC, merchant, and Elizabeth his wife, to William Cunnington of Charlestown, merchant, for £7000 SC money, lot on west side Bedons Alley adj .land of Phillip Tydings, Paul Townsend, devised by Peter Leg, late of Charlestown, to his daughter said Elizabeth Croft upon the death of his wife Mary now lately deceased. George Croft (LS), Elizth. Croft (LS), Wit: Willm. Johnson, Capers Boone Junr. Proved in Charlestown District by the oath of William Johnson 24 Jan 1778 before Geo: Sheed. Recorded 19 Feb 1778.

W-4, 182-186: Lease and release. 22 & 23 Sept 1777, Robert Brailsford of Charlestown, Gentleman, and Rose his wife, to Henry Cropp of same, for £500 SC money, 510 acres in St. Helena's Parish. (plat included dated 23 nov 1777 by John Linder, D.S.). Robt. Brailsford (LS), Rose Brailsford (LS), Wit: Jas Witter Junr, James Ballantine, John Linder, Jeremiah Brown. Proved by the oath of James Ballantine in Charlestown District before Geo Sheed, __ Jan 1778. Recorded 19 Feb 1778.

W-4, 186-191: Lease and release. 22 & 23 Sept 1777, Robert Brailsford, late of Parish of St. Bridget, London, Great Britain, Gentleman, but now of Charlestown, and Rose his wife, to Thomas Rivers, land granted 11 Apr 1715 to William Hodgson, several baronies. (plat included by James Peart, D. Surv.) Robt Brailsford (LS), Rose Brailsford (LS), Wit: Lambert Lance, William Fraser. Proved by the oath of Lambert Lance 26 Jan 1778 before Geo: Sheed. Recorded 19 Feb 1778.

W-4, 191-194: [first part missing] Cherokee Nation or tribe of Indians for a large and valuable consideration paid, by divers sorts of goods, by Richard Henderson, Thomas Hart, Nathaniel Hart, John Williams, John Luttrell, William Johnston, James Hogg, David Hart, and Leonard Henley Bullock of north Carolina, tract of land known by Transylvania, lying on the River Ohio and branches on Cantucky Chenoe, or what is called by the English Louise River, also a tract adjoining the same on a branch of the Cumberland River... land on Holston River, at Powells Mountain, line run by Col. Donaldson and Co.... Willm. Dry. Wit: Thos Shubrick, Charles Drayton. Proved in

SOUTH CAROLINA DEED ABSTRACTS 1773-1778

Charlestown District by the honble. Thomas Shubrick, 18 Feb 1778 before George Sheed. Recorded 21 Feb 1778.

W-4, 194-199: Lease and release. 15 & 16 ___ 1777, Archer Smith and Ann his wife, of Ninety Six District, to Samuel Dubois of Orangeburgh District, for £1683 SC money, 561 acres part of 600 acres granted to Archer Smith 4 Oct 1774 (originally granted to Wm. Cowden by Mathew Rowan, Gov. of North Carolina __ Sept 1753) at the mouth of Cowdens Creek. Archer Smith (LS), Anne Smith (LS), Wit: Willm. Currie, Abraham Pearce. Proved 10 Jan 1778 by the oath of William Currie before Michael Leitner, J.P., Recorded 12 Feb 1778.

W-4, 199-203: Lease and release. 17 & 18 Dec 1777, Samuel Dubois of Orangeburgh District, SC, to James Oliphant of Ninety Six District, for £2200 SC money, 561 acres part of tract granted to Archer Smith (originally granted to Wm Cowen), conveyed 15 & 16 of this instant by Samuel Dubois. Saml. Dubois (LS), Wit: Willm. Currie, Abraham Pearce. Proved 10 Jan 1778 before Michl. Leitner by the oath of William Currie. Recorded 26 Feb 1778.

W-4, 203-208: Lease and release. 14 & 15 Feb 1775, George Anson of Anson of Shugborough Manor in the County of Stafford, Kingdom of Great Britain, Esqr., by George Roupell of Charlestown, his attorney, and Richard Lambton of Charlestown, to Thomas Rivers of Granville County, for £742 SC money, 371 acres of Pine Land, part of barony number 10 (plat included). Richard Lambton (LS), George Anson by attorney George Roupell (LS), Wit: J. Simpson, Jas. Johnston. Proved in Charlestown District by John Colcock who proved the handwriting of James Simpson and James Johnston. Recorded 20 Feb 1778.

W-4, 209-214: Lease and release. 16 & 17 Ma-- 1770, Hannah Bradwell of St. Bartholomews Parish, Colleton County, widow, to Joseph Porcher of same, planter, for £2189 SC money, 200 acres on west side of the freshes of Edisto River adj. James Sadler and Thomas Burr, granted 7 May 1711 to Thomas Howard and conveyed by deed of sale 4 Dec 1714 to William Westbery and by said Westbery and Mary his wife 14 March 1716/17 to John Gwin deceased of whom Hannah Bradwell is heir at law and another tract of 198 acres granted to William Westbury 12 Jan 1716/17. Hannah Bradwell (LS), Wit: Joseph Law, John Coon, John Howard. Proved by the oath of Joseph Law before Saml Porcher, J.P. in Granville County, 17 March 1770.

Hannah Bradwell of St. Bartholomews parish, Colleton County bound to Joseph Porcher of same, in the sum of £4000 SC money, 16 March 1770 to make title to 200 acres. Wit: Joseph Law, john Howard. Proved by the oath of Joseph Law. Recorded 26 Feb 1778.

W-4, 214-218: Lease and release. 11 & 12 Dec 1777, Christopher Fitzsimmons of Charlestown, SC, to William Graham of same, lot in parish of St. Philip, Charlestown, adj. land of Mary Watson, John Morris, Cato Ash deceased. Christopher Fitzsimmons, Wit: Wm. Blacklock, William Valentine. Proved in Chas. Town District before William Nisbett by the oath of William Blacklock, 12 Dec 1777. Recorded 26 Feb 1778.

W-4, 218-222: Lease and release. 15 & 16 Jan 1778, William McConnico of South Carolina, executor of the will of Samuel McConnico of St. Marks Parish, to John Gabriel Guignard, merchant, 150 acres in Craven County granted 2 Dec 1774. William McConnico (LS), Wit: Th. Compton, Jas McCormick. Proved by the oath of Thomas Compton __ Jan 1778. Recorded 26 Feb 1778.

W-4, 222-227: Lease and release. 26 & 27 Feb 1772, Major Pierce Butler of Charlestown, Esquire, and Mary his wife (late Mary Middleton) to Alexander Rose of same, merchant, for £1000 SC money, 1000 acres in Craven county adj. land of Collo. Thomas Middleton deceased, Bulls River, Lt. Gov. Bull, on a marsha called Lewis's Marsh, by deed from Charles Lowndes Esqr., decd., then Provost Marshall to the late Capt. John Bull 6 __ 1755, also a plantation of 500 acres part of 5000 acres purchased out of Lowndes's patent by one Robert Thorpe in Prince Williams Parish, Granville County adj. Collo. Thomas ____, land formerly of Robert Thorpe, which was originally granted to one Samuel Jones and conveyed by said Capt. John Bull, which tracts were devised by the will of John Bull to his grandson William Middleton Esqr., decd, which became vested in his sisters the said Mary Butler and Mrs. Sarah Guerard, wife of Benjamin Guerard. Pierce Butler (LS), Mary

SOUTH CAROLINA DEED ABSTRACTS 1773-1778

Butler (LS), Wit: Francis Pinckney, Chs. Pinckney. Proved 7 Feb 1770 before John Troup, J.P., by the oath of Charles Pinckney, Esqr. Recorded 5 March 1778.

W-4, 227-232: Lease and release. 28 & 29 Feb 1772, Alexander Rose of Charlestown, merchant, to Major Pierce Butler of same, merchant, for £7000 SC money, 1000 acres in Granville County adj. land late of Col. Thomas Middleton deceased, branches of Bulls River, Lt. Gov. Bull, Lewis's Marsh, purchased by Rawlins Lowndes then Provost Marshall to late John Bull decd, 6 June 1775; 500 acres part of 5000 acres purchased out of Lowndes' patent, another tract of 997 acres in Granville County adj. other tract, adj. James St. John, granted to one Samuel Jones. Alex Rose (LS), Wit: Wm. Graves, Ch. Pinckney. Proved by the oath of Wm. Greaves __ Feb 1778 before John Troup, J.P. Recorded __ March 1778.

W-4, 232-237: Lease and release. 3 & 4 March 1772, Major Pierce Butler and Mary his wife (late Mary Middleton) to Godin Guerard, for £_000 [same tracts in preceding deeds, this lease and release in very poor condition]. Wit: Chs. Pinckney, Chs. Pinckney Junr. Proved 7 Feb 1770 before John Troup, J.P., by the oath of Charles Pinckney, Esqr. Recorded 5 March 1778.

W-4, 237-240: Lease and release. __ May 1774, Benjamin Garden and Amelia his wife to Godin Guerard, for £5000, tract in Granville County... Edmund Barnes & Elizabeth his wife to Benjamin Garden, 5 __ 1757. Benjn. Garden, Amelia Garden. Wit: Glen Drayton, Wm. Hazel.

W-4, 241-245: Lease and release. _____ 1775. Parker Quince and Susannah his wife of Brunswick County, ____, to Alexander Gillon of Charlestown, for £10,000 [?], lot on Church Street [deed fragmentary].

W-4, 245-250: Lease and release. Thomas Elliott of Berkley County and Sarah his wife to Alexander Gillon, lots 281 and 282 adj. land late of Samuel West, on the street leading to the Broad Path, also lot in Charlestown adj. lot of Schenkinghs Square. Thos Elliott (LS), Sarah Elliott (LS), Wit: Michl. Kalteison, Ann Lloyd, Franes Casper Hasonclever. Proved in Chas. Town District by the oath of Michael Kalteison, 23 Feb 1778. Recorded 5 March 1778.

W-4, 250-254: Lease and release. 9 & 10 Feb 1776, William Trusler of Charlestown, SC, butcher, to Hugh Giles of Parish of Prince Frederick, planter, for £50 SC money, plantation at Pedee of 50 acres adj. said Hugh Giles, Mr. McPherson, William Worrel. W. Trusler (LS), Wit: Thos Harvey, Jacob Bowman, Saml Hopkins. Proved by the oath of Thomas Harvey __ Feb 1778. Recorded __ March 1778.

W-4, 254-257: Lease and release. 20 & 21 Dec 1777, William Egger of South Carolina, planter, to Christopher Smithers of same, planter, for £500 SC money, 250 acres granted 27 March 174- to Ulric Egger adj. Conrade Engster, Leonard Meyer, John Eller, Hans Zwicher, John Zurcher, Hamptron Tobler, in township of New Windsor, which tract descends unto William Egger as son and heir to Ulrick Egger. William Egger (LS), Wit: Isaac Ste: Trezevant, Isaac Trezevant. Proved in Beaufort District by the oath of Isaac Stephen Trezevant who also attested that his son Isaac Trezevant was a witness, 21 Dec 1777, before Bellamy Crawford, J.P. Recorded 12 March 1778.

W-4, 257-260: Lease and release. 28 & 29 Jan 1777, John Burns, late of Parish of St. Marks, SC, yeoman, to William Lewis of same, yeoman, for £400 SC money, 100 acres on Rockey Creek a branch of Catawba River in Craven County granted 25 Sept 1766 to John Burns. John Burns (LS), Wit: Robert McClellan, Leard Burns, Martha Burns (M). Proved in Camden District before Philip Walker, J.P., by the oath of Leard Burns, 11 Sept 1777. Recorded 12 March 1778.

W-4, 260-264: Lease and release. 29 & 30 March 1769, Joseph Bee of St. Pauls Parish, Colleton County, SC, and Hester his wife, to Mary Hayne of said province, widow, for £4000 SC money, 433 acres in St. Pauls Parish on Ponpon River adj. land of Andrew Mayer, said Joseph Bee, Thomas Bee. (plat included, certified by Alexr. M. Forster). Joseph Bee (LS), Wit: James Donnom, Thomas Freer. Proved by the oath of James Donnom 31 July 1769 before Wm. Burrows. Proved 12 March 1778.

SOUTH CAROLINA DEED ABSTRACTS 1773-1778

W-4, 264-266: 30 March 1775, Herman Swertfeger of Saxagotha Township, yeoman, to Henry Patrick of Berkley County, Orangeburgh District, merchant, for £500 SC money, tract on Santee River adj. Jacob Skriner, granted to John Sandricur 5 __ 1742 the said John Sandricur married to Elizabeth Swertfeger who some time after departed this life intestate left no heir but his wife she dying also intestate the land descended to the said Herman Swertfeger heir at law to said Elizabeth. Herman Swertfeger. Wit: George Routledge, Daniel Haubigh. Proved before William Tucker, J.P. in Orangeburgh District, by the oath of Daniel Haubigh, 9 Apr 1775. Recorded 12 March 1778.

W-4, 266-268: 28 Apr 1775, Godlib Stabler and Barbara his wife of Berkley County, Saxagotha Township, Orangeburgh District, planter, to Henry Patrick, Esquire, of Saxagotha Township, merchant, for £500 SC money, 50 acres in Saxagotha Township adj. Jacob Zimmerman. Gottlieb Stabler (LS), Barbara Stabler (LS), Wit: William Fitzpatrick, Eleanor Fitzpatrick. Proved before William Arther, J.P., by the oath of William Fitzpatrick 24 May 1775. Recorded 12 March 1778.

W-4, 268-269: 8 __ 1759, Benjamin Burton of Town of Beaufort, on Port Royal Island, Granville County, SC, joiner, to John Smith of Charlestown, merchant, for £10 SC money, lot # 45 in Beaufort. Benjn. Burton (LS), Wit: John Gordon, Thomas Nethercliff. Proved in Beaufort District 6 Dec 1776 before Andrew Aggnew, J.P., by the oath of Thomas Nethercliff.

W-4, 270-273: 31 Jan 1772, John Frierson of Berkley County, SC, planter, and Ann his wife, to Isaac Motte of Charlestown, esquire, whereas Peter Herman Senr was possessed of five tracts of land and on his dying intestate the five tracts descended to his son and heir at law Peter herman Junr, who also died intestate and the said tracts became vested in Francis Murrel nephew and heir at law of said Peter Hermon Junr, and by his will dated 3 Sept 1754 devised to same to his godson John Frierson, now for £6500 SC money, tract of 230 acres on east side of Pooky[?] Swamp adj. Phillip Foullarts, Peter Girards; also tract of 560 acres adj. land of Peter Herman, Mr. John Gignilliat, Peter De St. Julien, four tracts which are contiguous; and another tract of 500 acres adj. land of Henry Noble. Jno Frierson (LS), Ann Frierson (LS), Wit: William Moultrie, John White. Proved by the oath of William Moultrie before Wm. Nisbett, 6 Feb 1778. Recorded 12 March 1778.

W-4, 273-276: Lease & release. 14 & 15 Nov 1774, John Pasehart and Magdalen Luesirin his wife of Ninety Six District, SC, to John Bert of same province, for £125 SC money, land on Sleepy Creek, waters of Turkey Creek, originally granted to said Magdalen Lusirin. Magdalene Lusirin (X), John Pasehart (X) (LS), Wit: Peter Dorst, Nicolas Glaser. Proved in Ninety Six District 15 __ 1774 before Benj. Tutt, J. P., by the oath of Peter Durst. Recorded 12 March 1778.

W-4, 276-278: Lease & release. _____ March 1774, Jacob Beilard, miller, to Jacob Guilleaudeau, peruke maker, for £___, 100 acres at Long Canes in Hillsborough Township adj. land of Daniel David. Jacob Beilard (mark), Jean David (LS), Susanne David (LS), Wit: John Delahowe, Charles Boucheneau. Proved in Charlestown District by the oath of Charles Boucheneau before Geo Sheed, 18 Feb 1778. Recorded 12 March 1778.

W-4, 278-282: Lease & release. 4 & 5 Feb 1778, Elizabeth Fidling of Charlestown, SC, widow, and John Fidling of same, to Thomas Hamett of said town, taylor, for £1200 SC money, part of lot in Charlestown number 37 in Bedon's Alley, Elliott Street, adj. land of Thomas Young. Elizabeth Fidling (X) (LS), John Fidling (+) (LS), Wit: Wm. Graham, George Flagg, James Gn. Williams. Proved in Charlestown District by the oath of James Green Williams 19 Feb 1778 before George Sheed. Recorded 12 March 1778.

W-4, 282-287: Lease & release. 4 & 5 Feb 1778, Elizabeth Fidling of Charlestown, SC, widow, and John Fidling of same, of the first part, Thomas Hamett and Charlotte his wife, of the second part, to Christopher Rodgers and Andrew Rutledge of Charlestown, of the third part, for £10 SC money, part of lot 37 on south side of Elliott Street. Elizabeth Fidling (X) (LS), John Fidling (X) (LS), Thos Hamett (LS), Charlotte Hamett (LS), Chris Rogers (LS), Andrew Rutledge (LS), Wit: George Flagg, Jas. Gn. Williams. Proved in Charlestown District by the oath of James Green Williams 19 Feb 1778 before George Sheed. Recorded 19 March 1778.

W-4, 288-291: Lease & release. 11 & 12 Feb 1777, George Cogdell of Craven County, Sc, planter, to Childermas Croft of same place, planter, for £5000 currency, 1000 acres in Craven County on

SOUTH CAROLINA DEED ABSTRACTS 1773-1778

Greens Creek adj. land of Meredith Hughes, Murreau Sarrazen, John Green, granted 29 May 1736 to Thomas Thompson, and said Thomas Thompson 9 & 10 June 1736 did conveyed to Meredith Hughes the above recited plantation, and said Meredith Hughes by his will did bequeath to his two sons Meredith Hughes and Henry Hughes, and said Meredith Hughes and Henry Hughes dying intestate William Hughes being the only surviving son and heir at law of said Meredith Hughes, conveyed 2 & 3 Apr 1765 to George Cogdell. George Cogdell (LS), Wit: William Greenwood, Levi Durant, Robt. Bruce. Proved in Charlestown District by the oath of Levi Durand, Esqr., before Geo: Sheed, 17 Feb 1778. Recorded 19 March 1778.

W-4, 291-295: Lease & release. 20 & 21 Oct 1774, Benjamin Coachman, John Harleston, John Allston and James Edmonds, to James Harley of Berkley County, planter, for £1783 SC money, 1783 acres in Berkley County on a Cypress Swamp made by a branch of Edisto River called Four Hole Creek. Benja. Coachman (LS), James Edmonds (LS), Jno Harleston (LS), John Allston (LS), Wit: Benja. Smith, Thos. Walter, James Coachman, Wm. Partridge. Proved 6 June 1775 before John Wright, J.P. in St. James Goosecreek, by the oaths of Benjamin Smith and William Partridge, 6 June 1775. Recorded 19 March 1778.

W-4, 295-299: Lease & release. 1 & 2 May 1776, James Harley and his wife Ann of St. Georges Parish, Berkley County, to Allen Miles of same, for £1330 SC money, 665 acres, being part of a tract originally granted to Capt. Tobias Fitch 22 Apr 1535 on south side of Four Hole Swamp in St. James's Parish, Berkley County adj. lands of Edward Perry, John Fullerton, James Lindsay, Frank. Hooks (plat included). James Harley (JH) (LS), Ann Harley (LS), Wit: Edward Perry, Elisha Mellard, John Fenwicke. Proved 29 May 1776 before Andrew Leitch, J.P. in Charlestown District, by the oath of Edward Perry. Recorded 19 March 1778.

W-4, 299-303: Lease & release. 1 & 2 Jan 1778, Jehu Willson of Parish of St. Paul, Gentleman, and Ann his wife, and Thomas Cater of Parish of Prince William and Rachel his wife, to Allen Miles of Parish of St. Paul Gentleman, for £6500 SC money, whereas said Ann Willson and Rachel Cater being two of the daughters and devisees mentioned in the will of Silas Miles, late of St. Pauls Parish, SC, deceased, are entitled unto an equal fourth part of the lands or a fourth part of the money to arise from the sale of the same, and whereas two of the daughters of said testator to wit Elizabeth the widow and relict of Press Smith, Esquire, deceased, and Susannah the wife of John McPherson of the Indian Land, gentleman, are infants under the age of twenty one years so that they cannot at present join in a full and complete conveyance, said Jehu Wilson and Ann his wife and Thomas Cater and Rachel his wife have agreed to sell their several undivided fourth parts of said premises; 394 acres in St. Pauls Parish, Colleton County, adj. land of Samuel Wainwright, James Nicholas, Robert miles, Allen Miles and 170 acres on south side of the Road from Rantowles' Bridge to Parkers Ferry adj. land of Robert Miles, Frederick Grimkie. Jehu Willson (LS), Ann Willson (LS), Thomas Cater (LS), Rachel Cater (LS) Wit: Josiah Miles, Robert Miles. Proved before Andrew Leitch, J. P., by the oath of Robert Miles, 23 Feb 1778. Recorded 19 March 1778.

W-4, 304-307: Lease & release. 17 & 18 May 1774, John Finder of Berkley County, SC, planter, to Conrad Kirsh of same, planter, for £805 SC money, 50 acres in the low grounds of the Congaree River on south side of sd. river, part of 250 acres granted to Frederick Rife 8 March 1775 adj. to heirs of Jon. Crofft, Ann Setterin. John Finder (JF) LS), Wit: Andreas Wagner (X), John Dill, Andreas Behringer [German signature]. Proved 23 Jan 1778 before Henry Patrick by the oath of Andrew Wagner. Recorded 19 March 1778.

W-4, 307-308: 21 Dec 1776, Abraham Ravot of parish of St. Mathew, Province of Georgia, planter, to David Giroud of Purisburgh in St. Peters Parish, Granville County, planter, for £6 sterling, lot number 66 containing one acre. Abraham Ravot (LS), Wit: John Bueche, John Forbes. Proved by the oath of John Buche 31 March 1777 before Rob. Dillon. Recorded 19 March 1778.

W-4, 308-313: Lease & release. 4 & 5 Dec 1777, James Postell of St. Bartholomews Parish, SC, Esquire, eldest son and heir at law of James Postell late of St. Georges parish, Esquire, deceased, and Thomas Smith, James Skirving Junior and John Postell, executors of the will of said James Postell, deceased, to honorable John Drayton of St. Andrews parish, esquire, for £10,687 s10 SC money, whereas said James Postell deceased was possessed of 1500 acres on the west side of

SOUTH CAROLINA DEED ABSTRACTS 1773-1778

Wateree River in Craven County and by his will dated 25 May 1770 did direct that his lands on the Wateree and Alltamaha Rivers should be sold by his executors on his son John's arrival at the age of 21 years which even hath since come to pass... tract granted to said James Postell 4 Sept 1759 (plat included). James Postell Junr (LS), Thos Smith (LS), John Postell Junr (LS), Jas Skirving Junr (LS), Wit: John Bishop, Wm. Miles, T. Pinckney Junr, Thos Elliott. Proved in Charlestown Dsitrict by the oath off Thomas Elliott 13 Feb 1778 before Geo: Sheed. Recorded 26 March 1778.

W-4, 313-315: Lease & release. 1 & 2 Feb 1770, Robert Harrison of Charlestown, Berkley County, SC, to Benjamin Farar of St. Matthews Parish, for £750 SC money, 150 acres in St. Marks parish adj. Luis Buckingham on Santee River originally granted to John Cameron 21 June 1765 also a tract of 50 acres on north east side of Wataree River in Craven County adj. Benjamin Dukes originally granted to James Lynah 4 June 1759. Robt. Harison (LS), Wit: Andw Broughton Sener, Andrew Broughton. Proved in Berkley County by the oath of Andw. Broughton Senr 15 March 1770 before Wm. Thomson. Recorded 26 March 1778.

W-4, 315-317: Lease & release. 1 & 2 Dec 1773, Richard Jackson of St. Marks Parish, Craven County, SC, to John Turner of same parish, for £1000 SC money, 120 acres on Gills Creek formerly called Patricks Creek part of 400 acres adj. estate of Thomas McPherson, Benjamin Farar, and land granted to Elizabeth Verditty now belonging to David Harp, said 400 acres granted to James St. John and conveyed to said Richard Jackson. Richard Jackson (LS), Wit: Benj. Farar, Eliz. Farar. Proved in Orangeburgh District before Ralph Humphries by the oath of Benjamin Farar, 19 July 1777. Recorded 26 March 1778.

W-4, 317-321: Lease & release. 8 & 9 Dec 1773, John Turner of the Congarees, Craven County, planter, to Benjamin Farar, of Saxagotha Township, Berkley County, for £1500 SC money, 120 acres on Gills Creek at the Congarees part of 400 acres at the time of the original survey bounded by lands of the heirs of Thomas Stittsmith, Thomas Brown, said 400 acres granted to James St. John 14 Feb 1735/6 and conveyed to Richard Jackson 14 May 1736 and conveyed to Ann January 1 July 1743 and conveyed to John Turner 7 Sept 1773. John Turner (LS), Wit: Alexr. Sterling, James Bunyie. Proved 5 June 1777 before Samuel Dwight, J.P., by the oath of James Bunyie. Recorded 26 March 1778.

W-4, 322-325: Lease & release. 20 & 21 Feb 1756, Abraham Penington of Berkley County, Sc, planter, and Mary his wife, to Jacob Penington of same, for £300 SC money, tract whereon the sd. Jacob now dwelleth, 200 acres on Indian Creek a branch of Collins's River. Abraham Pennington (LS), Mary Pennington (LS), Wit: John jones, Gilbert Gilder, William Cannon, John Fairchild. Proved by the oath of john Jones before John hamilton, J.P., 12 March 1756. Memorial entered in book No. 9, page 170, 15 Nov 1768. Recorded 26 March 1778.

W-4, 325-327: Lease & release. 21 & 22 Sept 1762, James Ronals of Berkly County, SC, & Agnes his wife, to Jacob Penington of same, for £50 SC money, 50 acres on Indian Creek adj. sd. Jacob's land, sd. Ronals land. James Ronals (+) (LS), Agnes Ronals (W) (LS), Wit: Reuben Flannegan, Wm. Hendrix (H), Issachar Willcocks. Proved 7 Oct 1762 before Edward Musgrove, J.P., by the oath of Isaachar Willcocks. Recorded 26 March 1778.

W-4, 328-329: Edward Hare of Berkly County, SC, by bond to John Paul Grimkie in the penal sum of £13,000 SC money, for the payment of £6500 to be paid before 4 Sept, lot in Charles Town, number 14 on north side of Broad Street... dated 4 Sept 1777. Edward Hare (LS), Wit: James Wright, John Mills. Proved by the oath of John Mills before Geo: Sheed, 14 March 1778. Recorded 26 March 1778. Mortgage satisfied 30 July 1779 before George Sheed.

W-4, 329-334: Lease & release. 1 & 2 May 1775, Henry Reeves of Christ Church Parish, and Charlotte his wife, to William Mackimmey of Charlestown, cooper, for £5100 SC money, 508 acres in Christ Church Parish (by a late survey) adj. lands of John Ward, now or late of said Henry Reeves, Peter Taylor on a branch of Wandow River (plat included). Henry Reeves (LS), charlotte Reeves (LS), Wit: Lewis Lesterjette, Geo. Jno. Fardo. Proved in Charlestown District by the oath of George John Fardo before Geo Sheed, 24 Feb 1778. Recorded 26 March 1778.

SOUTH CAROLINA DEED ABSTRACTS 1773-1778

W-4, 334-337: Lease & release. 22 & 23 Sept 1777, Gabriel Manigault of Charlestown, Esquire, to Col. William Thompson of same, for £2500 SC money, 500 acres on north east side of Congaree River in Craven County in the District of Camden adj. land of John Faust, land now of said William Thompson (plat included dated 4 July 1777 by Ralph Humphreys, DS). Gabriel Manigault (LS), Wit: William Banbury, Pet: Bounetheau. Proved by the oath of Peter Bounetheau Esqr., before Geo: Sheed, 28 Feb 1778. Recorded 26 March 1778.

W-4, 337-340: Lease & release. 13 & 14 Nov 1771, Rawlins Lowndes, Esqr., to Jacob Valk of Charlestown, gentleman, for £350 SC money, lot in St. Philips Parish on the Broad Road to and from Charlestown. Rawlins Lowndes (LS), Wit: Thomas Shubrick Junr, Wm. Chandler. Proved 18 March 1778 by the oath of Thomas Shubrick Junr before George Sheed. Recorded 26 March 1778.

W-4, 340-343: Lease & release. 1 & 2 July 1773, Jacob Valk of Charlestown, Gentleman, to John young of St. James Goose Creek parish, planter, lot in St. Philips Parish on the Broad Road to and from Charlestown adj. lot sold to Joseph Tippin. Jacob Valk (LS), Wit: Dandridge Clifford, Press Smith. Proved 6 Oct 1773 before Thomas Turner, J.P. in Charlestown District, by the oath of Dandridge Clifford. Recorded 26 March 1778.

W-4, 343-346: Lease & release. 1 & 2 Oct 1777, John Young of St. James Goose creek Parish, planter, to George Flagg of Charlestown, painter, for £500 SC money, lot in St. Philips Parish on the Broad Road to and from Charlestown adj. lot sold to Joseph Tippin. John Young (LS), Ann Young (X) (LS), Wit: James Culliatt, Paul Schlatter. Proved by the oath of Paul Schlatter before Geo: Sheed, 12 Feb 1778. Recorded 26 March 1778.

W-4, 346-350: Lease & release. 10 & 11 Apr 1777, Thomas Jones of Camden, Craven County, SC, to William Ancrum of Charlestown, Berkley County, merchant, for £560 SC money, 350 acres on Cane Creek a branch of Saluda River in Berkley County adj. Charles Robinson, John Savage, James Choples, John Dingles, ___ Hamilton, granted 10 Aug 1768, recorded in Book CCC, page 478. Thomas Jones (LS), Wit: John Wyly, William Rea. Proved 2 June 1777 by the oath of William Rea before Jno. N. Oglethorpe. Recorded __ Apr 1778.

W-4, 350-352: 11 Apr 1777, Thomas Jones of Camden, Merchant, to William Ancrum of Charlestown, merchant, for £1200 SC money, 29 lots in Camden, on Bull Street, Lyttleton Street, Market Street, Fair Street, numbers 363, 364, 365, 390, 391, 392, 393, 394, 375,376, 377, 540, 541, 542, 543, 544, 545, 614, 615, 616, 617, 618, 619, 620, 621, 622, 623, 624... conveyed to said Thomas Jones by Joseph Kershaw, John Chesnut, Eli Kershaw, William Ancrum, and Aaron Loocock 10 April 1777. Thomas Jones (LS), Wit: John Wyly, William Rea. Proved by the oath of William Rea before Jno. N. Oglethorpe, 2 June 1777. Recorded 2 Apr 1778.

W-4, 352-356: Lease & release. 5 & 6 June 1777, Ely Kershaw of Craven County, SC, esquire, to William Ancrum of Charlestown, for £10,700 SC money, 640 acres granted by North Carolina to John Westfield 22 May 1741 conveyed from John Westfield 13 March 1751 to John Kimbrough then by him 10 Jan 1754 to William Little, recorded in Anson County, then 14 January 1767 to Thomas Wade who conveyed 15 Aug 1772 to Ely Kershaw. Ely Kershaw (LS), Wit: Robert Lithgow, John Lyon. Proved before John Troup by the oath of Robert Lithgow 6 June 1777. Recorded 2 Apr 1778.

W-4, 356-358: 23 July 1777, Edward Martin, Esquire, Sheriff of George Town District, SC, to Thomas Hasell of Prince Georges Parish, Craven County, for £127 SC money... whereas Robert Dick of Sampit, planter, was possessed of 125 acres being half of 250 acres on north side of Santee River near Murrays Ferry adj. lands of Mr. Connor, and Roger Smith and Co., Thomas Hoddy, Timothy Crosby and James Oliphant did implead said Robert Dick in the court of common pleas and obtained a judgment. Edward Martin (LS), Wit: Abrm. Cohen, Joshua Pearson. Proved in George Town District before Paul Trapier 31 Dec 1777 by the oath of Joshua Pearson. Recorded 2 Apr 1778.

W-4, 358-361: 23 July 1777, Edward Martin, Esquire, Sheriff of George Town District, SC, to Thomas Hasell of Prince Georges Parish, Craven County, for £351 SC money... whereas Robert Dick of Sampit, planter, was possessed of half a lot of land in George Town, number 168, on Cannon Street and Duke Street, commonly called Borlands lott, and Roger Smith and Co., Thomas

Hoddy, Timothy Crosby and James Oliphant did implead said Robert Dick in the court of common pleas and obtained a judgment. Edward Martin (LS), Wit: Abrm. Cohen, Joshua Pearson. Proved in George Town District before Paul Trapier 31 Dec 1777 by the oath of Joshua Pearson. Recorded 2 Apr 1778.

W-4, 361-364: Lease & release. 19 & 20 Jan 1773, William Mason of Charlestown, SC, attorney at law, and Susanna his wife, to Gabriel Manigault of Charlestown, gentleman, for £2550 SC money, 690 acres in Berkley County composed of two several tracts adj. each other, 345 acres each originally granted to William Follingsby and by divers mesne conveyances descended to and became vested in said William Mason. Wm. Mason, Susannah Mason. Wit: Luis Peterman, John Hall. Proved in Charlestown District by the oath of John Hall before Geo Sheed, 5 March 1778. Recorded 2 Apr 1778.

W-4, 364-366: Honble William Dry to Charles Drayton Esqr., whereas by deed of grant 17 March 177, the Cherokee Nation or Tribe of Indians for a large and valuable consideration in divers sorts of goods by Richard Henderson, Thomas Hart, Nathaniel Hart, John Williams, John Luttrell, William Johnston, James Hogg, David Hart and Leonard Henley Bullock, tract of land or territory known as Transylvania on the River Ohio at the mouth of Cantucky Chenoe, Powels Mountain...one eighth to each person... on 20 Aug 1777 Leonard Henly Bullock of Granville county, north Carolina, conveyed to William Dry of County of Brunswick in the same state... now 14 Feb 1778 William Dry to charles Drayton of Charlestown, SC, for £5000 SC money. William Dry (LS), wit: Thos Shubrick, Wm. H. Drayton. Proved by the oath of the honble. Thomas Shubrick before Geo Sheed, 18 Feb 1778. Recorded 2 Apr 1778.

W-4, 367-370: Lease & release. 7 & 8 Oct 1772, Rev. Robert Smith and Alexander Gillon of Charlestown, executors of will of Richard Berresford, late of said town, esquire, to John Moore of St. Thomas's Parish, Esqr., for £3500 SC money, 523 acres in Berkley County which by his will 8 July 1772 appointed his wife Sarah Berresford during her widowhood executrix and said Robert Smith and Alexander Gillon, with Christopher Gadsden, Thomas Smith of Broad Street and his sons when they should attain the age of 21 years, executors... Robert Smith (LS), Alexander Gillon (LS), Wit: Wm. Gibbons, Peter Meurset, George Nixon. Proved by the oath of George Nixon before Geo Sheed 6 March 1778. Recorded 9 Apr 1778.

W-4, 371-373: Lease & release. 14 & 15 Feb 1777, James Witter of SC and Frances his wife to John Rivers of same state, planter, whereas James Witter hath purchased from James Ladson of Johns Island, gentleman, a tract allotted by a writ of partition made 14 Feb 1770, now for £6600 SC money paid by John Rivers, 300 acres on Johns Island, at the time of the original grant to Thomas Ladson deceased on Stono River adj. lands of John Raven, ____ Ladson deceased. James Witter Junr (LS), Frances Witter (LS), Wit: Joseph Rivers, Thos Rivers. Proved by the oath of Thomas Rivers, Esqr., 7 March 1778 before Geo: Sheed. Recorded 9 Apr 1778.

W-4, 373-378: Lease & release. 7 & 8 Oct 1772, Rev. Robert Smith and Alexander Gillon of Charlestown, executors of will of Richard Berresford, late of said town, esquire, to John Moore of St. Thomas's Parish, Esqr., for £560 SC money, lot number 70 on Prince Street in George Town, which by his will 8 July 1772 appointed his wife Sarah Berresford during her widowhood executrix and said Robert Smith and Alexander Gillon, with Christopher Gadsden, Thomas Smith of Broad Street and his sons when they should attain the age of 21 years, executors... Robert Smith (LS), Alexander Gillon (LS), Wit: Wm. Gibbons, Peter Meurset, George Nixon. Proved by the oath of George Nixon before Geo Sheed 6 March 1778. Recorded 9 Apr 1778. Sarah Berresford of Charlestown, widow of Richard Beresford, relinquished dower 3 Apr 1778 before Geo: Sheed.

W-4, 378-382: 13 Feb 1778, John Simmons of St. Bartholomews Parish, Colleton County, SC, planter, and Susannah his wife, to Samuel Wragg of George Town, Esquire, for £2800 SC money, town lott in Charlestown, number ___ on Union Street adj. land of John Poaug, which descended unto said John Simmons as eldest son of his father John Simmons late of Charlestown, deceased. John Simmons (LS), Susanah Simmons (LS), Charlotte Poaug (LS), John Poaug (LS), S. Wragg (LS), Wit: Isc. Hayne, Wm. Hill. Proved before Richard Hutson, J.P., by the oath of Isaac Hayne, 13 Feb 1778.

SOUTH CAROLINA DEED ABSTRACTS 1773-1778

John Poaug and Charlotte his wife acknowledge that the within lot of land mentioned were granted to the said Samuel Wragg and that said John Poaug will permit said Charlotte his wife whether married or sole to enjoy the rents, issues and profits, dated 16 Feb 1778. Wit: Jno Scott, Thos Waties. Proved in George Town District by the oath of Thos Waties 3 March 1778 before Job Rothmahler.

W-4, 382-386: Lease & release. 23 & 24 July 1777, Theophilus Hill of Craven County, Camden District, SC, planter, and Threesea his wife, to Paul Townsend, Esquire, for £2430 SC money, 810 acres in Craven County, Camden District, composed of three smaller tracts on Wateree River adj. lands of Joseph Kershaw, Esqr., Mr. McCord, James Parsons. Theophilus Hill (LS), Threesea Hill (LS), Wit: John Wyly, Hannah Oglethorpe (N). Proved 21 Feb 1778 by the oath of john Wyly before Jno. N. Oglethorpe, J.P. Recorded 9 Apr 1778.

W-4, 386-388: Lease & release. 11 Feb 1778, Joshua Curtis of Craven County and Sarah his wife to Ezekiel Self, planter, of same, for £200 SC money, 250 acres granted 10 Nov 1761 to William Clark in St. Marks parish, South west side of Pedee River adj. Alexander Thompson. Joshua Curtis (LS), Sarah Curtis (+) (LS), Wit: James Fletcher, John Dies (+). Proved in Cheraw District before Claudius Pegues, J.P., by the oath of James Fletcher. Recorded 9 Apr 1778.

W-4, 388-392: Lease & release. 7 & 8 July 1777, Joseph Huggins and his wife Elizabeth Sarah Huggins of Parish of Saint James Santee, Craven County, to Robert Daniell of Parish of St. Philips Charlestown, Berkely County, for £250 SC money, 311 acres in Prince Georges parish, Craven county granted to Marmaduke Bell 20 June 1764, and conveyed from said Marmaduke Bell to said Joseph Huggins. Joseph Huggins (LS), Wit: Elizabeth Sarah Huggins (LS), Wit: Saml Venning, John Jonah Murrell. Proved by the oath of Samuel Venning before John Troup, J.P., 27 Nov 1777. Recorded 9 Apr 1778.

W-4, 392-395: Lease & release. 9 & 10 Aug 1776, Jacob Rodgers of Camden District, SC, planter, to William Meyer of same, esquire, for £250 SC money, 300 acres on Cedar Creek waters of Congaree River, Craven County adj. John Everitt, John Cook, Robert Goodwyn, Martha Goodwyn, John Hamilton, Benjamin Farar. Jacob Rogers (R) (LS), Wit: Hollis Tims, Robert Hicks. Proved in Camden District by the oath of Robert Hicks before Phil. Pearson, J. P., 14 Feb 1778. Recorded 29 Apr 1778.

W-4, 395-398: Lease & release. 27 & 28 March 1776, Rachel Harper of Camden District, Craven County, to Jacob Ingleman of same, for £20 SC money, 20 acres granted to Rachel Harper on a branch the north side of Broad River, adj. David Edward, William Ballantine, Thomas Harbert, John Dunkly. Rachel Harper (RS) (LS), Wit: James Harper (X), Joshua Edwards. Proved in Ninety Six District by the oath of Joshua Edwards before Michl. Dickert, 24 Nov 1777. Recorded 29 Apr 1778.

W-4, 398-400: Lease & release. 25 Nov 1777, Jacob Ingleman of Camden District, and Mary his wife, to William Currie of Orangeburg District, for £20 SC money, 20 acres granted to Rachel Harper on a branch the north side of Broad River, adj. David Edward, William Ballantine, Thomas Harbert, John Dunkly, and conveyed 27 & 28 March 1776 to said Jacob Ingleman. Jacob Ingullmann (LS), Mary Inglemon (+) (LS), Wit: Edward Lane, Jacob Arney (I). Proved in Ninety Six District by the oath of Edward Lane before Michl Dickert, 24 Nov 1777. Recorded 29 Apr 1778.

W-4, 401-404: Lease & release. 21 & 22 Oct 1777, David Edward of Camden District, planter, and Jane his wife, to William Currie of Orangeburgh District, merchant, for £1000 SC money, 150 acres granted 6 Oct 1752 to Abraham Fining, above Saxagotha on the north east side of Broad River recorded in Book OO, page 118, by his bond 27 Apr 1750 for £100 made over to Barnet Livingston but said Abraham Fining died before the accomplishment of the conditions of said bond and said Barnet Livingston did on 13 Sept 1751 indorse and make over said bond unto Herman Geiger and said Herman Geiger died intestate and the right of inheritance devolved on his son John Conrade Geiger who by agreement with William Raiford deceased did assign to him 5 Sept 1761 but said Abraham Fining died intestate and without lawful heirs the right of inheritance devolved on his wife of widow Margaret who joined in the holy state of matrimony unto John ___ who for consideration of £100 granted unto Sarah Raiford and by virtue of lease and release 30 Sept and 1 Oct 1762 all that tract of 250 acres and said Sarah Raiford joined herself in the holy state of matrimony with Daniel Ellis and said Daniel Ellis and Sarah his wife by lease and release 26 & 27 March 1766 did make over 250 acres to David Edward. David Edward (LS), Jane Edwards (LS), Wit: John Ewing, Edward Nash. Proved in Ninety Six District by the oath of John Ewing 27 Nov 1777 before Michael Dickert, J.P. Recorded 29 Apr 1778.

W-4, 404-405: 24 Dec 1768, John Holman of Barkley County, planter, to Rev. John Nickles Martin of same, precher of the Gospell, for £400 SC money, 250 acres in Berkley County adj. land laid out unto Johannes Kunts, on Crims Creek. John Hollman (+) (LS), Christanna Hollman (O) (LS), Wit: Michael Dickert, Adam Sommer. Proved in Berkley County before Jonathan Gilbert, J.P., by the oath of Michael Dickert, 5 Jan 1769. Recorded 29 Apr 1778.

W-4, 406-407: 3 March 1778, Nicholas Martin of Charlestown, minister of the Gospel, and Anna Catherine his wife, to Michael Leitner of Orangeburgh District, Esquire, for £3000 SC money, 250 acres in Craven County on a branch of Broad River, originally granted to Francis Helo adj. Johannes Cant, Crims Creek, the residue of 121 acres was originally granted to the said Nicholas Martin adj. William Sours, Adam Simer's land, Bartholomew Minicks, John Hepps, and part on John Kounts land. Nicholas Martin (LS), Anna Catherine Martin [German signature] (LS), Wit: John Horlbeck, Henry Christoph Gafkan. Proved 13 March 1778 before John Thomas, J. P. in Ninety Six District by the oath of Henry Christoph Gafkan. Recorded 29 Apr 1778.

W-4, 407-409: 6 June 1772, Henry Culp and Barbara his wife of Parish of St. Mark, SC, to Jonathan Jones of same, yeoman, for £300 SC money, 250 acres granted 10 May 1768 to Robert Glover, on James McClure's spring branch, waters of a south fork of Fishing Creek in Craven County, conveyed to said Henry Culp 31 Sept 1768, Memorial entered in book I No. 9, page 189, 20 Oct 1768. Henry Culp (H) (LS), Barbara Culp (X) (LS), Wit: Alexander Brown, Nicholas Bishop, Ralph Baker. Proved before John Gaston, J.P., by the oath of Alexander Brown, 24 Sept 1772. Recorded 29 Apr 1778.

W-4, 409-412: Lease & release. 12 & 13 March 1778, Christopher Sheets of Charlestown, storekeeper, to Philip Eberhard of Orangeburgh District, planter, for £550 SC money, 100 acres in Berkley County on Cow Castell Branch a branch of Four Holes, waters of Edisto River in Orangeburgh Township, also 100 acres in Berkley County in the limits of Orangeburgh Township on Cow Castell adj. land of Christopher Sheets, Nicholas Shuller, Ulrick Bruner. Christopher Sheets (LS), Wit: David Kaufman, Paul Schlatter. Proved 14 March 1778 before Hopkin Price, J.P., by the oath of Paul Schlatter. Recorded 29 Apr 1778.

W-4, 412-416: Lease & release. 24 & 25 July 1775, Joshua Loper of SC to Darby Pendergrass of Charlestown, gentleman, for £50 Sc money, 40 acres in Craven County on north east side of Great Pedee River adj. Edward Drake, George Pawley, land granted to Elizabeth Murray, said tract granted to Joshua Loper 21 July 1775. Joshua Loper (LS), Wit: Winewood McKay, William Thomson, James Thomson. Proved by the oath of James Thomson before Geo Sheed, 12 March 1778. Recorded 29 Apr 1778.

W-4, 416-420: Lease & release. 24 & 25 July 1775, John Smith of Province of SC, to Darby Pendergrass of Charlestown, for £20 SC money, 100 acres in Craven County on north east side of Pedee River adj. Shorey Pawley, which said 100 acres was granted to John Smith 21 July last. John Smith (LS), Wit: Joshua Loper, James Thomson, William Thomson. Proved 12 March 1778 before George Sheed by the oath of James Thomson. Recorded 29 Apr 1778.

W-4, 420-422: Lease & release. 24 & 25 July 1775, James Thomson of Parish of ___ SC, to Darby Pendergrass of Charlestown, for £10 SC money, 400 acres in Craven County, Prince Georges Parish, north of Waccamaw River upon Cox's Swamp about two miles from North Carolina, which said 400 acres was granted to James Thomson 21 July 1775. James Thomson (LS), Wit: Sam. Perdriau, John Gambell. Proved 12 March 1778 before George Sheed by the oath of Samuel Perdriau. Recorded 29 Apr 1778.

W-4, 422-426: Lease & release. 19 & 20 June 1776, John Rivers Junior of James Island, Berkley County, planter, and Sarah his wife to William Croskeys of same, taylor, for £810 SC money, 52 acres on James Island in St. Andrews parish, Berkly County, part of tract formerly of William Screven late of James Island deceased, part of tract whereon John Rivers Junior now resides on Savannah Road (plat included, dated 10 Dec 1764 by John Pelot, Dept. Surv.). John Rivers Jur. (LS), Sarah Rivers (X), (LS), Wit: William Holmes, Peter Palmarin, Samuel Stent. Proved in Charlestown District by the oath of William Holmes 11 March 1778 before George Sheed. Recorded 29 Apr 1778.

W-4, 426-430: Lease & release. 14 & 15 Jan 1773, Jacob Gilder of Berkley County, planter, to Benjamin Chittey, late of county and province aforesaid, wheel right, late of the province of Maryland, for £150 SC money, 100 acres in the fork of Broad and Saluda Rivers on a small creek called Indian Creek waters of Santee River adj. Andrias Powers. Jacob Gilder (LS), Wit: James Lindsey, Jacob Farington, John Gilder. Proved 6 Feb 1773 by the oath of John Gilder before John Johnston, J.P. Recorded 29 Apr 1778.

W-4, 430-435: Lease & release. 17 & 18 Feb 1778, Godin Guerard of Charlestown, SC, esquire, and Anne his wife, and Jacob Guerard of same, gentleman, to Edward North and Edward Trescott of same, co-partners in trade, whereas John Guerard, late of Charlestown, deceased was possessed of tracts of land and several lots in Charles Town, and by his will dated 14 May 1764 did give to his son Isaac Guerard and his heirs the middlemost messuage or house and grand on the Bay of Charlestown, number 2, subject to a proviso in said will that if Isaac should die without issue then said lands should be equally shared between his sons Godin, Jacob & Joseph and his daughter Marianne, and said Isaac Guerard and Mariane Guerard are both dead under age the house and ground became vested in said Godin, Jacob and Joseph who is a minor, and said godin and Jacob Guerard have agreed to sell their parts, now for £14,100 SC money... Godin Guerard (LS), Ann Guerard (LS), Jacob Guerard (LS), Wit: Paul Schlatter, Jas. Culliatt. Proved by the oath of James Culliatt 19 March 1778 before George Sheed. Agreement also of E. North and Edward Trescot. Recorded 29 Apr 1778.

W-4, 436-438: Godin Guerard bound to Edward North and Edward Trescott in the sum of £14,100 SC money, to make title... dated 18 Feb 1778. Godin Guerard (LS), Wit: Paul Schaltter, Jas. Culliatt.

Jacob Guerard bound to Edward North and Edward Trescott in the sum of £14,100 SC money, to make title... dated 18 Feb 1778. Jacob Guerard (LS), Wit: Paul Schaltter, Jas. Culliatt.

Godin Guerard, as guardian of Joseph Guerard, minor, bound to Edward North and Edward Trescott in the sum of £14,100 SC money, to make title... dated 18 Feb 1778. Godin Guerard (LS), Wit: Paul Schaltter, Jas. Culliatt. Recorded 19 Apr 1778.

W-4, 438-442: Lease & release. 10 & 11 March 1778, Hezekiah Maham of St. Stephen's Parish, SC, planter, to John James Haig of Orangeburgh District, SC, esquire, for £3000 SC money, whereas Hezekiah Maham and John James Haig are joint owners of tract of 200 acres in Saxagotha Township, Orangeburgh District, conveyed by Michael Martz of Orangeburgh District, yeoman, to them, 24 & 25 Nov last past, recorded in Book T-4, page 505-506, now Hezekiah Maham conveys his moiety. Hezekiah Maham (LS), Wit: Andrew Dewees, Peter Lequeux. Proved by the oath of Peter Lequeux before Geo Sheed, 14 March 1778. Recorded 30 Apr 1778.

W-4, 442-445: Lease & release. 2 & 3 March 1778, Richard Withers of St. James Parish, Craven County, exr. of the will of Robert Murrell, late of Christ Church Parish, Berkley County, deceased, to Mark Huggins of George Town, Prince Georges parish, Craven County, vintner, £2100 SC money, whereas by grant 14 Dec 1739 to John Baker, 300 acres on north west side of a great marsh near a place called north point in St. James Parish, adj. land granted to Thomas Jones then belonging to said John Baker, and said John Baker conveyed 26 & 27 March 1741 to Robert Murell, and said Robert Murrell by his will dated 7 Apr 1759 did bequeath unto John Murrell all the above recited tract upon condition that should said John Murrell die leaving no heir then land directed to be sold. Ric'd Withers (LS), Wit: Jos. Hugins, Jos. Legare. Proved in Charlestown District by the oath of Joseph Huggins 10 March 1778 before Geo Sheed. Recorded 30 Apr 1778.

W-4, 445-448: Lease & release. 13 & 14 Feb 1778, John Stafford of Granville County, SC, and Susanah his wife, to Nathaniel Hall of Christ Church Parish, State of Georgia, for £2050 SC money, 100 acres on waters of Savannah River in Granville County adj. Edward Chevenaughs, John Peter Purry (now called Oglethorpes land), which said tract was granted to Thomas Noble and conveyed to Samuel Webster then to James Pou and by Pou to John Stafford, also 250 acres in Granville County on waters of Savannah River adj. John Smiths, John Peter Purrys, said John Stafford, Edward Chevenaugh, originally granted to sd. John Stafford. John Stafford (LS), Wit: Jane Smith, Theodore Gay. Proved by the oath of Jane Smith 21 March 1778 before Hen. Pendleton. Recorded 30 Apr 1778.

W-4, 448-451: Lease & release. 27 & 28 Feb 1778, Daniel Tharin of Charlestown, merchant, and Elizabeth his wife, to Jane Morand of same, widow, for £6000 SC money, lot on north side of Beresfords Alley adj. land of the estate of Richard Beresford deceased, Thomas Ham, Daniel Tharin. Daniel Tharin (LS), Elizabeth Tharin (LS), Wit: Jno Stevenson, Joseph Gaultier. Proved in Charlestown District by the oath of Joseph Gaultier 27 March 1778 before George Sheed. Recorded 30 Apr 1778.

W-4, 451-454: Lease & release. 11 & 12 March 1778, Darby Pendergrass of Charlestown, SC, gentleman, to James Moore of St. Peters Parish, SC, esquire, for £8400 SC money, 600 acres granted to sd. Darby Pendergrass 5 May 1773 in Prince Williams Parish, Granville County adj. Bartlet Brown, James Woods, Archibald Easley, Savannah River. D. Pendergrass (LS), Wit: Peter Bocquet Junr, Tho Winstanley. Proved by the oath of Thomas Winstanley 25 March 1778 before Geo: Sheed. Recorded 30 Apr 1778.

W-4, 454-457: Lease & release. 13 & 14 March 1778, James Moore of St. Peters Parish, SC, esquire, to Darby Pendergrass of Charlestown, SC, gentleman, by bond in the sum of £16,800 for the payment of £8400 SC money to be paid by 12 March 1781, mortgage of 600 acres granted to sd. Darby Pendergrass 5 May 1773 in Prince Williams Parish, Granville County adj. Bartlet Brown, James Woods, Archibald Easley, Savannah River. James Moore (LS), Wit: Tho Winstanley, Alexr. Forrester. Proved by the oath of Thomas Winstanley 25 March 1778 before Geo: Sheed. Recorded 30 Apr 1778.

W-4, 458-461: Lease & release. 27 & 28 Feb 1778, Philip Pettypool of St. Marks parish, planter, to John Gabriel Guignard of same parish, for £650 SC money, 93 acres in Craven county on north east side of Watcree River granted to sd. Philip Pettypool 25 Sept 1771. Phillip Pettypool (LS), Wit: David Reynolds, Josiah Gayle. Proved by the oath of Josiah Gayle before Nathl. Moore, J.P., 238 Feb 1778. Recorded 30 Apr 1778.

W-4, 461-465: Lease & release. 2 & 3 June 1767, Archibald Offutt and Lettice his wife of Berkley County, silver smith, to John Jaudon, planter, for £1300 SC money, two adjacent tracts, one of 700 acres adj. John Laten, the other 600 acres adj. Richard Blake, Charles Chovine.... granted to John Gaillard and he left it by will to his wife Mary Easter Gaillard who was afterwards wife of James Kinlock, Esqr., decd, and fell into the hands of Frances Kinlock their son, decd, conveyed to James Robert, then to John Robert, then to Elias Robert, then to sd. Archd. Offutt. Archd. Offutt (LS), Lettice Offutt (X) (LS), Wit: John Egan, Jno Leaten, Charles Gaillard. Proved by the oath of John Egan in Charlestown District before Geo: Sheed, 24 March 1778. Recorded 30 Apr 1778.

W-4, 465-469: Lease & release. 14 & 15 Feb 1778, John Jaudon & Ann his wife to St. James Parish, Craven county, planter, to Philip Dewees of Chs. Town District, planter, for £1200 SC money, 600 acres (joining a tract of 700 acres) adj. John Laten, on Hell Hole Swamp, granted to John Gaillard and he left it by will to his wife Mary Easter Gaillard who was afterwards wife of James Kinlock, Esqr., decd, and fell into the hands of Frances Kinlock their son, decd, conveyed to James Robert, then to John Robert, then to Elias Robert, then to Archd. Offutt, by original grants dated 28 June 1711. John Jaudon (LS), Ann Jaudon (LS), Wit: John Egan, Thomas Davis. Proved 24 March 1778 before George Sheed by the oath of John Egan. Recorded 30 Apr 1778.

W-4, 469-473: Lease & release. 14 & 15 Feb 1778, John Jaudon & Ann his wife to St. James Parish, Craven county, planter, to Philip Dewees of Chs. Town District, Inn keeper, for £1400 SC money, 700 acres (joining a tract of 600 acres) adj. John Laten, on Hell Hole Swamp, granted to John

SOUTH CAROLINA DEED ABSTRACTS 1773-1778

Gaillard and he left it by will to his wife Mary Easter Gaillard who was afterwards wife of James Kinlock, Esqr., decd, and fell into the hands of Frances Kinlock their son, decd, conveyed to James Robert, then to John Robert, then to Elias Robert, then to Archd. Offutt, by original grants dated 28 June 1711. John Jaudon (LS), Ann Jaudon (LS), Wit: John Egan, Thomas Davis. Proved 24 March 1778 before George Sheed by the oath of John Egan. Recorded 30 Apr 1778.

W-4, 473-477: Lease & release. 6 & 7 Jan 1778, William Ladson of Johns Island, SC, Esquire, exr. of the will of James Carson of Charlestown, esquire deceased, to William Fripp of St. Helena Island, SC, planter, for £8424 SC money, by virtue of lease and release 18 & 19 Feb 1773 made between Henry Stuart of parish of St. Helena in Granville County, planter, and said James Carson, deceased, of Parish of St. Johns Colleton tract of 748½ acres on Ladies Island in the parish of St. Helena in Granville County on Coosaw River, on Beaufort Creek adj. lands of Daniel and William Blake, Henry Stuart, half of three tracts of land conveyed for 1500 acres to said Henry Stuart by Charles Drayton of Charlestown, Doctor of Physick, 2 & 3 Oct 1772, and said Carson departed this life about the month of September last past having made will 22 Aug 1777 in which he authorized his executors to sell land upon Ladys Island, and it was found that said Carson was not seized of a legal estate of the plantation called St. Quintins, the said testator having nothing more than an equitable lien on the other moiety or half part of same plantation. William Ladson (LS), Wit: Jacob Cowen, Tho Winstanley. Proved by the oath of Thomas Winstanley 3 Feb 1778 before Wm. Mason, J.P. Recorded 7 May 1778.

W-4, 477-480: 14 March 1772, Daniel Ravenel Junr of Berkly County, SC, gentleman, and Charlotte his wife, to John Cook of same, planter, for £3500 SC money, 300 acres on Santee River adj. lands of Ralph Izard, Esqr., John Cook, half of 600 acres granted 22 Dec 1737. Daniel Ravenel Junr (LS), Charlotte Ravenel (LS), Wit: James Ravenel, Stephen Mazyck Junr. Proved 19 Dec 1774 before John Frierson, J.P., by the oath of Stephen Mazyck Junr. Recorded 7 May 1778.

W-4, 480-483: Lease & release. 30 & 31 March 1778, Margaret Cooler, formerly wife of Valentine Michael, and Charles Stover of Londonborough Township, SC, for £80 SC money, 100 acres in Londonborough Township, adj. Abraham Triets, John Adams, Philip Reiser, granted to Valentine Michael 22 Sept 1767. Margaret Cooler (mark) (LS), Wit: Eml. Abrahams, George Dener. Proved 31 March 1778 before George Sheed by the oath of George Dener. Recorded 7 May 1778.

W-4, 483-487: Lease & release. 26 & 27 Jan 1778, Ann Beatty of St. Bartholomews Parish, Colleton County, widow, to Major Samuel Wise of same state, for £14,000 SC money, 238½ acres (except the old burying place containing ¼ acre) in St. Bartholomews Parish adj. land of David Ferguson, Anthony Hiett, Edward Hext, land granted to Thomas Buer, also tract of 223 3/4 acres in St. Bartholomews Parish adj.land of said David Ferguson, John Beatty, Robert Hiett, John St. John, also 500 acres in St. Bartholomews parish adj. at the time of the original grant to land of Peter Rump, John Logan, Thomas Buer; said three plantations were bequeathed to Ann Beatty by her husband Francis Beatty late of St. Bartholomews Parish, planter, deceased, by his will 28 July 1773. Ann Beatty (LS), Wit: Jas Mayson, Wm. Print. Proved 28 Jan 1778 before John Troup by the oath of William Print. Recorded 7 May 1778.

W-4, 488-490: Lease & release. 27 & 28 July 1774, Benjamin Farar of Craven County to Rich Brown of same, for £600 SC money, 500 acres in Craven county on Cedar Creek adj. lands granted to Benj. Sims, Robt. Howell, estate of Jesse Goodine, John Everett, land said to have been surveyed for Mary Catharine Spiken, and land late the property of John Hamilton decd, also bounding inwards a tract of 50 acres called Rollinsons, originally granted to Wm. Mazyck 320 June 1764 and by him conveyed to sd. Benj. Farar. Benj. Farar (LS), Wit: Robert Goodwyn, Moses Vance. Proved 13 Aug 1777 before Wm. Meyer, J.P., by the oath of Robert Goodwyn. Recorded 7 May 1778.

W-4, 490-493: Lease & release. 15 & 16 June 1777, Capt. Richd. Brown to Major Samuel Wise, both of Craven County, planters, for £3500 SC money, 500 acres in Craven County on north east side of the congaree River on Cedar Creek adj. land granted to Benj. Sims, part of same tract now the property of Robert Nowell, estate of Jesse Goodwyn, Jno Everett, land said to be surveyed for Mary Cath. Spitzen, late the property of John Hamilton decd, including a tract of 50 acres called Rawlinsons, originally granted to William Mazyck 20 June 1764 and conveyed to Benja. Farar then to sd. Richd. Brown 28 July 1774. Rich. Brown (LS), Mary Brown (LS), Wit: Jas. Powell, john

SOUTH CAROLINA DEED ABSTRACTS 1773-1778

Russell, Henry Waylie. Proved in Cheraw District before Claudius Pegues, J.Q., by the oath of Henry Waylie, 9 July 1777. Recorded 7 May 1778.

W-4, 493-496: Lease & release. 22 & 23 Sept 1777, William Meyer of Camden District, SC, Esqr., planter, to Samuel Wise of district of Cheraws, for £2650 SC money, 250 acres, part of 300 acres granted 31 Aug 1774 to Jacob Rogers on waters of the Congaree River in Craven county adj. land of John Everett, John Cook, Robert Goodwyn, Martha Goodwyn, John Hamilton, Benjamin Farar, conveyed to said William Meyers 10 Aug 1776 being the northermost part of 300 acres. Wm. Meyer (LS), Winey Meyer (LS), Wit: Alexander McCartney, Andrew Petterson. Proved in Charlestown District by the oath of Alexander McCartney before Geo Sheed, 6 Apr 1778. Recorded 7 May 1778.

W-4, 496-498: Lease & release. 17 & 18 Oct 1778, Philip Pledger of Parish of St. David, SC, to Samuel Wish of same, for £200 SC money, 150 acres granted 31 Aug 1774 to Philip Pledger. Phil: Pledger (LS), Wit: Holden Wade, Calvin Spencer. Proved in Cheraw District before William Pegues by the oath of Calvin Spencer, 1 Nov 1775. Recorded 7 May 1778.

W-4, 499-500: 1 June 1775, Benet Taylor to Samuel Wise, for £200 SC money, 200 acres in Craven County on north side Pee Dee River adj. Wm. Hardicks, land granted to Archibald Guines, granted to sd. Bennet Taylor 9 Sept 1774. Bennett Taylor (LS), Wit: Zeph: Kinsley, John Peele. Proved in Charlestown District by the oath of John Peele before Jno Coram, 8 June 1775. Recorded 7 May 1778.

W-4, 500-502: Lease & release. 1 & 2 Aug 1775, John Jackson of Parish of St. David, SC, to Betty Wise of same, for £200 SC money, 150 acres granted 19 Aug 1774 to John Jackson, on south west side of Peedee River adj. Mr. Tomerlins. John Jackson (LS), Wit: Joseph Stanyarne, Joseph Pledger. Proved by the oath of Joseph Pledger 30 Jan 1776 before Jno Coram. Recorded 7 May 1778.

W-4, 502-504: Whereas Christopher Smith late of Charlestown, Shop keeper, by deed 11 & 12 Nov 1737 made by Wiliam Holman of Colleton County, planter, was in his lifetime and at the time of his death possessed amongst other lands 650 acres in Colleton County at the head of Cuckolds Creek, by grant to sd. William Holman 11 July 1733, and said Christopher Smith being so possessed by his will dated 23 July 1738 did devise said tract to his brother James Atkins and his friends John Daniel and to their heirs with directions that the said land should be sold and the money to arise therefrom be applied towards bringing up and maintaining his three children Benjamin, Elizabeth and Rachel Smith who were bastards and said Christopher Smith had at the time of his decease three lawful children named William Smith, Mary Smith wife of Emanuel[?] Smith of Charlestown taylor, afterwards married to William Bissett of Charlestown, and also Ann Smith afterwards married to William Mouatt since deceased, and said William Smith after the death of his said father assigned all his right to William Bissett with Mary his wife with the said William Mouatt and Ann his wife, on 18 April 1751 filed their bill in the court of chancery against said James Atkins as the surviving trustee of the will but before any determination, said James Atkins conveyed to William Garner of St. Pauls Parish 191 acres and after having by his will devised to his son William Atkins all the rest of his real estate... whereas the suit at present stands revived by the said Ann Mouatt, John Mouatt admr. of Mary Bissett, and others but said Ann Mouatt is willing to terminate the said suit so far as relates to the 191 acres conveyed to said William Garner and the share which the said William Atkins at present enjoys in said tract of 650 acres for the sum of £3500 SC money. An Mouatt (LS), Wit: Aedamus Burke, Robt. Testard, John Mouatt. Proved by the oath of John Mouatt 2 Apr 1778 before Jas. Parsons, J. P. Recorded 14 May 1778.

W-4, 504-507: Lease & release. 31 March & 1 Apr 1778, William Atkins of St. Bartholomews parish, SC, planter, residuary devisee of James Atkins of said parish, planter, deceased, to Henry Hyrne of same, esquire, for £7000 SC money, 330 acres in St. Bartholomews Parish on Cuckolds Creek adj. Thomas Hutchison, William Gardner. (plat included of "Mr. Joshua McPhersons General Survey and Division of Mr. James Atkins lands" dated 14 Apr 1764 by Jno. B. Girardeau, D.S.). William Atkins (LS), Wit: Robt Testard, Aedimus Burke, John Mouatt. Proved by the oath of John Mouatt 2 Apr 1778 before Jas. Parsons, J. P. Recorded 14 May 1778.

SOUTH CAROLINA DEED ABSTRACTS 1773-1778

W-4, 507-511: Lease & release. 18 & 19 Dec 1777, Samuel Ash of Charlestown, SC, Bricklayer, and Elizabeth Ash his mother, to Edmund Egan and Thomas Eustace of said province, state, and town, for £2960 SC money, whereas Cato Ash was possessed of certain lands, particularly of a town lott in Charles Town known as number 6, adj. James Stedman, Patrick Hinds, and being so possessed and dying without leaving any will, said Samuel Ash became lawful and true heir. Saml Ash (LS), Eliz'th Ash (LS), Wit: John Mouatt, Hampton Lillibridge. Proved by the oath of Capt. John Mouatt before Geo Sheed, 2 Apr 1788. Recorded 14 May 1778.

W-4, 511-515: Lease & release. 29 & 30 June 1777, John Drayton of St. Andrews parish, SC, and Rebecca his wife, to Christopher Williman of Charlestown, for £19,500 SC money, 1000 acres in Berkley County on the north side of Ashley River adj. lands of William Fuller, Landgrave Thomas Smith deceased, Richard Lambton, by lease and release 23 & 24 June 1760 released to said John Drayton. Jno Drayton (LS), Rebecca Drayton (LS), Wit: Susanna Perry, Henry Timrod. Proved in Charlestown District by the oath of Henry Timrod 3 Apr 1778. Recorded 14 May 1778.

W-4, 515-519: Lease & release. 27 & 28 Feb 1778, Richard Hutson of Charlestown, SC, esquire, to Christopher Williman of same, butcher, for £21,000 SC money, lot on east side King Street part of lot number 220 adj. lot of Mrs. Elizabeth Elliott, Richard Hutson, Mr. George Flagg. Richard Hutson (LS), Wit: Philip Meyer, Isc. Hayne. Proved 3 Apr 1778 before George Sheed by the oath of Philip Meyer. Recorded 14 May 1778.

W-4, 519-520: John McCay and Joseph McCay of St. Marks Parish, planters, bound to Christopher Willeman of Charlestown, butcher, in the penal sum of £60,000 SC money, for the payment of £30,000 on or before 25 March 1783, mortgage of eight slaves Bristol, Sampson, Davy, Ross and her child January, also Charlotte and her two children Jerry & Judy, and 100 acres on a branch of Black River, tract of 200 acres adj. lands of Robert Carter, tract on Lindsays Creek adj. lands of William Nelson, Benjamin Simmons, also stock of cattle. John MacCay (LS), Joseph McCay (LS), Wit: Henry Timrod, Christian Sigwald. Proved by the oath of Henry Timrod 3 Apr 1778 before Geo Sheed. Recorded 14 May 1778.

W-4, 520-523: Lease & release. 9 & 10 Apr 1777, William Tucker and Christian his wife of St. Marks Parish, to James Conyers of same, cooper, for ten shillings, 50 acres granted 27 Jan 1759 in Craven County adj. Wateree Swamp (surveyed for Thomas Jones) adj. land of said Thomas Jones, and by another grant 4 June 1759, 100 acres between the High Hills and Wateree River Swamp, adj. Robert Carter, Thomas Jones, total of 150 acres. William Tucker (LS), Christian Tucker Wit: Daniel Conyers, Godfrey Pringel. Proved by the oath of Daniel Conyers 24 Dec 1777 before Sam Nelson, J.P. Recorded 14 May 1778.

W-4, 523-527: Lease & release. 29 & 30 Dec 1777, James Conyers, planter, to William Richardson, planter, both of SC, for £3000 SC money, 50 acres granted to William Tucker on east side of Wateree River, adj. Thomas Jones, and another tract of 100 acres granted to William Tucker but surveyed for Thomas Jones between the High Hills and Wateree River Swamp, adj. Robert Carter, Thomas Jones and conveyed by William Tucker and his wife Christian to sd. James Conyers, also 150 acres in Craven County adj. Weston, Robert Carter, William Tucker, Thomas Jones, Thos Chadwick, granted to sd. James Conyers. James Conyers (+) (LS), Wit: Peter Mellet, Thomas Allison, James Rembert. Proved 21 Jan 1778 before Isham Moore, J.P. in Craven County. Recorded 14 May 1778.

W-4, 528-532: Lease & release. 29 & 30 Jan 1778, William Richardson of Parish of St. Mark, planter, to Thomas Eveleigh of Charlestown, merchant, for £5000 SC money, 50 acres granted to William Tucker on east side of Wateree River, adj. Thomas Jones, and another tract of 100 acres granted to William Tucker but surveyed for Thomas Jones between the High Hills and Wateree River Swamp, adj. Robert Carter, Thomas Jones and conveyed by William Tucker and his wife Christian to sd. James Conyers, also 150 acres in Craven County adj. Weston, Robert Carter, William Tucker, Thomas Jones, Thos Chadwick, granted to sd. James Conyers, total of 300 acres conveyed by James Conyers to William Richardson 29 & 30 Dec 1777. Wm. Richardson (LS), Wit: Wm. Doughty, Willm. Mansell. Proved 10 Feb 1778 before George Sheed, J.P. in Charlestown District, by the oath of William Doughty, Esqr. Recorded 14 May 1778.

SOUTH CAROLINA DEED ABSTRACTS 1773-1778

W-4, 532-534: 4 Feb 1778, William Dry to Thomas Eveleigh and James Wakefield, merchants, for £45000 SC money, whereas by deed of grant 17 March 177, the Cherokee Nation or Tribe of Indians for a large and valuable consideration in divers sorts of goods by Richard Henderson, Thomas Hart, Nathaniel Hart, John Williams, John Luttrell, William Johnston, James Hogg, David Hart and Leonard Henley Bullock, tract of land or territory known as Transylvania on the River Ohio at the mouth of Cantucky Chenoe, Powels Mountain...one eighth to each person... on 20 Aug 1777 Leonard Henly Bullock of Granville County, North Carolina, conveyed to William Dry of County of Brunswick in the same state, one sixty-fourth part... William Dry (LS), Wit: James King, Wm. Walton. Proved by the oath of James King before Geo Sheed, 6 Nay 1778. Recorded 14 May 1778.

W-4, 535-540: Lease & release. 2 & 3 Oct 1777, Michael Kalteisen, Esqr., of Ansonborough, SC, to Martin Pfeninger of Charlestown, for £2000 SC money... whereas James Brisbane and Rebecca his wife of the town and state aforesaid, gentleman, by lease and release 21 & 27 March 1767 conveyed to Alexander burn, all that part of lot marked with the letter F in the general plan of the lands of the late George Anson, Esqr., and said Alexander Burn hath since subdivided his said piece of said lot, and Godfrey Bohner deceased was possessed of a part of said lot which was conveyed to said Godfred Bohner by Alexander Burn 3 & 4 Sept 1772 adj. land formerly of Charles Grimball now of William Hopton, and Andrew Willson in the court of common pleas at August Term 1774 did recover a judgment for £129 s13 d4 to be levied on the estate of said Godfrey Bohner in the hands of Barbara Bohner admx, and by public sale 6 Apr 1775 to Michael Kalteisen. Michl. Kalteisen (LS), Wit: William Lowe, Robert Cameron. Proved by the oath of William Lowe 4 Oct 1777 before Hopkin Price, J.P. Recorded 21 May 1778.

Michael Kalteisen, Esquire of Ansonborough, SC, bound to Martin Pfeninger in the sum of £1000 SC money, to make title, 3 Oct 1777. Michl. Kalteisen (LS), Wit: William Lowe, Robert Cameron.

W-4, 540-542: 19 March 1778, William Wayne of Charlestown, SC, planter, and Esther his wife, to Paul Townsend of same place, esquire, bond in the penal sum of £12,000 SC money for the payment of £2000 on 19 May next, £2000 on 19 July next, and £2000 on 19 March 1779, mortgage of lot on side of an alley from Elliott Street to Tradd Street known as Bedons Alley. William Wayne (LS), Esther Wayne (LS), Wit: Wm. Glen Junr, Wm. Blacklock. Proved before George Sheed by the oath of William Blacklock 28 March 1778. Recorded 21 May 1778. Thomas Jones, exr. of the will of Paul Townsend, states that mortgage is paid off and satisfied, 2 Oct 1778.

W-4, 542-546: Lease & release. 1 & 2 May 1776, James Harley and his wife Ann of St. Georges Parish, Berkley County, to Edward Perry of Parish of St. Paul, planter, for £1330 SC money, 665 acres, part of a tract granted to Tobias Fitch 22 Apr 1735 on south side of a swamp known as Four hole swamp in St. James parish, Berkley County, adj. land of Allen Miles (being part of the original tract), said Edward Perry (plat included). James Harley (JH) (LS), Ann Harley (LS), Wit: Allen Miles, Elisha Mellard, John Fenwick. Proved 29 May 1776 before Andrew Leitch, J.P. in Charlestown District, by the oath of Allen Miles. Recorded 21 May 1778.

W-4, 546-550: Lease & release. 31 March & 1 Apr 1778, Peter Bounetheau of Charlestown, SC, esquire, and Elizabeth his wife, to Michael Kalteisen of Charlestown, for £11,000 SC money, land in Ansonborough adj. Paul Townsend, Peter Porcher, Richard Wainwright, on the Broad path, to the new fortifications. Peter Bounetheau (LS), Elizabeth Bounetheau (LS), Wit: J. Poaug, Alexander Gillon. Proved by the oath of John Poaug before Geo Sheed, 2 Apr 1778. Recorded 21 May 1778.

W-4, 550-552: 31 March 1778, Abraham Ladson of St. Andrews Parish, Berkley County, planter, and Elizabeth his wife, to Hopkin Price of Charlestown, esquire, for £8000 SC money, 800 acres in St. Andrews parish adj. Nathaniel Fuller, John Drayton, Esqr., Wiliam Chisholme, Col. William Cattell. Abram Ladson (LS), Elizabeth Ladson (LS), Wit: George Greenland, Wm. Print. Proved 6 Apr 1778 before George Sheed by the oath of George Greenland before Geo Sheed. Recorded 21 May 1778.

W-4, 552-556: Lease & release. 5 & 6 March 1778, Samuel Wise of Charlestown, SC, esquire, and Ann his wife, to Joseph Kershaw of Camden District, said Samuel Wise by bond in the sum of

SOUTH CAROLINA DEED ABSTRACTS 1773-1778

£20,000 SC money for the payment of £10,000 SC money, 238½ acres (except the old burying place of ¼ acre) in St. Bartholomews Parish, Colleton County, adj. lands of David Ferguson, Edward Hext, Thomas Buer, and a tract of 223 3/4 acres in St. Bartholomews parish adj. said David Ferguson, John Beatty, Robert Hiett, estate of John St. John, also 500 acres in same parish adj. land of Peter Rumph, John Logan, Thomas Buer, said tracts were bequeathed unto Ann Beatty by her husband Francis Beaty deceased and conveyed to said Samuel Wise by her 26 & 27 Jan last past, also tract of 500 acres in Craven County on north east side of Congaree on Cedar Creek adj. Benjamin Sims, Robert Howell, estate of Jesse Goodwin, John Everet, land surveyed for Mary Catharine Spitzen, John Hamilton deceased, including a tract of 50 acres called Rawlinsons, conveyed by Samuel Wise by Richard Brown and Mary his wife 15 & 16 June 1777. Saml Wise (LS), Ann Wise (LS), Wit: Jo. Ward, George Powell, George Chalmers. Proved by the oath of Joshua Ward, Esqr., in Charlestown District, before Geo Sheed, 16 March 1778. Recorded 21 May 1778.

W-4, 557-558: 26 June 1772, William Starling of Prince Williams Parish, planter, to George Warren of St. Bartholomews Parish, planter, for £5 SC money, 100 acres in Colleton County on Buckhead Swamp adj. George Warren, Joseph Glover, on 21 Feb 1772 granted to said William Starling. William Starling (LS), Wit: Alexius Mador Forster, John Bowler. Proved in Charlestown District 4 March 1778 by the oath of Alexious M. Forster before Joseph Glover, J.P. Recorded 21 May 1778.

W-4, 558-561: Lease and release. 2 & 3 Jan 1778, Hugh Stewart of District of Camden, SC, Blacksmith, to William Henderson of Sixth Regiment of SC foot, for £750 SC money, tract in Camden District on waters of Rocky Creek including the plantation of John Fondren at the Cross Roads, where the Saludy Road crosses the Fork Road that lads to Charles Town, 200 acres originally granted to John Fondren by Gov. Tryon of North Carolina, then supposed to lye in Mecklenburgh County, North Carolina, granted 28 Oct 1765, conveyed to Hugh Stewart by John Fondron 1 July 1769. Hugh Stuart (LS), Wit: Holey Bond (X), Zachariah Spiers, Elizabeth Wilson (+). Proved by the oath of Zachariah Spiers before Wm. Brown, 28 Feb 1778. Recorded 30 May 1778.

END OF BOOK W-4.

Page facing X-4, page 1: Plat. I have admeasured and laid off according to the last will and testament of James Crawford deceased unto Alexander Crawford son and legatee of the above deceased Crawford 130 acres of land, being half of tract bought by the above Crawford from Wm. McKeney and joining land run for Casper Culp. Certified 21 Feb 1778. Wm. Carsen Sur.

X-4, 1-6: Lease and release. 1 & 2 June 1775, Thomas Liston of Charlestown to Phillip Henry of same, for £1000 SC money, 1000 acres in Granville County near Savannah River adj. lands of John Wilds, Mary Southells, Hon. Andrew Irvin Esquire's Barony formerly William Wragg, estate of Lazarus Brown deceased known by the name of Perkins Bluff, granted 4 May 1775 to Thomas Liston. Thos Liston (LS), Wit: Lewis Lestarjette, Wm. Wightman. Proved 2 Apr 1778 before Geo. Sheed by the oath of William Wightman. Recorded 25 June 1778.

X-4, 6-11: Lease and release. 9 & 10 Aug 1775, John Howard of Charlestown and Margaret his wife, to Philip Henry of same, for £3000 SC money, 1000 acres near the waters of Saludy River adj. land of John Douglass, said John Howard, also tract of 500 acres on waters of Saludy adj. ____ Smith, John Douglass, Mr. Pope, also tract of 400 acres near the waters of Saludy adj. Aaron Weaver, said John Douglas, Charles Partin[?], said John Howard. John Howard (LS), Margaret Howard (LS), Wit: Wm. Roberts, T. W. Powell. Proved 19 March 1778 before George Sheed by the oath of Thos Warburton Powell. Recorded 25 June 1778.

SOUTH CAROLINA DEED ABSTRACTS 1773-1778

X-4, 12-16: Lease and release. 9 & 10 Aug 1775, Thomas Roche of Charlestown, gentleman, to Philip Henry of Charlestown, for £2000 SC money, 1000 acres on waters of Waccamaw River adj. Abraham Bellamy, John Stevens, also tract of 200 acres in Craven County on south side of Black River adj. William Graham, Thomas Roche, also a tract of 200 acres on south west side of Black River adj. land of Thomas Roche, all granted to said Thomas Roche 21 July 1775. Thomas Roche (LS), Wit: Jno Gilbank, G. H. Hartley. Proved 7 July 1777 before John Troup by the oath of John Gillbank. Recorded 25 June 1778.

X-4, 17-22: Lease and release. 9 & 10 Aug 1775, Walter Russell of Charlestown to Philip Henry of Charlestown, for £500 SC money, 1000 acres on a branch of Sandy Run in Berkley County granted to said Walter Russell 3 Apr 1775, also 1000 acres on Black Creek in Berkley County adj. unknown land, also 600 acres on High Hill Creek in Berkley County adj. Bernard Elliott, James Pearce, Simon Hooker, John Butler, Jacob Coleman, Ann Margaret Johnson, John Waggoner, which said two last tracts were granted to said Walter Russell 9 June 1775, also 150 acres on a small branch of Waccamaw River known as Simpsons Creek in Prince Georges Parish granted to Walter Russell 21 July 1775. Walter Russell (LS), Wit: Martin Pfeninger, Benjamin Wheeler. Proved 4 June 1778 before George Sheed by the oath of Martin Pfeninger. Recorded 25 June 1778.

X-4, 23-26: Lease and release. 15 & 16 Aug 1775, William Carter of Charlestown to Philip Henry of Charlestown, for £1000 SC money, 1000 acres in Berkley County on the head of great Bull Swamp granted to William Carter 3 Apr 1775. Wm. Carter (LS),Wit: John Coram Junr, Joseph Lancaster. Proved 29 May 1778 before George Sheed by the oath of John Coram Junr. Recorded 25 June 1778.

X-4, 27-31: Lease and release. 11 & 12 Sept 1775, Jacob William Harvey of Charlestown to Philip Henry of Charlestown, for £500 SC money, 250 acres, part of 500 acres in Craven County adj. Mr. Risks, Mr. Thompson, Joseph Allston, John Bozers, Alexander Resch, granted to Jacob William Henry 9 June 1775. Jacob Wm. Harvey (LS), Wit: Jno Gilbanks, Wm. H. Roberts. Proved 8 Apr 1778 by the oath of Thomas Elliott, Esqr., who attested to the handwriting of Jacob Wm. Harvey before Geo Sheed. Recorded 22 May 1778.

X-4, 32-37: Lease and release. 1 & 2 Oct 1775, Jeremiah Brower of Charlestown to Philip Henry of Charlestown, for £3000 SC money, 2400 acres on the head of Sandy Run Creek in Berkley County adj. Walter Russell, William Carter, ranted to Jeremiah Brower 9 June 1775, also a tract of 500 acres in Craven county on west side of Broad River adj. lands laid out for Thomas and Elizabeth Kinchard, William Farr, Isaac Simonson, John Feemster, George Bell, granted to Jeremiah Brower 15 Sept 1775. Jerem'h Brower (LS), Wit: Jonathan Clarke, Will Campbell. Proved in Charlestown District 23 June 1778 before John Troup by the oath of John Sturgeon who attested to the handwriting of Jeremiah Brower and William Campbell. Recorded 25 June 1778.

X-4, 38-40: Lease and release. 9 & 10 Nov 1775, James Oliphant of Charlestown to Philip Henry of Charlestown, for £10 SC money, 400 acres in Craven County on Clarks Branch of Wilsons Creek about Two miles from the mouth of the creek on the north side of Broad River ten miles above the Fish Dam Ford and a tract of 350 acres two miles north east of the Fish Dam Ford of Broad River on waters of Sandy River and Tereble Creek adj. James Moore, Thomas Hughes, Charles Nix. James Oliphant (LS), Wit: John Crawford, Willm. Templeton. Proved in Charlestown District by the oath of Thomas Harper who attested to the handwriting of James Oliphant 1 May 1778. Recorded 25 June 1778.

X-4, 41-43: Lease and release. 7 & 8 Oct 1775, John Wilson of Charlestown, merchant, and Mary his wife, to Philip Henry of same, for £1000 SC money, 1000 acres on waters of Saludy adj. Micajah Colley, said John Wilson, granted to John Wilson 1 July 1775. Jno Wilson (LS), Mary Wilson (LS), Wit: Rt. Ballingall, Jos. Bonneau. Proved in Charlestown District by the oath of John Bonneau before Geo Sheed 30 May 1778. Recorded 25 June 1778.

X-4, 44-49: Lease and release. 1 & 2 Sept 1775, Thomas Phepoe of Charlestown, and Elizabeth his wife, to Philip Henry of Charlestown, for £600 SC money, three tracts: (1) 500 acres in Orangeburgh District granted to John Gaillard Esqr., on a branch of Edisto River (2) 500 acres in Orangeburgh District adj. James Rantowle, John Nichols, Hans Balmes[?] land (3) 300 acres on

SOUTH CAROLINA DEED ABSTRACTS 1773-1778

Edisto River adj. land granted to Jacob Isler, Brand Pendarvis granted 23 June 1774 to Lt. Charles Taylor one of his majestys late companies of Foot in North America sold at public sale by James Haig, Esqr., Sheriff for Orangeburgh District by virtue of a judgment out of the court of common pleas at the suit of William Arther 10 Oct 1776, conveyed to Thomas Phepoe. Thos Phepoe (LS), Eliza. Phepoe (LS), Wit: Lambert Lance, Geo Carter. Proved 19 June 1778 before George Sheed by the oath of George Carter. Recorded 25 June 1778.

X-4, 50-55: Lease and release. 1 & 2 Sept 1777, Thomas Elliott of Charlestown, esquire, to Philip Henry of same, planter, for £1800 SC money, 350 acres in Craven County, St. Marks Parish, adj. ___ Yeats, John Bateman, granted to John Vaughan 4 June 1759; also 50 acres (surveyed for John Vaughan 13 Oct 1764) on east side Wateree River adj. William Helton, John Bateman, John Vaughan, granted 16 Jan 1772 conveyed by John Vaughan to Thomas Elliott 20 & 21 June 1775 (plats included). Thomas Elliot (LS), Wit: Elisha Poinsett, John Miller. Proved 10 June 1778 before George Sheed by the oath of Elisha Poinsett. Recorded 25 June 1778.

X-4, 56-62: Lease and release. 1 & 2 Sept 1777, Thomas Elliott of Charlestown, esquire, to Philip Henry of same, planter, for £2394 SC money, 300 acres, half of 600 acres in Berkley County, on south side Four Hole Swamp, adj. land of Edward Perry, Thomas Clarke, granted to Sarah Elliott 18 May 1773; also 897 acres being the half part of a tract of 1794 in Berkley County adj. John Mores, Abraham Woods, Henry Woods, Mr. Dunklin, Charles Bullard, granted to Sarah Elliott 27 Apr 1773 conveyed by Sarah Elliott to Thomas Elliott 13 & 14 Apr 1775 (plats included). Thomas Elliot (LS), Wit: Elisha Poinsett, John Miller. Proved 10 June 1778 before George Sheed by the oath of Elisha Poinsett. Recorded 25 June 1778.

X-4, 63-68: Lease and release. 1 & 2 Sept 1777, Thomas Elliott of Charlestown, esquire, to Philip Henry of same, planter, for £660 SC money, whereas William Elliott in his lifetime was possessed of 600 acres on Rocky Creek a branch of Stevens Creek in the district of Ninety Six adj. land surveyed for James Carson, and a tract of 576 acres on main branch of Horse Creek a branch of Savannah River in Ninety Six district, and a tract of 350 acres on Turkey Creek a branch of Savannah River in Ninety Six District adj. James Reynolds, John Purvis and land surveyed for ____ Humphreys, David Baty, granted to William Elliott 20 Feb 1775 and said William Elliott by his will dated 26 Feb 1775 did bequeath all his estate to his brother the aforesaid Thomas Elliott. Thomas Elliot (LS), Wit: Elisha Poinsett, John Miller. Proved 10 June 1778 before George Sheed by the oath of Elisha Poinsett. Recorded 25 June 1778.

X-4, 69-75: Lease and release. 1 & 2 Sept 1777, Thomas Elliott of Charlestown, esquire, to Philip Henry of same, planter, for £260 SC money, 500 acres surveyed 5 March 1773 on south side Tyger River on Youngs Creek also 800 acres surveyed 28 Feb 1773 in Craven County adj .John wood, John McWirter[?], George McWirter, David Lewis, also 500 acres surveyed 14 March 1773 on the springs of Cane and Dutchmans Creek the north side of Tyger River, also 500 acres surveyed 2 March 1773 in Craven County on the south side of Pacolet River on Sandy Run, also 1000 acres surveyed 8 Nov 1774 between Fair Forrest and Lawsons Fork or Chinkopen Creek, also 1300 acres surveyed 3 Nov 1774 in Craven County on waters of Lawsons Fork between Lawsons Fork and Pacolet River adj. land called the Pedlars, also 100 acres adj. John Baptist Bourquin, Cornelius Dupoin, Adrian Mayer, also 250 acres in Granville county adj. William Pugh, Adrian Mayer, John Vouchier, John Strohber, also 200 acres surveyed 19 March 1774 in Ninety Six District on south side Pacolet River granted 8 Dec 1774 to Thomas Elliott. Thomas Elliot (LS), Wit: Zach Cantey, Robt Lithgow. Proved 23 June 1778 before John Troup by the oath of Robert Lithgow. Recorded 25 June 1778.

X-4, 76-82: Lease and release. 1 & 2 Sept 1777, Thomas Elliott of Charlestown, esquire, to Philip Henry of same, planter, for £1920 SC money, 300 acres surveyed 28 Jan 1767 in Craven County on a fork of Rayburns Creek a branch of Saludy River; tract of 300 acres surveyed 3 Apr 1773 in Craven County adj. Ralph Humphreys land; a tract of 200 acres surveyed 24 Apr 1770 on waters of Bush River adj. George Derumple, Lewis Jones, James Young; 853 acres in St. Georges parish, Berkly County; 147 acres adj. Henry Wood, John Mores; 1000 acres in Granville County on the head of the three Runs on Tinkers Creek adj. Doct. Farrar, William Elliot; 1000 acres in Granville County on Tinkers Creek adj. Richard Halls; tracts originally granted 1 March 1775 to William

SOUTH CAROLINA DEED ABSTRACTS 1773-1778

Elliott and conveyed to Thomas Elliott. Thomas Elliot (LS), Wit: Zach Cantey, Robt Lithgow. Proved 22 June 1778 before John Troup by the oath of Robert Lithgow. Recorded 25 June 1778.

X-4, 82-83: 27 May 1777, Henry Hyrne of St. Bartholomews Parish, Esquire, to James Parsons of Charlestown, Esquire, for ten shillings, tract in St. Bartholomews Parish on south side of the southern branch of Ashepoo River at Hyrnes Landing. Henry Hyrne (LS), Wit: John Dilgare, Jacob Dilgare, James Ballantine. Proved in Charlestown District by the oath of John Delgare 5 July 1777 before Thos Hutchinson. Recorded 13 July 1778.

X-4, 83-86: Lease and release. 24 & 25 Apr 1778, Samuel Porcher of St. Peters Parish, SC, and Mary his wife, to Paul Porcher of St. Peters Parish, for £100 SC money, 150 acres in Craven County on east side of Broad River adj. land of Isom Dansby, granted to sd. Samuel Porcher 27 March 1772. Saml Porcher (LS), Mary Porcher (LS), Wit: James Moore, Peter Porcher. Proved 15 June 1778 before William Ross, J.P. in Beaufort District by the oath of Peter Porcher. Recorded 13 July 1778.

X-4, 86-89: Lease and release. 15 & 16 Feb 1775, William King of St. Andrews parish, James Island, planter, and Mary his wife, to George Rivers of James Island, St. Andrews parish, planter, for £521 SC money, Tindals Island on south west end of James Island, 51 acres and marsh adj. Stono River. Wm. King (LS), Mary King (LS), Wit: William Holmes, Henry Samways. Proved in Charlestown District before Isaac Rivers, J.P., by the oath of William Holmes. Recorded 13 July 1778.

X-4, 89-93: Lease and release. 17 & 18 Apr 1775, David Taylor of James Island, St. Andrews parish, Berkley County, ship wright, to George Rivers of James Island, planter, for £331 SC money, land granted 28 Apr 1733 to William Spencer of James Island, planter, 46 acres called Horse Island marsh land at the south west end of James Island, recorded in Secretary's office in Book AA, folio 156, and by several mesne conveyances became vested in Jonathan Evans and on 5 Jan 1754 [sic] he did make his will and Samuel Evans, William and James Screven, being his executors, did convey to John Ellis Senr, late of James Island, planter, and on 30 & 31 March 1747 conveyed to David Taylor of James Island, planter, and father to the above mentioned David Taylor, ship wright. David Taylor (LS), Wit: William Bradley, Joseph Rivers, Robt. Rivers. Proved by the oath of Robert Rivers before James Witter Junr, J. P. for St. Andrews parish. Recorded 13 July 1778.

X-4, 93-95: Lease and release. 24 & 25 Feb 1774, Ulrick Busser of Berkley County, to Henry Buzbee of Craven County, for £500 SC money, 150 acres on north side Broad River adj. John Frazer, surveyed 21 Nov 1749 granted 7 June 1751. Ulrich Busser [German signature] (S), Wit: William Frazer, Frederich Busser [German signature], Jacob Busser [German signature]. Proved 11 June 1778 before Jacob Richman, J. P., by the oath of Jacob Buser. Recorded 13 July 1778.

X-4, 95-98: Lease and release. 21 & 22 Feb 1775, Henry Buzbee of Broad River, Campden District, to Joseph Kennerly of Saludy River, Orangeburgh District, for £500 SC money, 150 acres on north side Broad River adj. John Frazer, surveyed 21 Nov 1749 granted 7 June 1751. Henry Buzbee (LS), Mary Buzbee (+) (LS), Wit: William Hunt, William Buzbee (+). Proved in Orangeburgh District by the oath of William Hunt before Evan McLaurin, J.P., 21 Feb 1775. Recorded 13 July 1778.

X-4, 98-101: Lease and release. 14 & 15 Apr 1774, Andrew Houser & his wife Catherine of Berkley County, SC, planter, to Richard Strother of province aforesaid, for £303 SC money, 150 acres granted 3 Sept 1754 on north side of Broad River adj. land surveyed for Edward Gregg, John Miller, granted to Christopher Phag and said Christopher Phag died intestate and the 150 acres devolved on his wife Catherine who is now Catherine Houser. Andreas Hauser [German signature] (LS), Catherine Houser (X) (LS), Wit: Wm. Fitzpatrick, Isom Joyner. Proved 15 June 1778 before Richard Brown, J.P. in Orangeburgh District, by the oath of William Fitzpatrick. Recorded 13 July 1778.

X-4, 101-104: Lease and release. 15 & 16 July 1774, Richard Strother and Rebekah his wife of Craven County, SC, to Joseph Kennerly of the province aforesaid, for £350 SC money, 150 acres granted 3 Sept 1754 on north side of Broad River adj. land surveyed for Edward Gregg, John Miller, granted to Christopher Phag and said Christopher Phag died intestate and the 150 acres

SOUTH CAROLINA DEED ABSTRACTS 1773-1778

devolved on his wife Catherine who married Andrew House and by them said Andrew and Catherine Houser sold to Richard Strother 14 & 15 Apr 1774. Richd. Strother (LS), Rebekah Strother (X) (LS), Wit: John Kennerly, John Baccus. Proved 16 July 1774 before Richard Winn, J.P. in the Dist. of Camden, by the oath of John Baccus. Recorded 13 July 1778.

X-4, 104-105: 4 Apr 1775, Maj. Andrew Bailie of the Kingdom of Ireland, to John Mitchell of County of Craven, SC, merchant, for £600 SC money, 640 acres in the county of Anson, province of North Carolina, on SW side Pedee River about a mile below Peter Henly, Esqr., granted to sd. Andrew Bailie 27 May 1760 a memorial entered in Book M. No. , page 13. Andrew Bailie (LS), Wit: John Ogle, M. D., Is. Mitchell. Proved in Cheraw District before Thomas Powe, J.P., by the oath of Doctor John Ogle, 2 March 1778. Recorded 13 July 1778.

X-4, 105-106: 4 Apr 1775, Maj. Andrew Bailie of the Kingdom of Ireland, to John Mitchell of County of Craven, SC, merchant, for £650 SC money, 400 acres in the county of Anson, province of North Carolina, on both sides Lynches Creek about three miles below John Strouds, granted to sd. Andrew Bailie 10 June 1761 a memorial entered in Book M. No. , page 13. Andrew Bailie (LS), Wit: John Ogle, M. D., Is. Mitchell. Proved in Cheraw District before Thomas Powe, J.P., by the oath of Doctor John Ogle, 2 March 1778. Recorded 13 July 1778.

X-4, 106-109: Lease and release. 29 & 30 Feb 1776, John Williamson of St. Davids Parish, Craven County, SC, planter, to John Mitchell of same, merchant, for £200 SC money, 100 acres on Thompsons Creek adj. land of Daniel Lundy, Johnson. John Williamson (LS), Wit: George Wright (X), Thomas Powe. Proved in Cheraw District before Wm. Dewitt, 6 March 1778 by the oath of Thomas Powe. Recorded 13 July 1778.

X-4, 110-112: Lease and release. 26 & 27 Sept 1777, Arthur Howell of Camden District, SC, planter, to Uriah Goodwyn and Francis Goodwyn of Orangeburgh District, for £300 SC money, 100 acres in Berkley County granted to Arthur Howell 30 Sept 1774 adj. land of Henry Patrick, Daniel Haubigh, recorded in Book TTT, page 218. Arthur Howell (LS), Wit: Robert Hicks, Robt. Howell. Proved in Camden District by the oath of Robert Howell before Philip Pearson, J. P., 27 Sept 1777. Recorded 13 July 1778.

X-4, 112-116: Lease and release. 1 & 2 June 1777, John Wragg of Charlestown, exr. of the will of Joseph Wragg deceased, to Judith Wragg of Charlestown, for £15,000 SC money, whereas Richard Lambton by deed 30 Aug 1768 between said Richard Lambton of Charlestown and Judith Wragg, widow and extx. of will of Joseph Wragg, esquires, deceased, and John Wragg son and heir of said Judith Wragg, said Richard Lambton agreed to convey to said Judith Wragg and her son John Wragg, and said Judith Wragg is since deceased and said John Wragg is become the acting executor, town lot on Broad Street in Charlestown adj. Doctor Ramsey, Henry Bedon now James Laurens, land formerly of the heirs of William Elliott lately to Elizabeth Darvil, also lot formerly belonging to the heirs of William Elliott. John Wragg (LS), Wit: Kath: Finlay, Joseph Darling. Proved before Jonathan Scott, J. P. for Charlestown District, by the oath of Joseph Darling, 4 June 1777. Recorded 20 July 1778.

X-4, 116-118: Lease and release. 15 & 16 June 1778, Henry Reeves of Christ Church Parish, SC, planter, and Charlotte his wife, to William McKimmey of Charlestown, cooper, for £5000 SC money, 235 acres in Christ Church Parish adj. land of said William McKimmey, John Ward, Doctor William Loocock, Hugh Swinton (plat included by Benj. Lord, D. S., dated 16 May 1778). Henry Reeves (LS), Charlotte Reeves (LS), Wit: E. Rutledge, Benj. Smith. Proved in Charlestown District by the oath of Benjamin Smith before Geo Sheed, 18 June 1778. Recorded 20 July 1778.

X-4, 118-121: Lease and release. 6 & 7 Dec 1777, William Allston of George Town, SC, planter, to John Nivian of same, tavern keeper, for £1000 SC money, half of lot in George Town, number 120 formerly property of Mrs. Margaret Webb and by her left to her son Charles Ash who lately sold the same to william Allston, on High Markett Street, Cannon Street. W. Allston (LS), Wit: Tho: Ousby, Tho: Tonnerton. Proved in George Town District by the oath of Thomas ousby before Paul Trapier, J. P., 8 Nov 1777. Recorded 20 July 1778.

SOUTH CAROLINA DEED ABSTRACTS 1773-1778

X-4, 121-124: Lease and release. 6 & 7 June 1777, Benjamin Farar of Saxagotha Township, Esqr., to William Bull the younger of said state, esquire, for £800 SC money, 150 acres in St. Marks parish on Santee River adj. Thomas Brown, ___ McDonald, Thomas Sumpter (plat included). Benja. Farar (LS), Wit: Lambert Lance, Joseph Guerard. Proved in Charlestown District by the oath of Lambert Lance before Geo Sheed, 18 May 1778. Recorded 20 July 1778.

X-4, 124-127: Lease and release. 15 & 16 Dec 1774, Richard Lambton, Esqr., of Charlestown, Berkley County, Sc, to Benjamin Farar of the Congarees in said county, for £200 SC money, 450 acres in St. Marks Parish on north side Santee River in Craven county opposite Amelia Township, granted to Charles Wright 18 Jan 1765 and by divers mesne conveyances became vested in the said Richard Lambton; also 250 acres adjoining the former adj. land now the property of Elias Buckingham, originally granted to said Charles Wright 23 Oct 1765. R. Lambton (LS), Wit: Thos Hutchinson, Jno Smith. P{roved 12 June 17754 before Ephraim Mitchell, J.P. by the oath of Thos Hutchinson. Recorded 20 July 1778.

X-4, 128-131: Lease and release. 24 & 25 Oct 1759, Thomas Slann (eldest son to Andrew Slann decd) of the parish of St. Pauls, planter, and Ann Slann (widow of said Andrew Slann), of Parish of St. George, Berkley County, to Ralph Izard of St. Georges parish, Berkley County, planter, for £300 SC money, 600 acres in St. James Parish on west side of Four Hole Swamp. Thos Slann (LS), Ann Slann (LS), Wit: James Sanders, Mary Waring, Ann Slann Junr. Proved by the oath of James Sanders before Benja. Waring, 26 Oct 1759. Recorded 20 July 1778.

X-4, 131-134: Lease and release. 19 & 20 May 1778, John Chambers of Charlestown, merchant, to Zephaniah Kinsley, merchant, and James Cook, carpenter, of Charlestown, for £14,000 SC money, lot in Charlestown, number 6 on south side of Tradd Street, also lot on the Bay Street adj. lot lately of Charles Elliott and now of William Greenwood, Charles Cotesworth Pinckney, Esqr., Fenwick Bull. Jno. Chambers (LS), Wit: David Baty, Anthony Farrasteau. Proved 22 May 1778 before Hopkin Price, Esqr., by the oath of David Baty. Recorded 20 July 1778.

X-4, 134-135: 15 Jan 1770, Edward Green of Province of SC, and Ann his wife, to William Willson for £150 SC money, 100 acres in County of Craven, SC, on Beaver Dam of Enoree River, patent dated 31 Oct 1769 to William Joyner and by him conveyed to Edward Green and Ann his wife. Edward Green (LS), Ann Green (X) (LS), Wit: John Johnston Senr, William Murray, Andrew McMechan. Proved 20 Jan 1770 before John Johnston, J. P. in craven county by the oath of Andrew McMoughon. Recorded 20 July 1778.

X-4, 136-138: Lease and release. South Carolina. 19 & 20 Dec 1772, Charles King of said province, and Charity his wife, to William Willson, tannar, for £255 SC money, 200 acres between Broad and Saludy Rivers near a creek called Indian Creek adj. Abraham Anderson, Charles King. Charles King (LS), Charity King (LS), Wit: John Lindsey, Abel Lewis, Robert Johnston. Proved 13 Jan 1773 before John Johnston, J. P., by the oath of Abel Lewis. Recorded 20 July 1778.

X-4, 139-141: Lease and release. 16 & 17 Jan 1774, Isaac Knighten of St. Marks Parish, SC, planter, to William Dinkins of same, planter, for £200 SC money, 82 acres in Craven County on east side Wateree River on the High Hills of Santee adj. William Dinkins, William Hilton, Henry Pitts, Joseph Howard, John Jarvis, Peter Matthews, James Furman, Francis Baty. Isaac Knighten (LS), Wit: John Gauling (Golden), Ann Paterson (X), William Stuard. Proved in Camden District 13 Jan 1778 before Nathl. Moore, J. P., by the oath of William Stuard. Recorded 27 July 1778.

X-4, 141-144: Lease and release. 1 & 2 July 1778, John James of St. Marks Parish, SC, planter, and Sarah his wife, to John Gabriel Guignard of same, for £1250 SC money, 62 acres in St. Marks Parish, Craven County, eastward of the Wateree River adj. land of sd. John James, on the public road, land of John Rodgers, said John Gabriel Guignard, part of 300 acres ranted to Sherwood James Senr, 23 June 1773 (plat included). John James (LS), Sarah James (LS), Wit: John Fabre, John James Junr. Proved 2 July 1778 by the oath of John Fabre before Isham Moore, J.P. Recorded __ July 1778.

X-4, 145-146: 14 Apr 1778, John Gibbes of Parish of St. Philip, Esquire, to Joseph Kershaw of Camden, merchant, for £1400 SC money, lot number 5 on Bay Street (plat included). John Gibbes

(LS), Wit: Geo Abbott Hall, John Douglass. Proved in Charlestown District by the oath of George Abbott Hall before Geo Sheed, 1 July 1778. Recorded 27 July 1778.

X-4, 147-149: Lease and release. 3 & 4 Oct 1775, James Smith of Charlestown, to William Downes of same, surveyor, for £20 SC money, 500 acres in Ninety Six District on waters of Enoree River on Coxe's Creek adj. Anguish Campbell, John Casey, Aaron Lynch, granted to sd. James Smith 15 Sept 1775. James Smith (LS), Wit: Henry Houseman, Wm. Edwards. Proved in Charlestown District by the oath of William Edwards 1 July 1778 before Geo. Sheed. Recorded 27 July 1778.

X-4, 149-153: Lease and release, indenture tripartite. 26 & 27 June 1778, Rev. Edward Jenkins of SC of the first part, Rev. Robert Smith, Rector of St. Philips Charlestown, Hopkin Price of Charlestown, Esquire, and Andrew Maybank of State of Georgia, Esquire, of the second part, and Susanna Jenkins wife of said Edward Jenkins, of the third part, for natural love and affection said Edward Jenkins hath to his wife, and for ten shillings, tract oat the Horse Shoe in St. Bartholomews parish, 500 acres, granted 18 Sept 1703 adj. James Postell, James Reid, William Clay Snipes, estate of said James Reid, also 300 acres at the horse shoe in St. Bartholomews Parish, granted to Susannah Reid adj. land of Isaac Hayne; also lot on Rivers Street or Dedcots Alley, part of lot number 142 in Charlestown; also 47 negroes [named], in trust. Edward Jenkins (LS), Robert Smith (LS), Hopkin Price (LS), Susanna Jenkins (LS), Wit: Catharine Sarazin, Thos Phepoe. Proved in Charlestown by the oath of Thomas Phepoe, Esqr., before Geo. Sheed 22 July 1778. Recorded 27 July 1778.

X-4, 153-157: Lease and release. 9 & 10 June 1767, Joseph Stone of St. Thomas Parish, Berkley County, SC, to Jacob Manrow of Christ Church Parish, same county, for £60 SC money, half of tract of 227 acres in St. Thomas parish adj. James Akin, Capt. Bonny now of James Akin, John Pagett or his heirs, Joseph Russell deceased, Cooper River, which was the plantation & dwelling place of Joseph Stone (father of Joseph Stone party to these presents), who by his will bequeathed to his son Joseph Stone and his son Benjamin Stone to be equally divided. Joseph Stone (LS), Wit: Rebekah Shrewsbury, Edward Shrewsbury, John Taylor. Proved in Charles Town District before John Poaug by the oath of Edward Shrewsbury 5 June 1778. Recorded 27 July 1778.

X-4, 157-158: 5 May 1778, Elias Jaudon of St. Peters Parish, Beaufort District, SC, planter, and Mary his wife, to William Atkins of Charlestown District, Parish of St. Bartholomew, merchant, for £500 SC money, 300 acres granted to Elias Jaudon 4 Dec 1771 recorded in Book KKK, page 160, on the head of Beaver Dam waters of Great Coosawhatchie Swamp, tract now known by the name of Bull head, St. Helenas Parish in Granville County. Elias Jaudon (LS), Mary Jaudon (LS), Wit: Elias Robert, Martin Shumann. Proved before Henry Gindratt, J.P. in Beaufort District, by the oath of Martin Shumann, 7 July 1778. Recorded 27 July 1778.

X-4, 159-163: Lease and release. 16 & 17 June 1778, William Bennie of Charlestown, SC, baker, and Rebecca his wife, to John Dart of Charlestown, attorney at law, for £11,500 SC money, lots in Charlestown, number 24 and 25, on Church Street adj. lots now or late belonging to Alexander Taylor and Francis Kinloch, William Hinckley, Christopher Rodgers, also part of lot number 261 on north side of Allen Street adj. land of Abraham Spidle, William Glen, also another part of lot number 261; also 123 acres in Granville County adj. land of the heirs of William Sanders deceased, Robert Brailsford, Thomas Shubrick, esqr. William Bennie (LS), Rebeka Bennie (LS), Wit: John Wragg, Wm. Mason. Proved in Chas. Town District by the oath of William Mason 20 June 1778 before Geo. Sheed. Recorded 3 Aug 1778.

X-4, 163-166: Lease and mortgage. 3 & 4 July 1778, Jacob Ernst of Charlestown, SC, to John Dart of same, attorney at law, in the penal sum of £8000 for the payment of £4000 before 1 January, lot number 161, on north side of Allen Street adj. land of Abraham Spidle, William Glen. Jacob Ernst (LS), Wit: Robert Jno Livingston, Edward Serjant. Proved before George Sheed by the oath of Edward Serjant 12 July 1778. Recorded 3 Aug 1778.

X-4, 168-169: Lease and release. 21 & 22 July 1778, Benjamin Wilkins of Charlestown, house carpenter, and Mary his wife, to Benjamin Darrell of same, gentn., for £5000 SC money, part of lot on south side of a Canal or Creek leading from old to new church street in Charlestown, adj. James Tousigers, Thomas Legares, John Rose. Benjn. Wilkins (LS), Mary Wilkins (LS), Wit: Joseph

SOUTH CAROLINA DEED ABSTRACTS 1773-1778

Robinson, Wm. Bell. Proved in Charlestown District by the oath of William Bell before Geo Sheed 22 July 1778. Recorded 3 Aug 1778.

X-4, 170-172: Lease and release. 15 & 16 June 1778, Isaac Odom and Hester his wife of Granville county, SC, to John Parkinson of Reachmount, Granville County, for £500 SC money, 150 acres in Granville County adj. Savannah River, James Cain, Isaac Odom. Isaac Odom (LS), Hester Odom (+) (LS), Wit: John Collins, Sabart Odom. Proved before John Troup, Esqr., by the oath of John Collins, 21 July 1778. Recorded 3 Aug 1778.

X-4, 172-174: 11 March 1778, John Harrison, Surgeon, and Susannah his wife of Charlestown, to Joseph Kershaw of Craven County, for £700 SC money, lot on east side of Church Street, number 64, adj. land now or late in the occupation of Charles Pinckney, also Mrs. Cooper, widow. John Harrison (LS), Susanna Harrison (LS), Wit: Joel Holmes, James Cook. Proved by the oath of Joel Holmes in Charlestown District before Geo Sheed 12 June 1778. Recorded 3 Aug 1778.

X-4, 174-177: Lease and release. 20 & 21 June 1777, Tacitus Gaillard of Berkly County, SC, Esqr., to William Ancrum of Charlestown, merchant, for £1000 SC money, tract in St. Matthews parish on south side Santee River, 100 acres being the eastmost part of 450 acres granted to Henry Blaymier 13 July 1737 adj. land of Henry Laurens, Esqr., John McWilliams, William Bull, Esqr. (plat included). Tacits. Gaillard (LS), Wit: Robert Lithgow, Wm. Arther. Proved in Orangeburgh District before Ralph Humphreys, J. P., by the oath of William Arther 21 June 1777. Recorded 3 Aug 1778.

X-4, 177: Joseph Hodge of Charlestown, bound to Robert Brailsford, in the sum of £1273 s5 SC money, for the payment of £636 s12 on or before 9 June 1779. Joseph Hodge for Wm. Whayman. Wit: James Rugge, Thos Arwin. Proved by the oath of James Rugge 23 July 1778 before Geo. Sheed. Recorded 3 Aug 1778.

X-4, 178-180: Lease and release. 6 & 8 June 1778, Joseph Hodge of Charlestown, attorney to William Whayman of London, Great Britain, to Robert Brailsford of Charlestown, by bond [see previous instrument], 693 acres (plat included, showing good rice land, part of the Mary Barony in Purrysburgh Township). for Wm. Whayman Joseph Hodge (LS), Wit: James Rugge, Thos. Arwin. Proved by the oath of James Rugge 23 July 1778 before Geo. Sheed. Recorded 3 Aug 1778.

X-4, 180-184: Lease and release. 12 & 13 Sept 1775, Andrew Reynolds of Long Canes in Granville County, SC, to Henry Rugeley of Charlestown, merchant, for £600 SC money, 300 acres on waters of Long Canes granted 20 Aug 1767 to Giles Williams the younger and by him conveyed to said Andrew Reynolds 21 & 22 July 1774. Andw. Reynolds (LS), Wit: Archd. Carson, Jas. Crandon. Proved 17 Apr 1776 before John Troup by the oath of Archibald Carson. Recorded 11 Aug 1778.

X-4, 184-187: Lease and release. 29 & 30 July 1776, William Moon of Craven County, SC, planter, to Rowland Rugeley & Henry Rugeley of Charles Town, merchants, for £200 SC money, 100 acres granted 12 July 1771 to William Moon in Craven County on a small branch of the Wateree Creek. William Moon (O) (LS), Wit: Jas. McFarland, Alexander Turner, Willm. McAllister. Proved by the oath of William MacAllester before John Troup 18 July 1778. Recorded 11 Aug 1778.

X-4, 187-189: Lease and release. 1 & 2 Aug 1776, William Moon of Craven County, SC, planter, to Rowland Rugeley & Henry Rugeley of Charles Town, merchants, for £175 SC money, 150 acres. William Moon (O) (LS), Wit: Domk. Craney, Willm. McAllister, Jesse Stevenson. Proved by the oath of William MacAllester before John Troup 18 July 1778. Recorded 11 Aug 1778.

X-4, 190-192: Lease and release. 20 & 21 Sept 1776, Thomas Gibson of Ninety Six District, SC, planter, to Rowland Rugeley of district of Chs Town, merchant, for £150 SC money, 250 acres in Ninety Six District granted 1 Feb 1768 to Thomas Gibson on north side Salludy River adj. land of Gideon Linicum. Thomas Gibson (T) (LS), Wit: James Calk, P. Waters. Proved 2 Oct 1776 before William Mayson, J. P., by the oath of Philemon Waters. Recorded 11 Aug 1778.

X-4, 193-195: Lease and release. 11 & 12 Nov 1776, Philemon Waters, late of Charlestown, but now dwelling on the Saludy River in Berkley County, planter, to Rowland Rugeley & Henry Rugeley, merchants, for £1200 SC money, 200 acres on south side Saludy River in Berkley County, granted to John Hak or Hack who conveyed the tract to sd. Philemon Waters 19 & 20 March 1771. P. Waters (LS), Wit: Johannes Ernst [German signature], Nancy Dawson. Proved by the oath of Nancy Dawson before John Troup, J.P., 18 July 1778. Recorded 11 Aug 1778.

X-4, 195-199: Lease and release. 18 Apr 177_, Joseph Helmes/Elmes and Ann his wife of Craven County, to Henry Rugeley, merchant, for £3000 SC money, 250 acres on Wateree Creek on west side of Wateree River granted to sd. Joseph _____ 3 Aug 1762. Joseph Helmes (I), Ann Helmes (X). Wit: Mawbery Helmes (X), Jas Crandon. Proved 7 May 1778 before William Nisbett, J. P., by the oath of James Crandon. Recorded 11 Aug 1778.

END OF BOOK X-4.

Indices prepared by James D. McKain

NAME INDEX

Abenor, Catharine 117
　George 117
　Jacob 117
Abercromby, James 155,157
Aberlain, Solomernier
　(Ellis) 160
Abian, John 15
Abney, William 213
Abrahams, Emanuel 27,
　31,32, 42,47,52,53,75,
　104,106,111,165,175,
　181,232
Ackerman, Carl Ludwig 174
Adam, David 195
　Frances 17
Adams, 77,159
　Abraham 195
　James 169,175
　John 45,137,232
　John Hans 11
　Richard 203
　Thomas 24,47,175,195
　William 17,132,184
Adamson, Alexander 7,10
　Dorothy 10
　Eleanor 102
　Eliz'th 102
　John 45,102,137,138
　Thomas 191
Addey, John James 68
Adie, James 60
Adler, Stolberg 119
Aggnew, Andrew 35,98,104,
　158,163,174,223
Agiular, Ephraim de 166
Agkettor, Daniel 77
Agner, John 158
Agnew, Andrew 86,193,197
Agnew, Samuel 101
Agnews, James 131
Agnice, Ana Mary 134
Aigner, John 80
Ainger, Joseph 46,86
Ainslie, Hannah 111
　John 62,184
　Mary 213
Ainsworth, James 135
Akin, Ann 159
　James 35,54,57,159,242
　Sarah (Bramer) 54
Aking, James 85
Albateslier, Peter 133
Alberson, Albert 27
Aldbright, Elizabeth 33
Alder, Williams 3
Alderage, Michael 70
Aldridge, William 90
Alexander, Ab'm 104
Alexander, Gorden 57

John Macknitt 196
John McKnitt 8,102
Jonathan 202
McCrea Jr. 57
Moses 15
Nathaniel 15
Rebeckah 165
Samuel 131
William 163,165
Alison, Andw. 174
　Hugh 8
　James Hugh 65
Allein, Mary 112
Alleison, Rachael 115
Allen, 184
　Andrew 61,115
　Ann (Savage) 61
　Eleazer 89,208,210
　Francis 139
　Gennins 71
　Gid'n 166
　Jacob 25
　James 208,210
　John 61,85,103,169
　Joseph 81,167
　Mary (Dick) 51
　Richard 51
　Sarah 208,210
　Susannah (Pawley) 81
Allenby, Anne 20
Allis, Stephen 53
Allison, Charles 200
　George 128,169,200,206
　Hector 191
　Richard 60
　Sarah (Reese) 211
　Thomas 211,217,234
Allston, Ann 81
　Charlotte 81,114
　Francis 218
　John 81,150,168,224
　Joseph 70,74,75,81,114,
　131,150,151,164,185,218,
　237
　Josiah 81,114,125,145
　Josias 81,115,125,150,
　168,218
　Rachel 185
　Sabina 150
　Samuel 81
　William 115,128,145,150,
　185,186,240
　Wm. Jr. 185
Alran, John 156
　John 17,39,46,59,203
Alston, John 20,70
　William 114
Alvan, John 45,86
Amey, negro 193

Amory, Jonathan 50
Amos, James 159
Amoss, James 111
Ancrum, 165,191
　George 2,27,94,160,166,
　188,210
　George Jr. 82
　John 50,94,166
　Mary (Hasell) 50
　Mary 94,166
　William 2,27,64,137,138,
　149,160,166,188,189,210,
　226,243
Andally, George 90
Anderson, Abel 144
　Abraham 47,241
　Alexander 202
　Andrew 4
　Ann (Bounetheau) 161
　Ann 27
　David 58,60,76,88
　Hugh 161
　James 43,51,171
　John 40,78,214
　John Jr. 76
　Rachel 116
　Robert 14,15,123,142,
　151,162,186
　Ruth 146
　Stephen 126
　William 22,34,39,94,116,
　126,147,150
Andrew, Thos 19
Andrews, Abraham 47,175
　Isham 170
　John 75,147
Ansminger, Peter 20
Anson, George 32,39,108,
　122,221,235
　George Lord 108
　Thomas 108
Anthony, negro 122
Arand, Peter 162
Archbould, John 182
Archdale, John 25
Ardis, Christian 95
　Mathew 95
Arendell, Benj. 124
Arledge, Isaac 173
Armstrong, James 8,45,54
　John 45,118
　Robt 37
Arney, Jacob 228
Arnold, Benj. 124
　John 18
Arran, Peter 162
Arrant, Conrad 215
　Philip 157

Arther, William 68,69,72, 76,83,110,118,119,176,223, 238,243
Arthur, William 37,59,126, 136,175,193,199,205
Arwin, Thos. 243
Asbill, Isaac 129
   John 129
Ash, Cato 10,104,221,234
   Charles 240
   Elizabeth 234
   Samuel 234
Ashby, Anthony 81
   Thomas 81
Asher, John 10
Askew, Leonard 159
Aspenal, William 42
Assey, John 120
Ather, Wm. 117
Atkins, 38
   Charles 25,102
   Francis 147
   James 2,3,160,178,233
   John 59,147
   Joseph 33
   Sarah 147
   William 3,242,233
Atkinson, John 30
   Joseph 192
   Robt. 33
   Thomas 49,72,117
Atwell, Benjamin 20,21
   Icabod 21,84,190
   Joseph 20
   Mary 20,21,24,84
Aubery, Saml 61
Audebert, John 163,183,185, 206,219
Audibert, John 191,192,199, 206
   Judith 191,192
Auger, 195
Aughtry, Zachariah 154
Auldje, John 151
Austin, Agnes 47
   Ann 35
   George 97,150
   Robert 89,149
Avant, Francis 120
   John 120
   Joshua 115
Averet, Benjamin 184
Avery, Joseph 109,179
Ayers, Aaron 59,147
   Mary 13
   Thomas 13
Ayrton, Francis 62

Baber, James 189
Baccus, John 240
Backler, Ezekiel 210
   Ezekiel Jr. 210
Backsell, Wm. 116

Bacon, Richard 217
Bacot, Peter 99
   Samuel 115,116
Badell, Leonard 98
Badger, Jonathan 26,28,41, 83,161
   Joseph 131
   Mary 161
   Samuel 26
Badley, John 49
Bagen, John 25
Bagshall, William 109
Bailey, Daniel 34,168
   George 73
   Richard 170
   Robert 73
Baileyson, John 25
Bailie, Andrew 240
Bain, William 212
Baird, Archabald 52,115,160
   Mathew 115
Baitman, John 137
Baker,108
   Aaron 135,201
   Benjamin 193
   Elisha 174
   Elizabeth (Elliott) 156
   Francis 66,95
   John 12,157,230
   Joshua 201
   Rachel 65,66
   Ralph 229
   Richard Bohun 17,156
   Richard Bohun Jr. 156
   Robert 156
   Sampson 141,164
   Samuel 204
   Thomas 13,73
   William 11,153,177,178, 214
Balducks, Richd. 154
Baldwin, Hester 25
Balfour, John 129,169,170
Ball, 63
   Alexander 119
   Ann (Waring) 101
   Ann 209
   Catharine 48,101
   Edward 88
   Elias 35,48,101,204
   Elias Jr. 35,48,185
   Elizabeth (Smith) 101
   Elizabeth 104
   Esther 49
   George 49
   John 35
   John Coming 48,101
   Joseph 106
Ballantine, James 220,239
   Mary 218
   William 31,162,218,228
Ballard, Jesse 36
Ballentine, Benjamin 77

   James 74
   William 18,122
Ballingall, Robt. 22,237
Balmes, Hans 237
Balzeher, Hans 2
Bambasine, Constantyne 167
Bampfield, Rebecca 44,80, 208,210
   William 44,80,87
Banbury, William 97,133, 193,226
Banester, William 82
Banks, William 75
Banner, Peter 201
Bannester, William 82
Bansall, Samuel 95
Barber, John 115
Barefoot, Melia 173
   Millie 173
   Newit 173
   William 173
Barefoutt, Noah 173
Barker, John 121
   Thomas 161
   Tim 54
Barkley, Agness 196
   John 196
   Robert 90,196
   Samuel 199
Barksdale, George 191
   George Jr. 191
Barnard, Edward 167
   Wm. 167
Barnes, Edmund 222
   Elizabeth 222
   John 24
Barnet, James 203
   John 10
   Joseph 24,54,99,196,199
Barns, Barbara 54,63
   Charles 63
   Jacob 54,63
   James 107
   Moses 54
   William 54,63
Barnwell, John 12,17,45
   John Jr. 124
   Martha 17,45
Barr, Isaac 217
   James 180
Barrett, Andw 122
Barringer, Hector 53
Barron, John 200
Barrs, Frederick 13
Barsh, George 28
Bartels, John 31
Barton, Mary 11
   Thomas 11,44,157
Baskins, William 15
Bass, John 109
   Moses 156
   Thomas 142

Thomas Jr. 142
Basset, Dorothy (Edwards) 49
  Mary 49
Bassnett, John 38,82
Bateman, John 238
Bates, 184
  Isaac 181
  John 60
  William 117
Baty, David 30,40,43,77,88, 99,105,216,238,241
  Francis 241
Bauers, Adam 130
Baxter, Arthur 138
Bayles, Maria Cayrel 190
Bayley, Daniel 34
  John 25,101
Bayshall, William 179
Beagler, Henry 127
  Martin 121,127
Beaird, George 71
  James 71
Beakes, Abraham 120
Beal, Hannah (Bull) 19
  John 202
  Othniel 19,91,113,144, 178
Beale, Fenwick 69,81
  Othniel 19,24,69,70,81, 202,209
Bealer, Chs. 116
Bean, John 138
  Robert 217
Bear, John 157
Beard, Ann 46
  George 82
  James 7,8,82
  John 42,46
  Jonas 53,76
  Mathew 82,90
  Robert 90,216
  Thomas 82
  Will/Wm. 90,169
Bearden, Ann 129,130
  Edmund 129,130
Bearfoot, Elizabeth 96
  Newit 96
  Noah 96
  William 96
Beasley, George 194
Beatey, Francis 37
  Hugh 37
  James 37
Beatty, Ann 232,236
  Francis 232
  Jean 101
  John 232,236
Beaty, David 77
  Francis 26,37,236
Beauchamp, Captain 188
Beaufain, Hector Barringer 53

Beck, Daniel 53
Beckman, Bernard 13
  John Frederick 173
  Michael 173
Becu, Abraham 165
Beddeley, John 190
Bedggood, John 130
  Nicholas 3
Bedingfield, 201
  Charles 1
  Henry 121
  William 141
Bedon, George 99
  Henry 240
Bee, Elizabeth 88
  Esther 122
  Hester 122,222
  John 37
  John Jr. 37
  Joseph 28,88,12?,222
  Rachel 161
  Thomas 2,95,96,103,113, 143,159,160,178,205,207, 212,222
  William 89,161
Beekman, Barnard/Bernard 69,81,115
  John 135
Beesley, Bethiah 48,60
Behringer, Andreas 224
Beilard, Jacob 223
Beird, George 201
  James 201
Belin, A. Jr. 114
  Allard 114,149,204,205
  James 204
  Margaret 204,205
  Mary 204
  Peter 117,120
  Sarah 204
  William 149
Belisario, Isaac Mendes 33
Bell, Benjamin 110,205
  Duke 187
  Frederick 180
  George 237
  James 136
  John 4,53,70,93,120,163, 176,177,187
  Marmaduke 4,228
  Mary 161
  Richard 147
  Samuel 130
  Thomas 54,126
  William 68,136,161,163, 198,199,243
  Zachariah 136,198,199
Bellamy, 22
  Abraham 237
Beller, Peter 162
Bellinger, Edmund 40, 46,116
  Elizabeth (Elliott) 116

  Elizabeth 40
  John 17,40
  Lucia 40
  M. L. 40
  Mary 40
  William 40
Bells, 125
Bellune, John 204
  Michael 114
  William 203,204
Belton, John 45,186,206
  Mary 206
  Wm. 206
Beltzer, John 33
Ben, negro slave 7
Benbow, Evan 132
Benenger, Abraham 134
Benet, Willm. 128
Benfield, John 40
Benis, John 81
Benison, William 20,157
Bennet, Samuel 195
  Tho 212
Bennie, Rebecca 242
  William 242
Benoist, Abigail 27
  Margaret 181
  Mary 27
  Peter 27,116,160
  Philip 195
  Samuel 181
Benson, John 39
Beraud, Matthias 191
Berenger, Hector 192
Beresford, Richard 1,21,26, 38,71,123,159,167,198, 201,205,211,231
  Sarah 1,123,167,198,211
  ____ (Foissin) 201
Berline, 184
Bernhard, John 62
Berresford, Richard 227
  Sarah 227
Berrie, James 160
Berry, James 22
Bert, John 223
Berwick, John 123,163,165
  Simon 12,165
Bery, 200
Besely, William 6
Besnard, John 110
Besset, Mary (Smith) 127
Beswick, John 90
Betchelor, David 38
Bettey, Thomas 16
Bettis, Ensunt 151
  Francis 151
Bettison, David 29
  Elizabeth 29
Bevill, William 203
Bewsers, George 12
Bhroad, Lucey 116
  Nicholas 116

Biddle, Thomas 41
Biddurph, Stephen 32,42
Bidggood, J. 133,185
  John 185
Bigham, James 73
  John 73
Bininger, Abraham 208
Bird, Sutton 11
Bishop, Abner 75
  John 225
  Margret 75
  Nicholas 171,229
Bissett, Mary (Smith) 233
  William 233
Black, George 205
  John 105
  Nathaniel 29
  Peter 1
  Robert 103,128
  Samuel 142
  Thomas 63
  Wm. 148
Blackall, Thomas 108
Blackland, Mary 135
Blackley, James Jr. 56
Blacklock, William 181,221, 235
Blackman, William 171,182
Blain, Patrick 200
Blair, Isabella (Gottier) 63
  Michael 128
  Robert 6,48,56,177,207, 214
  Wade 156
Blake, Daniel 25,49,59,108, 151,160,168,183,200,201, 204,207,232
  Edward 27,107,123,163
  Elizabeth (Izard) 49,204
  Elizabeth 11
  George 198
  John 53,122,123,194
  Joseph 101
  Richard 5,53,231
  Richard Jr. 5,53,220
  William 232
Blakely, Luke 29
Blakley, 149
Blalock, Lewis 211
Blamyer, Will. 191
Bland, George 197
Blanes, Michael 135
Blanton, Blarwell 211
  George 199,211
  Susannah 211
Blasingham, John 118
Blassengame, William 57,68
Blaymier, Henry 243
Blenco, Samll. 185
Blickenden, William 2
Blickendin, William 2
Blinco, Samuel 185

Bliss, Sarah 206
Blitchenden, Thomas 78
  William 2
Blitchington, John 32
Blith, Thomas 152,158
Bluler, Aron 155
Blyth, Joseph 172
Blythe, Thomas 160
Boatwright, 126
  Jno 128
Bobby, James 91,100
Bocquet, Elizabeth 50,158
  Peter 50,152,209
  Peter Jr. 50,158,199,231
Boden, Margaret (Eakins) 148
Bodett, John 4
Bodley, Ann 45
Bogan, James 194
Boggan, William 7
Boggs, Isabell 25
Bogs, Jas 25
Bohner, Barbara 235
  Godfrey 161,235
Boinest, Peter 38
Boisseau, James 51
Bolding, William 10
Boles, Susey 10
Bolin, Thomas 78,69
Bollison, Wm. 174
Bollough, John 27
  John Jr. 25
Bomer, Barbara 37
Bommer, Jacob 81
Bond, Abraham 126
  George Paddon 23,101
  Holey 236
  Jacob 117
  Jacob Jr. 23
  William 39
Bone, Godfrey 6
Boneau, Anthony 56
  Henry 88
Bones, John 184,219
Bonetheau, Peter 82
Bongardner, George 67
Bonhorste, Jacob 197
Bonijol, Isaac 86
Bonneau, 94
  Anthony 54,94,177
  Elias 140
  John 190,194,237
  Jos. 237
  Jr. 71
  Maria/Mary (Darby) 140
  Samuel 10
Bonnetheau, Peter 26
Bonnett, John 172
Bonney, Thomas 76
Bonny, Capt. 242
Booker, Joseph 2
Boomer, Jacob 69,81
  John 188

  Michael 186
Boone, Capers Jr. 220
  Charles 170
  Thomas 124,170,179
Booner, Michael 8
Booth, Charles 46
  John 46
  Mordecai 195
  Richard Wilbrahan 158
  Sarah 46
  Thomas 158
Bootwright, John 59
Boozer, George 16
Boquet, Peter 18,50,56
Borington, Henry 136
Boshart, Britta 118
  Rudolph 118
Bosher, Mary 208
Boss, Ann 198
  John 109,178,179,180,198
Bossard, Henry 126
Bostick, Jo'n 134
Boswood, Margrett 54
Bothwell, John 43
Botsford, Edmund 189,190
Botwright, Jesse 59
Boucheneau, Charles 223
Boudey, Robert 136
Bouneau, John 36
Bounetheau, Ann (Anderson) 161
  Elizabeth 235
  Peter 87,106,132,133, 147,149,150,161,188, 226,235
Bounty, Baresfords 36
Bouny, Thomas 87
Bourdeaux, Anthony 188
  Daniel 188
  Martha 188
  Nathl 188
Bourgett, Daniel 207
Bourke, Thomas 27,129,178, 195,203,214
Bourquin, Benedict 134
  Henery 39,133,134
  John 39
  John Baptist 110,238
  John Lewis 3,133
  Mary 133,134
Bours, Christian 151
Boutel, Cassimer 133
  Elisabeth 133
Bouyer, Michl. 168
Bowen, John 99,107
  Thomas 16,170
  William 16,46
Bower, Hans Jurg 118
  Jacob 114
Bowers, Adam 130
  George 130
Bowery, William 193
Bowie, John 2,21,83,89,105,

118,123,124,147,163,173
Bowler, John 236
   William 148
Bowles, John 75
Bowman, Amey 193,206
   Ann 174
   Barbara (Kerch) 2
   Daniel Orange 2
   Jacob 58,102,222
   James 93,166,184,188,
   193,206
   John 193,206
   Mary 206
   Matthew 184
   Milicen 93
   Ralph 59
   Robert 93,166,193,206
   Thomas 54,174
Bowra, Peter 12
Boyd, Ann 47
   David 47
   Henry 114,192
   James 17,57,74,79,131,
   180
   John 171,192
   Mary Jenet 35
   William 47
Boykin, Edward 189
   Saml 59
   William 58,75,131
Boyle, Catharine 85
   Charles 74,85
Bozers, John 237
Brabant, Daniel 133,206
   Isaac 133
   Wm. 86
Bracey, William 196
Bracher, Willm. 118
Brackley, Rachel 147
Bradberry, Francis 78
   Thomas 78
Bradley, Ann 45
   James 54,76,88
   John 44,121
   Samuel 118
   Thomas 118
   William 106,239
Bradwell, 108
   Hannah 221
   Isaac 21
   Jno 107
Brady, Edward 217
Brailsford, 162
   Joseph 31,103,104
   Robert 109,178,179,180,
   197,220,242,243
   Rose 220
Braly, John 212
Bramer, Mary (Marion) 54
Bramer, Sarah (Akin) 54
Brandford, William 99,110
Brandon, John 143
Branen, Michael 39

Branford, Ann (Horry) 107
   Elizabeth (Horry) 107
   Elizabeth 91,179
   William 56,91,107,120,
   209
Brannam, Susanna 39
   William 39,40
Braswell, Jacob 121
Bratton, John 215
   Mary 215
   Wm. 189
Brawford, James 31
   Samuel 31
Brazier, Mary Ann 52,63
   Zachariah 52,63,69
Breehl, George 138
Bremar, Fra's 200,201
Bremar, 94
   Francis 5,29,77,134,180,
   190,199
   J. 180
   James 54
   John 32,135,190,193,201
   Peter 125,190,201
Brenan, Eugene 30,40,123
Brent, James 144
Brewer, James 116
   Samuel 198
Brewton, Col. 28
   Mary (Izard) 49,204
   Mary 109,110
   Miles 7,19,49,58,98,109,
   110,117,159,187,204
   Robert 160
Brezina, Francies 118
Brian, John 18,159
   Mary 18
Briant, Jeremiah 94
Bride, Thomas 80
Briers, Richard 188
Briggs, Robert 34
Brimmingham, James 189
Brineau, Paul 143
Brisbane, Adam 37
   Adam Fowler 24
   Eunice 37
   James 20,24,111,112,235
   Rebecca 235
   Robert 35,61,193,195
   Sarah 112
   William 21,24,37,84
   William Alexander 24
Bristol, slave 234
Britton, Daniel 91
   Francis 120,139,155,157,
   164,198,203,204
   John 22
   Joseph 120,155
   Moses 132
   Phillip 157
   Stephen 132
   William 120,155,174
Broadway, Nicholas 117

Brock, Elias 79
Brockinton, James 159
   Rebecka 70
Brodie, John 77,216
Brolien, John 97
Bronkhart, Andrew 83
   Edward 72
   Rachel 72,83
Brook, Jacob 78
   Robert 195
Brooks, Job 171
   John 23
   Richard 127,130,167
   Thos 163
Broos, Peter 86
Broughton,56,103,164
   Andrew 77,184,199,225
   Elizabeth 204
   Thomas 67,70,204
   Thos Jr. 204
Brower, Jeremiah 237
Brown, 215
   Alexander 229
   Allan 6,214
   Andrew 59
   Archibald 130,131
   Barbara (Vanlerin) 7
   Barlet 135
   Bartlett 162,163,231
   Casper 31
   Charles 17,57,64,180
   David 35,161
   Edward 59,60
   Elien 111
   Esther 6,214
   Felix 171
   Francis 7
   George 75,127,135
   George Paddon 23
   Henry 13
   Hugh 50,198
   Jacob 7
   James 5,14,20,64,127,211
   Jean 22
   Jeremiah 220
   Jo. 211
   John 3,5,22,90,128,174,
   207,217
   Joseph 23,41,51,52,63,
   117,144,170,199,205
   Joshua 134
   Judith 215
   Lazarus 236
   Lazerous 126
   Margaret 94
   Mary (Easton) 50,198
   Mary 184.232,236
   Mourning 22
   Nathaniel 120
   Patrick 136,162
   Richard 58,86,101,136,
   175,184,203,215,232,236,
   239

Roger 28
Steward 10
Thomas 48,102,136,172, 184,225,241
William 29,47,64,105,155, 162,171,196,206,211, 236
Browne, Charles 74,103
Jackson 157
Browning, William 103
Bruce, Donald 49,119,126
John 136
Robert 47,224
Bruneau, Paul 11
Bruner, Ulrick 229
Brunson, David 13,155
Isaac 13,14
James 14
Josiah 82,201
William 155
Brunston, Josiah 82
Bruton, John 207
Bryan, Eliza. 200
Hugh 54
Hugh 82
James 107
Jonathan 163
Joseph 54
Katharine 31
Robt 85
Bryant, Robt. 85
Bryers, Laz'r 92
Brynan, John 5
Bryson, Hugh 73
Buch, John 114
Buchanan, John 148
Robert 199
Buche, John 208,224
Buckhalter, John 109
Michael 47
Buckhannon, John 219
Buckholds, Anthony 151
Henry 53
Buckholts, Anthony 151
Jacob 189
Buckingham, Elias 27,70, 241
Luis 225
Margaret 27
Buckle, Mary 38
Thomas 38
Buckloe, Richd. 171
Buckmyer, Daniel 42
Buer, Thomas 19,232,236
Bull, Fenwick/e 25,42,58, 68,91,92,100,112,116, 142,165,167,169,174,191, 241,202
Frederick 109,115,157, 158,175
Gov. 171,221,222
Hannah (Beal) 19
John 17,86,93,116,191,

207,221,222
Nathaniel 21
Stephen 3,54,90,110,162, 179
Thomas 191
William 19,24,30,64,69, 81,88,101,138,194,209, 211,241,243
William Jr. 181
Bullard, Charles 238
Edward 91,150,202
Bullion, Thomas 129,174
Bullock, James 29,103,206
John 34,121
Leonard Henley 227,235
Zachariah 54,79,117,135, 212
Bungardner, John 125
Bunkart, John 1
Bunsley, James 54
Buntricks, Nicholas 53
Bunyie, James 185,189,194, 204,225
Burch, Francis 143
Jonathan 49
Joseph 142,201
Burches, 142
Burchfield, John 211
Lucrecy 211
Burford, John 12,61
Burgess, William 79
Buris, 49
Burke, Aedimus 233
John 183
Thomas 156
Burkholter, Michael 72
Burkloe, Richard 171
Burkmire, Charles 46
Burkmyer, Charles 161
Burn, Alexander 160, 161,235
Andrew 207
Hannah 207
John 162,193
Samuel 207
Burnet, Daniel 163
John 163
Saml 114
Burnh, John 16
Burnham, Elizabeth 26
Elliot
Charles 26,70
Jonathan 26
Margaret 26
Mary, (Frost) 26
Nathaniel 26
Nicholas 26
Burns, Hugh 207
John 222
Leard 222
Martha 222
Mary 107
Peter 207

Burr, Thomas 221
Burrows, John 124
William 12,14,16,18,23, 32,35,62,69,81,89,96, 103,106,114,123,134,143, 146,190,193,208,210.220, 222
William Ward 103
Wm. W. 80
Bursell, Henry 167
Burton, Ann (Remington) 104
Benjamin 223
Elizabeth 141
Isaac 104
Joseph 95,102,203
Josiah 144
Thomas 141,150,164
William 143,144
Burzaglo, Elias 33
Busar, Jacob 117
Bush, Daniel 77
Isaac 189
John 105,137,189,220
Bushell, 180
Bussard, Rudolph 59
Busser, Frederich 239
Jacob 239
Ulrick 239
Bussey, Hezekiah 147
Thomas 134,135
Butler, Ann (Miles) 46
Elisha 39
Hugh 132
James Henry 50
John 237
Mary (Middleton) 221, 222
Mary Eliott 96
Peter 167
Pierce 109,199,221,222
Samuel 219
Sarah 185
Thomas 46,116,118,119, 150
Vallintine 202
William 46
Buttler, Thos 32
Buxton, Jacob 151
John 86
Samuel 86
Buzard, Rudolph 118
Buzbee, Henry 239
Mary 239
William 239
Buzbey, Nathan 114
Buzby, Henry 68
Buzzard, Rudolph 59
Byerley, Gasper 132
Byers, Robt. 31
William 30
Byrd, Saml 30

Caborn, Robert 131
Caddell, Alexander 126
Cade, William 156
Cadwer, Richard 60
Cahoon, David 141
  Ezekiel 88
Cain, Frances 67
  James 67,243
  Patrick 9
  Richard 97
  William 67
Caine, Daniel 11,143
Calcott, William 23,35,
  Willing 37
Calder, Archibald 54,127
Caldhun, James 39
Caldwell, Elizabeth 129
  James 146
  Jane 33,210
  Jean 33
  John 4,40,33,34,44,78,
    100,105,114,123,125,132,
    137,138,144,166,176,178,
    184,210,213,218
  Martha 33
  Moses 129
  Wm. 121
  Wm. Thos 114
Calhoon, James 39
  Hugh 123,175,212
  James 54,66
  Jannet 212
  John 88,126
  John Ewing 212
  Joseph 88,143
  Martha 212
  Patrick 9,67,88,110,114,
    126,143,147,174,175,189,
    212
  William 9,88,123,173,212
Calk, James 243
Callcote, James 156
Calmess, William 176
Calvert, John 5,133
  Wm. 151
Calwell, Henry 90
Cambel, John 217
Camber, Thomas 39,133
Cambridge, Tobias 7,109
Cameron, Alexander 15,42,
  51,72,89,92,126,163,189
  John 42,72,225
  Robert 235
Campbell, Alexander 45,147
  Anguish 242
  Anne 80
  Archibald 80
  Benjamin 148,207
  Danl 195
  Francis 74,172
  James 4,143
  Margaret (Wright) 93
  Martin 59,125

  William 135,237
Campble, James 46
Camron, Thomas 217
Canaday, Condice 67
  Silas 67
Cane, Bathsheba 174
  Frances 1
  James 1,141,174
  James Jr. 174
Canes, William 110
Cannon, Daniel 4,5,12,16,
  23,47,56,65,149,152,179,
  201,203
  Simcock 73
  William 95,225
  Daniel 201
Cant, Johannes 229
Cantey, Charles 12,21,31,
  61,81,153,170,175,199,
  210
  George 107,161
  James 161
  John 140,161
  Joseph 47,208,217
  Josiah 45,155
  William 161
  Zach 238,239
Cantz, Casper 12
Cantzon, John 5
Cape, Brian 140
  Bryan 62
Capers, Charles 38
  Elizabeth (Jenkins) 27
  Elizabeth 38
  Gabriel 220
  Mary 27,38
  Richard 26,27,38
  Thomas 26,27,38
  Wm 26
Capshaw, Essix 174
Cardie, Saml. 173
Cardy, Samuel 48,173,209
Carey, James 169
Cargill, John Jr. 176
  Thomas 79
Carion, Moses 180
Carlisle, Francis 117
Carmichael, James 116,150
Carmichel, John 37
Carne, Jane Elizabeth
  (Holmes) 80
  Samuel 69,81,115,157,
    172,193
Carnihan, Robert 217
Carpenter, Martha (Mann)
  213
Carr, A. W. 178
  Patrick 93
Carrel, Tarance 132
  Terrence 217
Carruth, James 88,212
Carsan, Archibald 129,203,
  214

  James 71,82
Carsen, Wm. 236
Carsey, John 194
Carson, Ann (Stuart) 186
  Archibald 179,216,243
  Charles 23
  James 124,186,232,238
  Jean 164
  William 23,104
Carss, William 95
Cart, John 20
Carter, George 238
  John 16
  Robert 118,234
  William 156,237
Carthey, Andrew 136
  William 136
Cary, James 18
  Jos. 147
  Mary 18
Casey, Abasel 102
  Abner 194
  James H. 72
  John 242
  Levi 194
  Moses 102
  Randolph 102
Caslick, Abm. 217
Cassell, Henry 153
Cassels, Benjn 76
  Henry 54,65,76,88,118,
    155,180,207
  Henry Jr. 65
Cassick, 25
Castillow, Mary 189
  Thomas 189
Castleman, 47
Caswell, Sarah 91
Cater, Rachel (Miles) 224
  Stephen 13, 103
  Thomas 224
Cates, Joseph 28,40,191
Caton, Thomas 26,73,171
Cattell, John 209,210
Cattell, William 110,111,
  177,209,235
Catterton, Ann 200
  Hannah 18,79,190
  John 75,79
  William 18,27,79,98,125,
    190,200,207
Cattle, John 209
Catton, Thos 115
Caudle, Hannah "Anna" 8
  Richard 8
Caulkings, Jonathan 114
Cavat, Susannah 14
  James 26,37
Caw, Rachl. 153
Cayson, James 131
Ceasetrunk, Henry 159
Chadwick, Thomas 195,234
Chaetabea, 93

Chalmers, George 236
  Lionel 51,53,199
Chamberlain, William 86
Chambers, Henry 71
  John 188,241
Chambliss, Peter 207
Champneys, John 13
Chandler, Isaac 99
  Wm. 226
Chanler, Isaac 158
Chapman, 99
  Giles 23,113
  Giles Jr. 23
  John 12
  Sarah 23,113
  William 20,21,84,91
Chappell, Henry 16
Chardin, Mary (Hutson) (Woodward) 162
Charles, Laurence 193
Charlotte, slave 234
Charlton, Thomas 118,119
Charnock, Thomas 52,63,69
Chateris, George 27,129,137
Cheney, John 116
  Martha 116
Cherry, John 146
Chery, George 84
Chesnut, John 82,119,137, 138,173,186,193,226
Chevenaughs, Edward 231
Cheves, Alexander 15
Chevilette, John 133,134
Chevillett, John 172
Chevillette, John 39,110
Chifelle, Phil. 215
  Philotheos 166
Chiffelle, Henry 113,134
  Phil. 29
  Philotheos 1,2
Childre, Thomas 215
Chiles, John
Chinners, Abraham 51,64
  Elizabeth 64
  John Sandiford 64
Chisholme, Wiliam 235
Chisolm, Alexr. 160,208
  John 98,141,151,163
Chittey, Benjamin 230
Chitty, Charles King 49
Chokters, Para 93
Chollet, A. 135,145
  Abraham 71,135,168,199
  Samuel 71,135,145,187, 199
Choples, James 226
Choupart, Daniel 152
Chovin, Alexr 91
  Charles 57,74,180
Chovine, Charles 231
Christie, Hepzibah (Rose) 7
  James 7
Churchill, Richard 60

Churne, Anthony 107
Clairman, John 74
Clandenin, Thos 189
Clark Alexr 175
  Ann 135
  Archibald 154,196,213
  Edward 120
  Elizabeth 172
  Henry 164,211
  James 15
  Jean 154
  John 91,151
  Jonah 164
  Malcom 16,86,159,181
  Robert 33
  Samuel 73,123,135
  Sarah 171
  Thomas 124,137,144,171, 173
  William 10,120,144,228
  widow 135
Clarke, Jonathan 237
  Jonathan Jr. 5
  Malcom 149,161,185,196, 214,220
  Samuel 15,181
  Thomas 107,238
  William 113
Clarks, 155
  William 201
Clary, Robert 170
Clatworthy, James 177,183
  Mary 183
Clayton, Isham 48,153,166
  John 130,153
Clehoin, William 154
Cleland, John 51,52,70,87, 160
  Mary 51,87
Clements, Benj. 118
  Edward 14
  Elizabeth 15
  Gabriel 60
Clemons, Robert 208
Clendinen, Thomas 189
Clifford, Dandridge 23,25, 29,30,226
  Martha 202,212
Clifton, Michl. 103
Clitherall, Elizabeth 188
  James 94,135,187,188,199
Clooker, John 39
  Sarah 39
Clowes, Chas. 158
Clyatt, Catharen 139
  Stephen 139
Coachman, Benjamin 168, 176, 224
  James 77,139,164,208,224
  John 49,112
  William 114,139
  William Poole 139
Coalman, Abner 36

Coates, Charles 118
Coats, William 36,125
Cobb, Samuel 86
Cobbs, Martha 39
Cobley, 53,86
Cochan, Robert 36
Cochran, 13
  Mary (Elliott) 26
  Cornelius 95
  Mary 26
  Robt 26,106
  Thomas 147,158,159
Cockeran, John B. 182
Cockerham, Bryan 149
  James 149
  Mary (Willson) 149
Cockfield, Barnaby 13
Cockran, Elizabeth 100
  William 149
Cocle, Catharine (Maclemar) 79
Coe, Edward 78
Cofer, Mary (Raven) 201
Coffey, William 54,66,163, 173
Cogdell, George 223,224
Cohen, Abraham 130,185, 226, 227
  Dina 51
  Isac Jr. 51
  Moses 51,52
  Robert 53
Cohune, Thos 34
Coil, Joseph 163
Coker, Bryan 115
  Thos. 22
Colcock, Charles 16
  Job 213
  John 16,32,40,89,102, 131,135,170,180,185,193, 197,204,210,221
  Willins 25
Cole, John 90,125,164
  William 112,180,181
Coleman, Christopher 77
  Jacob 43,237
  John 122,162,172
  Susannah 43
  William 74,76
Coles, Robert 127
Coleson, Daniel 83
Colhoun, J. Ewing 201
  John C. 124
  John E. 176
Colleton, Charles 100
  James 48,60
  John 48,60
  Peter 48
  Susanah 60
  Thomas 48,60
Collett, Richd. Jr. 175
  Thos 59
Colley, 197

Micajah 237
Collier, Robert 157,161
  Thomas 148
Collings, Robert 71
  Sarah (Johnston) 71
Collins, Absalom 14
  Ann 16
  Charles 80,171
  James 157,161
  John 243
  Jonah 24,36
  Jonas 24
  Joseph 16
  Mary 127
  William 16
Collis, Ann 90
  Elizabeth 90
  Thomas 216
Collson, William 83
Colman, Thomas 115,211
Colson, Abraham 17,215
Combes, William 59
Combest, John 217
Coming, John 48,50
Commander, Samuel 206
Committer, Lewis 2
  Ratchel (Kerch) 2
Compt, 115
Compton, Thomas 166,
  207,221
Conaway, Robt. 181
Conger, John 79
Conhary, Hugh 10
Conley, Charles 81
Conner, James 141
  Lewis 141
  Thomas 141
Connerly, Thomas 118
Conners, John 206
Connor, 226
  Thomas 112
Connors, John 180
Conroy, Hugh 10
Conyers, Daniel 234
  James 46,132,234
  John 180
Cook, 181
  Benjn. 137
  Come't 91
  Cornelius 100
  Edward 71
  George 26
  James 26,38,72,139,171,
    201,214,241,243
  John 29,45,136,147,184,
    204,215,216,228,232,233
  Sarah 72,201,214
  Thomas 184
  William 25,157
Cooke, Benjamin 142
  George 24,35,41
  John 117,138
  Jos. 147

Wilson 126
Cookson, William 131
Cooler, Margaret (Michael)
  232
Coombs, Wm. 59
Coon, Conrad 48
  John 221
  Peter 168
Coons, Pendrick 11
Cooper, 243
  Anthony 199
  Jacob 41
  John 117,160
  Jonathan 33
  Lucy 33
  Mary (Bee) 160
  Thomas 184,185,199
Coppick, Martha 105
Coram, Jno 177
  John 59,62,127,129,150,
    159,178,198,200,214,233
  John Jr. 237
Corbett, Margaret 26
  Richard 20,58,74,98,99,
    144,145,172
  Thomas 26,77,113,143
Corbin, Fran's 38
Cordes, Francis 38
  James 64
  John 53,64,146
  Samuel 64
Cordy, Saml 24
Corker, Thomas 39,70,172
Corly, George 130
Cormack, Alexander 28
Cornall, George 105
  Margaret 105
Corren, James 33
Correy, William 62
Corry, John 32
Corse, Timothy 15
Corslie, Pierce 116
Cossens, Edmund 28,30,40,
  182
  Edmund Godfrey 161,171
  Edward 144
  John 140
  Rachel 182
Cossings, George 46
Cosslett, Charles Mathew
  127
Cother, Bryant 115
Cotton, Thos 23
Couch, Capser 16
  James 129
Coulier, David 39
Coulter, Archibald 54
Councel, Betrix 6
  Hardy 6
  Henry 112
Council, Henry 141
Counsel, Hardy 129,177
Courage, Francis 57,74

Coursey, William 85,147
Courtonne, Ann 71
  James 25,71,105
Courturier, Isaac 21
Coutier, David 133
Coutrier, Philip 192
Couturier, Isaac 153
  Isaac Jr. 170
  Paul 127
  Peter 153
  Peter Jr. 153,170
Cowan, James 210
Cowar, Benja. 219
Coward, Benjamin 89,95
  Elizabeth 89,95
  James 89,95
  Joshua 89,95
  Willm. 202
Cowden, Wm. 221
Cowen, Jacob 232
  Wm 221
Cowper, Basil 82
  Mary 61
Cox, Elizabeth 86
  Ezekiel 127
  George 119
  John 35,86,142,168
  Joseph 162
  Thomas 11,100
Crabb, Robert 11,94,106
Craig, Alexander 120,121,
  142,143
  George 8
  James 9
  John 9
Crain, Elizabeth (Young)
  75
Crall, Ann 101
Crandon, James 169,179,
  214,243,244
Craney, Domk. 243
Cranick, Maryann 157
  Valentine 157
Crank, Jane 79
  William 79
Craswell, John 112,124
Crawford, 11
  Alexander 162,236
  Bellamy 75,78,185,197,
    207,222
  Daniel 29,53,64,215
  Edward 162
  James 210,236
  Jane 203
  John 68,86,87,103,151,
    173,185,195,237
  Robert 62,155,203
  Thomas 1,12,45,119,151,
    195
Cray, Joseph Scott 205
  James 103
  Moses 116
  Peter 116

Creech, Stephen 33
Creek, Peter 150
   Wm. 166
Creighton, Barbara 25
   Hugh 59
   Isaac 27
   John 6,25,187
   Thomas 146,202
   William 31,116,151,157
Creswell, Hector 125
Crieghton, John 2
Crim, George 18
   Peter 18,120
Crimps, John 23
Cripps, John Splatt 38,152
   Mary Abel Allen 161
   Mary Abel Allyne 216
   Robert 64,216
   William 1,178
Crips, John Splatt 211
Crockatt, James 159
   Robert 155,213
   Samuel 186
Crofft, Jon. 224
Croft, Childermas 27,223
   Edward 160
   Elizabeth 220
   George 125,150,178,180, 181,220
   Hill 54
   John 178
   Mary 220
   Peter 28,155,156
   Robert 27,28,38
Crofts, Edward 166
   John 204
Crokatt, Daniel 24,61
Croll, 20
   William 25
Crommer, Jacob 56
Cropp, Henry 220
Crosby, Timothy 41,131,161, 226,227
Croskeys, William 229
Croskry, William 183,184
Cross, John 141,154,161, 183,191
   Samuel 12,28,47,108,138, 197,207
   Sarah 183
   Susanna 138
Crossman, Bartholomew 72
Crosthwaite, William Ward 101
Crouse, Felix 68
Crowl, William 37
Cruise, Jesse 189
Cruser, Christopher 114
Crydon, Isaac 27
Cryer, Elizabeth 67
   Thomas 67
Cuetaws, Blue Salt King 93
Cuhun, George 25

Culliatt, James 186,187, 191,226,230
Culp, Barbara 229
   Casper 236
   Henry 8,188,229
   Peter 74
Cumming, Bejn. 123
Cummings, 77
Cummins, James 103
Cuningham, Jno. 67
   Robert 95
Cunningham, Andrew 31,87, 131,192
   David 136,173
   Jane 79
   John 118
   Patrick 74
   Robert 65,124,168,213
Cunnington, William 220
Currie, William 42,162,168, 218,221,228
Curry, Joseph 72,82,83,118, 159
   Josiah 82
   William 166,195,214
Curtis, John 153
   Joshua 228
   Moses 183
   Precillah (Wilson) 121
   Sarah 228
   Thomas 121
Cusack, Adam 17
Cuthbert, Dr. 46

DaCosta, Abraham 51
   Isaac 51,52,128,195
   Isaac Jr. 182
   Joseph 52
   Rebecca Mendes 166,176
Dabbs, Joseph 39
Dale, Oliver 44
Dallas, Dr. 94
Dalrymple, James 200
Dalton, 13
   Charles 46
   Darius 193
   Mary 193
Daly, John 108
   Peter 2
Damaris, Elizabeth (Moultrie) 104,111
Daniel, David 217
   Elias 147
   James 87,196
   Jesse 44,87,196
   John 88,233
   Robert 81,122,228
   Wm. 44
Danl, Isaac LeGrand 149
Danniley, 54,94
Dansby, Elizabeth 124
   Isom 239

   Jacob 124
Darby, Anna (Singletary) 140
   James 26,36
   Joseph 140
   Margaret (Elliott) 26
   Margaret 26,140
   Maria/Mary (Bonneau) 140
   Mary (Warnock) 140
   Michl. 71
Darbybe, Margaret 26
Dargan, Ann 98
   Jeremiah 132
   John 12,13,45,98
   Sarah 132
   Timothy 45,132,140
   William 115,132
Darling, Joseph 240
Darnall, John 72
Darquir, Moses 170
Darrell, Benjamin 242
   Edward 106,124,146,150, 176,181,182,212
Darrington, Jno. 87
Darson, Archd 179
Dart, 63
   Benjamin 153
   John 37,41,91,104,159, 197,198,242
   John S. 111
   John Sandfort 218
   John Sanford 104
   Sandford 117
Darvil, Elizabeth 240
Daseter, John 115
Dauboz, Henry 76
Daugherty, James 100
David, Daniel 223
   Daniel Abraham 39
   Jean 223
   Joshua 46
   Owen 203
   Susanne 223
Davidson, Alexander 70,144
   Alexander 70
   George 72,77,83,88,95, 103,106,108,110,124,138, 151,153,165,198,207
Davie, William 200
Davies, 217
   John 27,213
   William 10,90
Davis, Ann 99
   Chisby 60
   Christopher 70
   George 99,102
   James 73,149,154
   John 50,78,96,154
   Joseph 31
   Lightfoot Harrison 181
   Mark 20
   Martha 70

Robert 44
Thomas 58,231,232
William 79,99,103,126, 194
Davison, John 176
Davy, slave 234
Dawkins, George 7,8,18
George Jr. 218
Dawson, John 66,78,106,177
Nancy 244
Richard 29
Thomas 147
Day, Jesse 17
Nathaniel 61
Peter 116
William 174
De___, Benjamin 115
DeBeaufain, Hector Beringer 19
DeCosta, Sarah 52
DeFrance, George 190
DeGrey, William 179
DeLahowe, John 54, 214
DeLeighler, H. 89
DeMounge, Henry 205
DeSaussure, Daniel 12,86, 133,158
Lewis 158
Mary 133
Thomas 133
DeSurrency, Jacob 87
Deall, Wm. 147
Dean, Daniel 77
Thos 67
Dearington, John 103,215
Thomas 54,103,215
Deas, David 14,44,82,125, 159,174,198
Elizabeth 201
John 43,85,98,125,131, 201
Richard 127
Deason, Benjamin 215
Tereser 215
Debordieau, Joseph 54
Debous, Isaac 122
December, negro 110
Dedcott, 167
Deddurph, Stephen 37
Dee, Robert 109,158,180, 197
Deederys, Isaac 191
Defour, Francis 32,53,174
Deharriette, Benjamin 182
Delabere, John 78
Delahowe, Ann (Walker) 54
Ann 185
John 54,214,223
Delas, James 110
Delasaye, John 12
Delebare, Anne 12
John Kenard 12
Delegall, Phillip 202

Delesseline, John 107
Delgare, John 239
Deliesseline, Isaac 136,137
John 82
John Thompson 205
Deloach, Jesse 144,153
Michael 144,153
William 189
Deloatch, William 215
Denby, William 171
Dener, George 232
Denkins, Wm. 124
Denley, Margaret 58
William 58
Denman, James 182
Denneson, Robert 11
Dennis, Elizabeth 23
Hendrick 66
Henry 66
Mary 78
Samuel 78
Dennison, Isabella 11
Denny, John 36,37
Sarah 36,37
Derriman, John 19
Derumple, George 137,238
Desaussure, Daniel 46,163
Mary 86
Desel, Charles 136
Deston, Thomas 156
Desurney, Daniel 170
Saml. 170
Deveaux, Andrew 45,46,116
Jacob 17,45
William 17,45
Devo, Andrew 85
Devonald, Daniel 46,99
Dewees, Andrew 230
Cornelius 173
Philip 231
Sarah 173,174
Dewine, James 78
Dewitt, James 2
Sarah 2
William 30,138,164,170, 240
Dexter, Henry 131
John 5,69
Dezean, Frederick 110
DHarriette, Benjamin 89
Dick, Ann (Summers) 87
Ann 76,126,188
John 93,95,105,131
Mary (Allein) 112
Mary (Allen) 51
Robert 126,128,188,226, 227
Walter 153
Dicke, Edward 212
Dickert, Margarate 18,114
Margaret 11
Michael 7,8,11,18,20,56, 60,72,84,108,114,132,

147,148,176,218,220,228, 229
Dickey, Edward 123
Hector 102
Patrick 23
Dickinson, Adam 117
Benj. 60,176,177
John 117
William 41
Dicks, Robert 78
Thos 54
Dickson, David 27,132,142
John 62,102
Joseph 26
Margaret 62
Michael 62,196,217
Prudence 62
Robert 188
William 62,85
Didcotts, 19
Dies, John 228
Dightel, Hans George 60
Dildene, Harman 141
Dilgare, Jacob 239
John 239
Dill, John 197,224
Dillon, Patrick 62
Robert 123,125,224
Thos 22
Dingle, Benjamin 29
Joseph 29
John 226
Dinkens, Sarah 19
William 19
Dinkins, Asa 6
Sarah 14
William 6,14,241
Ditmore, John 17
Dixon, Christopher 160
Elizabeth 209
Thos 109
Dobbins, John 109
Joseph 192
Dobbs, Arthur 155
Gov. 68
Doby, John 213
Dodd, Margaret 210
Nathaniel 210
Dodge, Thos 157
Dodgen, Olley Man 40
Dodgeon, William 143,144
Doharty, James 202
Donaho, John 210
Donald, Peter 28,40
Donaldson, 220
Wm. 125
Donavan, Isaac 200
Dongworth, Henry 84, 102,135
Donnom, James 4,79, 101, 222
Donoho, James 107
Donom, Jas 19

Donovan, James 13,200
Donworth, Henry 73
Dooly, George 47
　John 7,11,34,47,53,65, 139
　Patrick 7
　Thomas 7,11,47
Dorchester, George 115,158
Dorman, Michael 22,145, 128
Dorrese, William 9
Dorrill, Eliza. 157
　Robt. 157
Dorris, William 51
Dorsius, John 158
Dorst, Peter 223
Dougherty, James 100
Doughty, Mary 47
Doughty, Thomas 47
　William 30,100,234
Douglas, George 10
　John 10
Douglass, James 202
　John 90,185,186,236,242
　Philip 15,45
　Thomas 165
Douxsaint, Paul 24,36,123
Dover, John 174
Dowland, John 39
Downes, Arthur 24,41
　Jonathan 147
　Walter 107
　William 30,97,99,143, 144,169,200,201,208,218, 242
Downs, Author 35
　Frances 14
　Henry 14,199
　Henry Jr. 14
　John 154
　Jonathan 95,105
　Sarah 105
　Walter 46,99
　William 209
Downworth, Henry 40
Doxsaint, Paul 101
Doyle, Garret 195
　John 217
　Patrick 195
Doyley, Daniel 90,155
Dozer, James 97
Drake, Edward 150,157,229
　Jonathan 16
　Mathew 157,161
　Saml 53
Drakeford, John 182,215
Drayton, 20,191
　Ann 213
　Charles 220,227,232
　Elizabeth (Waring) 30,31
　Elizabeth 213
　Glen 222
　John 209,213,224,234,235

John Jr. 139
Rebecca 234
Stephen 30,31,80,213
Thomas 17,41,80,213
William 139,161,209,213
William Henry 176,189
Wm. H. 227
Dreher, Godfrey 119
Drehr, Gottfird 119
Drenen, William 79
Drennan, John 90
　David 9
Dry, William 74,220,227,235
DuPont, Henry Lewis 158
Duball, John 78
Dubar, 183
Dubber, John Frederick 72
Dubois, Samuel 21,153,170, 221
　Susannah 153,170
Dubordieau, Josiah 24
Dubordieu, Joseph 70
Duborow, Susanna 102
Dubose, David 127
　Isaac 127
　Jemima 180
　Js. 27
Dubourdieu, Joseph 5,36,63, 218
　Mary 218
Duck, negro 110
Duckett, Joseph 194
　Josias 194
　Mary 72
　Thomas 72
Dudley, Charles 106
Dueits, Charles 191
Duesto, Moses 218
Dufour, Francis 33
Dufourth, Francis 28
Duhum, George 8
Dukes, Barbary 90
　Benjamin 225
　Joseph 90
　Michael 90
Dun, William 41
Dunavan, Cornelius 33
Dunavant, Cornelius 34
Dunbarr, Thomas 183
Duncan, David 183
　George 3,31,106,108,197
Dunkin, Nelson 73
Dunklin, 137,238
Dunkly, John 228
Dunlap, David 100
　George 10,99,100
　Gilbert 99
　John 95
　Robert 10,79
　Samuel 79,100
Dunlop, James 78
Dunn, Drury 12
Dunnam, Eben Jr. 198

Ebenezer 162,198
Jacob 198
John 198
Dunnoha, James 161
Dunrumple, George 95
Dupius, William 86
Dupoin, Cornelius 238
Dupoint, Abraham 36
Dupont, 138
　Abraham 38,164
　Cornelius 193
　Gideon 38,75,164
Dupre, Cornelius 38
　Jane 38
Dupree, Josiah Garnia 155
Dupuis, James 113
Dupuy, Jean 191
Duran, Susannah (Hext) 156
Durand, Levi 88,156,224
　Love 25
　Susannah (Hext) 155
Durant, Benjamin 147
　Hannah 76
　John 31,76
　Levi 224
　Susannah 156
　Thomas 202
Durborow, Benjamin 39, 102,126,
Duren, John 95
Durin, John 89
Durst, John 139
Dutarque, John 53,57,71,74, 131
　Lewis 185
Duvall, Lewis 75
　Michell 89
　Stephen 91
Dwight, Nathaniel 28,100
　Saml 50,66,94,164,166, 204,225
Dye, Thomas 154
Dyer, Elizabeth 94
　James 91,94,100,101

Eagner, George Jr. 19
　Jacob 153
　Mary 153
Eakins, David 148
　Margaret (Boden) 148
Earisman, 187
Earnest, Antony 68
Easley, Archibald 231
Easom, John 67,214
Eason, Isaiah 10
Eastland, Thomas 74
Easton, Caleb 1,50,198
　Mary (Brown) 50,198
Ebberson, William 29
Eberhard, Philip 229
Eberly, John 165,191
Edday, William 90

Eddings, Benjamin 116
　Elizabeth 116
Eden, James Gottier 157
Edes, Sarah 209
Edghill, Richd. 186
　Sarah 186
　Thomas 186
Edings, Benjamin 45
　Mary 45
Edmondeston, Moses 163
Edmonds, James 165,224
　Sarah 165
Edmonson, Jacob 153
Edmonston, William 189
Edwards, Abel 203
　Ann 30
　Benjamin 116
　David 218,228,229
　Dorothy (Basset) 49
　Jane 228,229
　John 7,49,58,60,110,120, 203
　Joshua 46,138,228
　Mary 58,210
　Mathew 92
　Mathey 21
　Robt 167
　Sarah 73
　Simon 30,97
　Thomas 41,124
　Uriah 73
　William 31,83,97,99,242
　William Newitt 30
Egan, Dennis 76,122,123, 151,152,194
　Edmund 125,173,234
　Eleoner 54
　John 4,11,47,54,65,76, 122,123,152,206,231,232
　John Jr. 123,194
　Thomas 123,194
Egger, Ulrick 222
　William 222
Eggerton, James 206
Egils, Mathew 157
Ehney, Frederick 16
Ehrhard, Abraham 143
Eiland, Abner 150
　Absalom 150
　George 150
Elders, John 58,171
　Thomas 171
Eleber, Jacob 13
Eler, Jacob 13
Elfe, Rachel 193
　Thomas 19,65,149,193
　William 149
Elkins, John 73
Elks, James 22,152,158
Eller, John 222
Ellerbe, Edward 57,148
　George 57
　John 57,148
　Sarah 57
　Thomas 57
Ellery, Thomas 48,54,60,185
Elliot/t, 31,106,146
　Amerinthea 156
　Ann/Anne 36,121,169
　Archibald 8
　Barnard 4,30,31,40,12, 135,153,156,171,177,219, 220
　Barnard Jr. 156
　Benjamin 17,23,35,99, 169,170,171,219,220
　Bernard 13,179,237
　Beulah 7
　Catharine 156
　Charles 17,19,109,125, 164,167,169,171,177,206, 241
　Daniel 8
　Elizabeth (Bellinger) 116
　Elizabeth 8,31,234
　Henrietta 26
　John 31
　Joseph 100
　Margaret (Darby) 26
　Margret 36
　Mary (Cochran) 26
　Mary 26,36
　Samuel 23,26,167,219
　Sarah 106,137,171,219, 222,238
　Susannah 220
　Thomas 3,7,24,28,42,82, 99,121,135,137,219,220, 222,225,237,238,239
　William 109,137,153,214, 215,238,239,240
Ellis, 218
　Daniel 7,8,160,178,229
　Edmund 11,22
　John 239
　Mary 49,165,191
　Sarah (Raiford) 228,229
　Solomernier (Aberlain) 160
　Stephen 70
　Thomas 36,48
Ellison, Robt. 8
Elmes, Joseph 244
Elmore, Mathias 78
　Sarah 95
　Stephen 78,95,105
　William 78
Elms, Ralph 24
Elvis, John 112
　Mary 112
Embree, John 95,105
　Moses 4
Emery, David 143
Emmerck, Andrew 122
Emmerks, Andrew 18
England, 121
English, John 197
Engster, Conrade 222
Enlling, Richard 59
Ernst, Jacob 32,242
　Johannes 244
Ervin, James 217
　John 54,217
　John Jr. 217
　Robert 217
Ervine, Robert 204
Esler, Samuel 124
Estridge, Richd 207
Eughstes, Thomas 11
Eustace, Susannah 165
　Thomas 33,34,165,234
Evance, Margaret 119
　Thomas 24,27,36,56,119, 177,187
Evans, 127
　Abel 15
　Catharine (Hollings-worth) 15,16
　Charles 1,153
　David 15,16,46,99
　Elias 104,111,165
　Evan 193
　George 137
　Hugh 61,89
　Jabez 172
　John 16,190
　Jonathan 239
　Philip 45
　Rowd. 11
　Samuel 239
　Thomas 15,45,71,122
　William 6,56,67,129,177, 214
Eveleigh, Thomas 7,100,109, 136,234,235
Everell, Benjamin 83
Everet/t, Jane 10
　John 182,232,233,236
　John Albright 10
Everin, Barbary 1
Everitt, John 228
Everson, William 41
Ewing, John 122,162,168, 218,229
Eycott, Ann (Wooley) 59
　Elizabeth 59
　John 59
　Richard 59
Eyering, John Adam 83
Eyrick, George 184

Fabian, John Jr. 36
　Joseph 48,56
Fabre, John 241
Fagans, Martha 4
　Phillip 4
Fagen, Patrick 132
Fairchild, Abraham 173
　Isabell 173

John 83,85,125,131,144,
  163,164,171,173,225
John Thos 173
Thomas 89
Falconer, T. 90
Fallerton, Robert 54
Fallows, James 33,42,43,198
Fanin, James 205
Fannin, Jacob 46
  James 46,79,148
  John 46,79
Fanning, James 79,174
  John 79
Faperet, Nancy 69
Farar, 111
  Benjamin 2,15,58,70,136,
    171,182,184,185,189,193,
    204,208,209,225,228,232,
    233,241
  Elizabeth 171,184,185,
    189,193,204,225
Fardo, G. 68
  G. F. 49,50
  G. J. 156,157,172
  George John 73,74,98,99,
    126,146,225
  J. 98
Faree, John 90
Farer, Field 77
Farewell, Henry 170
  Mary 170
Farie, William 61
Farington, Jacob 230
Faris, Denham 167
Farmer, David 166,195
Farnum, John 153
Farquahr, George 119
Farquharson, John 187
Farr, John 42
Farr, 97
  Thomas 40,41,91,122,160,
    199
  Thoms. Jr. 136,176,177
  William 237
Farrar, 126,238
  Benjamin 32,121,137
Farrasteau, Anthony 241
Farrel/l, Jane 146
  Thomas 146
Farrs, Thos 42
Faure, Peter 62
Faust, Casper 48,64,160
  Gaspar 160
  John 226
Faver, Elizabeth 54
  John 40
  Theophilus 54
Favewell, 74
Favier, John 40
Fayssoux, Peter 65,158
Feagin, Edward 218
Feares, Denham 202
  Mary 202

Fearis, Denham 40,59,97,98,
  202
Fechtner, Deodoris 36
Federolph, Nicholas 66
Fee, Hugh 11,65,118
  Margaret 11,53,65
  Sarah 11,53,118
Feemster, John 237
Felder, Henry 2,65,157
Felkland, Henry 159
Fell, Thos 130,138
Femster, Joseph 10
  Samuel 10
Fender, Mathias 130,195
Fenwick/e, Edward 24,37,
  139,209
  John 81,89,177,206,212,
    224,235
  Robert 8
  Sarah 8
  Thomas 139
Ferguson, 28,210
  Benjamin 18
  Charles 18
  Daniel 5
  David 4,101,232,236
  George 73
  James 3,90,206
  John 54
  John Horry 18
  Margaret (Stead) 73
  Martha (Ryley) 17,18
  Sarah 122
  Thomas 17,18,125,164,
    167,182
  William Cattle 18
Ferney, Thomas 127
Ferrell, Ann 6
  James 163
  Margaret 163
  Mary 163
Ferris, Abraham 108
Ferry, Champneys 123
Feulon, Chs. 160
Fewtrell, John 68,74,98,99,
  127
Fibben, Elizabeth 50
Fickling, George 121
  George Jr. 122
  Samuel 103
Fidling, Elizabeth 223
  John 223
Field, John 11
  Scots Old 153
Fields, John 67,101,102
  Sarah 101,102
Fifer, John 85
Fincher, Aaron 195,214
  Aron 166
  Francis 198
  Jesse 198,214
Finder, John 224
Findley, Robert 164

Fining, Abraham 228
  Margaret 228
Finks, 152
Finlay, Kath, 240
  Robert 141
Finley, Ann 207
  James 203
  Katharine 141
  Katharine Jr. 141
  Robert 141
  Samuel 84,85
  William 207
Fish, Joseph 118
Fishburn, William 22
Fisher, Brian 178
  Brice 177,214
  Ebenezer 8
  Edwards 115
  James 8
  John 2,3,32,61,77,88,
    105,119,132,133,138,142,
    179
  Micam 84
  William 104
Fitch, Beulah 7
  Jonathan 17
  Tobias 224,235
Fitchlin, Isaac 61
Fitsimmons, Christopher
  144
Fittig, Nicholas 33,106,175
Fitzgerald, Alexander 127
Fitzpatrick, Eleanor 223
  William 17,37,53,223,239
Fitzsimons, Christopher 7,
  65,22,221
  James 104,215
Flacks, James 161
Flagg, George 41,75,131,
  210,223,226,234
Flannegan, Reuben 225
Flavil, John 49
  Rebecca 49
Fleming, James 131
  Martha 96
  Patrick 37,59
  William 63
Fletchall, John 183
  Thomas 146,183
Fletcher, George 72
  James 228
  Thomas 136
  William 72,135,183
Fley, Frances 22
Flin/n, Edward 39
  John 180
Flint, Hannah 47
Florin, Lucas 191
Flower, 86, 197
Floyd, Alleys 132
  William 132
Flud, James 81

258

John 67
William 81,82,114,184,204
Fogartie, James 140,196
  Lewis 140
  Mary 106
  Mary Jr. 150
  Stephen 140
Foissin, Elias 201
  Elisa 38
  Pet'r 204
  ___ (Beresford) 201
Folk, Conrad 19
Follingsby, William 227
Fondren, John 174,236
Foost, William 69
Forbes, Ar. 49
  George 49,148,154
  Hannah 154
  John 135,190,208,224
Ford, 38
  Frederick 83
  George Jr. 192
  James 102
  John 30,75,86
  Sarah (Singleton) 192
  Sarah 36
  Thomas 17,30
  Tobas 215
Forest, George 34,168
Forester, Stephens 93
Forgartice, James 38
Forrester, Alexr 191,197, 205,231
  John Rowand 125
Forster, Alex M. 4,181,222
  Alexius Mador 37,213,236
  Henry 26
Forsyth, John 43
Forteath, John 47,179,138
Fortune, George 112,201
  John 94
Foskey, Bryan 197
Fost, William 68
Foster, Andrew 203
  Ann 10
  Artur 150
  Henry 10,18,37,114,154
  Isabella Hellena 203
  John 73,118,181
  Sarah 68,148,163
Fotheringham, 207
Foullarts, Phillip 223
Fouquet, John 172,210
Foust, Casper 137
  Gasper 160
  Peter 184
Fowler, James 144
  Nathan 97
  Oliver 213
Fox, John 63,119
  Joseph 104,139
  William 40,174,175
Francis, James 83,84

Vincent 132
Frank, Ann 39
  Ephraim 141
  John 164
Frankland, Admiral 66,180, 208,210
  Thomas 208,210
Franklin, Edmund 127
Franks, Nathan 145
Franks, widow, 22
Fraser, Alexander 35,96,161
  Don'd 78
  Jas. 167
  Mary 96
  William 205,209,220
Fraweek, George 211
  Leditha 211
Frazer, James 88
  John 239
  Robert 14
  William 239
Frazier, Alexander 23
Frederick, Andres 67
  Andrew 67,150
  John 164
Free Matt, negro 186
Freeman, Ann 210
  James 54,210
  John 88,101
  Joseph 39,53,136
  Wm. 183
Freemon, Joseph 11
Freer, John 28,35
  Solomon 100
  Susannah 28
  Thomas 222
Freman, Joseph 65
Fremouth, Hannah 126
  John 126
French, Alexander 25
  James 88
Frentz, John 97,98
  Margaret 97,98
Frewin, William 66
Freymouth, Hannah (Hopkins) 175
  John 126,175
Friday, David 193
  Jacob 37,105,193
  John 66
  Martain 37
Fridig, David 68,122
  Jacob 37,68,122
  John 122
  John Jacob 122
  Martin 122,162
Frier, Elizabeth 47
Frierson, Ann 223
  James 140
  John 127,153,170,181, 184,210,218,223,232
  Joshua 153
  Philip 184

Frink, 158
  Jabesh 141
  John 141
  Martha 141
  Nathan 141
  Nicholas 141
  Thomas 141
Fripp, William 232
Frisel, Gail 215
Frizell, Gail 215
Frizer, Joseph 197
Frost, Mary 209
  Mary, (Burnham) 26
Fry, John 103,108
  Mary 103
Frydig, Barbara 37
Fryer, George 18
  Martin 189
  Mary 189
Fulcher, Melchior 39
Fulk, Henry 83,119
Fulkard, Henry 159
Fulker, John 26
Fuller, 191
  Benjamin 61,209
  Catharine 181
  Katherine 182
  Lydia 182
  Nathaniel 80,181,235
  Thomas 122,160,181,182, 209,213
  William 12,41,61,181,234
Fullerton, John 10,164,182, 224
Fulmore, Jacob 162
Fulton, David 141
  John 78
  Thomas 188
  William 188
Furman, James 241
  Wood 6,14,22,42,45,87, 90,115,116,119,121,140
Furnace, William 46
Furney, William 46
Furquand, Paul 187
Fust, Casper 159
Futhy, Francis 113
  James 185
Fyfe, John 136,216
  Sarah 136
Fyffe, 51
  Ann (Summers)
  (Morrit) 188
  Ann/e 76,188
  Charles 160
  William 52,76,188

Gabel, Jno Michael 62
Gabell, Michael 62
Gaborial, John 131
Gadsden, Christopher 1,32, 51,123,161,167,201,211, 227

Gafkan, Henry Christoph 229
Gaillard, 107,120
  Alimus 120
  Ann 42,96,121,138
  Bartholomew 120,149,176, 177
  Charles 51,231
  David 101,127
  Frederick, 120
  Isaac 121,136,183,205, 210
  John 51,64,70,149,180, 231,232,237,
  Mary Easter (Kinlock) 231,232
  Mary Easter 122,180
  Sam 51
  Tacitus 11,21,40,42,96, 97,120,121,136,138,149, 183,207,209,210,243
  Theodore 11,51,71,120, 149,154
  Theodore Jr. 101,204
Galaven, James 112
Gallizer, Casper 13
Gallman, Henry 126,176,184
  Herman 136
  John 184
Galmon, Henrich 184
Galphin, George 167
Gambell, John 229
Gamble, Archibald 41
  Hugh 47
  James 131
  Robert 131
  William 131,151
Gambra, Michael 152
Gambrell, John 86
Gampert, Michael 153
Gandy, Robert 102
Gant, Israel 147
Gantter, George 109
Garden, 123
  Alexander 29,30,49,50, 89,208,210
  Amelia 222
  Ann (Stiles) 30
  Benjamin 29,208,210,222
  Moses 65
Gardner, Alice 98
  Edward 98,197
  George 24,174
  Jacob 174
  Lewis 203
  William 233
Garner, Melcher 89,156
  William 2,3,233
Garnett, Joseph 134
Garret, Edward 75
Garrett, Benjamin 23
Gartman, Bar'h 108
  Daniel 108

Garven, Ann 73
Garvin, John 185
Gaskins, Amos 97
Gasman, Henry 134
Gaston, Alexander 148
  John 54,73,83,84,93,94, 148,154,172,217,229
  Joseph 8,172
  Robt. 84
  William 148
Gates, George 115
Gauling, John 241
Gault, Robert 17
Gaulter, John 40
Gaultier, Joseph 202,231
Gaunt, Israel 7,59
Gause, Benjamin 112,201
  Charles 142
Gauthier, John Baptiste 134
  Theodore 134
Gautier, Anthoine/Anthony 3
  David 197
  Jane 3
  Mary (Peter) 197
Gaw, John 89,92,105
Gay, Hillery 110
  Theodore 231
Gayle, Josiah 13,231
  Harman 160
  Herman 137,228
  Hermon 219,220
  Hermond 148
  Jacob 66,193,220
  John 37,48,126,176
  John Conrade 228
  John George 51
  Margaret 219,220
  Mary 37
  William 220
Gender, David 192
Gendrat, Henry 18
Gendron, James 11
Gentry, Sarah 33
George, 93
  David 44
  Negroe 15
Gerdes, Henry 198
Gernett, Joseph 134
Geroud, David 39,128
Geroux, David 39
Gerral, Thomas 84
Gerrill, Gabl 171
Gervais, 54,66
  John Lewis 9,32,54,62, 66,102,103,136,191
Gibb, Robert 52,157
Gibbens, Peter 7
Gibbes, 2
  Benjamin 115
  Culcheth 64
  Henry 38
  John 162,241

Robert 28,125,212
William 119,123,139,163, 192,208
Gibbons, John 90
  William 90,227
Gibbs, John 212
  John Walters 200
  Robert 100,124
  Zachariah 129
Gibbson, Thos 161,168
Gibert, Lewis 40
  Peter 40
Gibes, Zach'h 174
Gibson, Daniel 25
  Elias 163,173
  George 85,189
  Gid. Jr. 156
  Gideon 5,53,156
  Gilbert 18,87,131,216
  Jacob 220
  Jeduthan 118,202
  John 5,13,18,38,206,207
  John Jr. 13
  Margarey 9
  Mary 215
  Patrick 9,173
  Roger 160
  Samuel 51,163,173
  Thomas 215,243
  William 63,173,182,198
Gickie, Wm. 169
Giger, Harmon 160
Gignillett, John Francis 122
Gignilliat, Benjn 21
  Francis 123,194
  Gabriel 21
  John 223
Gilbank, John 154,237
Gilbert, Ann 165,175
  David 6,19
  John 153
  Jonathan 60,229
  Julian 165,175
Gilchrist, James 85
Gilder, Gilbert 68,225
  Jacob 230
  John 4,68,230
  Reuben 196
Giles, Abraham 69
  Edward 189
  Hugh 155,162,222
  Jean 186
  John 6,25,127,186,187
  Newell 173
  Othn'l 127
  Sarah 162
  Thomas 181
Gilkey, Samuel 117
Gill, G. 154
Gill, James 59,87,184
Gill, John 58,59
Gill, Robert 52,155

Gill, Thos 155
Gillan, Francis 217
Gillard, James 123
  John 77
Gillaspy, Mathew 90
Gillbank, John 103,237
Gillespie, Francis 148
  James 69,215
Gilliam, Miles 196
  Robert 4
  Wm. 117
Gillison, Archibald 23
  Derry 190
Gillon, Alexander 1,18,21,
  26,38,50,123,136,152,
  167,201,211,222,227,235
  Mary 136,152
Gillum, Hannah 4
  William 4
Gilmer, John 72
Gimkey, Frederick 145
Gindras, Henry 134
Gindrat/t, Henry 185,192,
  199,206,219,242
Ginn, Scarborough 8
Girardeau, Isaac 117
  Jno. B. 233
Girards, Peter 223
Giroud, David 3,27,39,43,
  86,114,133,134,135,153,
  158,206,207,208,224
Gist, Sarah 214
  W. 53
  William 35,214
Gitsinger, Adam Frederick
  46
  George 198
Givens, Saml 117
  Wm. 10
Givins, Morris 37
Glasco, Robert 82
Glascock, Thomas 165
  William 165
Glaser, Nicolas 223
Glaze, John 56,66,168,175,
  176
Glazer, Frederick 75
  Jacob Frederick 75
  Mary 75
Glazier, Fredrick 37
Glebe, 13
Glegg, John 130,181
Glegney, Mary 8
  Samuel 8
Glen, John 60,96
  Margaret 159
  Martha 36
  William 3,31,159,209,242
  William Jr. 31,235
Glenn, Gov. 1
  William 197
Gless, Noah 82
Glover, Charles 97

Joseph 23,182,236
Robert 229
Widow 47
William 153
Goddard, Francis 120,155,
  163,164
Godfrey, Anthony 197,200
  Benjn 150
  Jane 83,197
  John 24,148
  Rebecca 197
  Richard 197
  Thomas 120,131
  William 85,86,128,134,
    149,197,200,206,207
Godin, Isaac 125,161
Goff, John 216
Goggins, William Jr. 186
Goin, Ann 73
Golden, John 241
  Thomas 100
  Thos. Knox 100
Goldie, John 119
Golding, Mathew 127
  Richard 210
  Thomas 192
Gole, John 31
Golfen, Dennis 7
Golightly, Culch. 29
Golsan, John 159
  Lewis 130,159,211
  John 130,150
  Lewis 2,130,150
Good, Hugh Mack 34
  Mackernnas 34
Goodbe/e, John 17,135
Goode, Mackerness 58
  Philip 11,47,53,65,117,
    147
  Thomas 179
Goodin, Robert 35
Goodine, Jesse 232
Goodman, Samuel 184,219
Goodwin, Abel 144,153
  Francis 132,136
  Jesse 236
  John 162
  Robert 19,136
  William 191
Goodwyn, Francis 240
  Jesse 114,182,232
  Martha 228,233
  Robert 128,130,131,171,
    172,228,232,233
  Uriah 240
  William 216
Goolsby, James 75
Gorden, Alexander 57
  Dd. 8
  James 91
Gordfrey, Thomas 68
Gordin, Lewis 11
Gordon, 68

Addam 147
Alexr 148
David 102
Elizabeth 146,148
Govin 146
James 70,113,120,155
John 61,118,132,146,223
Mary 148
Moses 54
Robert 10,148
Roger 110
Saml. 161
Thomas 61,146,198,217
Thomas Knox 22,50,107,
  111,157,172
William 76,88,146
Gorman, Henry 78
Gosling, Robert 135
Gossling, George 161
Gossman, John 202
  Mary 202
Goteare, Theodore 134
Gotier, Anthony/Antoine 3
  David 197
  Jane 3
Gotiere, David 3
Gotins, 78
Gotteer, Francis 155
  Isabella 155
Gottier, Francis 63
  Isabella (Blair) 63
Goudey, Robert 54,114,143,
  183
Gough, John 121,159,172,
  187
  Margaret 159
  Richard 52,153
Gould, William 20,58
Goulden, Thomas 100
Goun, George Adam 11
Gourdin, Isaac 70
  Lewis 11,149,154
  Marian 149
  Mariane 154
  Mary Ann/Maryann 11,
    154
  Peter 70,102,149,154
  Theodore 70,184
  William 51,149
Gourley, John 63
  Joseph 38,39,53,60,72,
    141,142
Gourly, Joseph 115,156,201
Goutier, Anthony 113
Gowdey, Robert 40
Gowdy, Robert 115
Grace, William 32
Graham, Arthur 155
  David 201
  John 56
  William 69,81,221,223,
    237
Grainger, Henry 60

Grame, David 110,166,188, 205
Gramlick, Adam 64
Grancer, John 158
Granlish, Thos 28
Granville, John Earle 214
Graves, James 197
  John 13
  Massey 197
  Thomas 197
  William 13,222
Gray, Ann 110
  Arthur 147,212
  George 72,77,83
  Isaac 95,135
  Jacob 34,44,110
  John 105
  Joshua 63
  Robert 104,129,169,170, 177,214,215
  William 147,186
Grayson, John 12
Greaves, William 139,183, 207
Green, Ann 5,241
  Comfort 208
  Daniel 25
  Dickerson 141
  Edward 241
  Jno. H. 181
  John 20,208,210,224
  Moses 208
  Richd Jr. 113
  Robert 208
  Susannah 152
  Thomas 78,144
  William 18,78,113,120, 135,156
Greene, Daniel 89
  Daniel John 197
  John 112
Greenland, George 235
Greenwick, slave 205
Greenwood, James 138,190
  William 86,90,200,224, 241
Greer, Joseph 23,116
Gregg, Edward 239
  John 25,52,188
Gregory, Jonathan 173
  Richard 173,191
Greneire, Peter Francis 167
Grenier, John 19
Greniere, John Francis 134
Grice, Robert 158
Grier, George 154,196
Grierson, George 213
  Katharine 213
Griffen, William 140
Griffeth, Matthew 46
  Joseph 61
Griffin, Anthony 44
  Richard 185

William 199
Griffith/s, Ann 1
  David 22
  Elizabeth 1
  Elizha 14
  Goodman 62
  James 1,87
  James Jr 1
  Mary 1
  Michael 1
  Samuel 1
  Thomas 113
  William 1
Grimball, Charles 235
  Elizabeth 57,74
  J. 26
  John 35,57,74,128,180, 191,206,219
  John Jr. 116
  Joseph 219
  Mary (Magdalen) 188
  T. 177
  Thomas 1,26,106,159
  Thomas Jr. 10,38,56,120, 146,172,177,188,202,210
Grimes, William 57
Grimke, Frederick 82
  John Paul 152
Grimkey, Frederick 95,111, 224
Grimkie, John Paul 187,225
  Mary 187
Grindlay, James 28,101,106, 194
Grisel, Gale 215
Grissendaner, Henry 3
Grobbs, Anthony 94
Gromer, Michael 120
Gromleish, Adam 150
Groob, Anthony 101
Grosman, Lewis 73
Grove, Samuel 186
Gruber, Charles 43,209
  Christian 30,92,97,98, 202
  Christian Gottlieb 161
  Samuel 105
Grumes, John 18
Grunsweig, Fredk. 208,210
Guerand, Anne 230
  Godin 230
  Joseph 230
  Sarah 182
  Benjamin 24,35,41,182, 221
  Godin 222,230
  Isaac 230
  Jacob 230
  John 35,96,230
  Joseph 230,241
  Mariane 230
  Sarah (Middleton) 221
Guerin, Francis 206

  Isaac 140
  Martha 140
  Mary (Elliott) 156
  Matheruin 186
  Mathurin 49
  Vincent 140
  William 125
Guerry, James 11
Guery, John 23
Guignard, 60
  John 116
  John Gabriel 27,135,221, 231,241
Guigneard, John Gabriel 38
Guilleaudeau, Jacob 223
Guilles, John 180
Guines, Archibald 233
Guiness, John 181
Guinn, John 197
Gullan, Thomas 82
Gunn, Henry 110
Gunter, John 108
Gurria, Jane 151
Guthrie, Robert 174
Gutt, Adam 32
  Elizabeth 32
Guttrey, John 61
Gutzman, John 91
  Mary 91
Guy/s, Rebeca 96
  William 82,96
Gwin, John 221

Hack, John 244
  Wm. 110
Hagans, Mary 90
  William 90
  Thos 202
Haggart, William 172
  Elizabeth (Marshall) 172
Haggett, William 115,157
Haggins, Mary 90
  William 90
Hagleman, Emanuel 31
Hagott, Elizabeth (Walter) (Marshall) 115
  William 115
Hahnbaum, George 8
Haig, 36
  George 115,126,128,153, 172,176,184,193
  James 238
  John James 119,195,230
  Susanna 193
Haigh, George 59
Hails, George 194,214
  Robert 71,102,194,204
  Thomas 194
Haines, Nicholas 58
Hainsworth, Henry 208
Hair, Elizabeth 18
Hairlock, James 211
  Sarah 211

Hairston, John 21
  Thos 21
Hak, John 244
Hale, John 45
  William 27,99,160,166
Haley, James 108,138
  Mary 191
Hall, Andrew 24
  David 61
  George Abbott 242
  George Archibald 36
  Henry 35
  John 8,54,75,94,125,129,
    199,227
  Mathew 144
  Nathaniel 231
  Richard 137
  Susannah 159,160
  Thomas Jr. 159,161
  William 15,25,73,159
Hallion, Elias 91
Halls, Richard 238
Halman, Conrad 48
Ham, Jacob 197
  Thomas 231
Hamelton, James 4
Hamer, John 124,125
Hameston, 145
Hamett, Charlotte 223
  Thomas 223
Hamilton, 226
  Alexander 71,205
  Ann 114
  Archibald 186
  David 73,205
  James 2,3,10,79,101,110,
    155
  John 9,10,24,33,77,115,
    130,139,144,145,175,176,
    182,183,194,195,225,228,
    232,233,236
  John Jr. 10
  Mary 101, 155
  Paul 90,91
  Robert 187
  Thomas 103
  William 44,144
Hamlin, Mary 56
  Samuel 56
Hammerton, James 74
  John 75,204
Hammond, John 74
  LeRoy 4,39,47,74,116,
    117,165,166,175,202,207
Hamond, Henry 172
Hampton, Edwd. 106
Hancock, Deborah 95
  Elias 95
  Elias Jr. 95
  George 219
  George Jr. 219
  Henry 141
  Joseph 127

Mary 95
Robert 95
Sarah 141
William 95
Handall, Jacob 158
Handlen, Thomas 63
Handlin, Thomas 152
Handyside, Mary (Hyde) 58
Hanersin, Barbara 33
  George 33
Hanhbaum, George 152
Hanisance, Jacob 130,172
Hankins, Dennis 22,112,141
  Masters 112
Hankinson, Robert 189
Hanna/h, James 63
  Robert 95,135,187
  William 124
Hanshaw, Joshua 109
Harbert, Thomas 18,219,228
Harbirt, Thos 18
Harbit, Thomas 7
Hardick, William 91,233
Harding, William 93
Hardridge, James 200
Hardstone, Joachim 134
Hardy, Mary 104
Hare, Edward 187,225
Harington, Henry William
  125
  William Henry 107
Haris, Moses 202
Harison, Charles 125
  Joseph 66
  Robt. 225
Hariss, Wm. 147
Harkey, Peter 134
  James 102
Harkness, George 126
Harleston, Edward 113,143,
  196,197,208,210
  Elizabeth 26,113
  Isaac 113,143
  John 21,26,35,48,113,
    143,196,208,210,224
  Nicholas 35,113,143,196
  William 113,143
Harley, Ann 224,235
  James 224,235
  George 150
Harlin, Ezekiel 201
Harp, David 225
Harper, Elinor 17
  James 84,228
  Rachel 228
  Solomon 17
  Thomas 69,81,237
Harrell, Martha 119
  Zachariah 119
Harrington, Henry William
  68,69,122,219
  Thomas 101
Harris, 167

Barton 202
Charles 88,159,165
Elizabeth 202
George 190
Is. M. 149
J. M. 140,166,195
James 178,202
James Martimer 88,126,
  165
John 15,212
Mortimer 211
Peter 108
Robert 18,37,79,99,154
Susannah 21
Thomas 1,15,21
William 15,51,83,117
Harrison, Carolina 197
  John 26,27,38,43,243
  Robert 225
  Saml. 153
  Susannah 26,243
Harriton, John 109,214,215
Harry, David 46,99,122,138
  John 120
  Mary 15,16
  Thomas 138
Harston, Joachim 190
Hart, Arther 97
  Arthur 1,7,39,59,163
  Christopher 193
  Daniel 117
  David 220,227,235
  Nathaniel 220,227,235
  Oliver 21,84
  Oliver Jr. 190
  Sarah 21,84
  Thomas 220,227,235
  William 132
Hartee, David 113,120
Harting, Mary 202
  Philip 202
Hartley, 78
  Daniel 23
  Elizabeth 16
  G. H. 168,237
  Henry 16,122
  John Newton 127
  Roger Peter Handyside
    22
  Stephen 178
  Thomas 36
  William 126
Hartlung, Philip 108
Hartly, Thos 167
Hartston/e, Joakim 18
  Catharine 43
  Joachim 53
Harvey, Alexander 12,14,42,
    43,44,90
  Arnold 128
  Charles 129,176
  Henry 128
  Jacob William 78,126,237

John 99,151,176
Mary 14,64
Thomas 192,222
William 12,14,99,139,
  192,214
William Henry 89
Hasell, Andw 56
  Elizabeth 193
  James 50
  Margaret (Summers) 87
  Margaret 76
  Mary (Ancrum) 50
  Sarah (Wright) 50
  Susannah (Quincy) 50
  Thomas 51,76,87,128,204,
    226
Hasonclever, Franes Casper
  222
Hatcher, Jaston 163
  Jemson 128
  Josiah 83
  Josiah Jr. 83
  Thomas 61
  Welmerth 61
Hate, John 12
Hatfield, John 25,41,143,
  181
  Sarah 25
Hathaway,/Hathway
  Thomas 212,216
Hatley, P. H. 215
  R. P. 40
  R. P. H. 199
  Roger Peter Handasyde
    103
Hatter, Elizabeth
  (Richardson) 110
  Elizabeth 111,198,201
  John 110,111,198,201
Haubigh, Daniel 223,240
  Joseph 160
Haul, Elisha 96
Hauser, Andreas 239
Hausihl, William 7,42
Having, Wm. 165
Hawke/s, Edward 64
  Robert 159
Hawkins, John 183,184
  Peter 199
  Philip 93,193
Hawser, Andrew 16
Hawthorn, John 62,112
Hay, Chs. 163
  David 48,58,128,154
  Dortch 154
  Elizabeth 131
  Hardy 131,154
  Howel 58,216
  John 21
  William 154
Hayes, Elizabeth 76
  John 31,76
  Isaac 85,192,197,227,

234,242
  Mary 197,222
Haynsworth, Henry 208
Hays, Gamaliel 135
  Henry 189
  John 153
  Sarah 46
  William 46
Hayse, John 76
Hayward, Dan 98
  J. 59
Haywood, Michael 183,184
  William 79
Hazel, Wm. 222
Hazelwood, Abraham 67
Head, William Ekan 97
Heard, 214
  Ann 22
  John 22,138,199,201
  Lydia 22
  Thos 22,168
Hearn/e, Eliz'h 114
  John 20
Heartstone, Joachim 43
Heath, John 216
Heathly, William 56
Heatley, Charles 149
Heatly, Chas. 132
  Mary 80
  William Jr. 132
Hector, negro 110
Heires, 131
Helmes, Ann 244
  Joseph 244
  Mawbery 244
Helo, Francis 229
Helterbrand, Daniel 130
  John Christopher 56,130
Helton, Isaac 6
  William 137,238
Hemele, Rachel 181
Henderly, Henry 86
Henderson, David Neilson
  186
  Edward 172
  James 50
  Richard 220,227,235
  Robert 140
  William 69,81,86,169,236
Hendlen, Thomas 205
Hendrick, Hance 102
  Hans 58
  John 118
  Sarah 200
Hendrix, Wm. 225
Henley, Elizabeth 85
  Leonard 220
Henly, Peter 240
Hennesley, Randal 34
Henrich, Philip 138
Henry, Ann 132
  Jacob William 237
  James 73,132,170

Philip 15,71,72,103,128,
  135,143,145,149,168,169,
  178,199,236,237,238
S. M. 199
Sarah Maria 199
Henson, Philip 28,40
Hepps, John 229
Heren, Andrew 159
Heriot, George 81,128
  Robert 52,76,87,110,128,
    129,160,168,177,178,181,
    218
Herman, Peter 223
  Peter Jr. 223
Hern/e, 47
  Wm. 109
Herons, William 135
Herring, William 191
Herriott, Robert 150
Heskett, George 140,165
  John 71,187
  Joseph 140
  Mary 140
Hesse, George 119
Hest, William 54,77
Heustess, John 122
Hewards, Dan 98
Hewat, Alex'r 151
Hewett, Andrew 24
Hewie, Robert 161
Hewitt, David 141
Hext, Alexander 24
  David 182
  Edward 232,236
  Hugh 42,155,156
  Philip 216
  Susannah (Duran) 156
  Susannah (Durand) 155
  Thos 23
  William 162,199
Heyward, Ann 27
  Daniel 27,78,162,168
  John 27
  Thomas 35,96,108,143
  Thomas Jr. 35,54
Heywood, Henry 53
Hibben, Andrew 157
Hicklin, Arthur Jr. 83
Hickman, Isaac 101
  Jacob 182
  Rachel 182
Hicks, George 1,70,87,211
  James 1
  John 1,124
  Robert 228,240
  William 125
Hide, Benjamin 91,94,100
  George 211
  Mary 171
Hiet/t, John 139
  Anthony 232
  Robert 232,236
Higdon, John 219

Higgenson, William 90
Higgins, Richard 108
Higginson, William 86
Higgs, James 88,165
   Wm. 49
Highler, Nicholas 66
Hiles, George 137
Hill, Charles 132
   Dominy 96
   John 98,116
   Jonathan 96,173
   Joseph 181
   Peter 67
   Theophilus 228
   Threesea 228
   William 150,217,227
Hillin, James 72
Hilton, Isaac 14
   William 241
Himeli, Rachel 211
Hinckley, William 242
Hincle, Jacob 197
Hinds, Ann 22
   Patrick 10,22,234
Hinson, Clayborn 39
Hirons, Simon 51,147
Hirst, Joshua 1,27
Hitchcock, Mildred 151
   Wm. 151
Hite, Jacob 83
   John Jr. 83
Hock, Johannes 32
Hoddy, Elizabeth 202
   John 202
   Thomas 202,226,227
Hodge, Joseph 179,180,243
   Sarah 184
   Thomas 51
Hodgedon, Susannah
   (Sansum) 27
Hodghison, Elisha 125
   John 109,178,179,180
   William 109,178,179,180,
   197,220
Hodsden, John 49,60,61,62,
Hodsdon, John 25
Hoff, Im 143
Hoffman, Jacob 67
Hogarth, William 43
Hoge, William 105
Hogg, James 190,220,227,
   235
   John 205
   Thos 62
Hoglow, Jacob 53
Holaday, Robert 54
Holbrook, Jacob 43
Holden, John 57
   John Jr. 121
   Margaret 195
   Thomas 166,195,198
Holiday, William 16,36
Holladay, Benjamin 210

   David 210
Hollingsworth, Catharine
   (Evans) 16
   Elias 20,127
   Evans (Catharine) 15
   George 33
   Isaac 146
   Jacob 106
   James 33
   Jean 33
   Joseph 33
   Samuel 15,16
   Thomas 146
   Valentine 99,203
   William 15
Hollman, Christanna 229
Holman, 184
   John 98,99,229
   Priscilla 99
   Thomas 98,115
   Wiliam 233
Holmes, Ann 183
   Daniel 100
   Elizabeth (Smith) 91
   Elizabeth 207
   Isaac 22,207
   Isaac Jr. 207
   James 183
   Jane Elizabeth (Carne)
   80
   Joel 22,243
   John Bee 208
   Joseph 54,66
   Rebecca 207
   William 11,230,239
Holsinger, John 51,62
Holson, Christopher 96
Holtons, William 210
Holzendorf, Frederick 39,
   86,134
   John 134,185,208
   John Frederick 133,134
   Mary 133
   William 114,133,153
Homes, Edward 70
   Rebeca 70
Hood, William 10
Hooker, Simon 115,145,237
Hookey, John 78
Hooks, Frank 224
Hoole, Joseph 47
Hope, George 127
   James 41
   Jean 41
   John 41,147
   Jude 127
   Wm. 99
Hopkins, David 130,190
   Frances 65
   Hannah (Freymouth) 175
   James 175,193
   John 86,150
   Samuel 65,135,208,210,

   222
   Sarah 86
   Wm. 191
Hopper, James 93
Hopton, John 25
Hopton, William 30,42,46,
   50,63,161,187,235
Horcks, Wm. 99
Horlbeck, Catharine 8,50
   John 8,18,149,229
   Peter 8,18,50,149
Horn, Alexander 7,24,104,
   215
   Hugh 179
   Peter 28,72,83,143,108
Hornes, Jacob 171
Horry, Ann (Branford) 107
   D. 107,140,176
   Daniel 94,95,120,205
   Elias 94,106,107,120,
   149,177,209
   Elias Jr. 82,107,110,
   131,176,177,179
   Elizabeth (Branford) 107
   Elizabeth 179
   Harriott 94
   Hugh 120,204,205
   James 120,205
   John 36
   Jonah 204,205
   Peter 106,107,120,204,
   205,214
   Thomas 94,107,110,176,
   177,179,204,205
   Thomas Jr. 107
   William Jr. 110
Horsey, Daniel 11,53,65
   Thomas 27,38,116,146
Hort, Alice 143
   William 143,210
Hotto, Isaac 3
Hottow, Charles 65
   Samuel 41
Houck, Edward 215
Hougard, John Ulrich 152
Houseal, William 168
Houseman, Henry 158,180,
   206,242
Houser, Andrew 239,240
   Catherine (Phag) 239,240
   Catherine 239
Howard, James 172
   John 221,236
   Joseph 241
   Margaret 236
   Robert 96
   Thomas 221
   William 58
Howe, William 172
Howell, Arthur 132,240
   Francis 212
   John 132
   Mary 132

Robert 132,232,236,240
Thomas 132,182
William 48,74,154
Howers, Col. 86
Howse, Elizabeth 88
Thomas 88
Hox, Frederick 31
Hoy, David 152
Hoyle, Richard 96,198
Hrabowski/y, Samuel 43,
  111,148,154,167
Hramblers, John 152
Hubbard, Humphrey 207
  Mathew 68
Hubert, John 184
Hudson, Elizabeth 85
  Isaac 85
  Samuel 121
  Thomas 135
  William 213
Hues, Patrick 101
Huffman, Jacob 67
Huger, Benjamin 20,52,122,
  157,178,213,214
  D. 95
  Daniel 66,94,120,205
  Isaac 20,171,201
  John 41,85,161,189,205
  Mary Esther 52
Huges, John 123
  Wm. 122
Huggins, Elizabeth Sarah
  228
  John 181,197
  Joseph 4,228,230
  Mark 20,187,230
Hughes, Edwd 79
  Goodridge 125,164
  Henry 224
  John 107,124,173,182,185
  Meredith 224
  Thomas 237
  William 138,224
Hughey, Saml 7
Hughs, Henry 49
  John 86
  Thomas 170
Hugins, George 220
Huguen, David 39
Huguenin David 39
Hull, Benj. 85
  William 200
Humbert, David 114
  David Peter 86
  Melchior 86
Humble, Christopher 173
Hume, John 97,128
  Robert 96
  Susanah 128
Humphreys, 238
  R. 119
  Ralph 118,137,159,189,
    193,194,204,216,226,238,

243
Richd. 117
Humphries, John 144
  Ralph 34,132,225
Hunger, John 85
Hunsinger, Michael 32,64,
  138
Hunt, Ann 37
  Catherine 57
  Daniel 30,50
  James 77
  Jesse 66,180
  John 4,6,21,37,46,89,144
  Joseph 12
  Martha 12
  Savannah 53
  William 239
Hunter, 179
  Dalziel 22,28,100,115,
    119,123,142,143,144,145,
    156,198
  David 13,84,85,128,135
  Daziel 112
  George 48,60,195
  Helen 64
  James 53,64
  John 95
  Nicholas 157
  Peter 77
  Susana 95
Hurgers, Henry 150
Hurlick, James 211
  Sarah Huney 211
Hurlock, James 211
  Vincent 166
Hurr, Jacob 189
Hurst, Jane 16
  Robert 16
Husbands, John 148
Huse, John 144
Hussey, John 29,212
Hustess, John 16,169,218
Hutchenson, Thomas 82
Hutcheson, Elizabeth
  (Pearce) 79
  George 79
Hutchings, N. W. 136
  Richard 9
Hutchinson, Elizabeth
  (Pierce) 92
  George 92
  John 78
  M. 204
  Mary 183,184
  Ribton 82
  Robert 183,184
  Thomas 4,181,193,239,241
  Wm. 123
Hutchison, James 30
  Robert 131
  Thomas 233
  William 9,148
Hutson, Christopher 210

Mary (Chardin)(Wood-
  ward) 162
Richard 162,165,227,234
William 116
Hutto, Ann 61
  Benjamin 61
  Charles 2,61,119
  Henry 138
  Isaac 61
  Jacob 61
  Susanna 61
Hutton, William 88
Hyde, Mary (Handyside) 58
  Mary 59
Hyrne, Henry 12,17,29,89,
  116,233,239
  Mary Ann 17

Iklar, John 98,163
Imer, Abraham 29,215
  Ann 29,215
Imrie, John 85
Inabnet, Margaret 112
Inabnit, Baltis/Baltus 3,
  112
  John 112
  Saml 112
Ingleman, Jacob 228
  Mary 228
Inglis, John 189
Ingullmann, Jacob 228
Inman, James 67
  Robert 56,67,214
  Thomas 56
Innis, Robert 63,69
Ion, George 25
Ioor, George 175
  John 66,108,175
  Thos 31
Irby, Charles 122,217
Irons, Simon 171,182
  Stephen 202
Irvin, Andrew 3,151,236
  John 160
  Robert 153
Irwin, John 21
  Robert 129
Isaacs, John 217
Isler, Jacob 238
Iten, Ann 163
Izard, 177,204
  Elizabeth (Blake) 49,204
  Elizabeth (Wright) 108,
    152
  John 108,111,152,199
  Joseph 29,49,204
  Mary (Brewton) 49,204
  Ralph 108,121,158,183,
    199,232,241
  Ralph Jr. 124
  Thomas 152
  Walter 152
  Wm. 120

Jack, negro 122
Jackson, 19
  David 6,13,144
  George 2,22
  Henry 29,162,200
  James 29,66
  John 22,58,59,200,233
  Joseph 171
  Mary (Willingham) 58
  Miles 59,161,171
  Reganal 29
  Richard 59,70,138,154,
    192,225
  Samuel 172
  Susanna 59
  Thomas 114
  William 165,217
Jacob/s, Israel 92
  John 86
  Joseph 79,80,92
Jamblers, John 152
Jamerson, 136
  James 136
James, Alexr. 24
  Benjamin 70,138
  Daniel 46
  Francis 45,210
  Howel 217,218
  James 203
  John 90,91,117,181,208,
    210,241
  John Jr. 195,196,241
  Philip 46,99
  Saml 217
  Sarah 117,242
  Sherwood 241
  Thomas 15,69,167,169,
    217,218
  William 5,122,138,190,
    203
Jameson, William 111,115
Jamieson, John 19
Jamison, William 184
Janeway, Ann 70
  James 87
  William 59,87,128
January, Ann 225
January, slave 234
Jarvis, John 241
Jasu, Jordan 11
Jaudon, Ann 231,232
  Daniel 53,123
  Elias 4,103,104,180,185,
    242
  John 123,194,231,232
  Mary 242
Jeachin, Stephen 105
Jeannerett, Henry 207
Jefferys, William 16
Jeffords, John Jr. 19,48
Jeffreys, David 175
  Nathaniel 117
Jehudi, Jacob 3

Martin 3
Jenkins, 23
  Benjamin 45
  David 95
  Edward 242
  Elizabeth (Capers) 27
  Elizabeth 38,107
  Francis 171
  George 119
  Jacob 57
  James 57,115
  James Jr. 68
  Jane 68
  John 57,68
  Joseph 45
  Susanna 242
Jenneret, Jacob 82
Jennings, Joseph 103
Jennis, Robert 52
Jenys, George 152
  Paul 108,152
Jerman, Edward 156
Jerry, slave 234
Jervis, John Lewis 166
Jesseret, Jane 160
Jessup, Robert 194
Jinkins, David 147
John, 93
  Enoch 6
  Jonathan 177,214
Johnes, John 113
Johns, Jacob 142
  Patience 142
Johnson, 240
  Ann Margaret 237
  Benjamin 116
  Eliza 172
  James 68,108,178
  Jane 68
  John 116,132
  Joseph 3,24,127,167,198
  Matthew 172
  Nathaniel 20
  Peter 185,219
  Robert 36,68,81,109,133,
    200
  William 219,220
Johnston, 150,204
Johnston, Andrew 52,70,
    113,133,169,170
  Archibald 70,81,115,145,
    162
  Charles 111,123,163
  Eliza 147
  James 16,17,19,49,56,65,
    78,106,111,126,151,170,
    198,221
  Jane 67
  John 32,77,88,118,128,
    135,144,146,164,194,230,
    241
  Nathl 179
  Peter 30

Richard 9
Robert 67,71,77,89,112,
    186,191,197,205,241
  Sarah (Collings) 71
  Thomas 79
  William 115,145,220,227,
    235
Johude, Martin 2
Joiner, Alexander 22
  John 67
  Joseph 16
Jolleys, Joseph 107
Jolly, Joseph 46
  Thos 31
Jones, Adam Cr. 13,62,101,
    173
  Adm. 173
  Ann 148
  Barclay 63
  Bartley 179
  David 40,124
  Edmun 38
  Edward 33,42,203
  Elizabeth (Palmer)(St.
    John) 127
  Elizth. 148
  Francis 118
  Fredrick 186
  Godfrey 129,214
  Jacob 129
  James 87,101,149,170
  John 23,30,88,98,225
  Jonathan 229
  Lewis 137,238
  Mary (Stevenson) 38,116
  Maurice 40
  Nathl. 148
  Rachael 129
  Ralph 10
  Rebecca 17
  Reuben 61
  Richard 60,109,215
  Samman 155
  Samuel 63,165,209,221,
    222
  Stephen 211
  Thomas 3,11,14,15,59,75,
    84,96,101,119,121,138,
    139,148,186,194,198,203,
    204,206,219,226,230,234,
    235
  William 17,20,69,128
Jonym, John 14
Joor, John 29
Jordan, David 109,138
  James 212
  William 62
Joseph, Israel 212
Joulee, John 212
Joy, Moses 208
  Richard 220
Joyner, Catherine 149
  Isom 239

John 124,144
Joseph 144,149
William 241
Judeth, 93
Judy, slave 234
Jugler, Ann 78
Juislen, Ed. 69
Julian, G. 158
  Peter 84
  Peter Jr. 85
Julien, Peter 85
  Peter Jr. 84
Jumper, Conrod 130
  Michael 30
Junes, John 157,161
Juno, negro 110
Jurdine, John 28
Jutz, Adam 31

Kagler, Andrew 153
Kalteisan, Michael 50,81, 235
Kalteison, Michael 8,18,50, 69,186,222
Karwon, Crafton 56
  Dingrel 147
  Mary 54
  Thomas 54,56,87,94
Kauffman, David 144,145, 229
Kaygleman, Emanuel 151
Kaylor, Daniel 185
Keall, Catharine (Rehm) 134,135
  Katherine 134
Keating, Edward 67,171
  John 133
Keaton, Edward 214
Keatt, David 190,206
Kebler, Mary 16
Keef, Arthur 169
Keeffs, Arthur 182
Keenan, John 182
Keeting, Edward 214
Keighley, John 38
  Peter 38,156
Keill/s, John 216
  Loudovick 133
Keisling, Hopson 33
  Stephen 53
Keith, Alexander 36,51,172, 177
  James 205
  William 29,215
  William Jr. 185
Keizor, Christian 66
Kell, John 54,84,93
  Philip 56
Keller, Esther 39
  Michael 24,70
  Thomas 32,39
Kelley, Edward 102
  Gersham 166

Kelly, Bryan 37
  Daniel 115
  Garad 45
  Gersham 144
  Gilles 151
  Jas 128
  John 111,167,184,187, 192,198
  Joseph 167
  Mary 111,167,192
  Neilson 128
  Samuel 4,7,95,100
  Winie 187
Kelsall, Roger 213
Kelsey, John 30,154
  William 152,156
Kelso, Joseph 18
Kemmel, Joseph 24
Kemmerling, Margaret 16
  Mathew 16
Kendall, Jacob Jr. 6
Kennedy, John 36
  William 33,42,195
Kennerley, James 117
Kennerly, James 137
  John 240
  Joseph 239
Kenny, William 5
Kerbey, Dorthy 174
  Wm. 174
Kerby, Charles 65
  Henry 45
  Thomas 65
Kerch, Barbara (Bowman) 2
  Frances (Owens) 2
  John George 2
  Ratchel (Committer) 2
Kerleys, George 94
Kermon, Benjamin 71
Kerr, Alexr 121
  John 169,200
Kersey, Susannah 199
Kershaw, 57
  Eli 82,226
  Ely 57,137,138
  Joseph 14,37,58,59,75, 137,138,147,173,186,226, 228,235,241,243
  Sarah 147,148
  William 198
Kesson, John 133
Kettle, Jacob 103
Keyser, Christian 56
Kidd, William 119
Killey, William Jr. 66
Killingsworth, William 15, 45,166
Killpatrick, Alexander 172
Kilpatrick, James 84
Kimbrough, John 226
Kincade, George 163
Kincaid, George 123, 190,193

Kinceler, Christian 119
  Conrad 83
  Harmon 83
Kincelor, Christian 83
Kinchard, Elizabeth 237
  Thomas 237
Kincler, Conrad 164
Kincsler, John 147
King, Benjamin 22,23,25
  Charity 144,176,241
  Charles 72,83,144,176, 241
  Cheroling 93
  Christopher 25
  Euchees 93
  George 42,83,121,184
  James 235
  John 70
  Joseph 20,60
  Mary 42,239
  Richard 97,101
  Tallafia 93
  William 239
Kings, George 154
  Patrick 65
Kinloch, Ann 52
  Francis 57,179,180,201, 242
Kinlock, Ann Isabella 52
  Frances 231,232
  Francis 74,123
  James 67,231,232
  Mary Easter (Gaillard) 231,232
Kinseler, Christian 68,69
  Conrad 68
  Conrode 68
  Harmon 68
Kinsler, Conrad 174
Kinsley, Zephaniah 54,233, 241
Kirby, Charles 53
Kirch, John 3
Kirk, Edward 33,42
  Moses 23
  William 86,152
  Will Jr. 153
Kirkland, Joseph 96
  Moses 44,60,70,76,87, 178,193,199,202
  Patience 44
  Richard 116,218
Kirkpatrick, James 148
Kirkwood, Eliz'h 124,173
Kirsh, Conrad 224
  John George 51,130
Kittleband, David 168
Kling, George 94
Knapper, Frederick 16
Knight, Jas. Jr. 170
  Margreat 208
  Wm. 69, 81
Knighten, Isaac 208,241

Margaret 208
Knighton, Thomas 208,210
　William 208
Knobeth, Elizabeth 36
　Frederick 36
　Martin 36
Knotts, Nathaniel 87
Knox, Robert 95
　Sarah 54
Koger, Joseph 94
Kohock, Thos 18
Kohun, Gasper 48
Kolb, Able 207
　Herman 118
　Jacob 39
　John 39
　Josiah 39
　Martin 94
　Peter 17,163
　Tillman 39
Kolp, Abel 138
Koon/e, Henry 70
　Casper 48
Kouche, Edward 109
Kounts, John 229
Kreidner, Catharine 106
　Frederick 106
Kroofin, Mary 39
Krozer, Peter 178
Kuhn, Gasper 48
Kunts, Johannes 229
Kuntzler, Conrad 119
Kysell, Conrad 27,32,33,42,
　43,52,53,64,83,174
　Esther 39
　Hester 52

LaRush, 156
Labbe, Anthony 84
Labruce, Thomas 139,164
Lacey, William 5,53
Ladson, 212
　Abraham 235
　Amelia 62
　Elizabeth 89,148,235
　Francis 80
　Isaac 209
　James 148,227
　John 89,200
　Margaret 200
　Mary 80
　Robert 23,96,109,148,
　　195,200,215
　Robert Jr. 148
　Thomas 148,227
　William 232
　Zacheriah 2,3
Laffette, David 110
　Peter 110
Lagers, Joseph 27
Laird, David 90
　Elizabeth 84
　Lodowick 84

Robert 84
Samuel 187
Lake, Thos 175
Lamar, Basil 150
　Jeremiah 214
　John 3,165,166
　Penelopey 147
　William 147
Lamb, Thos 115
Lamboll, Elizabeth 21
　Thomas 21,95,155
Lambright, John 4,101,155
　Sarah 101
　Wm. 155
Lambston, Richard 106
Lambton, Richard 56,57,71,
　124,162,221,234,240,241
Lamprier, Clement 208
Lampriere, Ann 208
Lancaster, Joseph 237
Lance, Lambert 47,99,108,
　193,205,207,209,219,220,
　238,241
Lancelot, Bland 61
Land, Glebe 36
　John 154
　Wm. 114
Landtrip, Hannah 166,214
　Thomas 166,214
Lane, Edward 228
Laney, Isaac 198
　Mary 156
Lang, Millicent 102
　Richard 58,102
　Robert 58,102,160
　Sarah 102
Langford, Ann (Shepheard)
　139
　John 139
　Nicholas 192
Languish, John 40
Lanner, Benjn. 150
Lard, Lodwick 187
　William 45
Larey, Darby 24,129,219
Laroach, James 90
Laroch, 150
Laroche, Daniel 63,69,156,
　178
　Thomas 156
Larrimore, James 9
Larrymor, Edward 23
Larse, Parce Choek 93
Lary, Mickeal 43
Lasey, John 113
Lasley, James 171
Lasman, George 197
　John Martin 197
Laten, John 231
Latham, Daniel 66,77,180
　Richard 15,108
　Thomas 66
Latour, Susannah 84

Latta, John 18,154,196
Lattimore, John 85
Laurel, William 136
Laurence, Augustus 143
　Henry 101
　Jona 77
　Stephen 77
Laurens, Eleanor 25
　Henry 25,31,49,54,75,76,
　　93,121,123,128,138,173,
　　190,193,204,243
　James 62,193,208,210,240
　John 25
Lavein, Peter 12
Law/s, Joseph 141,221
　Samuel 196
　William 88,138,174
Lawley, Joseph 81
Lawrence, Henry 66
　Jonathan 66,180,187
　Joshua 132
　Stephen 180
Lazowis, 20
LePoole, Peter 36,58,144,
　145
Leasey, John 102
Leaten, Jno 231
Ledbetter, Ephraim 98
　Nemiah 98
Lee, Edward 102
　John 131
　Maurice 186
　Thos 9
　William 22,124
Leech, John 216
Lefevre, John 219
Leftenent, Young 93
Leg, Peter 220
Legan, Samuel 123
Legare, Daniel 6,25,132,
　182,216
　Daniel Jr. 170
　Elizabeth 182
　Jos. 230
　Nathan 191
　Samuel 12,29,127,163,209
　Thomas 242
Leger, Peter 42,189,200
Legge, Edward Jr. 128
Legrand, Isaac 101
Lehre, Jacob 11
Leigh, Egerton 101,121
Leighton, John 211
　William 178
Leitch, Andrew 23,167,176,
　193,224,235
Leitner, John 110,205
　Michael 221,229
Leitz, Barnard 173
　Wm. 87
Lemer, Michael 124
Lemmon, David 124
Lemon, John 124

Lemprier/e, Clement 111,
  117,166
Lenard, John 83
Lennon, Thomas 210
Lenoir, Isaac 121
  Thomas 121
Leonard, Wm. 174
Lequeux, Peter 230
  Peter Jr. 5
Lerette, slave 205
Lesade, James 107
Lesesne, 140,185
  Isaac 56,122,164
  John 128,145
  Peter 133,145
Lesley, James 216
Lessle, James 22
Lessly, Davd. 3
Lestarjette, Lewis 236
Lesterjette, Lewis 225
Lette, 93
Levens, negro 110
Lever, Christiana 22
  Elizabeth 22
  Samuel 22
Leveston, Wm. 115
Levingston, George 91
  William 91
Levingstone, William 89
Leviston, William 52
Levy, Joseph 121
Lewis, Abel 241
  David 238
  Isaac 67
  John 10,67
  Judith 152,158
  Thomas 95
  William 36,107,222
Libecap, Mathias 193
Liddell, James 42
Liddle, James 128,135
  John 153
Lide, Ann 70
  Rebeca 70
  Thomas 57,68,70,148,163,
  170
Liebenhent, Henry 205
Lieutenant, Young 93
Lightwood, 66
  Edward 7,107
  Edward Jr. 123
  John 58
Lillibridge, Hampton 234
Linch, Captain 56
Linder, Jacob 171
  James 53
  John 53,98,114,190,197,
  208,220
  John Jr. 134
  Lewis 73,77,125,129,171
  Ludwig 61
Lindley, James 34,96
  Mary 34

Lindly, Jas. 4
Lindouws, Moses 21
Linds, Andrew 20
Lindsay, Barnard 210,217
  James 26,144,224
  Thomas 144
  Barnard 172
  Eleanor 172
  James 72,84,118,176,230
  John 241
  John Jr. 176
  Thos 84
Lines, Samuel 59
Linicum, Gideon 243
Lining, Charles 46
  Sarah 120,139
Linn, David 160,166
  Robert 117
  Valentine 95
  William 90
Linning, Charles 42
Linsey, James 26
  Joseph 168
  Thomas 72
Linwood, Nicholas 177,178,
  214
Lipham, Jacob 68
Liston, Thomas 236
Lithgow, Robert 79,137,189,
  193,226,238,239,243
  William 79
Little, John 153,194
  Penelephy 21
  William 17,21,226
LittleJohn, Rachel 4
Littleton, William Henry 70
Litz, Barnard 16
Livingston, Barnet 228
  George 117,169
  Henry 19
  Robert Jno 242
  William 9,51,62,92,169,
  194
Livingstone, William 105,
  176
Livington, W. 216
Livre, Robt 43
Llewellen, John 6
Lloyd, Ann 222
  Elisabeth 181
  John 10,91,126,128,131,
  170,220
  Martin 104,108,111,181
  Rachel 132
  Susannah 183
Lochon, Mary 165,191
Lockhart, David 202
Lockley, Henry 83,119
Locock, Wm. 201
Loe, William 161
Logan, George 61,167
  John 20,167,179,232,236
  William 1,16,61,152
Logue, John 86

Lohner, Jacob 130
  John 11
  Melicher 11
  Michael 11
Lomen, Michael 173
Long, Felix 13,38
  George 4
  John 134,212,218
  Mathew 13,15,142,212
  William 142
Loocock, Aaron 130,137,
  138,187,197,226
  Mary 197
  William 62,72,108,139,
  240
Looney, David 117
  Robert 117
Loosk, Jas. 110
Loper, Joshua 201,229
Lord, Andrew 49,77,102,
  189,216
  Ann 154
  Benjamin 101,154,171,240
  George 49,86
  John 164
  Peter 72,139,142
  Thomas 15,71,72,86,139
  William 6,50,94,166
Lorimer, Susannah 28
Lormiere, Lewis 171
Lott, Abraham Meurons
  167
Loundes, Charles 63
Lourigh, Michl. 122
Love, James 148
  John 65
Loveless, John 156
Low/e, Thomas 32,31
  William 114,186,235
Lowerman, John 172
Lowery, Robert 142
  William 23
Lowndes, Charles 82,221
  Edward 158
  Rawlins 4,12,66,152,156,
  179,201,202,203,205,216,
  222,226
  Rawlins Jr. 201
  Thomas 12,158
Lowrick, Michael 162
Lowry, Robert 151
Loyd, Ann 104
  Patience 121
  Thomas 94,121
Loyer, Adrian 19
Lucas, 182
  James 77
  John 99
  Joshua 107
  Joshua 99
  William 121
Lufft, George 108
Luke/s, Daniel 122

John 122
Luks, William 46
Lund, Benjamin 109
Lundy, Daniel 240
Lunn, Benjamin 179
Luptan, William 188
Lupton, 177
  William 51
Lusirin, Magdalen 223
Lusk, Elizbeth 196
  James 114
  Samuel 8,196
Luster, Negroe 15
Luten, Wm. 93
Luton, William 206,208
Luttrell, John 220,227,235
Luyton, William 47
Lyddal, Fenwick 178
Lykes, Arthur 13
Lyme, Andrew 95
Lynah, James 25,127, 184, 225
Lynch, Aaron 242
  James 26,209
  John 64
  Johnson 85
  Thomas 57,71,74,96,103, 122,131,157,170,179,215
Lyner, James 181
Lynes, Samuel 59,128,192
Lynn, David 72
Lyon, John 157,226
Lyons, Anna 87
  John 87
  Samuel 171

M'Donald, Ronald 90
M'Ginnis, Thomas 149
M'Kenzie, William 90
M'Millen, Agnes 78
  John 78
MacAllester, William 243
MacColough, Jams. 191
MacTeers, John 3
Macbeth, Alexander 125,182
Mace, Moses 48,56
  Rebecca 154,182
Mackelmore, John 6
Mackenzie, John 82,121
  Robert 123
  Robt Jr. 82
Mackie, James 30,114
  Jno 198
Mackimmey, William 225
Mackinen, Charles William 53
  Hellen 53
Mackintosh, 34
  Alexander 3,6,34,46,48, 69,71,122,129,138,177, 214
  Lachlan 33,103
Macklin, John 209

Mackreth, Hannah 31
Maclemar, Catharina 79
  Catharine (Cocle) 79
Macteer, John 21
Macter, Jno. 6
Maddock, Abraham 24
Mader, Richard 100
Magby, David 47
Magdalen, Mary 131
  Mary (Grimball) 188
Magee, Daniel 47
Mager, Adrian 39
Maginis, Abraham 79
Maham, Hezekiah 230
Maille, Peter 143
Main, Walter 216
Maine, Walter 77
  Wm. 49,169
Maker, John 43
Malden, John 150,164
Malphrus, Simon Jr. 141
Maltz, John Daniel 147
Man, 150
  Jno 209
Manderson, George 177,214
Maner, John 171
  Mary 141
  Mary Ann 171
  Samuel 141
  Thomas 214
  William 171,214
Manigault, G. Jr. 113
  Gabriel 23,24,51,69,81, 89,97,152,184,193,209, 226,227
  Gabriel Jr. 18,136,143
  Peter 13,16,42,54,64, 121,136,161,184,210
Mankin, Hilarius 11
Mann, Henry 210,213
  Henry Wickham 213
  Margaret (Wickham) 101
  Margaret 213
  Martha (Carpenter) 213
  Mary (Speitz) 213
  Nuby 63
  Sarah 213
  Susannah 123,198
Mannan, Derick 98
Mannin, Derrick 184
Manning, William 132
Manor, John 121
Manrow, Jacob 242
Mansell, Willm. 234
Mansfield, William Lord 172
Mantz, Elizabeth 44
Maples, Thomas 174
March, Patrick 171
Marchant, B. L. 103
Marchers, Patrick 214
Marden, John 103
Maret, Stephen 184

Marian, Elizabeth De. (St. Julien) 218
Job 218
Marion, 31,125,142,168
  Benjamin 115
  Francis 81
  Gabriel 21,82,126,128, 163,170,201
  Isaac 50,128,163
  James 54
  Job 126,192,193,204
  John 28,123,194
  Mary (Bramer) 54
  Peter 153,170
Marison, Andrew 72
Mark, John 184
  Larance 83
  Lorance 119
Markey, Patrick 71
Marley, John 28,56
Marlow, Robt. 201
Marry, Ralph 58
Marsales, Peter 91
Marsh, Samuel 44
Marshall, Elizabeth (Haggatt) 172
  Elizabeth (Walter) 157
  Elizabeth (Walter) (Hagott) 115
  George 32
  James 115,157,172
  John 130
  Tho's 58
  William 61
Martimore, Mary 110
Martin, Alexander 13
  Ann 13
  Anna Catherine 229
  Benjamin 71
  Edward 54,74,75,80,92, 185,204,226,227
  Eleanor/Elanor 169,191
  Elizabeth (Walker) 54
  Jacob 181
  John 98,126,166,170,175, 214
  John Nickles 229
  Josiah 7,83
  Laughlin 47,169,183,191
  Leonard 109
  Nicholas 229
  Robert 103,136,187
  Samuel 39
  William 58,60,73,74,83, 105
Martinangel, Mary 61
Martyn, Charles 125
Martz, Johannes 195
  Michael 195,230
Mashow, Henry 29
Mason, James 51,54,196
  John 179
  Richard 126,197

Susannah 227
W. 127
William 22,31,48,49,52,
78,80,81,92,126,157,189,
197,208,209,213,227,232,
242
Massey, Jane 84,90
Jos. 89
Phillip 89,90
William 62,203
Matawny, 93
Mathewes, Anthony 54
John Raven 178,207
Shadk. 211
Mathews, 71
Anthony 91
Benjamin 100
Daniel 109
George 100
John 91,125,172,179
Peter 19
Robt. 13
Wm. 187
Matlock, Stephen 102,109,
119
William 102
Matthewes, Charlotte 80
James 80
Matthews, John 81,122,168,
170
Peter 241
Matthison, Benjn. 14
Maul/l, David 3,76,87,93,
159,165
Maullare, David 3
Maverick, Samuel 147
Maxfield/s, John 82
James 102
Maxwell, William 64,161
May, James 154
John 151
Mayam, Hezekiah 195
Maybank, Andrew 242
Jos. 88
Mayer, Adrian 18,20,53,86,
113,114,128,133,134,135,
152,169,185,190,206,207,
208,238
Adrion 39
Andrew 222
John 85,87,103,141,215
Joseph 85
Laurence 215
Richard 85
Thos 85
William 85
Maynard, John 180
Mayne, Charles 162
John 162
Mayne, R. 117
Mayrant, John 53,57,74,180,
184,187
Susanah 94

Mays, 132
William 217
Mayson, Ann 39
James 24,39,40,54,58,60,
62,66,126,168,232
William 167,243
Mazick, J. 95
Mazyck, 50,149
Alexander 131
Benjamin 178,184,185
D. 111
Daniel 13,23,28,30,33,
96,143,182
Dl. 12,70,174,190
Dn. 165
Isaac 24,50,69,81,96,99,
143,152,209
Paul 96,182
Stephen Jr. 232
William 182,232
McAllilley, John 105
McAnair, Ebenezer 171
McAteer, William 176
McBee, Vardry 117,211
McBride, Hugh 68
James 124,173
John 68
William 68
McBurnet, James 84
McCall, Hugh 8
Jas. 174
John 12,31,157
John Jr. 31
Martha 12
McCane, 77
McCants, Hannah 17
James 82
John 219
Thomas 82
McCarey, Robert 93
McCarter, Moses 10
McCartey, William 105
McCartney, Alexander 233
Jane 23
John 23
McCarty, Cornelius 191
Margaret 105
Mary Ann 105
McCauley, John 56
McCaw, John 29
McCay, John 234
Joseph 234
McClain, Ephraim 63
McClane, Charles 73
Susannah 73
McClean, Ephraim 73
McCleanachan, Robt. 18
McCleary, Samuel 84,85
McCleland, Robert 126
McClellan, Robert 222
Thos 110,111
McClelland, Hugh 196
McClellon, William 147

McClendals, John 60
McClenehan, John 217
McCleskey, Agnes 143
Joseph 143
McClinton, Mary 94
McCluer, James 8
Wm. 84
McCluney, William 170
McClure, James 229
John 217
McCole, Adam 170
Joseph 170
McCollum, Henry 127
McComb, John 72
McConn, Robert 188
McConnell, George 124
McConnico, Samuel 221
William 135,221
McCool, John 136
McCord, 228
Charles 161,162
James 41
John 58,162,175
McCormick, 62
James 22,45,51,90,140,
221
McCottry, Robert 24
McCown, Alexander 73
McCoy, Daniel 133
McCracken, Arthur 37
John 211
McCrea, Alexander 57
Alexander Jr. 56,57
Thomas 57
McCreary, Mary 93,94
Robert 93,94
McCreest, Mathew 6
McCreevan, Duncan 212
McCulleys, James 84
McCulllough, James 84
McCullock, James 84
Thomas 154,155
McCullogh, Elizabeth
(Seawright) 101
John 205
William 202
McCullouch, James 8
McCullough, Janet 101
McCully, James 73
McCune, James 31
McCurdy, Robert 78,79
McCutchen, Robert 102,168
McDanel, James 132
McDaniel, Stephen 128,134,
206
McDaniell, John 112
McDaws, 198
McDoch, John 100
McDonald, 241
Adam 21
Archibald 5
John 5,94,170
McDoneld, Hugh 18

McDonnel, Hugh 18
McDougall, John 216
McDowel/l, Archd. 204
   John 63,83,84
McDugle, 138
McElhenny, Thos 169
McElroy, Dinah 118
   James 118
   Mary 155
McElveen, John 57
McElven, William 82
McElwee, David 51,62
McEwean, James 76,77
McFadden, Edward 188
   Isaac 188
   John 74,122,132
   John Jr. 122
   Robert 188
   William 74
McFadder, Hannah 84
   Robt 84
McFarland, Jas. 243
   Mordecai 183
McFarlanes, Mordecai 207
McFarlin, John 102
   Mordicai 154
McFersion, Thomas 171
McGaw, James 135
   John 135
McGee, Pattk. 169
McGere, Thos 74
McGill, James 30
   John 15
McGoraty, Patrick 189
McGowens, William 143
McGraw, Edward 66
   Willm. 66
McGrew, 184
   Peter 116
McGuckin, Bernard 94
McGuire, Peter 126
   Terence 126
McGuirman, Duncan 191
McHuges, 25
McHugo, Anthony 139
McIlraith, John 208
McIlwain, Andrew 146
McIlwean, James 135
McIntosh, Alexander 34
   Hugh 2
   James 108
   John 135
McIver, William 144
McIvor, 129
McKachey, Adm. 217
McKay, Charles 54,65
   Jeane 65
   John 65
   Joseph 54,118
   Katharine 54,65
   Martha 88
   Mary 54,65
   Saml 88

William 54,65
   Winewood 229
McKee, Adam 62
   Daniel 132
   John 62,203
   Saml 62
   Thos. 25
   William 102,202,203
McKellis, James 60
McKelver, James 12
McKelvey, Alexander 42
   Elexr. 15
   James 31,45,47,71,82,96,
      97,114,192,201
   Margaret (ONeal) 15
McKelvy, John 170
McKeney, Wm. 236
McKenney, 188
McKennie, Matthew 86
McKennys, Benjamin 143
McKensie, John 186,191
McKenzie, Robt 163
   William 4
McKeown, Robt. 30
McKewn, John 84
   Robert 11,47
McKey, Adam 62
   Jenny 62
   John Samuel 62
McKimmey, William 240
McKinnen, Charles William 53
McKinney, William 74
McKinnie, Mathew 20,43
McKinnney, Roger 102
McKintosh, Alexander 6,15,
      16,45,56,203
   Elizabeth 187
   Lachlan 117,187
McKissock, Neal 86
McKleroy, James 118
McKnight, Charles 73
McKown, William 26
McKoy, John 178,202
McLamore, John 6
McLaurin, Evan 168,239
McLean, Ephraim 73
   John 90,172
McLemore, Francis 6
McLeod, Norman 112
McLilly, John 8
McMahan, Jane 141
   William 141
McManus, James 162
   Thomas 162
McMechan, Andrew 241
McMeen, Francis 37
McMichael, George 61
McMillen, John 78
McMoughon, Andrew 241
McMuldrow, John 60
McMullan, Daniel 109
McMullen, Daniel 102

McMullows, John 30
McMurdy, Henry 112
McMurdy, Henry 54,142
   Mary 54
   Robert 95,105
McMurtry, Jean 83
   Samuel 83
McNeese, John 187
McNeish, John 38
McNichol, Sarah
   (Seawright) 118
   Sarah 194
McNichols, Elizabeth 205
   George 14
   John 138
   William 21,209
McNilage, Alexander 160
McPherson, 46,222
   Dennan 177
   Elizabeth 111
   Isaac 23,35,75,111,177
   James 213
   John 29,224
   Joshua 233
   Susannah 224
   Thomas 225
McQueen, Ann (Smith), 61
   James 93
   John 14,37,41,44,135
McQuiston, David 84
McRay, James 122
McTeer, John 25,168,169
McWatty, John 215
McWilliams, John 135,138, 243
McWirter, George 238
   John 238
Meadleton, William 86
   Wm. Jr. 86
Meadors, Jason "Juner" 74
Mean/s, James 18
   Rachel 18
   William 38
Meara, Michael 101,109
Meder, Richd 100
Meegees, William 5
Meek, Adam 37
Megee, James 115
Megerhoffer, Henry 134
Meggot, M. 124
Meigler, Nicholas 217
Mellard, Elisha 138,224,235
   George 139
   William 28,108,138
Mellet, Mary 14,76
   Peter 14,76,88,104,139, 234
Mellichamp, 97
Mellyard, William 73
Meloney, John 215
Melson, Anner 165
   David 165
Melton, Nathan 164

Melven, John 19
　William 19
Mercer, Eliz'th (Webb) 153
Merchant, 100
Merick, Nicholas 26
Merret, John Philip 53
Mertz, Lawrence 206
Meshow, Henry 41
　William 205
Metheny, John 215
Metscar, Henry 183
Mettrsel, Peter 167
Metz, Christopher 32
Meuratt, Peter 152
Meuron, Henry 114
Meurons, Abraham 167
Meurset, Peter 1,136,198,
　227
Meursot, Peter 38
Meverick, Samuel 38
Mey, Florian Charles 123,
　136,211
Meyer, Adrian 199,200
　Christian 54
　Conrad 62
　Jacob 172
　Leonard 222
　Philip 25,165,234
　Rudolph 130
　Robert 100
　William 56,130,172,228,
　　232,233
　Winey 233
Miars, Michael 215
Micco, Justonogcy 93
Michael, Ephraim 142
　Lewis 27
　Margaret (Cooler) 232
　Valentine 232
Michell, John 38,90,153
Michie, Alexander 151
　Charles 108,154
　Henrietta 151
　James 82,139
Mickie, James 58
Micklar, Daniel 102
Mickle, Joseph 118
Middleton, 98
　Arthur 108,177,200
　Collo. Thomas 221
　David 169
　Henry 44,108
　John 210
　Mary (Butler) 221,222
　Richard 93,128
　Robt 27
　Sarah (Guerard) 221
　Soloman 156
　Thomas 24,69,81,124,209,
　　222
　William 86,108,115,221
Miers, Michael 51
Mikell, Ann 138,162
　James 150,164

John 138
Milas, slave 205
Milbank, Catharine 10
　William 202
Milbrank, William 10
Miles, Acquilla 219
　Allen 89,168,176,224,235
　Ann (Butler) 46
　Ann (Willson) 224
　Aquila 134
　Edward 99
　Haswell 127
　James 210
　Jeremiah 89,96
　John 96,111,209
　Joseph 96
　Josiah 89,224
　Martha 111
　Rachel (Cater) 224
　Robert 89,168,176,177,
　　224
　Sarah 127
　Silas 177,224
　Susanna (Parsons) 96
　Thomas 96
　William 91,119,225
Milhous, Jane 100
　John 75,100,109,125,164
　Joseph 100
　Robert 100
　Samuel 100,101,119
Miller, Allexander 14
　Casper 61
　Catherine 62
　Charles 62
　Elizabeth 78
　Emanuel 102,203
　George 171
　Hannah 184
　James 202,210
　Jane 147
　John 8,93,166,168,193,
　　198,238,239
　John Weldrick 184
　Joseph 189
　Martin 8,91,92
　Mary 62,140
　Nathaniel 78
　Robert 147
　Samuel 188
　Stephen 30,36,60,62,140
　Susanah (Stead) 73,74
　Susannah 73
　William 73,126,169,177
Milligan, Joseph 2,26,146,
　　161,186,188,210
　William 43
Milligen, George 82
　Joseph 120
　Mary 82
Milling, David 209
Mills, John 8,95,106,185,
　　187,205,225

William 48,116,150
　William Henry 71,218
Milner, Ann 191
　Job 69,81
　John 89
　Solomon 19,191
Mims, Drury 219
Minear, Mary 141
　Samuel 141
Miner, William 67,121
Minick, Rebecca 103
Minicks, Bartholomew 229
Minor, Rueben 219
Minsing, Philip 8
Minter, Jno 48
　widow 179
Miolet, John 105
Miscampbell, James 123,
　124, 173
Miscombell, James 144
Miskelly, Edward 119
Mitchel/l, 77
　Anthy. 185
　Daniel 47
　David 32
　Edward 218
　Ephraim 31,48,71,77,81,
　　82,88,89,96,97,99,102,
　　112,116,119,124,150,151,
　　157,165,175,176,201,209,
　　241
　Isaac 33,34,210
　James 157
　Joab 86
　John 5,31,32,62,82,99,
　　115,123,138,145,162,163,
　　204,217,240
　Mark 86
　Mary 33,23
　Moses 180
　Robert 203
　Thomas 7,168,177,218
　William 2,3,5,22,28,31,
　　78,90,102,116,145,151,
　　216
Mitheringham, 132
Mock, Andrew 165
Moffett, Thomas 195,196
Mon Clair, Peter Abbast-
　ertier 39
Monaghan, Dav'd 107
Monahan, Daniel 99
　Daniel Jr. 99
　Thomas 99
Moncrieffe, John 129
Monelar, Peter 22
Money, Daniel 103,155
Monier, Moses 85
　Peter 85
Monk, John 3,138
Monohan, Daniel 138
Monroe, Daniel 186

Montague, Charles Granville 201
  David 25
  Gov. 1,194
  Samuel 19,158
Montgomery, George 57
  Henry 57,195
  Hugh 121
  James 57
  Margaret 57,195
  Samuel 93
  William 7,195
Moody, Catharine 8
  Ebenezer 8
  Joseph 8
Moon, William 243
Moor/e, 70
  Abraham 137
  Barbara 210
  Benjamin 210
  David 20
  Frankey 210
  Hugh 79
  Isham 14,135,181,195, 196,234,241
  James 3,31,131,231,237, 239
  Jethro 138
  John 36,54,84,85,137, 159,186,227
  John Jr. 5
  Joseph 9
  Nathaniel 14,104,117, 119,124,135,139,181,208, 210,231,241
  Rebecca 24
  Robert 215
  Roger 131
  Samuel 77
  Susannah 181,186
  Thomas 115
  William 14,71,113,210
Mooring, Daniel 199
Moragne, Peter 190
Morall, Daniel 158
Morand, Jane 231
Mordeth, John 87
More, George 203
Mores, John 238
Moret, Stephen 184
Morgan, James 125
  Lewis 20,207
  Mary 152
  Meldred 20
  Richard 169,192
  Thomas 69
  William 24,112,152,172, 186
Moris, Mark 191
  Wm. 93
Morral/l, Daniel 112,152
Morrel, Robert 29,146
Morrils, Thomas 204

Morris, Anthony 79,92
  Israel 216
  John 73,221
  Mark 160
  Martha 162
  Patrick 97
  Robert 196
  Thos. 51
Morrison, Samuel 119
Morriss, Robert 195
Morrit/t, Alice 188
  Ann (Summers)(Fyffe) 188
  Margaret 76
  Thomas 76,96,188
Morrow, John 93,125
  John Jr. 93
  Robert 125
  Samuel 93,212
  Thomas 125
Morse, Jno 195
Mortimer, Edward 149
Morton, Hugh 172
  Joseph 19
  Thos 93
Moseley, Fra. 195
  Sarah 175
  Wm. 175
Moses, Jacob 75
  Robert 119,181
Mote, Christian 172
  David 20
  Jacob 161
Motlett, Lewis 15
Motley, Abraham 113
Motly, John 113
Motte/s, Charles 161,219
  Isaac 186,187,223
  Jacob 19,24,28,36,89, 143,104,111,139
  Jonathan 34,44
  Mary 34
  Matthew 34
Mouatt, Ann (Smith) 233
  John 37,233,234
  William 233
Moultrie, Alexr 129,169
  Elizabeth (Damaris) 104, 111
  John 169
  Thos 49,169
  William 77,104,111,169, 223
Mounge, Henry De 110
Mountague, Samuel 192
Mouret, Jno 102
Mourey, Martha (Stephens) 79,80,92
Mouzon, Henry Jr. 42, 88,157
  Lewis 56,88
  Susanna Elizabeth 88
Mowett, John 2

Mrgill, Lewis 207
Muckenfuss, Michael 107, 175,183,202,208,210
Muckinfuse, Michael 97,98
Muckinfuss, Michael 106, 176
Muckleroy, James 11
Mulcaster, John 162
Mulkeys, Philip 135
Mull, David 90
Mullens, George 23
Mulligan, Joseph 177
Munck, Mary 185
Muncreef/f, Richard 43,80
  Susannah 43,80
Muncrieff, Richard 20
Munk, William 100
Munkey, Luke 141
Muray, James 45
Murdaugh, Josiah 166,198
Murdey, John 132
Murdock, Hameton 143
Murell, John 163
Murfe/e, John 219
  Malachia 5
  Mallichi 53
Murphew, James 59,186
  John 179
  Malachia 5
  Mallachi Jr. 103
  William 77,88
Murphy, 200
  James 5
  Malichi 59
  Mary 183
  Thomas 33,34
Murray, Ann 62
  Elizabeth 229
  James 64,87
  John 24,30,40,62,102, 125,135,136,145,183,187, 194,195
  Richd Donavan 52
  Thomas 214
  William 24,155,194,241
Murrel/l, 164
  Francis 223
  John 22,230
  John Jonah 228
  Robert 230
  William 6,7
Murrey, William 62
Musgrove, Edward 11, 120,225
Myers, Jacob 12,130
  John 141
  Mary 141
  Mordecai 185
Myles, Aquilla 36
  Eliz'a 36
Mylne, Robert 178

Nagerly, Gasper 7

Nash, Edward 229
  William 33
Naylor, Margaret 208,210
Neal, Charles 82
  George 178
  Jacob 193
  James 158
  Joseph 158
Neale, William 178
Neall, Thos 6,7
Nealy, Elizabeth 155
  John 155
  Samuel 114
  William 44
Ned, Old 93
Neel, Andrew 97
  Samuel 97
  Thomas 10,158,172,174
Neeley, George 79
  Hugh 102
  Samuel 8
Neely, Hugh 102
  Thomas 196
Negerlie, Margaret 65
  Peter 65
Neil, Andrew 51
  Sarah 51
Neill, Roger 63
Neilson, 111
  David 76
  Jared 111,184,208
  Josiah 82
  Reason 84
  Samuel 137
Neisbett, Saml Jr. 30
Nellson, Reason Jr. 182
Nelly, William 34
Nelson, David 118
  Hugh 90
  Jared 10,111
  John 47
  Joseph 91,94,100
  Mary (Sumpter) 111
  Mary 91,100,174
  Reason 73
  Rezon 179
  Samuel 47,234
  Samuel Jr. 46
  William 47,234
Nenson, Dorman 20
Neptown, Constantine 120
Nesbitt, William 143
Nesmith, Samuel 82,110,
    113,122,132,124
Nesser, Philip 192
Nethercliff, Thomas 223
Netmons, John Rodolph
    167
Nettles, Lucy 142
Neufville, John 89
Nevel, James 67
Nevill, Isaac 141
Nevin, John 97,133,195

Newbury, John 190
Newell, John 218
Newitt, William 173
Newman, Edward 21,153
  Joseph 30
  Samuel 4,65
  Solomon 117
Newsom, Solomon Jr. 4
Newsum, Solomon 4,166
Newton/s, 170
  Constantine 143
  Jane 132
  John 36,37,140
Neyle, Gilbert 157,161
  Sampson 24,29,30,36,50,
    157,161
Nicholas/es, George 40
  Henry 96,101,111,142,
    148,177,206
  Isaac 177
  James 206,224
Nichols, Henry 109,126
  Isaac 111
  James 177
  John 237
  Stephen 17
  Thomas 111
  William 85
Nicholson, 71
Nickels, David 93
  George 174
Niel, John 51
  Thomas 51
Nielson, Alexander 189
  Mathew 47
Niess, John 207
Nighton, Isaac 208
Nipper, John 113
Nisbett, William 3,5,13,17,
    25,30,32,33,41,42,43,49,
    58,78,94,97,101,103,104,
    109,112,117,125,126,128,
    142,143,152,158,168,180,
    186,187,199,190,205,208,
    209,218,221,223,244
Nivian, John 240
Nivie, Esther 48,177,214
Nivre, Esther 56
Nix, Charles 237
Nixon, George 123,198,227
Noah, John 24
Noble, Alexander 88,126,
    143
  Henry 223
  James 88,126,143,212
  Thomas 231
Nobles, Joseph 90
  Winifred 90
Noddings, George 76,123,
    182
Noes, Nicholas 182
Noland, Aunsbrey 61
Nolloboys, 165

John 3
Nollsbey, James 147
Noloboy, James 117
Nolphes, Simon Jr. 141
Nonemacker, Benedick 117
Norman, John 105
  Joseph 131
Norrell, James 37
Norris, Jno 213
  William 125,164,174
North, Edward 230
  Elizabeth 140
  John 33,44
  Richard 34,44
  Sarah 44
  Thomas 144
  William 140
Nother, Wm. 53
November, negro 110
Nowell, James 217
  Robert 232
Nuckols, John 79,117,211
Nufer, John Herman 91
Nuffer, Harman 104,108,111
Nuggelie, Peter 142
Nunry Mary 5
Nunry, Grifen 5
Nunry, Griffin 5
Nutt, John 40

OCain, Jeremiah 61
OCarrol, Anne 217
OHear, John 86,167
OHerins, Morris 94
ONeal, Charles 15,82,184,
    200
  Margaret (McKelvey) 15
ONeals, John 33
  William 33
Oakley, Thomas 39
Oats, Edwards 43
  Martin 16,51,104
Obrien, Thos 107
Oden, Thomas 202
Odingsell, Charles 116,168,
    198
Odom, Hester 243
  Isaac 243
  Sabart 243
Odum, Mary 112
  Richard 112
Offill, William 89,95
Offut/t, Archibald 57,74,
    123,194,231,232
  Lettice 231
Ogelbay, James 218
Ogier, Catharine 128
  Lewis 128,168,199
Ogilvie, Benjamin 97
  Charles 75,82
  Geo. 117
  Martha 97
Ogle, John 31,36,240

Robert 103
Oglesbee, Elijah 151
Oglethorpe, Hannah 228
  John N. 66,103,109,113,
    128,137,138,142,148,151,
    206,215,226,228
  John Newman 12,40,
    45,59,73,75,95,96,102,
    169,173, 198
Oldfield, John 150
  Scots 153
Oliphant, James 129,130,
  135,221,226,227,237
Oliver, George 165
  John 97,114
  Joseph 195
  Mark 220
  Peter 83
  Rachel 220
  Robert 75
  Thomas 25,75
Omar, James 69
Onsel, Abraham 95
Onsett, Henry 56
Oquin, Daniel 68
Oram, John 53
  Joseph 64
Orr, John 146
  Robert 98
  William 132
Osborn, William 184
Osborne, Thomas 23
Osbourn, Alexander 80
Osgood, Josiah 73
Oswald, 170
  William 192
Ott, Ulrick 159
Otterson, Samuel 132
Ottolinjke, Joseph 88
Ouldfield, John 67
Ousby, Thomas 240
Outerbridge, Mary 49
  White 19,49,122
  William 49
Owen/s, Frances (Kerch) 2
  James 86
  John 44,99,204
  Langford 17
  Thomas 43,218
  Wm. 8

Pace, Drewry 106
  James 113
Pack, Joseph 194
Pado, Abraham 176
Page, Thomas 18,27,133,134
Pagets, Francis 94,139
  John 54,94,242
Pagget, Francis 22
Pain, John 173
Paisley, Thos. 122
Palatine, John Carteret 109
Palmarin, Peter 230

Palmenter, Joseph 78
Palmer, Ann 54,104
  Charles 54,127
  Elizabeth (Jones)(St.
    John) 127
  Elizabeth 161
  John 11,42,104,115,139,
    162
  John Jr. 218
  Joseph 170
  Mary 151
  Robert 151
  Thomas 100,181
  William 151
Pamor, John 204,218
Panting, Thomas 209
Pardo, Abraham 9
Paris, James 105
Park, John 26,211
Parker, Elisha 219
  Elisha Harrison 219
  John 161
  John Jr. 192
  Sarah 139,204
  Timothy 9,51,54,63,66,
    123,124,163,173
  William 48,139
Parkins, Daniel 60
  David 60
  Patience 60
Parkinson, John 243
Parks, George 15
  Thomas 94
Parmenter, Benjamin 116
  Philemon 85
  Sarah 78
Parrish, Alexander 89
Parrock, Jno 195
Parsons, Anna 182
  James 54,62,96,101,109,
    112,114,124,125,126,142,
    143,156,167,169,191,194,
    214,228,233,239
  James O'Brien 96
  John 160
  Robert 71,122
  Robert Jr. 71,122
  Samuel 26,182
  Simon 16,122
  Susanna (Miles) 96
  William 122
Partin, Charles 236
Partridge, William 224
Paschart, John 223
Paslay, Robert 196
Paterson, Ann 241
Path, Ashley Ferry 91
Patrick, 171,188
  Alexander Kill 172
  Casimir 37
  Henry 13,37,56,69,70,
    153,159,160,184,196,217,
    223,224,240

John 103
Joshua 80
Luke 2
Mary 80
Robert 80
Robert Jr. 80
Patridge, William 38
Patterson, Thomas 3,6,21,90
Patton, Arthur 123,124,144,
  173
  James 8,9,10,14,62,74,
    90,104,114,146,154,196,
    203
  John 188
  Mathew 123
  Robert 154,217
  Samuel 175
  William 146
Pattrick, William 80
Patty, James 60
Paul, Archibald 8
  Barbary 28
  James 54
  John Jacob 28
Paulding, William 144
Pawderdussen, Alexr 150
Pawley, 181
  Ann 81
  Anthony 119
  Elizabeth Mary 63
  George 5,49,51,52,63,69,
    70,76,81,100,119,145,
    150,153,164,178,229
  George Jr. 52,63,100
  Hannah 63
  Mary 51,118,119
  Percival 81
  Percivell 150
  Sarah 62,100
  Shorey 229
  Susanna 49
  Susannah (Allen) 81
  William 118,119,150
Paxton, James 155
Paycom, John 29
Payne, John 96,186
  Joseph 121
  Philip 121
Peace, Isaac 98,120
Peacomb, Joseph 17
Peaglar, Martin 80
Pearce, Abraham 124,221
  Eleanor 124
  Elizabeth (Hutcheson) 79
  James 237
  John 21
  Offspring 13
Pearman, Thomas 49
Pearson, Enoch 132
  Jeremiah 142
  John 67,83,84,115,195,
    198,212
  Joshua 226,227

Philip 10,51,62,66,106,
  115,117,130,147,228,240
Peart, James 27,128,134,
  135,169,190,197,199,200,
  206,207,220
Peele, John 233
Pegues, Claudius 5,57,68,
  70,71,91,99,124,184,215,
  219,228,233
  Claudius Jr. 68
  William 125,184,218,219,
  233
Pelot, John 31,128,135,230
Pence, Elizabeth 92
Pendarvis, Brand 238
  Elizabeth 182
  John 2,89,182
  Josiah 134,135,169,190,
  200
  Thomas 182
Pender, John Arnel 154
  John Arnold 17
Pendergrass, Darby 112,120,
  142,159,161,180,201,203,
  229,231
Pendleton, Hen. 231
Penington, Abraham 225
  Isaac 72,83,84,176
  Jacob 72,83,84,176,102,
  225
  Jacob Jr. 72,84,176
  Mary 72,176
Penman, James 139
Pennington, Abraham 11,84,
  102
  Jacob 84
  Mary 225
Penny, William 40
Penrice, Edward 147
Penuce, William 117
Perdriau, John 204
  John Jr. 45
  Samuel 29,49,204,229
Perkins, Charles 60
  John 3,47,165,166
Peroneau, Arthur 207
  Henry 41,104
Peronneau, Alexander 107,
  120,207
  Henry 49,153,207
  Henry Jr. 192
Perrin, Wm. 85
Perroneau, Alexander 50,
  149
  James 102
  John 38
  Margaret 149
Perry, Edward 23,137,168,
  176,224,235,238
  Isaac 189
  John 31
  Joseph 160,200
  Mary 176

Richard 148
Susanna 234
Person/s, Collin 220
  John 220
  Philip 220
  Robert Jr. 71
  Simeon 71
  Simon 217
  Wm. 71
Peter, Charles Christopher
  197
  John 19
  Mary (Gautier) 197
  Mathias 22
  Michael 200
  Thomas 200
Peterman, Luis 227
Peters, John 29
  Solomon 131,150
Petigrew, Elizabeth 168
  James 168
Petrie, Alexander 151,193
  Elizabeth 193
  George 127
Petterson, Andrew 233
Pettypool, Philip 135,231
Peyer, J. L. 143
Peyrud, Gabriel 25
Pfeninger, Martin 235,237
Pfifer, John 67
Pfininger, Martin 99
Phag, Catherine (Houser)
  239,240
  Christopher 239
Phelp, Robt. 43
Phepoe, Elizabeth 237,238
  Thomas 11,12,18,21,27,
  31,50,63,69,81,89,94,
  125,129,152,182,205,213,
  237,238,242
Pheps, Joseph 90
Phifer, John 102
Philips, Benjamin 63,64
  Francis 32
  James 208,210
  John 186,217
  Stephen 174
Philp, Robert 111,164,193
Philport, Thomas 63
Phips, Arthur 148
Pickens, Gabriel 123,186
  John 14,42,147,210
  John Jr. 42
  Saphiah 123
  Zaruviah 123
Pickering, Joseph 28
Pickett, James 198
  Micajah 28,40
Pierce, Elizabeth (Hutch-
  inson) 92
  Ldw. 144
Pierons, Jacob 31,116,151
Pierson, Jeremiah 142

Pigg, John 93
Pillet, Daniel 134
Pinckney, 140
  Charles 16,29,40,41,48,
  49,60,116,161,189,222,
  243
  Charles Cotesworth 35,
  60,108,241
  Charles Jr. 16,108,222
  Cotesworth 108
  Deborah 131
  Elizabeth 29,49
  Frances Susannah 207
  Francis 222
  George Charles 60
  Hopson 2,13,41,126,166,
  170,175,186
  Roger 2,13,21,25,41,56,
  98,106,126,160,166,170,
  175,186,194,195
  T. Jr. 225
  Thomas 48,60
  William 48,60,106,131,
  174
Pinkney, H'n 99
  Roger 99
Pinson, 114
Pinson, Aaron 97
Pintard, Lewis 139
Pit, Sam 69
Pitchline, Isaac 146
Pitman, James 70
Pits, Henry 6
Pittman, Alice 90
  John 96,106
Pitts, Henry 241
Platt, Thomas 142
Pledger, Joseph 3,233
  Philip 1,3,87,112,141,
  154,233
Plunkett, John 73
Poaug, Charlotte 227,228
  J. 182
  John 28,47,121,141,182,
  227,228,235,242
  W. 207
Poffey, Sim 93
Poinsett, Elisha 152,238
  Joel 139
  Peter 64
Polard, James 152
Polk, Ezekiel 6,7,10,30,41,
  46,73,79,84,85,188
  Thos 30
Polks, George 25
Ponder, James 123
Pool/e, 74
  Thos 18
  William 52
Pooley, John 43
Pope, 236
  Barnaby 45,66,219
Popwell, John 72,135

Porcher, 13,149
  Isaac 15,38,67,82,149, 205,209,210
  Joseph 18,149,154,221
  Mary 239
  Paul 18,20,134,239
  Peter 77,195,235,239
  Pou Jr. 1
  Samuel 19,47,210,221,239
Port, Benjamin 203
  Frances 203
  Joseph 76,203,204
  Thomas 162,203,204
Porter Mary (Waldron) 13
  David 79
  Elizabeth 13
  George 13
  Thomas 13
  William 90,142
Ports, 202
  Joseph 87
Postell, Elijah 56,111,112
  James 1,2,115,156,172, 224,225,242
  James Jr. 123,225
  John 20,86,116,133,158, 160,164,185,208,216,224, 225
  John C. 133
  John Jr. 123,225
  Rosina 133
  Saml 31
  Susannah 111,156,157
Potter, John 22
Potts, Ezekiel 85
  George 85
  John 85,141,164
  Thomas 5,36,141,164,187
Pou, Gavin 32,54,115
  James 231
  Robert 54
Pough, Martha 78
  Willoughby 78
Pouncey, William 211
Pourquin, Henry 27
Powe, Thomas 240
Powell, Elizabeth 168
  G. G. 100
  Geo. Gab. 131
  George 122,125,236
  George Gabriel 109,149, 170
  Jacob 138,217
  Jas. 232
  Patience 125
  Sivility 125
  Thomas Warburton 168, 236
  Thos 82
Powers, Andrias 230
  George 51
  Henry 36
Powman, Thomas 174

Poythress, Edmund 162
Pratt, Thomas 129
Preel, George 33
Prells, 35
Prent, John 168
Pressley, David 9
Preston, Anthonoy 144
  Isaiah 144
  Thescilla 144
Prestwood, Betty 174
  Thomas 124,174,181,196
Price, Ann 192
  Eligah 100
  Henry 132
  Hopkin 7,11,16,20,24,35, 50,58,89,100,104,125, 126,138,146,147,155,159, 172,185,216,229,235,241, 242
  Hopkin H. 216
  John 171
  Jonathan 41
  Mary 41
  Richard 134,174
  Thomas 72,212
  William 111,167,192,202, 212
Prickett, Ephraim 44,147
  Rowland 105
Prielow, 46
Prince, Ann 58
  Charles 58
  Joseph 125,168
  Thomas 212
Pringel, Godfrey 130,234
Pringle, John 29,42,54,106
  Robert 24,61,69,81,82, 93,106,128,146,209
Print, William 14,23,35,38, 41,138,177,182,197,216, 232,235
Prioleau, Catherine 172
  Colonel 3
  Elijah 86,180
  Hext 210
  Philip 202
  Samuel 16,24,89,172,182, 188,209
  Samuel Jr. 172,201
Prising, Christian 39
Pritchard, Eliza Ann 93
  James 93,183,201
  Paul 181
Proby, Solomon 42
Proctor, Richard 64
  Sarah 102
Prosser, Stephen 142
Provost, John 25
Pruder, John 112
Puckett, Ephraim 117
  Timothy 14
Pugh, Evan 94
  William 238

Willoughby 18,86,133, 134,135,185,197,206,208
Purcell, Henry 87,178
  James 154
  Joseph 87
  Sarah 87
Purdy, Robert 23
Purry, John Peter 231
  Peter 82
Purse, William 210
Pursley, James 217
Purves, John 51,54,63,66, 73,85,147,149,171,179, 188
Purvis, Geo. 119
  John 72,238
Pury, Chs. 114
Pury, John Peter 39,114, 133,134
Pussell, John 165
Putatt, John 118
Pye, Peter 97,163
Pyer, Michl. 168

Quacon, negro 122
Quarterman, William 13
Quash, Robert 56
Quelch, Andrew 38,97,117, 166,218
  Elizabeth 218
Quich, Lewis 20
Quin, Hugh 214
Quince, Parker 50,94,126, 166,222
  Susannah 50,94,126,166, 222
Quincy, Parker 50
  Susannah (Hasell) 50
Quinn, Simon 100

Racliffe, Thomas 46,200
Radcliff/e, Thomas 13,42
  Thomas Jr. 13
Rae/s, Stephen 60
  William 76,87,204
Ragan, 133
  Wm. 174
Raggins, John 7
Ragnous, John 162
Raiford, Mary 219
  Philip 130,132,144
  Sarah (Ellis) 228,229
  William 228
Raines, Richd 113
  William 219
Rall, John 199
Ramadge, Chas 123
Rambo, Laurence 109,175, 215
Ramey, Samuel 63
Ramond, David 167
Ramsay, Robt 10
Ramsden, John 115,157

Ramsey, 240
Ramsey, Isaac 74,85
　Margaret 79
　Robert 79
　Sarah 74
　Wm. 112
Randall, Jacob Jr. 7
Randolph, James 98,136
　Jane 136
　Jno 102
Ranger, Anna Margaret 120
Rantowle, James 237
Raper, Robert 35
Rapley, Andrew 73,163
　Richard Andrew 9,10,44, 33,51,89,92,105,175,176
Rassnett, John 160
Ratcliffe, Samuel 219
Ratliff, Richard 97
Rattray, John 64,165
Rattrey, James 141
Rauster, Christian 168
Raven, Elizabeth (Vanderhorst) 127
　John 227
　Mary (Cofer) 201
　William 127
Ravenel/l, Charlotte 232
　Daniel 48,111,204
　Daniel Jr. 104,232
　Henry 204,218
　Henry Jr. 218
　James 232
　Mary (St. Julian) 218
Ravens, 212
Ravot, Abraham 39,224
Rawlinson, Benjamin 10
Rawsom, William 10
Rawston, Atherton 171
Rawstorne, Arthurton 30
Ray, Chrimas 175
　Isaac 175
　John 25,184
　Robt. 66
Raymond, David 167
　Joseph 167
Raymor, Nathal 103
Rea, William 138,208,210, 226
Read, Elizabeth 197
　Jacob 23,96,109,183,195, 215
　James 68
　John 58,102
　Robert 124,173
　Sarrah Margriller 31
Reagin, John 60
　Jonathan 60
Reagon, Elizabeth 20
　John 20,42
Ream, Hans George 56
Reardon, Timothy 40
Reaves, Henry 72

Recks, John 19
Redhead, Geo. 131
Redlisperger, Christian 26, 36
　Elizabeth 26
Redmon, Andrew 63
Redorfgrand, J. 143
Reed, James 41,57,68
Rees, Benjamin 12,13,14,15, 45
　Daniel 109
　Edwin 12
　Hugh 12,181
　Isham 12
　John 15
　Joseph 202
　Martha 137
　Roger 147
　William 12,13,14,15
Reese, Evan/Evans 211,218
　Sarah (Allison) 211
　Thomas 54
Reeve/s, Charlotte 209,225, 240
　Henry 139,167,209,225, 240
　Lewis 124,186
Rehm, Catharine (Keall) 134,135
　Frederick 134,190
Reid, Arthur 147
　James 97,131,161,184,242
　Susannah 242
Reily/ey, Miles 166,168
Reinauer, Leonard 134
Reine, Cornelius 190
Reinger, Anna Margaret 120
Reins, Cornelius 101,154
Reiser, Philip 232
Rembert, Abijah 14,45
　Andrew 54
　Andrew Jr. 13
　James 13,14,45,234
　Thomas 45
Remington, Ann (Burton) 104
　John 37,76,82,104
　John Jr. 138,200
　Margaret 104
　Ro't 37
　Sarah 200
Remley, Barbara 109,119
Remly, Barbara 108
　Martin 108,109
Remond, Jeremiah 158
Renerson, George 72,83
Rentz, George 6,21,94
　Margaret 94
Repault, 100
Repsommer, Pott 72
Resch, Alexander 237
Resor, Jacob 174

Ressinger, Fight 148
　John George 148
　Rachel 148
Reymonds, Joseph 39
Reynolds, Andrew 179,243
　David 218,231
　James 238
Reyquart, Christopher 220
Reys, Frederick 195
Rheffs, 48
Rhett, Mary (Wright) 50
　Sarah (Trott) 50
　William 50,144
Rhind, David 47,53,64,66, 75,207
Rhodes, 35
　Jno 174
　Wm. 170
Ribols, Elizabeth 125
Rice, James 216
　John 184
　Samuel 145
Rich, James 162
Richard/s, James 134
　James L. 122
　James Lytten 177
　Mary 27
Richardson, 184
　Arthur 119,135
　Edward 181
　Elizabeth (Hatter) 110
　John 75
　Richard 45,47
　Saml. 32
　William 135,218,234
Richbourg, Claudius 139
　Henry 184
　Rene 70
　Samuel 21
　Unity 139
Richburg, Claudius 104
　Henry 185
　Unity 104
Richerson, Amos 85
Richie, Mary 199
Richman, Jacob 239
Ricker, Elizabeth 136
Riddle, John 109
Riddlesparger, Christian 164
　Elizabeth 164
Riddlespurger, Christian 182
Rideout, Richard 218
Ridgdell, John 4
Ridlesparger, Christian 72, 171
Rife, Frederick 224
Rigen, Nicholas 208
Rigg/s, 60
　Alexander 193
　John 39,154
　Saml 25

Riley, Saml 167
Rilhover, George 121
Rilliette, Bartolemy 190
Rink, Christr. 158
Rintz, George 92
  Margret 92
Rippon, Isaac 19
Risener, George 53
Risk, 237
  William 160
Riss, John 56
Rits, Anthony 52,53
  Ietre 52,53
Rivers, Beulah 156
  Elizabeth 139
  George 239
  Henry 36
  Isaac 159,239
  John 2,227
  John Jr. 229,230
  Joseph 227,239
  Rebecca 28
  Robert 21,28,239
  Sarah 229,230
  Thomas 190,197,200,220, 221,227
Rives, Wm. 115
Rixey, John 146
Roach, Henry 190
  John 86
  Patrick 142
  Wm. 160,166
Robbers, John 76
Robenson, Alexander 143
  James 44
Robert, Elias 123
  Elias 35,57,74,162,179, 185,192,206,219,231,232, 242
  James 57,74,103,104,179, 180,231,232
  John 57,74,103,179,180, 231,232
  John Elias 57
  Jonah 154
  Josiah 149
  Judith 57,74
  Peter 57,74,103,104,149, 154
  Sarah 57,74
  Sarah Jr. 35
Roberts, Aaron 28
  Chas 146
  Isabella 167
  Jacob 75
  James 31
  John 123,160,194
  Moses 28,143
  Obadiah 216
  Owen 209
  Reuben 191
  Thomas 4,165,167
  Thomas Jr. 165

William 46,236
Wm. H. 237
Robertson, Alexander 142
  Anthony 142
  Archey 54
  Daniel 97
  Hannah 14
  James 14,17,53,85,178
  John 56,155,160
  Robert 151
  William 101
Robeson, John 189
Robins, Joseph 63
Robinson, Archibald 10
  Charles 226
  Hanah 163
  James 163
  John 34,207
  Joseph 54,73,78,79,118, 242,243
  Lily 54,63
  Matthew 212
  Richard 165
  Wm. 168
Robison, Archibald 10
  Margaret 10
  Sarah 10
  Wm. 189
Robson, James 178
Roche, Francis 132
  Jordan 28
  Mathew 64
  Thomas 237
Rodgers, Christopher 223, 242
  George 3,117,165,166
  Jacob 228
  James 203
  Jean 199
  John 97,117,241
Rodland, Mary 113
  Maryan 113
  Nicholas 113
Rodolph, 86,197
Roe, James 1
Rogers, Benjamin 69, 122, 149
  Christopher 151,152,156
  Eliz'th 151,152
  George 39
  Jacob 233
  James 203
  Jane 199
  John 17,22,90,147
  Mary 62
  William 9,62,90
  Winifred 90
Rohdes, Wm. 35
Rohte, Peter 32
Rolain, James 159
Role, John 61
Rolison, 182
Rolla, Hans 52

Rollers, John 76
Rolleson, Benjn. 10
Rollinson, Abegal 174
  Abigail 40
  William 40
Rollison, Obigal 174
Romney, Andrew 48
Ronals, Agnes 225
  James 102,225
Roper, Joseph 63
Roquemore, Jaquar 8,9
Rosborough, Alexander 47
Rose, Alexander 117,139, 221,222
  Francis 107,110,120,209
  Hepzibah (Christie) 7
  Hezekia 146,147,190
  Hugh 86
  John 23,26,160,193,242
  Robt. 125
  Thomas 38,139
  William 108
Rosewell, John 77,88
  Walter 66
Ross, Arthur Brown 75
  Hannah 75
  Isaac 135,142
  James 105
  John 107
  William 118,239
Ross, slave 234
Rossel, J. T. 54
Roth, Christian 65
  William 43,73
Rothmahler, Ann 106
  Job 4,5,52,54,80,92,106, 112,130,133,178,181,185, 188,204,216,218,228
Roupell, George 12,108,221
Rout, George 131,218
Routledge, George 223
Roux, James 180
Row, Nathaniel 144
Rowan, James 188
  John 131
  Mathew 17,154,221
Rowe, Christopher 3,32,36, 61,62,67,90,112
  Samuel 54,112
  Walter 215
Rowell, Hubert 130
  John 192,206
Rowlain, James 84
Rowlin, Peter 41
Rows, Arthur 151
Roya, Willm. 218
Royall, John 121
Roye, George 138,217
Rudall, Wm. 151
Rudhall, Wm. 139,151
Rudnall, Wm. 139
Ruff, George 56,67
Rugeley, 109

Henry 101,129,179,203,
  214,243,244
R. 100,127,129,176,200,
  215
Rowland 4,12,15,27,40,
  61,118,125,126,129,152,
  155,156,165,168,169,177,
  178,179,199,201,202,203,
  214,243
William 1,6,7,8,10,12,
  13,15,18,20,21,22,23,24,
  25,27,28,29,30,31,35,36,
  37,38,39,40,41,42,43,44,
  45,49,52,54,56,64,65,66,
  67,69,70,71,72,75,76,77,
  81,82,83,84,85,86,88,90,
  91,96,97,99,103,104,105,
  106,110,111,112,113,115,
  116,117,119,120,121,123,
  124,142,143,144,145,146,
  148,149,150,151,152,154,
  155,156,157,158,160,161,
  164,165,167,170,171,172,
  174,176,215
Ruger, Christina 98
  William 98,194
Rugge, James 243
Rumley, Andrew 217
Rump/h, John 31,116,150,
  151
  Peter 232,236
Rush, Abraham 104
  Barbara 104
  Frederick 104
  Herman 127
  Mary 104
Rushurt, John 200
Russ, Jonathan 3,71,211
  Joseph 71
  Thomas 152
Russell, 54,66
  Charles 132
  Elizabeth 133
  Jeremiah 139
  John 40,86,105,133,174,
    203,232,233
  John Jr. 6
  Joseph 159,242
  Nath 82
  Walter 237
  William 54,106
Russes John 28
Rutledge, Andrew 212,223
  E. 192,240
  Elizabeth 96
  Hannah 118
  Hugh 44,90,213
  J. 37,106
  John 2,7,9,12,29,30,35,
    42,48,54,62,96,126,184,
    192,194,212
  Sarah 119
Ryan, Benj. 202

Lacon 201
Ryley, Barnabay 17,18
  Bryan 17
  John 17,18
  Laurance 23
  Martha (Ferguson) 17,18
Rylie, Bryan 187
Ryly, George 150

Sabb, Morgan 149
  Thomas 105,174
  William 184
Sacheverall, Thomas 17,91
Sacheverell, Thos 37
Sacheveull, John 4
Sachweiller, Melchior 116,
  151
Sadler, Isaac 5
  James 221
Saffold, Daniel 79
  Reuben 79
  William 79
Sallegia, 93
Sallens, Robt. 47
Salley, John 19
Sallisbury, Andrew 106
  Pettegrew 106
Salmon, Nathaniel 169
  Wm. Jeanes 161
Salsbery, Andrew 10
Salters, Richard 98
Saltus, Henry 13,50
  Jenry 13
  Mary 13
  Richard 175,199
Salvador, Francis 33,89,
  105,166
  Joseph 9,10,33,89,92,
    105,166,175,176
Samet, Lenard 217
Sampson, slave 234
Sams, Robert 90
Samways, Henry 239
  John 107
Sandel, John 88,174
  Peter 88,174
Sanders, Abraham 100
  Ann 178
  Henry 137
  James 5,156,178,210,241
  John 156,161
  Lawrence 101
  Peter 117,143
  Roger 121
  Thomas 73,89,92,105
  Thomas Martyn 202
  William 23,171,178,215,
    242
Sandricur, Elizabeth
  (Swertfeger) 223
  John 160,223
Sandys, William 178,180,197
Sansum, John 27

Susannah (Hodgedon) 27
Santee, James 11
Sarah, negro 121
Sarazin, Catharine 242
Sarazin, Jonathan 69,81,166
Sarrazen, Murreau 224
Sarrazin, Jonathan 81,126,
  127
  Morreau 69,81
Sartor, John 146
Satchwell, George 58,59,128
Satterwhite, John 74
Satur, Abraham 156
Saunders, F. 197
  Francis 197
  James 5
  John 71
  Laurence 170
  R. Parker 169
  Roger 77
  Sarah 170
  Wm. 169
Sausey, Gabriel 39
Saussey, Catharine 43
  David 39,43
Savage, Ann (Allen) 61
  Ann 83,127
  Edward 19,107
  Jeremiah 99,179,197
  John 12,15,22,34,54,61,
    67,83,114,118,121,126,
    127,136,137,142,152,162,
    173,183,226
  Martha 66,183
  Samuel 60,58
  Thomas 107
  William 66,183,207
  William Jr. 127
Savery, James 59
Sawyer, Elisha 111,167
Saxby, George 24,69,81,203,
  209
Saxon, Yancey 30
  George 30
Saxweller, Melchior 31
Sayler, Jacob 130
Schetterle, John 8
Schitz, Susannah 186
Schlatter, Paul 11,16,20,
  23,35,50,68,126,146,186,
  187,191,226,229,230
Schmidt, John Barnard 32
Schober, Anna Margaret 42
Schuckall, Henry 136
Schultz, Henry Ephraim 146
Scott, 184
  Archib'd 205
  Arthur 93
  Benjamin 67
  Dorcas 48
  James 14,44
  Jno 228
  John 6,19,35,43,48,53,

65,100,165,183,184,214, 217
John Jr. 165
Jonathan 35,240
Mary 20,42,76,159
Peter 20,42,200
Samuel 53,65
William 61,76,126,159, 171,175,209,219,220
William Jr. 204
Scottow, Joshua 83
Mary (Smith) 83
Screven, Benjamin 113
Eleanor 21,84
Elisha 70,113,178
Elisha Jr. 113
Hanah 178
James 198,239
Joshua 70
William 21,190,203,230, 239
Scriven, Elisha 69
William 46,52,84
Scudder, John 96
Scurlock, Philip 109
Se, Che 93
Seabrook, John 24
Jos. 45
Seal, Anthony 142
Sealy, John 29,116,147
William 78
Seaman, George 170
Searight, Robert 30
Searson, Thomas 128,134
Searth, Jonathan 88
Seastrunk, Henry 159
M. Magdalen 159
Seawright, Elizabeth (McCullogh) 101
George 42,66,217
James 62,101
Sarah (McNichol) 118
Secheverals, 142
Seirs, Mary 34
Self, Ezekiel 228
Seller, Mathew 122
Mathias 160
Sere, Noah 32
Serjant, Edward 242
Setterin, Ann 224
Sewell, Edward 129
Seywald, Christian 33
Shackelford, William 51,160
Shackleford, Willm 178
Shakespear, John 167
Shaley, John Wolfgang 66
Shapland, John 2
Sharp, James 22,130
Jeremiah 75,93
Wm. 168,210
Sharrod, Elizabeth 115
Shaw, John 207
Joshua 58

Saml 89
Shecut/t, Abraham 98,163
Mary 163
Shed, George 56
Sheed, George 26,41,49,84, 94,102,111,129,130,131, 133,135,136,137,138,139, 140,144,147,159,160,161, 180,181,182,183,185,186, 187,190,191,192,193,194, 197,205,206,207,208,209, 210,211,216,218,219,220, 221,223,224,225,226,227, 229,230,231,232,233,234, 235,236,237,238,240,241, 242,243
William 36,94
Sheedy, Geo. 21
Sheekle, Adam 83
Sheets, Christopher 186,229
Sheier, Paul 32
Shepheard, Alexander 139
Ann (Langford) 139
Charles 167
Thos 167
Sheppard, John 78
Sherly, Catharine 67
Sherrod, Alexander 115
Sherss, Christopher 18
Shetts, Christopher 191
Sheuer, Paul 62
Shewmake, Daniel 78
Shieder, John 2
Shiffell, John Lowes 192
Shillins, John 193
Shingelton, 144
Benjn 167
John 18
Shinhur, Solomon 97
Shirley, Thomas 111,167, 192,202,212
Casper 62
Shivers, John 121
Shlapper, Conrad 146
Shockley, Prudence 146
Thomas 146
Shoemake, Volantine 121
Shorters, John 206
Shower, George 3
Shram, George Barnard 67
Shrewbury, Edward 93
Shrewsbury, Edward 242
Rebekah 242
Shubrick, Jacob 87
Richard 186
Thomas 179,186,220,221, 227,242
Thomas Jr. 4,7,12,29,35, 226,203
Shular, George 67
Shuler, Barbara 120
Shuller, Nicholas 229
Shumake, John 71,162

Shuman/n, Peter 171
Martin 242
Shutterling, John 209
Sigwald, Christian 25,42, 47,132,209,234
Sill, Daniel 162
Simer, Adam 229
Simes, Benjamin 97
Simmerly, Jacob 76
Simmons, Benjamin 234
Ebenezer 100
Henry 8
James 100
John 32,42,150,202,207, 227
Maurice 64
Samuel 39,94
Susannah 227
Vincent 132
William 88,124
Simon, Samuel 54
Simond, Peter 68,110
Simons, Anthony 14
Edward 153
Eleanor 168
Keating 153
Maurice 51,66,68,75,107, 139,199
Patk. 125
Peter 48,114,119,153, 168,218
Simonson, Isaac 237
Simpkins, Arthur 44
Simpson, 106,169
Barbara 20
Elizabeth 24,62,194
Gilchrist 160
Hugh 126
James 17,19,20,66,100, 144,152,168,213,217,221
James Gilchrest 122
James Gilchrist 164
John 19,111,156
Sarah 122,123,164,182
Thomas 10
William 24,62,98,129, 142,144,146,160,194,196, 211
Sims, Benjamin 182,232,236
Jacob 150
Rebecca 70
Thos 70
William 79,185,199,211
Sincklear, James 181
Singellton, Benjamin 131
Singelton, John 192
Richard 67
Singletary, Anna (Darby) 140
Benjamin 140
Singleton, Christopher 195
Daniel 192
Martha 98

Mary 195
Mathew 45
Mathias 195
Matthew 135,181,195,196
Richard 27,56,77,135,192
Robert 135,195
Samuel 192
Sarah (Ford) 192
Thomas 16,148,149
William 192
Sinkfield, Francis 44
Sinkler, 145
  James 199
  James Jr. 191
  John 167
  Peter 51
Sinquefield, Aaron 63
  Francis 63,150
  William 4,62,63
Sistrunck, Henry 159
Sizemore, Henry 74
Sizer, Charity 211
Sizzer, Charity Huney 211
  Sarah Huney 211
Skeen, 11
  Alexander 23
Skelly, William 42
Skinner, Alexr 169
Skirving, James 19,37,64,
  169,216
  James Jr. 224,225
Skottowe, Thomas 5,112
Skreene, John 194
Skrene/s, John 20,123
Skrine, John 57,74,82,180,
  204,214
Skriner, Jacob 223
Skudder, Thomas 74
Slann, Andrew 19,20,58,241
  Ann 241
  Ann Jr. 241
  Peter 20,58
  Thomas 241
Slappey, Casper 216
  George 196
Sleigh, Samuel 94,105
Sleighen, Britta 118
Sleys, Ulrick 148
Slight, Oldrick 53
Slon, James 95
Smelie, Wm. 19,20
Smiser, Paul 24,186,191
Smith, 189,202,236
  Abraham 182
  Ann (McQueen), 61
  Ann (Mouatt) 233
  Anne 221
  Archer 75,112,172,221
  Benjamin 24,69,81,89,
    143,171,186,187,188,196,
    209,224,233,240
  Benjamin Wragg 187
  Bostian 157

Caleb 93
Charles 74,83,117,166
Christopher 49,233
Daniel 192
David 189
Ebenezer 15,16
Elizabeth (Ball) 101
Elizabeth (Holmes) 91
Elizabeth 61,71,82,129,
  224,233
Emanuel 233
Felix 159
George 7,8,56,94,97,112,
  118,120,127,133,181,185,
  186,187
Henry 6,101,209
Jackson 160
James 22,31,104,113,124,
  126,129,140,142,143,148,
  176,201,219,242
Jane 231
John 4,12,22,42,61,67,
  71,82,91,188,203,223,
  229,231,241
Josiah 106,146,150,171,
  180,181
Josiah Jr. 12,97,106,181
Martha 131,183
Mary (Besset) 127
Mary (Bissett) 233
Mary (Scottow) 83
Mary 22,158,168,187,196,
  209
Melchior 32
Messor 62
Philip 121,175,182
Press 29,30,143,180,224,
  226
Rachel 233
Ralph 28,40,75,130,166
Rignal 36
Robert 1,17,36,38,87,
  123,167,181,201,207,211,
  227,242
Robt. Arrow 116
Roger 9,99,128,153,188,
  226
Samuel 83
Sarah 140,208,210
Thomas 1,6,35,36,49,81,
  89,123,125,133,138,152,
  161,162,164,167,186,187,
  201,208,209,210,211,224,
  225,227,234
Thomas Loughton 98,187,
  188
William 1,6,7,22,38,77,
  122,131,158,179,183,188,
  196,202,233
Smithers, Christopher 222
Smyser, Paul 37
Smyth, John 212
Snead, Robert 74,75

Sneashe, 94
Snees, Conrad 165,175
Snees, Elizth. 175
Sneider, Michael 12
  William 12
Sneither, Jacob 16
Snelgrove, Henry 107
  John Jr. 107
Snell, Adam 120
Snellgrove, Freeman 145,
  161
Snelling, Henry 59,61,114,
  128,192
Snells, Henry 150
Sness, Elizabeth 165
Sneyder, Hendrick 107
Snider, Jacob 51,62
  Michael 130
  William 51,62
Snipes, 119
  William Clay 242
Snow, Francis 113
  George 129,132
  James 113
  Margaret 120,155
  Thomas 129,132
  William 113,120,155
Sommer, Adam 229
Sommers, Humphrey 104,
  155
  John 156
  Susanna/h 104,155
Sorsby, Samuel 191
Soulegre, John 35
  John James 139
Sours, William 229
South, Hardy 77
Southells, Mary 236
Southwell, Edward 193
Soverance, John 218
Spann, John 163
  William 163
Spear/s, Charles 142
  Jacob 184
  James 129,130
  Johan Jacob 184
  Sarah 142
Speed, G. 18
Speer, Ann 119
  Robert 119
Speissiger, John 146
Speitz, Mary (Mann) 213
Spencer, Calvin 148,233
  Joseph 187
  Saml 91,195
  William 239
Spidel, Abraham 52
Spidle, Abraham 8,242
Spiers, Zachariah 236
Spiken, Mary Catharine 232
Spikes, 106
Spillock, Comfort 166
  Drury 166

Spires, William 129
Spits, John 16
Spitzen, Mary Catharine 182,232,236
Spooler, Catharine 167
  Margaret 167
  Philip 167
Spooner, Ephraim 58
Sporg, Hans 162
Springer, Cooper 102
Spullock, Robert 166
Spurgen, John 130
Spurgin, Elizabeth 102
  John 102
Spurlock, Benjamin 184
Spyer, John 121
St. John, Audeon 164,184, 205
  Autoen 110
  Elizabeth (Jones) (Palmer) 127
  Elizabeth 47,152
  James 25,47,70,127,152, 184,205,222,225
  John 232,236
  Mary 164
St. Julian/en, Mary (Ravenel) 218
  Elizabeth De. (Marian) 218
  Peter De 223
St. Martin, John 181,211
St. Peair, Lewis 40
St. Pierre, Lewis de 124, 190,173
Stabler, Barbara 223
  Gottlieb 223
Stack, Wm. 205
Stafford, John 141,231
  Robert 151,163
  Susanah 231
  William 82
Staley, Peter 130,159
Stallings, Elias 53,65
  Frederick 53,65
  James 53,65
Stallion, Elias 100
Stamburger, Christina 138
Stanyard, James 167
Stanyarn/e, Archd. 167
  Benjamin 91
  John 170
  Joseph 36,233
Stapf, Lewis 3,6,21,90,92
  Margaret 6,21,92
Stapler, Abraham 157
Staples, Abrm. 203
Stark, Jeremiah 144
  Robert 125,126,189
  Thos 72
Starling, William 236
Starmonth, James 97
Starns, Ebenezer 85

Stead, 127
  Benjamin 30,31,117
  Margaret (Ferguson) 73
  Susannah (Miller) 73,74
  William 73
Stedham, Benjamin 93
Stedman, James 234
Steed, Wm. 169
Steedman, Elizabeth 102
  James 102
Steel, Aaron 72
  John 187
Steen, John 78
Stell, Robert 155
Stent, Samuel 230
Stephen, Aaron 83
  Adam 83
Stephens, Andrew 1
  Ann 37
  Jesse 141
  John 79,80,92
  Martha (Mourey) 79, 80,92
  Martha 37
Sterling, Alexr. 225
Stevens, Aaron 83
  Cotton Mather 130
  Daniel 43,130
  Jervis Henry 169
  John 237
  Katharine 130
  Margarett 124
  Mary 127,143,169
  Richard 124
  Robert 131
  Samuel 73
  Willm. 39
Stevenson, Abigail 116
  James 50
  Jesse 243
  John 145,231
  Mary (Jones) 38,116
  Mary 116
  Mary Jones 27
  Noah 193
  Peter 27,38,116
  William 183
Steward, Charles Augustus 7,99,148,149,151,162,163
Stewart, Adam 144
  Ann 198
  Henry 104
  Hugh 236
  Jane 198
  Jas 213
  John 13,149
  Robert 106
  Thos 198
  William 102
Stiles, Ann (Garden) 30
  Benjamin 90
  Copeland 30
Still, John 138

Stillman, Augustine 21
Stirk, Benjamin 60
  Hannah 60,61
Stitt/s, Agness 111
  William 181
Stittsmith, Thomas 225
Stobo, Jacob 191
  James 2,94,105,169
  Mary 106,171
  Richard Park 69,81,106, 171,209
Stockton, Newberry 85
Stoll, David 21
Stone, Benjamin 139,242
  Joseph 85,139,242
  Thos 69,81
Story/ey, 99
  Charles 11
  Elizabeth (Warnock) 11
  John 4
  Marey 4
Stoutenburgh, William 25, 54,107
Stoutenmire, Martin 138, 217
Stover, Charles 232
Strain, Thomas 72
Stratford, Richard 195,196
Strawder, George 23
Street, Guignard 172
Stribling, William 142
Strick, James 64
Stringer, Francis 189
  Lucretia 189
  William 165
Strobel, Daniel 3,90
  Gasper 26
  Mary Elizabeth 90
Strober, John 78
Strobhar, Jacob 39
  Susannah 86
Stroble, Frederick 97
  Gasper 36
  John 97
  Margaret 97
  Obillia 36
Strohber, John 238
Stroman, Ballezor 31
  Baltazer/Baltzager 116, 151
Strong, Charles 47
Strother, Catharine 147
  Charles 150
  Francis 137
  George 13,103,147,150
  Jeane 137
  Jeremiah 147
  John 147,152
  Rebekah 239,240
  Richard 137,239,240
  William 98,148,149
Strouble, Gasper 164
Stroud, John 240

Joshua 59
Sarah 73
William 73
Stroup, John 193
Strozer, Peter 178
Struthers, William 69
Stuard, William 241
Stuart, Alexander 45
  Ann (Carson) 186
  Daniel 101
  Francis 186
  Henry 186,232
  John 128
  Robert 126
Sturgeon, John 158,190,237
Sturly, James 208
Sturtz, John 112
Stynwinder, Eberhard 28
Suestrunk, Henry 159
Sullivan, 20
  John 206
Summerford, Jeffery 39
Summers, Adam Jr. 132
  Ann (Dick) 87
  Ann (Morrit)(Fyffe) 188
  Elizabeth 59
  James 76,87,188
  John 59,77,88
  Margaret (Hasell) 87
Summervell, James 47
Summerville, James 47
Summott, Lenud 76
Sumott, Lenud 87
Sumpter, Mary (Nelson) 111
  Thomas 93,111,187,241
Sumter, Thomas 36,184,206, 208
Supre, Josiah 59
Suptan, William 75
Surveyor, D. 192,193,220
Sustrunk, Casper 159
  Gospar 159
  Henry Jr. 159
Sutliff, Abraham 139,140
Sutton, John 16
  Richard 173
Swabb, Mathews 28
Swadler, Abraham 216
  George 216
  Mary 64,216
Swaine, Thomas 4
Swallow, William 69,81,103
Swann, Robert 214
  Samuel 85,214
Swearingham, Joseph 42
Sweney, Richard 135
Swertfeger, Elizabeth (Sandricur) 223
  Elizabeth Herman 223
  Herman 223
Swighard, Gerorge 117
Swillevin, Owen 214

Swindershine, Nicholas 42
Swint, John 8,128,150
Swinton, Alexander 4,5,164
  Elizabeth 4,5
  Hugh 131,139,240
  Margaret 4,5
  William 4,63,69,125,164, 178
Swykard, George 117
Syfritt, Alexander 174
Sym, David 28
Syme, Elizabeth 110
  John 36,85,110,111,117, 189,197,201,214
Synes, Samuel 114
Sypit, Alexander 88

Tagert, John 211
Talbird, Henry 174,202
Tamplett, Elisha 205
Tanner, John 44
Tapley, Adam 124
  Edna 124
  Joel 196
  Mary 124
Tarar, Benjamin 82,70
Tate, Alexr Jr. 154
  James 196
  Jesse 211
  William 211
Tateman, Daniel 195
Taton, Anthony 86
Taylor, Alexander 106,146, 172,242
  Andrew 25
  Bennett 233
  Charles 238
  Christopher 22,185
  David 239
  Elias 141
  Jacob 153
  James 48,58,87,160,184
  John 16,48,242
  Jonathan 4
  Mary 74,160
  Michal 147
  Peter 89,150,225
  Reuben 1
  Robert 124,144,173
  Thomas 115,184,193
  William 74,188
Teabout, Junes 82
  Sarah 111
  Tennis 116
  Tunes 111
Tead, William 143
Teague, Elizabeth 23
Teal, John 113
Tear, William 113
Tebout, Tennis 116
Teel/e, Charles 64
  Edward 64,113
  Rebekah/Rebecca 64,113

Telebach, George 152
Telfair, Edward 71
Templeton, William 130,237
Tennent, Susannah 139
  William 139
Terrel/l, Anne 6
  Joshua 69
  William 6
Terrick, Jacob 162
  John 162
Terry, Champness 34,39
Terry, David 100
Testard, Robt. 233
Tetes, William 69
Thacker, Abraham 33
Tharin, Daniel 6,25,156,231
  David 6
  Elizabeth 231
Thayler, Emanuel 116
Theith, Will 82
Thesson, John 24
Theth, James 66
Theus, Eve Rosanna 66
  Jeremiah 4,12,66,203
  Randolph 110,127,205
  Simeon/Simon 66,142
Thills, Phillip 33
Thippy, Henry 128
Thomas, Abel 109
  Archibald 36
  Daniel 118
  Edwd. 186
  Isaac 109
  James 116,127
  John 12,30,34,77,212, 213,229
  John Jr. 183
  Lambel 155
  Martha 30
  Mary 109
  Patrick 44
  Robert 30,212
  Stephen 190
  Susannah 128
  Willm. 53
Thomerson, John 136
Thomlinson, Jno 63
Thompson, 237
  Alexander 47,228
  Andrew 161
  Ann 94
  George 112,201
  Hugh 102,163,170
  James 22,23,30,94,105, 144,151,201
  John 154,196
  John Jr. 70
  Jonathan 166,176
  Joseph 95,105
  Michael 142
  Moses 104,139,184
  Robert 94,163
  Samuel 99,154

Sarah Ann 191
Thomas 224
William 16,31,32,58,86,
  121,135,144,145,159,171,
  185,201,226
William Jr. 191
Thomson, Adam 202
  Andrew 152
  Archd. 36
  Elizabeth 201
  George 193
  James 98,151,153,174,
    201,207,219,229
  John 102,202
  Joseph 78
  Molly 202
  Moses 80,208
  Moses Jr. 80
  Walter 152
  William 2,16,74,149,182,
    191,220,225,229
Thornton, Mark 151
Thorpe, Robert 221
  Samuel 104
Threadcraft, Elizabeth 75
  George 75
Thweatt, David 116,165
Tidyman, Philip 24
Tier, Richard 140
Tierney, James 176
Tiffit, Nicolas 176
Tighe, Charles 70,185
Tillet, Giles 129
Tillett, Constant 30
  Giles 30,135
Tilly/ey, James 32,65
  Joseph 142
  William 112,142
Timmons, John 7,212
  Richard 200
  Samuel 212
  Thomas 200,212
  Thomas Jr. 200
Timothy, Peter 115
Timrod, Henry 234
Tims, Amos 217
  Hollis 228
Timsly, 70
Tindall, Mary 148
  Robert 148
Tines, Samuel 75
Tinley, Giles 148
Tippin, Joseph 226
Titmore, Elizabeth 17
  John 17
Tobias, Jacob 43,94,104,111
Tobler, Hamptron 222
  Ulrich 112
Tod/d, John Jr. 64
  Thomas 30,40,77,88,105,
    129,130,179,185,216
  William 31,32
Toland, Brian/Bryan 14,74

James 14
Janerett 14
Toles, John 3
Tollason, Daniel 78
  Sary 78
Tomb, Alexr. 202
Tomerlins, 233
Tomkins, Francis 184
  Stephen 184
  Thomas 184,219
Tonnerton, Tho. 240
Tooly, Robt. 93
Toomer, Anthony 75,172,
  198
  Benjamin 193
  David 54
Torrans, John 182
Totton, Jane 175
Tousigers, James 242
Towagger, James 104
Town, Little 93
Townsend, Daniel 43
  Ezekiah 54
  Ezekiel 18,21,63,94
  John 99,198
  Paul 19,99,116,135,146,
    194,220,228,235
  Stephen 147,157
  Thomas 93,99
  William 157
Townshend, 41
  Daniel 14,44
  Paul 160
Towsigger, James 215
Trail, James 19,23,64,107,
  111
Trammell, Thos 78
Trapier, Benjamin 54,76,87,
  152,158,204,218
  Elizabeth 152,158,216
  Judith 76,87
  Paul 51,67,76,87,120,
    126,128,131,133,152,158,
    168,177,178,204,214,216,
    226,227,240
Traweek, George 211
Tread, William 143
Trescot, Edward 38,39,230
Tress/es, Barbra 56,130
Treutle, John Adam 64
Trezevant, Isaac 222
  Isaac Stephen 222
  Theodore 115,117
Triets, Abraham 232
Triggs, John Jr. 157
Trott, Nicholas 50,208,210
  Sarah (Rhett) 50
  Sarah 165,191,208,210
Troup, Frances Charlotta
  117
  Henry 160,166
  John 5,6,13,17,18,21,23,
    26,27,29,32,36,41,42,46,

47,60,63,71,84,88,94,
  101,104,109,111,117,125,
  126,127,128,129,131,132,
  133,136,142,151,152,154,
  160,166,169,171,173,174,
  178,179,183,185,187,188,
  189,191,193,194,195,198,
  200,203,204,206,207,210,
  214,220,222,226,228,232,
  237,238,239,243,244
Trushet/t, Charles 134
  David 133,206
  Mark 75
Trusler, William 149,222
Tryer, Godfrey 83
Tryon, Gov. 46,76,236
  William 63,78,80,85,129,
    141
Tucker, Benjamin 29
  Christian 234
  Daniel 128,129
  John 42,162
  Ruth 42
  Thomas 197
  W. B. 12
  Warner 142
  William 16,77,87,106,
    118,119,153,154,160,175,
    195,203,223,234
Tufts, M. 100
  Mary 100
  Simon 26,91,100
  Simsor 107
Tuke, John 47,85
Tunis, John 157,161
Turbevell/e, Charles 86,135
Turblefield, William 82
Turk, John 34
Turnball, Patrick 3
Turnbull, Patrick 2,89,200
  Robt. 199
Turner, Alexander 243
  Ann 75,108
  Edward 119
  James 54,107,108,131
  John 70,95,104,119,131,
    163,215,225
  Joseph 163
  Samuel 33
  Thomas 5,10,15,39,47,48,
    53,58,59,63,65,75,90,93,
    108,120,123,143,149,152,
    156,160,161,165,175,201,
    202,226
  Vinuas 142
  Wm. 36,60
Turnipseed, Beat 72
Turpin, Hugh 183
Turquand, Paul 138
Tutt, Barbara 105
  Benjamin 73,95,105,149,
    223
Tweed, Alexander 27,63

James 27
Twist, Robert 155
Twitty, William 79
Tydings, Phillip 220
Tyler, Saml 203,204
Tyserman, Dorothy 24
  Philip Jacob 24

Uckerman, Carl Ludwig 174
Uldrick, John 72,73,171
  John Christian 73
Ullmer, Adam 120
Ulmer, Adam 4
  Jacob 28
Ulrick, Margaret 50
Underwood, Isaac 169
Utsey, Isaac 120

Vachier, John 208
Vaigneur, John L. 199
  Mary Ann 199
Valentine, William 66,103,
  221
Valk, Jacob 11
  Jacob 16,20,22,23,24,25,
  29,35,36,37,41,50,58,67,
  73,126,136,146,181,186,
  191,198,226
Van Bebber, Henry 17
  Jacob 54
Vanai, Frances 86
Vanal, Mathew 37
Vanbibber, Jacob 86
Vance, Moses 232
Vanderheiden, Peter Ganet
  133,152
Vanderhorst, Arnoldus 127
  Elias 49,86
  Elizabeth (Raven) 127
Vanderkeyden, Peter Ganet
  134
Vanlerin, Barbara (Brown)
  7
Vann, John 9
  Joseph 178
Varambo, Francis 54,94
Varnado, Leonard 61
Varnet, Elizabeth 61
Varnodo, Isaac 61
Varnon, Mary 202
Vauchier, John 134,208
Vaughn/an, Agnes 85
  Arabela 105
  Evan 69,70
  John 137,238
  Robert 105
  Thomas 69,85
  Walter 100
  William 75,86
Vaun, John 64
  Judith 64
Vaux, William 131
Velstine, John 102

Venderdusen, Alexander
  181
Venning, Saml 228
Verdier, Andrew 12,78
Verdilly, Elizabeth 192
Verditty, Elizabeth 58,59,
  128,225
Veree, James 24
  Joseph 219
Vereen, Wm. 164
  Wm. Jr. 164
Vergereau, Peter 139
  Susannah 139
Vernezobee, Daniel 110
Vernezobre, Daniel 3
Vernod, Francis 101
Vernon, John 201,202
  Mary 201
Verree, James 79,80,91,92
  Joseph 93,190
Vickeridg, Eliza 35
Vickers, John 27
Videau, Henry 94
  Peter 103,215
Vier, Wm. 166
Vies, Jacob 95
Vilet, Negroe 15
Villard, Ann 152
Villepontoux, Benjamin 77,
  120,208
  Jane 77,208
Vines, John 141
Vinson, Mary Ann 64
Virgent, George 180
Vivian, John 133
Volentine, William 54
Votier, Francis 86
Vouchar, John 207
Vouchier, John 238
Vouloux, James 37
  Jaques 37
  Louise 37
Vovers, 197
Voyer, 86

Wactor, George 66
Waddell, Charles 132
Waddingham, Rebekah
  180,181
  Samuel 150,180,181
  Sarah 180,181
Wade, Holden 91,233
  John 63,195
  Thomas 3,6,7,59,74,91,
  128,143,151,162,172,195,
  226
Wadeson, Richard 84,137
Wadlington, James 72,83
  Thomas 23,72,83
  Thomas Jr. 72
Wagerman, George 114
  Ludwick 114
Wages, James 138,218

Waggoner, John 237
Wagner, Andreas 224
  Andrew 224
  John 8,19,23,35,53,80,
  126,132,133,158,175,176,
  193
Waid, Thomas 215
Waight, Abraham 136
  Abraham Jr. 136
  Benjamin 136
  John 136
  John Jr. 136
  Mary 136
Wainwright, Richard 116,
  235
  Samuel 111,115,172,224
Waites, 114
  William 114,161
Waits, Abraham 212
Wakefield, James 168,235
Waldron, Mary (Porter) 13
Walker, 158,202
  Alexander 35,143
  Ann (Delahowe) 54
  Benjamin 24,62,194
  Elizabeth (Martin) 54
  Elizabeth 54
  John 125,136,156,161,188
  Joseph 25
  Martha 76
  Mary 114
  Philip 18,222
  Richard 175
  Richard Jr. 76
  Robert 146
  Sanders 59
  Thomas 54,185
  William 114,124
Wallace, Alexr 105
  Annisbell 63,64
  James 169
  John 57
  Oliver 40,63
  Richd. 121
  Robert 149
  William 67
Walley, William 60
Walling, William 102,171
Walls, Benjamin 61,154
Walter, Elizabeth
  (Marshall) 157
  Elizabeth (Marshall)
  (Hagott) 115
  John 115,157
  Richard 168,177,199
  Thomas 13,204,224
Walton, Geo. 71,82
  Jno 165
  Wm. 235
Walzer, Gabriel 114
Ward, 33,201,202,214
  Elizabeth 123,149
  James 110,127

John 27,49,72,109,113,
  139,141,164,189,225,240
Joseph 143,165,191,200,
  201
Joshua 27,64,82,100,113,
  164,174,185,194,207,212,
  236
Thos 151
William 123,175
Warham, Charles Jr. 159
  David 191,207
Waring, Ann (Ball) 101
  Ann 185
  Benjamin 185,186,241
  Elizabeth (Drayton) 30,
    31
  Elizabeth 163
  John 31,76
  Joseph 199
  Josiah 30,31
  Mary 241
  Richard 101,108,185
  Thomas 80,112,191
Warley, Christianna 35
  Jacob 35
  Jacob Jr. 35
  Melchior 8
Warner, Wm. 122
Warnock, Abraham 4,11,180
  Ann 180
  Charles 4,11,180
  Charles Jr.11
  Elizabeth (Story) 11
  Elizabeth 4
  Joseph 140
  Mary (Darby)
  Samuel 126,127
Warren, George 236
  John 78
  Lott 165
Warring, Josiah 30
  Robert 37
Watchman, slave 205
Waters, Joseph 87,204
  Mary 129,197
  Philemon 59,85,129,194,
    197,243,244
  Thomas 1,85
  Wm. 8
Wates, Thomas 173
Waties, Dorothy 112
  Jno 51
  John Jr. 204
  Thos 51,228
  William 49,112,126,128,
    141,164
Watkins, Moses 63
  William 17
Watser, Gabriel 134
Watson, 193,217
  Ann 63
  James 78,106
  John 76

Mary 207,221
Michael 23
Samuel 78
Thomas 23,87
Wm. 73
Watt, Saml 83
Wattkins, Moses 54
Watts, Benjamin 101
Wattson, 188
  Lott 112
Waughan, Walter 100
Waughup, James 155
Wawsaw, Andrew 195
Way, Parmenas 198
Waylie, Henry 233
Wayman, Edward 43
Wayne, Esther 235
  William 104,144,235
Weakley, Thomas 102
Wealth, Peter 1
Weatherly, Isaac 100,191
  Wm. 100
Weathers, John 115,145
Weaver, Aaron 236
  Henry 16,126,176,193
  Maurice 30
Webb, Charles 190
  David 126,153
  Eliz. 18
  Eliz'th (Mercer) 153
  James 17
  John 120,127,149,152
  Jolly 94
  Joseph 76
  Margaret 240
Webber, Mary 190
Weber, Henry 193
  Mari 190
Webster, Henry 2
  Samuel 231
Weedingman, Barbara 118
  John 118
Weedinman, Johannes 118
  John 73
Weems, Henry 163
Weers, William 47
Weighter, Martin 217
Weir, James 157
Welch, Elizabeth 15
  James 15
  John 15
  Patrick 114
Welches, 101
Wells, Benjamin 142
  Charles 35
  David 176
  John 12
  John Jr. 204
  Joseph 179,190
  Philip 23
  Robert 111,155,156,188
  Samuel 113
  Thomas 157

William 18,27,134
Wellstead, John 15
Welshing, Hans William 32
Wershing, George 75
Wertz, Martin 67
West, Charles 80
  Esther 201
  John 107
  Mary 164,174
  Samuel 222
  Sarah 140
  Wm. 164,174
Westbery, Mary 221
  William 115,221
Westcot/t, John 140,194
Westfield, John 6,16,48,56,
  57,67,68,71,122,129,177,
  214,217,226
Weston, James 132
  John 168
  Marian 185
  Plowden 25,102,125,126,
    163,164,174,185
Wetstone, John 31
Wever, John 37
Weyman, Edward 64
Weymouth, Viscount 64
Whary, Samuel 171
Whatsman, John 116
Whayman, William 179,180,
  243
Wheeler, Benjamin 157,237
  Henry Jr. 214
  John 22,90
  William 90
Whelchel, Francis Jr. 78
Whetstone, Barbara 115,145
  Henry 31,115,145
  John 115
Whilden, John 132
Whitaker, Benjamin 32
White, Agnes 84
  Alexander 110
  Anthony 52,54,63,139,
    160,170,218
  Barbara 110
  Blake Leay 24,27,115,145
  Bryan 210
  Edwd 74
  Elizabeth (Wilkins) 93
  Elizabeth 27,115,145,189
  Hugh 154
  James 60
  Jere 166
  Jeremiah 117
  John 25,27,30,39,40,63,
    140,154,189,195,218,223
  John Jr. 220
  John Plowman 175
  Joseph 59,60,218
  Mary 155
  Reuben 60,135
  Samuel 197

Stephen 84
William 39,60,68,86,93,
110
Zachariah 106
Whitefield, 13
George 9
Whiteside/s, Hugh 8,47,114,
155
William 76,87,96,204,217
Whitsetts, 170
Whitt, Blakely 84
Whitter, Frances 227
Wickham, Margaret (Mann)
101
Nathaniel 101,204,213
Nathaniel Branchhurt 101
Richd 101
Wicolett, David 3
Wier, John 84
Saml 121
Wigfall, Benjamin 56,88
Martha 56
Wigg, Richard 27
William Hazzard 86,197
Wiggin, Samuel 190
Wightman, William 236
Wikoff, Isaac 206
Pere 206
Wilbrahan, Randle 158
Wilbun, Judith 195
Wilds, Abel 45,46
John 236
Wilkenson, Christopher 42
Wilkes, 160
Wilkes, John 162,166,176,
178,179
Wilkeson, John 95,105
Wilkie, Jane 41,131
Wilking, William 36
Wilkins, Alexander 98
Benjamin 242
Elizabeth (White) 93
James 93
Jonathan 78
Mary 242
Wilkinson, B--- 200
Christopher 19
Edward 156,162,183
Elizabeth 19
Morton 19
Wilks, 202
Will, slave 205
Willcocks, Issachar 225
Willcox, Joseph 200
William, Jacob 150
Robert 189
Williams, 184
Andrew 51,54
Ann 78
Anthony 160
Calep 59
Daniel 34,44,58,72,102,
127

David 21,94,144,154,189,
190,193
Ezekiel 131
Francis 141
Frederick 87
Giles 124,243
Grace 171
Hardy 171
Henry 83
James 131,155,178,186,
202
James Green 223
John 15,29,30,33,34,44,
49,50,117,132,146,168,
217,220,227,235
John Mortimer 38,155,
160,166,201
Joseph 209
Martha 1
Mary 155
Micajah 78,126
Moses 155
Nimrod 58
Philip 159
Pryde 207
Richard 164
Robert 14,44,86,97,101,
104,154,167,190
Robert Jr. 9,13,14,16,
28,40,43,64,123,160,164
Samuel 1,34
Thos. 154
William 23,144
Williamson, Andrew 9,51,
52,54,62,63,66,89,92,
123,124,163,173
Benjamin 28
Champernoun 28,29,215
Hennery 28
John 28,41,240
Joseph 28,100
Richard 28
Thomas 216
William 23,28,35,104,
127,215
Williford, Saml 150
Williman, Christopher 234
Jacob 33
Willingham, Joseph 57,74,
76,122,180
Mary (Jackson) 58
Mary 76
Willison, Samuel 210
Willson, Andrew 235
Ann (Miles) 224
David 76
Grace 76
James 131,149,188
Jehu 224
John 180,188
Mary (Cockerham) 149
Robert 54,76,193
Thomas 116

William 150,241
Wilson, Alexr 121
Algernon 177
Andrew 104
Archibald 83,188
Daniel 62,137
David 65
Elizabeth 236
Francis 7
George 91
Henry 15
Hugh 93
Jain 7
James 83
John 36,237
Mary 237
Precillah (Curtis) 121
Ralph 189
Robert 54,65,69,81,160,
217
Roger 54,65
Thomas 54
William 54,127,144,181
Wincorne, Samuel 90
Thomas 90
Windham, Reuben 150
Windle, John Hand 11
Windsor, Shad 128
Wingate, Edward 141
Wingfield, John 195
Wingood, John 218
Winingham, Edward 58
Thomas 58
Winn, 13
John 87,142,151,187
Priscilla 219
Richard 30,219,240
William 136
Winnes, Richard 199
Winningham, 67
Henry 67
Joseph 123,194
Mary 67
Winslow, Edward 58
Winstanley, Thomas 30,33,
97,112,161,169,231,232
Winter, Frederick 1,8
Winter, Jacob 28
Wirxam, James 17
Wise, Ann 235,236
Betty 3,233
John 88,211
Mary 211
Richard 211
Samuel 20,22,58,68,91,
232,235,236
Thomas 88,211
Wm. 151
Wish, Benjn 156
John 66
Samuel 233
Wishart, Isaac 122
James 122

Wisser, William 38
Withers, Francis 117,205
  James 197
  Richard 230
  William 188
Witherspoon, David 56,160
  Gavin 56,155,184,217
  James 160
  James Jr. 56
  John 118,137
Witten, George 194
  Peter 77
  Robert 194
  James 227
  James Jr. 220,227,239
  John 179,197
  Thos 24
Witts, Martin 185
Wiver, Henry 16
Wofford, Jos. 129
  W. 211
  William 7,86
Wolf/e, Ann 54
  Jacob 54
  Jacob Jr. 54
  Mathias 109
Wolrich, 46
Womack, Jacob 135
Wood, Bartholomew 83,84
  Benjamin 65
  Francis 201
  George 56
  Henry 12,61,137,153,238
  James 7,65,66,211,212, 216
  Jane 65
  John 65,238
  Jonathan 65
  Joseph 65,66,79
  Martha 65
  Peter 65
  Rebecca 65
  Robert 73
  Sarah 65,66
  William 184
  William Jr. 216
Woodbery, John 107
Woodcraft, 170
  Richard 94,105
Wooddall, William 72,84
Woode, Andrew 148
  Frame 148
Woodin, John 35,36
  Thomas 35,38
Wooding, John 35
Woodrop, William 195
Woods, Abraham 238
  Andrew 148
  Frame 205
  Isable 205
  James 63,231
  John 123
  Joseph 205

  Sarah 64
Woodward, John 37,29
  Mary (Chardin)(Hutson) 162
  Richard 162
  Thomas 219
Wooley, Ann (Eycott) 59
  John 59
Woolf, Henry 216
Wooten, John 218
Workman, John 47
Worrel, William 222
Wosbery, William 200
Wournel, William 38
Wrag/g, Ann 103
  Jacob 50
  John 6,25,103,115,125, 134,141,155,191,206,240, 242
  Joseph 43,50,63,106,152, 158,208,210,240
  Judith 240
  Mary 125
  Samuel 131,181,227,228
  William 22,30,31,75,115, 125,172,236
Wrand, Esther 159
  Hester 159,180
  Sarah 159
  William 159
Wright, Abraham 93
  Alexander 56,108,152,162
  Carney 184
  Charles 71,73,241
  Elizabeth (Izard); 108, 152
  George 240
  George Jr. 58,102,
  Gov. 106
  Hannah 5
  Henry 104
  Jacob 11
  James 1,5,57,74,180,187, 200,225
  Jermain 73
  John 20,46,116,121,173, 200,224
  Joseph 20,60
  Margaret (Campbell) 93
  Mary (Rhett) 50
  Mary 24,46
  Rebecca 200
  Richard 24,50
  Robert 24,43,73,85,112, 132,184
  Sarah (Hasell) 50
  Thomas 102
  William 6,11,19,20
Wunderly, John 133,134
Wurst, Henry 112
Wurster, Henry 112
Wurtz, Henry 116
Wurtzer, Henry 31,151

Wyatt, Joseph 103,112
Wylie, James 94
  Peter 94
  William 74
Wyly, James 165
  John 84,119,138,147,198, 226,228
  Saml 10

Yarborough, Francis 34
  John 154
  Lewis 154
  Moses 34
Yates, Joseph 13,150,164
  Thomas 22,119,192
Yeadon, Richard 202
Yeats, 137,238
  David 169
Yeomans, William 89
Yonge, Francis 160
  Susannah 160
You, Thos 27
Young, Anderson 75,113, 114,208
  Ann 226
  Benjamin 81,128,150,168, 170,185,202,218
  Elizabeth (Crain) 75
  Francis 70,148,160,164, 170
  Henry 167
  Isham 70
  James 34,137,238
  John 28,76,143,211,226
  Joseph 62
  Martha 168,218
  Mary 140
  Mathew 110
  Simon 59
  Thomas 36,155,164,223
  Thos Jr. 190
  William 3,60,140,214
Younge, Francis 167
  Henry Jr. 167
Youse, Samuel 94

Zahler, Jacob 3,90
Zahn, Jacob Christopher 42, 136,137,205
Zimmerman, Jacob 114,223
  Philip 74
Zinn, Cronimus 215
  Valentine 105
Zon, Henry 32
Zuberbuhler, Sebastian 134
Zubly, David 195
Zurcher, John 222
Zwicher, Hans 222

PLACE NAME INDEX

Abittons Creek 55,78
Abners Creek 196
Accabee 153
Addisons Creek 181
Alexr Creek 77,216
All Saints Parish 66,70,
 141,218
Allen Street 50,242
Alligator Branch 142
 Pond 215
Allisons Creek 41
Allstons Creek 81
Altamaha River 175,225
Amelia County, Va. 64,
 87,165
Amelia Township 14,15,16,
 28,31,42,43,47,58,66,80,
 94,102,106,115,121,125,
 127,132,135,138,145,149,
 171,172,174,210,211,217,
 218,241
Anna Kitt Parish, Ireland
 111
Anson County NC 7,17,
 18,59,68,73,78,79,124,
 128,151,155,170,184,
 195,226,240
Ansonborough 32,41,48,63,
 75,106,122,131,146,161,
 180,235
Anthonys Bluff 133
Aposce Creek 19
Archdale Street 8
 Square 25
Archer Creek 12,45
Arencaster 59
Ashepoo 116,185
 River 40,89,239
Ashley Ferry 153
 Ferry Path 91
 River 12,61,73,91,98,
 107,112,115,123,125,139,
 153,161,163,172,181,234
Augusta County Va. 117,
 188
Augusta Ga. 167,171,214
Bacons Bridge 73,112
Bakers Creek 179
Balinaclough, Ireland 101
Baltimore Md. 47
Bartins Run 218
Bartletts Buildings 115,157
Bay of Charlestown 187,230
 Street 1,2,241
 Swamp 11
Beach Creek 98,115
 Hill 73
Bear Bluff 19
 Creek 108
 Swamp 80
Beards Branch 35

Beaufort 12,45,82,98,109,
 130,163,174,186,197,214,
 223
Beaufort Creek 232
Beaufort District 17,64,75,
 78,86,98,103,104,133,
 141,144,151,153,158,163,
 174,185,192,193,197,201,
 202,206,219,222,223,239,
 242
Beaufort River 78
Beaver Creek 56,102,168,
 178,202
Beaver Dam 112,143,217,
 241, 242
Beaver Dam Branch 54,77,
 135,190,207
Beaver Dam Creek 1,20,
 132,154,179,200
Bedons Alley 220,223,235
Bee Tree branch 135
Beechhill 13
Bees Creek 191
Belfast Township 9,51,124,
 144,173
Bell Branch 142
 Mont 130
Bells Creek 136,199
 Mill Creek 198
Beresford Alley 231
 Creek 181
Berkley County 1-244
Big Beaver Creek 168
 Creek 23,60
 Meadow 214
 Saltcatcher Swamp 38
 Wolf Creek 94
Black Creek 4,5,237
 Mingo 27,92
 Mingo Creek 24,63
Black River 27,47,52,54,63,
 65,88,118,119,140,143,
 144,150,152,155,166,169,
 184,188,196,206,234,237
Black River Swamp 131,183
 Swamp 82,127,141
Blakleys line 149
Bluff Beech Creek 179
 Head 140
Boonesborough 11,22,53,62,
 65,118,199
Borlands lott 226
Boston Mass. 26,83
Boundary Street 42,46
Bourdeaux Township 27
Brents branch 7
Briar Creek 151
Bristol England 10,109,179
Broad Path 65,106,160,222,
 235
Broad River 4,6,7,8,10,11,

 18,20,23,25,31,35,41,44,
 48,53,55,56,61,63,66,67,
 68,69,70,72,73,78,83,84,
 85,102,105,107,108,114,
 117,118,120,122,127,132,
 135,137,143,144,146,148,
 158,162,168,169,170,174,
 176,194,196,199,205,217,
 218,219,228,229,230,237,
 239,241
Broad Road 4,36,111,121,
 131,132,152,156,173,191,
 201,203,226
Broad Street 1,19,22,35,37,
 59,62,66,71,77,123,152,
 166,167,176,187,188,193,
 201,205,207,211,225,227,
 240
Brotherhood Plantations
 189,190
Broughton St 31
Browns fork 137
Brunswick County 114,222
 County NC 50,74,94,166
 County Va. 220
Brunswick NC 227,235
Buck Creek 103,145
Buckhalters Creek 109,214
 Mill Creek 47
Buckhead Swamp 236
Bucks County Pa, 71,122
Buffaloe Swamp 175
Buffelo Lick Creek 174
Buflow Creek 128
Bull Head 103,242
 Street 26,93,226
Bullocks Creek 73,79,85,99,
 198,199,214
Bulls River 221,222
Bum Swamp 119
Burks County Ga. 189
Burlington 92
 NJ 79,91
Burns Alley 160
Burrasus Neck 116
Burrows Neck 147
Bush Creek 4,59,60,78,95,
 100,105,199
Bush River 7,27,59,137,200,
 238
Cacaw Swamp 36
Cain Creek 79,210
 Gall Branch 185
Cainhoy 140
Calhoun Creek 212
Camden 58,100,119,137,138,
 147,186,218,226,241
"Campden Precinct" 67
Camden District 12,16,17,
 28,41,45,46,47,54,62,64,
 73,74,80,83,84,85,86,87,

88,93,95,96,102,104,105,
109,113,117,118,119,122,
127,128,130,131,132,136,
137,138,139,140,144,146,
148,151,153,159,169,170,
171,174,181,182,184,186,
188,190,195,196,198,199,
202,203,205,206,208,211,
213,215,216,217,219,222,
226,228,233,235,236,239,
240,241
Camp Creek 9,17,99
Cane Creek 10,20,226,238
  Gall branch 185
Cannon Creek 56
  Street 226,240
Canteburg River 105
Canteys 157,161
  Creek 157,161
Cantucky Chenoe 220,
  227,235
Capers 160
Captain's Creek 30
Carans Branch 173
Carteret Street 197
Catawba Path 151
Catawba\Cataba River 9,37,
  41,79,94,99,118,146,213,
  217,219,222
Catfish 17
  Creek 164,191
Cattles Creek 65
  Swamp 72
Cecil County, Md. 189
Cedar Branch 119
  Creek 20,32,228,232,236
  Pond Branch 157
Charles Folk 85
  Street 53,55
Charlestown 1-243
  Creek 59
  District 1-243
Charlestown Neck 4,12,36,
  38,48,75,87,93,113,116,
  123,143,161,179,190,191,
  196,202
Cheeves Creek 188
Chehaw 12
"Carraw" District 1
Cheraw District 16,39,53,
  57,60,68,69,70,71,72,91,
  107,122,125,129,138,141,
  142,148,151,154,162,167,
  169,170,177,184,195,207,
  214,217,218,219,228,233,
  240
Cheraw Hill 170
Cherokee Line 200
  Nation 227,235
Chester County 158
Chesterfield County, Va.
  138
Chevees Creek 83

Chickesaws 59
Chilsbury Estate 204
Chinkopen Creek 238
Christ Church Parish 5,23,
  25,38,72,88,97,117,132,
  139,143,147,155,156,157,
  160,166,167,172,191,197,
  201,208,214,218,220,225,
  230,240,242
Christ Church Parish Ga.
  88,231
Church of St. Philip 89
Church Street 25,29,36,91,
  128,136,152,187,207,222,
  242,243
Clarks Fork 85
Clouds Creek 76,87,105
Cockholds Creek 2,13
Coffee House 127
Colhons Creek 167
Colleton County 1,2,3,4,6,
  11,13,17,19,21,22,23,24,
  25,28,29,31,33,34,35,36,
  37,38,39,40,41,43,44,45,
  46,51,52,55,61,62,66,67,
  73,74,79,85,89,90,94,95,
  96,100,101,102,103,105,
  106,109,110,111,114,117,
  119,121,122,123,125,128,
  131,136,139,142,144,146,
  148,149,150,152,153,155,
  156,160,163,164,165,167,
  168,170,172,175,177,181,
  182,183,185,197,200,205,
  206,212,213,214,216,221,
  222,224,227,232,233,236
Colleton Square 22,55,136,
  172
Colleton Tract 232
Collins River 72,83,84,176,
  225
Colonel's Creek 45
Columbus Street 193
Comande District 8
Combahee 162
  Plantation 108
  River 12,108
Combraw Creek 160
Commings Street 192
Congaree 37,53,62,70,126,
  130,136,150,154,172,184,
  189,192,225,236,241
Congaree River 10,12,16,33,
  40,48,51,56,58,59,87,
  115,121,130,131,132,136,
  147,159,160,171,174,184,
  193,203,216,220,224,226,
  228,232,233
Cooks Creek 181
Cooper River 16,50,60,67,
  139,159,185,204,242
Coosahache 191
  Bridge 191

Coosahatchie Swamp 119
Coosaw River 232
Coosawhatchie 128,134,185,
  190,206,207,219
Coosawhatchie River 4
  Swamp 35
Copuis 122
"Cornacre" 166
County of Down, Ireland
  111
  of Middlesex, 178,
  179,194,197
County of Middlesex,
  England 89,105,176
County of Stafford, England
  221
County Palatine of
  Lancaster 158
Cow Castell Branch 229
Cowdens Creek 221
Cowpen 140
  Tract 213
Cowpers Hill Plantation 82
Cox's Creek 242
  Swamp 229
Cracker Neck 189
Craven County 1-244
Cravens Bastian 35
Creek Indian Nation 93
Crimps branch 39
Crims Creek 122,229
Cross Roads 236
  Street 165
  Swamp 126
Crowders Creek 80
Crown Inn 186
Cuckolds Creek 233
Cuffy Town 43,52
  Town Creek 149
Cumberland County,
  England 89
Cumberland River 220
  Street 47
Cummings Point 196
Curltail creek 110
Cusau River 11,104
Cypress 49,204
  Creek 185
  Swamp 30,168,174,224
Danes 115,157
Daniel Creek 50
Darkdale, England 178, 179
Darthdale 109
Davids folly 68
Dawfuskee Island 61
Days Creek 61
Deans Creek 35
Dedcots Alley 242
Deer Creek 71
Dewees Island 173
Dinwidde County, Va. 117
Dorchester 8,49,58,73,101,

108,111,115,158,183
Dorchester Plantation 108
Douglass Swamp 4,11,180
Drake Street 190,191,209
Dry Branch 153
  Creek 205
  Swamp 12,45
Dublin, Ireland 63
Duck Branch 4
Duke Street 226
Duncans Creek 187,194
Dutch Church Alley 50
Dutchmans Creek 200,238
Dwights Island 163
East Florida 4
Eastern Bay 13
Edinburgh, Scotland 106, 146
Edisto 3,54,103,116,151
  Island 45,127
Edisto River 2,19,31,32,67, 88,90,93,95,110,119,138, 139,142,150,152,153,157, 160,198,221,224,229,237, 238
Egham, County Surry England 179
Elex Creek 77
Ellery St. 49
Elliott Street 223,235
English Santee 160
Enoree 39,97,176
  River 23,35,75,86,95, 129,130,135,146,194,196, 199,241,242
Euhaws 108
Eutchee path 93
Ewhaw Creek 116
Exeter, County Devon England 157
Exeter, England 161
Fair Lawn 48
  Lawn Barony 60
  Street 226
Fairforest 18,109,129,174, 238
Fairforest Creek 11,26,30, 37,76
Fairforest Waters 135
Fawn Branch 216
Fergusons Creek 135
  Ferry 111
  Swamp 77
Fish Dam Creek 146
  Dam Ford 237
Fishing Creek 8,47,63,74, 102,114,154,155,188,189, 196,213,229
Flat Creek 215
  Rock 218
  Rock Creek 95,182
Fork Creek 153

Island 94
  Road 236
Fort Boone 55,66
Four Hole Creek 224
  Hole Swamp 11,26,36,38, 42,67,77,103,108,135, 137,157,171,208,235,238, 241
Four Holes 229
Frederick County Md. 72
  County Va. 72,83,176
Fredericksburgh 30,121,137, 186
Free School Lands 185
French Church 85
  Mans Creek 130
Friend Street 47,152
Frigate Randolph 216
Front Street 31,128,190, 191,216
Garrens Creek 140
George Street 48,116
Georgetown 5,41,51,52,54, 63,68,69,76,78,79,87,91, 101,110,126,128,129,130, 131,133,150,157,177,178, 181,185,188,198,204,214, 216,218,220,226,227,230, 240
Georgetown Creek 202
  District 4,24,48,52,54, 74,80,81,92,127,128,130, 133,139,141,144,150,155, 156,157,164,167,168,181, 184,185,188,202,203,204, 216,226,227,228,240
Georgetown River 69,126-,178
Georgia 15,16,25,45,60,64, 78,79,88,100,139,150, 166,175,178,198,242
Gilders Creek 86
Gilford County NC 7
Gilkeys\Gilkies Creek 55, 79,117
Gills Creek 110,205,225
Gloucester 59
  County 59
Goose Creek 6,16,25,26,31, 38,46,52,56,89,101,115, 121,131,143,158,161,169, 190,196,209,224,226
Goswell Street, London England 109,197
Granies Quarter Creek 67, 102,109,119
Granny's Quarter 215
Granville County 1,3,4,6,8, 9,10,12,13,14,15,17,18, 19,20,21,25,26,27,29,30, 35,38,39,42,43,46,47,50, 51,55,57,61,62,63,64,66, 67,71,72,74,75,77,78,82,

83,85,86,90,91,93,94,95, 97,98,100,103,104,105, 110,112,113,114,116,117, 119,121,123,124,126,127, 128,129,130,131,133,134, 135,137,141,142,143,145, 146,147,149,150,151,152, 162,163,165,166,167,171, 173,174,175,178,179,180, 185,186,188,189,190,191, 192,197,198,199,200,201, 202,206,207,208,210,212, 213,214,215,219,221,222, 223,224,231,232,236,238, 242,243
Granville County NC 227-,235
Great Branch 73
  Britain 192,212
  Bull Swamp 237
  Coosahacke Swamp 103
  Coosawhatchie Swamp 219, 242
  Great Falls 1
  Linches Creek 104,128
  Marshes 20
  Ogechee 93
Great Pedee River 71,91, 113,138,184,203,219,229
Great Pond 217
  Road 6
  Rocky Creek 123
  Salcahache 103
  Saluda River 117
  Stephens Creek 214
  Swamp 200
Greens Creek 224
Guignard Street 165,172,191
Guilford County NC 33
Gun Bluff 45
  Bluff creek 12
Hainers creek 148
Half Way Swamp 47
Halfway swamp creek 60
Hallifax County Va. 58,102
Hampstead/Hamstead 76-,87, 93,190,191,193,209
Hanahs Creek 217
Handysides Lake 216
Hanover Square 124
  Street 193
Hard Labour 55,66
  Labour Creek 9,55,66, 163,173
Hard Labour River 51
Harleston 26,113,143,196
Hazell Street 66,94,126,180
Hell Hole Swamp 57,180,-231
Henleys Creek 115
High Hill Creek 42,43,162,

294

237
High Hills 45,195,234
High Hills Santee 6,14,15, 19,90,98,124,135,147, 195,196,208,210,241
High Markett Street 240
Road 38,153,154,161
Sole 174
Street 63,69,130
Wadon 116
Hills Creek 127
Hillsborough Township 174, 190,191,223
Hilton Head 202
Hobcaw Barony 177,178
Point 177
Hobshaw 181
Creek 211
Hogskin Creek 183
Holston River 220
Home Swamp 169
Horns Creek 165
Hors Pen Bay 94
Horse Creek 120,198,238
Island 12,17,239
Pen Branch 136
Savannah 111
Shoe 242
Shoe Creek 216
Shoe Inn 109
Shoe Savannah 29,41,110
Horsepen Bay 105
Creek 43
Howard's Creek 7
Hughes Creek 107
Hunters Street 55
Creek 172
Husbands Creek 148
Husper Creek 193
Hutchins's Cabin 85
Hyde Park 48
Hyrnes Landing 239
Indian Creek 72,102,225, 230,241
Indian Field Swamp 24,182
Hut Branch 97
Landing 71
Town 110
Inverness, England 179
Ireland 240
Island of Bermuda 27,49
of Grenada 3
of New Providence 205
Iwamlow 158
Jack on the ashes Camp 74
Jacks Creek 47
Jacksonborough 6,21,92
Jacksonburgh 1,2,22,167
Jacksons Creek 8,48,219
Jacob Creek Bridge 125
James Island 20,64,139,161, 197,230,239
Jeffers Creek 25,39,60,142

Johns Island 36,100,212, 227,232
Johnston's Island 113
Johnstons Creek 134,135-,200
Jopsham in County of Devon 157,161
Jumpers Land Creek 30
Kain Hoy 157
Kensington 48,204
Kensington Plantation 52
Keywaw River 100
King Street 1,7,10,18,19, 22,35,50,59,65,84,91,92, 104,111,167,186,178,192, 198,202,208,210,212,234
King William County Va. 195
Kings Bounty 189,201
Kings Creek 31,84,85,144, 158,174
Kingston Township 23,58
Knavesdale Parish 109
Ladys Island 104,232
Lancaster Pa. 26,165
Latham 158
Lawsons Fork 216,238
Lazowis land 20
Leadenwah Creek 90
Leicester 109
Lemon's Swamp 125,164
Lenneaus Ferry 194
Lewis's Marsh 221,222
Lick Branch 129
Creek 151
Lime Street, London 175
Lincolns Town, England 158
Lindsays Creek 234
Linshes Branch 199
Lions Creek 217
Littenwaw Creek 19
Little Buffaloe Creek 174
Cherokee Creek 199
Flat Rock Creek 89
Lynches Creek 23
Ogechee 93
Peedee 42,88,112,174
Peedee River 112,159
Little River 3,23,27,33,44, 58,74,98,110,112,114, 126,129,143,151,152,158, 167,178,187,199
Little Saludy River 23,44, 76,87,116,164,174,219
Little Stephen Creek 155
Turkey Creek 148
Lockabor 189
Log Creek 33,44
London England 9,10,27,30, 31,33,40,68,79,82,86,89, 92,105,108,109,110,117,

129,158,162,166,172,175, 177,178,179,193,214,243
Londonborough 232
Long Bay 22
Bay Waccamaw 115,145
Bluff 170
Branch 105
Long Cane 9,13,88,128,135, 179,183,186,223,243
Long Cane Creek 11,14,15, 21,22,53,55,66,72,101, 110,114,123,135,147,163, 165,169,174,189,199,200, 212
Long Cane Rode 155
Long Cane Settlement 10,15, 33,112,114,126,142,143, 145,147,163,175,212
Long Marsh 11
Lorill Hill 163
Louisa County Va. 207
Louise River 220
Lowndes's Patent 221,222
Loy Creek 149
Lunenburg County Va. 7
Lynches Creek 70,85,129, 151,155,162,169,180,195, 206,215,219,240
Lynches Pasture 180
Lyttleton Street 226
Maidens Meadow 85
Main Swamp 88
Maple Swamp 143
Marin Lodge 43
Market House 62
Place 49
Street 6,226
Marks's Creek 184,219
Marrs Bluff 38
Mary Barony 243
Maryland 230
Masson 152
Mathews Branch 100
Mathis's bluff 35
McCowans corner 155
McPhersons branch 219
Mealy Spott 141
Mecklenburg County NC 8,10,14,18,26,30,37,63, 67,76,90,99,102,105,118, 141,154,155,165,196, 215,217,236
Meeting House St. 104,155
Street 186,191,215
Mepkin High Land 204
Middle Temple, London England 179
Middlesex County, England 9,115,124,157,166,176, 177
Middlesex, England 109, 208, 210

295

Mill Creek 77,207
　Hill 115,157
Millers Waggon Road 129
Mitchells Creek 26,37
Mitheringham 132
Moore Creek 23
　Street 149
Morgans branch 151
Morris' Nook 7
Mount Hope 64
　Hope Swamp 140
　Parsons 112,142
Mountain branch 136
Muddy Branch 196
　Creek 129,132
Mudlick 209
　Creek 33,34,44,74
Murrays Ferry 226
　Creek 149
Musgrove 133
Naked Creek 1
Nassau Street 193
Neck Creek 99
Neds Branch 187
New Barn Tract 177
　Bourdeaux 190
　Church Street 159,161
　River 200
　Three Runs 131
　Town 205
　Windsor 105,207,222
New York NY. 139
Newfoundland 187
Newmans branch 132
Ninety Six 9,11,24,31,34,
　39,40,53,54,58,62,65,89,
　92,102,105,115,116,136,
　183,194,201
Ninety Six Creek 33,34,77,
　136
Ninety Six District 7,9,13,
　15,21,23,31,33,34,44,51,
　52,55,58,60,62,63,66,67,
　70,72,73,74,75,76,78,79,
　83,85,86,87,89,92,95,97,
　100,101,103,105,108,112,
　114,116,117,118,119,123,
　124,125,127,132,135,141,
　142,144,146,147,148,149,
　150,155,163,164,165,166,
　168,172,173,174,175,176,
　178,183,186,187,188,189,
　190,194,195,196,198,199,
　200,201,202,203,207,211,
　212,213,214,216,217,218,
　219,220,221,223,228,229,
　238,242,243
Nismes France 12
Nobles Creek 150,175
Norens Creek 147
Norfolk Street 115,157
North Edisto River 77
North Point 230

Northamton 111
Northumberland County
　109
Northwest Fork 165
Oglethorpes Barony 82
Okaty Creek 75
Old Barn Tract 177
　Cape Fear Road 218
Old Church Street 50,128,
　104,144,149,155,166,186,
　188,191,215
Old Quarter House 6,25
　Town 107
　Town Creek 107
Onslow County NC 87
Orange Garden 193
　Street 27,145
Orangeburg 2,3,5,9,31,32,
　33,49,54,61,65,72,83,88,
　102,112,115,116,119,138,
　142,145,150,201,229
Orangeburg District 32,33,
　36,54,59,61,63,67,70,77,
　81,83,86,87,88,90,112,
　114,119,121,122,125,127,
　129,130,132,137,138,142,
　146,147,149,150,157,159,
　161,162,166,168,171,173,
　184,189,195,211,216,218,
　221,223,225,228,229,230,
　237,238,239,240,243
Ox Creek 145
Oyster Point 49
Pacolet River 77,85,103,
　108,118,172,216,238
Pages Creek 209
Palmetto Branch 7,59
Parker 111
　Ferry 224
Parking Creek 22
Parsons Point 181,211
Parts Creek 76
Patricks Creek 225
Pawleys Creek 81
Pearse's Swamp 193,206
Pearsons Island 121
Pedlars 238
Pee Dee 1,69,91,135,154,
　206,217,222
Pee Dee River 3,5,6,7,11,
　15,16,17,20,38,39,41,45,
　46,53,56,57,58,59,67,68,
　69,70,86,87,96,99,100,
　103,107,113,115,120,122,
　124,129,135,139,141,142,
　148,150,154,155,156,157,
　162,163,164,170,177,185,
　190,191,201,203,204,214,
　219,228,229,233,240
Peech Tree branch 135
Peigulars branch 171
Pen Branch 77
　Branch River 77

Creek 93
　Swamp 157
Pennys Creek 42,128,-
　135,169
Perkins Bluff 236
Persimmon branch 219
Peters Creek 61,181
Philadelphia Pa. 79,92,206
Pinckney Street 64
Pine Tree Creek 186
Pinetree 165
Piney Creek 163
Pit Creek 51
Plimouth, Massech. 58
Plumfield 15
Pocotaligo Bridge 35
　River 46,55,116
Point Comfort 131
　Hope 181
　Plantation 50
Pon Pon 22,73,92
Pon Pon River 1,2,3,31,61,
　119,151,167,222
Pond Bluff 81
Pooky Swamp 223
Porcher 13
Port of Plymouth, New
　England 58
Port Royal 109,178,179,214
　Island 35,78, 193,223
　Street 82,186
Portsmouth in Piscatigua,
　New England 130
Potatoe Creek 187
Powels Mountain 220,227,
　235
Prince Frederick Parish 4,
　5,17,24,27,54,57,69,70,
　74,76,82,113,127,131,
　132,140,150,157,160,161,
　162,163,180,183,184,185,
　217,222
Prince George Parish 4,20,
　22,38,51,52,63,69,70,76,
　87,100,106,107,112,114,
　117,118,119,120,123,126,
　128,133,142,143,144,145,
　149,151,152,158,162,163,
　168,177,178,179,180,185,
　187,188,198,201,202,203,
　204,209,218,226,228,229,
　230,237
Prince Street 54,68,218,227
Prince William Parish 3,4,
　13,14,17,21,27,35,42,46,
　47,54,53,65,75,90,103,
　106,108,123,133,166,168,
　190,193,197,219,221,224,
　231,236
Private branch 143
Publick Land Place 89
Pudding Swamp 217
Purrysburg 3,18,19,27,29,

296

39,43,53,86,98,110,113, 114,128,129,133,134,135, 143,152,153,158,167,185, 190,192,197,199,206,207, 208,215,224,243
Quarter house 59,65,121
Queen Street 77,104
Queensborough 70,113,120, 155,157,162,164,203
Quince Street 68
Rabins Creek 34
Raeburns Creek 137
Raibourn Creek 193
Raifords Creek 131,132
Ramptons branch 119
Rantowles' Bridge 224
Rapers Alley 197
Rawlinsons 232
Rayburns Creek 238
Reachmount 243
Red Bluff 150,164
Redbank Creek 163
Reed Street 209
Reedy Creek 88,174
   River 58,96,199
Reybournes Creek 199
Reyburns Creek 23
Rhettsberry 50
Rhode Island 26
Rice Hope 163
Richmond 129
   County Ga. 207
Rileys corner 23
River May 202
   Ohio 220,227,235
   Pond 103
   Street 242
   Swamp 138
Road River 67,68,79,199
Roan County NC 7
Rockey branch 194
   River 134,190,210
   Spring 88
Rocky Creek 8,40,54,73,84, 93,110,116,124,147,154, 172,217,222,236,238
Rollinsons 232
Rosses Creek 212
Round about 170
Rowan County NC 26,37,- 104, 139,212
Rowlins Neck 41
Russells Creek 128
Salcacha River 182
Salem on Black River 118
Salop, England 97
Saltcatcher 160,165,166, 168,175,198
Saltcatcher River 3,90,125
   Swamp 4,164,182
Saluda 37,39,178,194,210, 237

Saluda River 1,4,9,10,11, 19,20,22,23,24,31,33,35, 37,39,42,44,53,56,58,59, 60,61,62,67,72,83,85,96, 97,100,102,107,108,109, 110,114,119,122,124,126, 129,135,137,144,147,148, 162,163,168,175,176,194, 196,199,200,213,217,226, 230,236,238,239,241,243, 244
Saluda Road 236
Salvadors 21
Sameat creek 76
Sammy's Branch 166
Sampit 69,226
   Creek 78,126,178
   River 133
Sand Hills 163
Sandy Creek 14,171,181
   Island 185
   River 127,237
Sandy Run 3,33,77,110,186, 199,237,238
Sandy Run Creek 237
   Run Swamp 47
Sanes Creek 199
Santee 11,24,29,36,51,53, 57,74,76,94,101,106,115, 120,122,123,139,146,149, 154,157,161,179,187,194, 206,208,210,228
Santee River 4,12,13,14,25, 28,29,42,47,51,57,58,64, 66,71,74,76,81,82,87,88, 93,94,96,97,98,104,106, 110,111,114,119,120,121, 122,123,130,135,138,139, 144,145,146,149,153,157, 159,160,162,164,166,171, 172,174,176,177,181,184, 192,193,194,195,204,205, 206,209,211,213,217,218, 223,225,226,230,232,241, 243
Santee River Swamp 21,149, 181,217
Sapola District Ga. 122
Savannah 7,97,184,211
   Back River 215
   Creek 51
Savannah Ga. 3,19,53,60,61, 71,82,98,134,152,189,206
Savannah Hunt 53
   Old Town 95
Savannah River 1,8,9,21,35, 39,44,52,53,62,63,65,71, 72,73,74,75,77,82,85,86, 91,94,100,105,106,109, 113,123,128,131,134,141, 143,149,150,151,153,162, 165,167,173,179,186,189, 190,197,199,200,201,207,

210,212,231,236,238,243
Savannah Road 230
Sawney Creek 14,30,97,118
Saxe Gotha 12,51,58,59,66, 83,87,98,114,115,119, 122,126,136,153,159,160, 162,172,175,176,184,189, 193,195,223,225,228,230, 241
Schenkinghs Square 222
School house Street 116
Scotch Creek 23,59,113,147
Scull Creek 202
Second Creek 67
Seder Creek 150
Sedge pond 214
Shanks Creek 98
Shaw Fork 95
Sheep Island 12,17,45
Ship Charming Sally 112,- 201
Shugborough Manor 108
Simons Creek 185
Simpsons Creek 237
Sink Branch 22
Six Mile Swamp 188
   Miles Creek 34
Sleepy Creek 74,85,173,223
Small Woods Island 110
Smithfield Plantation 71
Smiths Barony 20
   Ford 6
   Valley NY 139
So Fork Road 217
Sochasta 168
   Creek 168
Sochorsta Creek 125
Soho 124
Solomans Lodge 69,81
Somerset County 109
South Bay Street 163
   Edisto River 156
   Pacolet River 216
Spoon 28
Spoon's Savannah 17
Spring branch 108,229
Spur Creek 13
Squirrel Street 48,63
St. Andrew Parish Church 209
St. Andrew Parish, London 115,157,175
St. Andrews Parish 12,40, 49,61,80,89,91,98,99, 100,106,107,110,119,120, 139,148,153,161,169,171, 181,197,209,219,220,134, 224,230,235,239
Sa. Ann Parish 124
St. Bartholomew Parish 1,2, 3,4,6,17,22,29,37,55,66, 73,89,90,92,94,101,106, 109,121,126,148,152,153,

160,163,167,170,182,192, 197,200,213,216,221,224, 227,232,233,236,239,242
St. Brides, London 109,178, 179
St. Bridget Parish, London 220
St. Clemant Parish 115,157
St. David Parish 1,3,7,15, 16,38,39,57,60,68,69,70, 72,85,99,124,127,148, 151,153,154,156,162,190, 198,219,233,240
St. David Parish, Ga. 150
St. Denis Parish 36,54,85, 103,139,215
St. George Parish 2,8,13, 24,29,49,56,58,66,71,72, 73,90,101,103,108,111, 115,124,129,137,138,152, 158,164,168,171,176,177, 182,183,185,199,204,207, 208,235,238,241
St. George Parish Ga. 224
St. George Parish Bermuda 27
St. George Parish England 9
St. Helena Island 100,232
St. Helena Parish 17,29,75, 78,86,98,103,104,108, 113,130,158,169,174,185, 186,190,191,193,199,200, 202,206,207,220,232,242
St. James Parish 6,11,16, 25,26,29,31,38,46,51,52, 53,56,57,74,76,82,89,94, 101,106,115,120,121,122, 123,131,139,146,149,154, 157,161,166,169,176,179, 192,194,206,209,224,226, 228,230,231,241
St. John Parish 11,21,31, 48,60,71,77,81,82,90, 100,101,104,111,113,114, 121,136,143,153,170,181, 182,194,196,197,198,201, 204,218,232
St. Lukes Parish 116,146
St. Marks Parish 4,5,6,8, 10,12,13,14,15,16,17,19, 22,25,28,30,31,40,44,45, 46,47,54,57,59,66,67,73, 74,75,76,82,83,84,88,93, 95,97,99,104,109,111, 113,114,115,117,118,119, 121,124,129,131,135,137, 139,140,142,143,146,147, 154,155,157,159,161,165, 169,171,172,173,178,180, 181,183,184,187,188,192, 193,195,196,200,202,204, 205,206,208,211,213,215,

217,218,221,222,225,228, 229,231,234,238,241
St. Martin Parish 9,177
St. Martin Parish England 214
St. Martins Creek 211
St. Mathews Parish 2,15,28, 31,32,39,42,61,62,64,67, 69,74,81,111,114,121, 127,130,132,135,138,142, 148,150,154,136,161,166, 171,183,184,185,205,207, 209,210,214,224,225,243
St. Michaels Parish 35,145, 157,171
St. Michaels Parish Church 24
St. Pauls Parish 7,13,17, 23,24,36,42,48,66,89, 101,111,117,122,136,149, 153,156,160,163,164,168, 169,176,177,182,205,206, 222,224,225,233,235
St. Pauls Parish Ga. 7,13, 93,165,167
St. Peters Parish 3,18,20, 29,43,60,64,78,82,86, 113,128,133,134,144,153, 158,167,185,191,197,199, 206,207,208,215,219,224, 226,231,239,242
St. Philip Parish Ga. 39
St. Philips Church 90,242
St. Philips Parish 16,22, 29,30,36,43,48,49,50,65, 75,87,102,104,116,126, 152,156,160,161,192,208, 210,221,226,228,241
St. Quintins 232
St. Stephens Parish 10,51, 64,70,126,127,149,153, 170,199,205,210,218,230
St. Thomas Apostle County Devon 157
St. Thomas Parish 36,54,56, 62,84,85,87,88,94,103, 110,139,140,157,158,159, 173,181,185,201,211,214, 215,227,242
St. Thomas Parish NC 151
Stafford County 108
Stell Creek 63
Stephens Creek 3,9,44,51, 52,55,62,66,72,83,85,97, 117,121,124,147,165,173, 178,179,202,238
Stevenses Swamp 120
Stolls Alley 24
Stoney Fork 8,196 Run 128,134
Stono 28,29,40,97,111,215 Bridge 206
Stono River 100,122,160,

177,197,219,227,239
Stony Run 206
Sugar Creek 75,135
Sunbury Ga. 213
Surry County NC 79
Susey Boles Branch 10
Sweet water 75
Swifts Creek 135
Tarrapen waters 213
Tereble Creek 237
The Distillery 117
Thickety Creek 18,46,55,78, 79,143,211
Thompsons Ford 199 Creek 74,148,151,240
Three Runs 137,238
Tigar River 35,61
Tilley Swamp 112,142,201
Timicau Island 173
Timothy Creek 169,177
Tindals Island 239
Tinkers Creek 74,137,238
Tipperary, Ireland, 25
Tobys Creek 86,135
Tocco Swamp 88
Togoloo Trading Path 134
Toms Creek 220
Town Gates 201
Tradd Street 14,28,41,43, 44,58,155,156,171,188, 193,208,210,216,235,241
Transylvania 220,227,235
Trotts Point 208,210
Truchets Plantation 75
Tryon County NC 6,7,10,26, 30,55,73,78,79,84,85,91, 129,158,174,198,211,216
Tupelo Head 196
Turkey Creek 5,10,23,30,40, 97,148,217,223,238
Turtle River 175
Twelve Mile Creek 90
Twenty Five Mile Creek 113, 135,136,142
Tyger River 7,11,26,120, 129,130,132,135,141,166, 168,194,195,198,199,212, 214,217,238
Union Street 43,60,104,187, 197,209,227
Unity Alley 159,180
Upper cane brake 117
Virginia 175,217
Vyniard Lott 190
Wabbecaw Creek 120
Waccamaw 6,28,74,81,100, 117,125,143,150,157,161, 164,168
Waccamaw Neck 22,81,119, 145,186,218
Waccamaw River 23,74,81, 112,126,128,138,141,142,

144,145,152,163,177,178,
201,213,214,229,237
Wackindaw Creek 160,166
Wacondaw Creek 117
Wadbecan Creek 177
Wadmalaw River 164
Wadmalaw Island 19,90
Wake County NC 195
Wakendau Creek 132
Wallnut Creek 199
Wambaw Creek 94
   Swamp 11,101
Wampee pond 71
Wando/w River 26,38,139,
147,166,181,201,211,214,
225
Wandow 166
Wandower 160
Wappoo 139,197
War Hall Plantation 89
Warrior Creek 39,75,86
Wassamasaw 77,133
   Swamp 18
Watboe 181
Watco's Creek 211
Wateree 118
   Creek 168,191,243,244
   Neck 142
Wateree River 6,10,14,22,
39,40,45,67,75,82,86,96,
98,102,106,119,121,135,
137,139,142,173,174,181,
186,191,195,202,203,210,
215,218,220,225,228,231,
234,238,241,244
Wateree River Swamp
115,234
   Swamp 234
Wattohan Creek 94
Waxhaw 10,62,99,146
   Creek 62,154,203
Wexhaws 196
Waxhaws NC 99
Webbs Creek 183
Weektee Lake 213
Wehaw 160
   Creek 52
Welch Neck 45,99
Welch Tract 1,5,6,15,16,17,
20,46,48,53,56,58,67,69,
71,87,101,122,129,138,
154,203,207,214,217
Welches Creek 101
West Creek 105,125,164
   New Jersey 92
Westminster 166,176
Weymouth 170
Whippys Swamp 103
White Oak Creek 84
   Point 163
Whitehaven 89
Widow Weaver's ferry 119
Wild horse Creek 177

Wilkersons Creek 169
   Swamp 77
Williams Creek 19,168
   Old Field 98
Williamsburg 56,57,82,110,
121,124,152,153,155,160,
217
Williamsons Creek 108
Willow Creek 72
Wilsons Creek 39,237
Wilthington County 59
Windzor Street 3
Winyaw 5,49,51,52,69,76,
110,133,149,157,163,178,
181,198,202,209
Winyaw Bay 213
Withington Parish 59
Wood Street 51,54
Youngs Creek 238
   fork 60

OCCUPATIONS INDEX

Attorney/Barrister 9,10,12,
  20,25,27,32,33,41,43,44,
  49,63,79,83,87,89,92,97,
  106,108,109,111,121,124,
  128,136,146,151,157,158,
  159,161,165,166,175,176,
  178,179,192,195,205,207,
  212,214,221,227,242,243
Baker 8,16,17,22,24,32,65,
  146,151,192,198,242
Blacksmith 8,26,67,72,84,
  96,97,98,106,107,111,
  110,116,127,141,186,236
Boat Builder 39,46
Bookkeeper 109
Bookseller 111
Breeches Maker 126,131
Brewer 125
Bricklayer 8,36,43,75,104,
  126,155,163,164,198,234
Butcher 8,33,131,124,150,
  222,234
Cabinet Maker 65,88,105,
  136,138,149,157,193,198,
  207
Carpenter 3,6,7,19,21,22,
  28,29,37,39,47,49,64,76,
  80,84,87,90,93,102,121,
  131,147,148,155,159,176,
  178,190,191,196,205,208,
  241
Chairmaker 118,140
Chief Justice 22,50,107,
  172,179
Clerk 94,139,189,190,208,
  210
Cooper 22,43,46,67,68,98,
  99,105,132,225,234,240
Cordwinder 10,22,36,40,142,
  148
Creek Indian 93
Deputy Surveyor 11,27,31,
  32,42,53,65,77,83,84,
  124,128,125,134,135,169,
  175
Deputy Surveyor General
  101
Distiller 66
Doctor 146
Doctor of Medicine 150
Doctor of Physic 28,40,55,
  158
Factor 210
Farmer 7,11,97,129,216
Freeholder 21,68,110,122
Governor 1,28,30,36,46,63,
  68,76,78,80,85,106,122,
  155,171,180,194,201,221
Governor of NC 7,129,141
Gunsmith 19,89,90,123,180
Hatter 95,162,218

House Carpenter 27,43,79,
  83,91,116,129,152,168,
  242
Indian Trader 115,172,184
Innholder/Keeper 6,8,25,28,
  30,32,38,42,43,52,109,
  138,143,147,231
Interpreter 93
Jeweller 24,126,130,135
Joiner 19,26,29
Justice and Secretary NC 87
Justice of Court of Common
  Pleas 107
Labourer 59,61,63,65,74,
  120,172,184
Landgrave 40,60,109,116,
  133,161,179,180,197,209,
  234
Leather Breaches maker
  101
Lt. Gov. 19,169,221,222
Magistrate Ninety Six
  District 132
Mantuamaker 31
Mariner 49,55,78,111,126,
  169,180,198
Master of Court of Chancery
  23,123,208,210
Master of Free School 95
Master of Ship Charming
  Sally 112,201
Mayor 109,157,158,162,166,
  176
Merchant 1-244
Messenger of his Majestys
  Council 95,106
Miller 33,51,123,223
Millwright, 26,59,109,125
Minister of the Gospel 79
Notary Public 10,33
Organ Maker 146
Overseer 97,194,196
Painter 226
Peruke Maker 79,92,98,223
Physician/Practitioner of
  Physic 15,26,103,108,
  110,111,112,127,169,188,
  193,194,199,201,215
Pilot 91,197
Planter 1-244
Post Master 208
Precher of the Gospell 229
Provost Marshall 2,13,41,
  63,82,98,90,106,126,155,
  160,166,186,194,221,222
Public Register 18,79
Receiver of Quit Rents 37
Rector 29,49,50,59,208,209,
  210,242
Register 7,111,158
Ropemaker 97

Sadler 9,11,17,21,29,35,49,
  62,66,79,198,202,204
Sail Maker 21
Sawyer 143
Schoolmaster 9,27,36,142,
  154
Scrivener 29
Secretary of the Province 5
Sheriff 21,25,74,75,120,
  125,126,146,159,177,189,
  198,202,204,210,218,226,
  238
Ship Carpenter 38,123,163,
  182,195,196
Shipwright 85,93,178,239
Shoemaker 16,18,48,60,61,
  77,98,119,131,183,186,
  192,197,207,208
Shopkeeper 22,33,37,42,51,
  90,100,152,160,169,180,
  186,198,212,233
Silver Smith 57,69,74,81,
  135,231
Simner 66
Storekeeper 82,136,195,229
Student at law 212
Sugar Baker 25,106,165
Surgeon 8,76,110,243
Surveyor 26,31,35,72,94,99,
  116,128,134,150,179,183,
  193,200,201,206,214,219,
  230,242
Tallow Chandler 65
Tanner 8,63,95,104,105,155,
  241
Tavern Keeper 39,40,52,72,
  76,83,92,108,133,134,
  137,151,171,174,182,199,
  202,214,240
Taylor 3,14,25,28,45,69,76,
  77,83,87,89,90,92,93,
  101,106,130,134,139,146,
  151,165,184,190,216,223,
  229
Tin Plate Worker 90,105
Tobacco Spiner 126
Trader 34,59,148,181,230
Turner 63
Vendue Master 172
Victualler 22,83,91,97
Vintner 95,137,143,230
Watchmaker 22
Weaver 8,46,54,187,195,217
Wharfinger 77,179
Wheelwright 4,5,65,88,102,
  145,146,230
Wine Merchant 108
Winyaw 110
Yeoman 9,10,17,32,47,
  51,59,62,66,71,72,78,83,
  84,99,103,104,113,120,
  155,163,170,173,189,195,
  212,219,222,223,229,230

Heritage Books by Brent H. Holcomb:

Bute County, North Carolina Land Grant Plats and Land Entries

CD: Early Records of Fishing Creek Presbyterian Church, Chester County, South Carolina, 1799–1859

CD: Kershaw County, South Carolina Minutes of the County Court, 1791–1799

CD: Marriage and Death Notices from The Charleston [S.C.] Observer, *1827–1845*

CD: South Carolina, Volume 1

CD: Winton (Barnwell) County, South Carolina Minutes of County Court and Will Book 1, 1785–1791

Early Records of Fishing Creek Presbyterian Church, Chester County, South Carolina, 1799–1859, with Appendices of the Visitation List of Rev. John Simpson, 1774–1776 and the Cemetery Roster, 1762–1979
Brent H. Holcomb and Elmer O. Parker

Kershaw County, South Carolina Minutes of the County Court, 1791–1799

Marriage and Death Notices from Columbia, South Carolina Newspapers, 1838–1860; Including Legal Notices from Burnt Counties

Marriage and Death Notices from The Charleston Observer, *1827–1845*

Winton (Barnwell) County, South Carolina Minutes of County Court and Will Book 1, 1785–1791

South Carolina Deed Abstracts, 1773–1778, Books F-4 through X-4

South Carolina Deed Abstracts, 1776–1783, Books Y-4 through H-5

South Carolina Deed Abstracts, 1783–1788, Books I-5 through Z-5

www.ingramcontent.com/pod-product-compliance
Lightning Source LLC
Chambersburg PA
CBHW062001220426
43662CB00010B/1194